Praise for TRIUMPH WITHOUT VICTORY

"The most comprehensive book written about the Gulf
conflict to date . . . *Triumph Without Victory* also offers
a vivid combat history woven from interviews with
soldiers after the war's conclusion . . . It is a book
that needed to be written."
—PETER ARNETT, front page,
Los Angeles Times Book Review

"Instant history can't come much better than this
powerful mosaic of the Gulf War, written almost like
a mystery novel about chaos on a wartime roller
coaster . . . Full of new insights and detailed,
credible revelations."
—BENJAMIN F. SCHEMMER,
Armed Forces Journal International

"A readable volume that will bring greater understanding to a six-month war . . . Gulf War veterans in particular will enjoy the book."
—JAMES M. MORRIS, Professor of History, Christopher Newport College, *Newport News*

✠

"Excellent journalistic history that is unlikely to be surpassed."
—COLONEL RICHARD SWAIN, *Army*

✠

"This book goes a long way toward putting flesh—and blood—on the vast but generally superficial coverage of the Gulf crisis . . . *Triumph Without Victory* does a great job in blowing away the image of a flawless and bloodless 'Nintendo war.' The chapters on the ground war, particularly, read like a techno-thriller novel, only better."
—OTTO KREISHER, *The San Diego Union-Tribune*

✠

"Thorough enough to be considered the first 'definitive' history of the Gulf War."
—LIAM O'MALLEY, *The Boston Phoenix*

"This book avoids flag-waving, unbounded patriotism and slanted writing. It's just the facts—and plenty of them . . . *Triumph Without Victory* is the best book written about the war to date . . . It fills in many gaps and is a demonstration of what reporters do best: seek the truth."
    —RICK R. SMITH, *The Raleigh News & Observer*

"Triumph Without Victory is such an incredible story that it's sometimes easy to forget it's non-fiction. In many ways, it reads better than a Tom Clancy novel."
    —BOB ELLIS, *Detroit Free Press*

TRIUMPH WITHOUT VICTORY

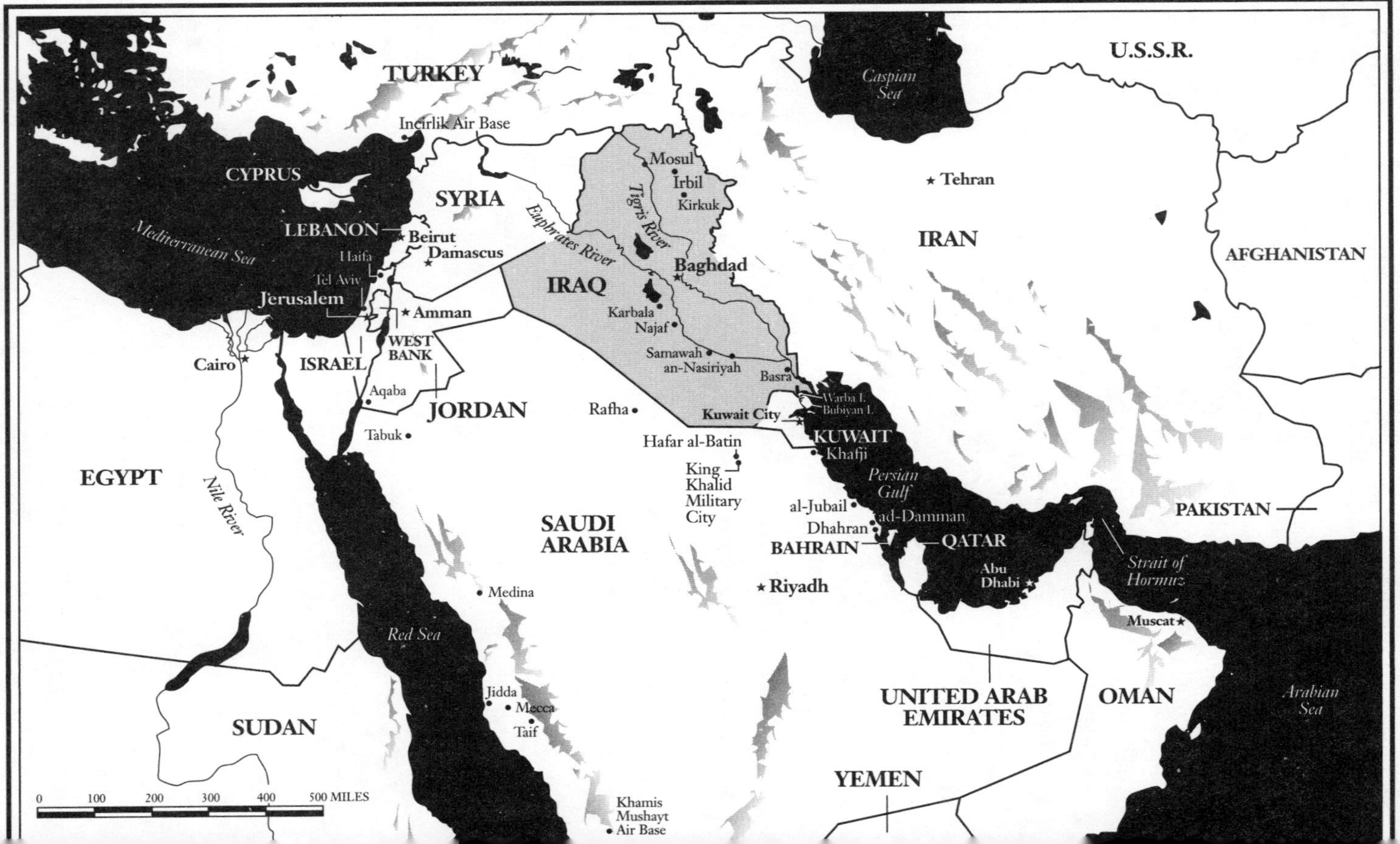

U.S.S.R.
Caspian Sea
TURKEY
Incirlik Air Base
CYPRUS
Mosul
Irbil
Kirkuk
Tehran
SYRIA
Tigris River
Euphrates River
Mediterranean Sea
LEBANON
Beirut
Damascus
IRAN
AFGHANISTAN
Haifa
Tel Aviv
Baghdad
IRAQ
Jerusalem
Amman
Karbala
Najaf
WEST BANK
Samawah
an-Nasiriyah
Cairo
ISRAEL
Basra
Aqaba
Warba I.
Bubiyan I.
JORDAN
Rafha
Kuwait City
Tabuk
KUWAIT
Hafar al-Batin
Khafji
King Khalid Military City
EGYPT
Persian Gulf
Nile River
al-Jubail
ad-Damman
SAUDI ARABIA
PAKISTAN
Dhahran
QATAR
BAHRAIN
Strait of Hormuz
Abu Dhabi
Riyadh
Medina
Muscat
Red Sea
UNITED ARAB EMIRATES
OMAN
Arabian Sea
Jidda
Mecca
Taif
SUDAN
YEMEN
0 100 200 300 400 500 MILES
Khamis Mushayt Air Base

U.S. NEWS & WORLD REPORT

TRIUMPH WITHOUT VICTORY

The History of the
Persian Gulf War

TIMES BOOKS

RANDOM HOUSE

All rights reserved under International and Pan-American
Copyright Conventions. Published in the United States by Times
Books, a division of Random House, Inc., New York, and
simultaneously in Canada by Random House of Canada Limited,
Toronto.

This work was originally published in hardcover by Times
Books, a division of Random House, Inc., in 1992.

Library of Congress Cataloging-in-Publication Data

Triumph without victory : the history of the Persian Gulf War /
U.S. News & World Report.
p.   cm.
Originally published: 1st ed., c1992. With new pref.
Includes index.
ISBN 0-8129-2145-3 (pbk.)
1. Persian Gulf War, 1991.   I. U.S. News & World Report, Inc.
DS79.72.T75 1993
956.704'42—dc20   92-35768

Manufactured in the United States of America
9 8 7 6 5 4 3 2
First Edition

To the victims

"Any soldier worth his salt should be antiwar."

—GENERAL H. NORMAN SCHWARZKOPF

CONTENTS

Contents

LIST OF MAPS

List of Maps

PREFACE
TO THE
PAPERBACK EDITION

SINCE *Triumph Without Victory* was first published in January 1992, little has come to light that, in our judgment, requires us to revise in any substantial way our portrait of why and how America went to war in the Persian Gulf. It is true, of course, that since the war's end the world has learned a great many more details of the strategic, political, and military origins of this extraordinary conflict. We now understand better, for example, just how the Reagan and Bush administrations' gestures of friendship—some would say appeasement—in the decade preceding the Iraqi dictator's seizure of Kuwait may have encouraged Saddam Hussein's geopolitical ambitions. And, thanks to United Nations inspectors and Iraqi defectors, we now have chilling evidence of just how close Iraq's Western-educated scientists—aided by American money and technology—came to building nuclear weapons. What is perhaps less well understood is how the Gulf War turned out not to be the jewel in the crown of George Bush's forlorn re-election campaign, but became a nagging reminder of misbegotten diplomacy abroad and political opportunism at home.

The public euphoria and patriotic fervor that swept across an America exultant in the wake of the Gulf War faded even more swiftly than the yellow ribbons that had adorned the trees, bushes, and fences of Desert Shield and Desert Storm. The streets had barely been swept clean of the debris from the last of the ticker-tape victory parades when America awoke with a gigantic hangover. Persistent recession and growing unemployment gnawed at the country's vitals. The President who could do no wrong suddenly could do nothing right: George Bush, bewildered, watched his approval rating in the polls plunge from just over 90 percent during the war to only 35 percent as he began seeking re-election.

Those who had hoped that the humiliation of Iraq's military forces on the battlefields and the chokehold of international economic sanctions would somehow lead to the ouster of Saddam Hussein were sorely disappointed. Two years of sanctions have visited extreme hardship on millions of ordinary Iraqi citizens, but the turmoil and suffering seem only to have strengthened Saddam Hussein's grip on the levers of political power. Although his military strength today is only 40 percent of what it was before the Gulf War, that smaller force has been efficiently reorganized and is as busy as ever killing Kurds in the north and Shiites in the south, while a vastly larger and more heavily armed presidential guard of 7,500 troops keeps the peace in Baghdad and Saddam in power.

The messy end of the Gulf War has become even messier. A nagging scandal continues to prompt an important question: How much credit can George Bush properly claim for leading the allies to war against the very enemy that he and his aides helped to strengthen and nurture? Investigators in Congress and the media have revealed that Bush, both as Ronald Reagan's Vice President and later as President himself, was so determined to make a friend of Saddam Hussein that in the years before the Gulf War he intervened personally to ease the way for American companies to sell sophisticated technology and equipment with obvious military implications to Iraq. And Bush, we learned, championed the granting of some $5 billion in American commodity loans to Iraq, despite warnings from the experts that Saddam Hussein would never repay the loans and that he was diverting some of the money to the purchase of weapons—weapons that would soon be turned against America and its allies.

That soft line on Iraq had been the Reagan-Bush policy for more than a decade, dating from Iraq's eight-year war with the Ayatollah Khomeini's revolutionary Iran. American policymakers took to heart an old Arab proverb—the enemy of my enemy is my friend—and steadfastly ignored evidence that their new friend, Saddam Hussein, was doing such unfriendly and uncivilized things as using poison gas on Iraqi Kurds, destabilizing Lebanon with extensive weapons shipments, providing money and material support to some of the world's most dangerous terrorists, and pursuing his own obsessive quest for nuclear weapons, poison gas, and missile delivery systems for both. Washington also apparently hoped that befriending Saddam would help to moderate his behavior and bring Iraq into the family of peaceful nations.

As late as the end of October 1989, when international bankers and the U.S. Agriculture Department had already cut off all lending to Iraq because it had fallen so far behind in repayments, Secretary of State James Baker telephoned Agriculture Secretary Clayton Yeutter to complain that Agriculture was balking at loaning another $1 billion to Iraq that President Bush personally wanted to see go through. Baker was operating under a top-secret National Security Directive signed by the President just days before that specifically ordered even closer U.S. ties with Iraq. Yeutter caved in. Baker aides then pressured the last holdouts, the Treasury Department and the Federal Reserve, into approving the loan "on foreign policy grounds." By early 1990, Iraq had spent the first $500 million installment of that loan and was demanding that the rest be paid.

Assistant Secretary of State John H. Kelly declared in a March 1990 letter to his bosses that "we have explicit presidential authority for expanding trade with Iraq," and urged them to put the heat on federal nuclear regulatory officials who were refusing to clear exports of sensitive technology to Iraq. In May 1990, faced with growing evidence of fraud and mismanagement and diversion of funds for military purchases, the Agriculture Department again suspended the Commodity Credit Corporation loans to Iraq, and again was pressured by White House and State Department policymakers to release the last $500 million. As late as July 9, 1990, three weeks before the invasion of Kuwait, April Glaspie, the U.S. Ambassador to Iraq, was assuring Iraqi officials in Baghdad that the Bush administration was doing everything it could to get the second installment released to them. Such prewar policy decisions cost the American taxpayers an estimated $2 billion in loans Iraq will never repay, let alone the cost of the war that followed.

Since the original publication of this book a number of writings have appeared that deal with one or another aspect of the Gulf War. If we were to rewrite the book now we would want to enlarge or compress sections to take account of them; but we have found no reason to reconsider the general interpretation of the book or the treatment of significant details in it. The book is therefore reissued with only a few corrections of technical errors that slipped by in proofreading.

In *Triumph Without Victory*, we have tried to combine battlefield-level detail with command-level history. We believe we have written a sweeping and authoritative chronicle of war and politics that will stand the test of time and further revelation. We invite our readers to judge.

—PETER CARY
BRIAN DUFFY
JOSEPH L. GALLOWAY
U.S. News & World Report
Washington, D.C.
January 16, 1993

PREFACE

IT WAS the global village's first prime-time war, a see-it-now, hear-it-now electronic spectacular that filled the world's television screens with images of battle in the age of the microprocessor and the memory chip. However, despite the technological wizardry of the Persian Gulf War, to the armies of correspondents who descended on the Middle East in search of history in the making, the story they had anticipated finding often seemed as elusive as a desert mirage. Instead of the human story of men in battle, they found the banality of antiseptic official briefings and the shackles of restrictive press pools. Instead of high drama, they found a war that was all but invisible.

The result was that for all the torrent of words that poured out of reporters in Saudi Arabia, Iraq, and Kuwait before and during the war and in its melancholy aftermath, the complete story of why and how it happened has gone largely untold. In a sense, most of what should have been the first drafts of history have turned out to be incomplete and, in some instances, misleading.

In this book, the editors and staff of *U.S. News & World Report* have sought to connect the dots and fill in the blanks that until now have hobbled our understanding of what by any measure was an extraordinary episode in modern warfare and diplomacy in the closing years of the twentieth century. Given the fresh perspective offered even by a limited passage of time, this book is less a journalistic reprise of familiar events than a true second draft of history, a richly textured, comprehensive, and authoritative narrative of the Gulf conflict. It is based on a harvest of primary sources and original reporting. It endeavors to tell the story of the genesis of the conflict with Iraq, of the diplomacy that resulted in the creation of an extraordinary coalition of nations, and of the planning and prosecution of the war itself.

Long before the first American warplanes appeared in the dark skies over Baghdad, *U.S. News* realized that if war did break out, censorship, secrecy, and logistical complications would prevent the complete story from being pieced together until after the fighting ended. Nevertheless, starting in November 1990, we began the process that has now resulted in this book. With the cease-fire in March 1991 came a relaxation of the wartime secrecy that had so constrained the press while the fighting was in progress. To retrace the origins of the conflict we looked to the public record—the myriad speeches, resolutions, and acts that preceded the outbreak of war. We then revisited the intricate diplomacy that created the mass alliance of nations that agreed to oust Saddam Hussein's forces from Kuwait. Our correspondents crisscrossed the Middle East, Europe, the Soviet Union, and the United States, interviewing most of the key protagonists who participated in the decision to go to war against Iraq. Statesmen and soldiers alike were interviewed. In all, more than 600 interviews were conducted all over the world in the months after the war ended. A trove of new information was unearthed as a result, some of it startling. Among the key revelations:

· On the final night of the war—within hours of the cease-fire—two U.S. Air Force bombers dropped specially designed 5000-pound bombs on a command bunker fifteen miles northwest of Baghdad in a deliberate attempt to kill Saddam Hussein. This, despite President Bush's repeated denials that Washington had ever targeted Saddam Hussein personally.

· The decision to seek United Nations involvement was part of a larger, more cynical strategy of the Bush administration to circumvent Congress, to bypass the constitutional authority of Congress—and only Congress—to declare war.

· During the very week King Fahd was persuaded to invite U.S. troops to Saudi Arabia in order to defend his monarchy from the alleged threat of an Iraqi invasion, a U.S. intelligence officer who was secretly sent to Kuwait by General H. Norman Schwarzkopf reported that Iraq had begun withdrawing its crack Republican Guard divisions from Kuwait entirely.

· Several weeks before Baghdad was bombed on January 17, 1991, U.S. intelligence agents successfully inserted a computer virus into Iraq's military computers. It was designed to disable much of Baghdad's air-defense system.

· Because of the Pentagon's policy of refusing to permit reporters to freely accompany troops into battle, the four-day ground war was both sanitized and largely invisible. For the first time, the actual battles as they unfolded are recounted in vivid detail, based on scores of postwar interviews with the combatants themselves.

· The largest tank battle of the war, which has previously gone unreported in any detail, conclusively demonstrated the superiority of American tanks and fighting doctrine over that of the Soviets. As a whole, the battles of the ground war showed that American military doctrine—emphasizing speed, maneuverability, and deception—clearly outclassed the plodding tactics of the Iraqis, who had been taught by their Soviet advisers.

· The size of the Iraqi army in the Kuwait Theater of Operations was probably much smaller than claimed by the Pentagon. On the eve of the war, Iraq may have had as few as 300,000 soldiers there—less than half of the 623,000 claimed by General Schwarzkopf, or the 540,000 estimated by the Pentagon.

· Iraqi military casualties were probably far lower than the 100,000 calculated by the Defense Intelligence Agency. In fact, the number of Iraqi soldiers killed in action may have been as small as 8,000. However, civilian casualties may have been as high as 70,000.

· In official reports, the Pentagon has admitted that of the 148 American servicemen and women who perished on the battlefield in the Gulf conflict, 35—or 24 percent of the total killed in action—were victims of friendly fire. But that figure does not tell the whole story. Eleven more Americans were killed when unexploded Allied munitions blew up, raising the rate of casualties caused by friendly action to 31 percent. Another 18 American soldiers were killed by unexploded enemy ordnance. Most soldiers said that the thousands of unexploded mines and bomblets they encountered, especially friendly ordnance, were more dangerous than enemy fire.

A word about sources. As is standard in journalism, we began this project with the information already available in the public record. We then supplemented and, where necessary, corrected the record. Our sources for the events described in this book have been the people directly involved. In a great many instances, we have been fortunate enough to acquire multiple accounts of certain events. In the best of circumstances, these sources were able to provide us with accounts derived from notes taken either during or immediately after certain events took place. Throughout, we have maintained a simple rule. If the speaker recalled a quotation directly and we could corroborate it with someone else present at the time, we have used the account verbatim. These are represented in the book between quotation marks. Similarly with accounts derived from the notes of those present, where we could corroborate the statement with either the speaker or someone else present, we used the statement verbatim. Where corroboration was not possible for certain statements—either by the speaker, by other participants, or by a notetaker—we have considered it appropriate to use such statements, but they are not represented as verbatim, or direct quotations. They appear without quotation marks.

In an undertaking of this size and scope there are inevitably more people to thank than time and space allow. Still, we would be remiss if we didn't take this opportunity to thank at least some of the many people who contributed to this book.

President Bush took time from his hectic schedule to respond at length to a number of questions about critical points in the conflict with Iraq. We should especially like to thank Secretary of Defense Dick Cheney, Chairman of the Joint Chiefs of Staff General Colin Powell, National Security Adviser Brent Scowcroft, and White House Press Secretary Marlin Fitzwater. In addition, General Carl Vuono, former Army chief of staff, and General Gordon Sullivan, current Army chief of staff, provided valuable insight on Pentagon planning for both Operation Desert Shield and Operation Desert Storm.

We were fortunate to have had the firsthand accounts of Egyptian President Hosni Mubarak, Turkish President Turgut Ozal, Israeli Prime Minister Yitzhak Shamir, and dozens of senior diplomatic and military officials in more than a dozen countries. We also interviewed and reinterviewed ranking officials at the United Nations, the site of some of the most important diplomatic actions throughout the Gulf crisis. Wherever possible, we have identified these officials by name and title; where they have insisted on anonymity we have taken pains to describe the nature of their involvement in these events as precisely as possible.

Our efforts to interview many people in Iraq, particularly those in decision-making positions within the government, were limited. Despite our reporting efforts in Iraq before, during, and after the war, the government of Saddam Hussein made it virtually impossible to shed meaningful light on its calculations before the invasion of Kuwait, during the ensuing conflict, and in the aftermath of the war. In conversations after the war, many ordinary Iraqis expressed anger and disenchantment with Saddam's rule; others with the violence inflicted on them by the American-led coalition. The Iraqi people remain fearful of retribution, and without exception, they insisted on anonymity. Their sentiments are reflected here, but the motivations of their government, at least for now, remain shrouded in secrecy.

Our deepest gratitude goes to the literally hundreds of officers and soldiers who fought in Desert Storm and later shared their stories with us. We sought out those who actually planned the key operations, fought the key battles, and flew the key missions. We recorded their thoughts while memories were still fresh. We should like to especially thank Army Captain H. R. McMaster, commanding officer of Eagle Troop, 2nd Armored Cavalry Regiment, for providing a copy of his personal journal of the battle of 73 Easting; Major General Barry McCaffrey, commanding general of the 24th Infantry Division (Mechanized); and all the officers and troops of Victory Division who permitted *U.S. News* reporter Joseph L. Galloway to accompany them on their charge to the Euphrates River. Among the division's officers who were particularly helpful were: Major General Terry Scott, Colonel John Van Alstyne, Colonel John LeMoyne, Colonel Paul Kern, Colonel Ted Reid, Colonel Burt Tackaberry, Lieutenant Colonel Tom Leney, Lieutenant Colonel B. J. Craddock, Lieutenant Colonel Chuck Ware, Major Tom O'Brien, and Major Ben Freakley.

Thanks also to the officers and men of the 1st Cavalry Division, the First Team, who were generous with their time and hospitality both in the Saudi desert and at their home base in Fort Hood, Texas, among them Major General John Tilelli and Colonels Leon LaPorte, Randolph W. House, and John Sylvester. We are grateful, too, for the hospitality in the Saudi desert of Lieutenant Colonel Walter "Skip" Sharp, commander of the 1st Squadron 7th Cavalry, and Sergeant Major Gilbert Ortiz. In addition, Captain Chris Blockhus, Lieutenant Blake Wallace, Command Sergeant Major Bob

Wilson, and Sergeant First Class Andy Anderson gave generously of their time under the trying conditions of war. Lieutenant Colonel John F. Feeley, Jr., interrupted his first leave in a long, busy year to describe the heretofore untold story of his experiences behind enemy lines in Kuwait and Iraq.

Special thanks also to Captain Gerald S. Davie, commander of Alpha Troop in the 4th Squadron, 7th Cavalry, for recounting the story of his troop's encounter with the Tawakalna division of the Republican Guard; to Colonel Roger Scearce, chief of Host Nation Activities for Lieutenant General William G. Pagonis, for the many hours spent explaining the logistics of Operations Desert Shield and Desert Storm; to Colonel James McDonough, director of the School for Advanced Military Studies at the U.S. Army Command and General Staff College; and to Lieutenant Colonel Larry Icenogle, public affairs officer at the U.S. Army War College.

In the 1st Infantry Division, we are grateful to Lieutenant Colonel Pat Ritter and his men of 1st Battalion, 34th Armor, as well as the commanders and men of the 2nd Battalion, 34th Armor, and 5th Battalion, 16th Infantry, for spending many hours describing the battle of Norfolk. In the 1st Armored Division, thanks to Colonel Montgomery Miegs, Lieutenant Colonel Keith Alexander, Lieutenant Colonel Thomas Strauss, and Major Kenneth Fugett, for explaining their operations. In the 2nd Marine Division, thanks to Major General William Keys, commanding general; Colonel Ron Richard, operations officer; Colonel Larry Livingston, commanding officer of the 6th Marine Regiment; and the men of 2nd Battalion, 2nd Marines, of 1st Battalion, 8th Marines, of 1st Battalion, 6th Marines, and of the 2nd Light Armored Infantry Battalion who painstakingly relived their days of battle.

In the 37th Tactical Fighter Wing (F-117A), Tonapah Air Force Base, Nevada, thanks to Colonel Alton Whitley, wing commander; Lieutenant Colonel Barry Horne, operations officer for 415th Tactical Fighter Squadron; Major K. D. Boyer, chief of mission planning; and Captain Marcel Kerdavid and Sergeant Bobby Shelton, public affairs. In the 416th Bombardment Wing (B-52), Griffiss Air Force Base, New York, thanks to Captain David Ross, First Lieutenant Raffaele Moretti, Major Ian MacInnis, and Captain Tom Jacobson.

We would also like to express our appreciation to Captain Russell Handy of the 1st Tactical Fighter Wing at Langley, Virginia, and to Specialist Michael Moore of the Public Affairs Office of the 82nd Airborne

Division at Fort Bragg, North Carolina. In addition, special thanks are due to Major Mike Worden of the 23rd Tactical Fighter Wing for sharing his combat experiences.

For assistance with reporting the story of the GBU-28 bomb constructed to kill Saddam Hussein, we thank Major Dick Wright, the GBU-28 program manager; Dr. Mario (Mike) Caluda, deputy director of the laboratory and senior scientist and engineer at Eglin Air Force Base, Florida; Captain Ernie Staubs, the financial officer of the GBU-28 program; and Dr. John Collins, who was responsible for all computer-simulated testing of the special bomb.

Finally, a special acknowledgment to General H. Norman Schwarzkopf, who twice met privately with *U.S. News* early in the air war, answered all of our questions fully and frankly, and then graciously opened doors for our reporter throughout his command. "I know what you want," the general said. "And I'm going to give it to you." He was as good as his word.

Our conversations with these soldiers served to remind us that the true cost of war, whether endured by victor or vanquished, is always to be measured in shattered human lives. To them all: our profoundest gratitude.

Almost by definition, newsmagazine journalism is a collective effort. But when the reporting assignments range from the recesses of the Kremlin to the major capitals of Western Europe to the inner sanctums of official Washington and from dozens of critical points in the Middle East to scores of military posts in the United States and overseas, the number of correspondents, writers, editors, and designers who necessarily become involved multiplies astronomically. Moreover, when a book of this scope and seriousness must be produced on a forced-march schedule, the dimensions of the tasks at hand mandate the involvement of a still larger staff.

The principal reporting was conducted by Peter Cary, Brian Duffy, Joseph L. Galloway, Kenneth T. Walsh, Bruce B. Auster, Mike Tharp, Elizabeth Pezzullo, Susan Pastrick, Douglas Pasternak, Jeff Trimble, David Makovsky, and Richard Z. Chesnoff. Other correspondents involved in the global reporting effort were Matthew Cooper, Steven V. Roberts, David Lawday, Robin Knight, Warren Bass, Louise Lief, Carla Anne Robbins, Jim Impoco, Linda Robinson, Henry Trewhitt, and Serge Trifkevic.

The portfolio of distinguished maps that grace this book was created by cartographer David Merrill working under the direction of *U.S. News* art director Rob Covey. The magazine's library staff, directed by Kathleen L. Trimble and Kate V. Forsyth, provided valuable background and source material. They were assisted by Kathleen Flynn, Anne Bradley, Brent Short, Carol Hook, Penny E. Pendergrass, Lee Neville, and Toni Ritucci Vanover. Ron Wilson devoted time and effort above and beyond his normal duties in speedily transcribing the many interviews that were tape-recorded for this project. Kathleen Phillips directed her corps of indefatigable fact-checkers, including Tim Kennelly, Rick Newman, and John Sellers, who performed the critical service of helping reporters and writers avoid error. Whatever mistakes that may have found their way into the book are in no way their responsibility.

The idea for this book first germinated in the fertile mind of Harold Evans, president and publisher of Random House and former editorial director of *U.S. News*. It was nurtured into reality by Editor-in-Chief Mortimer B. Zuckerman, who was convinced that *U.S. News* could build on its record of reporting prior to and during the war to produce a first-rate history. Led by co-editors Michael Ruby and Merrill McLoughlin, the magazine won admiration for its weekly coverage of the Gulf War just as the staff was beginning the prodigious efforts that went into the reporting, writing, and editing of this book. At *U.S. News,* the overall project was managed by Mel Elfin. Kathy Bushkin, Susan Riker, and Priscilla Totten provided invaluable assistance in keeping the project on track.

In Steve Wasserman, editorial director of Times Books, we were blessed with both a gifted editor and an understanding friend. He gave shape, tone, and direction to what in the beginning often seemed an inchoate concept. His colleagues at Times Books and at Random House are to be thanked as well, especially Peter Osnos, publisher of Times Books, Marge Anderson, Nancy Inglis, Mitchell Ivers, Annik La Farge, Naomi Osnos, and Della Smith. In addition, the meticulous and supremely intelligent contribution of Trent Duffy, copy editor *extraordinaire,* is gratefully acknowledged.

Above all, this book is the result of the talent, energy, and dedication of Brian Duffy, its editor and principal writer, and Peter Cary, who reported and wrote the chapters on the war. As the project developed, it was decided that the book, unlike the weekly magazine, would benefit by having a single authorial voice. Working with mountains of reportage and background materials and on a schedule that often required them to write thousands of words a day, Duffy and Cary, with the invaluable assistance of their colleagues, were able to write a book that combines a dramatic journalistic sensibility with the rigorous demands of modern historical scholarship. In this sense, *Triumph Without Victory* is perhaps a new form of historiography, and we hope that it may help to set a new standard for newsmagazine journalism.

—THE EDITORS
U.S. News & World Report
Washington, D.C.
January 16, 1992

TRIUMPH WITHOUT VICTORY

PROLOGUE

A T 7:19 P.M. on February 27, 1991, less than twelve hours before hostilities against Saddam Hussein's army would end, a U.S. Air Force C-141 transport plane skidded to an abrupt halt at a darkened military air base deep in the Saudi Arabian desert. Even before the enormous cargo plane came to a stop, an Air Force weapons specialist, clutching classified videotapes in his hand, was scrambling from his seat toward the forward exit. On the tarmac, a jeeplike vehicle known as a Humvee waited to carry the specialist to a high-security hangar.

In the cargo hold of the C-141 aircraft were two highly unusual bombs, the product of a crash Air Force development program that had begun on January 19, just after the start of the Allied air campaign against Iraq. President George Bush had repeatedly insisted that the commanders of Operation Desert Storm were not out to "get" Saddam Hussein, that it was not U.S. policy to personally target leaders of other countries for assassination—indeed, as Bush well knew, it was against the law. But these two bombs, the first two of their kind ever to be manufactured, had been designed expressly to accomplish that end. They were built to penetrate the deepest, most hardened bunkers where Saddam and his most trusted aides were likely to be hiding. Previous air strikes on the hardened bunker at one of Saddam's several palaces in central Baghdad had, in the words of Lieutenant General Charles Horner, the overall air commander for Operation Desert Storm, only "dug up the rose garden." The new bomb was dubbed by the workers who built it as the "bunker-buster." Its official name was Glide Bomb Unit-28 (GBU-28).

U.S. intelligence officials had never had precise information about the whereabouts of Saddam Hussein. But on January 16, the first night of the air campaign, Lieutenant General Horner and his senior air staff had made certain that the pilots of the F-117A Stealth fighters, the only aircraft assigned to bomb targets in central Baghdad, delivered their 2000-pound bombs onto every known Iraqi command bunker. The generals of the U.S. Central Command, which planned and prosecuted Desert Storm, had hoped and expected that Saddam Hussein would be inside. "Now that would not have targeted Saddam Hussein," Horner said. "But it targeted key command-and-control facilities, and he should have been present for duty."

The two special bombs were built to give George Bush a final shot at Saddam Hussein. Longer and harder than the 2000-pound ordnance delivered by the Stealth fighters earlier in the war, these particular bombs weighed in at 5,000 pounds. They were designed to pierce hardened concrete and explode only when they had penetrated to a certain depth, where the cavernous command center was likely to be.

Although President Bush and his generals have asserted that they did not target Saddam Hussein, numerous officials familiar with the classified development and production program that had resulted in the manufacture of these new bombs insisted that the bombs were expressly designed for precisely that purpose. A senior Central Command officer who was intimately involved in the decision on where (and on whom) to target the two new bombs said there was no question about their purpose: "I would be lying to you if I told you they weren't meant for Saddam." Indeed, so obvious was the intended purpose of the new bombs to the people involved in their production that the machinists who sculpted the bomb casings at the Watervliet Arsenal in upstate New York had chalked the words "the Saddamizer" on the first bomb they produced.

As early as October 1990, Al Weimorts, the chief engineer of the Armament Directorate at Eglin Air Force Base in Florida, had begun work on a new, deep-penetrating bomb. "We understand quite well what it takes to penetrate targets—what it takes in terms of fusing, survivability, explosives, and all," Weimorts said. Ideally, a deep-penetrating bomb should be long, slender, and heavy, and be dropped from a high altitude. The United

States would need to establish total air superiority to get a clean shot over the intended target. "Just three days into the air war, it looked to me like that was possible," Weimorts said. "So I sketched out something that we could carry high, and it would be heavy." Weimorts called it the GBU-28 (GBU was a standard acronym employed by the Air Force, meaning "glide-bomb unit"). The GBU-28, Weimorts said, was a much bigger, more destructive version of the 2000-pound GBU-27 that the F-117A Stealth fighter pilots had dropped on targets in downtown Baghdad. Yet it would need to have the same outside diameter as the GBU-27, so that it could be mounted readily on the F-111F bomb rack. That meant constructing a longer bomb, and, at this late stage, it would have to be a crash program. Making such a bomb from scratch would take years, but someone thought of using old hardened-steel howitzer barrels. After a search, several of the 7500-pound barrels were found at the Watervliet Arsenal near Albany, New York.

On Friday, January 25, technicians at Watervliet had begun working around the clock on the supersecret project. At 9 A.M. on Monday, February 11, a team of officers from the Air Force's Tactical Air Warfare Center's Armament and Avionics deputate had begun formulating operational concepts for the GBU-28. Six days later, the first bomb body had been delivered from Watervliet to Eglin Air Force Base. It measured nearly nineteen feet long. It was so big that Eglin's normal bomb-loading equipment was useless. The big bomb had to be lowered by crane into a deep hole in the back of the high-explosive research and development facility at Eglin and packed with explosives by hand. The bomb had then been subjected to ten days of operational and computer testing. On February 26, two such bombs had finally been loaded on the C-141 transport plane and shipped to Saudi Arabia.

Knowledgeable officials said the target chosen to be attacked on February 27 represented their best guess as to where Saddam Hussein might be. The hardened bunker was located at the al-Taji Air Base approximately fifteen miles northwest of Baghdad. Several stories deep and some 200 feet square, the bunker had been struck three times by 2000-pound bombs delivered by F-117A Stealth fighters, suffering little apparent damage. U.S. Air Force and intelligence officials believed that Saddam might well assume that on the final night of the war it was his safest refuge.

The pilots who were chosen to deliver the bombs were given this information. Within minutes after landing in the C-141 transport plane, the

Air Force weapons officer, who was from the 431st Test and Evaluation Squadron at McClellan Air Force Base, was briefing two other weapons officers and two F-111F pilots from the 48th Tactical Fighter Wing, giving them the details of arming, releasing, and aiming the bomb. Outside the briefing room, technicians had loaded one GBU-28 under one of the F-111F's wings, loading an MK-84 2000-pound bomb under the other in order to try to balance the aircraft. Even then, the aircraft tilted to one side. The other F-111F was similarly loaded. The pilots would have to guide the bunker-buster bombs onto their targets with their laser-guidance controls.

Their briefing completed, the two pilots and their weapons officers climbed into their cockpits as their crew chiefs completed hasty preflight checks. The two big bombers roared off into the night. Several hours later over Baghdad, the first F-111F flew over the Iraqi bunker, and the weapons officer released the four lanyards that secured the GBU-28 to the bomb rack. Right behind the first F-111F, the second pilot crossed the target and released his big bomb. With their laser controls, the two F-111F weapons officers guided the bombs directly onto the target area, a small section of the bunker's roof immediately around an air duct. One after the other, the 5000-pound bombs crashed through the roof. Several seconds later, smoke began billowing from the six entranceways to the underground facility. The bunker, finally, had been destroyed. It would take another several hours, however, before U.S. officials discovered that Saddam Hussein had not been inside.

It was almost as if the use of the big new bomb was a metaphor for the war and its conclusion, many senior Pentagon officials later said. The bombs had been rushed into production, from drawing board to completion in a matter of weeks. That was many times faster than the normal production schedule for any previous Pentagon weapon. The bomb performed exactly as its inventors wished. It was a technological triumph. But the attempt to kill the Iraqi leader had failed. It had ended, like the entire conflict, in a hollow victory.

CHAPTER I

SADDAM INVADES KUWAIT

FROM INSIDE their air-conditioned apartments, behind the thick plate glass designed to shut out the killing heat, the percussions sounded muffled at first to the residents of Kuwait City. Some said the explosions began an hour before sunrise, others even earlier. All agreed the noise came out of the north.

About an hour after the first explosions, at 5:30 A.M., a pale sun rose above the horizon and the heat began to shimmer just above the desert floor. Some forty minutes later, with near parade-ground precision, soldiers swept through the capital of the tiny oil-rich emirate. The date was August 2, 1990. The invasion of Kuwait had begun.

At 6 A.M., Ibrahim Boukhumssen awoke, stretched, and turned on the radio. He was greeted with the terse announcement that Iraqi armored units had crossed the border into Kuwait. He was not surprised; nearly everyone had known for days about the Iraqi units poised across the border. Like most Kuwaitis, however, Boukhumssen was convinced that if the Iraqis did come south, they would do so to capture the Rumaila oil field and maybe a small island or two in the Gulf, areas of long-standing dispute between the two countries. But the news was different—and more alarming. Iraqi soldiers, with their tanks, attack helicopters, and jet fighters, were expected to enter Kuwait City within minutes. Boukhumssen threw on his clothes, got in his car, and drove into the center of Kuwait City. When he switched on the car radio, he heard a voice with a pronounced Iraqi accent: "There is a revolution in Kuwait. The palace is occupied. The emir has escaped."

Boukhumssen's heart jumped. He was among a growing number of young Kuwaitis who had hoped to urge more democratic measures on the Sabah family, who had ruled Kuwait for more than two hundred years. With Iraqis shooting Kuwaitis in the street, however, the very independence of his country—much less its internal political arrangement—was in peril. Later, back at home, Boukhumssen saw that nearly everyone was awake. People stood on the sidewalks in tight knots, talking intensely. Their anxiety and uncertainty were palpable.

By 6:30 A.M., the gold souk had been looted, and a Palestinian businessman had seen an Iraqi tank smashing into the display window of an expensive downtown department store. But by and large the Iraqi soldiers appeared to be maintaining a strict discipline. They clearly had been given explicit orders. Some buildings the soldiers stormed right past; others were to be occupied; still others, like the Foreign Ministry, were destroyed.

The Kuwaitis nevertheless mounted a spirited resistance. Shortly after 6:30, the fight had concentrated around Sheik Jaber al-Ahmed al-Sabah's opulent Dasman Palace. The emir himself had fled in a royal limousine minutes earlier, south across the border to Saudi Arabia. Despite his absence, many of the emir's palace guard took up defensive positions. In the firefight that ensued, the emir's younger brother, Sheik Fahd al-Ahmed al-Sabah, was mortally wounded. Some Kuwaiti fighter pilots managed to get to their French-built Mirage jets at al-Jaber airfield, south of the capital, and they began strafing the Iraqi troops besieging Dasman Palace and the Defense Ministry. Elsewhere downtown, in the high rises and the more expensive detached homes arrayed along the harbor and the waters of the Persian Gulf, the distant percussions were replaced by the staccato of machine-gun and small-arms fire, punctuated by the deep bass of Iraqi bazookas.

Downtown the fight was intense. Caryle Murphy, a *Washington Post* reporter who was the only American journalist in the emirate, had a bird's-eye view of the invasion from her seventh-floor room in the Kuwait International Hotel, just a few blocks away from the palace. A diplomat told Murphy he had seen Iraqi soldiers dragging fallen comrades across a street near Dasman Palace under withering fire from Kuwaiti soldiers. There were long bursts of heavy machine-gun fire, and the explosions of mortars echoed from the walls of buildings across the littered thoroughfares. (Murphy would later win a Pulitzer Prize for her courageous reporting, smuggling dispatches out through friends and acquaintances before she finally fled, disguised, to Saudi Arabia.) As Murphy watched, artillery shells exploded at the base of the emirate's distinctive water towers, just across from the palace and down the street from the American embassy. Within minutes, thick columns of brown smoke were billowing into the pale blue sky. In the center of the city's business district, armored personnel carriers filled with Iraqi troops crunched through the streets, flanked by Soviet-built T-72 tanks. Iraq's forces had reached the very heart of the emirate.

In another room at the same hotel, another American, U.S. Army Major John F. Feeley, Jr., was also awakened by the sound of explosions. A graduate of West Point, Feeley resembled a stereotypical California surfer. Tanned, with blond hair and sculpted good looks, he had a passion for open-water sailing. He was also possessed of other, more intellectual, passions. Feeley had a master's degree from the University of California at Berkeley in Chinese and Japanese studies. He had returned to West Point as a professor of Chinese history and gone on to the Armed Forces Staff College at Norfolk, Virginia, and then to the Pentagon's National Training Center in Fort Irwin, California, where he was an instructor in tank warfare. In July 1989, he was at Fort Irwin wondering where he would be posted next.

"Beirut," he was told.

Feeley was flabbergasted. Was it because of his desert-warfare training at Fort Irwin?

No, the Pentagon deskman told him, it was because "you're a Mideastern specialist." The man said he had the records right there in front of him on the computer screen.

"I guess the computer had burped," Feeley said. "Instead of coming up with the designator Foxtrot, for Far East[ern specialist], it came up with Golf, which is Mideastern specialist. So I became a Mideastern specialist." He never made it to Beirut, though; instead, Feeley was assigned to the staff of General H. Norman Schwarzkopf at the headquarters of the U.S. Central Command, just outside Tampa, Florida.

On July 28, 1990, under orders from Schwarzkopf, Feeley arrived in Kuwait City carrying a briefcase crammed with classified intelligence documents. His mission: to brief W. Nathaniel Howell, the American ambassador, on the threat to Kuwait from Iraq. Feeley was also to brief senior Kuwaiti officials. Just before 4 A.M. on August 2, having gotten off the phone with his colleagues in Florida just three hours earlier, Feeley was jolted awake. "Explosions," he would later remember. "I looked out my window and saw flashes across the horizon. It was like lightning, except it was coming from the wrong direction. It was coming from the ground up."

Following instructions he had left with them earlier, the Marine guards at the U.S. embassy telephoned Feeley minutes later to confirm the invasion. Feeley shaved quickly and ran up the street from the hotel to the embassy. For the next several weeks, at considerable personal risk, Feeley and members of the embassy's defense attaché's staff roamed the streets of Kuwait City, using walkie-talkies to keep in touch with Americans throughout the country, gathering reports of Iraqi troop movements, and checking those against what other sources had reported. "We set up a little war room of our own inside the embassy," Feeley later recalled. From there, he would report to General Schwarzkopf in Tampa. Schwarzkopf thought so highly of Major Feeley's reports that he would later award him the Legion of Merit, the Pentagon's second highest award for meritorious service, which is usually reserved for colonels and generals. For more than a month after the invasion, Feeley would remain inside Kuwait. He was Schwarzkopf's "Deep Throat."

As the sun climbed higher into the summer sky, a sense of stunned disbelief seemed to climb with it. By now, Iraqi soldiers were going house to house in some neighborhoods, checking for Kuwaiti soldiers and government officials. All other citizens were instructed to return to their homes and stay indoors.

Many Kuwaitis had never expected an invasion, despite the smoke, the soldiers, the shelling, and the edgy days of worry about reports of Iraqi forces massing on the border just sixty miles north of the capital. Almost no one imagined that the invading troops were the spearhead of a much larger force.

Saddam Hussein had reviewed the invasion plans for the last time the evening before and had given his commanders their final orders. He had left nothing to chance. Advance Iraqi scout units had crossed the border well before midnight in jeeps and armored personnel carriers. The first

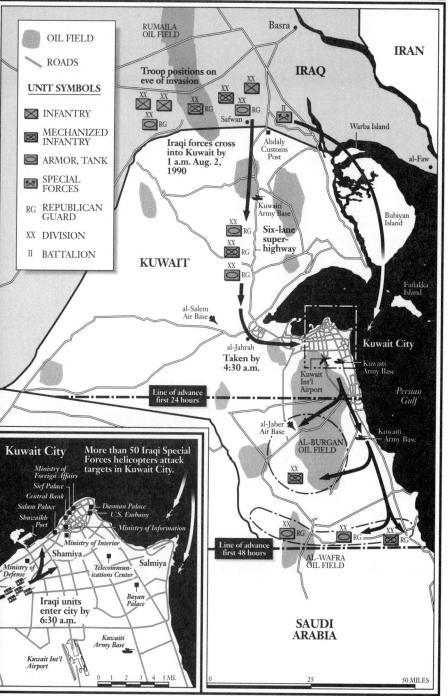

DAVID S. MERRILL

INVASION ROUTE OF IRAQI FORCES ON
AUGUST 2 AND 3, 1990

tanks and artillery crossed the border just two hours later at the customs post of Abdaly, where the six-lane superhighway from Basra flowed into Kuwait. All across the ragged frontier east to the port town of Umm Qasr on the Persian Gulf, tanks, armored personnel carriers, and trucks were moving south at the same time.

The Iraqis did not even have to face the small force normally in position north of Kuwait City. Kuwait's three brigades, all ground units, were ordinarily deployed north, south, and west of the emirate's capital. The brigade deployed to the north was the weakest, with an officer corps comprised largely of Kuwaiti shopkeepers. To the south and out of harm's way was the royal brigade, the one that participated in parades. All three brigades had some supporting anti-tank battalions, but none was a match for any of the units Saddam could throw at them. As it turned out, however, this small force was not available for the defense of the emirate. On July 28, the brigades' commanding officers notified their troops that they would be given unscheduled leave. Incredibly, with tensions as high as they were with Iraq, the Kuwaitis were leaving the door to the emirate's capital unlocked and unguarded. U.S. officials who spoke with senior Kuwaiti military officials before the invasion said the leave was granted so that the three brigades would not be seen by Saddam as a provocation. According to one Pentagon official, "The decision among the Kuwaitis, was 'We do not want to irritate him any more than he needs to be.'"

Saddam's invasion force exceeded 100,000 men. Most were from his eight divisions of the Republican Guard, the elite force created by the Iraqi leader toward the end of his war against Iran. It was the Republican Guard that reversed the Iranian tide of victory in that bloody eight-year quagmire, and Saddam made sure they were well paid and better fed than his regular troops. Loyal and well trained, they were said to be extraordinary fighters. Despite the resistance thrown up by Kuwaiti soldiers and a gaggle of palace guards, the emirate never stood a chance against Saddam's elite forces.

At 8:25 A.M., three Iraqi jets flew low over the fight raging around Dasman Palace. Some Iraqi soldiers lay dead in the street, but even more Kuwaitis were falling. Kuwaiti policemen had joined the fighting downtown, in several instances engaging Iraqi soldiers in furious hand-to-hand combat. In front of the American embassy, Kuwaiti National Guard units were confused about what they should do. "They thought that a lot of the Iraqis were Saudis coming up to help," Major Feeley said. "So they had to be told several times, 'No, no, no.' " Feeley and the embassy's Marine guards grabbed pencils and paper and drew the Iraqi military insignia for the Kuwaitis. The Republican Guard insignia was a triangle, and each division had its own emblem inside. The Americans told the Kuwaitis to shoot anyone wearing that insignia on his shoulder. The Kuwaitis quickly caught on. After the T-72 tanks that had been in front of the embassy left to engage the Kuwaiti resistance elsewhere, several Republican Guard officers approached the Kuwaiti National Guard troops. The Kuwaitis checked and double-checked the insignia on the soldiers' uniforms. Then they grabbed the men, took them to the nearby beach, and shot them, leaving their bodies in the sand. "Well, now we are in big trouble," Feeley remembered thinking.

By 10 A.M., any Kuwaiti up on a rooftop could see three large fires burning. One was at Dasman Palace. The second was at Bayan Palace, another of the emir's showplaces. The third was near the Defense Ministry. More Iraqi heavy attack helicopters swarmed through the humid air. Just before 10:30 A.M., fifteen Iraqi helicopters roared over Dasman Palace. By noon the Kuwaiti resistance around the palace was all but finished. Two hours later only the odd gunshot rent the air.

It did not take long for the bad news to sink in. Late in the day, an elderly man watched as several youths fired shotguns at an Iraqi tank. The rounds bounced off. "It's all over," the man mumbled. "It's all over."

The audacity of Saddam Hussein's blitzkrieg, his determination to swallow the whole of Kuwait, stunned most observers. In the weeks and months prior to the invasion, there had been signs of the Iraqi dictator's intentions. But with the collapse of communism in Eastern Europe, few wanted to look for new troubles. Besides, Saddam had recently ended eight bloody years of war with Iran. His country was deep in debt and his exhausted people longed for peace.

Once Moscow's most important client in the region, Saddam had forged a de facto alliance with the West over the course of the past decade. From the moment of Islamic fundamentalism's victory in neighboring Iran, Saddam Hussein and his secular Baath Party were seen as a counterweight to the radical Shiites in Tehran. Despite the fact that Iraq harbored and financed some of the world's most deadly terrorist organizations, and despite its own public policies, in 1983 the Reagan administration took

Baghdad off its list of state sponsors of terrorism. In the following years, diplomatic ties were restored. Shortly after that, hundreds of millions of dollars in U.S. subsidies for big grain purchases were approved. Iraq would soon become the largest importer of American rice and the fifth biggest importer of American wheat.

In addition, Iraq purchased a host of high-tech hardware, much of it with potential military applications. Because of this "dual-use" potential, some goods and equipment were expressly forbidden to be exported to Iraq. These included precursors to lethal chemical mixtures that could be used in bombs, high-speed centrifuges that could be used to enrich uranium to weapons-grade quality, and a handful of advanced computer software programs. But as Saddam's purchasing agents found ways to buy what they wanted, Washington preferred to look the other way. At the urging of Lieutenant Colonel Oliver North, the White House even slipped Baghdad satellite intelligence data on the disposition of Iranian troops. The Iraqis, in return, provided intelligence on Palestinian terror groups; but, according to experts, the material was "useless junk." Only a handful of officials at the Pentagon protested.

Washington, nonetheless, was persuaded that it could work with Baghdad. In October 1989, President George Bush signed a presidential directive outlining U.S. policy toward Iraq. Despite concern about Saddam's continued human-rights abuses among his own people, Washington intended to pursue "normal relations" with Baghdad. Quiet diplomacy was thought to be the best way to achieve stability in the volatile, oil-rich Gulf. On January 17, 1990, Bush reaffirmed the administration's desire to seek expanded trade with Iraq, as well as more guarantees from the U.S. Export-Import Bank, which would also help improve relations with Baghdad. All this was in America's national interest, said the President. Secretary of State James A. Baker III also urged more credits for Iraq. The diplomats who worked for him were instructed that while Iraq should be dealt with sternly on questions relating to its human-rights abuses, on all other matters Saddam was to be encouraged that he had a friend in Washington. It was a policy of deliberate opportunism. "We knew what he was, he wasn't an altar boy," said a senior administration official. "We thought, rightly or wrongly, that it was better to engage than not."

In mid-February 1990, John H. Kelly, the assistant secretary of state for Near Eastern and South Asian affairs, visited Baghdad to talk with Saddam. Kelly would later be criticized by some for failing to anticipate the drift of events in the Gulf and for shunting the blame for the failure of American diplomacy onto his ambassador in Baghdad, April Glaspie. Others thought that much of the criticism was unfair. Widely respected within the foreign service, which he joined in 1964, Kelly had served as ambassador to Lebanon from 1986 through 1988, and he had been known as a man with a nose for trouble. During the Reagan administration, for example, Kelly had given an early warning to Secretary of State George Shultz on some of the pitfalls of foreign-policy issues. In the Bush administration, however, despite his elevation to the post of assistant secretary, Kelly appeared to lack the authority of past assistant secretaries of state.

This state of affairs was partly the result of how George Bush and his inner circle preferred to operate. Bush would typically consult a handful of key advisers before making important decisions; government bureaucracies, even at the most senior levels, were largely irrelevant. Kelly's influence also had been circumscribed by Secretary of State Baker's insistence on appointing Dennis Ross to head the State Department's influential Policy Planning Staff. A highly regarded young expert on both Middle East and Soviet affairs, Ross had been a Bush adviser during the 1988 presidential campaign. He had been expected to stay at the White House with Bush, perhaps even as the President's adviser for national security affairs, but in the event he had turned it down. When Baker insisted on Ross coming to State, Ross made it clear that he, and not the assistant secretaries, would run the Soviet and Middle East portfolios.

In his three-hour conversation with Saddam Hussein in Baghdad, Kelly recalled, "We spent the biggest part of the time discussing superpower relations. He reacted to talk about Afghanistan, the Arab-Israeli dispute, how we saw the future of the Soviet Union. He was an intense personality—not a trace of a sense of humor. He told me the Soviet Union was finished as a regional power." Saddam went on to say that, now that the United States was the lone superpower, it had five years to resolve the Arab-Israeli conflict. Kelly reflected later that classified American intelligence estimates had indicated that five years was about how long it would take Iraq to develop weapons of mass destruction.

Less than a week after Kelly's return to Washington, Saddam Hussein flew from Baghdad to Amman. The occasion was the first anniversary of the Gulf Cooperation Council, a regional common market comprised of, among others, Egypt, Iraq, Jordan, and North Yemen. Jordan's King Hussein had laid on a lavish welcome. Between speeches there was considerable pomp. Despite the king's generous hospitality, the gathering broke up a day earlier than expected.

While President Hosni Mubarak of Egypt and others publicly cited the press of business at home as the reason for their premature departure, their aides and advisers privately mentioned the Iraqi leader's strident address to the council. In the world according to Saddam, the unraveling of communism in Eastern Europe and Mikhail Gorbachev's desperate plight in Moscow meant that the world was suddenly left with a single superpower. Saddam's explanation surprised his fellow Arab leaders. The United States, Saddam said, "with its known capitalist approach and its imperialist policy . . . will continue to depart from the restrictions that govern the rest of the world." With the retreat of their Soviet protector, Arabs would be in greater jeopardy than ever; Israel could be expected to embark on "new stupidities." Moreover, "the country that will have the greatest influence in the region through the Arabian Gulf and its oil will maintain its superiority as a superpower without an equal to compete with it. This means that if the Gulf people, along with all Arabs, are not careful, the Arabian Gulf will be governed by the U.S. will. If the Arabs are not alerted and the weakness persists, the situation could develop to the extent desired by the United States; that is, it would fix the amount of oil and gas produced in each country and sold to this or that country in the world."

At the Central Intelligence Agency, experts in the Office of Near East and South Asia Analysis noted the speech. Over at the White House, Peter Rodman, a former aide to Henry Kissinger and perhaps the most experienced Middle East hand on the National Security Council staff, was sufficiently alarmed by Saddam's rhetoric that he sent a memo to his boss, Brent Scowcroft, President Bush's adviser for national security affairs. In his spacious office on the sixth floor of the State Department in Foggy Bottom, John Kelly was also bothered by the speech. Beyond worry, however, there would be no response from official Washington.

Within the State Department's Policy Planning Staff, there was some unease about America's Iraq policy. Two junior aides, Stephen Grummon and Rick Herrmann, had written papers early in 1990 questioning the administration's policy. One paper, titled "Containing Iraq," had gone to Dennis Ross, who thought it had merit. But his attention was elsewhere. U.S.-Soviet relations were paramount. The reunification of Germany was proceeding more rapidly than anyone had imagined. Iraq, despite the signs of trouble, would just have to wait.

On April 2, 1990, Saddam announced that Iraq possessed chemical weapons. "By God," he declared, "we will make the fire eat up half of Israel if it tries to do anything against Iraq." Many Arabs thrilled to the sentiment. Jordan's *al-Ra'i* newspaper said Saddam had spoken for the entire Arab world in the only language that Israel and "the remnants of colonialism" could understand. Saudi Arabia's leading daily, *Assharg al-Awsat,* hailed the Iraqi leader's "extremely firm" warning. And in Egypt, a senior analyst in a pro-government think tank summoned up references to the late Gamal Abdel Nasser and applauded Iraq's newly "credible deterrence" to the "real" American-Israeli threat. Among the Arab states, only Syria, Iraq's sworn enemy, kept silent.

Despite the hyperbole of his public pronouncements, Saddam had been at some pains to ease suspicions of untoward intentions. In late March, he had telephoned King Fahd in Riyadh, seeking to resolve any possible misunderstandings with the Saudis. If Fahd would send an emissary to Iraq, Saddam would send a message to President Bush, Prime Minister Margaret Thatcher, and other world leaders. The king dispatched Prince Bandar bin Sultan, the son of the third-ranking royal figure in the kingdom and one of his most trusted emissaries.

Bandar was a larger-than-life figure. With his elegant Savile Row suits, his vast ski chalet in Aspen, and his ready wit, Prince Bandar was at home almost anywhere on the globe. The Saudi ambassador to the United States, he was also employed by King Fahd almost as a diplomat without portfolio. On instructions from the king, Bandar flew from Washington to Baghdad on April 5. An Iraqi plane then took him to the mountain city of Mosul in northern Iraq. Saddam wanted Bandar to reassure Bush and Thatcher that he desired good relations with both of their countries. In addition, he said, he had no intention of attacking Israel.

On April 11, however, in the obscure English Midlands port of Teesport, British Customs agents seized eight huge steel tubes, each more than a yard in diameter. Made to precise specifications by the renowned Sheffield Forgemasters, the tubes were labeled on shipping documents and bills of lading as petroleum pipes. Their destination: Baghdad. In fact, they were components of an allegedly deadly supergun. Designed by an errant genius named Gerald Bull, the tubes were fabricated to slot into a gun barrel 130 feet long—a weapon that, if it worked, would be capable of delivering artillery shells, perhaps filled with Saddam's chemical weapons, nearly anywhere in the Middle East. Some experts have suggested that the tubes may have been intended to slot together to form a missile launcher for intelligence-gathering satellites.

The discovery of the tubes in Teesport prompted concern in capitals all over the world. Within days of the seizure, officials in Athens, Istanbul, London, and Naples seized more Iraqi-bound equipment: triggers that could be used for a nuclear weapon, a huge cylinder for an artillery system, and seventy-five tons of forged steel for the supergun assembly.

Just two weeks before Customs descended on the loading dock at Teesport, Gerald Bull was entering his apartment in the Brussels suburb of Uccle when someone fired two 7.65-millimeter slugs at point-blank range into the back of his skull. The $20,000 in cash in Bull's trouser pockets remained untouched. Bull's family charged that he had been murdered by agents of Israel's Mossad. Israel denied it. Bull was a man with many enemies, none of whom stepped forward to take credit for his murder.

In Washington, the debate over Iraq within the intelligence community intensified. Despite incomplete and often conflicting evidence, some senior analysts began urging a revision of the official estimate as to when Iraq was expected to build a nuclear weapon. Since Israeli jets had destroyed the Osirak nuclear reactor in 1981, the estimate had been in the range of five to ten years. Nearly a decade later, however, some analysts at the Pentagon, the CIA, and the State Department wanted the estimate revised to between three and five years; some even thought that Baghdad could develop such a weapon in only two or three years.

As always, the truth was hard to come by. The challenge for a good intelligence officer was to take bits and scraps of data, assess their meaning, and then try to come to some larger conclusion. With Iraq, this was especially difficult. Thanks to the extraordinary secrecy enforced by Saddam's totalitarian methods, no one outside Iraq knew for sure when he would have the bomb, but much of the available evidence strongly suggested it would be sooner rather than later.

When Robert Gates, the President's deputy adviser for national security affairs, convened a meeting of the so-called Deputies Committee on April 16, it was the first time in the Bush administration that Iraq received such high-level attention. The Deputies Committee comprised Gates and his counterparts from the State Department, the Pentagon, and the CIA. The deputies were not empowered to make decisions, but they wielded enormous influence. At the meeting, Robert Kimmitt, the under secretary of state for political affairs, argued that Iraq's behavior warranted cutting off credits from the U.S. Export-Import Bank. However, Kimmitt didn't like the idea of leaving this decision to Congress; if and when Iraq reformed, it should be the prerogative of the executive branch to rescind the decision. But the members of the committee could reach no consensus on rescinding Baghdad's Ex-Im credits, which had grown to nearly $250 million since 1987.

Meanwhile, on April 12, five senators, led by Robert Dole, the minority leader, had met with Saddam Hussein in Mosul. The senators delivered a letter condemning Iraq's quest for chemical and nuclear weapons. But, according to Iraqi officials who secretly taped the meeting and later released a transcript, Dole wanted to let Saddam know that not everyone in Washington was against him. Indeed, Dole's home state of Kansas had benefited from improved relations with Baghdad, shipping thousands of tons of wheat in taxpayer-subsidized deals. Dole added that a recent Voice of America editorial that compared Saddam to the recently deposed Romanian president, Nicolae Ceaușescu, had been a mistake. He told the Iraqi leader—incorrectly, as it turned out—that the editorial writer had been fired. (However, John Kelly did denounce the Voice of America broadcasts and instructed U.S. Information Agency officials to clear all Voice of America editorials in writing with the State Department.) Not to be outdone, Alan Simpson, Republican from Wyoming, told Saddam with some sympathy that his problems in Washington were due to a "haughty and pampered" press.

Just days after the senators returned to Washington, John Kelly was still eager to convince congressional skeptics of the basic wisdom of the administration's policy of "engagement" with Iraq. Under questioning by the Senate Foreign Relations Committee, Kelly conceded that Saddam's behavior since February had "raised new questions about Iraqi intentions in the region." But sanctions, he argued, would impede the United States from exerting any kind of "restraining influence" on Baghdad. This was the heart and soul of the administration's policy, a policy the administration believed was as tough as possible. "No one," said a senior official, "had a tougher policy toward Iraq than we did except Israel. If we had imposed sanctions, we would have been alone, and the sanctions, obviously, would have been meaningless. Even right before the invasion, we would have been alone. Not even the Kuwaitis were interested."

But what was so tough about the policy? While the State Department had used admirably strong language in condemning Saddam's human-rights abuses, in the year before the invasion of Kuwait, despite the growing indications of ominous designs emanating from Baghdad, there were no stern warnings issued from Washington. The taxpayer-subsidized flow of grain to Iraq continued unabated. Regardless of the concerns of a few experts in the Pentagon and the CIA, more and more high-tech goods with obvious military applications found their way onto ships and planes bound for Baghdad. It was certainly true, as administration officials pointed out, that only Israel had a tougher policy toward Iraq. But that was because much of the rest of the world was falling all over itself to buy Saddam's oil or to sell him weapons.

For their part, the Kuwaitis seemed remarkably unperturbed by Saddam's blustering right up until the invasion. On July 17, Saddam delivered a blistering speech commemorating the Baath Party's takeover of Iraq in 1968. Not all Arabs, Saddam said, had been behaving as brothers. The myth of the Arab world had been exposed time and again: the bitter rift between the impoverished have-nots in Egypt, Algeria, Iraq, and elsewhere, who scrambled to avoid starving, and the greedy haves in the Persian Gulf emirates and Saudi Arabia, who spent their millions on Mercedes-Benzes and gleaming mansions. Thwarted by Iraq's massive military force from working their will in the Gulf, the imperialists (America and Israel) had taken to economic sabotage, Saddam charged. Some Arabs, some of the greediest Gulf Arabs, had conspired with the imperialists.

In point of fact, Iraq had enormous debts. American intelligence officials estimated that the eight-year war with Iran had cost Iraq something on the order of $500 billion. Despite its vast oil revenues, Iraq had been left with a debt of some $80 billion, roughly 150 percent of its annual gross national product (America's own troublesome budget deficit at the time amounted to just over 5 percent of its GNP). Of the $80 billion Iraq owed, about $30 billion was due in short-term notes in Europe, the United States, and Japan. There was no way Saddam could pay it out of his own pocket.

The Iraqi leader knew this. And so, in his speech, he blamed deflated oil prices, and specifically those members of the Organization of Petroleum Exporting Countries (OPEC) who exceeded their production quotas. Artificially low oil prices, Saddam said, were a "poisoned dagger" thrust into

Iraq's back. The hands gripping the dagger were the United Arab Emirates (UAE) and the Sabah family in Kuwait.

The accusations could not have come as a total surprise to Kuwait and the UAE. The day before Saddam's speech, Tariq Aziz, his foreign minister, had sent a detailed list of grievances to the Arab League accusing Kuwait and the UAE of "direct aggression" against Iraq. Besides producing oil above and beyond the OPEC quotas, Kuwait was accused of slant-drilling into the Rumaila oil field, which straddled southern Iraq and northern Kuwait, thus stealing $2.5 billion of oil that rightfully belonged to Iraq. Sheik Jaber al-Sabah and his family advisers in Kuwait City refused to take the charges seriously. They still believed that Saddam could be bought off with a couple of billion dollars. "They weren't alarmed at all," said a senior State Department official. "They made no special requests of us."

Sheik Zaid ibn Sultan, the crafty old Bedouin who ruled the UAE, felt differently. Hours after hearing of Saddam's speech, he was on the phone to Washington requesting a joint military exercise. The Pentagon, ever alert for potential staging bases in or near the Gulf, leapt at the opportunity. By the next day UAE fighter pilots were conducting "short notice" maneuvers with aircraft from the Joint Task Force Middle East, under the command of Rear Admiral William Fogarty aboard the USS *LaSalle* in the Indian Ocean.

Sheik Zaid's caution would prove well founded. On July 20, just three days after Saddam's speech, a military attaché from a Western embassy was driving north in the Iraqi desert along the highway from Kuwait City to Basra when he came upon hundreds of Iraqi military vehicles. The attaché counted more than 2,000 trucks and armored personnel carriers. He was able to identify the troops and vehicles as belonging to two of Saddam's armored Republican Guard divisions. Four days later, Washington was able to flesh out this eyewitness report. On July 24, William Webster, the Director of Central Intelligence, and Richard Stoltz, his deputy director of operations at the CIA, went to the White House for an emergency meeting. They presented President Bush with the first hard evidence of Iraqi actions. American spy satellites had photographed the movement of the two Republican Guard armored divisions, the Hammurabi and the Medina Luminous, from their bases in central Iraq to within a few miles of the Kuwaiti border. These were the same two divisions the Western attaché had spotted. Analysts working overtime at the National Photographic

Interpretation Center in the Washington Navy Yard had confirmed the information, which had then been sent by courier to CIA headquarters at Langley, Virginia. There specialists in the agency's Office of Imagery Analysis had reconfirmed the data from the electronic-imaging satellites. With White House approval, the information was now disseminated to select embassies throughout Washington.

Suddenly, the Kuwaitis were jolted awake. OPEC ministers were scheduled to meet in Vienna on July 26 and 27. The stakes were high and they were obvious. At the moment, the benchmark Brent crude was selling for $14 a barrel on the international market. Saddam wanted $25. That kind of shock hadn't been felt since the early 1970s. It would be ruinous for economies the world over. Baghdad seemed bent on exercising a wildly disproportionate influence within the oil cartel. It was feared that Saddam could conceivably dictate price and production numbers for the entire Persian Gulf. If he one day grew tired of oil at $25 a barrel, he could simply have it raised more. Concern over Iraq grew in at least a dozen major capitals.

Among all of the heads of state made anxious by Iraq's actions prior to August 2, few expended more energy or took greater risks than Egypt's President Mubarak. The same day CIA Director Webster was showing President Bush the satellite photographs of Iraq's Republican Guard divisions massing near the Kuwaiti border, the Egyptian president secretly flew from Cairo to Baghdad to see if he could mediate the dispute between Saddam Hussein and the Sabah family. In Baghdad, Saddam was waiting with a car, a large British-made sedan with the steering wheel on the right. Saddam wanted to drive himself. Both leaders had a retinue of aides, but Saddam left them behind as they drove to one of the Iraqi leader's several presidential palaces. This one was not too far from the airport, Mubarak remembered, and it overlooked a lake.

At the palace, Saddam once again dismissed the aides. He and Mubarak met alone for three hours. "I kept trying to ask him, What are your intentions, why this tension between Iraq and Kuwait?" Mubarak pressed Saddam about the movement of Republican Guard divisions toward Kuwait. Saddam said it was nothing to be concerned about: It is a usual thing that we do. Mubarak would not be put off. "I asked him a clear, direct, definite question: 'Do you have any intentions for any combat action against Kuwait?' " Again, the Iraqi leader told him not to worry. The troop movements, Saddam said, were merely designed to throw a scare into the Sabahs: They are terrified, frightened, and that is enough.

After lunch, Saddam once again personally drove Mubarak back to the airport. Mubarak told Saddam that he intended to go to Kuwait next. He could carry a message directly to the Sabahs for the Iraqi leader. Saddam, Mubarak said, seemed only mildly interested, but he did have a request: Don't tell them now that I am not going to do anything. Let them be terrified for a while. Mubarak countered with a proposal: If Saddam would send a delegation to a third country, and if the Kuwaitis would send a delegation, it was possible the two sides could resolve their differences without violence. The third country need not be Egypt, Mubarak said. Why not the Saudi port city of Jidda? It would be a neutral location, and besides, it was one of the most tolerable places in the region during the broiling summer heat. Saddam agreed.

The plane trip from Baghdad to Kuwait City took only an hour and fifteen minutes, but by the time Mubarak landed, Iraqi Foreign Minister Aziz had already issued a press release on the meeting between the two presidents that morning. The two leaders had not discussed the issue of Kuwait, the statement said. The talks had been confined to matters affecting bilateral relations. An aide intercepted the statement from a wire-service machine on Mubarak's jet just as it began its final approach to Kuwait City. The aide handed the statement to the president. "I was very, very upset," Mubarak said. "So quickly like this. How could you explain it?"

At the airport, Sheik Jaber al-Sabah led the delegation meeting Mubarak. As soon as greetings had been exchanged, an aide to the emir presented a Mubarak adviser with a copy of the Aziz statement. Then Mubarak spoke. Ignore the Aziz business, he said. Saddam has no intention of invading, "but you should be very flexible so as to come to a conclusion on this problem." What did President Mubarak think the Iraqi leader wanted? "I laughed," Mubarak said, "and told them very frankly, 'It seems he needs some money.' "

The emir could not have been surprised. He had recently concluded a meeting with Saadoun Hammadi, Iraq's minister of state for foreign affairs and one of the few Shiites in Baghdad's predominantly Sunni regime. Hammadi had been blunt, even insulting, the emir told Mubarak. Give us $10 billion, he demanded, and give it to us now. The emir told Mubarak that even Kuwait could not come up with that kind of money that quickly.

Mubarak then proposed the meeting in Jidda. Kuwait would have to send a delegation if it wanted to reach any kind of agreement with Iraq and avoid trouble. The emir agreed. Mubarak then flew off to meet with King Fahd. The Saudi monarch also thought the Jidda meeting would help. The meeting was set for August 1. Elated, President Mubarak briefed the international press. Saddam, he told the reporters, "had no intention of invading Kuwait."

Just hours after CIA Director Webster had showed the pictures of Iraqi Republican Guard divisions to the President, Margaret Tutwiler, the State Department's official spokesperson, held a regular noon briefing for reporters. "We do not have any defense treaties with Kuwait," she said. "And there are no special defense or security commitments to Kuwait." However, "Iraq and others know that there is no place for coercion and intimidation in a civilized world."

On the following day, July 25, April Glaspie, the U.S. ambassador to Iraq, an Arabist and a respected professional with twenty-five years' service in the State Department, spent more than an hour in the Foreign Ministry, explaining the Tutwiler statement and insisting that a copy of it, and of the announcement of the military exercise with the UAE, be delivered to Saddam. Shortly thereafter, she was summoned to go to the president's office immediately. Finally, after more than two years in Baghdad, Glaspie was to meet the Iraqi leader; Saddam had always been unavailable to her. She had no time to request instructions from Washington.

With Foreign Minister Aziz present, Saddam Hussein received the American ambassador coolly. He had the Tutwiler statement and the announcement of the U.S.-UAE exercise in his hand. "I have summoned you today to hold comprehensive political discussions with you," the Iraqi leader said. "This is a message for President Bush." Saddam knew that Glaspie was scheduled to leave Baghdad for vacation in a day or two. The Iraqi leader seemed to want to use the American ambassador as a high-level courier to the White House. He proceeded to recount the history of U.S.-Iraqi relations, the break in ties between 1967 and 1984, the reestablishment of diplomatic ties during the war with Iran, America's desire for a sure and steady flow of oil, America's meddling in the Middle East, America's bias toward 3 million Israelis at the expense of 200 million Arabs, Iraq's readiness to fight any foe over a matter of honor, regardless of the cost, and America's inability to accept "10,000 dead in one battle."

Baghdad later released a transcript of this meeting, which Glaspie said was incomplete and misleading. Many months later, the State Department released some of the cables Glaspie sent afterward. The two accounts differ sharply. Senior State Department officials familiar with these events said that the Iraqi version was about three-quarters accurate. The State Department said it intends to comport with established diplomatic procedure regarding conversations between ambassadors and heads of state, and has refused to release Glaspie's own "memcon," the memo of conversation diplomats file as a matter of course with the State Department after meetings with officials of foreign governments.

As released to the Senate Foreign Relations Committee months later, Glaspie's cables provided some insight into American policy. "We can never excuse settlement of disputes by any but peaceful means," Glaspie told Saddam, according to one dispatch. She went on to raise the dispute with Kuwait "in the spirit of friendship, not in the spirit of confrontation." Such a statement was perfectly proper, of course, from an ambassador to the head of a nation with whom the United States still maintained diplomatic relations and whose stated policy was to seek improvement in those relations. What was perhaps less called for was Glaspie's stating to Saddam that "we have no opinion on the Arab-Arab conflicts, like your border disagreement with Kuwait."

Toward the end of Glaspie's meeting with Saddam, the Iraqi leader was called away for an urgent telephone call. It was Hosni Mubarak, he told her when he returned. The final arrangements for the meeting between the Iraqi and Kuwaiti delegations in Jidda were all set. It would be followed, Saddam said, by another meeting in Baghdad, "for deeper discussion. When we meet and we see that there is hope, then nothing will happen. But if we are unable to find a solution, then it will be natural that Iraq will not accept death, even though wisdom is above everything else. There, you have good news." Aziz added, "A journalistic exclusive."

On August 1, Sheik Saad al-Sabah, Kuwait's crown prince, met in Jidda, at the edge of the Red Sea, with Izzat Ibrahim, vice-chairman of Iraq's Revolutionary Command Council. Ibrahim was a lackey, albeit a well-connected one with a daughter married to Saddam's oldest son, Uday. Saddam had authorized him to deliver a blunt message, stand up from the negotiating table, and walk out of the room. In the event, Ibrahim added a wrinkle of his own, according to several participants in the meeting. "I am a sick man," he said, standing up and thereby indicating that the meeting had come to a close. "I am ill, I am going to Medina for prayers." Instead, he went straight back to Baghdad, arriving at 1 A.M. Iraq's T-72 tanks were already rolling south.

CHAPTER 2

WASHINGTON REACTS

S EVEN THOUSAND miles west of the Kuwaiti emir's beleaguered Dasman Palace, a secure telephone rang at 8:30 P.M. in the East Wing of the
White House. Brent Scowcroft, President Bush's national security adviser,
accepted the call. Because eight hours separated Kuwait City and its
daybreak invasion from the East Coast of the United States, the date in
Washington was still August 1.

Robert Kimmitt, the under secretary of state for political affairs and one
of James Baker's most trusted and influential aides, was on the line from his
home. A tall man with a ready smile, Kimmitt was overseeing most of the
day-to-day operations of the State Department while Secretary Baker was
in Irkutsk, in the Soviet Union, the next-to-last stop in a diplomatic
odyssey that had begun in Indonesia and would end in Ulan Bator, Mongolia.

Just before he telephoned the White House, Kimmitt's own phone had
rung with news from the State Department's round-the-clock operations
center. Ambassador Nathaniel Howell was reporting gunfire in the downtown area of the emirate's capital, the desk officer told Kimmitt. The
invasion of Kuwait, Kimmitt told Scowcroft and Bush in the brief telephone conversation, was now a matter of fact.

Richard Haass was with the President as well. Although his tumble of
sandy blond hair made him look younger than his thirty-nine years, Haass,

the National Security Council staff director for Middle East affairs, had considerable responsibilities. Bush wanted answers, and he wanted them immediately. (This was the same President, after all, who had phoned the CIA's twenty-four-hour operations center in the middle of the night during the U.S. invasion of Panama. Had Noriega been caught? A startled desk officer gulped once, then told the President that they were still working on it.)

What do our analysts say? he asked Scowcroft and Haass. What are our options? Perhaps, he wondered, an eleventh-hour warning "would help" Saddam understand the consequences of a full-scale invasion and occupation. No one knew. The President wanted action. "Find out exactly what's going on," he instructed his aides. "What's our intelligence community saying?"

From past briefings, the President knew that neither the CIA nor the Pentagon had spies inside Iraq. But Bush, as a former Director of Central Intelligence, also knew that even if they had, the chances were slim that any spy could answer the most difficult question in the espionage business, which had to do with intent, with predicting what someone would do at a given time. "At most," said a senior intelligence official who monitored the Iraqi invasion as closely as anyone, "a handful of people in Baghdad probably knew what Saddam was going to do before he did it." Said another Bush adviser: "The President was smart enough to know what you could expect in a situation like this and what you couldn't."

Despite the lack of intelligence, General H. Norman Schwarzkopf's war planners had anticipated the Iraqi threat two weeks before. At 4:30 P.M. on July 17, Schwarzkopf's Central Command headquarters at MacDill Air Force Base near Tampa, Florida, received a flash bulletin from the Defense Intelligence Agency (DIA) in Washington. This was the same day that Saddam had delivered his blast at Kuwait and the United Arab Emirates, accusing them of thrusting a "poisoned dagger" into the back of the Iraqi nation by exceeding the OPEC production quotas and driving oil prices down. It wasn't the speech itself that triggered the flash, however. Analysts working for Walter P. Lang, the DIA's intelligence officer for the Middle East and South Asia, had flagged a rather large movement of troops in southeastern Iraq. The Iraqi military maintained a large training facility in the area. Lang had concluded, according to numerous sources, that while the movement was probably a routine exercise, Schwarzkopf's Central Command ought to know about it.

Like other senior intelligence officers, Lang knew that in January 1990 General Schwarzkopf had ordered a computerized command post exercise (CPX) to explore possible responses to an Iraqi invasion of the Arabian peninsula. Its code name was Internal Look. A senior officer who was deeply involved in the running of the exercise said, "Schwarzkopf wanted to have an exercise to test the war plan as it was developing so that we could refine it." In deference to the sensibilities of the State Department, however, Iraq was never named in the exercise. In both of the two scenarios that were sketched out, Iraqi forces were labeled "red" and American forces were "blue." In the first scenario, Schwarzkopf's planners assumed a red invasion force of five to seven divisions. The second scenario assumed a red force of some thirteen divisions, flooding south through Kuwait and on to the vast Saudi oil fields. "Our dilemma," recalled one officer involved in the exercise, "was: How do you handle that kind of scenario? What would you do in order to get them stopped, or if you had to take it back? So that was the whole exercise."

The exercise was hardly the result of any special prescience on Schwarzkopf's part. Months before, the colonels and generals who peopled the cloistered halls and offices of the Pentagon's directorate for plans and operations had begun looking at precisely the same threat. Reporting to the Joint Chiefs of Staff, the directorate was headed by Lee Butler, a wiry Air Force three-star general. Sharp, intense, a man given to staring people squarely in the eyes when he listened to them, Butler was worried about Iraq's million-man army. If Saddam's intentions were truly peaceful, as he had insisted at the end of his war with Iran, why did he need such a large force?

When Colin Powell had been appointed chairman of the Joint Chiefs by President Bush in 1989, he had taken an immediate liking to Butler. In the "tank," the soundproofed, second-floor conference room in the Pentagon where the Joint Chiefs met, Butler would brief Powell and the others on "kill-coefficients" for exotic new Air Force weapons systems. Butler adored such euphemisms, loving the military jargon even more than most of his colleagues. According to several people present during these briefings, Powell would often interrupt Butler, smiling, but wanting clarification. What, exactly, would the new weapons system do to the enemy, the chairman wanted to know: "Lee, are you telling me it will kick his ass?" Powell was enormously pleased that Lee Butler and his staff were already focusing on the Iraqi threat.

Schwarzkopf's Internal Look computer exercise was based on a preexisting Pentagon plan, code-named 1002-90. "Ten-oh-two," as it was known, was purely a Central Command product. In coordination with the Joint Chiefs directorate for plans and operations, all of the ten military commands were required to have a host of contingency plans at the ready at all times. Each command was assigned a different series number. The Pacific Command, for instance, ran 5000 series plans. Central Command ran 1000 series.

Plan 1002-90 spelled out the biggest threat Schwarzkopf's soldiers would ever be called upon to deal with. Since the creation of the Central Command in 1983, Plan 1002 had been designed to counter any and all threats to the vast oil reserves of the Arabian peninsula. Plan 1002-82, for instance, was designed to deal with the threat of a Soviet invasion of Iran. Later plans anticipated that the threat would come from Iran itself. In 1002-90, and in Internal Look, Schwarzkopf had ordered that the focus shift to Iraq. But the plan had not been reviewed yet by the Pentagon's Joint Chiefs, or by a single policymaker. The 1990 version of 1002 provided a new concept for operations. But many of the details had not been worked out. The plan, for example, did not have an offensive component.

With Lang's flash on July 17, Schwarzkopf's planners began to scramble. Saddam's Republican Guard divisions in the Iraqi desert south of Basra were acting just like the red forces in the Internal Look computer exercise. In fact, the parallels were eerie. "It was something like Twilight Zone," said Major John Feeley, the Central Command intelligence officer who would be dispatched to Kuwait City just days before the invasion. In late July, Feeley's job had a certain schizophrenic quality to it. In the exercise, he was responsible for briefing on the actions of the red forces. He was also charged with keeping his bosses apprised of the movements of Iraq's troops in the desert. "I would brief the computer game," Feeley said, "and then I would turn right around and brief the real situation as it was developing. Sometimes I would get them mixed up. I had to keep thinking, Okay, the computer did that; no, *this* is the real thing over here!" At Central Command headquarters, some senior planners and intelligence analysts believed that Saddam's concentration of forces on the Kuwaiti border was a genuine harbinger of trouble. "You could tell it wasn't a training exercise," said one planner involved in the work after July 17. "Everything was there except his corps artillery."

Saddam's lack of artillery was seen by Schwarzkopf's planners as a dog that didn't bark. "If you looked at the Kuwaiti army," said one senior official, "you didn't need a whole lot of artillery to overthrow it. So there's probably some good reason why his artillery wasn't there. He didn't need it is the basic reason." The lack of artillery, in other words, didn't mean there would be no invasion. The Kuwaiti armed forces comprised only 50,000 men, 245 tanks, 430 armored personnel carriers, 72 pieces of artillery, 35 combat jets, and 18 armed helicopters.

The Central Command planners knew their views would receive a thorough hearing at the very highest level of the Pentagon. Months before Saddam Hussein began making belligerent noises in the Gulf, General Schwarzkopf had been scheduled to deliver his biannual briefing to the Joint Chiefs of Staff. Picking a date at random, someone had penciled Schwarzkopf in for August 1.

At the sylvan Langley campus that houses the five directorates of the Central Intelligence Agency, analysts monitoring the activities of Saddam Hussein through the summer of 1990 also believed that an invasion was likely. Winston Wiley, the head of the CIA's Persian Gulf division, had about three dozen analysts working for him. Half were assigned to monitor Iran and Iraq, the rest to the Arabian peninsula itself. Like Schwarzkopf's planners and intelligence specialists, Wiley's experts were predicting trouble.

Besides gathering information from spies, from satellites, and through other means, the CIA analyzed what the information meant and then attempted to predict what would happen next. The agency produced hundreds of Secret, Top Secret, and Classified papers every day. One of the most important was the National Intelligence Daily. The NID, as it was called, was delivered to senior policymakers and intelligence officials throughout the government. On July 19, the NID had carried a full-page report headlined "Baghdad Is Threatening Effective Sanctions Against UAE and Kuwait." The CIA analysts wrote, "If Baghdad believes its threats are not working, it will probably make threatening gestures along the Iraq-Kuwait border."

On July 24, the NID reported that "Iraq now has ample forces and supplies available for military operations [inside Kuwait]." The following day's NID was headlined "Iraq-Kuwait: Is Iraq Bluffing?" The report stated: "Kuwait has reduced the alert level of its military forces, and reporting suggests [that] Kuwait believes Iraq is only bluffing. The Kuwaitis are probably mistaken. . . . Unless Kuwait moves to meet Iraq's demands quickly, Saddam Hussein will step up the pressure." Despite the analysts' prescience, none of their intelligence provided definite clues to Saddam's intentions. Nevertheless, the photoanalysis specialists at the National Photographic Interpretation Center and at the CIA's own Office of Imagery Analysis had come up with enough data to worry some of the President's closest advisers. In addition to the movement of the Republican Guard's elite Hammurabi and Tawakalna divisions hard on the Kuwaiti border, by late July American spy satellites had also identified the heavily armored Medina Luminous division positioned on Kuwait's western flank. That division's T-72 tanks stretched in a line for miles. A fourth Republican Guard division, the Baghdad, was normally based in southeastern Iraq; the satellites now showed it farther south than usual. More ominously, the photos revealed pontoon-bridging equipment, as well as hundreds and hundreds of heavy tank carriers that would enable Saddam's heavy armored divisions to race far south before depositing the tanks in the sand to begin the real work of an invasion.

The purpose of all of this analytic effort, in the context of a bureaucracy as vast and complicated as that in engaged in protecting U.S. national security, was to bring the weight of its influence to bear on a very small number of people. In the administration of George Bush, this was an exceptionally small number of people indeed. On many issues—particularly those involving foreign policy, where aides said he felt especially surefooted—the President was his own adviser. When he wanted outside counsel, or if he wished merely to bounce an idea off someone, George Bush turned to a handful of his most senior aides. The most critical were the other members of the so-called Big Eight: Vice-President Dan Quayle, Secretary of State James Baker, Secretary of Defense Dick Cheney, Chairman of the Joint Chiefs of Staff General Colin Powell, National Security Adviser Brent Scowcroft, Deputy National Security Adviser Robert Gates, and Chief of Staff John Sununu. In addition, CIA Director William Webster was also an important participant in many critical meetings. The Big Eight dealt with the most pressing issues. Just below them, their deputies dealt with other concerns. Among the foreign-policy professionals at State, the Pentagon, and the CIA, the fear was that if it didn't make it to the deputies' level, the problem didn't really exist.

At 9:30 on the morning of August 1, exactly eleven hours before Bush took the call from Bob Kimmitt telling him of the Iraqi invasion, the deputies reviewed the past few days of the Iraq crisis in detail. In that session, Richard Kerr, the deputy director of the CIA, pointed out that the signals out of Baghdad were not reassuring. Just the day before, the Iraqi government newspaper *al-Jumhuriya* had boasted: "Iraq attends the Jidda meeting to regain its rights and not to hear new talk about 'fraternity' and 'solidarity,' which mean nothing."

As a young Soviet analyst, Kerr had been thrown cold into the tumult of the Cuban Missile Crisis. He had monitored many more crises overseas since then, and colleagues said he had a kind of sixth sense for the way such events moved and developed lives and energies of their own. To Kerr, everything coming out of Iraq smelled bad, and he told the deputies so in no uncertain terms. "Dick Kerr said the Iraqis were ready to move," recalled a participant in the meeting. "He said they would go." Gone were the "probablys" the CIA analysts had thought it wise to include during the past several weeks in the NID.

At the Pentagon, the same day the deputies were meeting around Secretary Baker's mahogany conference table, General Schwarzkopf had delivered his scheduled biannual briefing to the Joint Chiefs. There was a certain ritual to such briefings. As a matter of tradition, the briefer was given the hot seat at the middle of a long polished table, directly across from the chairman of the Joint Chiefs. On either side of the chairman, according to the protocol, sat the director of the Joint Staff and a senior assistant. The other service chiefs and their top aides ringed the table. More aides occupied the deep leather chairs along the walls.

A senior official present that morning recalled Schwarzkopf's presentation with some amazement: "Instead of giving a sort of generalized status of command of what his forces are and where they are and what his readiness problems are and whatnot, he came in with a very focused briefing on Iraqi military dispositions today, where the Republican Guards are. And he had satellite photography that [was only] a day or so old."

Frantically updating Plan 1002-90 and pulling some of the more useful elements from the Internal Look computer exercise, Schwarzkopf's planners had cobbled together a comprehensive response to Iraqi movement. "We had four immediate options, which we could have executed as a deterrent to show Saddam the U.S. was serious about its commitment in the

Persian Gulf," a Central Command planner said. The first was to redeploy the USS *Independence* carrier-battle group. The *Independence* had left San Diego in July after routine maintenance for another tour in the Indian Ocean. After Saddam's "poisoned dagger" speech on July 17, Baker and Kimmitt had argued that the Pentagon's chief of naval operations should order the *Independence* to the Persian Gulf. General Powell and Defense Secretary Cheney had resisted then; Schwarzkopf's planners now put the *Independence* option at the top of their list. At the moment, however, the carrier-battle group was still in the Strait of Malacca, 3,495 miles away. The second option was to move more B-52 bombers into the strategic U.S. base at Diego Garcia, 2,500 miles from Iraq in the Indian Ocean. The bombers, renowned for their "rolling thunder" raids in Vietnam, would be within striking distance of Kuwait. They could send a powerful signal. A third option was to move five of the maritime prepositioning ships out of Diego Garcia and into a holding pattern off Oman or even into the Persian Gulf. A squadron of five such ships would carry enough food and ammunition to supply the 16,500 troops of the 1st Marine Division for thirty days of combat. Moving them near the Gulf would be the first step needed to launch a counterinvasion of Kuwait from the sea. The fourth option was to move the F-15 jet fighters of the 1st Tactical Fighter Wing out of Langley Air Force Base near Norfolk, Virginia, over to Saudi Arabia.

The chiefs were not overwhelmed. What evidence was there that the Saudis would accept American F-15s? The presumption had to be that they would not. That left three options, two naval and one air. None, the chiefs thought, was very good. Schwarzkopf returned to his headquarters in Tampa that afternoon. For the first time in two weeks, his planners broke off early, quitting for the day at 3 P.M. For the moment, they thought, there was nothing more to be done.

Later that evening, after the call from Kimmitt to the President, the atmosphere changed dramatically. In the situation room in the White House basement, Scowcroft and Richard Haass were furiously working the phones. Scowcroft was able to reach nearly all of the rest of the Big Eight. At CIA headquarters in Langley, Deputy Director Kerr ordered Winston Wiley to his seventh-floor office and told him to set up an Iraq task force immediately. Within the hour, technicians were plugging computers into prewired sockets beneath the raised floor of the agency's Operations Center conference room. Ordinarily the conference room was used for staid meetings around a long polished table. While some technicians were moving the banks of secure phones and computers into the center, others were putting the table and chairs into storage, where they would remain for months. After double-checking with Kerr, CIA Director Webster confirmed the worst of the bad news by a videolink hookup to Scowcroft: A "massive invasion," he said, was now under way.

Jim Baker had learned of the invasion soon after it had been confirmed by the CIA. Baker and a clutch of senior aides were quartered on the second floor of a handsome guest house in the city of Irkutsk, a thriving metropolis of some 550,000 people in Soviet Asia just west of Lake Baikal. Baker was conferring with his opposite number, Soviet Foreign Minister Eduard A. Shevardnadze, when an aide from the State Department's Bureau of Diplomatic Security approached Margaret Tutwiler, Baker's confidant and chief spokesperson. Tutwiler was outside the guest house chatting with Jack Matlock, the American ambassador to Moscow, when the security officer gave her a hand-held radio. On the other end was an official from the State Department's command post, which had been established for the Baker visit to Irkutsk. Quickly, the officer read Tutwiler an urgent message from the State Department's twenty-four-hour operations center. The message stated that Kuwait had been invaded by a large number of Iraqi forces. Tutwiler wrote the message down quickly, and she and Matlock rushed inside to inform Baker. Baker relayed the news to Shevardnadze. That cannot be true, Shevardnadze said. He instructed a senior aide to check on the report immediately. Word soon came back that the report was true.

Shevardnadze told Baker that he needed to return immediately to Moscow to confer with Gorbachev and other members of the Supreme Soviet. Baker himself was scheduled to leave soon for Ulan Bator. The visit was of enormous significance to the Mongolians, and Baker was reluctant to cancel it. Instead, he instructed Dennis Ross and Robert Zoellick, two of his closest advisers, to go to Moscow aboard Shevardnadze's plane and begin talks with Soviet officials about how the two superpowers might issue a joint statement condemning the invasion by Iraq. Baker and Shevardnadze were both aware of how critical the Soviet response would be. Baker had worked assiduously to cultivate the Soviet foreign minister, and the two men had genuinely become friends. The relationship would be of utmost importance now.

. . .

Just before 10 P.M., an hour and a half after the call from Kimmitt to the President, the State Department received an urgent call from Ambassador Howell. The Kuwaitis, Howell told Kimmitt and John Kelly, were requesting American military assistance. Despite the fact that the United States had no defense treaty with Kuwait, and despite the fact that the Kuwaiti minister of foreign affairs had once boasted that "the people of this region are perfectly capable of preserving their own security and stability," senior officials at the White House, the State Department, and the Pentagon had begun to consider months before what might be done to defend Kuwait. The Kuwaitis, Howell noted, were insisting the Americans say nothing publicly should they decide to send tanks and soldiers into the emirate. It was a preposterous demand. Howell was told to inform the Sabah family that their request was wholly inappropriate.

About an hour later, Howell phoned back. The Kuwaitis, he said, would very much appreciate American military assistance, and upon reflection the Sabah family had decided that they would not object if the Americans announced their help publicly. By now, however, the request was more than a little late. Even as Kimmitt and Kelly listened to the report from Ambassador Howell, Sheik Jaber al-Sabah and Crown Prince Saad al-Sabah were already fleeing Kuwait in a royal limousine.

Kimmitt rang the switchboard at the U.S. Mission to the United Nations. Find the ambassador quickly, he instructed. Thomas Pickering, one of the most highly regarded members of the foreign service, was at that moment at New York's elegant Carlisle Hotel. The British envoy to the United Nations, Sir Crispen Tickell, was retiring from Her Majesty's diplomatic service to assume a teaching post at Cambridge. Pickering and his wife, Alice, were hosting an intimate farewell supper for Tickell and his wife, Penelope. Discreetly, the Carlisle's maître d' summoned the American ambassador to a private phone. The time was 10:10 P.M. Kimmitt was brief. The farewell dinner for Ambassador Tickell and his wife would just have to wait for another time.

Kimmitt then called Secretary Baker, who was now in Mongolia. They had discussed the role the United Nations might play in the Iraq-Kuwait dispute. Baker was insistent that the United Nations was of paramount importance. President Bush would come to use the United Nations as a critical element in his drive to push Iraqi forces out of Kuwait, but "the idea of using the U.N. as aggressively as we did was Baker's," a senior U.S. official said. "And it was resisted very strongly by our friends across the river [in the Pentagon]. And people in the White House objected." Kimmitt knew all about the objections. Early on, Powell worried that the United Nations would be of limited use, that it would hamper the President and his war planners just when they most needed the freedom to respond quickly and effectively. Among the Big Eight, Scowcroft, Gates, and Sununu shared these concerns, senior administration officials said. Despite the objections, Kimmitt and Baker plunged ahead.

Kimmitt next conferred with Scowcroft over the videolink. The President, Scowcroft said, also wanted the United Nations Security Council to denounce the Iraqis as soon as possible. Bush and Baker were convinced that such a denunciation by the council would send a strong, unambiguous message. But what if the Security Council would not cooperate? The Soviets were a big question, the Chinese even more so. Both could veto any U.S.-sponsored resolution. Then there were the nonaligned members. It was anyone's guess what they might do on such an issue.

Ambassador Pickering began working to convene an immediate emergency session. He phoned the Kuwaiti mission. An alert switchboard operator tracked down the Kuwaiti ambassador, Saud Nasir al-Sabah, at the posh Russian Tea Room, on West 57th Street near Carnegie Hall. It was now nearly four hours since the invasion of Kuwait had begun. The Kuwaiti envoy to the United Nations had heard nothing of it, however. It was left to Pickering to tell him. "I've got bad news," he told the Kuwaiti. Then he urged the envoy to get to the United Nations as quickly as possible. Pickering then set to work drafting language for point 1 of the resolution, condemning the Iraqi invasion of Kuwait. Point 2 demanded that Iraq withdraw its forces "immediately and unconditionally" to the positions they had occupied on August 1. (There would be considerable discussion on this point: rather than appear to take sides in the border dispute between Iraq and Kuwait by identifying a fixed point in either Iraqi or Kuwaiti territory, it was decided to specify a retreat to the pre–August 2 position of Saddam's forces.) Point 3 called for immediate and intensive negotiations between Iraq and Kuwait to resolve their outstanding differences over the border issue and the question of drilling in the Rumaila oil field. Point 4 was U.N. boilerplate: the Security Council would meet again, as and when necessary, to deal with events in the Gulf as they unfolded. Pickering finished the draft and reread it carefully. A secretary at the United Nations would later assign the document a number: Resolution 660.

In Washington, Brent Scowcroft used the videolink system in the White

House Situation Room to convene an emergency meeting of the Deputies Committee. It was not yet 11 P.M. Kimmitt informed the others about his call to Pickering and the now imminent meeting of the Security Council. Next, Dick Kerr stressed the need to freeze Iraqi and Kuwaiti assets. That would prevent Saddam from looting the Kuwaitis' bulging bank accounts across Europe and the United States. Estimates placed the Kuwaitis' total overseas investments somewhere near $100 billion. Some said it was considerably higher. Either way it was substantial. Kuwait profited more from such investments than from the revenue derived from the selling of their oil. The deputies also figured that Saddam would not hesitate to steal every last dollar.

The administration knew that Iraq used some of Manhattan's biggest banks to handle its financial affairs in the United States. What was not yet known, according to Treasury and CIA officials involved in the effort to locate Baghdad's assets, was that the same banks controlled the accounts for as many as fifty of Iraq's embassies around the world: payroll, construction and maintenance accounts, plus other funds that could have been diverted to more nefarious purposes.

In the coming weeks and months, Saddam would threaten to unleash terrorists on the nations arrayed against him. It did not strike many people as an empty threat. The Iraqi leader harbored some of the world's most dangerous thugs. But there would be no successful Iraqi-inspired acts of terror throughout the war. Some U.S. and Western intelligence officials believed the reason may have been the frozen assets. With his embassies' access to easy money blocked, Saddam's terrorists may have been unable to finance and mount a major attack abroad. There may simply have been no money for renting safe houses, setting up bank accounts, and buying weapons and explosives. Before and during the war, police and intelligence agencies would stop and detain a number of suspected Iraqi terrorists, but the most serious attempts at terrorist action occurred far from Washington, Paris, and London, in places like Manila and Jakarta.

The President had finally gone to bed. But at the Pentagon, no one was getting any sleep. Just after 2:30 A.M. on August 2, Lieutenant General Tom Kelly, the operations director for the Joint Chiefs of Staff, was handed a phone by an aide in the Crisis Situation Room. It was Colin Powell. Better tell Schwarzkopf to beat it back to Washington, he said. He was to be in Powell's office by 7 A.M. The general said he would be there.

At the White House, Scowcroft finally dozed off on the couch in his office around 4 A.M. Boyden Gray, the White House counsel, woke him just forty-five minutes later. The order freezing the assets of Iraq and Kuwait was ready for the President's signature. George Bush was a notoriously early riser, but 5 A.M. was early even by his standards. It didn't seem to matter. Scowcroft handed the President the papers. Bush signed them quickly.

An hour later, the Security Council agreed to condemn the invasion of Kuwait. The vote was 14–0; only Yemen failed to participate. The Yemeni envoy, it seemed, was nowhere to be found. General Schwarzkopf, meanwhile, was airborne, watching a weak sun peeking through thin clouds, still thirty minutes from Washington.

•

CHAPTER 3

THE PENTAGON MOBILIZES

I N T H E hours before dawn on August 2, not far from Washington, D.C., analysts at the National Security Agency, which eavesdropped on electronic communications around the globe, were already listening in on radio communications between Iraq's invading Republican Guard divisions consolidating their grip on Kuwait City. By the time General Schwarzkopf arrived at the Pentagon for his meeting with Colin Powell, the small staff of officers in the Pentagon's National Military Intelligence Center had overwhelming evidence of the size of the invasion force. They also had an idea of the quality of Saddam Hussein's battlefield commanders, though it would take some time to make sense of it. Schwarzkopf's war planners, who were most familiar with the capability of the Iraqi military, were the first to understand the early signs of ineptitude on the part of Saddam's generals. As impressive as the tank charge south from Iraq to Kuwait City was, the Iraqi generals had made a fundamental error once they arrived. "They did a really dumb-shit thing there," said a senior Central Command planner who reviewed all the intelligence data on the invasion and the subsequent disposition of Iraqi forces in Kuwait. "They got all bogged down trying to get through Kuwait City. Any armored-mechanized commander would tell you that the thing you don't want to do is go into a major metropolitan area with your armored forces, regardless of the reason. You just cut it off and let your trailing reserve infantry clear the thing; the armor keeps going." In fact, Saddam's Republican Guard tank battalions would spend nearly three days getting through Kuwait City. It would be a full four days before a force of eight divisions reached the Saudi border.

Plan 1002-90 had assumed that Saddam would target the big Saudi industrial belt that stretches from the port city of al-Jubail south along the Persian Gulf to ad-Dammam. Schwarzkopf's planners had figured Saddam's forces could invade Saudi Arabia in just eight to ten hours, hurtling down the four-lane coastal highway with just armed reconnaissance units. In the event, it took a lot longer, and his troops inexplicably halted at the Kuwaiti-Saudi border.

Why didn't Saddam go all the way into Saudi Arabia when he had the chance? What were his real intentions? After all, if he had wanted only to resolve the dispute over the Rumaila oil field in northern Kuwait, he could have simply occupied that corner of the emirate. To solve the historic problem of Iraqi access to the waters of the Gulf, Saddam might also have occupied Warba or Bubiyan, the tiny Kuwaiti islands at the far north end of the Gulf. In either case it would have been unlikely that President Bush would have responded with military force. Any United Nations condemnation almost certainly would have lacked the clout of the unanimity that Resolution 660 had engendered. Saddam could probably have kept his ill-gotten gains at little cost except some short-lived international criticism.

Perhaps Saddam really believed he could devour Kuwait and pay no penalty. Clearly, he believed America had no stomach for military action. The United States, he had told Ambassador Glaspie, was not the kind of nation that could absorb 10,000 casualties in an afternoon, as Iraq had done during the course of its war with Iran.

Perhaps it was less Vietnam and more Lebanon he had in mind. In 1983, President Ronald Reagan had sent the Marines to war-ravaged Beirut, declaring the mission to be in America's "vital interest." Then a fanatic in a dynamite-laden truck careened into a barracks near the international airport, killing 241 American soldiers, and suddenly the U.S. interest in Lebanon wasn't so vital after all. The Marines were withdrawn, and an Arab diplomat smirked that America "lacked the breath" to contend with the furies of the Middle East. Saddam, evidently, shared that view.

Now, America's mettle was once again being tested. The gauntlet had been thrown down. George Bush saw the invasion of Kuwait as a challenge to America's post–Cold War leadership. But was it worth risking American lives? Critics of the administration said that George Bush had woken up on third base and assumed he had hit a triple. Within the administration—especially in its early months, with the collapse of communism in Eastern Europe, the electoral triumph of Violeta Chamorro over the Sandinistas in Nicaragua and the quick-hit U.S. invasion of Panama—there was a kind of smug gloating about "how many pieces we're picking up around the board." With the exception of Panama, however, the new administration could claim little credit for such successes. There was a real sense, even among some insiders, that the Bush team had somehow had it too easy for too long. For several of the Joint Chiefs and their senior aides, the critical question was: What would the Bush team do when the going got tough?

From the start, Brent Scowcroft, who would become the most influential figure after Bush in guiding the administration's policy during the crisis, pushed hard for some kind of military force that could be deployed quickly. This issue would be put to General Colin Powell point-blank on August 2. And this time it would be the President himself asking the questions.

General Schwarzkopf entered the Pentagon through the electronically controlled doors of the building's river entrance shortly before 7 A.M. The security guard waved as he stepped through it, and Schwarzkopf turned right, down the Pentagon's E-Ring corridor to Powell's office. Visitors were sometimes surprised at the location. Just a few steps down the E-Ring from the river entrance, the office of the chairman of the Joint Chiefs of Staff was passed by thousands of people, military and civilians, every day. Some suggested that the chairman's office should have been on an upper floor, in a corner location. Powell, however, liked the spot he was in just fine. It saved his wasting time when darting in and out of the building for this or that meeting downtown. An aide greeted Schwarzkopf in Powell's outer office, and the chairman quickly ushered him into the inner sanctum, calling for coffee as he closed the door behind him. The regular meeting of President Bush and the other members of the National Security Council would begin less than an hour later, at 8 A.M.

Powell was worried. Plan 1002-90 may have been the basis of a decision to commit forces to the defense of Saudi Arabia, but it was hardly more than a sketchy outline of what those forces would do once they got there. It had no offensive component. And it never contemplated a coalition of forces. In the judgment of some of the staff of the Joint Chiefs, Plan 1002-90 was little more than a glorified Tip-fiddle. This was military shorthand for

Time-Phased Deployment List. Every military operation had a Tip-fiddle. But all it generally states is which units are to be deployed in what order. Powell felt 1002-90 was much more than a Tip-fiddle. "There was an operational plan," Powell said. "At least I had one in my mind, and Norm had one in his mind. And it was based on a plan. But every plan ultimately results in a glorified Tip-fiddle until we get the forces there." Plan 1002-90 may not have been all that the Pentagon brass desired. But it was all Powell and Schwarzkopf then had to bring to tell the President what his options were in dealing with the threat from Iraq. Still, it could have been worse. There could have been no Plan 1002-90. In fact, there could have been no Central Command at all.

Schwarzkopf's command was one of the ten American military commands. Some, like the recently created Transportation Command responsible for moving troops and matériel to crisis points around the globe, had a command staff but few other assigned personnel. Among the fighting commands, the Southern Command, headquartered in Panama, had a command structure and 8,000 troops. The Central Command, with no permanent troops assigned to it, was headquartered at a sprawling Florida air base half a world away from the threat it was intended to counter.

The Central Command's origins spoke volumes about the history of American policy toward the Persian Gulf and Southwest Asia. For years the policy had amounted to no policy at all. Washington had long been content to leave the Persian Gulf to the British. After the Second World War, Britain had maintained a substantial military presence in the region, and it had kept up its close political and economic ties to key oil-producing states. In 1968, however, London announced that it would be withdrawing its forces from the Gulf. Washington responded primarily with offers of arms sales to its "twin pillars" in the region, Iran and Saudi Arabia. The Pentagon, taking its cue from the policymakers' priorities, paid little more heed to the Gulf until the Carter administration. "One of the great untold stories of this whole thing," said a veteran Army official, referring to the Iraqi invasion of Kuwait and the American response, "is how much George Bush owes Jimmy Carter."

In the second week after Carter's inauguration, Zbigniew Brzezinski, the new national security adviser, initiated a complete review of American strategy toward every region of the world. It would result in a presidential review memorandum known as PRM-10, which concluded that "the United States is unprepared to respond to crises in the Third World, and specifically in the Persian Gulf."

Brzezinski recruited William Odom to be his military assistant on the National Security Council staff. As a graduate student at Columbia University, Odom had taken Brzezinski's course "The Dynamics of Soviet Politics." Having risen to lieutenant general over the course of a brilliant Army career, Odom was regarded as one of the Pentagon's most knowledgeable experts on the Soviet Union.

Odom wanted to use PRM-10 as a kind of club to force changes in the way the United States projected power in the world. Samuel Huntington, a classmate of Brzezinski's from Harvard whom Brzezinski had lured down to Washington to help direct the research and writing of PRM-10, agreed. In August 1977, Odom and Huntington produced a detailed analysis of specific problems in East-West relations. The most important part of the analysis was what Huntington called the crisis confrontation question: Where was the most likely point for a U.S.-Soviet confrontation? The answer: Iran and the Persian Gulf.

At the Pentagon, however, the Persian Gulf seemed to be no one's direct concern. Global maps showing responsibilities of the various American military commands divided Southwest Asia roughly down the middle. One half was the worry of the European Command, then based in Stuttgart, West Germany. The other belonged to the Pacific Command, headquartered in Honolulu. On a visit with Odom to Pakistan, as he flew across the imaginary boundary separating the two Pentagon commands, Brzezinski got a firsthand look at the problem. "We were on a White House plane," Odom recalled, "and suddenly there's an F-14 off our wing. Was it ours? If not, whose?" The pilot couldn't be contacted. The pilot of the White House jet anxiously queried Stuttgart. There were frantic phone calls but no answers. The same was true of Pacific Command headquarters in Honolulu. "To this day," Odom said, "I'm not sure we know whose plane that was up there."

Concerned by the potential for trouble in the Gulf, Brzezinski and, finally, President Carter pushed the Pentagon for answers. They joined Odom and Huntington in advocating a new unified command for the Middle East and Southwest Asia. Pushing the Pentagon bureaucracy was not easy. Odom wrote several memorandums emphasizing the need for a new command in the Gulf and sent them across the Potomac to the

Pentagon. Nothing happened for a while. Then finally in late 1979, there was a reply. No new command, Defense Secretary Harold Brown said. Instead, the Pentagon would create a Rapid Deployment Joint Task Force. The beginnings of the task force were hardly auspicious. In December 1979 Brown traveled to Tampa's MacDill Air Force Base to make it official. The new task force would be headquartered underground in a grubby bunker its command staff dubbed "the mole hole." However, the task force outgrew these quarters almost immediately and was transferred into a grim complex of trailers above ground, on the south side of the base. The task force's headquarters staff would eventually grow to nearly 300 people, but it would have no forces. In the event of trouble, it would be assigned units from the 82nd Airborne Division and 101st Airborne Division (Air Assault), as well as three brigades of Marines. It would also be able to call up elements of the 24th Infantry Division (Mechanized) and several tactical fighter wings and airlift squadrons.

Many in the Pentagon worried that the airborne divisions, which traveled with no heavy tanks, were not equipped to fight the heavy Soviet-type armored divisions of Iraq and Syria or, in the worst scenarios, Soviet troops moving toward the waters of the Gulf through the Zagros Mountains of Iran. Except for the 24th Infantry Division (Mechanized), American heavy Army units were not assigned to the new task force. They were committed to the defense of Europe, and the task force was not authorized for any new combat units.

The new task force had a respected soldier as its first commander. Marine General P. X. Kelley had plenty of experience in the Middle East. Perhaps more important, he had served with all four of the U.S. services during his career. "This was the first time in history," Kelley said, "that we had ever put together a standing joint task force that consisted of all four of the services. We concentrated immediately on Middle East contingencies." Kelley arranged for maritime prepositioning ships to be based at Diego Garcia, in the Indian Ocean. Then he began running exercises at the Army's vast training center for desert warfare at Fort Irwin, California, the same place George Patton had trained his army for the North Africa campaign.

Regardless of the creation of the new task force, Washington's ability to respond effectively to potential trouble in the Gulf was still limited. More needed to be done. Laboring over the initial draft of Jimmy Carter's State of the Union address over the Christmas holidays in 1979, Brzezinski tinkered with the idea of a "regional security framework" for the Persian Gulf. Secretary of State Cyrus Vance and White House Counsel Lloyd Cutler saw the draft afterward and took the phrase out. It implied too deep a commitment, they felt, one the United States could not make good on.

Brzezinski would not be put off, though. In the final draft of the State of the Union address, he had penciled in the three words "regional security framework." He considered them essential to American policy. On January 23, 1980, President Carter made it plain that the United States would brook no meddling in the Gulf. "Let our position be absolutely clear," he told the joint session of Congress and the national television audience. "Any attempt by any outside forces to gain control of the Persian Gulf region will be regarded as an assault on the vital interest of the United States of America. Any such assault will be repelled by any means necessary, including military force."

The United States began to extend its reach throughout the Gulf region. Bob Murray, the deputy director of international security affairs at the Pentagon, led a quiet U.S. delegation to Saudi Arabia, Oman, Somalia, Egypt, and Kenya to talk about "host-country support" for U.S. forces. The term meant different things to different people: bases, joint exercises with U.S. troops, prepositioning of American military equipment for fast use in times of crisis. Murray found receptive listeners everywhere. In Oman, the sultan told Murray that he had had a largely Iranian security force to protect him. Now, however, in the aftermath of the Ayatollah Ruhollah Khomeini's toppling of the shah, he was worried about the force. Murray told the sultan about the 25,000 American soldiers that could be mobilized in P. X. Kelley's Rapid Deployment Joint Task Force. "They could be in Oman before breakfast," Murray boasted, recalling his host's reaction. "When the sultan heard this, he got a big smile on his face and became very happy."

In Egypt, the first Bright Star joint exercise with U.S. troops took place in November 1980. It involved 1,000 U.S. soldiers and cost American taxpayers $25 million. It set an important precedent. When, less than a year later, Egyptian President Anwar Sadat was assassinated by members of the Muslim Brotherhood opposed to his signing the Camp David accords with Israel, the pace of the Bright Star exercises quickened. Eventually, there would be more than twenty-five Bright Stars, involving tens of thousands of U.S. troops.

By the time the Carter administration departed Washington, no one on

Ronald Reagan's transition team had any illusions about the potential for trouble in the Persian Gulf. But no one knew quite what to do about it either. What happened next was one of those common but often critical occurrences that drive policymakers to distraction and make either villains or heroes out of nameless bureaucrats.

Lieutenant Colonel Chris Shoemaker, who had been recruited from the Pentagon to the National Security Council staff by Bill Odom, had stayed on as a member of the National Security Council staff transition team. Like Odom and Brzezinski, Shoemaker was a believer in the idea of a new unified command for the Gulf region. President Reagan's new national security adviser, Richard V. Allen, had asked that all of the sixty-three national security directives signed by Jimmy Carter be reviewed. The task fell to Shoemaker.

It was a golden opportunity. On the last day of his administration, Jimmy Carter had signed four such directives. The last was PDNSC-63, which spelled out the need for a Persian Gulf security framework and emphasized the need for a new unified command. This was Brzezinski's brainchild, but Shoemaker had written the document. Shoemaker put Carter's PDNSC-63 at the very top of the pile of national security directives he passed on to Allen for Reagan's approval. President Reagan signed it a short time later. The new administration renamed it NSDD-4, for National Security Decision Directive 4.

Less than a year later, on August 23, 1981, Secretary of Defense Caspar W. Weinberger signed an order converting the Rapid Deployment Joint Task Force to the U.S. Central Command. The headquarters staff would be expanded from nearly 300 to 800 people. A permanent headquarters facility would be established at MacDill to replace the grimy old trailers P. X. Kelley had inherited. Crisis planning for the Persian Gulf region would begin immediately. By January 1983 a true unified command would exist. "The real thought work for the Persian Gulf had been done," said Les Denend, a National Security Council staffer in the Carter administration who joined the Joint Chiefs staff as an Air Force colonel in the Reagan administration. "The Reagan administration just adopted it all after a relatively short review."

General Powell and General Schwarzkopf were the direct beneficiaries of these past preparations. They now had less than thirty minutes to get to the White House for the 8 A.M. meeting with the President and the other members of the National Security Council. They would go in with what they had, even if it was a glorified Tip-fiddle, and hope for the best. Powell reviewed the maps, plans, and options a final time. He and Schwarzkopf were under no illusions about the stakes involved. George Bush had already told aides that the crisis was "big time."

The President's objective was clear. "He thought that the aggression should not stand," recalled a senior adviser who spoke with Bush on the night of the invasion and then again early the next morning. "Especially in a place we had staked out as our vital interests. The invasion would not be allowed to stand. That was the President's strong view."

"I did feel early on that the aggression by Iraq could not—must not—go unchallenged," Bush said. "The overriding reason for this was the fact that bold and naked aggression could not be permitted to stand. I worried that Saddam's intentions went far beyond taking over Kuwait. With an attack on Saudi Arabia, he would have gained control over a tremendous amount of the world's oil supply. But the bottom line was that aggression could not stand. If he was permitted to get away with that, heaven knows where the world would have gone and what forces would have been unleashed."

Some officials familiar with the President's thinking in the aftermath of the invasion were troubled, however. The Iraq crisis had blown up like a powerful summer thunderhead, with almost no notice. To be sure, the intelligence community had issued warnings, but they were necessarily ambiguous, and the administration had been caught flat-footed. Having to come to terms quickly with the threat from Iraq now, Bush was understandably troubled by its implications. According to several advisers who spoke with the President during the early days of the crisis, the President's worst nightmare was of American troops being slaughtered while landing in the desert, with Iraqi forces unleashing chemical weapons on Saudi runways and in Saudi ports just as the troops were disembarking. Another version of his nightmare, these officials said, was of American soldiers being returned home in body bags, their bodies and faces horribly disfigured by the same kind of chemical burns suffered by Iraqi Kurds after Saddam ordered them gassed toward the end of the Iran-Iraq war. Bush had told friends he could vividly recall the news photographs of those gruesome scenes. He described chemical weapons as a coward's violation of the warrior's code, which requires that noncombatants be spared.

The Pentagon's war planners also worried plenty about the Iraqi chemical threat. But they knew that chemicals are notoriously inefficient. Even a slight breeze could render them virtually harmless. The gassing of the Kurds that had left such a vivid impression on the President, for example, had been wildly exaggerated. After Saddam Hussein had ordered the gassing of the Kurdish village of Halabja, in March 1988, more than 4,000 people had been reported killed; the number was actually closer to 2,000, intelligence officials said. In any case, some of the Pentagon brass were concerned that the size and scope of any military response be governed more by its objective and less by narrower concerns. Whether or not Saddam would use his chemical weapons fell into that category, they felt.

At the White House, Powell and Schwarzkopf were quickly ushered into the Cabinet Room. William Webster, the Director of Central Intelligence, was present. Bob Kimmitt was also there, sitting in for Secretary of State Baker. So were Dick Cheney, the secretary of defense, and Paul Wolfowitz, the under secretary of defense for policy. John Sununu, the rumpled chief of staff, Nicholas Brady, the secretary of the treasury, and James Watkins, the energy secretary, were already present. Richard Darman, the director of the Office of Management and Budget, and Boyden Gray, the White House counsel, joined the group. Thomas Pickering, the ambassador to the United Nations, was among the last to arrive, having just caught a shuttle from New York after the 6 A.M. Security Council vote on Resolution 660.

As Schwarzkopf began laying out his maps and arranging his slides, Bush arrived with Scowcroft. And then Marlin Fitzwater, the press secretary, led a small group of White House reporters, photographers, and TV people in. The President's aides thought he should appear on the morning newscasts condemning the invasion of Kuwait. Suddenly aware of the cameras, Schwarzkopf scrambled to retrieve the maps and slides.

A reporter asked the President how he planned to respond to the Iraqi aggression. Would he authorize the dispatch of American troops to the Gulf? "I'm not contemplating such action," Bush said. His tone was firm. Just hours before, however, Scowcroft had been strongly urging a military response. Along with the others, Schwarzkopf waited and wondered. Whatever happened, he thought, it would be the President's call.

Once the reporters were dismissed, Scowcroft began summarizing the events of the past twenty-four hours. Bush asked Webster for the latest intelligence on the invasion. The CIA's photoanalysts had confirmed an attack force of more than 100,000 men, all from Saddam's elite Republican Guard divisions. Webster told the President that the threat to the Saudis was real but not imminent. The heavy concentration of Iraqi armored units in downtown Kuwait City would slow any move further south.

Bush told Brady and Webster he was pleased at how fast they had located and frozen Iraq's assets. But more needed to be done. Other nations had to take similar action. Kimmitt said that they were already working on it at the State Department, and Bush indicated he would make several calls himself. He wanted as much pressure as possible brought to bear on Iraq immediately. That meant economic sanctions.

What did it look like in the Security Council? Bush had served as U.N. ambassador, and he knew how difficult it could be to get the fifteen members of the Security Council to agree on almost anything. Pickering assured the President that there was sentiment among the members for additional action against Iraq.

Watkins, Brady, and Sununu discussed the impact of the invasion on the world oil markets. With the overnight invasion, Saddam Hussein was in a position, they believed, to control nearly 10 percent of the world's known oil production. There was some evidence the U.S. economy was already beginning to tip into a recession. The higher prices Saddam could conceivably command would surely accelerate that movement.

Bush wanted to talk about possible military options. The Air Force KC-10 tankers dispatched to the Gulf two weeks before for the exercise with the United Arab Emirates had been moved to fields in Saudi Arabia, Secretary Cheney reported, and Colonel John McBroom, the commanding officer of the 1st Tactical Fighter Wing at Langley Air Force Base near Norfolk, Virginia, had been ordered to tell his F-15 fighter pilots to be ready to fly at a minute's notice.

General Schwarzkopf followed the discussion closely. Not a short hitter in the lot of them, he thought. No posturing, no dumb questions. Scowcroft was clearly a driving force. But Bush was his own man. General Powell concluded his remarks on the Iraqi invasion, then introduced Schwarzkopf. There were basically two ways to go, Schwarzkopf said.

The first was with retaliatory strikes from the air. Attack aircraft could be flown off aircraft carriers in the region. Targets could include the Iraqi army in Kuwait, strategic or military facilities in or around Baghdad, or economic targets like pipelines. Responding to an earlier question from Dick Darman, he noted that pipelines could be repaired quickly. In any case, the United States could not launch enough carrier-based strikes to do much more than make Saddam mad; his military and his economy would not be badly hurt, and it would almost certainly not be enough to persuade him to leave Kuwait. On the plus side, this was a quick, strong response that would send a message loud and clear to Saddam and his henchmen. Powell opposed the idea. "There was no point in doing a retaliatory strike," he recalled much later. "You either reverse an invasion or you don't. But to go pinprick at something had no relevance." Not only might it heighten the risk of attack on Saudi Arabia, Powell concluded, it would achieve exactly nothing.

The second way to go was Plan 1002-90. It was, Schwarzkopf conceded, purely a defensive plan. It would take time, months in fact, to put into operation. But if the Saudis would grant permission to accept the 200,000 military personnel required by the plan, Schwarzkopf could guarantee the defense of the House of Saud.

There was a final slide in Schwarzkopf's briefing kit. It showed in detail, with numbers, the offensive capability of Saddam Hussein's military machine. If the President should decide to move to an offensive capability, Schwarzkopf said, "it will take a lot longer than what I am showing you [in 1002-90] in terms of the time lines of the defense." Months later Schwarzkopf would recall, "My only point was to illustrate that the offensive was a lot different than the defensive." The point was duly noted. Perhaps for that reason, after Schwarzkopf concluded, the discussion drifted back to the subject of oil. The President was scheduled to depart shortly for Aspen, where he was to deliver a speech. The meeting broke up. Nothing had been decided.

CHAPTER 4

POWER
AND PRINCIPLE

IN IRKUTSK at the time of the invasion, Secretary of State James Baker had pressed Eduard Shevardnadze hard for the Soviets to cut off arms sales and deliveries immediately to Baghdad. The Soviet foreign minister had agreed that something had to be done. With his approval, Moscow had already issued a statement criticizing the invasion. In the Security Council meeting in New York, Yuli Vorontsov, the Soviet ambassador to the United Nations, had vigorously supported Resolution 660.

Moscow was in a delicate spot. On the one hand, Baghdad was its most important client in the Gulf. For years, however, the Soviets had also been working assiduously to cultivate ties to other Gulf states, particularly the oil-rich emirates. But Kuwait had been the only one to respond to Moscow's overtures: in 1963, the Sabah family had agreed to establish an embassy in Moscow. Since then, relations had warmed. By 1979, Kuwait was receiving Soviet arms. Later it would welcome Soviet technicians and advisers. During the Iran-Iraq war, Kuwait persuaded the Soviets to protect its tankers. On May 17, 1987, the U.S. frigate *Stark* was hit by an Iraqi missile, killing thirty-seven American sailors. For the men in the Kremlin, as for the men in the White House, Kuwait's practice of playing one superpower off the other was a dangerous game. Nevertheless, Shevardnadze's number two at the Foreign Ministry, Aleksander Belonogov, delivered a stern Soviet statement to Ghafil Jassim Hussain, the Iraqi ambassador. "The Soviet government is convinced," the statement said, "that a swift and unconditional withdrawal of Iraqi forces from Kuwaiti territory would make it possible to end the dangerous tension in the Gulf. The sovereignty . . . of the state of Kuwait must be fully restored and protected." It was not a condemnation, but the Iraqi ambassador was surprised by the strong language.

Shevardnadze wanted something even tougher. Back in Moscow after the long flight from Irkutsk, he held a series of meetings with the Kremlin leadership. The reaction from Politburo hard-liners was immediate—and fierce. "You will have [Iraqi] blood on your hands," Shevardnadze was told, according to two senior U.S. officials who spoke with the Soviet foreign minister after the sessions.

As complicated as its relations were with the states of the Persian Gulf, Moscow had much bigger worries on the eve of the Iraqi invasion, and in many ways the Soviet role in the crisis would develop into a kind of magnifying glass on the shape of the world after the Cold War. Gorbachev's diplomatic behavior might have surprised the cold warriors of the West, but it flowed logically from the Soviet president's established foreign policy. In the midst of the deepening social and economic chaos of the Soviet empire, the Kremlin under Gorbachev had realized that its foreign policy was being crafted from a position of weakness, not strength. Economically, it was obvious that the Soviet system could not compete with that of the West; it was falling farther and farther behind each year. Ronald Reagan's cherished Strategic Defense Initiative, the "Star Wars" anti-missile defense, and a host of other twenty-first-century American weapons programs promised that the Soviet military, too, was doomed to second-rate status. It was Shevardnadze who understood the significance of this gloomy reality most clearly. The Soviet Union was no longer capable of playing a direct role in all the world's business. But it could continue to play on the great stage through other means. A web of security and economic arrangements, Shevardnadze believed, would preserve Moscow's status as at least a partner of the West in world affairs. Early on, it had been Shevardnadze's vision, for instance, to replace the insupportable Warsaw Pact with the notion of a "common European home." Neatly, by implication, such a home precluded the need for NATO.

According to several of his senior advisers, Shevardnadze realized that Iraq's invasion of Kuwait might well be a disaster for the Soviet Union. For several years, Moscow had pursued a foreign policy aimed at working to quiet selected trouble spots around the globe and settling disputes with neighbors amicably. Allowing the Warsaw Pact to collapse, a move that many saw as making a virtue of necessity, had nevertheless reaped enormous goodwill for Gorbachev and his men in the Kremlin, and a newly friendly West was beginning to increase trade and other forms of economic cooperation with Moscow. If Saddam Hussein, by his rash act, were permitted to throttle the world economy by driving oil prices higher, inflation would quickly rise and the world economy—not just that of the United States and Europe—would tumble into a deep recession. Moscow too would suffer, and badly.

The crisis must therefore be ended quickly, Shevardnadze argued to members of the Politburo. Underlying his concerns for the Soviet economy was a more specific strategic concern. The last thing Moscow wanted to see in the Persian Gulf and the Middle East was a military conflict that could produce a power vacuum in the region, allowing Washington to assert itself completely over events there. Not everyone in the Kremlin agreed that the way to prevent such an outcome was to support Bush against Baghdad, as Shevardnadze urged. Doing so would mean jettisoning ideological baggage, baggage that a lot of the men in the Kremlin had grown fond of. They would not part with it happily.

Before leaving Ulan Bator, James Baker had taken a final call from Dennis Ross in Moscow. A senior administration official said that Ross told Baker "that he had taken it as far as possible" with his Soviet counterparts at his level. The Americans and the Soviets were very close on draft language for a joint statement. Baker was needed to close the deal. It was already 2:30 A.M. August 3 in Ulan Bator. Baker would have to return to Moscow. He did not know what the Soviets would say once he got there, but it had to be something of significance. "You simply do not invite the secretary of state to come all that way," explained a senior U.S. official, "if you've got nothing to say."

Baker knew just how much was riding on Shevardnadze's shoulders. "They weren't the closest friends in the world," said a senior adviser to the secretary of state. "What there was was a genuine respect, [a feeling that] this was someone you could work with and trust." Shevardnadze was risking a lot in going to bat for Baker. And Baker wondered how much the Soviet would be able to do in the end. The weight on Baker's shoulders was no less obvious to Shevardnadze, aides to the Soviet foreign minister said. This was the biggest crisis of George Bush's still young presidency, and Baker's job was to try to find a way to resolve it.

Stepping off his State Department jet at Moscow's Vnukovo VIP Terminal, Jim Baker looked exhausted. Waiting on the tarmac for him, Eduard Shevardnadze cut an impressive figure. With his handsome mane of silver hair and his confident manner, Shevardnadze looked every inch the respected senior diplomat he was, one of the most important figures on the world's diplomatic stage. With members of the press scribbling rapidly on all sides of him, Shevardnadze spoke in forceful and uncompromising terms. Despite its long relationship with Baghdad, and notwithstanding the 7,830 Soviet citizens working in Iraq—most of them engineering and other technical personnel assigned to military projects—Moscow was urging a worldwide halt to deliveries of arms to Saddam Hussein.

Shevardnadze had evidently won the day. But Baker and his aides knew there would be other battles to fight, battles in which Shevardnadze would risk his entire career.

Back at the Pentagon, Schwarzkopf began considering his commanders. First among them was Lieutenant General Charles A. Horner. The commanding officer of the 9th Air Force, which included all U.S. fighter bases east of the Mississippi River, Horner was the Central Command air boss. Horner received his summons from Schwarzkopf while in midair. Screaming northeast along the Atlantic coast in an Air Force F-16 fighter he was piloting, on his way to Langley Air Force Base in Virginia, he was ordered to return immediately to Shaw Air Force Base in South Carolina. From there, he was to go to Tampa.

At the headquarters of the U.S. Central Command, a senior official said, the former Vietnam ace put on something of a show. Much decorated, Horner had flown forty-eight missions over South Vietnam. He had also completed seventy missions over Hanoi, attacking surface-to-air missile batteries. In the Central Command's cramped war room, Horner's battlefield experience was immediately evident. "He came into the war room and sat down with us to put together the air campaign," a senior official remembered. "He had a yellow notepad and a pencil, and he was just putting the sucker together. I mean, that was before the first airplanes had ever deployed, before the first Air Force airplane ever got there. In about two or three hours, as I recall, [he] laid out the conceptual outline of the plan for the air campaign. And it did not change a whole lot." Horner's plan for what would come to be known as Desert Shield and, ultimately, Desert Storm called for the most massive concentration of air power in history. In an era when the Pentagon routinely produced much less significant products with teams of experts armed with high-speed computers, Chuck Horner would design the air campaign for Desert Shield with a pencil and a yellow notepad.

In addition to Horner, Schwarzkopf had a shortlist of commanders. Lieutenant General Walter E. Boomer, a laconic North Carolinian and Vietnam veteran, would lead the Marines. John J. Yeosock, a lean, cigar-chomping son of the Pennsylvania coal country, would become Schwarz-kopf's commander for all U.S. Army ground troops. Major General William G. "Gus" Pagonis, would be given the task of organizing the nightmarish logistics for all operations. Short and intense, the wisecracking Pagonis would quickly gain a reputation for doing whatever it took to get the job done. One senior U.S. official would dub Pagonis Schwarzkopf's Milo Minderbinder, in tribute to the fictional supply wizard of Joseph Heller's *Catch-22*. Major General Robert B. Johnston, an exacting officer of Scottish descent, would be chief of staff. The Navy commander would be Vice-Admiral Henry Mauz, Jr. The commander of the U.S. Seventh Fleet, Mauz would be placed in charge of all naval operations. He would also be directing the U.S.-led naval blockade of Iraq. If the President was going to ask him to go to work, Schwarzkopf thought, he could hardly have asked for a better team to work with.

George Bush and Brent Scowcroft were scheduled to depart for Aspen within minutes. Bush was to deliver a speech at the prestigious Aspen Institute. Before the President left, Scowcroft felt he needed to emphasize the importance of doing something more to respond to the invasion of Kuwait.

We do not have the option to appear to be doing nothing, Scowcroft had said during the morning meeting, according to several of those present. Just before the meeting adjourned, Bush had echoed the point in much the same language. Scowcroft followed Bush into the Oval Office to find out how hard the President was prepared to push.

Scowcroft was an unlikely warrior. Balding, just five-foot-eight and 130 pounds, he barely filled out the dark blue pin-striped suits he favored most days in his West Wing office. To casual acquaintances, Scowcroft seemed a delicate and professorial man, too soft-spoken to be threatening, too shy to be aggressive. The appearance was misleading. In the weeks and months ahead, Scowcroft would do more than anyone besides Bush himself to move the nation toward war. At sixty-five, just a year younger than the President, Scowcroft shared many of Bush's most deeply felt beliefs. Like Bush, Scowcroft had been profoundly influenced by the Second World War, and later by the Cold War. Like Bush, Scowcroft had also had an early brush with his own mortality: Bush had narrowly escaped injury when his Navy bomber was shot down by Japanese fighters in the South Pacific in 1944, Scowcroft had been seriously injured when his Air Force jet crashed on a training mission in New Hampshire in 1948. Scowcroft had remained in the service, retiring finally as a lieutenant general. That background, Scowcroft's nuanced understanding of foreign affairs, and the government experiences both men had shared beginning in the administration of Gerald Ford all counted enormously with Bush. There was no one on whom the President would rely more heavily in the coming months.

In the Oval Office, both men agreed that the invasion could not go unchallenged. The President seemed firm. The two men then met briefly with Boyden Gray. If they decided to select one of Schwarzkopf's military options, Bush wanted to make sure he had the necessary legal authority on which to act. Scowcroft viewed the meeting with Gray as a positive sign.

On his Air Force jet en route to Aspen, Bush went immediately to the telephone. Some of his aides made light of it, not because they thought it was silly or unproductive, but because George Bush was so obviously compulsive about his telephone diplomacy. It was a hallmark of the Bush presidency, however. Just as the President prided himself on taking time to write hundreds of personal notes to friends and acquaintances no matter how busy he was, he believed that establishing strong personal relationships with key world leaders was vital. One on one in certain situations, he was convinced, he could do better than rooms full of bureaucrats, diplomats, and other so-called experts.

Bush had already called Ankara, and the result had been quite positive. Turgut Ozal, the Turkish president, had quickly agreed to help. Ozal believed that a strong bond with Washington would help Turkey, already a member of NATO, gain full membership in the European Community. Turkey had long been the "sick man of Europe," and for years Turks had been ambivalent as they looked first to Europe, then to the Orient. Ozal was certain that the future lay toward the north. And he had marshaled a considerable bit of history to make his argument.

Since the fourteenth century, the Ottoman forebears of the modern Turks had made their capital in Europe, not Asia. The Ottoman capital had been in Adrianople; in 1453, it was moved to Constantinople, now called Istanbul. Although the empire of the Ottomans would continue to expand through the Middle East, the Ottoman capital would remain in Constantinople, the southeastern ledge of Europe, hard by the Bosporus. Centuries later, Kemal Atatürk, the founder of the modern Turkish state, pushed his countrymen further toward the West by personally emulating Western habits. He also gave Turkey a constitution, making it the first secular state in the Muslim world.

Ozal saw himself as firmly within this historical tradition, and he wanted to knit his country more closely into the weave of a fast-changing Europe. The nascent multinational move against Iraq presented a golden opportunity, he felt, but only for a statesman with the vision to seize it. Ozal was not a man who missed many chances. "President Bush called me especially to talk about the pipeline," Ozal said, "because the embargo would depend on the closure of the pipeline. It was the critical element." Any embargo the United Nations imposed on Baghdad would be meaningless if Ozal decided to keep the pipeline from Iraq through Turkey open. And, despite his friendship toward the West, Ozal had a good reason to keep the pipeline open: Iraq owed Turkey $750 million. It could pay the money back only with oil revenues. Bush knew this and wanted to see how Ozal wanted to proceed. Ozal recalled: "I suggested to him that the U.N. should take a decision right away about the embargo. In that case, it would not be difficult for us [to shut the pipeline]." It was the answer Bush wanted. With the invasion of Kuwait, Bush would put some of his valued personal relationships to the test.

Half a world away, as Bush was flying west to Aspen, President Mubarak and King Hussein were meeting in Alexandria. They were both worried and agitated by Saddam's duplicity. "I said, 'Your Majesty, what is this? I cannot believe what is going on,'" Mubarak recalled. "This is a disaster. We are at the end of the twentieth century. Nobody will accept this in the whole world."

The king told the Egyptian president that he had spoken with Saddam earlier that day and that the Iraqi leader had assured him his soldiers would begin to leave Kuwait soon—but only if there was no condemnation of the invasion and talk of outside interference. "You know us," the king quoted Saddam as saying. "If the result is going to be a position of condemnation and accusations and a tough stance that might pave the way for outside intervention, then we will tear each other's eyes out." King Hussein told Mubarak that it was critical that there be no hasty condemnation of the invasion at the upcoming meeting of the Islamic Conference in Cairo. The meeting was to be attended by the foreign ministers of nearly all of the Arab nations. "It was very, very important, knowing these people [the Iraqis] as we do," the king said, "that nothing happen at this meeting. This was a problem that could not be solved by foreign ministers, at any event."

Their conversation was interrupted: Bush was on the line. King Hussein spoke with the President first. The king said that he requested time, perhaps two days, to try to arrange a solution. He told Bush about Saddam's promise to withdraw from Kuwait soon. According to two senior aides, Bush told the king: "I'll give you the extra time, forty-eight hours. Let's see what you can do with it." Their conversation lasted a full nine minutes before the king handed the receiver to Mubarak.

With both leaders, George Bush had cultivated strong relationships. He had gone fishing with the Jordanian monarch and watched a Baltimore Orioles game with the Egyptian president. With the onset of the Iraq crisis, Bush told his advisers, he felt he could rely on both leaders to work in concert with the United States. "What is the situation?" Bush asked, according to Mubarak. "Could you both work to find a solution peacefully?" Mubarak told Bush that they were trying to do just that.

But already, Mubarak felt a certain reluctance on King Hussein's part. President Mubarak remembered his reaction: "The king sat. He did not show any sign of enthusiasm to do this. I picked up the phone and asked to contact Saddam Hussein. In the presence of the king."

The call to Baghdad went through quickly. Mubarak said: "Hello, President Saddam, I have King Hussein with me. I would like him to come to you to discuss two points, and on the basis of these two points, we are ready to ask for a limited summit to find a solution to the problem." Mubarak didn't want to talk details over the phone, both because the lines to and from Baghdad were not secure and for fear of having Saddam reject the proposal before it could be presented to him in person. Mubarak said that

Saddam agreed to talk with the king, and the monarch got on the phone to arrange details of the meeting. They decided to convene the next day.

George Bush was hard at work on the Air Force jet. He had agreed to deliver a speech to the Aspen Institute long before anyone had concerns about Saddam Hussein devouring Kuwait, and the White House speech-writing machine had cranked out a workmanlike address. It spoke of balancing the continued need for a strong military with the administration's determination to spend less money on defense in the post–Cold War world. There was no reference in the address to a "new world order." But neither was there any reference to the invasion of Kuwait. Brent Scowcroft thought that it would be a glaring omission not to mention it, and he told the President so. Bush agreed. Scowcroft and Roman Popadiuk, a trusted aide, began to rewrite the President's speech. Scowcroft preferred to write longhand on legal-size yellow pads. This was how he kept the notes of Bush's phone calls with world leaders. It was also how he tinkered with the prose of the President's speechwriters.

Scowcroft thought for a while about the points the President should stress. Clearly, the invasion of Kuwait illustrated the hazards of the post–Cold War world Bush had planned to talk about in Aspen. It also illustrated the need for America to remain strong. With the President's voice in mind, Scowcroft started writing: "The brutal aggression launched last night against Kuwait illustrates my central thesis: notwithstanding the alteration in the Soviet threat, the world remains a dangerous place with serious threats to important U.S. interests wholly unrelated to the earlier patterns of the U.S.-Soviet relationship. . . . These threats, as we've seen just in the last twenty-four hours, can arise suddenly, unpredictably, and from unex-pected quarters. U.S. interests can be protected only with a capability which is in existence, and which is ready to act without delay."

Popadiuk liked the addition Scowcroft showed him. But he felt the point about the need for a strong military could be strengthened. With Scow-croft's approval, Popadiuk scratched the following insert immediately be-hind the other: "The events of the past day underscore also the vital need for a defense structure which not only preserves our security but provides the resources for supporting the legitimate self-defense needs of our friends and of our allies. This will be an enduring commitment as we continue with our force restructuring. Let no one, friend or foe, question this commitment."

Scowcroft took the two additions to Bush. The President scanned them quickly and nodded his approval.

George Bush did not have the same warm relationship with Margaret Thatcher as Ronald Reagan had had, but the two were close. Like Reagan, Bush genuinely admired the conservative revolution the British prime minister had directed from 10 Downing Street, and seeing her was one of the reasons he had looked forward so eagerly to his visit to Aspen. Thatcher was to be awarded the Aspen Institute's prestigious Award for Statesmanship. She had come to Aspen a few days early to vacation.

Margaret Thatcher, for her part, was equally keen on seeing Bush. Thatcher had watched with concern as Bush had grown closer to Helmut Kohl, the German chancellor. The reunification of Germany and the fall of Communist regimes throughout Eastern Europe seemed to have put a damper on London's "special relationship" with Washington.

For both leaders, it was an important meeting. Henry Catto, the American ambassador to the Court of St. James's, had been a trustee and chairman of the Aspen Institute, and he and his wife, Jessica, had a showplace country home in nearby Woody Creek. Margaret and Denis Thatcher had been guests of the Cattos before, and after Bush had agreed to speak at the institute, the Cattos had invited him for a casual get-together with the British prime minister.

On the morning of August 2, the Cattos awoke to the news of the invasion of Kuwait, and Henry Catto immediately called Scowcroft. Yes, the national security adviser assured him, the President still intended to come to Aspen. The Cattos made plans accordingly. Bush arrived in Aspen in the early afternoon, and the two leaders met in the great room of the Cattos' main house. With mountain views flooding through floor-to-ceiling windows and an enormous flagstone fireplace dominating the room, it was a fabulous setting, one marred only by the constantly ringing telephone. He was summoned several times to the phone, interrupting his conversation with Thatcher. Bush took the calls in the Cattos' bedroom. There were calls from Yemen's President Ali Abdullah Salih and from King Fahd in Jidda.

For weeks afterward, several White House aides believed that it was Thatcher who had emboldened Bush to respond vigorously to the Iraqi threat; others disagreed. "[The President] needed no steel in his spine," Catto said. "His eyes were flashing, and he was clearly not going to put up with this kind of thing." Others present said it was more complicated than that. Bush's thinking, a close adviser said, "had already evolved significantly by the time he met with her. But I think what she did is underpin the conclusions that he was beginning to reach about the significance of this event. This was not like an attack by Rwanda into Burundi or something like that."

Mrs. Thatcher told Bush that it was appalling how the Iraqi leader had lied about his intentions just prior to the invasion. Thatcher and Bush both had a high regard for Hosni Mubarak. In the days before August 2, Mubarak had gone to extraordinary lengths to avert a conflict, staking his prestige and reputation on a peaceful solution. "Don't worry," Mubarak had told Bush in a phone call just two days before the invasion, according to a senior administration official briefed on the conversation, "[Saddam] has assured me that this is just a quarrel and nothing's going to happen." Mubarak was outraged now, Bush said. And he was too. Thatcher shared the sentiment.

Thatcher and Bush discussed how they might proceed. The British prime minister, according to senior U.S. officials, believed strongly that the United Nations could provide the necessary cover for any military response. Article 51 of the U.N. Charter provides that any member of the world body can invite any other member to bring military force to its aid in times of crisis. There was no question, Thatcher said, that the Kuwaiti emir would invite the United States and Britain in; in fact, he had already issued a blanket invitation for just about anyone to come to his aid. All we need, Thatcher said, is to cite Article 51. But within the innermost councils of the Bush administration, recalled a senior official privy to discussions with the President after the invasion, "no one knew anything about Article 51." It would, nonetheless, soon become an important tool. Tom Pickering and William Webster had also come to Aspen separately to attend sessions of the institute. An aide to Webster had carried one of the CIA's high-security scrambled fax machines to Aspen, and he and Pickering took turns using it to keep in touch with developments in Washington and New York. Already, within the Security Council there was a sense that the United States might well respond to Iraq's aggression under the aegis of Article 51.

No one knew for sure what would happen next, but Pickering recalled that he did little to squelch speculation about Article 51. It would prove highly useful later on, a kind of sword of Damocles hanging over the deliberation of the fifteen members of the Security Council.

Publicly, Bush kept calm. "We're not ruling any options in," he told a press conference in the Cattos' luxuriant garden shortly after a light lunch of sandwiches and coffee. "And we're not ruling any options out." Between his conversations with Scowcroft and Thatcher and his phone calls with leaders around the world, though, Bush was gaining a deeper understanding of just what his options were.

The United Nations would clearly be critical to the imposition of economic sanctions against Iraq. But more important at the moment was the defense of Saudi Arabia. Schwarzkopf had made his point about the vast difference between offensive and defensive plans. Plan 1002-90 was purely defensive. Any attempt to move troops into Kuwait under Article 51 would mean a radically different operation. It would also take a great deal more time. "The issue was whether to dispatch forces to defend the kingdom of Saudi Arabia," recalled a senior Bush adviser, "and to create a context against which sanctions could work. That was our initial hope. The initial strategy of August, which was our strategy through the next few months, was to deny Saddam a chance to expand his aggression into the kingdom or anywhere else—in a sense, to limit the damage to what he'd done and then, against that backdrop, to put in place the sanctions to tighten the screws."

Thatcher had emphasized the priority of defending the Saudis. But would the Saudis allow themselves to be defended? King Fahd was as proud as he was rich. Would he allow American soldiers with their rock 'n' roll and their raunchy magazines into his hermetically sealed, highly conservative society? Bush had first met Fahd when he was Gerald Ford's Director of Central Intelligence and Fahd was crown prince (and had run the Saudi intelligence service for thirteen years). The relationship had blossomed, and Bush had continued to cultivate Fahd during his eight years as Reagan's vice-president.

During his telephone conversation with President Bush from Jidda, the Saudi monarch was very nervous, a senior U.S. adviser recalled. He asked what American intelligence was saying about Saddam's intentions. Bush replied that his advisers believed there was a threat to the kingdom. Bush and Scowcroft felt that Fahd would see the wisdom of American intervention. The conversations with King Hussein, President Mubarak, President Ozal, and President Salih had all been positive. All seemed to appreciate the gravity of the situation. That was a starting point. The invasion of Kuwait was not yet twenty-four hours old, but already a sense of shared interests was beginning to emerge—one that would result, ultimately, in the creation of a remarkable coalition of thirty nations. It would not be created easily, and once created, it would be subjected to enormous strains. But that it would be born at all its participants would later come to regard as a near miracle of mutual interest and dogged diplomacy.

Back in Tampa, the anxiety was acute. "We kind of went through a lot of goat-roping around," a senior planner said. "A million questions is the best way to describe it, because even though we had 1002-90, which was what Internal Look was based on, it wasn't appropriate for this situation." Not only had 1002-90 never been subjected to high-level review, even some of Schwarzkopf's experts believed it specified too small a force structure to guarantee the defense of the Arabian peninsula. "Mass confusion, almost hysteria" was the way one planner described the days immediately after the invasion. Moreover, no one either at the Pentagon or in Tampa knew what the President would do. But some wanted to be ready to move as soon as they got the word. For that reason, some of Schwarzkopf's senior headquarters staff began pushing Lieutenant General Tom Kelly to issue a "warning order." Such an order would alert individual military units that there was a mission or a deployment order that they might have to respond to in the near future and that they should be ready to move on extremely short notice.

At Fort Hood, Texas, the 1st Cavalry Division already had all its gear on specially designated railcars. The division had been scheduled for months for a series of grueling exercises at the Army's National Training Center in Fort Irwin, California. Schwarzkopf's planners knew that fighting a war in the Saudi desert would require a great deal more than what the 1st Cavalry would be bringing to California. But they argued that a warning order, plus the good fortune of having so much equipment already on railcars, would give them a good jump if the President told them to start moving forces. In the Pentagon, the Joint Chiefs of Staff opposed issuing the warning order. Central Command officers pushed harder. Finally,

General Kelly had had enough. "Well, you're not getting a fucking warning order," he shouted on the line. "So forget it!"

On August 3, after returning from Aspen, Scowcroft opened the regular 8 A.M. meeting of the National Security Council. Scowcroft had sought to chair the morning meeting the day before, but the President had jumped in and run things himself. By mutual agreement that would not happen this time. Perhaps it would be better, Scowcroft had urged the President the evening before, if he took the lead in the next morning's meeting. "In order to have a free debate," Scowcroft had told Bush, "let me make the argument. People will be more willing to criticize me than you." This way, Scowcroft suggested, Bush could sit back, having not shown his hand, and get the benefit of the other players' "unvarnished advice."

Scowcroft began the meeting with a simple premise. As hard as it might be for the United States to respond to a crisis so far away, the invasion of Kuwait had to be considered unacceptable. All the participants in the meeting were familiar with an analytical paper on world oil reserves prepared by economists in the CIA's new Office of Resource, Technology and Trade. The impact of Iraq's invasion of Kuwait, Scowcroft said, according to several people present, was bad news not just to the economy of the United States but to that of the world. Therefore, no matter how difficult it was, the United States would have to respond. And the only response that would guarantee results, Scowcroft said, was force. The President remained silent.

Scowcroft opened up the discussion. Defense Secretary Cheney said that he agreed that a military response was required. General Powell seconded the sentiment. "My visualization was that we had to get something over there rapidly and get the American flag in the ground," he later said. "I was reasonably sure in my own mind that although Saddam Hussein was willing to go to war with Kuwait, and was quite prepared to go to war with any regional actors who wanted to get in the way, it certainly couldn't have been in his mind to go to war with the United States of America. And therefore we had to get the United States of America there. And we had to do it rapidly before he realized we weren't there—or how badly we weren't there."

Powell was followed by Lawrence Eagleburger, Baker's deputy secretary of state. A career foreign-service officer, Eagleburger had risen higher than any professional diplomat in the State Department. Like Scowcroft, with whom he had worked in the blue-chip consultancy established by Henry Kissinger, Eagleburger wielded a kind of special influence. Over the course of his more than two decades in the foreign service and through a variety of postings overseas, Eagleburger had found himself in the thick of hundreds of foreign-policy dilemmas. He was a man who some thought would favor quiet talk over wielding a big stick. But now he was urging a military option.

Finally, the President spoke. He agreed with Scowcroft and Eagleburger on the need to use force. He was, aides said, becoming increasingly convinced that Saddam Hussein would not respect anything short of military action. The President mentioned his conversation with King Fahd the day before. The question was whether the Saudis would accept a sizable American military presence such as that called for by Plan 1002-90.

General Powell indicated that Schwarzkopf and General Kelly were working on an "options package" for the President. They would be ready to present it shortly. Bush said that the next day would be fine. He would be leaving for Camp David that afternoon. Powell, Cheney, and Schwarzkopf could all take the helicopter out to the presidential retreat in Maryland's Catoctin Mountains the following morning. For the President and his senior advisers, it would be a working weekend, the first of many.

Camp David sits atop a heavily wooded peak nearly 2,000 feet above sea level in the Catoctin Mountains. Built in 1939 by the National Park Service, it was a favorite among bird watchers. In 1942, within months after the bombing of Pearl Harbor, President Franklin Delano Roosevelt had come for a visit to High Catoctin, as it was then called. Roosevelt decided that the rustic site would make a splendid weekend retreat. He selected 6,000 acres and named the place Shangri-La, after the mountain utopia in James Hilton's novel *Lost Horizon*. After Dwight D. Eisenhower moved into the Oval Office, he changed the name to Camp David, in honor of his new grandson. Not all presidents have been truly enamored of the rough charm of the place. Ronald and Nancy Reagan had used it as a getaway from the capital, but aides said they never really warmed to it. George and Barbara Bush, by contrast, genuinely loved Camp David. They tried to spend as many weekends there as they could.

On the morning of August 4, Bush and his advisers gathered in the compound's sprawling Aspen Lodge. This was the presidential residence, named by Mamie Eisenhower for the Aspen trees of her native Denver (however, the walls of the Aspen Lodge were native red oak, milled from the trees of the surrounding hills of the Catoctins). The meeting in the lodge's conference room began at precisely 8 A.M. Of the hundreds of meetings the President would convene to discuss the Iraq crisis, aides said that only two or three were absolutely critical. This would be one of them.

President Bush sat at the middle of the long beige table, directly across from General Powell. To Powell's left was Scowcroft, and to Bush's left sat Schwarzkopf. Elsewhere around the table were Cheney, Paul Wolfowitz, Vice-President Quayle, John Sununu, William Webster, Marlin Fitzwater, Richard Haass, and Lieutenant General Charles Horner. James Baker was also there, having flown most of the previous day from Moscow after his meeting with Shevardnadze. With the exception of Quayle, who wore a tie, the group was dressed in casual shirts and sport jackets. Bush wore a white windbreaker with the seal of the Group of 7, a souvenir of the recent economic summit of the world's seven biggest economic powers.

After a few brief remarks by Powell, Schwarzkopf took the floor. Munching pastries and doughnuts and pouring refills from steaming pots of black coffee, Bush and the others listened carefully. Schwarzkopf based his talk on Plan 1002-90. Using color and black-and-white slides, much of it high-resolution satellite photography less than a day old, he outlined the Iraqi order of battle. It was clear that Saddam's battlefield commanders had allowed themselves to get bogged down in Kuwait City. But other slides, of the desert south of the capital, showed long lines of Iraqi tanks raked hard along the Kuwaiti border. That border, Schwarzkopf pointed out, was less than 300 miles from Riyadh and the gleaming palaces of the House of Saud. If the President so ordered, Schwarzkopf continued, he could have 2,000 to 3,000 American soldiers on the ground within twenty-four hours. One brigade of the 82nd Airborne Division was always on alert. The Division Ready Brigade, or DRB, could be scrambled immediately. More troops would follow. Within two to three weeks, Schwarzkopf said, the President would have a force of 40,000 soldiers in the desert. Almost all would be light forces, however—infantry packing shoulder weapons and Marines driving lightweight and small-gunned M-60 tanks. They would certainly not be capable of countering Saddam's heavy Republican Guard divisions with their top-of-the-line Soviet tanks. Schwarzkopf's elite heavy force, General Barry R. McCaffrey's 24th Infantry Division (Mechanized), with their M1A1 Abrams tanks, would take longer to deploy, even with the Navy's new Fast-Sealift Ships.

Schwarzkopf quickly summed up the defensive component of Plan 1002-90, summing up the work his staff had done over the past several weeks. Fully implemented, the war plan would require probably a quarter of a million American soldiers. It would take roughly four months to get them and their equipment into place. Even that, he said, would mean a sealift and airlift operation of historic dimensions—much larger than the requirements for the D-Day landing at Normandy. And that assumed a minimum of problems en route. That, Schwarzkopf said, was just for defense.

Schwarzkopf pointed out that Saddam's force of a million men was the fourth largest military in the world. But, while the force was large, it was not uniformly good. Poorly paid conscripts—many of them Shiites who had little love or loyalty to Saddam's Sunni Muslim regime—were little better than cannon fodder. Where Saddam packed a real punch was with the eight divisions of his Republican Guard, with his chemical weapons, which he could launch on short-range missiles, and with his superior South African–manufactured artillery.

Schwarzkopf noted that conventional military theory called for a force of at least three to one to drive an opponent out from a dug-in position. Some U.S. Army doctrine manuals called for forces of up to six to one. Nevertheless, Schwarzkopf said, Baghdad was already isolated internationally. Everyone in the room anticipated they would get the U.N.-backed embargo of Iraqi oil. The Japanese had already given the administration indications that they would participate (they would make good on the promise a day later). Like the United States, Britain and France had frozen the assets of Saddam's regime, and the European Community was working on broad sanctions that would be approved before the day was out. With the promise from Turgut Ozal to close the pipeline across Turkey once the United Nations approved the embargo, it was already beginning to look like the Iraqi economy was being fitted for a noose. Despite Iraq's ability to manufacture many spare parts for its military machine, Schwarzkopf said, the international chokehold would, over time, seriously reduce the ability of its military forces. By the time he had an offensive capability in place, Schwarzkopf said—and he emphasized that this could take nearly a year—Iraq's forces would be considerably weakened. Better American tactics, better equipment, and vastly superior air power would also work to reduce the textbooks' three-to-one ratio considerably.

But there were obstacles. Prying the Iraqi forces out of a place like Kuwait City would almost certainly require nasty, house-to-house fighting, which would mean lots of casualties. American munitions reserves were low: there was a real risk of a shortage if and when shooting started. Also, both defensive and offensive plans would mean calling up large numbers of reserves. Everyone in the room understood that such a call-up would be political dynamite. Pulling people off their jobs, separating families—these things would upset assembly lines, splinter communities. They would bring the Gulf conflict home to America in a way that would make even the nightly television news broadcast seem remote. But reserves would be critical, Schwarzkopf said, especially pilots. They would be the backbone of the massive airlift necessary for just the defensive component of 1002-90.

Schwarzkopf was asked about an air-power option alone. A mud soldier and proud of it, Schwarzkopf believed that the infantry represented the very best of the American military. Still, to the President and his aides listening intently, Schwarzkopf gave the air-power option a fair evaluation. Then he turned the briefing over to Lieutenant General Horner, his air commander. With the availability of Saudi bases, Horner said, plus American carriers in the Gulf and the Red Sea, he would be able to put up several hundred combat sorties a day. The Iraqis, with vastly inferior numbers, training, and pilots, would be chased from the sky in a matter of days, perhaps less. Horner had supreme confidence in his men and their flying machines.

At almost exactly 9 A.M., their briefing completed, Schwarzkopf and Horner were excused from the room.

A vigorous discussion ensued. Powell and Cheney believed that if Plan 1002-90 meant anything, it meant defense. And defense meant ground forces. Air power, Powell pointed out, had never won a war by itself. If the objective of this operation was to protect the kingdom of Saudi Arabia, Powell continued, air power alone would not do it.

Over the course of Colin Powell's distinguished career, his detractors have called him a political general. The youngest chairman of the Joint Chiefs of Staff in history, he was given the job by President Bush, leapfrogging more than thirty other more senior four-star generals. When Operation

Desert Shield began, Powell had held the chairmanship for a little more than a year. As the nation prepared for war, however, what it needed more than anything else in its top military post was a general who understood the art of the possible, someone who would make sure that if war came, the job would be done right.

The road to the chairman's suite of offices at the end of the General Omar Bradley corridor on the E-Ring of the Pentagon began in Harlem. "I was across the street from Fort Apache," Powell likes to say today. Powell's parents, who were immigrants from Jamaica, expected him to go to college, and in 1954 he was accepted by New York University and City College of New York. NYU cost $750 a year back then while City College cost just $10. The choice had been easy. Powell entered the City College of New York as an engineering major. It was only after he matriculated that he discovered he had no aptitude for engineering. Eventually, Powell joined the campus Reserve Officer Training Corps (ROTC). He had signed up, Powell said, because he liked the look of the uniforms of the unit he selected, the Pershing Rifles. It was not long after that he discovered he did have an aptitude for soldiering.

As the nation's top military officer, Powell is acutely conscious of the debt he owes to the black soldiers who came before him. The walls of his office near the river entrance of the Pentagon—with its secure telephone lines and four rows of wall-to-wall bookshelves packed with everything from his collection of mugs to biographies of William Tecumseh Sherman and George C. Marshall and a shotgun given to him by Mikhail Gorbachev—are lined with paintings of the Buffalo soldiers, black troops who fought in the West around the turn of the century. The anteroom of his office is dominated by a print from the movie *Glory*, which tells the story of the 54th Massachusetts, the black unit that fought in the Civil War. Powell does not apologize for the fact that the military is disproportionately made up of minorities. In speech after speech he has challenged American business to offer the same opportunities for minorities that the military provides.

In many respects, Colin Powell models himself on General George C. Marshall, the architect of the Army that defeated the Germans and Japanese, who cherished power only insofar as it enabled him to do his job. During the Second World War, Marshall dearly wanted the D-Day command, but he refused to lobby for it. President Roosevelt agonized over whether to select Marshall to command the invasion of Europe, but in the end he picked General Dwight D. Eisenhower because he found that he could not do without Marshall in Washington. Powell's career developed in much the same way. "He is not a reluctant suitor," said one top administration official close to Powell. "But he gets jobs not by running for them, but by doing a good job where he is." Like Marshall, Powell's bottom line is getting the job done. In the conflict in the Persian Gulf, and in his tenure as chairman prior to that, even most critics of the Pentagon conceded that Colin Powell has used his immense power wisely and well. "His genius," said a colleague, "is understanding at a gut level the politics of Washington and how national security policy is made." Herein lies the basis for the allegation that Powell is a "political" general.

The few detractors there said that Powell calibrated his counsel to superiors in order not to ruffle feathers. Champions—and Powell has many—said that the chairman simply deplored ambiguous arguments and inconclusive discussions that left politicians with convenient pillars to hide behind. Like a lot of the brass in the Pentagon, Powell remembered Vietnam and the forlorn commitment, with little public support, to a badly planned military campaign whose objectives seemed murky at best. There would never be another Vietnam as far as he was concerned. If the President was going to send American soldiers to fight a desert war halfway around the globe, Powell wanted to make sure that the mission's objective was clear in everyone's mind and that he had the forces he needed to do the job and the time necessary to get them into place and ready to fight. "Clearly, some of this comes out of the Vietnam experience, particularly the guidance part of it," Powell later said. "But I also don't walk around with a big V burned into my forehead. A lot of this comes out of thirty-three years of military training and experience. It's the kind of thing that I would expect any captain in any infantry school would be able to figure out. And it's more common sense than it is Vietnam experience. When you go to war and you have the possibility of bringing enough force to bear that the outcome is ordained, you are an idiot to do it any other way."

Powell reemphasized the amount of time that Schwarzkopf had said he would need; this would not be another Panama, he said, done in a day. Then there were Saddam's chemicals and the hostile desert environment.

He wanted the implications made obvious. "This is not the minor leagues," Powell told the President and his advisers gathered around the long table. "This is the NFL."

Brent Scowcroft, for one, did not need to be convinced. If they were serious, Bush's national security adviser agreed, it would mean deploying ground forces. To some in the room, whose responsibility to the President straddled the arenas of domestic politics and foreign policy, this was cause for concern. In public-opinion surveys conducted immediately after the invasion of Panama and the capture of Manuel Antonio Noriega, the President's approval ratings had soared. But suppose this turned out to be more messy? It was certainly, as Schwarzkopf and Powell had taken pains to point out, a much bigger, more long-term commitment. That could mean trouble. It could also mean, as it had meant after Panama, triumph. "Isolationism is still just below the surface [in the United States]," reflected a Bush adviser who was present at the Aspen Lodge meeting. "There is no question about that, but I think that if we succeed this time, the next such crisis might not take all this much agony. In other words, if potential aggressors believe in advance that the civilized world is going to behave in a certain way, then they will tend to tailor their actions." That was the hope anyway. But was the game worth the gamble?

What did the President think? According to several participants, Bush insisted that he saw stark parallels between the crisis in the Gulf and the reaction of the nations of Europe in the late 1930s to the threat and bluster of Nazi Germany. The Saudis and the other nations of the Gulf, Bush told his advisers toward the conclusion of the Aspen Lodge meeting, had to be persuaded to reject "the appeasement option."

But would they? To several of the advisers, this was the crux of the problem. "The real question," recalled one participant, "was working out the diplomacy with the Saudis." There was no good offshore option, as Powell had stressed. And deploying forces from the sea was not something Schwarzkopf and his planners were anxious to do. "The big question over the meeting," this adviser said, "was whether the Saudis were going to be willing to involve themselves with us."

Bush and several of his advisers had reason to believe they would. The day before Prince Bandar bin Sultan, the gregarious Saudi ambassador to the United States, had been invited to meet with Scowcroft in his spacious suite a few steps down from the Oval Office. The mood in Saudi Arabia, Bandar knew, was very near panic. Nevertheless, King Fahd was not of a mind to accept American assistance if it was going to be just a token gesture. The king had been embarrassed once, and badly, during the Carter administration. Scowcroft knew the story well. When the shah of Iran had been driven from the Peacock Throne, Jimmy Carter had dispatched a squadron of F-15 fighters. Even before the F-15s had landed in Saudi Arabia, the White House had announced that none of the planes was armed. That will not do this time, Bandar told Scowcroft. Not at all.

Scowcroft assured the Saudi envoy that the President was contemplating something far more serious. But the king would have to open the gates. Near the end of the meeting, Bush had poked his head into Scowcroft's office. Some days the President did this as many as a half-dozen times. This time he knew Bandar was there and wanted to assure him of his personal commitment to the House of Saud. In fact, he wanted Bandar to see for himself. General Powell and his people were already working on a massive operations plan, Bush said. He wanted Bandar to have a look at it—the satellite photos, the deployment list, everything. Scowcroft and Cheney would arrange the details, the President said. He shook hands with Bandar and then left almost immediately for Camp David.

Bandar had arrived in Dick Cheney's third-floor Pentagon office late on Friday afternoon. "The President," Cheney told Bandar, "has instructed me to brief you on what the United States can do to help the kingdom defend itself." With Cheney, gathered around his small conference table, were General Powell, Paul Wolfowitz, and Richard Haass. All knew the Saudi envoy well. None doubted his importance in whatever King Fahd might decide. Cheney was businesslike in his presentation. With Powell, Wolfowitz, and Haass chiming in briefly, the defense secretary showed Bandar the satellite photos of the Iraqi order of battle. The Iraqi tanks south of Kuwait City were within miles of the Saudi border. Bandar knew the speed and range of the best of the Iraqi armored force.

The photos hit home. A former fighter pilot in the Saudi air force, Bandar knew an attack force when he saw one. There could be no question about the threat to the kingdom. Next Powell showed Bandar the latest revisions to Plan 1002-90. The numbers had seemed to serve as a hammer, driving home the point made by the satellite images: 2,000 to 3,000 troops almost within hours after the king gave the go-ahead; 40,000 a few weeks later; maybe a quarter of a million all told.

Bandar was impressed. Bush had already indicated his support for the plan. This was no squadron of unarmed F-15s. The Saudi envoy said he would speak with King Fahd directly. He promised to be specific about the threat to the kingdom and to urge Fahd to invite the Americans in.

Just after 10 A.M., as the meeting in the conference room of the Aspen Lodge adjourned, Scowcroft asked several of the principals to stay behind for a few minutes. What was Bandar's promise really worth? he wanted to know. Baker, Cheney, Powell, and Webster had doubts. The Saudis had bought their way out of trouble before. Even with the best will in the world on the part of Bandar, King Fahd might be persuaded by other senior advisers in Riyadh that the threat from Iraq was bogus, that perhaps it was all some sort of scheme to get the Americans inside the kingdom and astride their precious oil reserves.

According to several of his advisers, Bush was even more concerned than anyone else about the Saudis' willingness and ability to stand firm. He related the substance of his conversation with King Fahd from the telephone call from Colorado. It had been ambiguous, at best. The President promised to call again.

It was nearly noon when this smaller meeting broke up, and Bush and Scowcroft escorted the others outside to their helicopters. The Aspen Lodge was about a half mile southeast from the landing pad, and as the President and his aides walked toward it, Richard Haass and several others spotted Chris Evert riding in a golf cart toward the compound's tennis courts. Bush had invited the tennis star to Camp David for the weekend.

"Does anyone want to stay and play tennis?" the President asked. His aides, taken aback by the request, shook their heads no and walked the rest of the way to the helipad in silence.

Back in the Aspen Lodge, Bush and Scowcroft called King Fahd at his summer palace in Jidda. How serious were the Saudis? The call went through quickly, and Scowcroft listened in on an extension, taking notes on a yellow pad in his elegant, cursive hand. Bush pressed Fahd. With the threat to the kingdom, would Fahd accept American assistance? The king seemed eager, Bush and Scowcroft noted. When are you sending this team to brief me? the king asked. Bush looked at Scowcroft blankly. Scowcroft hadn't discussed anything like that with Bandar; it must have come up with the Saudi ambassador later on. With Scowcroft vigorously nodding his head, Bush promised that the team would be departing from Washington very shortly. The request from Fahd was a good sign, though. Promising to talk again soon, Bush hung up. The President and his national security adviser were winging it. He and Scowcroft just looked at each other. Now they had to figure out who to send to talk to Fahd. First, however, George Bush had a tennis date. If no one else would volley with Chris Evert, then he would, by golly. She was his guest, after all.

CHAPTER 5

KING FAHD ISSUES
AN INVITATION

B Y T H E time he boarded his Air Force jet on Sunday afternoon for the long trip to the Persian Gulf, Dick Cheney had solved the mystery of where King Fahd's notion of an American briefing team had come from: none other than Prince Bandar. True to his word, the Saudi envoy had urged Fahd to consider inviting American forces into the kingdom. Bandar was convinced that the threat to His Majesty and the kingdom was real. Fahd had said he would like to see the satellite intelligence photos for himself. Thus was the briefing-team idea born. Only Bandar had forgotten to tell the Americans about it.

Still, President Bush was grateful for the Saudi ambassador's intercession with Fahd. After consulting with Scowcroft, the President asked Cheney to lead the mission to Jidda. The three of them then quickly agreed on the composition of the team. The defense secretary would be accompanied by Paul Wolfowitz, General Schwarzkopf, Lieutenant General Horner, Robert Gates, Scowcroft's deputy for national security affairs, and Pete Williams, Cheney's press secretary. Also included was Charles W. Freeman Jr., the U.S. ambassador to Saudi Arabia. (A veteran China hand, Freeman had translated for Richard Nixon on his historic mission to Beijing. Since then, the chain-smoking diplomat had become fluent in Arabic and had been given the critical posting at the sprawling embassy compound in Riyadh. Freeman had been in Washington for consultations with the State Department. Learning of the Cheney trip, he hitched a ride back to the kingdom on the Air Force jet. As it turned out, it would be a mutually beneficial coincidence. Freeman had studied the royal family closely, and during the course of the long flight, Cheney would tap him for advice about how best to approach the king and his advisers. Long after that, in the trying months before and even during the war, Freeman would also become a valued confidant of General Schwarzkopf.) Rounding out the team were Sandra Charles, Richard Haass's deputy on the National Security Council staff, Art Hughes, a key deputy to Paul Wolfowitz at the Pentagon, and a senior military analyst from the CIA's Office of Near East and South Asian Analysis.

As for Prince Bandar, after his Friday afternoon meeting with Cheney and Powell in the Pentagon, he had had his private jet refueled and then left for Jidda. Since then, he had remained in almost constant touch with Scowcroft by phone.

Washington did not know it, because most of the phones from Kuwait City had gone dead, but things in the U.S. embassy compound, normally run so efficiently by Nathaniel Howell, were beginning to look worse. Even though embassy personnel had finally made the Kuwaiti National Guard units understand whom they should point their guns at, no one believed they could hold off the Iraqis indefinitely. There were just too many. The embassy staff's fears were confirmed late in the day on August 3. "I was looking at the TV [security] cameras," Major John Feeley remembered. "And the next thing we saw was our guards in their underwear—B.V.D.s, Fruit of the Loom, whatever, that's what they were in, completely stripped—and running down the street in their bare feet. And so we lost our guards."

The embassy was now fair game. "A group of Republican Guard infantry . . . surrounded the embassy and threatened to come over the wall," Feeley said. "So we were buttoned up the first night [after the invasion], and then the second night and then the third night, with this threat every night of 'We're coming over, and if you resist, we're going to take out everything that's in there.' "

Saddam's commanders knew which government buildings they wanted to occupy, and which ones they wanted to destroy. For some reason, however, they did not seem to know that the walled compound just down the street from the Kuwait International Hotel was the American embassy. The evident lack of understanding served to raise the level of fear inside the compound. "The fourth [night after the invasion]," Feeley said, "was a fairly tough night because we were convinced they were coming over. They had threatened enough already, they had gotten everything [in downtown Kuwait City] cleaned up. And so we were all set up, as the Marines said, to rock 'n' roll. We hadn't had any sleep, and we pretty much thought that the majority of the military folks weren't going to make it through the night." The plan was for Feeley and the Marine guards to defend the civilian personnel inside. There was a heavy steel vault in the chancellery, and that would have afforded protection.

Before that, though, Feeley and the others planned on making it very tough for the Iraqis. Armed with shotguns and big .357 Magnum handguns, the military people planned to fight. So did some of the civilians. Many of the embassy staff had been able to locate flak vests. The Marines would do the heaviest fighting, and if Iraqi troops came over the wall, the plan was to back steadily toward the vault in the chancellery, the Marines providing covering fire. "We were going to do some other things," Feeley said, "when they finally got to the door, and that would have kept them out for a while." The soldiers planned to use tear gas on the invaders. Besides the stifling heat to contend with, then, the twenty-odd Americans in the embassy compound each had a gas mask. Everyone practiced putting them on. If Feeley and the Marines fell and Iraqi troops got into the chancellery, however, Ambassador Howell's only option would be to surrender and take his chances with Saddam's soldiers. But on August 4, and then again on the fifth, despite the mounting fears, no Iraqi soldiers came over the wall.

With the details of the Cheney mission finally sorted out, Brent Scowcroft decided to get a few hours' rest. Before the invasion of Kuwait, he had made a point of ducking out of his West Wing office for afternoons and evenings to look after his wife. Brent and Marian Scowcroft had been married for nearly forty years, and despite the varied demands of his years in the Pentagon, at the White House and as a business partner with the peripatetic Henry Kissinger, Scowcroft had always been able to carve out enough time for his wife and a daughter, now grown. Now, however, Marian Scowcroft was suffering from acute diabetes, and her husband was finding it ever more difficult, even in these early days of the crisis, to break away to be with her at her bedside.

With Bush due to return from Camp David shortly and Cheney just about to depart, it looked like a good opportunity to get away, and Scowcroft summoned Richard Haass to his office. He knew the President would want a briefing as soon as he stepped off his helicopter onto the South Lawn of the White House. Haass was the most junior of Bush's foreign-policy advisers intimately involved in the Kuwait crisis, but Bush and Scowcroft placed a lot of trust in him. A former Rhodes scholar, Haass was a quick study, and he knew how to cut to the heart of things. It was a trait Bush valued highly. Scowcroft had no compunctions about asking Haass to brief the President in his stead.

In his cluttered office in the Old Executive Office Building next to the White House, Haass spent a few minutes checking the latest information coming out of the Gulf. There were no troop movements, despite the Iraqi promise to withdraw. Growing numbers of atrocities were being reported. It was bad news all around. Haass typed quickly. He got out to the South Lawn just as the corpsmen in their dress uniforms were lowering the stairs from the big olive-drab-and-white helicopter with the Marine Corps seal on the side. Bush was dressed in a gray suit, dark tie, and white shirt. As the rotor wash from the helicopter died, Haass's hair spilled across his forehead. He handed the President his hastily typed notes and waited. Bush scanned the words quickly, but, typically, he wanted an oral briefing. "What have you got?" he asked. The situation on the ground was extremely bad for the Kuwaitis, Haass said. The reports of atrocities inside the emirate were mounting. Saddam's front-line troops were still very far south in the Kuwaiti desert.

Roped off in a specially designated area, the White House press corps was waiting. Bush strode toward the knot of reporters briskly and was immediately peppered with questions. Would the President authorize the use of force to counter the invasion of Kuwait? Was a military option now under consideration? Bush declined to answer specifically. His options, he said, were "wide open." Moreover, he charged, his anger evident, Saddam Hussein had lied once again: there had been no movement of his troops from Kuwait.

But what would the President do? The reporters pressed him.

"Just wait," Bush shot back. "Watch. And learn." Preparing to disengage from the journalists, his wife Barbara waiting for him a short distance away on the lawn, the President concluded: "I view very seriously our determination to reverse out this aggression. This will not stand. This will not stand! This aggression against Kuwait." Then he spun on his heel and left.

Bush seemed to have made up his mind. Suddenly, the stakes seemed very high indeed. "His demeanor in those ten minutes signaled it wasn't business as usual," an aide recalled. "I think anybody watching that, anybody there at the time, came away saying, 'This is really big. This is really different. This is serious.' And I think that for a lot of people it was kind of a punctuation mark in this crisis. We knew that by Cheney going there, we were basically moving into the next stage. We knew we were crossing the Rubicon, [but] we didn't know where it was taking us."

At 38,000 feet over the Atlantic, Dick Cheney knew precisely where his Pentagon aircraft was taking him, and he was not at all disturbed by the President's remarks. After Bob Hall, Pete Williams's deputy in the Pentagon's public-affairs office, had heard Bush on CNN, he had phoned his boss aboard Cheney's plane to report the comments. Williams in turn had relayed the news to Cheney. "Good," the Pentagon chief had told his press secretary. "That's exactly what he should have said." Cheney was not at all worried about his President. What concerned him was the mission ahead. Even with Saddam Hussein's tanks less than three hundred miles from his palace in Riyadh, King Fahd would not be thrilled by the idea of accepting thousands of American troops. It would be an enormously difficult sales job.

To several of Bush's closest advisers, it seemed inconceivable that Fahd would recognize the seriousness of the Iraqi threat and then do nothing about it. To some, whose view of Saddam Hussein was largely one-dimensional, prefaced usually with the label "thug" or "murderer," the problem was analogous to the twilight world of organized crime. Even the motivations seemed the same: money, turf, and pride. Citing those motivations, one family (headed by Saddam in Iraq), had declared war on another (the Sabahs in Kuwait). In such a situation, the last thing to expect was that a third family (the Sauds), fearing more violence, would call in the Feds. More natural was for one family, presented with an offer it could not refuse, to buy off the other. Failing that, everyone would go to the mattresses, and when the shooting finally stopped, the turf would be redivided. All the families would be losers.

Despite his family's great wealth, King Fahd well knew how recent was the emergence of Saudi Arabia as a state. It was not until 1932, for instance, that Saudi Arabia had any international political identity. Fahd's father, King Ibn Saud, had challenged several other Bedouin chieftains for control of much of the Arabian peninsula and won. The leader of a puritanical Muslim sect known as the Wahhābis, he would come to preside over a vast desert kingdom whose peoples belonged to dozens of different sects and whose borders had shifted time and time again. Elsewhere in the eastern Mediterranean and the Persian Gulf region, borders had been drawn by British and French imperial overlords who had carved up the remnants of the defeated Ottoman empire in the aftermath of the First World War. If King Fahd could find a way to come to terms with Saddam, a brother Arab after all, why should he risk armed conflict over some lines in the sand drawn by arrogant Europeans nearly three-quarters of a century ago?

In the middle of a broiling afternoon on Monday, August 6, Ambassador Pickering had made it clear to his Security Council colleagues what kind of support was building behind the anti-Iraq movement. Making a point of specifically citing Article 51, the U.S. envoy also called upon other articles of Chapter VII of the United Nations Charter. Very broadly, the articles gave the U.N. powers to "protect and restore peace and security." Under those two umbrellas, Pickering urged the imposition of a full economic and military embargo against Iraq. If he got it, all 159 members of the world body would have to adhere to it. Word had already begun to leak, meanwhile, of a massive naval blockade, to be led by the United States.

For some U.N. members, however, doing the right thing would sting. Together, Iraq and Kuwait produced four million barrels of oil a day. Japan imported a half-million barrels of oil a day from Iraq and Kuwait, amounting to 12 percent of its total daily consumption. Brazil imported just over 30 percent of its oil from the two countries.

In the Security Council, everyone knew the stakes. It had been an elaborate dance, and it would get more elaborate still. Meeting at the elegant French mission to the United Nations in midtown Manhattan, the five permanent members of the Security Council had agreed to support the draft of Resolution 661, which spelled out the terms of the economic and military embargo. But Pickering knew that nothing in the Security Council was ever really done until the votes had been cast publicly and recorded.

The seven members of the so-called nonaligned movement on the council were critical. If they bolted, China might well follow. And the Chinese had a veto. Pickering worked assiduously to prevent that outcome, and to win them over. When the balloting was finally completed on Resolution 661, Pickering had pitched another shutout. The vote was 13–0. Only Yemen and Cuba had abstained.

In Ankara, without missing a beat, Turgut Ozal said, "We will obey the U.N. embargo." He then announced that Turkey's council of ministers would convene immediately. "Three hours after that," the Turkish president recalled, with evident satisfaction, "we closed the pipeline."

On the day after the invasion of Kuwait, George Bush and his advisers had discussed a two-pronged effort against Iraq: sanctions and force. They had the one. Now they would see about the other.

"The coalition became essential from the very first days," Bush said. "Unilateral U.S. response to Saddam's invasion could well have gotten us crosswise with the Soviet Union, with other Arab countries, and even with Europe. It was essential that other countries join in, and that the United Nations be involved. Some of that related to what we ourselves could do, or what I could get Congress to accept. But the aggression was so clear, and contravened so directly the U.N. purpose, the U.N.'s stated objective, that we all felt we could and must get the United Nations to pass a resolution. In so doing, not only could we bring together the coalition that would commit forces, but major powers such as China would be committed. So there were 'philosophical underpinnings' for our insistence on U.N. action and on forming the coalition that would bear the military burden."

Dick Cheney had never been the type to leave anything to chance. On the long flight from Washington, he had put his team through its paces. He wanted to make sure each presentation had as big an impact on the king as possible. To keep things as simple and unencumbered as possible, he had decided to scrap the briefing by the CIA's military analyst. The man was an impressive briefer, but Cheney had concluded that the information on the satellite photographs in which Fahd reportedly was so interested would be more effective coming from Schwarzkopf. He had also decided to include Robert Gates, Paul Wolfowitz, and Ambassador Freeman.

The meeting occurred on the evening of August 6. When Prince Bandar escorted the group into the royal family's private council room, the Americans saw that Fahd had kept his own group deliberately small. With him were Prince Saud al-Faisal, the Saudi foreign minister. Like Bandar, the prince had attended Princeton University, where he had majored in petroleum economics. Many diplomats regarded him as the most knowledgeable and impressive of Fahd's inner circle. Also in attendance at Fahd's side was the Saudi crown prince, Abdullah ibn Abdul Aziz, who was every bit as conservative as the king. A handful of other influential princes flanked the monarch, but they would say nothing during the session.

Fahd opened with some brief but evidently heartfelt remarks, according to two of the Americans present. Several took notes during the course of the meeting, as did two of the Saudi princes. The king told Secretary Cheney that he had a close and valued relationship with President Bush and with the United States. He was pleased that the President had sent such a distinguished team to brief him and his advisers on the recent events in Kuwait. With Bandar translating fluidly, the king concluded his remarks and then indicated that he and his advisers were very interested to hear what Secretary Cheney and his colleagues had come such a long way to tell them.

Cheney began by conveying the President's personal greetings, but he cut very quickly to the threat posed by Saddam's forces. The President, Cheney said, "stands personally behind the American security guarantee." Saddam's "lies, deceit, and naked aggression" had put nearly all the world against him, Cheney continued. Even the Soviets, the defense secretary emphasized, had agreed to cut off arms supplies to Baghdad, and Secretary of State James Baker would be talking to Moscow in the next day or so about imposing tougher measures against Iraq. Beijing, Tokyo, the European Community were all moving in concert, and the United Nations had acted forcefully and would continue to work to isolate the government of Saddam Hussein. An embargo would take time to work, however, Cheney said. It would not stop Saddam's tanks from dashing south into the Saudi oil fields—or even to Riyadh, if he were so inclined. He emphasized the two-pronged strategy that President Bush had discussed with his advisers: sanctions and a defensive force for the Arabian peninsula. A defensive force would protect the kingdom from further Iraqi aggression, and eventually the worldwide embargo would force Saddam Hussein's grip on Kuwait to loosen. Saddam could not hold out against that kind of pressure forever. Ultimately, he would have to negotiate or withdraw.

As Bandar had predicted, the king was extremely interested in seeing for himself the product of the Americans' billion-dollar spy satellites. Cheney turned to Schwarzkopf for the presentation. The general kept his remarks as brief as possible. On the flight over, he and Cheney had discussed how they should approach the king. Making predictions was to be avoided at all costs, Cheney said, and Schwarzkopf had agreed. The important thing was to emphasize the size of the Iraqi invasion force—much larger than anything Saddam had needed simply to conquer Kuwait. The other thing, drawing the obvious lesson from the speed of the August 2 invasion and the quality of the Republican Guard armored divisions, was the speed with which they could be inside Saudi Arabia once they decided to move.

"We don't know what he is going to do," Schwarzkopf said, with Bandar interpreting again for the king and his advisers. But Saddam could have his tanks deep inside Saudi oil fields, the general said, "easily within forty-eight hours."

According to some of the Americans present, Fahd was impressed by the satellite photos and by the argument on the size of the Iraqi force. Why should Saddam attack Kuwait, the king asked, "such a small country, with such a large force?"

Schwarzkopf had not completed his briefing, but Cheney saw an opening, and he used it to reemphasize the point about speed. It was true that they could not say with certainty what Saddam's intentions were, the defense secretary said; but it was also true that "he could move faster to attack than we could to defend." The message was clear: if you're going to ask for American help, you better do it sooner than later.

Schwarzkopf resumed his pitch, laying out the components of Plan 1002-90. He never used the number of the plan, and he spoke only of its defensive component. Nor did he mention the plan and its recently concocted offensive element. And since none of the Saudis thought to ask, he never gave the total number of troops required. Some things were better left unsaid. Using an 8½-by-11-inch notepad with holes already punched to slip it into a conventional three-ring binder, Schwarzkopf flipped from page to page methodically. Each page showed an updated phase of the American deployment. Engrossed, the Saudi princes watched the pages turn. The first American forces, a couple of thousand, could be deployed immediately, Schwarzkopf said, flipping the page. The rest would follow as quickly as possible. Four months after the initial deployment, the American force would be able to handle anything Saddam decided to throw at it. Finished, Schwarzkopf resumed his seat.

It would be up to Cheney to close the deal. This was where the sales job got tough. Before Cheney's departure, President Bush had urged him to stress the need for the Saudis to reject the "appeasement option." Cheney had modified the language. "If this invasion of Kuwait is not countered," he told the king and his advisers, according to notes taken at the meeting by a member of the American delegation, "the consequences for the king-dom of Saudi Arabia will be grave." With American forces, the king would be able to defend the kingdom. Should the combination of force and the worldwide embargo against Baghdad both fail to persuade Saddam to back down, Cheney continued, Saudi and American forces together would be enough to defeat him.

King Fahd, according to two people present, responded to this with interest. King Hassan of Morocco, an old and dear friend, had already promised a contingent of Moroccan soldiers, he said. Hosni Mubarak of Egypt might well do the same, and the other members of the Gulf Cooper-ation Council would surely contribute forces. Fahd did not say it, but it was clear that the presence of other Arab forces with the Saudis and the Americans would make his decision more palatable to his conservative coreligionists, who opposed inviting American troops at all costs.

Cheney expressed satisfaction at the idea of inviting other friendly forces. "Excellent," the defense secretary said. But he wanted to reempha-size the point about doing whatever they did quickly. We cannot wait, he told the king, until Saddam is about to cross the border. It was 7,000 miles to the United States. If American forces were going to come to assist with the defense of the kingdom, they would have to start moving immediately. Once the threat had vanished, Cheney concluded, making a point that Ambassador Freeman had stressed and would continue to stress to his nervous Saudi counterparts in the weeks and months ahead, the American forces would leave. They would not stay, Cheney promised, a minute longer than they were needed.

Throughout the presentation by the Americans, Crown Prince Abdullah had seemed the most resistant of all Fahd's advisers. An archconservative with a constituency of rural and urban fundamentalists, Abdullah had been "vehemently opposed" to any joint action with the Americans, Saudi sources said, and he had led the argument against such action in Jidda during the royal family's debates even before Cheney left Washington. At Cheney's promise to leave when asked, Abdullah ibn Abdul Aziz muttered something barely audible. It was an aside to the other Saudi princes that the American delegation could not make out, and Bandar did not translate. There was a rather lengthy colloquy between the king and the crown prince. Fahd abruptly ended it and turned to the Americans. The Saudi monarch had spoken with President Mubarak, he said, with Sheik Zaid of the United Arab Emirates, and with the displaced Kuwaiti emir, Sheik Jaber al-Sabah. "One has to ask," Fahd said, "why Saddam Hussein creates these forces. . . . It is not just his aggression against Kuwait. . . . [He] aspires to something larger." Concluding, he said that "the United States has no ulterior motive. . . . If we were to do anything with our friends from America, it would be only in defense—not as aggressors. . . . The most important thing is to protect our country." The Americans, Fahd said, were welcome. He mentioned again getting other Arab nations to bring their forces in—he would see to that himself.

"This has been a historic meeting," Cheney said, according to a note-taker. It has indeed, replied the king.

Once Cheney and his delegation had been ushered from the royal presence, late on August 6, a driver had taken them back to the State Guest House. The other members of the Cheney team who had not been present for the meeting with the king were electrified by the good news. One of the Pentagon's STU-III secure telephone units was plugged into a push-button phone in the guest house. Operated by a key, the STU-III plugged into just about any conventional phone line, scrambling the conversation to foil electronic interceptors. When the call came through to the Oval Office, Cheney was put on the President's speakerphone. His words came out, as if by magic, unscrambled on the other end. The king had agreed to invite the Americans in, Cheney reported. The deployment could begin as soon as possible.

Bush said that was terrific, "great news." Margaret Thatcher, who was also in the Oval Office at the time (having stopped by on her way back to London from Aspen for a "diplomatic refueling stop," as one senior U.S. official put it), simply beamed.

Cheney then requested the President's approval for Powell and Schwarzkopf to issue the deployment orders to begin implementing Plan 1002-90.

"You got it," Bush said. "Go."

Within minutes of the phone call from Cheney, the Central Command in Tampa was alerted to the news. The planning room in the Central Command headquarters looked nothing like the nerve center of a nation preparing to embark on a major military venture. It measured just ten feet wide by about fifteen feet long. Two big chalkboards were mounted against one wall. Measuring four feet by eight feet, the chalkboards would be used to keep tabs on which units were being deployed when. A long table ran down the middle of the room, and smaller tables were shoved into the corners. The furniture was nondescript.

What mattered were the phones. A red phone was the secure line to General Tom Kelly's people in the Pentagon's Crisis Situation Room. There was an STU-III, one of the third-generation models of the Pentagon's Secure Telephone Unit device that could scramble phone calls from anywhere around the world. On the long table was also a multiline STU-III for General Schwarzkopf's planners. In a cramped back office off the planning room were two more red phones and five more STU-IIIs. Every phone in both the long room and the back office was busy, a senior Central Command official recalled, "all the time."

Working the phones was the only way to get things done. "We really couldn't leave because it was all in our heads. *None* of this was on paper. The deployment orders were on paper, but in order to get a deployment order out, you had to coordinate all the details on the phone. There wasn't time to send an alert order, get a commander's estimate back and a course of action, and all that crap."

Some of Tom Kelly's senior staff had complained that Plan 1002-90 was a glorified Tip-fiddle. In the chaotic planning room at the headquarters of the Central Command, this seemed like a joke. "We didn't have a Tip-fiddle," the senior Central Command official said. "Just didn't have it. It was nonexistent, and so we were massaging the deployment sequence, making adjustments as soon as force list decisions were made in the Pentagon. The end result was a total jump-through-the-hoop situation—the ultimate crisis situation!"

At Langley Air Force Base near Norfolk, Colonel John McBroom was among the first to get the word from General Schwarzkopf's harried planners. The commanding officer of the 1st Tactical Fighter Wing,

McBroom was a "right stuff" kind of guy, a well-muscled fighter pilot whose idea of a good time was pushing state-of-the-art aerodynamics to their absolute limit. McBroom's young fliers admired him—some even said the Air Force had no fliers the equal of their commanding officer. Since August 2, McBroom had had his pilots on standby alert. The word from the Pentagon galvanized them into action. "We had a general recall at about 6 P.M.," McBroom recalled, "and I tell you what, this whole base, we were prepared to go."

McBroom had already prepared a "small package" of eight to ten F-15 Eagles in the event he got orders to move. When the orders did come through, however, he was told that a full two squadrons were to go. "We got word to go with forty-eight [aircraft]," McBroom said, "because it was going to be a war. Now that's quite a change."

The order set Colonel Richard Cwynar, McBroom's deputy commander for resources, into a blur of nonstop activity. Some of it seemed awfully mundane, but important nevertheless. "Basically," Cwynar said, "once the units get the word they're going, they have to get their people ready. And that involves a lot of personal preparation, making sure their shots are up to date, that they've got their finances taken care of, that they have a power of attorney for their family, that they have a will."

First, of course, they had to find everyone. McBroom remembered locating one of his fliers at a family reunion. There was a sudden rush of emotion, McBroom said, then "he was gone. They were saying good-bye to him. Just walked out of the family reunion. You're getting deployed!"

At midnight on August 6, the roads around the 82nd Airborne Division's home base at Fort Bragg, North Carolina, were choked with cars, blades of headlights stabbing into the dark. At 2 A.M., Staff Sergeant Robert England recalled, the All Americans division, as it was known, got orders, along with most of the rest of his brigade, to report to the ammunition depot on the far side of the base. Orders were issued to begin loading equipment in preparation for an immediate deployment from Pope Air Force Base nearby. Only no one had told the soldiers where they were going, England said. By 4 A.M., Sergeant England's brigade was in Fort Bragg's marshaling area, and the rumors were flying. There had been trouble in the Philippines on and off. There had been five coup attempts against the government of Corazon Aquino, plus sporadic attacks on American military personnel stationed at Clark Air Base and Subic Bay Naval Station. "Maybe there was a threat to our bases, that type of thing," Sergeant England remembered thinking. "Maybe we were going to the Philippines, but not to perform anything but a defensive role."

At exactly 7:55 A.M. on Tuesday, August 7—a little more than fourteen hours after the Central Command staff had issued its execute order—Sergeant England's brigade lifted off from Pope on two commercial aircraft arranged by planners of the U.S. Transportation Command. News reporters had gathered on the side of Pope airfield where the the Air Force's enormous C-5B and C-141 transport planes normally depart from, and so they missed the departure of the first American soldiers for the Saudi desert. For the soldiers of Sergeant England's brigade, the commercial aircraft were a blessing. The seats were much more comfortable than those they would have had on the military transports. Still, it was going to be an eighteen-hour flight. And only once they were airborne would they find out where they were really going. Saudi Arabia, who would have figured?

The man who would become the Milo Minderbinder of the Saudi desert took the phone call from the Army's chief of staff, General Carl Vuono, in his kitchen. Vuono told him that he had "twenty-four hours to get over there," Major General Gus Pagonis recalled. "He said, 'Pick twenty guys,' so I sat down at the kitchen table and wrote down twenty names. My wife called a few. I told them all to report to Fort McPherson. That's the greatest thing that happened to me—that I could send out a call to twenty guys, and they dropped everything and showed up, no questions asked. One guy had waited twenty years for a special assignment, but he came. My wife wrote their wives later to explain." What would nearly defy explanation is how Pagonis and the rest of his far-flung colleagues would pull off the largest logistical deployment in the history of modern warfare.

In the message center of the Military Sealift Command headquarters at the dusty old Washington Navy Yard, the computers suddenly chattered to life. Colonel Rick Fields looked at the flood of messages in disbelief. No one had even bothered to see whether the "Tip-fiddle" specified in the Central Command's Plan 1002-90 was even "transportation feasible." At the headquarters of the Pentagon's Transportation Command at Scott Air Force Base in Illinois, Lieutenant General Hansford T. Johnson was similarly nonplussed. He had heard that the mission to Saudi Arabia was to be called Operation Desert Shield. What it sounded like to one of Johnson's logistics men was something very different entirely: "Dunkirk in reverse."

CHAPTER 6

DESERT SHIELD: FORGING THE COALITION

I N BAGHDAD, on the same day Cheney met with Fahd in Jidda, Saddam Hussein had summoned Joseph Wilson to his office. The deputy chief of the U.S. mission in the Iraqi capital, Wilson was the ranking American diplomat in April Glaspie's absence. After her meeting with Saddam Hussein on July 25, Ambassador Glaspie had gone ahead with her plans to return to the United States. She had hoped to deliver Saddam Hussein's message to President Bush as soon as she arrived in Washington. As it happened, she was on a layover in London when the invasion occurred. Secretary of State Baker and John Kelly, his assistant secretary for Near Eastern and South Asian affairs, believed that it would send a disastrous signal to have Glaspie return to Baghdad. She had thus gone on to Washington, leaving Wilson to deal with Saddam.

A no-nonsense diplomat, Wilson, like Glaspie, found himself doing far more listening than talking with the Iraqi leader. First, there had been a brief photo session. Then Saddam got down to business. As he had with Glaspie, Saddam recounted for Wilson the unhappy history of relations between Washington and Baghdad. He also pointed out that Iraq had signed a nonaggression treaty with the Saudis just a year earlier and that "Iraq respects its commitments." The Americans, Saddam said, were using this supposed threat to the kingdom as a pretext to put their soldiers into the Gulf. As for Kuwait, it was Wilson's feeling that the Iraqi leader regarded the invasion of Kuwait as a "done deal."

In Washington, on August 7, President Bush, flanked by Margaret Thatcher and Manfred Woerner, the secretary general of NATO, made a strong statement approving the imposition of the embargo by the United Nations. From the Pentagon, word of preparations for the naval blockade had begun to leak, as had some details of Secretary Cheney's mission to Jidda. At the State Department, it was announced that Secretary Baker would be departing shortly for Turkey and then for Brussels, where he would meet with the foreign ministers of most of the NATO members.

It did not take an astrologer to tell where events were heading, and the world's financial markets were already signaling their alarm. By the time the closing bell had sounded on Wall Street on Monday, August 6, the Dow Jones industrial average had plunged almost 94 points. Uptown at the New York Mercantile Exchange, the price of a barrel of benchmark Saudi crude had jumped $3.56 to $28.05—the highest level in five years. Across town at the Pan American World Airways building, a press release was issued stating that Pan Am's management would be raising air fares to cover the cost of higher jet-fuel prices; the airline was merely following similar moves by Northwest and several other major air carriers. In Washington, the benchmark 30-year Treasury bond lost nearly six dollars per $1,000 of face value. The dollar, by contrast, went higher, fueled by speculation that a military clash in the Gulf would drive investors to the American currency as a safe haven.

The sense of alarm was hardly limited to the United States. Ninety minutes after the opening bell in Tokyo on August 7, the 225-share Nikkei average tumbled 1,264.25 points to 27,335.28, a drop of nearly 5 percent, reflecting the decidedly serious implications of the Iraqi embargo for Japan's heavily oil-dependent economy. In Paris, London, and Frankfurt, stocks took a similar pounding, and trading volumes were unusually high.

Throughout the crisis, the numbers would continue to jump, but already the leaders of some of the OPEC nations were moving to calm the volatile markets. For example, King Fahd announced that Saudi Arabia would increase its production of oil to help make up for the supplies lost as a result of the embargo. In Caracas, Venezuelan officials pledged to Vice

President Quayle that they, too, would begin producing oil above and beyond their OPEC quota.

The phones in Tampa never stopped ringing. Having arranged for the refueling of McBroom's two squadrons of F-15s and the departure of troops from the 82nd Airborne Division from Fort Bragg, Schwarzkopf's men still had to figure out how to move McCaffrey's heavy 24th Infantry Division (Mechanized) from Fort Stewart, Georgia, and General J. H. Binford Peay's 101st Airborne Division (Air Assault) from Fort Campbell, Kentucky. More units were backing up rapidly behind them, too. And all of this had to be coordinated with Lieutenant General Tom Kelly's staff in the Pentagon's Crisis Situation Room, as well as with the Military Sealift Command and the Military Airlift Command—both of which reported to Lieutenant General Hansford Johnson's Transportation Command headquarters staff.

Schwarzkopf's staff was trying to construct a real Tip-fiddle from scratch and on the run, but they were having trouble. "One of the problems we had communications-wise," one Central Command planner said, "was that we didn't have enough phones. And so what happened after the morning on the eighth of August is that our red line, which is the secure telephone going to the Joint Chiefs of Staff, was converted into an open hot line. And then the damn thing was used almost constantly twenty-four hours a day talking to the JCS; every phone in the place was in use every minute of the day, it seemed. But that's kind of how it started. It was a madhouse but necessary in order to get everyone moving."

At one point early on, the Marine Corps watch officer at Twenty-nine Palms, California, got an urgent call from Tampa. Twenty-nine Palms was the home of the 7th Marine Expeditionary Brigade. According to Plan 1002-90, the brigade was to fly by C-5 transport planes to the Gulf. There it would hook up with the five maritime prepositioning ships based at Diego Garcia in the Indian Ocean. Thanks to other orders just issued, the ships would be moving very shortly toward the Gulf, the official remembered telling the watch officer. "Hey, you need to alert the 7th MEB advance party. We're deploying."

"How fast?" The Marine was thoroughly professional.

"Twenty-four hours," the official said. "Here's the warning order, here's where you're going to go, here's what we think is going to happen, and I will get back to you with details as quick as I can."

The official in Tampa hung up, but was summoned to the phone again a few minutes later. It was the Marine watch officer from Twenty-nine Palms. "He was very thorough," the official remembered. "He called back just to ascertain if this was an authentic phone call or not, because it could have been some hoaxer calling up, I suppose."

The Marine also said he wanted to relay some preliminary information. "We're going to have our advance element and our advance party ready in twenty-four hours," he reported. He sounded pleased at his efficiency.

"Wrong," Schwarzkopf's man said. In the intervening ten to fifteen minutes, the Marines' departure time had been reduced to seventeen hours.

"Holy shit!" the Marine said. Then he slammed down the receiver. Somehow he had just lost seven hours.

On Wednesday, August 8, President Bush publicly announced the deployment of American forces to the Persian Gulf. Equating the mission with the "struggle for freedom in Europe," Bush was careful to assure the public that the action was being taken to "assist the Saudi Arabian government in the defense of its homeland." Despite his call for "the immediate, unconditional, and complete withdrawal of all Iraqi forces from Kuwait" and the restoration of Kuwait's "legitimate government," the President told reporters that troops were not being sent to force the Iraqis from Kuwait. The economic sanctions imposed by the United Nations were intended to drive the Iraqi army out of Kuwait, Bush said. The soldiers' mission was purely defensive.

From the tentative conclusions of the earliest meetings after the invasion of Kuwait, Bush had settled on a policy with two clear objectives. The President had come to his decision outside the councils of his senior aides. In the meetings over the past several days, he had listened carefully, advisers who were present said. He had insisted from the very start that the invasion of Kuwait should not go unchallenged. But he had been uncertain about how the United States should respond. Scowcroft's counsel had moved him closer to a decision to use American military might, if the Saudis would accept it. Margaret Thatcher's words apparently reinforced Scowcroft's stance. In many of the other meetings, however, the argument had gone back and forth: oil prices, economic implications—these were only a few of the many factors that clamored to be taken into account. It was the habit of this particular President, however, for better or worse, to listen to advice and then to arrive privately at a decision himself. Thus was the decision made to send American soldiers halfway around the world.

For all its risk, Bush and his cadre of advisers believed the policy would work, that its mission was well defined, its objective within reach. To be sure, if Saddam Hussein's armed forces came south, the American forces just landing in Saudi Arabia would be dangerously exposed. But General Schwarzkopf's planners were already scrambling to beef up the American presence. Once that occurred, the Americans would be able to guarantee Saudi Arabia's defense. The prospect of a multinational ground force serving with the Americans was welcomed, but it would take time to pull it together. Thatcher had already pledged several warships to the U.S.-led naval blockade, and France, Spain, and a host of other nations would soon follow suit. International support was building almost hourly. Once the naval blockade against Iraq had been announced officially, it had received almost immediate approbation from the international community. In addition, Greece had allowed American warplanes to enter its airspace, and Turkey had given the go-ahead for U.S. pilots to fly combat air-patrol missions against Iraq out of the NATO air base at Incirlik. Soon Turkey would also move a sizable force of its own troops and aircraft down onto its border with Iraq, compelling Saddam to leave a number of his divisions on Iraq's mountainous northern frontier. Still more nations were joining the embargo of Iraqi oil and military equipment. With such extraordinary international cooperation, Bush's second objective, of persuading Saddam to withdraw his soldiers from Kuwait, seemed within reach.

Employing a classic carrot-and-stick approach (but with far more of the former), Bush would offer billions in aid and forgiven loans to help construct the coalition of nations against Saddam Hussein. The final accounting would be staggeringly high—in terms of both actual dollars and compromised principles. For example, after years of pressure from the United States, Colombia would quietly be allowed to renounce its treaty agreements to extradite major drug traffickers to the United States. Malaysia, another member of the U.N. Security Council, would get a break on textile import quotas. Syria, a brutal regime given, as the administration well knew, to state-sponsored terrorism, would move closely into the orbit of the United States and receive a payoff of billions in aid from the Saudis. Even China would support Washington. Some observers thought this was the least Beijing could do given Bush's kid-glove response to the slaughter of the dissident students in Tiananmen Square in June 1989. As for Turkey,

Turgut Ozal had long wanted to resell a number of American-made F-16 fighter jets to Egypt. According to U.S. officials, Ozal received the necessary permission, although the deal would take nearly a year to become final, earning Ankara millions in hard cash.

At this early stage, both the administration's policy and its objectives had the full support of the military leaders who would be charged with carrying out the mission. Despite reports that suggested reluctance on his part, General Colin Powell has said he was fully behind the policy, as well as with the process through which it had been developed. "I think we were blessed with a group of political leaders, a President, and a secretary of defense who . . . allowed the military to participate in the decision-making process from the very beginning, and allowed me as chairman to be a part of the inner sanctum," Powell said. "When discussions were going on, the secretary of defense and I were there to make sure that the military input was there in the beginning and not sort of after the fact, after political judgments had been made. So there was, as close as possible, integration between political issues and political thinking and military issues and military decisions."

Despite his penchant for operating alone, the President wanted advice from his chairman of the Joint Chiefs, and sought it at every turn. Later, during the war itself, Bush would not interfere with his generals. This was no Lyndon Johnson, picking targets for his bombers from the Oval Office. (LBJ boasted on more than one occasion to visitors that his fliers could not "bomb an outhouse" without his okay.) Bush wanted none of that. Lieutenant General Gary E. Luck, the commander of the 18th U.S. Airborne Corps, whose divisions included the 1st Cavalry, the 82nd Airborne, the 101st Airborne (Air Assault), and the 24th Infantry (Mechanized), said he and his colleagues could not have been more pleased. George Bush, said Luck, "was a hero to all of us. He did not tie us down."

"Thank God," Saddam Hussein announced, soon after learning of the American military deployment and taking the occasion to announce the annexation of Kuwait as Iraq's nineteenth province, "we are now one people, one state that will be the pride of the Arabs." In the Iraqi capital, many people greeted Saddam's words by dancing in the sun-baked streets and splashing water from fountains on one another. Celebratory gunfire split the air, and an official statement was issued above Saddam's signature:

"My fellow citizens, history has proved that Kuwait is part of Iraq." But what the statement didn't note was that in 1899, the Sabah family had signed a treaty that established Kuwait as a separate protectorate of the British empire. But still Baghdad coveted Kuwait, unable to forget the old Ottoman years when it had been a part of a province governed from the city of Basra. After Kuwait had gained its independence from Britain, in 1961, Iraqi troops had sought to conquer the new country. British forces had stopped them, but now, nearly thirty years later, Saddam Hussein seemed determined to renew (and enforce) the Iraqi claim.

For the Sabahs, Baghdad's act was an unexpected betrayal. A cornucopia of oil, Kuwait had always been more a family corporation with hereditary stockholders and managers than a normal nation-state. Throughout Iraq's eight years of war with Iran, the Sabahs had been Saddam's most ardent cheerleader and generous financier. As long as Saddam and his Arab generals were bent on killing Persians, the Kuwaitis had been happy to pay him to do so.

State Department officials who served in the Persian Gulf region doggedly defended the government of the Sabah family, even though Kuwait boasted a virulently anti-Israel policy, and even though the Sabahs had briefly cut off oil shipments to the United States after the Six-Day War in 1967. Kuwait, they said, was the most democratic of the emirates, which was true, as far as it went. Since 1963, however, the Sabahs had twice suspended the country's constitution. And never had the emirate treated its large disenfranchised population of Palestinian guest workers with anything much above contempt.

The latter issue afforded a good propaganda point for Saddam. But even he did not bother to use it as a justification for his invasion. The truth was that Saddam had no use for the Kuwaitis. As long as they had paid into his protection racket during the war with Iran, they were valued. But now that the war had ended and the debts from it were ever more onerous, Kuwait was a fiction that no longer had to be respected.

Just days before the invasion, Marwan Qassem, Jordan's foreign minister, had met with the emir and encouraged him to do whatever was necessary to avoid further conflict with Iraq. If it was a question of resolving the border dispute by a few kilometers, a high Jordanian official quoted Qassem as saying, why not do it? The emir flatly refused. The Jordanian official, who was present at the time, recalled: "His answer was something to the effect that our constitution [which was still suspended] forbids us to give an inch of territory to anybody." But what if Saddam invaded, the Jordanian persisted? "The response was, well, if he wants to come across, let him come across. The Americans will push him out."

The emir was right. It was largely to restore the rule of this myopic man and his wealthy family—and to preserve the regime of his fellow monarch and his family of 4,000 princes in Saudi Arabia—that George Bush had decided to dispatch hundreds of thousands of American soldiers.

In Kuwait City at the end of the first week after the invasion, something unexpected happened: Saddam Hussein had begun moving his elite Republican Guard divisions north—back to Iraq. "It was sometime around the ninth [of August]," John Feeley recalled. Feeley, who knew more about Saddam's military than any other American in Kuwait—who was more knowledgeable on the subject, in fact, than anyone else in Kuwait—was not sure exactly where the Republican Guard divisions were being redeployed. He did know they were gone. "They were headed out of Kuwait," Feeley said. "They went back up to the area where they ended up staying for the next six months." Other analysts placed the withdrawal of the Republican Guard force about ten days later.

King Fahd had invited American forces into Saudi Arabia because he was worried about an Iraqi invasion. The CIA's satellite photographs showed a large Iraqi force massed in the Kuwaiti desert not far from the Saudi border. That, in turn, worried General Schwarzkopf's staff. A senior Central Command officer explained: "In spite of 1002-90, which was the scenario for [our response to] an invasion of Kuwait and Saudi Arabia, the Iraqi force that actually went in there was a hell of a lot bigger than what 1002 had envisioned. We [had been] talking twelve, fourteen divisions, max, and only two or three or maybe four going down into Saudi Arabia. Well, they ended with six or eight down on the Saudi Arabian border within four days." Schwarzkopf, for one, was absolutely convinced that Saddam had designs on the kingdom. "I don't think there is any question at all," Schwarzkopf later told David Frost in a televised interview, "that he would have attacked Saudi Arabia." But without his Republican Guard, his best trained, most elite force?

Although the Republican Guard had spearheaded the invasion of Kuwait, other divisions followed. The divisions Saddam had farthest south in the Kuwaiti desert were equipped with heavy tanks. They were first-echelon mechanized-infantry and armored divisions, U.S. military and intelligence officials said. A senior Pentagon official said they included Saddam's 12th Armored Division, which was far to the west, where the Kuwaiti desert ended and the Iraqi desert began. Ranged east along Kuwait's southern border with Saudi Arabia were Saddam's 5th, 10th, 11th, and 17th Divisions. Like the 12th, these were first-echelon units. The 6th Division, a decidedly second-echelon unit, rounded out the force arrayed along Kuwait's southern border facing the Saudi oil fields.

However, none of these divisions was remotely the equal of the Republican Guard divisions. Would Saddam have attempted an invasion of Saudi Arabia with his Republican Guard divisions so far to the north? The Iraqi leader had told Jordan's King Hussein that he was prepared to pull his forces out of Kuwait. On the face of it, there was no reason to believe him. With so many divisions so far south, as King Fahd pointed out to Secretary Cheney in Jidda, it was far more force than he needed to take over Kuwait.

But an attack on Saudi Arabia—the very premise of which constituted the justification for American intervention? "We still have no hard evidence that he ever intended to invade Saudi Arabia," a senior Central Command officer conceded months after the war ended. "We believe he did. But none of the captured documents or prisoner debriefs has come up with anything hard [indicating an attack on the Saudi oil fields]."

Wars often begin with uncertainties and faulty assumptions. In this conflict there was considerable evidence indicating that the kingdom of Saudi Arabia was not in jeopardy. But with an unpredictable character like Saddam making the decision, no one could be sure. More to the point, after the invasion of Kuwait, no one wanted to be wrong.

In Cairo, one week after the invasion of Kuwait, Hosni Mubarak was immensely frustrated. Although Saddam had agreed to accept a visit from King Hussein, the trip arranged by Mubarak had not gone well. Mubarak had insisted that if the proposed Jidda meeting between the Kuwaitis and the Iraqis were to have any chance of success, Saddam would have to agree to two conditions beforehand. First, withdraw from Kuwait. Second, allow the Sabah family to return. After that, with Egypt, Saudi Arabia, and Jordan doing some arm-twisting, the Kuwaitis would have to listen to Saddam's complaints and offer some form of redress. The only problem, as Mubarak recalled it, was that King Hussein had bungled the mission. "I asked him,

'What about the two points?' He told me, 'I didn't discuss the details.' I said, 'Your Majesty, I cannot hold myself back.' " Finally, Mubarak had to do something.

With Mubarak's blessing, the Arab League had issued a bland statement denouncing the action by Iraqi troops in Kuwait. That had angered Saddam even further, but Mubarak nevertheless requested, through the Iraqi ambassador in Cairo, that he send a delegation to a summit of the Arab League. With the Iraqis present, the Egyptian president believed, and the pressure that could be brought only in a summit-type forum, perhaps a solution could still be reached.

Saddam dispatched Taha Yasin Ramadan to Cairo. An erstwhile bank cashier, the Iraqi envoy evidently had been authorized to adopt a hard line with Mubarak. The Iraqi leadership had the lowest possible regard for the Egyptian president. "Clumsy, a fool" were the words Foreign Minister Tariq Aziz used to describe Mubarak to Secretary of State James Baker, according to a notetaker during their last session in Geneva before the war.

It was evident as soon as he got off the plane in Cairo on the morning of August 10 that Ramadan intended to bully the summiteers. A very nervous Sheik Jaber al-Sabah had come to Cairo, at last, to talk. But when the Iraqi plane disgorged one hundred uniformed soldiers, each carrying a fully loaded Kalashnikov machine gun, Mubarak thought he had made a grievous mistake in asking Ramadan or any other Iraqis to the summit. "I was terrified that they might do something to the emir of Kuwait," the Egyptian president recalled. "Are they coming to fight the summit? Really, one hundred! We took them far away, and we put the whole delegation in a special residence." The Sabah family was staying in one of the big luxury hotels downtown, and the heavy Egyptian security detail was instructed not to let any of the Iraqi delegation anywhere near them. "They could shoot the emir, kill him and get rid of the whole family," Mubarak worried. "And then we would be accused of having not secured everything. We were terrified of that."

Once settled in his special residence, Ramadan requested a meeting with President Mubarak, and they agreed on a time. Ramadan showed up a half hour late, offering no apologies. Then, Mubarak recalled, incredulous, as if there had been nothing specific on their agenda, "he asked me w' ` I wanted to discuss."

Mubarak indicated he was interested in talking about the inder of Kuwait.

The Egyptian president said he remembered Ramadan's answer very clearly: "He told me, 'There is nothing called Kuwait.' . . . He said, 'No, it is Iraqi soil. There is nothing called Kuwait!' " Clearly, Mubarak thought, the summit would be a complete and utter failure.

In fact, that's precisely what it was. Once the summit was convened, Mubarak saw no reason to waste time. He called the roll of the twenty Arab nations. The proposition on the floor was whether to send a multi-Arab force. Initially, Mubarak had thought such a force might be enough without the Americans. He had given up that notion days before, however. Now the proposal was to have the Arab force join the Americans already arriving in Saudi Arabia. Gravely, Mubarak called the roll. The final vote was 12–8 in favor. Arabs would send soldiers to fight a brother Arab—an action without precedent for the Arab League. "The Iraqi delegation left the summit," Mubarak said. "All of us heads of state, and them insulting us with the nastiest words you could ever imagine!"

It had ended as badly as it might have. Afterward, King Hussein disputed some of the points made by President Mubarak concerning his mission to Baghdad, but he said he had had no real illusions about the way things would finally turn out. Saddam had been in desperate financial straits for some time, and things had lately gone from bad to worse. In the king's presence, Saddam had begun talking in extremes, and he had used an old Arab expression on more than one occasion. It worried the king considerably. The expression, the king said, translated as follows: "Cutting throats is preferable to starving people."

In Tampa, General Schwarzkopf's planners and intelligence officers were working virtually without sleep, "hot bunking" it, grabbing two to three hours at a time in MacDill's Bachelor Officers' Quarters before getting up to go back to work again: when one bunk was vacated, another exhausted officer would tumble into it. Schwarzkopf believed that a "minimum deterrent force" of at least 40,000 troops was needed immediately. He wanted reinforcements for those high-risk advance units, and he wanted them right away. His staff, it was true, had had no indication of any move by Saddam Hussein's forces south into the Saudi oil fields. But they had to be prepared for such a possibility. "We figured they could attack with four divisions," a senior Central Command officer said. "They could have reached Dhahran in two days. They could have done it."

Planning on how to counter such an attack would determine, in some instances right down to the brigade level, which units needed to be put on planes and fast-sealift ships first. "General Schwarzkopf had a very difficult task," said Colonel Daryl Bottjer, the head of the crisis-action team at the headquarters of the Military Airlift Command at Scott Air Force Base in Illinois. When Schwarzkopf wanted something moved, Bottjer was often the man who would have to move it. "He's looking at several armored divisions and mechanized-infantry divisions and a sophisticated air force. And he needs to put in a ground force that will block the Iraqis from moving into Saudi Arabia. But that force has to be placed there in such a manner, at specific numbers and types of equipment and with enough speed so that if Saddam Hussein went south, that force would have a reasonable chance of surviving until they could be reinforced."

Publicly, General Powell and Defense Secretary Cheney expressed confidence that the first troops in the desert were out of harm's way. "I think they are pretty secure," Powell told a Pentagon news conference on August 8, in response to a reporter's question. "Even though these aircraft and ground troops are just arriving, the *Independence* is in a position to provide support, as is the *Eisenhower* battle group. So we have the ability to cover these movements."

Technically, that was true. The two aircraft carriers and the warships in their battle groups would have provided some protection, but not much. "If [Saddam] had come across with four or five divisions," a senior aide to Schwarzkopf said, "it would have just been a running delay. We'd have shot and moved, shot and moved, shot and moved and just kind of traded space for time. But with a light force like the 82nd being foot mobile, they would have had to pull back into an enclave on the coast and rely on the carrier planes and the naval gunfire to support them. . . . So the 82nd would have been trapped on the beach somewhere." Others were more pessimistic. If Saddam had come south with heavy tanks, General Luck said, the brigade from the 82nd Airborne Division would have been a mere "speed bump."

In many respects the history of the Gulf War was made up of a series of critical turning points. Had Saddam gone only part of the way into Kuwait, had the Bush administration failed to garner U.N. support for condemning the invasion, had the Americans absorbed several hundred casualties in the days immediately after the invasion—any one of these events, and others later, could have changed the outcome of the conflict dramatically.

Nations join with one another and act in concert for only one reason: self-interest. Nevertheless, in building the coalition that would ultimately go to war against Saddam Hussein, it did not hurt that the nations of the world were being asked to line up against a villain straight out of Central Casting. "You just could not fathom," said a senior Bush administration official, "how much Saddam helped to build the coalition and hold the coalition together."

The Iraqi leader's behavior was almost always as baffling as it was counterproductive. After the stunning success of his blitzkrieg invasion, Saddam Hussein did nearly everything wrong. He couldn't even keep his story straight. Iraq's first announcement of the invasion of Kuwait had been at pains to praise the brave "students" and "revolutionaries" who had summoned assistance from Baghdad to throw the corrupt Sabah family out of power. When these "students" were trotted out for the world, however, two of them spoke with decidedly Iraqi accents. It was an obvious sham, and Saddam soon gave it up. Next, on August 8, came the announcement of the "provisional government" of Kuwait. Unfortunately, every one of the new ministers was an Iraqi. This ploy was so blatant a fraud that when Thomas Pickering stood up in the well of the U.N. Security Council the following day to condemn this latest outrage and declare the annexation of Kuwait "null and void," there was no objection. When the balloting was completed, U.N. Resolution 662 had passed unanimously. This time even Cuba and Yemen had voted to condemn Iraq.

And still Saddam made matters worse. Less than a day after the Security Council vote, he had ordered the borders of Iraq and Kuwait closed, trapping more than one million Asian and Arab guest workers, as well as several thousand Westerners. Many of those Westerners detained in Iraq and Kuwait would soon become hostages, but according to several close advisers, George Bush knew the perils of becoming consumed by the plight of hostages. He had seen firsthand the damage Ronald Reagan's obsession with hostages had caused in the Iran-contra scandal. More important, he believed that it was morally repugnant to barter with a despot like Saddam. While the State Department would refrain from referring to the Westerners in Iraq and Kuwait as hostages, Bush would use the term bluntly. Nevertheless he would refuse to allow the hostage issue to affect the larger decisions he would face in the confrontation with Iraq.

The Arab League vote to send troops to join the American-led force had taken place on August 10. In response, the Iraqi leader called for a "holy war" against the Western forces already beginning to arrive in the Saudi desert. In a statement read over Radio Baghdad, Saddam threatened to turn Kuwait into "a graveyard" if any attempt was made to liberate the emirate. It was the sixth time in the eight days since the invasion that Iraqi press statements had used the graveyard image.

Apart from Bush's own remarkable efforts in pulling together the global anti-Saddam coalition, no one was more gifted at this task than his secretary of state, a diplomat who combined the hard-sell skills of an aluminum-siding salesman with the polish and charm of the high-priced corporate advocate he had once been. In his native Houston and in Washington, James Addison Baker III had acquired a reputation as a consummate dealmaker. The odd thing about Jim Baker was how late he had stumbled into the political arena. In late 1969, a highly successful corporate lawyer, Baker was trying to decide whether he should seek the congressional seat being vacated by George Bush for a Senate run. In January 1970, however, his wife, Mary Stuart, was diagnosed with cancer. She was dead within a month. The loss devastated Baker, who was left with four boys, all under the age of sixteen. While a run for Bush's old seat—and if he won, a move to Washington—was simply out of the question, helping Bush was not. The two-term congressman was challenging Lloyd Bentsen, another Texan who would rise to a position of immense influence in the Washington of the 1980s. Bush wound up losing the race, but in Jim Baker he gained a lifelong friend, his best.

For his part, Baker gained a new lease on life. Nearly three years after Bush's loss to Bentsen, Baker married a handsome divorcée named Susan Garrett Winston. Two years later, with his four children and her three, the Bakers moved to Washington, where he joined the administration of Gerald Ford. Less than a year later, the Bakers added an eighth child to their Washington household with the birth of Mary Bonner Baker.

After Gerald Ford was defeated by Jimmy Carter in 1976, Baker made his first and only run for elective office. In his attempt for the attorney generalship of Texas, he was defeated by a Democrat, but friends said that his infatuation with the world of politics was confirmed once and for all. Baker himself confessed later to having "been bitten by the political bug." Eight years with Reagan had just made the infection worse, and although many in Washington suspected that Baker harbored presidential ambitions, friends insisted that the position of secretary of state was "the only job he ever wanted."

Months after the invasion of Kuwait, the debate in Washington would heat up about the effectiveness of the sanctions against Iraq, and Bush would seriously begin to contemplate doubling the American force in the desert. It would almost certainly mean war. War meant uncertainty, and in uncertainty lay the seeds of failure. It was then that some of the President's closest advisers would complain privately that Baker was seeking to put some distance between himself and his old friend's seemingly imminent decision to use offensive force. Failure was not an outcome that Jim Baker had much use for. And quagmire was not a word that appeared in his political dictionary.

In August 1990, however, there was no evidence of any such division between the President and his secretary of state. For the moment, Scowcroft was clearly Bush's guiding influence. In the weeks ahead and through the fall and winter, few people would invest more time and energy than Baker in helping to construct the coalition against Iraq. After all, it had been Baker's idea to use the United Nations as the focus of diplomatic action against Saddam. It would be Baker's job to sell the coalition to individual leaders around the world.

Despite the early evidence of strong international support, at the Pentagon, many senior officials worried the concept of a coalition like an old bone. Perhaps the United States wouldn't be able to put it together. At the State Department, however, senior officials trumpeted Baker's sales techniques and lawyerly closing skills. They were true believers. "No one," said a senior administration official who is a confidant of the secretary of state, "is better than Jim Baker one on one."

Notwithstanding the insularity of the most senior levels of the Bush administration, coalition building was not the exclusive province of the President and his secretary of state. John Kelly, the assistant secretary of state for Near Eastern and South Asian affairs, would play a critical role. Kelly believed that if any Arab leader was inclined to oppose Saddam, it might well be Hafez al-Assad, Syria's ruthless dictator, an astute reader of the geopolitical map. With the Soviet Union struggling with its own internal problems, Assad knew he could no longer count on his chief patron. After twenty years, the Soviets had said they were going to shut off the cash pipeline to Damascus. Assad was fond of quoting Arabic sayings, among them this favorite: "Do we want grapes in the vineyard, or do we want to fight the vintner?" Assad, Kelly felt, would want the grapes. On August 13, Kelly saw Assad in Damascus. Hardly one of the world's most voluble figures, Assad said enough to satisfy Kelly. If there was going to be a military coalition arrayed against the hated Saddam Hussein, Assad would not be left out.

Of all the leaders of the Arab world, Jordan's King Hussein was in the most difficult position. A good 60 percent of his subjects were Palestinian. Stateless and mostly impoverished, the Palestinians bore no love for Kuwait. The Sabah family had been glad to have Palestinians come to the emirate and tend their gardens and remove their trash. But Palestinian workers had been forbidden to bring their families with them. Once their guest-worker visas had expired, they had been forced to leave; there were, it seemed, plenty more Palestinians willing to work cheap. On August 12, Saddam Hussein announced that he would do whatever was necessary to resolve the crisis in Kuwait, if Israel would withdraw from the occupied territories of the West Bank and the Gaza strip and if Syria—his true archenemy—got out of Lebanon. The speech complicated matters for King Hussein. Suddenly, Palestinians in Jordan were volunteering to drive to Iraq and fight side by side with Iraqis. Not only had the king infuriated Mubarak, his halfhearted public defense of Saddam shortly after the invasion had enraged George Bush. The king had been a friend, Bush told several senior advisers; he had thought he could trust him, and he had been badly disappointed to learn that he could not. Bush appreciated the difficulty of the king's position, aides said. Jordan lay between the bristling border of Israel and Saddam's Scud missile launchers in western Iraq. Any air conflict as a result of the Gulf crisis would almost certainly involve Jordanian airspace. Still, Bush felt, the king should have seen how wrong it was to side with Saddam.

There was also the matter of money. The Jordanian port on the Gulf of Aqaba was Iraq's principal maritime outlet. Aqaba handled, on average, 500 ships a year and 2,300 tons of cargo daily. At least half that was taken by truck to Baghdad. In return for Jordan's expeditious handling of Iraqi cargo, Amman received a daily shipment of 35,000 barrels of fine Iraqi oil, at the hard-to-beat price of $2 a barrel. King Hussein knew he would pay a heavy price if he joined the Iraqi embargo. But he might ultimately pay a heavier price if he did not. Jordan, the king emphasized after several days of uncomfortable silence, understood its obligations to the United Nations: the port of Aqaba would be closed. Still, it would be some time before traffic to Aqaba was really shut off, and then only because of pressure from the American-led flotilla, not from the Diwan, the elegant hilltop complex of the Hashemite royal court in Amman. There would also be cheating and leakage through the Jordanian "back door" across the desert. Even with Jordan's less-than-full cooperation, however, the international embargo against Iraq would prove to be one of the most effective ever undertaken.

For Eduard Shevardnadze in Moscow, it had taken almost no time after James Baker's departure for the battle with the hard-liners to begin. It started out nasty, and it would only get worse. In urging the Kremlin to join with the West in cutting off Baghdad economically and militarily, Shevardnadze had not just turned a relationship of more than two decades on its head, he had taken on some of Moscow's most well-entrenched bureaucratic infighters.

The Soviet military was particularly alarmed. Arms deals with the oil-rich Middle East had been a particularly lucrative source of hard cash. Between 1986 and 1990, for example, Soviet arms sales to the Middle East had totaled about $17.5 billion. By most estimates, Baghdad had been closer to Moscow than Damascus had. Hundreds of senior Soviet military officers had served in Iraq at one time or another as technical advisers, and many had maintained close ties with their counterparts in Saddam Hussein's military machine. In the Supreme Soviet, conservative deputies, nearly all of them from the military, would charge that Shevardnadze wanted to send troops to the Gulf. Shevardnadze would hotly deny the charge, but the seed would eventually bear fruit: the loyalties of the foreign minister, a Georgian, would come to be seen in some quarters as suspect.

The suspicion began in the Soviet foreign-policy community, generally thought to consist of the foreign ministry, the military-industrial complex, the Communist Party's International Department, the KGB, and Gorbachev's inner circle of presidential advisers. "The internal diplomacy," said a senior Soviet diplomat involved in the debates, "was much more difficult than the external dealings." Trade organizations, especially those dealing with the export and import of oil and the sale of oil-extraction equipment, howled in protest over Shevardnadze's actions. For its relatively small size, Baghdad maintained a brisk trade with Moscow and several of the fifteen

Soviet republics. From its elaborate embassy complex at 12 Pogodinskaya Street, in a quiet central Moscow neighborhood, Saddam's representatives routinely presided over hundreds of millions of dollars in trade deals.

Shevardnadze may have been able to contend with the trade organizations, and perhaps even with the irate military, but he found himself bucking much of his own foreign ministry as well. While Shevardnadze viewed the Gulf crisis through the lens of warming East-West relations, within the ministry's influential Middle East department the conflict was viewed in the traditional terms of the Soviets' long-standing support for the more radical constituencies within the Arab world. One reason for this was that the Middle East department and, to a large extent, the entire foreign ministry, were dominated by *arabisti,* diplomats whose careers had been built on pushing the pro-Arab, anti-Israel line espoused by the Soviet Union for four decades. It made little sense, they argued, to throw out a valued twenty-year relationship with Iraq and gamble on a still nascent bond with the West that was fraught with difficulties and possible traps.

The main proponent of this view was Yevgeny M. Primakov, a former *Pravda* correspondent in the Middle East who would play a crucial role in the tense, last-minute diplomacy just before the war broke out. As Gorbachev's personal envoy, Primakov would shuttle back and forth between Baghdad and Moscow with proposals aimed at averting conflict—but only at the cost of some concessions to Saddam that George Bush was not prepared to make.

Skepticism about cooperating with the United States in the Gulf seemed to be shared by many ordinary Soviets. For decades public opinion had had no effect on Kremlin decision making. That had changed. Under growing pressure from an evolving democracy movement, the unpredictable forces unleashed by Gorbachev's policy of glasnost, and a public made restive by declining living standards, the Supreme Soviet had to be attentive, if not wholly responsive, to the public mood. The debacle of Afghanistan had left many people uneasy about the prospect of deploying fighting troops outside the Soviet Union—and in particular to the Muslim south.

For these reasons, just a week after the invasion of Kuwait, the Kremlin announced only that "the Soviet Union stands for coordinated actions within the Security Council of the United Nations." Still, Bush and Baker were enormously pleased by the Soviets' decision to cut off arms supplies to Baghdad immediately. They hoped to persuade Moscow to participate in the Allied military force they were just beginning to build—even if it was the mere token presence of a single Soviet warship in the multinational naval flotilla. It was not to be, however. The Kremlin statement concluded: "At this time, there is no question of taking part in a multinational force or sea blockade outside the confines of the United Nations Security Council."

However, with the passage of Resolution 665, on August 25, the Security Council would impress the seal of the United Nations on the American-led naval flotilla. The Soviet delegate, Yuli Vorontsov, would vote in support of the measure (as would all the others except Cuba and Yemen). The Soviets still would send no warships. Moscow had evidently decided it would not restrain Washington's hand in the "new world order" Bush had asked them to help construct. But it would not reach out to actively help either.

CHAPTER 7

PREPARING FOR WAR

W HEN NATIONS go to war, nothing is simple. Few knew better than H. Norman Schwarzkopf the truth of that maxim. In Tampa, in the days prior to his August 25 departure for Riyadh, the burly four-star general was like a man possessed, reaching into a half-dozen different logistics and planning problems at once, pushing, always pushing for more, and faster. He had spoken of a "minimum deterrent force" of 40,000 soldiers, but knew that in the event push came to shove he would need many, many more. He would have to be prepared. His President expected no less.

Sometimes, aides and colleagues said, General Schwarzkopf seemed to revel in his many apparent contradictions. He would deny it again and again, but some aides said he had a terrible temper that manifested itself in towering, coruscating fits of rage and frightening desk-pounding diatribes. Almost always, however, especially in the early days of the Desert Shield deployment, the general's rages were born of a kind of tenderness. It was a given that good generals put the needs of their soldiers first; with Schwarzkopf, aides said, his soldiers' safety was an absolute passion. He wanted them protected, and he didn't care much whom he had to walk over to see that it was done. But there was another side to the general. Some of the same aides who marveled at the depth of Schwarzkopf's emotional commitment to his troops would also later criticize their chief as being something of a megalomaniac and a self-promoter. Indeed, some of his counterparts among the Pentagon's general-staff officers had long held that view.

In two tours of duty in Vietnam, Schwarzkopf had won three Silver Stars and several other medals. He had also confirmed once and for all the difference between a field command and a desk command. In 1965–66, Schwarzkopf served as an adviser to the Vietnamese Airborne Division. It was, he said, the best year of his life: "When they slept on the ground, I slept on the ground. What they ate, I ate it. I was truly serving a cause I believed in." In his second tour, in 1969–70, Schwarzkopf divided his time between a staff job at U.S. Army Vietnam headquarters and command of a battalion of the American Division. "I hated it in the rear," Schwarzkopf said. "It was a cesspool. I went out to my battalion, and I never went back to the rear except when ordered. . . . You saw the worst there; the commander was living in luxury and his focus was on things like the reenlistment rate. It was a nightmare."

Schwarzkopf held to these views with a fierceness and intensity that was hard to conceal. As it turned out, it didn't much matter, for over the course of his career in the Pentagon after Vietnam, he made no real effort to make a secret of them. Sitting behind a desk in the Pentagon, Schwarzkopf said on numerous occasions in a variety of forums, was not fit work for real generals. In 1974, he underscored the point, volunteering for a deputy command of a brigade in faraway Alaska. "Anything," a friend said, "to get out of the building and get a command. He loved it."

And still he rocked the boat. The deputy commander of the Grenada invasion in 1983, Schwarzkopf went public afterward with his criticisms of the Pentagon's planning for the operation. For many of those involved in the invasion, the story (perhaps apocryphal) that summed up the Keystone Kops quality of the planning was when one young soldier had to use his mother's telephone credit card in a pay phone to get in touch with his commanders over a public line. Schwarzkopf's complaints struck some at the time as grandstanding. But others who knew the general well said that his motivation was pure. And at its heart, once again, was the sacred duty senior officers had to their soldiers in the field. In Grenada, Schwarzkopf felt, the brass had let the grunts down.

Schwarzkopf had nothing but contempt for any officer who took his responsibilities to his soldiers lightly. A student of the Civil War, he was fond of quoting General Robert E. Lee. "The military is the only calling

I know," Lee wrote in a letter home, "that demands that you kill those you love the most: to be a good commander, you must love your soldiers; to be a good commander, you must send them out to die." Schwarzkopf saw plenty of people die in Vietnam, and he blamed many of the Pentagon's senior officer corps at the time for those deaths. "All you have to do is hold your first soldier who is dying in your arms, and you have that terribly futile feeling that 'I can't do anything about it, the life is literally flowing out of this young man, and I can't do anything about it.' Then you understand the horror of war. Any soldier worth his salt should be antiwar."

Although he had continued to add stars to his shoulder board, earning his fourth in November 1988, Schwarzkopf never quite shook the reputation as being somehow different, a kind of moral scold just a bit out of sync with much of the rest of the general staff. For that reason, at the time he was given the commander-in-chief's job at the Central Command in Tampa, many on the Pentagon's general staff believed that Schwarzkopf's days were numbered. For all the efforts that had gone into its creation, Central Command was considered a backwater, the Pentagon's ugly-duckling command. It had to have been particularly galling for Schwarzkopf, who loved nothing better than mixing it up with his troops: the Central Command had no troops assigned to it. Among the general staff, Pentagon officials said, it was widely known that Schwarzkopf would take his retirement at the earliest possible opportunity. Then came Kuwait. Now there could be no thought of retirement. He had a kingdom to defend and, just possibly, a war to prosecute.

Schwarzkopf could issue the orders to move, but executing them would require extraordinary effort. Fortunately, on August 2, even before receiving a phone call from General Powell, Hansford Johnson, the commander-in-chief of the U.S. Transportation Command and the Military Airlift Command, had assembled a crisis-action team under the direction of Colonel Daryl Bottjer. Scott Air Force Base in Illinois would become the nerve center of a military airlift operation that would surpass by far the intensity of the Berlin airlift in 1948 and the prodigious long-haul resupply efforts that kept American troops in beans and bullets during the height of the Vietnam War.

Bottjer was the focal point of the sudden activity at Scott. For nearly twenty-four hours a day, he would be confined to a room surrounded by floor-to-ceiling maps and enormous TV-like screens that could track as many as 200 aircraft at a time on their individual flight paths from the United States to the Persian Gulf. Bottjer had been notified by Lieutenant General Johnson on August 4 that he might have to move fast. His "execute order" had come nearly seventy-two hours later—less than ninety minutes after Dick Cheney's phone call to the Oval Office reporting the invitation from King Fahd. "What transpired after that," Bottjer remembered, "was an insatiable thirst for lift that grew exponentially as the hours went by."

After arranging for the two commercial aircraft to pick up the soldiers from the ready brigade of the 82nd Airborne Division at Pope Air Force Base in North Carolina, Bottjer dispatched one of the Military Airlift Command's C-141 StarLifters to Dhahran with enough of his own people on board to run a good-sized airport. The C-141 took off at 6:25 P.M. on August 6 from McGuire Air Force Base in New Jersey. Aboard were teams of operations people, air-traffic controllers, loadmasters, logistics managers, communications specialists, and intelligence officers. This Airlift Control Element team, as the Pentagon called it, had arrived in Dhahran before anyone else. Now, at least, Bottjer was ready to deal with the demands that would come flooding into his headquarters.

And flood they did. A senior Central Command officer helping to coordinate the airlift remembered inundating Bottjer's staff with orders. With the C-141 StarLifter barely airborne out of McGuire Air Force Base, the Central Command began to demand planes, planes, and more planes. The commercial aircraft for the initial cadre of the 82nd's ready brigade had already been tapped. But Schwarzkopf now wanted the rest of the 82nd Airborne following right behind. "We activated forty aircraft," an officer said. "Twenty-five 747s, eight DC-8s, one L-1011, five DC-10s, and one 707. And that was just to haul the 82nd." Bottjer's staff set to work, and soon planes began moving. At its height, officers involved in the airlift would dub it "the aluminum bridge to the Middle East." With American aircraft landing in the desert as often as every ten minutes, it wasn't much of an exaggeration.

The airlift was just one component, albeit a very large one, of an enormously complicated military operation. What Schwarzkopf really needed to protect his soldiers were the big M1A1 Abrams tanks with their 120-mm cannons of Major General Barry McCaffrey's 24th Infantry Division (Mechanized). There was no way in the world the heavy armor of the 24th Division could be gotten to the desert by air. It would have to go by ship, as would the other heavy divisions that would be needed.

That job fell to the Military Sealift Command. There was just one small problem. On October 1, 1988, the Pentagon had established the new Transportation Command at Scott Air Force Base. In theory, this new unified command, with its headquarters staff of some 500 personnel, was tailor-made for the sudden deployment. In theory, it would coordinate all the transport responsibilities of sea and air and provide a clearinghouse of information for Major General William G. "Gus" Pagonis, the Central Command chief of logistics. However, in practice, according to Navy officials, the Transportation Command had a headquarters staff that was oriented almost exclusively to the needs of airlift. Lieutenant General Johnson was a respected Air Force commander who also was chief of the Military Airlift Command. Colonel Bottjer had done a formidable job getting the airlift operation moving. But Schwarzkopf wanted Barry McCaffrey's big battle tanks, and that was a sealift job.

So where was the sealift? On August 9, Jerry Peschka, fleet operations director for the Military Sealift Command in Washington, might have been pardoned for wondering the same thing. A burly, bespectacled Navy captain with a penchant for off-color jokes, Peschka, together with his staff, was in an awkward position. An aide to Peschka remembered receiving a phone call from a Marine officer on Lieutenant General Johnson's staff. The order, the aide recalled, was short and sweet—and absolutely bereft of specifics: "Start the sealift." Peschka's aide pressed the Marine for details. Which units were to go first? Where? The Marine had no further information. He had been instructed to pass along the order, and so he repeated it again. "Start the sealift!" Adding insult to injury, Peschka was informed that "C-Day," the official start of the sealift, had been August 7. He was already two days late.

Sometimes, movement creates its own order. Rick Fields was an Army colonel who worked with Peschka as director of plans and programs. He had a safe in his office that contained the contingency plans of most if not all of the ten U.S. military commands. Fields checked his safe. Sure enough, he did have a Central Command operations plan for a sealift deployment to the Gulf. But it was nearly two years old and specified a wholly different conflict, sending soldiers and tanks to the other side of the Persian Gulf. Schwarzkopf's planners gave a version of Plan 1002 to Colonel Fields, but it was an earlier draft, and it made some radically different assumptions. One was that there would be a warning time of thirty days. Another was that the combat force would comprise 200,000 reservists. "That would make my task absolutely phenomenal," Fields recalled. "The only thing on my mind was 'How do I get out of this building?'"

Fields took a deep breath and started working the phones. He had friends in McCaffrey's Division, and rumor had it that it would be the first of the heavy armor dispatched to the desert. Fields called McCaffrey's headquarters at Fort Stewart, Georgia, with what he thought was a simple question: What are you guys taking with you? He remembered the answer clearly. "Everything." That would require at least seven of the Navy's fast-sealift ships, Fields figured. Massive commercial container-cargo vessels that could manage a rapid 33 knots in open seas, the ships had been purchased by the Navy in the aftermath of the failed 1980 hostage-rescue attempt that had ended so tragically in the Iranian desert. The ships, known as FSSs, would have to be gotten to the port of Savannah as quickly as possible. They were scattered in Navy ports from Jacksonville, Florida, all the way to Beaumont, Texas. At the moment, none even had full crews with them. Once the ships were brought to Savannah, they would be loaded up with the big tanks and Bradley fighting vehicles of the 24th Division (Mechanized). It would then take the vessels eleven days to deposit McCaffrey and his division in Saudi Arabia.

McCaffrey, however, was not about to wait for the ships. That was someone else's job, and he simply assumed it would get done. General Schwarzkopf would ultimately assign the 24th Division the role of the "point of the spear" in the ground assault against Saddam Hussein's forces, and the assignment would come, according to a senior Army official, "precisely because of Barry McCaffrey." Some said the U.S. Army had no finer warrior. McCaffrey, in any event, had few peers. Hearing the news of the success of the Cheney visit to Jidda, he had simply assumed that the 24th would be the first heavy division to be deployed, and he had ordered his one "ready brigade" to load up and head for Savannah. The orders to move would simply have to catch up with them. "It was the old Stonewall Jackson adage," recalled a senior Central Command official, who laughed with relief over McCaffrey's presumption. "The guy who starts first usually wins the battle. That's the kind of guy McCaffrey is, and he showed it even before the war ever got started. He's sitting down there in Georgia, and he's twelve hours ahead of the orders process."

Back at Military Sealift Command headquarters, the demands on Colonel Fields and his staff kept mounting. Schwarzkopf's planners were now calling for the 1st Cavalry Division and the 3rd Armored Cavalry Regiment. In addition, the Air Force needed to move equipment and spare parts and the Marines were clamoring for transport of tanks, guns, food, and fuel. Fields and Peschka, it was increasingly obvious, would need more ships. Together they did some quick figuring. The entire U.S. sealift fleet consisted of 128 ships. Of these, the 8 FSSs would be the stars. But there were also 11 other prepositioning ships based at the tiny island of Diego Garcia in the Indian Ocean and in several ports in the Mediterranean. Ready to sail on short notice, these ships were crammed with gear for Army and Air Force personnel, who could link up with the ship en route to a destination, saving a great deal of deployment time. The Marines had 13 prepositioning ships, similarly loaded with tanks, food, fuel, and ammunition. All could be moved quickly; some were already in motion. Behind them, the bulk of the fleet, the so-called ready reserve force, consisted of 96 ships. A semi-mothballed lot of dry-cargo and refrigeration ships, they were maintained by the Maritime Administration and stored all over the country. Seventeen of the ready-reserve fleet were roll-on, roll-off container ships, or ro-ros— perfect for loading tanks, Bradley fighting vehicles and other heavy equipment quickly. But just to get under way, Peschka knew, the ro-ros had to be towed to the nearest port, where a crew would have to feed them fuel and water, stoke the boilers, and test all of the creaky old operating systems.

First, however, there was the priority of the 24th Division. Schwarzkopf's planners had emphasized it, and Major General McCaffrey's people had told Fields they were bringing everything. Fields had figured seven FSSs for the job. When Peschka learned what "everything" was, he thought again. "Everything" would require ten ships, minimum.

Jerry Peschka was the right man in the right place. At the age of eleven, laid up with polio in his home in New Mexico, he had begun to read about the sea. He had dreamed of little else ever since. As a young man, he had longed to become the captain of a ship in the U.S. Merchant Marine. Poor eyesight, however, had kept him out of the Merchant Marine Academy in Kings Point, New York; he had gone on to Oregon State University where, at graduation, he obtained a commission in the U.S. Naval Reserve. Almost from the start, he had seen the Military Sealift Command as the place he wanted to be. Soon, he was running the busy Military Sealift Command shop in Pusan, South Korea, where he never passed up a chance to visit a Merchant Marine ship that happened into port. Eventually, he was transferred to a new posting in the Mediterranean, where he had absorbed a wealth of information through firsthand contact with ports in Africa and the Persian Gulf. Some of the ports he had visited personally, having captained a fleet oil-supply ship in the Gulf. By the time Peschka assumed the job of fleet operations director for the Military Sealift Command in Washington, he knew the dry docks, repair facilities, and ship-chandlery outfits up and down the Gulf. For instance, he knew that the Saudi port of Dammam had an enormous pier nearly two miles long with heavy cranes scattered at regular intervals. He also knew which of the Gulf's dingy ports would be able to accommodate any obscure need of the U.S. Navy.

Peschka also believed that, no matter how chaotic the Persian Gulf deployment seemed in its opening hours and how harried he and Rick Fields might become, a lean operation was best. In a spacious room on the top floor of one of the Military Sealift Command's two redbrick buildings in the Washington Navy Yard, Peschka's command post was determinedly low-tech. Signs identifying individual team leaders hung from chains of paper clips from the ceiling. Like nearly everyone else in the Pentagon, Peschka felt he was naked without access to CNN. He had a television, but no access to cable TV. Peschka authorized Marge Holtz, the Military Sealift Command's public-affairs officer, to buy some insulated copper wire, which a technician then ran over to Peschka's command post from a cable-wired room across the hall. For keeping track of the ships that would be picking up, ferrying and unloading the soldiers and supplies for General Schwarzkopf, Peschka's staff propped big, white, plastic-coated boards against the walls. Markers were available nearby to track every new development. The notion that Peschka might prefer markers to computers would later be received with considerable grumpiness by the high-tech types back in Transportation Command headquarters in Illinois. Peschka was perfectly content with the markers and the big boards, however. In fact, they would work just fine.

Not everyone would respond with such efficiency. When Schwarzkopf's planners called Fort Hood, Texas, to check on the readiness of the 6th Cavalry (Air Combat) Brigade, they got bad news. Regarded by many as the Army's premier combat-aviation unit, with a full component of nearly sixty of the ungainly-looking but deadly Apache anti-tank aircraft, the unit was expected to deploy to the Gulf in ten days.

Impossible, came the reply from Fort Hood. The brigade was low on biological and chemical gear, they had just come off a training exercise, so they were not 100 percent up to speed with pilots. And they were in tough shape on spare parts. They had fifty-four of their fifty-nine available Apaches ready and thirty-five of the efficient Charlie-model scout aircraft, but the unit had no Hellfire missiles. Without the Hellfires, the Apaches would be doing no tank killing. The Hellfire anti-tank missiles were stored at an ammo dump outside of Anniston, Alabama. For that reason, and with all the unit's other problems, it might take as long as thirty days to deploy.

A Central Command staffer said he could not believe the reply. He recalled the time: 11 A.M. on August 9; and the first aircraft of McCaffrey's 24th Division were ready to take off in exactly 2½ hours for Savannah for loading on FSSs. The 6th Cavalry couldn't hustle and do the same? To Schwarzkopf's key staffers, the stakes were obvious. The brigade from the 82nd Division was being described as a "speed bump" for Saddam's tanks, and in the cramped planning room, over the constantly ringing phones, Schwarzkopf was screaming for tank killers. "I don't give a shit who it is," a senior staffer quoted Schwarzkopf as saying. "I just want Apaches to kill tanks. And that's what I want—tank killers!" In the end, he got his killers.

Schwarzkopf's planners hit the phones. The 4th Battalion of the 229th Aviation Regiment was available. Someone else suggested the aviation brigade from the 2nd Armored Division in Germany. That would get more Apaches to the desert quickly. Meanwhile, the 1st Cavalry Division, an M1A1 tank and Bradley fighting vehicle force also from Fort Hood, needed a third brigade to replace their "roundout" brigade of National Guardsmen. The Tiger Brigade of the 2nd Armored was selected, and the 1st Cavalry Division now had three maneuver brigades.

There seemed to be no end to the things that had to be moved. Uniforms, for example. At considerable cost, the Pentagon had commissioned new uniforms for its desert-warfare troops. The soldiers called them "chocolate chips," because of their mottled design. However, the Pentagon did not have enough of them to outfit Schwarzkopf's soldiers. The Pentagon's Defense Logistics Agency had long-standing contracts with two plants in Puerto Rico and another in Philadelphia to crank out jungle-green fatigues. Could they handle a rush job and switch to the sand-colored fatigues? They could. The logistics agency placed the order for 400,000 chocolate chips.

From the Pentagon, Admiral Frank Kelso, the chief of naval operations, ordered the USS *John F. Kennedy* and the seven ships in its carrier-battle group to prepare to depart immediately from the East Coast for the Mediterranean. The aircraft carrier alone had enormous provisioning needs. A call went out to the Pentagon commissary in Norfolk, Virginia. With its escort ships, the *Kennedy*'s shopping list was Brobdingnagian: 185,000 pounds of hot dogs, 250,000 pounds of chicken, 300,000 pounds of french fries, 400,000 pounds of hamburger, and 2 million fresh eggs.

For the troops already arriving in the desert, there were fuel and water needs to be anticipated also. The average armored division burned between 550,000 and 600,000 gallons of fuel a day. Among some aircraft units, anticipated fuel needs topped a million gallons a day. Drinking water was a critical need. On their first day in the desert, in the brutal 120-degree weather, sixty-five fliers and support personnel assigned to the 1st Tactical Fighter Wing had collapsed from heat exhaustion. The only sure remedy was to keep the fluids coming. Water needs for the troops would eventually exceed 236 million gallons a month.

To defend themselves, the American soldiers would obviously need ammunition. By mid-August, ammo was coming, almost literally, from all points on the compass. The Pentagon had a huge ammunition dump in Guam. There were other dumps in Europe and at bases in the Indian Ocean. Within days, thanks to the combined efforts of Central Command headquarters staff in Tampa and Jerry Peschka's Military Sealift Command staff in the Washington Navy Yard, more than eighty ships loaded with ammunition would be steaming toward Saudi ports in the Persian Gulf.

Of all the elements in the early days of Operation Desert Shield, almost none was more important than emergency medical supplies. An Iraqi attack, especially one involving chemical weapons, might mean large numbers of casualties. The number of fatalities could be reduced if good medical care were immediately available. To be prepared for the worst, the Defense Logistics Agency had placed a rush $2 million order with a Maryland company called Survival Technology, Inc., for more than 400,000 kits containing atropine, a poison-gas antidote. Each soldier would be issued two or three of the kits, along with a gas mask, rubber gloves, and a special uniform. For treatment of more serious victims of a chemical-weapons attack, Admiral Kelso's staff had activated the U.S. Navy hospital ships USNS *Comfort* and USNS *Mercy* on August 10. By August 15, the *Mercy* was already en route to the Gulf, and Schwarzkopf's planners had issued orders that would eventually result in the establishment of fourteen full-fledged military hospitals in the Gulf. (Army units even loaded up their old

MASH medical tents from Vietnam, although it would prove a waste of time and effort—in the killing heat, the antiquated MASH equipment would fall apart and have to be junked.)

At the time, the Pentagon had no idea how much all this was costing American taxpayers. One highly regarded think tank, the Washington-based Center for Defense Information, estimated the bill for deploying 50,000 troops with their equipment at $14.6 million a day. In the end, that number would go much, much higher.

At the Military Airlift Command, Colonel Bottjer and Lieutenant General Johnson referred to the blur of activity in the second and third weeks of August as the "initial surge." In Tampa, a senior official directing the flow of men and matériel to the Gulf would look back on the deployment in awe. "Everything," the officer said, "was really flowing." In truth, the world was witnessing a rapid and massive military movement of historic proportions.

At 5 P.M. on August 23, Major General Gus Pagonis had water on the brain. Every day since arriving in Saudi Arabia late on August 7, the logistics wizard of Desert Shield had a new problem to solve. Today's problem was water: drinking water, chilled for overheated soldiers; water for showers, water. "Two days before, it had been 'feeding, sheltering and transportation,'" Colonel Roger Scearce, a senior aide to Pagonis, recalled. "Every day it was something else, and it just never stopped."

Neither did Pagonis, who would later be awarded a third star for his performance in the Gulf conflict. But with just the two, Gus Pagonis was the most senior American military commander in Saudi Arabia until General Schwarzkopf's arrival. For his first three days in Saudi Arabia, however, Pagonis did not even have an office. In the 120-degree heat, he had worked out of the back of a stifling Chevrolet Blazer, plotting out the essential logistics that could mean the difference between a successful military deployment and an embarrassing failure. As in Hannibal's time, an army still moved on its belly. And if Pagonis couldn't make sure that there was food to eat, cooks to prepare it, trucks to deliver it and water, juice, or soda to wash it down with, things would come to a grinding halt even before the first bomb burst over Baghdad.

Pagonis knew the costs of failure, and he never let up. He had arrived in the desert with a staff of just four, and he pushed them relentlessly.

Lieutenant Colonel Thomas Ehlinger was his contract specialist. Whatever U.S. forces needed to buy or rent, Ehlinger handled the details. Colonel Jack Tier was Pagonis's initial chief of staff, and Colonel Steve Koons was his transport expert. Lieutenant Colonel James Ireland was Pagonis's executive officer, and anything that wasn't handled by someone else usually fell to Ireland to straighten out. All four men were younger than their commanding officer, but at the end of another twenty-hour day, when they were ready to fall into bed exhausted, Pagonis was still going strong.

By August 13, Pagonis had more staff. These were the officers whose names he had scratched down at his kitchen table after getting the order to move from General Vuono. To Pagonis's exhausted group of four, the new arrivals had come not a moment too soon. Scearce said that by the time he arrived, "Tim Ireland looked like a cadaver, and the others were also pretty beat." But not Pagonis. A physical-fitness buff, he rose daily at 5 A.M., ran three to four miles, then settled in for paperwork before the real workday began. At lunch, he either swam or played basketball. But his health consciousness did not extend to his diet. Pagonis was a junk-food junkie. He loved Oreo cookies, and his main staples in the desert were Snickers bars and Diet Pepsis. Wherever Pagonis went, an aide accompanied him with a cooler full of the chilled diet sodas and candy bars.

In the view of Schwarzkopf, there was no one more willing to break china to get things done creatively than Pagonis. He eventually moved his staff into a dingy recreation room adjacent to an indoor swimming pool in Dhahran and dubbed the place the Logistics Operations Center. There he held two meetings a day. The first was a small morning meeting of Pagonis's immediate staff. The second was a much bigger meeting, the one-hour "stand-up" that began at five in the afternoon. Pagonis's aides would stand to report on the day's successes and failures.

Pagonis often made it up as he went along. He had run three massive annual NATO exercises in Europe, moving large armies across vast distances, but every new operation presented new problems. An early one here was latrine facilities. Pagonis wanted to know why they couldn't simply build latrines like they had in Vietnam. His only engineer at the time was a young captain. At one of the afternoon meetings soon after his arrival, Pagonis asked the captain whether he had served in Vietnam.

"No, sir," the man said, "But I saw the movie *Platoon*." The walls echoed with laughter.

"What does that have to do with anything?" Pagonis replied, laughing too.

"Well, they had a shitter in the movie that I remember," the captain said. "You want me to design you one of those?"

"Yeah, yeah, do that!" Pagonis shook his head, chuckling.

Sometime later, the captain's design in hand, an aide to Pagonis found a Saudi vendor who agreed to build the latrines. Within days, the aide recalled, "that's all you saw rolling out of the gate [from Dhahran] and down the road, because all the Saudis had gone south to Riyadh, and the only people on the road were our people trucking hundreds of showers and shitters going up and down the highway. They went all over the desert; they were delivered everywhere. They were a big morale builder."

Literally everything that the soldiers would need once they arrived in the desert would have to be procured by Pagonis and his small staff. Ninety percent of the American soldiers deployed in Desert Shield and later in Desert Storm would arrive on military aircraft, with only their weapons and a few personal belongings. Everything else, from ammunition to bottles of sunscreen, would have to come through Gus Pagonis and his staff.

In order to keep tabs on the thousands of separate items moving at any given moment, Pagonis ordered his staff to set up a simple system. Each officer was required to keep three boards or posters near his workplace, updating them daily. Some of the staff wrote on cardboard, in pencil; one officer took an unhinged door, leaned it against his desk, and used a grease pencil. The first chart listed "siggies," or significant actions taken that day. The next was called "three-up, three-down." It chronicled the three biggest achievements and the three biggest problems of the staff officer that day. The last was called "lessons learned." Its purpose, as the Americans gradually became more familiar with the very different Saudi way of doing things, was to prevent the staff from making too many of the same mistakes twice.

Pagonis himself was an obsessive user of index cards. Blue three-by-five cards were a trademark. Anyone, even the lowest private, who dropped a blue card into Pagonis's in-box would receive an answer (aides said he answered most within the hour). "It was his info base," Colonel Scearce said. "He had the ability to manage down to the truck if he wanted to, in terms of who got the next Toyota four-by-four that rolled off the boat. And you had to be prepared to talk at that level of detail."

In his first days in the desert, food had come first on Pagonis's list. King Fahd had promised to supply the American and Allied forces with both food and fuel. At least at first, the arrangement for fuel was simple: the Americans would simply drive up in their vehicles to a Saudi depot, gas up, then sign a chit. Food turned out to be slightly more complicated. The king had commissioned a fabulously wealthy Saudi businessman named Zahir Masri to make sure the soldiers had everything they needed. The Masri family owned what was described as the largest farm in Saudi Arabia and had warehouses throughout the country. For years, they had supplied the Saudi military with its provisions.

However, the Masris had no idea what to expect from the Americans. For several days, Zahir Masri came to the Logistics Operations Center asking to see Major General Pagonis. Despite his letter from the king, the American soldiers had refused to let him in. "Here's this little guy running around in a sheet," a senior aide to Pagonis recalled. "[The guards] said, 'You want to feed 200,000 people? Get out of here.' Nobody believed him."

Masri persisted, and finally Colonel Scearce learned of Masri's efforts and located him in the lobby of the opulent Oberoi Hotel in Dhahran. "He showed me the letter from the king," Scearce said. "He showed me his brochures from his company, Astro Foods. And we set about devising a plan right there to feed the 82nd Airborne and the follow-on forces." Scearce put Masri together with another of Pagonis's staff, Chief Warrant Officer 4 Wes Wolfe.

Although most soldiers of Desert Shield and Desert Storm would never know his full name, let alone his title, Wes Wolfe became something of a legend to the troops. To feed the Saudi army, Masri had basically made sure that his people butchered enough lamb and supplied enough rice to keep the soldiers happy. To deal with the Americans, Wes Wolfe told Zahir Masri, things would have to be done differently. American soldiers liked pizzas, Wolfe said. Masri nodded. He would arrange for pizzas. What about french fries? And hot dogs? Masri nodded again. He understood. What American soldiers really liked, Wolfe went on, were hamburgers. Again Masri nodded. The Saudi and the American began discussing how they could provide hamburgers and hot dogs and pizzas and french fries to the soldiers who would be spread out across the endless desert. Wolfe suggested mobile mess halls. Masri liked the idea.

In fact, the mobile mess halls would become one of the more ubiquitous icons of the American presence. In honor of Wes Wolfe's inspired notion,

Zahir Masri dubbed his burgers "wolfburgers" and the mess halls "wolfmobiles." Like a fashionable new restaurant, wolfmobiles very nearly became the victims of their own success. In the months before the war, soldiers and brass alike driving a dizzying variety of military vehicles and aircraft would descend on the wolfmobiles for snacks, wolfburgers, and fries. An occasional Apache or a Black Hawk helicopter created immense storms of swirling dust, their crews jumping out with orders for wolfburgers to go. Bradley fighting vehicles dropped in for fast food. "The most bizarre thing I saw was a huge road grader pull up to one," Scearce said. "I never did see a tank stop though." Out of his own seemingly bottomless pockets, Zahir Masri paid for the wolfmobiles to be built and then stocked. "I don't know how he was paid by the Saudis," Scearce said, "but I know the U.S. taxpayer didn't pay for that. . . . Masri was a major, major unsung hero."

Within the first ninety days of Desert Shield, Pagonis and his staff would move 1.3 million tons of equipment, including 12,000 tanks, 67,000 wheeled vehicles, 115,000 tons of ammunition, 55 million pounds of mail, 117 million bottles of drinking water, and an untold amount of lumber, fuel, toothbrushes, tires, bandages, fan belts, caps, shoes, shoelaces, tents, grills, T-shirts, baseballs, and assorted odds and ends.

It was for the soldier, Pagonis told his staff time and again: make it happen. The miracle was that it did.

Even at this early stage in Operation Desert Shield, there were many in Washington who believed that George Bush's real reason for deploying American soldiers to the Gulf was not the stated one. On a shimmering summer afternoon in the third week of August, the President told a large assembly of military officers from the steps of the Pentagon's river entrance that Saddam Hussein was a threat not just to the world's oil supply but to "our way of life." Comparing the Iraqi dictator to Hitler, he said, "A half-century ago, our nation and the world paid dearly for appeasing an aggressor who should, and could, have been stopped. We are not going to make the same mistake again." Bush's policy, at least officially, had not changed. Its public objectives were the defense of Saudi Arabia and, through the exertion of economic pressure, the withdrawal of Iraqi forces from Kuwait. But to many of the men in uniform listening to him, it sure sounded like war.

By the middle of August, American intelligence analysts had several new developments to consider. On August 12, the first Westerner, a Briton named Douglas Croskery, was shot dead by an Iraqi soldier in Kuwait City. Working his network of radio contacts around the emirate, Major Feeley had kept his superiors in Tampa and Washington informed of the growing number of rapes, beatings, and other assorted attacks. The toll was appalling. The murder of Croskery, however, was the first indication that Saddam's soldiers were willing to kill their Western hostages in cold blood. That made Saddam's previously announced August 24 deadline for the closure of all foreign embassies in Kuwait City seem all the more ominous.

Saddam's next move surprised nearly everyone, especially his old enemies in Tehran. On August 15, without warning, the Iraqi leader announced that his soldiers would withdraw immediately from Iranian territory. All Iranian prisoners of war held by Baghdad would be summarily released. In addition, Iraq was renouncing any and all claims to the Shatt-al-Arab, the slender waterway that separated Iran from Iraq. To Winston Wiley, the man in charge of the Persian Gulf task force at the Central Intelligence Agency, this last offer was astonishing. Control of the Shatt-al-Arab was the main reason Iraq had gone to war with Iran in the first place. Suddenly, Saddam Hussein had turned his back on eight years of blood and bitter strife as if they had never happened. It was a worrisome sign, many analysts believed. "That war was over," explained a senior U.S. intelligence officer. "[Saddam] was looking at a new one. And he didn't want a third front with Iran."

The analysts worried over Saddam's intentions. On one of its regular passes over the Iraqi divisions crouched on Kuwait's southern border with Saudi Arabia, an American spy satellite captured several high-resolution images of Saddam's soldiers loading and unloading artillery rounds. These were conclusively identified as containing chemical weapons. Some of the shells were being fed into the maw of Saddam's big G-5 artillery pieces. Designed and made in South Africa, the G-5 was quite simply the finest and most lethal artillery piece in the world. It had both greater range and accuracy than anything in the American artillery arsenal. Was the loading of chemical weapons, in plain view of the satellites Saddam knew were watching, more "posturing" to warn the Americans away? The last time the word had been used was during the secret and inconclusive debate over Saddam's intentions for the two divisions of Republican Guard forces massed on the Kuwaiti border in late July. Few people were willing to advance the argument again now. Posturing it may well have been. But no one at the CIA, the Pentagon, or Central Command in Tampa could be sure. If Saddam was loading chemical weapons, it had to be assumed that he intended to use them.

By August 22, the forward headquarters of the United States Central Command in Saudi Arabia was up and running and awaiting further orders from its commander-in-chief, General H. Norman Schwarzkopf. On the same day, one of the most important orders of the entire Gulf adventure was issued. "It was exactly 1:35 [P.M.] on the twenty-second," a senior planner recalled. "That's when the decision was made to roll in the F-117As." However, some pilots and F-117As, which would become the undisputed aces of the air campaign against Iraq, had already arrived in Saudi Arabia. The order to deploy went to Colonel Alton Whitley's 37th Tactical Fighter Wing at Nellis Air Force Base in Nevada (Whitley would himself drop one of the first bombs on Baghdad in the air war, crippling a critical communications complex on the first of twenty-nine successful combat bombing missions). Although most pilots scoffed at the idea of a "surgical" bombing campaign, Colonel Whitley's Stealth fighters would show that with so-called smart laser-guided bombs and state-of-the-art anti-radar aerodynamics, it was possible for the very best pilots to deliver extraordinarily precise strikes on a repeated, high-percentage basis.

Even in these early days in August, Schwarzkopf and his planners had understood the importance of an air war. Conferring long-distance over a secure line to Lieutenant General Chuck Horner in Riyadh, Schwarzkopf wanted to know what Horner was doing to "eliminate the Iraqi ability to reinforce in the Kuwait theater of operations." With his dime-store pencil and ubiquitous yellow legal pad, Horner had already sketched the broad outlines of the air war. Now he was starting to fill in the innumerable details to guarantee total and complete Allied air superiority. Eventually he would design an "air-tasking order" of almost unfathomable complexity. There would be multiple AWACS aircraft flying at the highest altitudes. They would perform the critical job of air-traffic control, keeping the many American and Allied warplanes out of one another's way while en route to their separate targets. Below them would be hundreds of fighters, bombers, ground-attack aircraft, and electronic-jamming planes. These would come from the carriers in the Persian Gulf and in the Red Sea, as well as from a half-dozen different air bases in the desert. American pilots would be flying alongside Saudi, Kuwaiti, British, French, and Italian airmen. Communications would have to be flawless; nothing could go wrong. Working with intelligence analysts from the Air Force, the Central Intelligence Agency, and the Defense Intelligence Agency, Horner's staff began working on a master target list that by late August included 200 major Iraqi defense and weapons facilities. From there, recalled a Central Command official deeply involved in the targeting plans, "We just kept building and building and building." When Horner and his staff were finally finished, not long before President Bush gave the go-ahead for the air war, the air-tasking order for Desert Storm would run to more than 400 pages.

CHAPTER 8

THE CONFLICT INTENSIFIES

ONE OF Dick Cheney's abiding passions was fishing. In the little spare time he had as secretary of defense, Cheney enjoyed poring over catalogues of exotic fly-fishing gear. What he liked even better, however, was getting out on a good trout stream and putting the gear to work. Long before Saddam Hussein invaded Kuwait, Cheney had scheduled two weeks of vacation for the middle of August. He had planned to spend the time fishing in Wyoming. George Bush had made a point of going ahead with his vacation plans, conscious of not wanting to be held hostage to a crisis, as had Jimmy Carter. Bush had departed resolutely for his family's vacation home at Kennebunkport, Maine. Cheney had told aides that the President's calm sent an important signal to the nation, but it was not one he felt he could emulate. Having personally ordered tens of thousands of soldiers, airmen, and sailors to the Persian Gulf, Cheney thought it would look bad if he turned around and went off for a couple of weeks of trout fishing. The fish would just have to wait, Cheney told his wife, Lynne; he was going back to the Gulf.

In Saudi Arabia, Cheney would see firsthand the controlled chaos involved in moving an army as well as an armada. Some of the troops and some of their commanders seemed bewildered by the desert; others were still trying vainly to cope with the oppressive heat. While Powell and Cheney had said publicly that the danger of heavy American casualties in an Iraqi attack was declining daily, aides said Cheney privately believed the numbers would still be very high. Cheney had the deployment numbers in his head. At the moment, there were some 35,000 American troops either on the ground in Saudi Arabia or en route. There were another 20,000 sailors and naval aviators on American ships nearby. And more were coming.

There would also be more bases for his people to use. Cheney had made a point of seeing Sheik Zaid during his brief swing through the Gulf, and the leader of the United Arab Emirates had agreed to allow U.S. forces to use military bases on his territory. After weighing Cheney's pitch for several days, Qatar would follow suit. The emirates' decisions would expand the network of bases the Allied forces could rely on over the coming months.

Cheney also knew that, in order to give Schwarzkopf the personnel and equipment his staff was calling for daily, the President would have to call up significant numbers of reserves. Schwarzkopf had briefed Bush and his advisers on the need for reserves at Camp David on August 4. It was time now for the President to issue the order. Upon his return, therefore, Cheney, accompanied by Powell, flew to Kennebunkport to see what George Bush wanted to do.

The President knew the political risks of calling up large numbers of reservists, but he assented. If Schwarzkopf said the reservists were necessary, Bush told Cheney and Powell in Kennebunkport, he would issue the summons for them. The orders had already been forwarded to him. On August 17, after Bush had left for his Maine retreat, typists in the Office of the Assistant Secretary of Defense for Reserve Affairs had finished making the final changes on orders for the call-up of as many as 200,000 reservists. A Pentagon courier had been dispatched to Kennebunkport to deliver the packet. Naturally, there would be changes. At first, the number to be called up was closer to 80,000. Based on his conversations in Saudi Arabia, Cheney figured 50,000 reserves would be needed immediately. Those reservists were the first to get the call; the rest would be summoned later.

While Bush was confident of Schwarzkopf's need for so many reservists, he was not entirely happy about calling them away from their jobs and sending them to a distant desert. Already, an American family had suffered its first loss in the execution of Operation Desert Shield. On a darkened runway in the desert, a well-liked Air Force staff sergeant named John Campisi had been run down by a big Pentagon truck and killed. Sergeant

Campisi left a wife and four children behind in California. Even without direct conflict with Iraq, the President knew that there would be more deaths besides that of Sergeant Campisi. Should it come to war, the Defense Department's classified estimate of casualties, which varied widely depending on the assumptions of the type of conflict, was as high as 30,000. In the coming weeks, wild rumors would report that the Pentagon had shipped 50,000 body bags—or 70,000, or even 100,000—to the Persian Gulf. In fact, the Pentagon, seeking to put the pain of Vietnam behind it, no longer used the term "body bags." The official euphemism was now "body-remains pouches." The Pentagon would eventually send just 16,000 of them to the Gulf. Bush's generals could call the bags whatever they wanted. The President knew that if the number used even approximated 16,000—let alone 30,000—a war in the Gulf would be a political disaster. "Another Vietnam" would be the phrase on the lips of millions of Americans.

In this respect it turned out that Bush's best ally was Saddam Hussein himself, who seemed to possess an unerring capacity for giving ordinary Americans reasons to detest him. There were some 6,500 Americans and Britons in Kuwait, and a little more than 13,000 Westerners in Iraq and the emirate combined. On August 16, Saddam had ordered all Americans in Kuwait to report to the Kuwait International and two other big hotels in downtown Kuwait City. Saddam's spokesmen referred to the Americans and some other Westerners in Kuwait as "restrictees." By August 22, a number of Americans, Britons, French, and other Westerners had been taken from their hotels and moved to Iraqi defense installations. These unfortunate people would become so-called human shields. "You are going to receive some American bodies in bags," the Iraqi leader said in a prepared statement specifically addressed to Bush. Americans by the millions were outraged.

Privately, aides said, Bush was furious, but outwardly his administration was maintaining a studied calm. Despite some counsel from aides that he temper his remarks, Bush decided to vent his disgust at a man he regarded as an out-and-out criminal. At a gathering of the Veterans of Foreign Wars in Baltimore on August 20, the President called on Americans to make "personal sacrifices . . . to protect our world from fundamental evil." Given the events of the past few days, Bush said, there could be no flinching from the quality of the evil emanating from Baghdad. "We have been reluctant to use the word 'hostage,' " Bush told the VFW audience. "But when Saddam Hussein offers to trade the freedom of those citizens of [the] many nations he holds against their will in return for concessions, there can be little doubt that, whatever these people are called, they are, in fact, hostages."

Back in Kennebunkport, in his meeting with Cheney and Powell two days after the VFW speech, Bush confided that he was worried about the hostages. Not just for their own sake, though their safety, he said, was important. But also because their presence in Baghdad would inevitably complicate things if Saddam attacked Saudi Arabia or ultimately refused to divest himself of Kuwait. The presence of American hostages was surely a complicating factor, one of only several that had the potential to worsen the conflict. For now, it was a war of words. But for many of the American military personnel en route to Saudi Arabia, the big question was whether and when war would break out.

In the three weeks since Saddam Hussein's Republican Guard divisions had rolled into Kuwait, Israel had been the unpredictable factor in the ever complicated diplomatic arithmetic arising from the Gulf conflict. If Saddam could draw Israel into the conflict—if Israel would allow herself to be drawn—it would complicate things enormously for the Arab members of the anti-Iraq coalition. Privately, the government of Prime Minister Yitzhak Shamir had given assurances to Washington that it would do nothing to exploit any conflict that grew out of the invasion. Equally privately, senior Bush administration officials had asked the Shamir government to stay out of any fighting. On August 27, at one of the new absorption centers that had been created to assist the thousands of Soviet immigrants arriving each month with the abrupt transition to new lives in Israel, Prime Minister Shamir sought to reassure the Americans of his nation's cooperation. Israel, Shamir said, "has no interest in attacking any Arab state—not even the most extreme among them. . . . [Israel] wants to live in peace with all Arab states."

It was an important gesture on Shamir's part. Relations between Washington and Jerusalem had chilled considerably since Bush had become President. Many Israelis and their supporters in the United States believed that George Bush and James Baker, a former oilman and a native Texan, were emotionally more disposed to the Arab point of view on some of the critical questions in the Arab-Israeli conflict. In his fitful efforts to jump-start the peace process during the months prior to the invasion of Kuwait, Secretary Baker had spoken with Eduard Shevardnadze about how the Soviets might play a role in Middle East peacemaking, a role commensurate with Moscow's recently more constructive behavior in the region. This was not inconsistent with Baker's adherence to the peace-process philosophy espoused by his predecessor, George Shultz. The United States, Shultz had said, would agree to a "properly structured" peace conference "at the appropriate time." The problem was not only the objections of the Shamir government, but the fact that Baker had spent the first eighteen months of the Bush administration telling the Soviets and the Europeans that the "appropriate time" had not yet arrived. Against this backdrop, the Shamir statement was important, signaling a willingness to cooperate with the United States in its policy against Iraq.

Typically, however, the gesture was quickly undermined. In separate remarks on August 27, Israeli Defense Minister Moshe Arens delivered himself of more troublesome thoughts about Iraq and Saddam Hussein. "If he remains in his post," Arens said, in a televised interview, "and if the weapons in his possession remain in his possession, then there will be room for worry among us, the whole region, and the whole world. I hope this will not be the outcome." In principle, the statement was absolutely unobjectionable. It was, in fact, perfectly in line with what many officials in the Bush administration were saying privately and with what the President himself would say publicly again and again. Given the delicacy of the moment, however, some senior administration officials thought the Arens statement was unnecessary.

Israel's position was a difficult one, though, something not everyone in the Bush administration truly understood. While the Shamir government had angered President Bush with its policy of building new settlements in the occupied territories, it was also true that Israel had far more at risk with an unrestrained Iraq than the United States did. Again on August 27, for instance, Zevulun Hammer, Israel's education minister, had sent a letter to every Israeli school principal. "We are opening the school year with special preparations," the letter said, "in the event of an emergency." On the first day of class, Israel's one million schoolchildren would be instructed in the proper way to don gas masks. In the coming weeks, during the daily chemical-warfare drills, children would walk rapidly to the upper floors of their school buildings. Gas, the children were told, was heavier than air and would therefore concentrate on the lower floors. Given the stark qualitative difference in the levels of risk, the Israelis were understandably worried.

As they had been for some time. The signals emanating from Baghdad during the early months of 1990 had troubled a handful of Middle East and intelligence specialists in Washington, but the concerns had never risen to the most senior levels of the State Department or the Central Intelligence Agency or to the National Security Council staff. In Israel, by contrast, Iraq was already at the top of Shamir's list. "After the Iran-Iraq war," said General Dani Rothchild, the deputy director of military intelligence, "Israel began to ask, 'Where is Iraq going?' "

By January 1990, General Rothchild and his colleagues had the glimmerings of an answer, and they did not like what they saw. Israeli intelligence officials had confirmed the movement of more Scud missile launchers into far western Iraq, in an area labeled "H-2" and "H-3" on Israeli military maps. Fired from H-2 and H-3, the Scuds could easily reach Haifa, Tel Aviv, and Jerusalem. The Israeli air force immediately began keeping a much closer watch on the Scud launchers in H-2 and H-3.

Next came Saddam Hussein's virulent anti-American speech to the Gulf Cooperation Council in February 1990. This speech had worried Assistant Secretary of State John Kelly, analysts in the CIA, and some of the Middle East specialists on the National Security Council staff. But it alarmed Israeli officials even more. Israeli intelligence officials said that Saddam had pressed Egyptian President Hosni Mubarak to sign a defense treaty with Iraq. The Iraqi leader said he was worried about an Israeli attack on western Iraq. More ominously, the Israeli officials said, Saddam had spoken almost mystically of having seen "the lights of el-Quds" from the council's meeting site in Amman. El-Quds was the Arabic for Jerusalem.

Saddam's "scorch Israel" speech in April increased the concerns about Iraqi intentions. "You have to take the words seriously even if they sound crazy," Shamir said. "We had to start getting ready. From then on until the start of the war, we saw no sign of him backing down."

There were other interpretations among Israeli officials. General Dan Shomron, the chief of staff of the Israeli defense forces, took Saddam's remarks at face value. Saddam had said he would use his chemical weapons only if he was attacked by Israel. General Shomron said he interpreted this to mean that if the Israeli air force moved to take out the Scud launchers in H-2 and H-3, Iraq would retaliate—something it had not been able to do after Israeli jets destroyed Saddam's nuclear reactor at Osirak in 1981. If Israel left the Scuds in H-2 and H-3 alone, Shomron said, there was no reason to assume Iraq would attack. In an interview with the mass-circulation daily *Yediot Ahronot* just days after Saddam's speech, Shomron had tried to calm things down. "I do not see any danger," he told the newspaper, "of escalation [of hostilities] in the Middle East."

In Washington, Shomron's opinion carried considerable weight. At the State Department, some officials felt that the general's comments would be helpful if seen in Iraq. "We took that statement and passed it on," a senior U.S. official said. "April Glaspie gave it to Tariq Aziz. It was understood well in Baghdad."

But one could never be sure about such things. There were some unconfirmed reports that Prince Bandar bin Sultan, the Saudi ambassador to the United States, had acted as a go-between for Saddam, extracting a pledge from the Shamir government not to launch a preemptive attack on the Iraqi Scud launchers. The Israeli prime minister said that was not true. "We never said we wouldn't be the first [to attack]," Shamir insisted. "We said we would not hit. We said, on our own will, that we would not hit [the Scud launchers] so as to give [Saddam] an alibi."

Technically, then, there was no specific Israeli pledge to Saddam not to strike first. But for its own political reasons, the Shamir government had decided to sit tight and let Saddam make the first move, if he were so inclined. Reuven Merhav, the director general of the Israeli foreign ministry, traveled quietly to Cairo in April to convey the news. The Egyptians then passed the word on to Baghdad.

Despite the confidence of General Shomron that Saddam would not attack Israel if he were not attacked first, senior Israeli military officials were worried that the Iraqi leader would do something. The concerns were not shared, these officials said, by their counterparts in Washington.

Just as relations between the Bush administration and the Shamir government were distinctly chilly at times, Israeli and American military officials in early 1990 were having a difficult time of it. Shamir described the military-to-military bond as "poor." Senior military planners from both nations met twice a year, and it just so happened that the next session had been scheduled for April 1990 at the Pentagon.

It was a tense meeting. Iraq had come up almost immediately, and the American side accused the Israelis of "overestimating" the threat from Saddam. David Ivri, the director general of the Israeli defense ministry who led the Israeli delegation, recalled later that the American response to Iraq's recent actions seemed timid. Ivri was a former chief of the Israeli air force, and had been in charge of the Israeli bombing of the Osirak reactor. Ivri now told his American counterparts that Israeli concerns nine years earlier had been similarly dismissed. Once again, he said, Israel was being accused of exaggerating. Privately, Ivri thought that the United States was missing the signals coming out of Baghdad because it was so preoccupied with the wrenching internal conflict in the Soviet Union. Publicly, he made the case that his Pentagon colleagues should begin paying closer attention to Iraq immediately. When you have one million men under arms, Ivri said, concluding his remarks, and you don't demobilize because you have no civilian jobs for your soldiers, you have to find new challenges for them, new military adventures. The American side thanked Ivri and his colleagues, but there had been no agreement.

Things had continued pretty much in that fashion until the second half of July, when Moshe Arens could stand it no longer. A former aerodynamics engineer, Arens was variously regarded as brilliant, irascible, and humorless. As the Israeli defense minister, Arens was afforded ample opportunity to display all of those traits, often at the same time. Concerned that Washington was still not sufficiently impressed by what was going on in Iraq, Arens telephoned Cheney at the Pentagon. He wanted to see him as soon as possible. Cheney agreed to see Arens. The meeting occurred in Cheney's third-floor office on July 19. The American defense secretary was impressed by Arens's colleagues. The Israeli defense minister had brought the head of military intelligence for the Israeli defense forces as well as the chief of the Mossad, the Israeli intelligence agency. The Israeli team had maps, photos, documents—all pertaining to secret Iraqi production facilities designed to provide Saddam Hussein with nuclear weapons. The maps and photos together identified the size and locations of several small facilities spread out around the Iraqi countryside. Within these installations, Arens told Cheney, the Iraqis had set up a sophisticated network of high-speed centrifuges of the type that could enrich uranium to weapons-grade level. It was essentially the same argument advanced by some analysts in the CIA and the Defense Intelligence Agency (DIA), but Arens and his team had what looked like hard evidence. CIA and DIA analysts had been pushing for the U.S. intelligence community to revise its official estimate on when Saddam might have the bomb. Five to ten years seemed hopelessly optimistic. The Arens material would somehow have to be checked, Cheney had thought at the time. In and of itself, it was not conclusive.

After the invasion of Kuwait, Cheney came to believe that the Pentagon would need to coordinate closely with the Israelis. Nevertheless, like nearly every other senior adviser to President Bush, Cheney did not want to give the Israelis everything they knew, or even to alert them to what actions they were considering. There was far too little trust for that, both Israeli and American officials said.

Still, Cheney thought, some form of improved communication was absolutely essential. The Israelis swore by the principle of retaliation. A tiny state, Israel could deter attacks only by ensuring that any such action would be countered with even more terrible force. That was the fundamental principle on which the security policy of the Jewish state had been constructed. Arens stated the case more forcefully than most Israeli officials. But with every member of the Shamir cabinet, retaliation was an article of faith.

Cheney said that sudden military action by Israel would not only do grave damage to the coalition Bush and Baker were working to cement together; it would also be potentially dangerous to the American military. With more than 35,000 American soldiers in the Gulf, and American aircraft in the skies constantly flying combat air patrols, Cheney wanted to make sure they would not be running into—or worse, be fired upon by—Israeli fighter jets.

In late August, Cheney met with David Ivri to see what could be done about the problem. It was the first time, according to U.S. and Israeli officials, that the term "disconfliction" came up. Disconfliction was shorthand for a problem that kept air force officials from both sides awake at night: How to prevent Israelis from shooting down Americans, and vice versa? In Israel's 1967 war with Egypt, an American intelligence-gathering ship named the *Liberty* was in the waters of the Mediterranean off Israel when it was attacked by Israeli jets. It had been a tragic case of mistaken identity. In his meeting with Cheney, Ivri said he wanted desperately to avoid a "flying *Liberty*." What could be done to guarantee there would be no accidents? Ivri pressed for "real-time" satellite data from the Americans and for an exchange of each nation's airplane identification, or IFF, codes. These electronic codes are issued from the transponders of military aircraft—"identify, friend or foe."

Cheney appreciated Ivri's concern, but there was still the matter of trust.

The plain fact of the matter was, according to knowledgeable U.S. and Israeli officials, that there was simply too little trust by the Bush administration and its Pentagon commanders to turn over some of the nation's most sensitive military secrets to the Israelis.

Nevertheless, Cheney believed some steps could be taken to improve matters. The defense secretary ordered improved reporting of U.S. intelligence data to the Israelis. (Even on the eve of war, the Israelis would still not be receiving "real-time" American satellite intelligence, but in the months prior to the commencement of the air war, there was better coordination between the two nations' military-intelligence communities.) For his own part, to make sure there would be no miscommunication at the very top of the Israeli and American militaries, Cheney ordered a secure, direct line installed that would enable him to reach Defense Minister Arens at any time of the day or night. The communications link was assigned the code name HAMMER RICK. In the Pentagon, at the White House, and in the State Department there were strong objections to the installation of HAMMER RICK. If disclosed, the critics said, it would appear as if the United States was coordinating much too closely with the Israelis. So sensitive was HAMMER RICK that while the secure communications equipment was transported to Israel shortly after the Cheney-Ivri meeting in late August, the telephone apparatus would remain in a locked vault in the U.S. embassy for months.

With the President in Maine, Secretary of State James Baker taking a vacation in Wyoming, and the Pentagon preoccupied with the enormity of the Desert Shield deployment, Washington in late August seemed almost deserted. Perhaps it was for that reason that the Kurdish leader Jalal Talabani could find no one to talk to. Talabani did not think so, however.

During the course of Iraq's years of war with Iran, Talabani had led a guerrilla army in northern Iraq that so angered Saddam Hussein with its audaciousness that he issued a death sentence for the Kurdish leader. Talabani's forces had been attacked by Saddam's chemical weapons. Toward the end of the war, between 1986 and 1988, Talabani's forces had joined with those loyal to the successors of another esteemed Kurdish warrior, Mulla Mustafa Barzani. Together, they ignited a spirited Kurdish resistance movement centered in the city of Kirkuk. They were so successful in Iraq's northern mountains that Saddam had been forced to divert tens of thousands of his soldiers from the effort against Iran in the south.

A week before his visit to Washington, Talabani had met in Damascus with the leaders of a number of other dissident Iraqi groups. The Syrian leader, Hafez al-Assad, would have liked nothing better than to see Iraq dissolve into anarchy, and he had agreed to host the gathering of Iraqi oppositionists. But anarchy wasn't quite what Talabani and his fellow rebels in Damascus had in mind. The Kurds from the north and the Shiites from the south—many of whom swore allegiance to a ninety-year-old holy man named Mohammed Baqer Hakim—had agreed to work together to destabilize the Baghdad government. The opposition groups knew that alone they would have no success in removing Saddam; if he were toppled somehow during the current conflict, however, the Kurds and Shiites were prepared to work together to create a new government. Before leaving Damascus, they had signed a document pledging to seek national elections for a democratic successor to Saddam.

In Washington, however, Talabani got the brush-off. Unofficially, senior bureaucrats at the State Department, the Central Intelligence Agency, and the Pentagon had been informed of Talabani's visit. None wanted to talk with him. "We were concerned about the violations of the Kurds' human rights," a senior Bush adviser explained later. "But we did not want to get involved in anything like the creation of a new Kurdish nation."

For the Kurds, it was a familiar story of opportunism and betrayal. For more than a thousand years, the Kurds had been sold out, their lands carved up into multiple regions, their lives crushed when their presence became inconvenient. "The Kurds," said Mulla Mustafa Barzani, who was spirited out of Iraq to the United States in 1975 as he was dying of cancer, "have no friends." Certainly he had little reason to value the "friendship" of the United States, which had cynically aided the Kurds in the early 1970s only to cut off all aid in 1975, the moment Saddam and the shah of Iran ended a border dispute.

The Bush administration would not deal with the Kurds. The Shiites from the south had even less luck. Before the invasion of Kuwait, the premise of Washington's pro-Iraq policy had been breathtakingly simple: if Baghdad, however repellent its ruler, would continue as an effective foil to the radical Shiites in Tehran, then it was deemed to be in America's interest to support Saddam. Helping Shiites in Iraq was the last thing the United States intended to do.

Nevertheless, President Bush would be at some pains to distinguish between the Iraqi leader and his unfortunate people. "We have no argument with the people of Iraq, and indeed we have only friendship for the people there," Bush would declare in a speech in late November. In February 1991, with the war already launched and soldiers dying, Bush would be more specific: "And there is another way for the bloodshed to stop, and that is for the Iraqi military and the Iraqi people to take matters into their own hands and force Saddam Hussein the dictator to step aside."

But in late August 1990, and indeed right through the course of the war and its aftermath, the Bush administration steadfastly refused to even talk with the very people they were urging to "take matters into their own hands." That way lay potential disaster for the nascent anti-Iraq coalition, administration officials believed. The Saudis wanted a Sunni military dictatorship in Baghdad, albeit without the unruly Saddam. Syria, which had since pledged several thousand troops to the coalition, wanted a solution best described as Iraqi anarchy, with Kurds, Shiites, and Sunnis all vying with one another for power. Jalal Talabani left Washington a disappointed man whose disappointment would only grow deeper with the passage of time.

CHAPTER 9

BUSH SEIZES
AN OPPORTUNITY

G EORGE BUSH'S advisers and his friends and family were worried. Despite the several weeks the President had already spent at the eleven-acre compound in Kennebunkport that had been in the Bush family for four generations, the sixty-six-year-old chief executive was wearing down visibly by the end of August. "He just could not recharge the batteries," a close adviser said. The presence of family, of grandchildren, and the brisk salt air blowing in across the rocks of Walker's Point had all failed to restore the President. He was increasingly obsessed by the deepening conflict with Saddam Hussein, aides said. On hearing good news, the President was naturally delighted. But when he encountered problems or setbacks or learned of some new outrage from Baghdad or Kuwait City, as he often did, Bush's mood turned dark. The hostage issue had worn on him heavily. So, too, had the mounting cost of the massive military operation he had approved. Richard Darman, the director of the Office of Management and Budget, had told the President that deployment costs for Operation Desert Shield had escalated to $28.9 million a day—more than double what they had been in the early days of the month. Over the next six months, Darman reported, assuming there was no conflict with Saddam Hussein's forces, America's taxpayers would have to pay some $3 billion to feed, fuel, and maintain its large fighting force in Saudi Arabia.

Nevertheless, Bush was convinced that a hard line—a vigorously enforced embargo and a determination to use force if that failed—was the only way to persuade the stubborn Iraqi leader to leave Kuwait. Some of his closest advisers, however, had professed discomfort with the President's two-pronged policy. Defending Saudi Arabia and employing an economic vise to force Saddam out of Kuwait were both laudable goals, these advisers agreed. But even if they were met, the United States and its allies would still have failed to deal with the long-term threat posed by Saddam Hussein to the Persian Gulf and the rest of the Middle East. Several aides had pushed the argument hard. Could Washington and its allies content themselves with restoring the Sabah family to power in Kuwait City, they asked, while leaving Saddam in Baghdad with his million-man army and his chemical and biological weapons intact? And what of his nuclear program? Vice-President Dan Quayle was among those who were especially alarmed by the intelligence that had been provided by Israeli Defense Minister Moshe Arens in mid-July. Among the President's men, Quayle was the most hawkish. He argued that the administration's ultimate objective should be to defang Saddam Hussein's military machine, and especially to destroy his weapons of mass destruction. Quayle and most of Bush's close advisers had met frequently in Kennebunkport to discuss the Iraq crisis. Quayle had been supported by Defense Secretary Cheney, Under Secretary of Defense Paul Wolfowitz, and Robert Gates, the President's deputy adviser for national security affairs.

Just before seven in the morning on August 23, the President called Brent Scowcroft in his room at the Nonantum Resort just down the road from Walker's Point. Bush had decided to chase the bluefish, which were running, and he wanted to know if Scowcroft would join him aboard his speedboat, the *Fidelity*. Scowcroft dutifully agreed. He was used to the President's spontaneous suggestions for one outdoors adventure or another. Like the President, Scowcroft too was exhausted. In the days immediately after Iraq's invasion of Kuwait, Scowcroft had set up house in his spacious suite near the Oval Office, catching occasional catnaps on his white sofa, his shoes and suit jacket discarded. Concerned aides would peer in occasionally and find Scowcroft curled in a fetal position beneath a blue-and-red afghan, only his head and black-stockinged feet peeking out. Soon after August 2, Scowcroft had come down with a severe cold and a 102-degree fever. Bush ordered Scowcroft to accompany him to Camp David for the weekend, where he decreed that the general was to do nothing but rest. Scowcroft had slept for most of the two days. The

President genuinely admired Scowcroft. He knew all about Marian Scowcroft's illness, but Scowcroft himself never spoke of it. While he slipped away from the White House every chance he could to be with his wife, he was always there when the President needed him. Colleagues said Scowcroft handled the Gulf conflict with a physical toughness and stern mental discipline that deeply impressed Bush.

As they headed out into the Atlantic, Bush told Scowcroft that he had been thinking hard about the Gulf conflict. He wanted to review where they were and what might happen next. With a Secret Service agent and a Coast Guardsman as their only company, Bush and Scowcroft attached lures to steel leaders at the end of heavy-test lines, then dropped the lines over the boat's stern and planted the poles firmly in their metal holders. With their fishing lines playing out behind them, the sea breeze blowing gently, and the Maine sun shining brightly, it was a gorgeous morning.

Bush confessed that he was worried by the enormous risks inherent in the conflict with Iraq. Unless much of it was borne by allies, the cost of the operation would be an enormous burden on an already strained federal budget. The lack of support from King Hussein, a friend, had been a bitter pill. But he worried most about American casualties. Cheney and Powell had given him classified estimates of casualties as high as 30,000 dead in the event of a war with Iraq. Despite the risks, Bush said, there could be real opportunities for American leadership abroad, after the conflict with Iraq was resolved. Bush outlined his vision. It was not simply the "window of opportunity" the Middle East specialists talked about. He was thinking instead about the meaning of the coalition that had begun to form against Iraq. It was a dramatic example of how diverse nations could come together to address a common problem, he said. At home, he saw a kind of post-Vietnam "maturity" among the public. The mood had manifested itself, Bush told Scowcroft, in the strong support reflected in the recent public-opinion polls on American policy in the Gulf.

Scowcroft listened quietly, the twin engines of the *Fidelity* burbling in the background. He knew that Bush's belief was not the result of a sudden epiphany; pieces of it had been falling together for months. A large part of the President's conception had to do with the startling changes in the Soviet Union and Eastern Europe. Along with Scowcroft, Cheney, and Gates, Bush had been skeptical of Mikhail Gorbachev's intentions. After months of probing and testing, however, Bush had come to believe that the Soviet leader had truly determined to let go of his end of the Cold War rope. The past few weeks had deepened his sense that he had been correct about the Soviets. The courage of Eduard Shevardnadze in facing down the Kremlin hard-liners and Gorbachev's support for the resolutions against Iraq in the U.N. Security Council were among the more obvious examples of a fundamental shift by the Soviet leadership, Bush said; in the bad old days of the Cold War, such cooperation would have been impossible to imagine. Bush told Scowcroft that the Gulf conflict had helped to crystallize some of his ideas about foreign policy, even about the United Nations. One historical era was ending, another was being born. A new world order was in the making, and the President believed that America would help to shape it.

Meanwhile, the problem posed by Saddam Hussein would have to be resolved. While it was true, as the President had pointed out, that the Soviets had been helpful (as had the entire international community), there was still the thorny matter of the hostages. Bush and Scowcroft agreed that no matter how wrenching their plight became, the actions of the United States would not be determined by a blackmailer ready to sacrifice the lives of hostages. Bush said that he had taken seriously the concerns Quayle, Cheney, and Gates had raised about the administration's limited objectives in the Gulf. Besides the defense of Saudi Arabia and the commitment to force Iraqi troops out of Kuwait, Bush talked about the need to do something that would guarantee the security of the Gulf states once the conflict was ended. This was a profound commitment, Scowcroft observed, a significant stretch beyond the objectives the President had publicly outlined to the nation, and to his own military commanders, in giving the go-ahead for Desert Shield.

Would it mean eliminating Saddam? Scowcroft said that he thought it made little sense to try to remove Saddam from power because his successor would almost certainly be another Baath Party thug, a Sunni Muslim who would be just as detestable as Saddam to the Shiite majority in the south of Iraq and to the Kurds in the north. Trying to topple Saddam, Scowcroft argued, would also cost the lives of many Americans and Allied soldiers. He said that he had learned a powerful lesson from the American invasion of Panama only nine months before: American forces had had a great deal of trouble locating and capturing Manuel Antonio Noriega. While the worst of the human-rights abuses in Panama had ceased after Noriega's removal to a Miami prison cell, drug trafficking and government corruption had continued to flourish. Changing political leaders was difficult enough, Scowcroft believed; changing societies was nearly impossible.

Bush spoke again of the idea of international cooperation, saying that as a result of the crisis in the Gulf, the United Nations might finally assume the role that had been designed for it at its founding in 1945: to stop international aggression through concerted action. In pursuing that end, Bush said, despite the efforts of many skilled and dedicated diplomats, the United Nations had showed itself to be one of the world's most feckless organizations. That might now all be in the past. In moving against Iraq, the disparate members of the Security Council had been firm and resolute. They had acted with dispatch. This could be made to happen again and again. After all, the Soviet Union was no longer using its veto to block American action. Many of the old ideological obstacles had crumbled over the past eighteen months. There was now real opportunity for superpower cooperation, Bush said, and the good news of the Iraq crisis was that it would demonstrate to the world the potential for such action. Bush told Scowcroft that Saddam Hussein was just the kind of villain who would force "civilized nations" to see the importance of stopping another Hitler. If it were handled properly, the outcome of the crisis would deter other international brigands from "naked aggression" and set the stage for further international cooperation. Scowcroft agreed. With that, Bush steered the speedboat back toward shore, satisfied with both the conversation and the three bluefish, including a sleek fourteen pounder, he and his national security adviser had somehow managed to catch.

On September 3, Major General Barry McCaffrey watched with satisfaction as his soldiers from the 24th Infantry Division (Mechanized) rolled their Bradley fighting vehicles and M1A1 tanks off of the USNS *Regulus* in the Saudi port of Dhahran. His division was as well prepared for a desert war as it could be. The *Regulus* and eight of the Navy's FSSs had moved the division halfway around the world in just over two weeks. The ships had managed thirty-two knots as they crossed the Atlantic and the Mediterranean, then pushed through the Suez Canal before entering the Red Sea, crossed the Arabian Sea, and on into the Gulf of Oman and the waters of the Persian Gulf. "We have never, ever done anything like this," McCaffrey exulted, smiling as he watched the clouds of diesel fumes rise from the tanks and from the other vehicles rolling out of the belly of the *Regulus* and onto the bustling wharf.

For General Norman Schwarzkopf, McCaffrey's big tanks were a godsend. Since Schwarzkopf arrived in Saudi Arabia on August 25, he had prayed every night that the M1A1s would get there quickly. To protect against Saddam's Scud missiles, Patriot missile batteries had been installed in the busy port areas of Dhahran, al-Jubail, and ad-Dammam. But Schwarzkopf wanted the big tanks. He wasn't taking anything for granted. While a senior intelligence official had told President Bush in late August that "our Muslim friends feel he cannot last more than a few weeks," Schwarzkopf knew how shaky that intelligence estimate really was. He also knew that despite denials from Washington, knowledgeable American and Arab officials said that the Sabah family had had discussions with an unnamed interlocutor for Saddam and had offered to pay some $2 billion to settle the dispute over the Rumaila oil field and Bubiyan Island. In Washington, administration officials had said publicly that they would not agree to such a deal. Privately, senior United States officials acknowledged that such a settlement would have been accepted by the United States as part of subsequent negotiations between Kuwait City and Baghdad, after Iraqi withdrawal from the emirate.

Still, Schwarzkopf worried about the possibility of an Iraqi charge into Saudi Arabia. He had been relieved when the 7th Marine Expeditionary Brigade had arrived in the Gulf on August 24. Schwarzkopf arrived a day later. After the shock of the alert given to the Marine watch officer at Twenty-nine Palms, California, in early August, the 7th MEB had moved out on several of Colonel Daryl Bottjer's enormous C-5A cargo aircraft. In the increasingly complex choreography of the Desert Shield deployment, the 16,000 leathernecks of the 7th MEB had "married up" with their prepositioning ships already steaming from the U.S. base at Diego Garcia. With the air advantage, the Marines had beaten McCaffrey's division to Saudi Arabia. However, their smaller M-60 tanks were no match for Saddam's heaviest armor. With the arrival of McCaffrey's big tanks, while suddenly the odds were not quite even, at least they were no longer as lopsided. From now on, there would be no more talk of American "speed bumps" in the Saudi desert.

In the first week of September, at the Military Airlift Command in Illinois and at the Military Sealift Command in the Washington Navy Yard, respectively, Colonel Bottjer and Captain Jerry Peschka felt overwhelmed whenever they contemplated how they would do the job of moving so many soldiers and so much equipment to the Gulf so fast. Bottjer had been heartened by the number of reservists who had volunteered during the hectic weeks of August. Many of the pilots in the Air Force Reserve and the Air National Guard were well-paid commercial pilots who normally volunteered to fly military cargo planes once a month or so. After the announcement of the Desert Shield deployment by President Bush, many reserve pilots volunteered for longer stints, sacrificing their paychecks. "Even that was insufficient in numbers," Bottjer said. "And therefore we started calling up reserve units. But as we started calling up those units, even that was overwhelmed by the airlift system."

After conferring with Bottjer and representatives of most of the U.S. commercial air carriers, Lieutenant General Hansford Johnson, the head of the U.S. Transportation Command, had activated the Civil Reserve Air Fleet. It was the first time in its thirty-eight-year history that the civil air fleet had been called upon to assist the Pentagon with a military operation. Even though most of the commercial carriers had few planes to spare during the tail end of a busy summer tourist season, they came through with the necessary aircraft. The commercial pilots, many of them tested veterans with flying experience in Vietnam or Korea, were astonished by the scope of the operation. "You could have walked across the Mediterranean on the wings of the C-5s, C-141s, and commercial aircraft," recalled Mike Carlozzi, an American Trans Air pilot with twenty-five years of commercial experience who flew his first mission to the Gulf just days after Lieutenant General Johnson activated the civil air fleet.

By early September, the military airlift fleet and the civil air fleet had flown more than 2,000 missions to the Gulf, delivering 106 million pounds of cargo. Because of the limited landing space in Saudi Arabia, there had been enormous stackups of U.S. aircraft over the desert. Gradually, new landing strips were cleared, but the flow was anything but smooth at times. "We got through it. It worked," Bottjer said. "[But] it was taking a hose with about an eight-inch opening in the United States and going down to a two-inch opening in Saudi Arabia."

At times, the hose had seemed as if it would burst from the pressure. Amazingly, it never did. One reason was that many of the flights from the United States to Saudi Arabia were routed through Europe, and General John Galvin, the commander of all the NATO forces in Europe, had thrown all his resources into the breach. Galvin had been on holiday with his younger brother in New Hampshire when he had received word of the invasion of Kuwait. After just twenty-eight hours there, on learning of the news from the Gulf, he ordered his pilot to prepare to fly him back to Brussels. In the meantime, he telephoned Powell and Schwarzkopf to see how he could be of service.

NATO would prove a key link, not just in the early deployment, but even more so afterward, when President Bush decided to order the U.S. Army's VII Corps from Germany to the desert to double the size of the American force in Saudi Arabia. In the early days after the invasion, however, with the civil air fleet beginning to fly missions, it was Galvin's job to provide support wherever it was needed. "Right from the beginning, I got my commanders together," Galvin recalled. "I said, 'Whatever Norm asks for, we say yes. We find out the nature of the request later. So the answer is "yes, what's the question?" And that has been our motto: 'You call, we haul.'"

Things were not quite so simple at the headquarters of the Military Sealift Command. The ready reserve force of ninety-six Navy ships had proven less than ready. "For the most part, the time line was met," a senior aide to Schwarzkopf said. "But it wasn't one hundred percent. We had a lot of problems with the reserve-fleet shipping. You know, boilers wouldn't work and just broke down. Just all kinds of problems. These things sit in mothballs for years and years and years, boilers go to hell—just one thing after another." It meant that Peschka would have to go out and lease ships. An old law designed to protect U.S. shipping required the Navy to hire from the U.S. merchant fleet first before turning to the foreign market. But the U.S. merchant fleet was just a shadow of what it had been during the Second World War, when it had performed heroically. The American shippers that were still in operation and interested in the Pentagon's business were asking $20,000 for a charter to Saudi Arabia. Foreigners were charging an average of about $8,000 for the same trip.

The law was the law, however, so by early September, Peschka and his headquarters staff were paying the higher prices of the American merchant fleet. Before all was said and done, Peschka would hire 46 U.S.-flagged and 210 foreign-flagged vessels to ensure that Schwarzkopf's tanks, trucks, and ammunition got to the Gulf. Some of the ships had seen better days, and Navy officials doubted whether some of their rheumy-eyed old captains could even find their way to the Gulf. They were a sorry lot, some of them, and inasmuch as they conjured up images of "McHale's Navy," it made it all the more amazing when they groaned into Saudi ports 7,000 miles away, their cargo more or less intact, their arrival more or less on schedule. It was to be one of the many small miracles of the American intervention in the Gulf.

By the first week of September the initial surge of deployment had ended, and General Schwarzkopf's "minimum deterrent force" of 40,000 soldiers was in place. The rest of the force for Desert Shield was en route to Saudi Arabia, and the chaos of August had settled into something very much like a routine.

As Plan 1002-90 was becoming a reality on the floor of the Saudi desert, no commander was more in evidence than Gus Pagonis. It was his job to make sure that America's fighting forces had everything they needed so that if and when they were called upon to go to war there would be no question about their readiness. In the earliest days of the deployment, there were no American truck drivers, so Pagonis authorized his staff in the Logistics Operations Center to go out and find some. U.S. Army officers fanned out across Dhahran, al-Jubail, and ad-Dammam, and within days they assembled a corps of earnest if somewhat bewildered Koreans, Pakistanis, Filipinos, and Indians. "I called them the Pakistani Truck Battalion," said Colonel Roger Scearce, who was then Pagonis's chief of staff responsible for coordinating with the Saudi authorities. "We gave them all a desert camouflage baseball cap and a T-shirt with the Desert Shield logo on it, and suddenly they were part of the team."

Lieutenant Colonel Tom Ehlinger, Pagonis's contract specialist, arranged for a fleet of rental trucks, and a team of Army specialists spray-painted them with the legend "Rented to the U.S. Army, Op. Desert Shield." Pagonis assigned a lieutenant colonel and a sergeant to the newly formed truck battalion, who would all muster just like regular troops every day. The punishment for having a truck unsafe or unready to drive? The driver was prohibited from driving that day, and pressure from other drivers in the battalion kept maintenance problems from recurring. There was nothing in the Army regulations that specifically allowed the creation of the Pakistani Truck Battalion, but neither was there anything specifically prohibiting it. Both before and during the war, the ragtag band of truckers would provide a vital link with American and Allied soldiers in far-flung forward positions. Eventually, American drivers would come to supplement the foreigners, but the job of moving Schwarzkopf's army was so big that it could never have been done without Pagonis's unorthodox recruits. "We always worried that once the war started, they wouldn't drive," Scearce said. "But they drove as long as our guys did. They were great, great soldiers. We were prepared to give them chem masks. We fed them, billeted them. They were good people."

Pagonis had assigned an American soldier to accompany each of the foreign drivers, and the Muslims among the Pakistani Truck Battalion would stop their trucks to pray to Allah five times a day, as specified in the Koran. That was fine with the American GIs. It was the sixth stop—the one for brewing tea—that flustered some of the soldiers. "They would always build their fire in the shade, and the only shade was under their truck trailer," Scearce recalled, laughing. "So you had these guys building little fires with their propane heaters under a truck loaded with artillery ammunition or explosives. And this guy is under the truck cooking his tea, and the GI is out there in the sand a ways away because he knows that truck is going to go boom. Never lost one, though. They were a great team."

Toward the end of the first week of September, James Baker embarked on his second long diplomatic odyssey of the Iraq conflict and President Bush departed for a summit with Soviet President Gorbachev in Helsinki.

The costs of Desert Shield were becoming increasingly worrisome. Grateful for Mubarak's help in forming the Allied coalition, Bush had decided to write off $6.7 billion of Egypt's staggering military debt to the United States. The gesture did not go unnoticed. Other members of the coalition had begun to signal an interest in similar treatment, and budget analysts in the State Department began to worry that Washington would soon be faced with requests to write off tens of billions of dollars of debt.

On September 5, the day he was to depart for Saudi Arabia, Baker met with Israeli Foreign Minister David Levy in his office at the State Department. According to knowledgeable American and Israeli officials, the meeting was difficult. Baker told Levy that he was trying to get several Patriot missile batteries delivered to Israel on an expedited basis. Levy thanked Baker, but aides said he knew Baker had other things on his mind. Baker continued: I want you to know first that I am going to Damascus. It will only be for two hours, but I am going with my eyes wide open. We are realistic. Why don't you stop off in Israel while you are in the region? Levy asked. It was a source of pain and chagrin to the government of Yitzhak Shamir that the secretary of state had never visited Israel. Baker promised Levy that he would visit Israel once the conflict with Iraq had been resolved. We do not want to live in the shadows, Levy replied. I know, Baker said, but now is not the time to come. Levy told Baker that he had had a telephone call from Shamir earlier that morning. Shamir had instructed Levy to ask Baker that Israel receive the same treatment as Egypt on debt reduction. Levy said: Camp David says that we should be treated equally. We are erasing the Egyptian debt because it is essentially worthless, Baker replied. However, we do not want to set a precedent that other countries might follow. There is a saying around here: You stand where you sit.

State Department officials were already weighing what some called the hidden costs of the Gulf venture. Jordan, despite its continuing vacillation, was requesting millions of dollars in assistance so that it could respond to the needs of the thousands of refugees staggering out of the Iraqi desert and into temporary camps just inside the Jordanian border. In Eastern Europe, the jump in oil prices had been particularly cruel. Having thrown off the weight of Communist regimes and begun to move toward more market-driven economies, the Eastern European nations had been left gasping by oil prices that hovered near $30 a barrel. Beginning January 1, 1991, they would be obliged to pay for all of their oil imports in hard currency. If something was not done, inflation would soon be out of hand and the new and fragile democracies would be in real danger. In the State Department, many of the desk officers who handled Eastern Europe wondered how much the United States would be able to help. On the other hand, they wondered, how could Washington afford not to?

CHAPTER 10

THE JEDI KNIGHTS

B Y SEPTEMBER 25, the Central Intelligence Agency's photoanalysts estimated, Saddam Hussein had 430,000 troops in and around Kuwait, four times the number he had used to invade and conquer the country. These forces were digging in. The thousands of photographs taken each week by the American spy satellites that crisscrossed the desert every two hours revealed a large military force arranged unambiguously in a defensive posture. The high-resolution imagery detailed recent construction of elaborate anti-tank defenses, command bunkers, and other fortifications, as well as mines strewn by the thousands across the desert and on the emirate's beaches. Despite Schwarzkopf's fears, Saddam's army looked nothing like an offensive force ready to move at a moment's notice into the Saudi oil fields. But neither did it appear eager to head back to Baghdad any time soon.

CIA Director William Webster approved the dispatch of weekly reports on the effectiveness of the sanctions that had been imposed on Iraq in early August. The classified assessments went to the President, the Pentagon, and the State Department, as well as to the Senate Select Committee on Intelligence and the House Permanent Select Committee on Intelligence. "In the short or medium term," the CIA's analysts reported, sanctions seemed unlikely to drive Saddam out of Kuwait. A former prosecutor, federal judge, and FBI director, Webster was blasted by Democrats on

Capitol Hill. "Flip-flop," charged Representative David McCurdy, the new chairman of the House intelligence panel. But it was not. The American intelligence community now had nearly two months of observable, measurable data, and none of it suggested that Saddam Hussein was willing to back down. By every measurable standard, the CIA's analysts concluded, the embargo imposed by the United Nations and enforced by the American-led naval flotilla had begun to bite. The only problem was that the sanctions were biting the Iraqi people. Saddam and his small coterie of confidants, as well as the leadership and rank and file of the Republican Guard, were well insulated against privation of any sort. For that reason, the agency's analysts were not hopeful that the economic sanctions and the naval embargo would persuade Saddam to get out.

The report documented considerable smuggling into Iraq. For example, there was leakage of goods and foodstuffs across Iraq's long eastern border with Iran. There was simply no way to police smuggling activity through the narrow, tumbled valleys of the Zagros Mountains. Along Iraq's shorter frontiers with Turkey to the north and Jordan to the southwest, there was also some smuggling activity. Iraqis still had money, and profits were to be made.

Moreover, Saddam seemed to go out of his way to antagonize Bush and the coalition. He was playing a dangerous game with the Western hostages, pledging to move them to strategic sites around Baghdad. Iraqi television had begun running a nightly program on Saddam's "guests." The program featured an off-camera host who fielded previously screened questions from three well-coached "guests." To President Bush, the show was not reassuring.

Saddam's behavior, never ordinary, struck many observers as increasingly bizarre. The CIA had commissioned a psychological profile of the Iraqi leader, one of three such studies Schwarzkopf would be presented with by the U.S. intelligence community in the coming months. Israel's military intelligence analysts had also authorized a profile of Saddam. Shamir asked that an English translation of the report be sent to the White House, the CIA, and the Pentagon's Defense Intelligence Agency. More than two hundred pages long, the secret report was entitled "Saddam Hussein: A Psychological Profile." Like the American studies, the Israeli profile drew on much old information, marshaling it to bolster increasingly grim conclusions about the Iraqi leader's intentions. Many American intelligence officials believed that Israelis tended toward alarmist views on certain subjects, especially Syria and Iraq. Still, their profile of Saddam was considered enlightening. One instance cited in the profile dated from 1964. After the Baath Party's ouster from its brief nine months in power the year before, Saddam had gone underground as the leader of a small terrorist cell. Holed up in a house in a Baghdad suburb and surrounded by hundreds of policemen, he was armed with only a pistol and a small amount of ammunition. A demand for his surrender was made. Saddam refused. In a futile gesture of pride and resistance, he fired every last bullet at the constabulary force before turning himself in. According to Israeli General Dani Rothchild, Saddam was not a man to bow to pressure. The harder he was pushed, the harder he would kick back.

On Sunday morning, September 16, General Powell picked up his *Washington Post* and there, emblazoned across the top of the front page, was the headline "U.S. to Rely on Air Strikes If War Erupts." The article relied heavily on quotes from General Michael Dugan, the Air Force chief of staff. Dugan was one of the most widely respected generals in the Air Force, a close friend of John McBroom and many of the service's best and brightest commanders and fliers. But in the course of a long swing through the American air bases scattered across the Saudi desert, he had spoken to a handful of reporters about the planning and paramount importance of the air campaign.

To his defenders, Dugan had done nothing more than articulate a view widely held among the Air Force brass, who believed there was no finer place to fight a war than in the desert of Saudi Arabia. To be sure, the gritty sand of the desert played havoc with million-dollar aircraft, but as far as seeing the enemy and being able to kill him, top Air Force officials were convinced that an air war with Iraq would very quickly turn into a lopsided affair. Already some officers were talking of a "turkey shoot."

For Colin Powell and Dick Cheney, the Dugan gaffe was unforgivable. In meetings with the President, both men had stressed the importance of cooperation, of a multiservice effort in the Gulf. If the conflict with Iraq ever turned violent, Powell and Cheney said, every service would have to play a part. The idea that air power alone could achieve victory, as Dugan had suggested, was a dangerous and foolish idea. Dugan's remarks, however, had infused the chimera of a victory through air power alone with new life. While Cheney regarded Dugan as one of his most able generals, he felt he had no choice but to fire him.

However, the concept of a victory through air power alone lived on. As Congress prepared to adjourn for the year, it was debated in Capitol Hill cloakrooms as a sensible, even seductive, option if the economic sanctions ultimately failed. On October 2, both the House and Senate adopted resolutions supporting the President. Both stopped emphatically short of endorsing the use of force, however. Both Sam Nunn, the influential chairman of the Senate Armed Services Committee, and Les Aspin, the chair of the House Armed Services Committee, believed that the administration should allow the sanctions plenty of time to work. But they suspected that neither Bush nor his advisers were inclined to give the sanctions much time. The momentum pushing the President toward war had already begun to build. And with Bush's approval ratings in the public-opinion polls at an historic high, no Democrat was prepared to seriously challenge the President.

Five days later, on October 7, Jerusalem erupted in a kind of mad violence that claimed the greatest number of casualties in a single day in the Jewish state since the Six-Day War. On the Old City's Temple Mount, Islam's third holiest shrine, the al-Aqsa mosque, stands hard against the Western Wall, Judaism's most holy place. A group of Palestinians had been hurling stones down from the top of the Temple Mount onto Jewish worshippers at the Western Wall below when a jumpy Israeli border policeman dropped a tear-gas grenade. Chaos ensued. More stones flew as the Palestinians turned viciously on the outnumbered policemen. The police retreated to regroup, and then returned in a murderous rage, firing at random, their weapons on full automatic. By the time the shooting ended, 17 Palestinians had been killed and nearly 150 wounded. Within two weeks, an Israeli commission of inquiry issued a report on the tragedy, blaming the Palestinians for inciting the violence and exonerating the police entirely. It would take a courageous Israeli magistrate named Ezra Kama another nine months to contradict several key points of the earlier investigation. The damage to the fragile Allied coalition, meanwhile, was severe.

Yassir Arafat, the chairman of the Palestine Liberation Organization (PLO), had been trying ever since the invasion of Kuwait to link Iraq's intransigence to the Arab-Israeli dispute. He knew, of course, that Saddam had offered to pull his troops out of Kuwait only after the Palestinian problem had been resolved. (Palestinian support for Saddam had the effect of crippling the Israeli peace movement, which had as its centerpiece the idea of coexistence between the two peoples.) Saddam's invasion might also boost Palestinian morale. For months the *intifada*, the violent uprising led by stone-throwing youths in the occupied territories, had been flagging. At the United Nations, PLO representatives had tried desperately (and unsuccessfully) to establish some kind of linkage between the Palestinian question and the Iraqi occupation of Kuwait. There were few sympathizers. Now, as a result of the Temple Mount violence, the Israeli-Palestinian conflict suddenly flared anew.

Saddam Hussein was quick to exploit the opportunity. On October 8, he announced that he had a new missile that could reach deep within Israel's borders. He would not hesitate to fire it, he said, when "the day of reckoning comes." Saddam called his new missile the Hijara, or "stone."

The danger that Israel might be drawn into the conflict was real. Bush knew that Israeli involvement might well undermine the coalition and close the "window of opportunity" for an Arab-Israeli peace that might open briefly once the conflict with Iraq was resolved. Thus, in New York on October 8, Thomas Pickering, the U.S. ambassador to the United Nations, voted with the four other permanent members of the Security Council to condemn Israel "and particularly the excessive Israeli response" to the Temple Mount incident. The resolution also expressed regret that Jewish worshippers had been attacked. The United States also supported a second Security Council resolution condemning the Israeli violence and calling for a United Nations fact-finding mission to go to Jerusalem.

Israeli officials were livid. Since the earliest days of the construction of the anti-Iraq coalition, Israel had felt itself politically isolated, held at arm's length by the Bush administration and viewed as a potential coalition-buster by the rest of the anti-Iraq alliance. The United Nations actions dramatically intensified this sense of isolation, and among many senior Israeli officials, there was a seething anger directed toward Bush and Baker. Many Israeli politicians complained that Washington had sold out its most trusted ally in the Middle East. Worse, in the words of a senior official in Prime Minister Shamir's office, it seemed as if the United States was "beginning to pay off Saddam in Israeli political coinage." As for the fact-finding mission, Shamir said that it constituted an "unwarranted intrusion" into the internal affairs of Israel. Coming on the heels of the Security Council's condemnation, many Israeli officials believed, any "fact-finding mission" would surely be a kangaroo court.

Shamir, however, was well aware of how high the stakes were. Just as he would later shock his fellow hard-liners, urging restraint at critical moments during the war when other influential members of the Israeli inner cabinet were pushing for military action, Shamir saw the bigger picture clearly. "There were all sorts of thoughts," the prime minister said. "It was in Saddam's interest that we start some provocation, so he could transform the war into an Iraqi-Israeli one. We made an explicit decision not to let him do that."

Still, the violence on the Temple Mount came at an unfortunate moment. Bush and some of his senior aides had already privately begun laying the groundwork to secure United Nations approval for Allied military action against Iraq. If it came to a showdown, Bush and Baker were insistent that the Security Council authorize Allied military action in advance. This was not only for philosophical reasons bound up with the President's conception of a new world order, but also for domestic political reasons. As a senior aide to Baker put it, obtaining United Nations approval first "would also box the Democrats in very nicely."

For the next fifty days, however, Temple Mount would be center stage in the Security Council. "It was a fantastic powder keg," Pickering recalled. "It was a terrible time for us. We did not want to see the [U.N] focus on the Iraq-Kuwait situation shift." In Washington, the worry over Temple Mount was acute. "We were desperate," said a senior State Department official, "to get the question off the radar screen." Until the storm over Temple Mount subsided, any action seeking the blessings of the U.N. Security Council for military action against Saddam would have to wait.

Meanwhile, the President was growing impatient. In a meeting during the second week of October with his senior advisers, Bush had wanted to know if Saddam Hussein's army could be ejected from Kuwait with the forces already committed to General Schwarzkopf under Plan 1002-90. Several advisers said that it seemed as if Bush was raising the question in the most speculative way. But if the President of the United States wanted an answer, Defense Secretary Cheney and General Colin Powell intended to see that he had one. No one was happy about providing such a briefing, least of all the officials from the U.S. Central Command.

When Schwarzkopf learned of the request, he flew into a rage, according to several of his aides. He had been as explicit as he could have been in spelling out the differences between the defense of Saudi Arabia and an offensive plan that would push Saddam Hussein out of Kuwait. How could anyone have missed the point? he demanded. With so much still to be done in the desert, Schwarzkopf felt he could not leave Riyadh to return to Washington. On Tuesday, October 9, he sent Major General Robert B. Johnston instead. The chief of staff of the Central Command, Johnston was fifty-three years old, a classic, detail-oriented staff officer who knew the ins and outs of every facet of Desert Shield. Schwarzkopf knew the operation had a decidedly personal dimension for Johnston: like Pagonis and a handful of other commanders, Johnston had a son in the desert, a junior officer in a Marine infantry battalion. Schwarzkopf had a lot of respect for Johnston, a mud soldier like himself. If there was anyone who could brief the President about the Central Command's military thinking, Schwarzkopf believed, it was his chief of staff.

On the morning of October 10, General Powell greeted Johnston in his Pentagon office. The two went almost immediately down the hall to the "tank," the Joint Chiefs' conference room on the second floor. Secretary Cheney was there with Paul Wolfowitz, General Tom Kelly, and a handful of other brass. Powell welcomed the Johnston visit. Many senior officials in the Pentagon, and several key advisers in the White House, believed that Powell was reluctant to move to an offensive capability. Powell, they felt, was an advocate of a containment policy that would provide for the defense of Saudi Arabia while allowing the sanctions against Iraq to bite harder. Powell disagreed with that characterization of his thinking. Within the Pentagon, the deployment for Desert Shield had been a source of concern. Since early August, Powell had kept Cheney and Bush apprised of the progress of the deployment, bringing them up to date at least once a week on the numbers of tanks, troops, aircraft, and ships as they arrived in the Gulf. Powell was concerned about the long lead times it required. As he had emphasized in the meeting with the President and his advisers at Camp David in early August, the operation specified in Plan 1002-90 would take months to carry out. Powell had just returned from the Gulf two weeks earlier, and he had seen for himself how well Schwarzkopf's forces were shaping up. But they were still no match for the huge force Saddam Hussein had in Kuwait.

As he listened to Johnston's briefing in the "tank," Powell was already looking to the future. "We made sure the President understood that at some point in the fall we would be coming back to him to say, 'What do you want to do?' And as we entered October, we were reaching that point. The buildup was going well. I had looked ahead with Norm, and we knew exactly when we would hit the full defensive buildup. It would be sometime in the first week of December. But you can't wait until the first week of December to decide you want to keep going; you have to make judgments before that."

The Johnston briefing would ignite a firestorm of controversy. There would be a heated debate about the merits of the plan Johnston would outline that morning, and some senior administration officials would later attempt to use it to claim credit for the war plan that ultimately humiliated Saddam Hussein's forces. The truth of the matter was at once more prosaic and enlightening. Johnston had been instructed to brief an offensive plan based on the defensive force the President had authorized under the terms of Plan 1002-90. Following his orders to the letter, Johnston did just that. The plan was a model of conventional military thinking. "It wasn't a bad plan in the sense that there were any military flaws," recalled a senior officer on the Joint Staff who was present. "But it wasn't quite up to the speed that the chairman was expecting."

Johnston and Schwarzkopf were well aware of the problems with the plan they had been ordered to brief. Johnston had concluded by pointing to a chart listing all the problems with the plan. The problems, Cheney recalled, seemed insurmountable. "Nobody was happy with the plan at that point," he said, "including the Central Command." Powell and Schwarzkopf agreed that Johnston had detailed only a Potemkin plan. "It was never a recommendation," General Schwarzkopf said. "We were asked how you would do it [invade Kuwait] if you had to do it right now. And this was the only thing that we had available. But it was certainly not the recommended plan." Powell, for his part, remembered it as a bit of helter-skelter. "This was a very short-notice briefing. . . . General Johnston made it clear when he briefed it that it was a preliminary view and [that] a lot more work had to be done." Schwarzkopf did not yet have all the forces the President had already authorized. CIA and Pentagon analysts were still studying the desert terrain to see how and, indeed, if it would support heavy tanks maneuvering at high speeds. The Defense Mapping Agency had still not even completed its charting of the territory in many parts of the Kuwait

Theater of Operations. "I considered it a first cut," Powell said, "and I never considered it a plan we would execute." Significantly, the plan focused almost exclusively on air power. It was a four-phase plan.

For the air plan, Lieutenant General Chuck Horner had begun work in early August with Brigadier General C. Buster Glosson and his small team of "fraggers," or target specialists. "The [first] objective," said a senior Central Command officer who participated in the sessions and reviewed the air-tasking order as it was being put together, "was to eliminate [Iraqi] leadership, command, and communications, their ability to reinforce. . . . Phase two of the strategic air campaign was to gain and maintain total air superiority. We thought that would probably take about six to nine days. Phase three was the attrit-to-combat ratio, and here we were concentrating on the Republican Guard. And then Phase four was the ground-campaign plan." This last phase called for a straightforward, "force-on-force" offensive against the very heart of the Iraqi defensive lines. It was, with almost no modifications, the same plan the Central Command headquarters staff had briefed to Schwarzkopf on August 24.

The plan was wholly inadequate to deal with the much larger Iraqi force Saddam Hussein had moved into Kuwait since then. "Johnston came back not just to brief the ground plan," Powell emphasized. "He came back to brief the whole plan. And he briefed the entire air campaign, which was most of the briefing, because early on we had an air option. And so if the President was so hot for war, he could have gone for war then. But it was only an air option. . . . It was at the tail end of that briefing that we showed the preliminary ground plan based on some work done by staff folks on very short notice. And it was tagged onto the end of the air campaign, but it was caveated as being a preliminary first look. And some people got more excited about it than perhaps they should have been."

One reason there was so much concern about the war plan briefed by Johnston was that it would have to be presented to the President. A meeting had already been scheduled with Bush for the following day.

In Riyadh, Schwarzkopf had begun his own planning for a ground war against the Iraqi army. For inspiration, he turned to a small cell of military theorists. They were part of a select group known within the Pentagon as the Jedi Knights, after the characters in George Lucas's hit film *Star Wars*.

Their origins went back to the late 1970s, when an obscure group of young officers and military thinkers considered outsiders and mavericks began to meet in military classrooms and over beers in officers' clubs. They wrote papers, read them to one another, and then argued about them. They read obscure German texts and studied long forgotten battles. One group even began skipping Friday beer nights at the large Marine Corps base at Quantico, Virginia, in order to drive thirty miles to Alexandria, where they met in a living room of a town house to argue over battle tactics some more. In the end, this group of men changed the way the Army and the Marine Corps conceived, planned, and trained for war.

In the Army, the officers who pursued these new ideas were derided at first as Jedi Knights for their bright-eyed, wunderkind approach to warfare. In the Marine Corps, they were known pejoratively as "maneuverists." They were linked to another, larger group of critics of Pentagon weapons-buying practices known disparagingly as the "military reformers," a loose federation of whistle-blowers and activists who advocated simple low-tech weapons over expensive high-tech ones. Eventually, many senior officials would come to embrace the ideas of these new thinkers, but others bitterly resisted them. As a group they would lay the groundwork for a new fighting doctrine. Within the group several individuals would play key roles.

One was John Boyd, an Air Force colonel who radiated intellectual intensity. A fighter pilot during the Korean War, Boyd went on to become a senior instructor at the Tactical Fighter Training Center at Nellis Air Force Base in Nevada before he retired. There, his students had dubbed him "forty-second Boyd" for his habit of contending, always correctly, that he could beat them in any air-to-air combat duel in forty seconds.

At Nellis, Boyd had refined his theory of air combat, teaching young pilots to start their second maneuver while their opponent was still trying to react to their first. He applied his ideas to later work he did assisting with the design of F-15 and F-16 fighters; he believed the new aircraft needed to be able to move from one maneuver to another faster than enemy aircraft. Boyd had also begun to see applications of his theory in all modes of conflict. Boyd had turned his theory into a six-hour lecture called "Patterns of Conflict." He suggested that pilots and soldiers go through a four-stage cycle as they fight: observing the opponent; orienting to the new challenge; deciding on the next move; and acting on the decision. He called it the "OODA loop" and talked about his theory to anyone in the military who would listen. To many who heard him, Boyd became something of a guru. People began to talk of "getting inside the enemy's decision-making cycle," getting inside his OODA loop.

But there was more to Boyd's theory than clever acronyms. He had researched battles where smaller and less powerful forces had beaten larger ones by using superior tactics, strategy, and speed of maneuver. He had studied the battles of the ancient Persians, the Spartans, and the Greeks, the maneuvers of Genghis Khan, the writings of T. E. Lawrence, the blitzkreigs of the Germans, and the winning tactics of Civil War generals. He had found cases where forces had conquered their opponents by attacks from unexpected quarters that disoriented and confused the enemy so they could not react in time to the attack. For Boyd, the ideal campaign was one where one side so terrorized the other, so psychologically manipulated him, that the opponent surrendered before ever engaging in battle. The ideal war, Boyd felt, was one in which no battle was fought.

Boyd's ideas appealed strongly to an elite group, a handful of military-affairs specialists. While Boyd was lecturing, they were arguing in Congress and the Pentagon that smaller and cheaper weapons were often better than bigger and more expensive ones. They believed that because in a war with the Soviets in Europe the attrition rate of men and machinery would be very high, the United States would need more reliable, less expensive, low-tech weaponry. There was nothing wrong with so-called smart weapons, of course, but they had to be based on sound principles. More important, they had to work. These men championed such weapons as the small, fast, and agile F-16 Falcon attack fighter and the ugly A-10 Thunderbolt "Warthog" tank killer.

Although Bill Lind had never served in the military, he did know military history and strategy. By the age of thirteen, he had read the writings of Carl von Clausewitz. By 1974, he was a staffer for Senator Robert Taft, Jr., on the Armed Services Committee. A specialist in naval affairs, Lind gravitated toward the study of Marine Corps tactics. By the early 1980s he was regularly publishing articles in the Marine Corps *Gazette*, a forum for wide-ranging thinking, where he laid out his arguments for what came to be called "maneuver warfare." Its central thesis was that battles could be won by speed, cleverness, and deception rather than by the simple application of overwhelming brute force.

In the Marine Corps, these ideas were not readily accepted. Of all the services, the corps prided itself on its guts. But a few Marines thought

Lind's thinking had merit. Lieutenant Colonel Mike Wyly was one of them. Wyly had commanded an infantry company during two tours in Vietnam. Later, he had studied at the Marine Corps Command and General Staff College. Two past wars had influenced his thinking: the Yom Kippur War of October 1973, a conflict whose blistering speed of maneuver and destructive weaponry shocked many American military tacticians; and the Russo-Finnish war of 1939–40, in which the Finns had used small, mobile units of ski-troopers to chop up the invading Russians, inflicting losses of perhaps ten times their own before capitulating. In 1979, as Bill Lind was pursuing his concepts of maneuver warfare and John Boyd was explaining OODA loops to anyone who would listen, Wyly was teaching the tactics of speed, deception, and maneuver at the Marine Corps' Amphibious Warfare School in Quantico. Late that year, Lind published an article in the Marine Corps *Gazette* entitled "Victory or Attrition: What Are We Fighting For?" After reading it, Wyly telephoned Lind. "I said, 'I'm not sure what I'm for,' " Wyly recalled. "And he said, 'I'm not sure what I'm for either, but there is a man who has an alternative. He's a retired Air Force colonel named John Boyd.' "

Wyly invited Boyd to speak at Quantico, and Boyd delivered his six-hour lecture. That was the first time Wyly or his students had heard Boyd's theory of conflict, and for some it struck them with all the force of an epiphany. They were looking for a better way, and here was a man with answers. "A cadre of fifteen or twenty of us stayed into the night, talking and arguing," Wyly said. "There was a feeling of real excitement." Soon the group was getting together on Friday nights at Bill Lind's town house in Alexandria, Virginia. Between sessions they studied, wrote papers, and then shared them, seminar-style. "Marines don't debate well," said Wyly, "but we found this subject exciting." Their ideas soon began to spread through the corps.

In the Army, a major change in war-fighting doctrine was also under way, spearheaded by a small corps of officers. The charge was led by a short, pugnacious general named William DePuy. In the mid-1970s, General Creighton Abrams, the Army's chief of staff, began trying to repair the damage done by the Vietnam War by creating two new commands. The first, called FORCECOM, was a standing army for combat. The second, the Training and Doctrine Command (TRADOC), was DePuy's command.

Having quickly realized that the Army's fighting doctrine had become useless and irrelevant, DePuy gathered a dozen highly regarded senior officers and found space for them in a boat house at Fort Monroe, in southeastern Virginia. He instructed the officers to begin working on a new theory of war fighting for the Army. The officers came to be called the Boathouse Gang.

After some time, they returned to DePuy with a new doctrine. It was summarized in a new version of the Army field manual, number 100-5, or FM 100-5 (or just 100-5). In 1976, DePuy had it published with a camouflage cover—lest there be any doubt that it was the Army's definitive manual for waging war.

FM 100-5 represented a bold step forward. It took lessons learned from the firepower and swiftness of the Yom Kippur War and applied them to the modern battlefield. It stressed using the concentrated firepower of the combined arms of all units to strike at an advancing Soviet army in Europe, and to hit the enemy again and again, to slow him down and wear him out as he tried to advance across the Continent. After the Boathouse Gang finished writing the manual, teams of generals traveled to Army bases around the country, explaining and selling its contents to the rest of the corps.

At the U.S. Army's Command and General Staff College at Fort Leavenworth, Kansas, a lieutenant colonel with the unlikely name of Huba Wass de Czege realized that while DePuy's so-called active defense might appear to work in theoretical tests, it was impractical on a battlefield. Born in Hungary, Wass de Czege was a product of West Point. He had commanded a rifle company in Vietnam, been wounded, and received a Silver Star before becoming an instructor at Leavenworth. FM 100-5 neglected the counterattack component of defense, Wass de Czege said: "And it never addressed what to do with large units, how to run a military campaign. It was missing the human dimension."

Boyd had also read FM 100-5, and he didn't like it either. "You don't want to hit the enemy head-on," he said. "You'll cave a lot of heads, you'll lose a lot of bodies." He began campaigning to get the manual changed. "Fighter pilots come in the back door to shoot," he said. "We've got to teach this to the Army."

By 1979, there had been enough criticism of FM 100-5 that Army Chief of Staff Edward C. "Shy" Meyer wanted it revised. It was an ironic if not wholly welcome compliment to DePuy that his revolutionary manual stirred such debate within the Army that it was changed again within three years. The job fell to Wass de Czege.

Consulting a group of like-minded officers and friends, Wass de Czege began reworking the manual to stress all the things he believed were missing: counterattack, turning battles into campaigns, the human dimension of warfare. The new manual stressed deception, fluidity, and adaptability. It cited two key battles as examples. The first was the Battle of Vicksburg in May 1863. The second was far less well known. This was the Battle of Tannenberg in August 1914. Both were dramatic illustrations of the effectiveness of mobility, speed, surprise, and flexibility on the battlefield. "Setting a pace of operations so rapid that his enemies could not follow his activities, [General Ulysses S.] Grant defeated the forces of Generals [Joseph] Johnston and [John] Pemberton in five engagements," Wass de Czege wrote. "He covered 200 miles in 19 days, capturing the city of Jackson and driving the defenders of Vicksburg into their trenches." Commenting on the Battle of Tannenberg, which was fought by the armies of Germany and Russia, Wass de Czege wrote that the conflict was "a closer parallel to the fluid conditions, rapid maneuver, and calculated risks of future operations."

Wass de Czege has since said that while the ideas in the new FM 100-5 came from the studies and advanced thinking of himself and his Army colleagues, he credits Boyd and Lind with keeping the ideas of maneuver warfare in the forefront of military debate in the 1970s and 1980s and challenging America's military theorists to think creatively. The revised manual was finished in 1982. The same year, Wass de Czege set up the Army's School for Advanced Military Studies, whose graduates adopted the name of Jedi Knights.

It was the 1982 version of FM 100-5 that energized the Marine Corps. By then, an iconoclastic general named Alfred Gray had been named commandant. Gray was familiar with maneuverist thinking in the corps, and as commander of the 1st Marine Division, he had decreed that the fluid and flexible style would be his style of fighting. When he saw the new version of FM 100-5, he decided that the Marine Corps needed something similar, although even more fundamental and shorter. He called on a young captain named John Schmitt, who had just finished writing a Marine Corps manual on ground combat. Schmitt consulted Wyly, Lind, and Boyd. He studied Clausewitz and Sun-tzu, the 4th-century B.C. Chinese strategist and philosopher. He had numerous meetings with Gray, since this was really to be Gray's book. What emerged in 1989 was a slender, elegantly written classic called "Warfighting. FM FM 1." The manual is to Marine Corps combat what Strunk and White's *Elements of Style* is to writing. The tactics of daring and deception would form the bedrock of the military's new fighting doctrine. And the doctrine of the maneuverists and the Jedi Knights would find its greatest champion in General Norman Schwarzkopf.

Within days after his arrival in Riyadh, Schwarzkopf received a telephone call from Carl Vuono. The two had met as teenagers when they were cadets at West Point in the 1950s. Now the chief of staff of the Army, Vuono was an avuncular man with deep-set, beaglelike eyes. He was a year younger than Schwarzkopf, but had risen more quickly through the ranks. Like Schwarzkopf, Vuono remembered the pain of Vietnam ("the low point," he had called it) and had determined to remain in the Army, to rebuild it, to make it better. Nearing the end of a distinguished career, Vuono saw the Jedi Knights as one of the most promising signs that his Army had finally shaken off the incubus of Vietnam. Without pressing the matter on Schwarzkopf—whom he knew was one of the Army's most difficult and dedicated soldiers—Vuono asked whether the commander would like to have some graduates from the School for Advanced Military Studies (SAMS) assigned to his headquarters staff in Riyadh. This school, established by Wass de Czege in 1982, marked the Pentagon's institutionalized acceptance of the Jedi Knights' war-fighting theories.

Schwarzkopf said he would be pleased to have the SAMS graduates. Just over two weeks later, three majors, a colonel, and a British lieutenant colonel stepped off a military jet into the baking heat of Riyadh. An advance element of the Jedi Knights had reached ground zero. They went to work immediately. They were billeted together and given a handful of liaison officers among the senior Central Command staff. Schwarzkopf gave the Jedi Knights brief but heady instructions—to think broadly on how they might achieve the Allied objective—and told them that whatever they needed, they would have. For the next two weeks, as they struggled to come to grips with the complexities of an offensive plan that would succeed in driving the massive Iraqi force from Kuwait, they would hear nothing from Schwarzkopf.

Working under the guidance of their senior colonel, the five Jedi Knights were authorized to ask their designated contacts anything, but they were not allowed to tell the Central Command staff what they were working on. Traditionally, Pentagon war planners went about their business by focusing on a basic calculus known as METT-T (this stood for Mission, Enemy, Terrain, Troops, and Time). But in the Gulf crisis, the number of troops available for an offensive operation, the terrain, and the intention of the enemy force were all largely unknown. Nevertheless, the small Jedi Knight team began to explore a number of options for a ground attack. They considered an attack up the coast toward Kuwait City, another attack at the "elbow" where the Saudi border is closest to Kuwait City, and a third option, attacking around the Wadi al-Batin, where the Kuwaiti frontier meets the borders of Iraq and Saudi Arabia. For each option, the five war planners weighed the costs and benefits—and the risks of failure. The process was not easy because the options that offered some of the greatest potential for gain carried with them the greatest risk of failure. Soon after they came to grips with the complexity of the task before them, these five Jedi Knights would be joined by more converts to the movement begun by John Boyd, Bill Lind, and their colleagues. Working with Schwarzkopf's regular planning staff and with planners assigned to the Joint Chiefs of Staff, the Jedi Knights would dramatically shape the outlines of Operation Desert Storm.

The five Jedi Knights in Riyadh had their first meeting of substance with their Central Command boss at the end of the first week in October. By all accounts, Schwarzkopf was the boldest soldier in the room. Even as his chief of staff, Major General Robert Johnston, was preparing to deliver his "up the middle" Washington briefing that would cause so much consternation, Schwarzkopf was considering the array of tentative plans by his Jedi Knights that would have his heaviest forces swinging far to the west. It was not thought through yet, and there was no way Johnston could brief the idea in Washington. But Schwarzkopf recognized its potential. It would have to be fine-tuned, the huge logistics problems addressed and ironed out. But even then the potential for such a plan—for outflanking an Iraqi army schooled almost exclusively in defensive warfare—was so obvious it was an inspiration. All it would take to make it happen was for President Bush to give Schwarzkopf twice as many soldiers as he had.

Schwarzkopf told aides that if he were asked to lead an offensive to eject Saddam Hussein's army from Kuwait, he would need the U.S. Army's entire VII Corps from Europe. The VII Corps comprised the 1st, 2nd, and

3rd divisions. All these were armored. Among the heaviest forces in the American military, they were equipped with the newest M1A1 main battle tanks. Unlike many of the M1 tanks already in the desert, the M1A1s of the VII Corps had overpressurized cabins, which were presumed to provide a highly effective defense against Iraq's chemical weapons. They also had tougher armor.

On the morning of October 11, Defense Secretary Cheney and General Powell escorted Major General Johnston to the White House to talk to the President about the Central Command's thinking on an offensive capability. The briefing occurred in the Situation Room. Vice-President Quayle, Secretary of State Baker, and National Security Adviser Scowcroft were also present. According to several participants, Scowcroft was sharply critical of Johnston from the earliest moments of the briefing. "The air campaign was accepted . . . ; it was not changed," said a senior official on the Central Command staff who attended the briefing. "The ground campaign was changed by Brent Scowcroft, and I don't give a damn what anybody says. I sat there and heard the discussion. He said, 'Why are you going force-on-force? Why don't you go around and come in from the side?' "

Near the end of the meeting, Johnston raised the issue of deploying the VII Corps from Germany to Saudi Arabia. The addition of the three heavy divisions would provide the Central Command with a true offensive capability. President Bush asked Johnston how long it would take to move the VII Corps from Europe to the Saudi desert. "At least a couple of months, sir," Johnston replied. There were no two ways around it, then: a true offensive capability would require several more months and the use of ground forces. While using air power alone to confront Saddam Hussein still appealed to some of the President's key advisers, Powell was dead set against it, and so was Cheney. As for Scowcroft, the retired Air Force general never wavered on one point: if you're going to throw Saddam Hussein out of Kuwait, he argued, you're going to need to use your soldiers on the ground.

The next day, General Tom Kelly, the operations director for the Joint Chiefs of Staff, called one of his senior planners at home. Kelly told the man that he had just spoken with Cheney. "I want you to get some guys together," Kelly said. "Mr. Cheney has called, and he wants us to develop some feasibilities."

The feasibilities Cheney wanted Kelly to work on were stimulated by his return flight from the Persian Gulf. Cheney's Pentagon aircraft had flown over the broad, empty desert of western Iraq. He told several aides that that had prompted him to begin exploring the options for an attack on Iraqi forces from its western desert.

On Saturday, October 13, Kelly met with his planners in an electronically secure conference room in the Pentagon known as a tactical-operations center. Kelly felt a bit uneasy about discussing military options with his Joint Staff planners without Powell being present, but Cheney had asked for a briefing on Monday and Powell was out of town. Kelly and his planners would have to have some answers by then on the feasibility of an Allied attack deep into western Iraq. "Logistics was the big thing," said one of the participants in the meeting. Once an American-led force had attacked so deep, could it be continually resupplied with food, fuel, and ammunition?

General Powell returned on October 14 and was briefed on the planners' new assignment from Cheney. Powell told the planners to begin thinking about a plan of attack into Iraq from the northern border of Saudi Arabia, but not nearly as far west as Iraq's borders with Jordan and Syria. "Powell was the one who started bringing us back in a little bit further," one of the planners recalled.

"The supportability [of the operation] was the big thing," another senior Pentagon planner said. "We got logisticians in, and there was almost an attitude on the part of Mr. Cheney and General Powell of 'You've shown me this; now prove to me that it can be done.' We got it figured out down to how many trucks it would take to get all of the supplies out there. How do we get the water out there? We looked at everything. There was [an oil] pipeline that ran down the side of the Tapline Road north in the Saudi desert. We looked at whether we could reverse that thing and start shooting water back up the other way. We had some folks from CIA come in and tell us, 'That's stupid, you can't do that.' So we looked at everything, how much water it would take, how to get all the supplies out there, how much supply you would have to have built up before you could start an offense. And we had it all down to some pretty good numbers that we were satisfied with. And basically what it showed, I think, especially to Mr. Cheney, was that it was feasible to do it."

On October 15, Kelly's planners presented several options to Cheney. In the past forty-eight hours, Kelly's experts had worked almost nonstop. One option involved seizing a large sector of the western Iraqi desert and offering to trade it for the withdrawal of the Iraqi army from Kuwait. "This would have helped with the [Scud missile] threat against Israel," a senior planning official said. "But in coordination with the services, basically, it seemed too difficult to do." Another option called for an American force to drive straight north from the Saudi border into central Iraq south of Baghdad. Yet another option, as the planners heeded Powell's advice to bring the lines of attack farther east, called for deep strikes into southern Iraq west of Basra. These options were a far cry from the plan Johnston had outlined just days earlier. Five days later, Kelly's men briefed their options to Scowcroft. The President's adviser for national security affairs was so intrigued by the options being contemplated by the Joint Staff planners that he took a White House limousine over to the Pentagon to hear about them firsthand. The new plans were not yet ready to be presented to Bush. But participants in the meeting said that Scowcroft left the briefing saying he was pleased and very impressed.

Also on October 20, General Powell boarded one of the Pentagon's executive jets at Andrews Air Force Base. It was time for another trip to the desert. Powell had heard from Carl Vuono, who had returned from the Gulf nearly two weeks before, that Schwarzkopf was not a happy man. The command performance to brief an offensive plan to the President had made him angry. The trip to the desert would serve three purposes. First, Powell could assure Schwarzkopf in person that the entire administration was behind him, that he enjoyed the full faith and confidence of President Bush and Secretary Cheney. Second, Powell would be able to examine the precise requirements for building a true offensive capability. And third, he would be able to spend some time with the troops. Like Schwarzkopf, Powell believed it was important for the troops to be able to see and talk to the people who made the decisions that governed their lives. There were few things, Powell knew, that could boost soldiers' morale more quickly.

The next day, Powell met Schwarzkopf at his headquarters in the Saudi Ministry of Defense and Air in downtown Riyadh. The two generals, both dressed in desert camouflage uniforms, greeted each other warmly. Schwarzkopf briefed Powell first on the state of the Desert Shield deployment. It was going well, he said. They were on time, maybe a day or two behind schedule at the most. Powell wanted to know Schwarzkopf's requirements for an offensive force. He also wanted to talk about the planning for an offensive against the Iraqi forces in Kuwait. Unlike others in the administration, Powell was confident that Schwarzkopf's planners would ultimately come up with a winner.

Many people in the Pentagon and in the Bush administration would later attempt to claim credit for the so-called Left Hook, in which the bulk of Schwarzkopf's ground forces would drive deep into Iraq, striking Saddam's army on its long, exposed western flank. In fact, the plan had many fathers. Dick Cheney was among the first to raise the notion of an attack from western Iraq. General Powell had refined that notion, drawing the lines of attack farther east and closer to the Kuwait-Iraq border and the Republican Guard divisions clustered south of Basra.

Those were just the broad conceptual outlines of the plan, however. Like Cheney and Powell, Schwarzkopf was deeply impressed by the possibilities of a fast, deep strike with the bulk of his forces into south-central Iraq. But it was not until the Jedi Knights in Riyadh began working with Schwarzkopf's regular planning staff and trading ideas with General Kelly's planners on the Joint Staff that a true war plan began to emerge. In many respects, several key participants explained, it was as if three sets of plans were emerging independently. But as the Allied force moved closer to war, critical elements of the three plans began to merge into one unified plan.

It was this plan that had to take account of such things as the enormous logistical obstacles of a fast, deep strike into Iraq and the uncertainties about whether the desert terrain would support the heavy M1A1 tanks of Lieutenant General Frederick Franks's VII Corps and Major General Barry McCaffrey's 24th Infantry Division (Mechanized).

"We were still learning about the terrain," Powell said. "We had a lot of work to do on the terrain. We had to do a lot of work on operational analysis of the battlefield and of the enemy. And so a lot of give-and-take went back and forth. The logical, obvious plan emerged from that." Schwarzkopf was especially concerned about the terrain. He had the satellite imagery and a host of other intelligence, but the question of the desert terrain remained unanswered. If he could be sure that the desert would not swallow his tanks, and if the President would give him the forces to build a true offensive force, then he knew what he wanted to do.

Saddam Hussein had left his right flank, to the west of Kuwait, completely exposed, Schwarzkopf explained. If the desert would support fully loaded M1A1 tanks, he had a viable plan of attack. "I said, 'All right,' "

Schwarzkopf recalled afterward, " 'if [the Iraqi enemy] stays in this con-figuration that he's in right now, and the terrain over there on . . . his right flank is in fact trafficable, we have a wonderful opportunity to cut off and destroy his forces.' " Powell said that this had the makings of a good offensive plan, as long as Saddam didn't redeploy his forces and cover his flank. Powell would not interfere with the nuts and bolts of his battlefield commander's war planning. He was confident that with the efforts of the Joint Staff in Washington and the Jedi Knights in Riyadh, Schwarzkopf's team would get the job done.

Powell noted that the Central Command was already confusing Saddam Hussein's commanders in Kuwait, who seemed to be expecting an attack from the sea. Schwarzkopf wanted to do everything he could to encourage such thinking. A few weeks before Powell's arrival in Riyadh, Schwarzkopf had ordered the Central Command's naval chief, Vice-Admiral Henry Mauz, to begin rehearsing large and very visible amphibious operations. Just after dawn on October 1, with Mauz monitoring events from the bridge of the USS *Blue Ridge*, his command ship, leathernecks from the 4th Marine Expeditionary Brigade and sailors from the USS *Okinawa*, USS *Ogden*, USS *Fort McHenry*, USS *Durham*, and USS *Cuyuga* embarked on the first major amphibious rehearsal operation of Desert Shield. The operation took place just off Ras al-Madrakah, in Oman. It would have been hard for Saddam, even with his limited intelligence capabilities, to have missed it. The operation was given the code name Camel Sand, and Schwarzkopf told Powell that he had ordered up another big amphibious rehearsal to take place in mid-November. Confident that he had Saddam's battlefield com-manders thoroughly alarmed, Schwarzkopf wanted to keep them focused on the sea. The second operation was to be called Imminent Thunder.

Powell turned the discussion to the force structure Schwarzkopf would need for an offensive capability. He wanted to leave nothing to chance, he said. If the President was going to order them to go after Saddam's forces in Kuwait, they were going to go in with everything they had. When he returned to Washington, Powell told Schwarzkopf, he would tell Secretary Cheney and the President to authorize the deployment of the VII Corps, as Schwarzkopf had suggested in an earlier discussion. But Powell said he wanted more. If Schwarzkopf agreed, he would also move another Army division to the desert. Powell suggested the 1st Infantry Division (Mech-anized), known throughout the Army as the Big Red One. Powell said he also wanted more naval forces. The Air Force capability should be reexamined as well, he said. He also wanted to give Schwarzkopf another division of Marines. Schwarzkopf was enormously pleased. He and the chairman of the Joint Chiefs spoke the same language.

On October 31, Powell and Cheney went to the White House with their wish list. Kelly's planners, who had conferred with the planners in Riyadh, had come up with seven attack plans. None called for an attack on Baghdad, but some were highly ambitious. One called for an invasion by a large U.S. Marine force through Jordan into western Iraq. Another called for a Marine amphibious invasion through Bubiyan Island at the northern end of the Gulf, cutting off the Iraqi army in Kuwait from the north. That was rejected because it would inevitably result in a high number of casualties. Two others called for launching offensive strikes from eastern Syria and southern Turkey into Iraq; these were rejected primarily for political reasons.

Of the seven plans devised by the Joint Staff planners, Powell and Cheney agreed to brief only three to the President and his senior advisers. All three involved variations of an American-led attack on Iraq from the western desert. "It all went back to the chairman's philosophy," a senior Joint Staff planner said. "He believed that we did not want to take any action where we're going to have to rely on the Iraqis' reaction to it. We wanted to force him, to destroy him when we made the decision to do so. And the plan that eventually evolved did that. It was not just cut off [the Iraqi army in Kuwait] and sit and wait. It was, 'We're going to take it to him.' "

The discussion with the President and his advisers was lengthy. But none of those present said they had any doubt about what the President intended to do. "He never hesitated," Cheney said. "When it was time, when we said, 'Look, Mr. President, we're going to want to send a total of six aircraft-carrier battle groups. We've got one Marine division over there now; we're going to want to send another one. We want to send another division [the Big Red One] from Kansas. Et cetera, et cetera." The VII Corps was already a given, Cheney said. But Bush did not hesitate when he learned of the size of the offensive force. The initial order called for a doubling of the number of troops, to more than 400,000. But Bush knew the numbers would almost certainly exceed 500,000. "He never blinked," Cheney remembered. "He signed off on it, and he said, 'Do it.' " Aides said that Bush had been leaning more and more in recent weeks toward a decision to double the American force in the Gulf. He was not committed to war, but he wanted to keep all his options open. If he was going to have to use offensive force against Saddam's army in Kuwait, he was going to make sure his commanders had every tank and soldier they needed.

"I became convinced early on that, if diplomacy failed, we would indeed have to use force," Bush later told *U.S. News.* "I kept hoping that the use of force could be avoided. I cannot pinpoint all of this to a certain date, but I was determined from the very beginning that aggression would not stand, and as the military planners went forward, I was more and more convinced that we could use force and be successful. Various plans changed from time to time, and they were improved as the situation became clearer and clearer to our military. Many felt that Saddam would finally come to his senses and see that he could not prevail, and that he would pull out of Kuwait unilaterally to comply with the resolutions of the U.N. But he never did that. He miscalculated, and he underestimated our determination."

For the moment, the President and his advisers agreed to refer to the larger force as the "enhanced option," and they would not announce it for several days. General Powell understood the politics of euphemism as well as anyone, but he tended to favor a more plainspoken idiom. "I don't believe in doing war on the basis of macroeconomic, marginal-analysis models," Powell said. "I'm more of the mind-set of a New York street bully: 'Here's my bat, here's my gun, here's my knife, I'm wearing armor. I'm going to kick your ass.' "

CHAPTER 11

BAKER MOUNTS A DIPLOMATIC BLITZKRIEG

NOVEMBER 3 BROUGHT brisk winds and a hint of snow as James Baker's State Department airplane lifted off the tarmac at Andrews Air Force Base, taking him on a diplomatic odyssey to twelve countries, some of which he would visit twice. In a year that would see Baker cover more than 200,000 miles on visits to thirty countries, this would be the longest, the most grueling, and by far the most important of his many diplomatic missions.

According to some of his closest advisers, President Bush still held out hope that economic sanctions and the threat of military action might yet persuade Saddam Hussein to pull his army out of Kuwait. But, relying on the counsel of Brent Scowcroft, Dick Cheney, and Colin Powell, the President had decided to keep "all his options open" by authorizing the deployment of an offensive force to the Persian Gulf. As a result, on the same day Baker was taking off from Andrews Air Force Base, hundreds of specialists from the VII Corps in Germany and the 1st Infantry Division (Mechanized) at Fort Riley, Kansas, were preparing their M1A1 tanks and Bradley fighting vehicles for the long trip to the Saudi desert. If he decided he needed to use it, the President would have his offensive capability. But Bush was determined he would not use military force without the prior approval of the international community, and it was Baker's job to secure the approval of key nations. He knew that he had his work cut out for him.

Baker's trip came at a delicate time. The violence on the Temple Mount had complicated things enormously in the Security Council. Still, both Bush and Baker were reasonably confident that, given time, they had a good chance of securing a favorable vote on the use of military force. In that calculus, of course, Saddam Hussein was a key factor: he continued to hold hundreds of Westerners hostage in Baghdad and Kuwait City. Refugees had trickled out of the beleaguered emirate with eyewitness accounts of rapes, dismemberment, torture. There was little doubt of Saddam's villainy. Bush emphasized this again and again. For weeks, he had pounded away at Saddam Hussein, calling him morally evil, a man capable of the vilest sorts of crimes. The President had begun reading Martin Gilbert's *The Second World War*. Aides said that Bush had remarked that Hitler's Death's Head regiments in Poland had committed crimes "hauntingly similar" to those the Iraqi soldiers were committing in Kuwait. Some of the Iraqis' crimes, Bush said, were even worse than what was done by the Nazis. "Outrageous acts of barbarism," Bush described the Iraqi atrocities on November 1. "I don't think Hitler ever participated in anything of that nature." The comparison was extreme, but Bush stuck by it, telling *U.S. News* months after the war had ended: "Yes, I felt and properly stated that Saddam was like Hitler. There were some critics of this—quite a few, if one goes back and reviews the clippings. But that's the way I felt about it. Having said that, it was clear to me that the goal was the removal of Iraq from Kuwait. What we tried to do was make clear to the people of Iraq, and even to the Iraq military, that the dispute we had was not with them, but with their leader who ordered the invasion."

Still, many Americans were uncertain about the President's policy. In mid-October, a *Washington Post*/ABC News poll had showed that 70 percent of the respondents believed that the United States should "take all action necessary, including the use of force," to oust Saddam Hussein's army from Kuwait. That same survey, however, reported that only 46 percent supported a military attack in the event the embargo failed to persuade Saddam to get out of Kuwait peacefully. Muddying the waters further, the polls showed that the public had little confidence that economic sanctions would work.

Baker was well aware of the ambivalent public mood. He had seen the President's approval rating slide from a near historic high of over 80 percent in late August to just over 50 percent in early November. And there was every indication, Baker told friends, that things were going to get worse. Just before he departed for the Gulf on November 3, Baker took Dick Cheney and Bob Teeter, Bush's pollster, fishing for a few days in Wyoming. As they hunted trout and bantered back and forth, the three men knew they must somehow reverse the downward slide in the public's approval ratings for the Gulf deployment. In terms of domestic politics, Teeter pointed out, the Democrats had finally begun to sense an opportunity in the Gulf crisis. Although Congress had adjourned on October 28, some key committee chairmen in both the House and Senate had begun hinting that they would hold hearings to examine the administration's Gulf policy.

Cheney and his top generals worried that any congressional debate would inevitably send the wrong signal to Saddam Hussein—"the ultimate CNN watcher," as Powell called him. If Saddam thought Washington was divided by the Gulf crisis, this most isolated of political figures might well draw the wrong conclusion and decide to remain in Kuwait. Baker said that the United States could not afford to get too far out in front of the international community. If he could work the issue in one-on-one sessions during his forthcoming trip, Baker told Cheney and Teeter, Security Council approval of the use of force against Saddam would render the Democrats' actions impotent. More important, it would keep the Allied coalition strong as the prospect of war with Saddam loomed larger. That was the objective of the long trip, Baker said.

On November 4, after a brief stop in Bahrain, Baker visited Dhahran, where the single largest concentration of American military personnel was. As reporters from around the world took down his every word, Baker addressed the American troops. The conflict in the Persian Gulf had entered a "new phase," he said. "While we are still seeking a peaceful, political, and diplomatic solution, we have to, I think, put ourselves in a position where we would be able to exercise any options that might be available. I don't think we can—nor should we—rule out the use of force."

Over the next few days, on his visits to Cairo and Ankara, Baker made the same argument, and in both President Hosni Mubarak and President Turgut Ozal, he found a receptive audience. Typical of both the tight scheduling and the sometimes impromptu nature of the Baker trip, the secretary of state squeezed a critical meeting into his Cairo visit. China's foreign minister, Qian Qichen, had been scheduled to come to Cairo, but his itinerary had suddenly changed. Baker caught up with him in the VIP lounge of the Cairo airport. The United States would be seeking Security

Council authorization in the very near future for the use of force against the Iraqi troops in Kuwait, Baker told Qian, according to aides accompanying the secretary. The nature of the Gulf conflict had changed, and the Security Council would have to face up to its responsibilities in the Gulf. The Chinese foreign minister listened impassively. He made no promises, but neither did he threaten to use the Chinese veto.

On November 9, just days after the midterm congressional elections, George Bush sent the clearest signal possible that the United States was serious about using its military force in the Gulf. "I have not ruled out the use of force at all," the President said, "and I think that is evident by what we're doing here today." A reporter asked whether the doubling of the American force in Saudi Arabia from 200,000 soldiers to more than 400,000 meant that the administration had given up on sanctions. "I hope that the sanctions will work," Bush replied, "within a two-month period."

Few people noticed it at the time, but Bush had just telegraphed his own rough timetable for when the conflict with Iraq would have to be resolved. His closest advisers stressed that the President still believed that sanctions coupled with the more ominous military threat might yet persuade Saddam Hussein to get out of Kuwait. "From the start," a senior Bush adviser said, "he was prepared to do everything he could to resolve this peacefully. He has been in warfare . . . and he knew that war meant war deaths and casualties. Doubling the force was not a move to war."

That still left the question of the United Nations. If the enormous American military force in the Gulf was to be a truly convincing threat to Saddam Hussein, Bush wanted a clear signal from the Security Council that he could use it if he had to. "I think one of the major successes [of the Allied action against Iraq] has been the ability to have world opinion totally on our side because of the U.N. action," Bush said, in announcing the doubling of the U.S. force. "The peacekeeping function of the United Nations has indeed been rejuvenated by the actions of the Security Council."

There was another compelling reason to turn to the United Nations. Because of growing nervousness at home about the use of the American military force against the Iraqi troops in Kuwait, Bush wanted the political cover that only a Security Council resolution could give him. Already, he had begun to feel the heat from his decision to deploy another 200,000 troops to the Gulf. On Capitol Hill, influential Democrats were furious over the timing of the announcement. It had everything to do with domestic political considerations, they charged, and very little if anything to do with military factors in the Gulf. Immediately, Sam Nunn, the Georgia Democrat who chaired the Senate Armed Services Committee, announced that he would convene hearings. The hints of a showdown with the administration had become a reality, and the Democrats promised to come out fighting.

In Moscow on November 9, James Baker found himself squarely in the middle of the pitched battle that had been raging since early August between the Soviet hard-liners who urged solidarity with Iraq and the "new thinkers" allied with Shevardnadze who believed it was important to cooperate with the West. Gorbachev had dispatched Yevgeny Primakov, the foreign ministry's most influential *arabist,* as his personal emissary to Baghdad. Primakov said he believed it was possible that Saddam could be persuaded to remove his soldiers from Kuwait. The West was making it impossible, however, with its hard demands.

As Gorbachev's envoy to Saddam, Primakov would make several trips to Baghdad, emerging as the key player on the Soviet side as the world moved closer to war. On the face of it, the inclusion of Primakov in Gorbachev's inner circle of advisers made perfect sense. Like Bush, Gorbachev was a man who placed great faith in personal relationships in the resolution of differences. Primakov had known Saddam Hussein for more than twenty years. The relationship went back to 1968, when the Baath Party had come to power in Baghdad and Primakov was covering the Middle East as a correspondent for *Pravda.* Since then, Primakov had worked hard to maintain a broad range of contacts throughout the Arab world, and he had put them to good use advising Gorbachev as the Soviets were maneuvering their way out of Afghanistan.

Primakov was a formidable adversary to Shevardnadze. Aides to Baker had heard that the situation in Moscow had become even more complicated for Shevardnadze. According to Kremlin sources in Gorbachev's retinue, the Soviet leader had been frustrated by his foreign ministry's inability to talk Saddam Hussein out of Kuwait during the early stages of the crisis. This was the Arab leader with whom Moscow had maintained such close relations, after all. The criticism did not extend to Shevardnadze himself, the Kremlin sources said; Gorbachev continued to hold his foreign minister in high regard. Nonetheless, resorting to Primakov had certainly undermined Shevardnadze.

Baker wondered how receptive Gorbachev would be to his plea for Soviet support of a Security Council resolution authorizing the use of force against Saddam. Now, ninety-nine days after the invasion of Kuwait, he would have a chance to find out. The meeting with Gorbachev took place in the Soviet president's dacha outside Moscow. As Gorbachev listened attentively, Baker said that unless Saddam was convinced that the United States and its allies would use the military force arrayed against him, it was unlikely that the Iraqi leader would budge. A Security Council resolution authorizing Allied military action would turn up the heat under Saddam. Therein lay the real hope for a peaceful solution to the crisis. Gorbachev made no commitments in response, beyond a profession that Washington and Moscow would have to continue to cooperate closely. As the meeting drew to an end the Soviet leader raised two fingers to Baker and held them together, saying "We must stay like this."

For the moment, at least, Shevardnadze seemed to be prevailing. At a concluding news conference with Baker in the gilded entry hall of the Osobnyak State Guest House, Shevardnadze expressed confidence that the Soviet Union and the United States would work together to resolve the conflict with Iraq. While his message was addressed to the reporters assembled before him, it was directed at his opponents in the Kremlin: "I would advise against looking for some differences between the Soviet Union and the United States."

The United Nations resolution Bush and Baker intended to seek authorizing the use of force against Iraq was becoming increasingly important. Public support for the President's Gulf policy had begun to erode even further. The November 9 speech announcing the move to an "offensive military option" had alarmed many Americans, who began to fear the prospect of war. In mid-November a survey conducted for the Times Mirror Company showed that for the first time in his presidency, Bush's overall approval rating had slid below 50 percent. Many people seemed confused as to just why it was that hundreds of thousands of troops were being sent so far away. Senate Minority Leader Bob Dole spelled the word out on the floor of the Senate: "o-i-l." On November 13, after meeting with

Joe Clark, the Canadian foreign secretary, Baker echoed the sentiment: "The economic lifeline of the industrial world runs from the Gulf, and we cannot permit a dictator such as this to sit astride that economic lifeline. To bring it down to the level of the average American citizen, let me say that means jobs. If you want to sum it up in one word: it's jobs."

In Tokyo just days earlier, Vice-President Quayle had returned to his argument for the administration's Gulf policy, further muddling the administration's message. American soldiers were in the desert, Quayle said, to contain Iraq and prevent Saddam Hussein from using his weapons of mass destruction. Eventually, Bob Teeter's polling would show that concern over Saddam's potential for nuclear weapons was a real "hot button" issue with the American people. Bush, Baker, and Cheney would quickly conclude that it would be Iraq's putative nuclear threat that would enable them to forge a domestic consensus for war with Iraq.

On November 18, Baker consulted with Shevardnadze once again. They were both in Paris for a meeting of the Conference on Security and Cooperation in Europe, as were their presidents. "It was really late at night," a senior aide who accompanied Baker said. "He and Shevardnadze met for what seemed like the hundredth time. And that's when [Baker] first showed him what [the resolution] would look like in writing." Baker had kept no notes during his hectic travels, but the resolution he had in mind was not complicated. He had written it out in longhand, the aide said. It was the first time the critical language had been put on paper. It called for Iraq to comply with the terms of Resolution 660, the first Security Council response to the invasion of Kuwait. This meant that Iraqi forces would have to withdraw to the positions they had occupied prior to August 1, and that Baghdad would have to begin negotiations with the Sabah family over all outstanding differences between Iraq and Kuwait. It also authorized United Nations members to use "all necessary means" to enforce compliance with Resolution 660, as well as all other resolutions passed by the Security Council against Iraq. Shevardnadze could not commit to it, he said. President Bush would be dining with Mikhail Gorbachev at the residence of the American ambassador the following evening. Shevardnadze suggested that the two leaders would have to take the matter up then. This was a matter for the two presidents to decide.

On the evening of November 19, Gorbachev was ushered through the imposing wrought-iron gates at the entry to the American ambassador's ornate residence in the Rue du Faubourg Saint-Honoré. Bush and Gorbachev greeted each other warmly. The dinner proved a bitter disappointment for Bush, however. Gorbachev could not say yes. Consultations should continue, the Soviet leader told Bush. No firm decision on a Security Council resolution was possible in Paris. Bush had wanted the Soviet agreement badly. He was scheduled to leave the next day for a critical tour of several Middle East capitals, and he'd planned to spend Thanksgiving with the troops in Saudi Arabia. It would have helped enormously to have a Soviet pledge in his pocket authorizing Allied military action. With Gorbachev's stalling, many of Bush's closest advisers worried, Primakov and the *arabisti* would have more time to work on the unsteady Soviet leader.

This would be Shevardnadze's fateful trial. The next ten days would be the most difficult period Moscow would experience in the entire conflict with Iraq. While Baker accompanied Bush to the Middle East, a bitter debate raged day and night in the Kremlin crisis room, a cavernous, wood-paneled chamber where the Politburo had convened in secret in the days before perestroika. Shevardnadze threw everything into the fight, and according to all accounts, it became increasingly personal, with the *arabisti* and other hard-liners charging that the Soviet foreign minister wanted to send Soviet troops to fight in the desert. "There will be blood on your hands," Shevardnadze was told, according to two knowledgeable officials.

On November 23, continuing his diplomatic odyssey, Baker arrived in Sanaa, the capital of Yemen. Baker had no great expectations that he would secure Yemen's support, but planned to argue for it anyway, pointing out the millions of dollars in aid the Yemeni government stood to lose from Saudi Arabia and other members of the anti-Iraq coalition if they voted against a Security Council measure authorizing Allied military action. Baker spoke for three hours with President Ali Abdallah Salih. Yemen's leader rejected Baker's plea bluntly. "We do not support the presence of foreign forces in the region," he said. "We think there can be an Arab diplomatic solution, but unfortunately these foreign forces are complicating the problem."

Baker's visits to Colombia and to other members of the U.N. Security Council were more successful. By November 27, when the representatives of the five permanent members of the Security Council convened in New York to discuss the American proposal for a resolution authorizing Allied military action against the Iraqi army in Kuwait, Baker was confident that he had the minimum nine votes needed for passage. But China or the Soviet Union could veto it.

In Baker's meeting with the permanent members of the Security Council on November 27, Primakov pushed hard to postpone a vote. Baker told Primakov he would not hear of a delay. The United States held the Security Council's rotating presidency in November. On December 1, the presidency would be transferred to Yemen. A Security Council vote on the U.S.-sponsored resolution could then be delayed through December. That was unacceptable, Baker said. Primakov then insisted on a deadline for the withdrawal of the Iraqi army from Kuwait. This resulted in another long debate. Baker was prepared to accept a deadline as late as January 30. Others pushed for earlier dates. The Soviets argued that Saddam would need considerable time to withdraw such a large force. Finally the delegates settled on a deadline: January 15. Baker wanted to make sure this was acceptable to all five of the permanent members. The Chinese delegate, Ambassador Li Daoyu, assured him that it was. It seemed there would be no veto. Baker requested that the Security Council vote take place two days later.

Baker himself presided as president of the Security Council as it convened on the evening of November 29. Wearing a dark banker's suit and a navy tie against a white shirt, the secretary of state wasted little time in calling for a vote on United Nations Resolution 678. One by one, the ballots were cast. Among the five permanent members, the votes were called. France, Britain, and the Soviet Union voted yes. When China was called, at first there was silence. China, Ambassador Li then announced, would abstain. Baker was confident of the yes votes of eight of the nonpermanent members of the Security Council. That left Cuba and Yemen as possible no votes. While Cuba's vote was a foregone conclusion, some of Baker's aides suspected that, realizing the cost of its potential isolation, Yemen might have had a change of heart. But Yemen had had no such thing. When the Yemeni foreign minister voted no, applause could be heard from some onlookers in the gallery. Angry, Baker scrawled a note and handed it to an aide to deliver to the Yemeni ambassador, Abdalla Saleh al-Ashtal, later. It read, "That is the most expensive vote you have ever cast."

With the abstention of China, the final tally was 12–2. The Bush administration had at last won the blessing of the international community to use military force. It had also made an adroit end run around Congress, sidestepping the issue of the President's constitutional right to take the country into war without a congressional declaration. The administration seemed convinced that it could substitute a U.N. resolution for a congressional declaration. It was also confident that it could buffalo any opposition.

After the Security Council vote, Bob Kimmitt, the under secretary of state for political affairs, caught the last shuttle from New York to Washington. He had worked hard to cement the coalition together and to round up the necessary votes in the Security Council. As Kimmitt settled into his seat, Bill Bradley, the Democratic senator from New Jersey, came aboard. Spotting Kimmitt, Bradley said, "It looks like you had a good day." "Pretty good," Kimmitt replied. "We feel like we now have a strong basis in international law for the use of force." Bradley chose his words carefully: "Don't think this automatically means that we will support that." Kimmitt chuckled. "Well, senator," he said, "I know what a strong supporter of international law you are."

For the Bush administration, it was a heady moment. Four hundred thousand troops were either in or en route to the Saudi desert, the United Nations had given Washington a green light, and only now did some members of Congress begin to fear the dogs of war. Congress might kick and scream, but Bush and his men had already set the terms of debate.

Nevertheless, the administration was beginning to receive more criticism of its Gulf policy. The day before Resolution 678 was passed by the United Nations, Senator Nunn had opened hearings on the administration's Gulf policy. Two former chairmen of the Joint Chiefs of Staff, General David Jones and Admiral William J. Crowe, Jr., had strongly urged that the administration allow the sanctions to work longer before they resorted to military action. Their views were echoed by other distinguished diplomats. Richard Murphy, assistant secretary of state in the Reagan administration for Near Eastern and South Asian affairs, George Ball, an under secretary of state in the Kennedy and Johnson administrations, and Paul Nitze, a deeply conservative arms-control adviser to several administrations, were all convinced that economic sanctions would eventually work against Saddam Hussein. "We can outlast him," Nitze said. On the op-ed pages of the nation's major newspapers, the commentary, which had largely been favorable to the administration, began to turn negative. In the streets of the nation's major cities, demonstrations, some attracting hundreds of thousands of protesters, were mounted. For the first time since the invasion of Kuwait, ordinary Americans seemed to awaken to the prospect of war. And, for the first time, the administration's policies and plans began to come under fierce public scrutiny.

CHAPTER 12

"BLINK, SADDAM, BLINK"

GEORGE BUSH'S political advisers had been after him for weeks to do something to calm the public's growing fears. On Friday, November 30, they finally succeeded. In a morning news conference at the White House that was billed as "an address to the nation," Bush intoned: "We are in the Gulf because the world must not and cannot reward aggression. And we are there because our vital interests are at stake. . . . And we're in the Gulf because of the brutality of Saddam Hussein." In a final effort to avoid war, the President said, he was offering to have Secretary of State Baker visit Baghdad to look Saddam "in the eye" and explain that America and its allies were deadly serious about the January 15 deadline imposed by the Security Council. There should be no doubt, Bush said, about his desire "to go the extra mile for peace."

In addition, he was inviting Tariq Aziz, Iraq's foreign minister, to come to Washington during the week of December 10 for talks at the White House. The President said that he earnestly hoped that Baker would be able to meet with Saddam Hussein in Baghdad "at a mutually convenient time" between December 15 and January 15. "I will be prepared, and so will Secretary Baker, to discuss all aspects of the Gulf crisis," Bush said. "However, to be very clear about these efforts to exhaust all means for achieving a political and diplomatic solution, I am not suggesting discussions that will result in anything less than Iraq's complete withdrawal from Kuwait, [the] restoration of Kuwait's legitimate government, and freedom for all hostages." If Iraq was unwilling to comply with all three of those terms by January 15, Bush continued, America and its allies would be obliged to resort to force. "[But] this will not be another Vietnam," the President promised. "This will not be a protracted, drawn-out war. . . . If one American soldier has to go into battle, that soldier will have enough force behind him to win and then get out." Even as he was speaking, Bush noted, dozens of ships loaded with American M1A1 tanks from the VII Corps in Germany and the 1st Infantry Division (Mechanized) in Kansas were steaming toward Saudi Arabia. The United States was not bluffing.

Noting Bush's love for his five grandchildren, a reporter asked whether the principles at stake in the Gulf were so important that he would risk one of their lives, as he was asking hundreds of thousands of American parents to risk the lives of their own children. Removing his glasses and leaning over the lectern, the President repeated that America's "vital interests" were at stake in the Gulf. Saddam Hussein's aggression against Kuwait had violated fundamental principles of international law. As for American casualties, Bush said he still held out hope that there would be no war: "I will do my level best to bring those kids home without one single shot fired in anger." If Saddam forced the allies to eject his army from Kuwait, however, the alliance would have the advantage of a superior military force. That was precisely why he had authorized the additional U.S. forces to be deployed to Saudi Arabia. If the overwhelming American and Allied firepower did not persuade Saddam Hussein to withdraw his army from Kuwait, it would ensure that Allied casualties would be limited. As to the conclusion of hostilities should they occur, Bush pledged that "there will not be any murky ending."

In the White House that evening, Bush told congressional leaders that he welcomed their scrutiny of his Gulf policy and that he looked forward to working with Congress in the coming weeks. But he warned them that if Saddam Hussein refused to withdraw from Kuwait by January 15, he would not need to consult Congress before committing the American military forces in the Gulf to war. Privately, Bush had told his advisers that he would welcome a congressional vote supporting the administration's policy. But, after the meeting with the congressional leaders was concluded, Bush was convinced the votes just weren't there. Even members of his own party had been skeptical of Bush's promise that a war in the Gulf would be quick and relatively painless. "History is littered with the bones of optimists and generals," said Senator William Cohen, the Maine Republican, "who thought they were headed for a short war."

In Camp David's Aspen Lodge on the morning of December 1, Bush was seated at the long conference table, surrounded by his most senior aides. He wanted to review the Gulf crisis's military and political dimensions before leaving on a week-long trip to South America. Brent Scowcroft was present, along with Defense Secretary Cheney, Jim Baker, and General Powell, who had brought along all of the service chiefs to brief the President.

Powell began by saying that the planning for offensive operations had begun to progress rapidly. Schwarzkopf's people were working with the Pentagon's Joint Staff on an ambitious concept, and they were still refining it. If the President authorized an offensive operation, Powell said, it would start with a lengthy and destructive air campaign that would target strategic sites in and around Baghdad, knock out Saddam Hussein's command-and-control network, and punish the eight Republican Guard divisions, the heart of Saddam's strength. Next a ground campaign would occur that featured a lightning-fast charge on Saddam's exposed western flank. The brunt of the fighting would fall to Major General Barry McCaffrey's 24th Infantry Division (Mechanized) and the three heavy armored divisions that would be commanded by Lieutenant General Frederick Franks. Meanwhile, there would be some deliberately obvious activity in the Gulf to convince Saddam's commanders that the main attack would come from the sea. Details of the Marine attack through the Iraqi defensive lines in southern Kuwait were still being worked out. It was an enormously complicated military operation, Powell concluded, and the VII Corps and the 1st Infantry Division had not even arrived yet in Saudi Arabia.

Bush was pleased. The Pentagon had come a long way from the "up the middle" plan briefed by Major General Robert Johnston seven weeks before.

The conversation turned to the political dimensions of the crisis. There had been no response yet from Baghdad to Bush's offer to meet with Tariq Aziz in Washington and to send Baker to Iraq to meet with Saddam. Bush's advisers agreed that the offer alone had had a significant effect at home, however. It shows that we're willing to do the utmost to achieve a peaceful solution, Baker said. Bush said that while he was concerned by the reaction of Congress, the law was clear. As commander-in-chief, he had the legal authority to order military action without seeking congressional authorization. There could be no backing down from that principle, he insisted. Cheney agreed. They would have to state their case firmly. It was also important to say clearly why the administration believed that sanctions alone would not, in all likelihood, persuade Saddam to withdraw. There was no credible evidence showing that the sanctions were working. Indeed, Bush was reminded, CIA Director William Webster was scheduled to testify to the House Armed Services Committee, where he would tell the panel that the agency's best estimate was that Saddam Hussein's ground forces in Kuwait could maintain their current state of readiness for as long as nine months, despite the sanctions. Saddam's air force, however, would begin feeling an effect within three months. Everyone agreed that even three months was too long to wait. The President said he was confident that the political climate would eventually turn in the administration's favor.

In Jerusalem on Sunday, December 2, the Israeli cabinet convened at 2 P.M. All its members were deeply troubled by Bush's unexpected offer to send Baker to Baghdad. The trip, said Yuval Neeman, the hard-line science minister, was tantamount to "Chamberlain and Munich." Others, too, including many allies, feared that Bush would find a way to cut a deal with Saddam. Virtually no one was convinced that a visit by Baker to Baghdad was a good idea.

The Israelis were not alone in their concerns, then. They just had more to fear from Saddam than anyone else. Prime Minister Yitzhak Shamir and Foreign Minister David Levy refuted Neeman's remarks publicly. But both men were deeply concerned. Levy telephoned William Brown, the American ambassador. According to several officials briefed on the conversation afterward, it was a testy exchange.

I did not know about the Bush announcement in advance, Levy said. I have defended it, but I am truly worried. Levy noted that Boutros Ghali, the Egyptian minister of state for foreign affairs, had already issued a statement saying that the Egyptian forces in the coalition would defend Saudi Arabia, but they would not participate in any invasion of Iraq. Saddam may leave Kuwait, Levy told Brown. But he will emerge from the conflict strengthened. It is the deal of the century. I sometimes wonder if it was planned this way, and whether Egypt was a part of it. I might be wrong.

Brown did more listening than talking. He noted Levy's concerns and tried to put them to rest. The conversation ended inconclusively.

Many of Shamir's most trusted advisers believed that their problems with Washington lay not so much with Bush and Baker as with Scowcroft. "Scowcroft and the NSC kept thinking that somehow we were going to screw things up for the Americans in Iraq by going preemptive," a senior Israeli defense ministry official said. "There are times we even benefit by such thinking. They always think the worst about us there [at the National Security Council]. If we don't do the absolute worst, then they think we are *tzadikim* [the righteous ones]."

On Monday, December 3, *USA Today* released a poll that showed that Bush's approval rating had climbed to 57 percent, up six points from two weeks before. The President's offer to have Baker travel to Baghdad was working, Bush's political aides said, at least with a majority of the public. Congress was proving more difficult to sway. On Tuesday, members of the House Democratic Caucus voted 177–37 in support of a resolution declaring that President Bush should not initiate any offensive military action in the Persian Gulf without the formal approval of Congress.

On Wednesday, Saddam Hussein agreed to accept a visit from James Baker. A day later, he asked the Iraqi National Assembly to approve the release of all Western "guests" in Iraq and Kuwait, and the National Assembly complied. Few of Bush's advisers believed that Saddam would actually let the hostages go. But at exactly 9 P.M. on December 9, an Iraqi Airways Boeing 747 chartered by Joseph Wilson, the deputy chief of mission of the U.S. embassy in Baghdad, departed from Saddam International Airport for Frankfurt, Germany, with 325 people aboard. These were the first of Saddam's hostages allowed to leave Iraq in significant numbers. Many more would follow.

In Washington, Bush's men were relieved. The President had insisted that no matter what Saddam did with his human shields or any of the other people the Iraqi leader was detaining illegally, American policy would not be swayed by it. Many senior officials had worried that the administration would never be able to keep that pledge. "It would have been, in all candor, double tough to start bombing a place when you have three thousand Americans in there," a senior aide to Baker said. With the unexpected release of the hostages, however, Washington and its allies were spared from facing a decision many of the President's advisers believed he would never have made. "Can you imagine starting to bomb?" a senior administration official asked. "Of course, the Iraqis had put the hostages in places that would be hit. And, of course, they would give the file footage [to the media]. Of course it would ricochet back in here. . . . It would have made it—not only for us, but for the French, the British, everybody—tougher. But what did Saddam give us? He gave us a playing field!"

But Saddam had not given Bush an acceptable date for Secretary Baker's visit to Baghdad. He said that the only time he could see Baker was January 12, just three days before the United Nations deadline. Brent Scowcroft told the President that it was impossible for Saddam to remove a dug-in force of more than 430,000 soldiers from Kuwait in just three days. The offer was a ruse, he, Cheney, and others argued; if the Iraqi leader truly intended to get out of Kuwait, he would have to offer another, earlier date.

On December 20, Eduard Shevardnadze shocked the world by resigning as Gorbachev's foreign minister. As he rose in the Congress of People's Deputies to announce his resignation, Shevardnadze made it clear just how dire was the predicament that his country faced. The Soviet Union, he said, pointing a finger at his critics, was rapidly sliding toward dictatorship.

In Washington, the news came as a severe blow. Just ten days earlier, Shevardnadze had been in Houston conferring with Baker. Despite their friendship, Baker told aides, the meeting had been one of his most difficult. Moscow badly wanted a United Nations Security Council resolution calling for an international peace conference on the Middle East. After pushing this idea for years, the Soviets believed they were now entitled to American cooperation, given their cooperation with the United States on the Gulf crisis. Baker had told Shevardnadze that the timing was wrong and had pressed the Soviet foreign minister to commit a token Soviet troop contingent to the multinational military force in the Gulf. Shevardnadze had resisted vigorously. Hadn't Baker understood how serious the criticisms of him were within the Supreme Soviet and the Congress of People's

Deputies? Shevardnadze had repeated that while Gorbachev supported the objectives of the anti-Iraq alliance, it was impossible for Moscow to send a single soldier to the Arabian peninsula at this time.

In Riyadh, meanwhile, General Schwarzkopf stated publicly that a war against the dug-in Iraqi forces in Kuwait could last as long as six months, predicting that Saddam's soldiers would put up a "tough fight." The morale of the Iraqis was one of the factors Bush and his commanders worried about. Saddam possessed a huge army. But how well would it fight?

Two days after the Schwarzkopf statement, Lieutenant General Calvin A. H. Waller, the deputy commander of the American-led forces in Saudi Arabia, told reporters that with so many of the American heavy forces just arriving in Saudi Arabia from their bases in Germany and Kansas, the Allied military coalition would not be ready to fight by the January 15 deadline. A more realistic date, Waller said, when all units would be fully ready for combat, was February 1. Waller likened his situation to that of a football coach preparing for the game of his life. "If the owner asks if I'm ready to go," Waller said, "I'd tell him, 'No, I'm not ready to do the job.' "

Waller's statement infuriated Bush's closest advisers. "This is not the message we are trying to send now," fumed a senior administration official. In the Pentagon, the anger was greater—even among some senior officers who knew and respected Waller.

With President Bush's direct approval, the Pentagon embarked on a highly secret operation known within the administration as "Blink, Saddam, Blink." In early December, the administration recognized that it needed to send a consistent message to Saddam that it was serious about its threat to use military force and that the Iraqi army must withdraw from Kuwait by January 15. "Blink, Saddam, Blink" was primarily a public relations effort, but it had an operational component as well. For example, the administration discovered that the Iraqi currency was not printed inside Iraq; the Iraqis relied on two other countries to do the printing for them. Washington was able to persuade those countries to print counterfeit Iraqi currency, which was then distributed to Kurdish leaders, who flooded the market with worthless bills.

The statements by Waller and Schwarzkopf puzzled Bush. Before he left for Camp David on December 21, the President had questioned Scowcroft and others about the conflicting signals coming from his generals in the Gulf. There had been no good answers. Cheney and Powell were in the Gulf, Scowcroft said; in fact, Waller had spoken to the group of reporters traveling with the two men. Bush said he wanted to see his defense secretary and the chairman of the Joint Chiefs of Staff as soon as they returned to Washington.

In the meantime, once settled in at the Aspen Lodge, Bush began working the phones. Gorbachev was among the first of his calls. In his conversation with the embattled Soviet president, aides said, Bush assured Gorbachev of his support. When the conversation turned to the Gulf crisis, Bush said that he was hopeful that Saddam Hussein would recognize how impossible his situation was and give the order for his army to begin withdrawing from Kuwait. Bush then made dozens of other calls, some to old friends to wish them a happy holiday, others to members of Congress. The President still had a lot of friends on Capitol Hill, and even though he did not believe he was obliged to consult with Congress before authorizing military action in the Gulf, he told aides that it was important to keep key members apprised of events.

On Christmas Eve morning, Dick Cheney and Colin Powell stepped onto the helipad at Camp David and climbed into a waiting golf cart to cover the half mile to the Aspen Lodge. "Colin and I had gone out [to the Gulf] to spend a couple of days over there," Cheney said. "[We] went over to review the campaign plan, especially the air war, in great detail. We looked at how they were doing with the ground-war deployments, but that was down the road." At the lodge, Bush and Scowcroft were waiting, eager to hear about the visit. Cheney had talked to the President earlier about the comments of Waller and Schwarzkopf, telling Bush not to worry. Schwarzkopf's people were still scrambling to put the plan for the ground campaign together. The Marines were still bickering among themselves about which units would breach the heart of the Iraqi defensive lines; despite the danger, every Marine unit was fighting to be included.

The President was interested in the plan for the air campaign, since that was to be the start of an offensive operation against Saddam Hussein. Could the air war begin soon after the United Nations deadline expired? he asked. Cheney and Powell told the President that it could begin the minute the deadline expired or anytime thereafter. "We had the fifteenth [of January]," Cheney said. "But we hadn't picked a date yet to actually start the

[air] campaign. And the more we thought about it, the more we concluded that we wanted to do it as soon after the fifteenth as we could. We didn't want to let a lot of time pass."

Later that day, a White House aide telephoned Camp David with news from Baghdad. Scowcroft took the call. Saddam Hussein had just recalled his ambassadors from Washington, Tokyo, all of the major European capitals, and a few other selected capitals. He also announced that if war broke out and Iraqi forces were attacked, he would retaliate against Israel immediately.

On Christmas Day the President's mood was decidedly subdued.

On the evening of December 25 in Geneva, Barzan Ibrahim welcomed an elegantly dressed Parisian man into a warm study in a handsome building in the city's diplomatic quarter. Barzan Ibrahim was Saddam Hussein's half brother. A former Iraqi security chief with a well-deserved reputation for brutality, he had been sent to Geneva as Iraq's permanent representative to the United Nations Conference on Human Rights. The irony was not lost on the Iraqi's guest. "I was rather embarrassed," said Edgard Pisani, the former director of the Institut du Monde Arabe in Paris and a trusted adviser of French President François Mitterrand. Since the end of October, Pisani had been acting as a behind-the-scenes emissary for Mitterrand. He did not believe the Bush administration knew what it was getting into in the Persian Gulf conflict. "The world community thought that since the occupation of Kuwait was illegal, you had to return to the original situation and free Kuwait before any talking could be done," Pisani said. "That was the basis for the entire conflict. [But] Saddam Hussein wanted to be treated as a possessor. He was ready—I can confirm this—he was ready to let go of what he had taken, but only in exchange for something. The world community told him, 'Let it go and we can negotiate.' But negotiate what? No one ever told him."

Pisani had first met Barzan Ibrahim six weeks before. "It was two stern monologues," Pisani recalled. "Him very stiff, me not very flexible." Pisani told Barzan that Saddam had to realize that the Americans, the French, and the British were serious. The coalition was powerful enough to crush Iraq. Barzan had listened, but "in the end," Pisani recalled, "he simply said, 'It would perhaps be useful for us to see each other again.' " With Mitterrand's blessing, Pisani and Barzan had met again in Geneva, in early December, immediately after the release of the first Western hostages from Baghdad. "He told me that he had seen his brother," Pisani said, "that he had explained the Western point of view to him, and that [Saddam] had found our conversation very interesting."

Now, with a brisk wind blowing off Lake Geneva, Pisani repeated the argument to Barzan. "I told him that it had to be understood that there was only one way to peace. Iraq had to take it alone and in the first instance make the gesture of announcing its decision to evacuate Kuwait. No discussion was possible without that precondition. . . . It was the precondition for any negotiation." Barzan's only response was to thank the Frenchman stiffly for his counsel. Leaving Geneva, Pisani felt no confidence that the meeting had amounted to anything.

On December 27, the *Baghdad Observer* ran an editorial that asked: "Time is running out? Who says so? The U.S. administration has to realize that there is no loss of face in admitting the error of the rush [to] war or in opening the door for just equitable dialogue." The next day, Saddam delivered a tougher message. The Iraqi leader had sent his diplomats back to their posts in Washington, Tokyo, and Europe. "We are ready for a serious and constructive dialogue," Saddam said, "based on mutual respect and the rejection of the course of hegemony and arrogance, which the American administration tries to impose on us." He continued to insist, however, that any discussions about Iraqi forces leaving Kuwait would have to be linked with negotiations over Israeli withdrawal from the West Bank and Gaza. Saddam was unwilling to compromise on that point. Iraq, he said, "is ready to [make] any sacrifice in the battle it wages against the United States and its allies."

Budimir Loncar, Yugoslavia's federal secretary for foreign affairs, arrived in Baghdad that same evening. Loncar was representing the Non-aligned Movement. Before leaving Belgrade, he had consulted with Secretary of State Baker, U.N. Secretary-General Javier Pérez de Cuéllar, and most of the foreign ministers of the member nations of the European Community. In the final weeks before the January 15 deadline imposed by the Security Council, no foreigner would spend more time with Saddam Hussein than Loncar.

"Tariq Aziz met me at the airport," Loncar said, "[which was] the first favorable sign." Loncar had known the Iraqi foreign minister for years, and he immediately noted the studied formality of the greeting. Aziz was wearing a military uniform. Over dinner, Aziz spoke nearly nonstop for two hours, at pains to detail Iraq's historical claim to Kuwait. Loncar said, "At that dinner, I muttered only three sentences. I thanked him for his hospitality, I said that I had listened attentively to his statements, and I told him that I would present him with the purpose of my mission the following morning."

Aziz was more hostile the next day. "He was much more aggressive in his demeanor," Loncar said. "He took exception to my arguments." The session was broken off three times over the course of nearly eight hours. "It was me who asked for the interruption of the third round of talks," Loncar recalled. "I said that on substantive issues I wanted to talk with President Hussein himself."

The following day, December 30, Saddam Hussein dispatched several government cars for Loncar and his small delegation. They were taken directly to Saddam's official residence and ushered almost immediately into the Iraqi leader's presence. Loncar and his colleagues were not even subjected to a security check at the gate. "Saddam was in his field marshal's uniform," Loncar recalled. "He had a pistol, too, a firm handshake, direct eye contact. . . . He unbuckled the belt with the pistol and put it next to him." The talks were under way. Loncar began by outlining the long and productive relationship between Yugoslavia and Iraq. Trade had been brisk, and there had been few problems. Saddam said that he valued the relationship highly. "The worst thing that can happen to a man," he said, according to a note taker, "is to lose a friend. Especially a close, trusted friend. And that applies to countries too." Like Aziz, Saddam recounted Iraq's historical claim to Kuwait. He went on to describe what he called Kuwait's "economic diversion." He charged the Kuwaitis with stealing oil from the Rumaila oil field, an act, Saddam said, of "aggression." How could Iraq sit by and tolerate this? If Iraq had not responded to the theft by Kuwait, it would become "a trunk with strangled branches that would fall to the ground one day. . . . Every man is entitled to face his dignity, even when he faces the abyss," Saddam said. "The people of Iraq are ready to pay the price of their dignity."

The United States was the only superpower left, Saddam continued. It was an open question whether the Americans would behave responsibly, or whether they would seek to hold the entire world in their hands. "It is not in the interest of the world," Saddam said. "It is not in the interest even of the United States [for the Americans] to become masters of the Middle East oil fields. In this way, [the United States] could become a power without a compass. Such a power could bring the world to the brink ... [so that] when Iraq defends its homeland, it is defending the liberty of all."

Loncar replied, "Three years ago, this crisis would have acquired such global dimensions that it would have become a contest between the two blocs in the end. Now all this has changed. One can no longer count on the existence of two antagonistic blocs." Saddam nodded his agreement. Then he interrupted, "But exactly because the balance is disrupted, because the USSR is out of the game, this is an opportunity to start establishing a new counterbalance to the United States."

The discussion had lasted nearly two hours. Saddam had made what Loncar thought might be a genuine offer. "I am ready to make a concession," Saddam said. "But the other side has to make one." Loncar wanted to pursue the issue. He asked Saddam that their aides be dismissed. The Iraqi leader agreed. Only Tariq Aziz remained, serving as translator. "I asked what I could do, in concrete terms," Loncar said. "I drew his attention to the specific role that could be played by the European Community." Earlier that day in Paris, foreign ministers of the European Community had announced that they would convene an emergency meeting January 4 in Luxembourg. When Saddam asked if the EC would be willing to work on a peaceful solution to the crisis, Loncar replied that he thought it would. But if there was war, Saddam said, the EC would side with the United States. Loncar agreed that that was so. This would not be good, Saddam replied. If he would make a gesture, Loncar told Saddam, the EC could issue a statement forcefully urging a peaceful solution to the crisis. But the Iraqi leader had to move first. Saddam returned to the question of the Palestinians. Loncar realized then that the discussion with Saddam had been fruitless. He was ushered out of the presidential residence a short while later.

On New Year's Eve, Saddam Hussein visited his soldiers in Kuwait. Wearing a military uniform with a pistol stuck in his belt, the Iraqi leader defied the United States and its allies just on the other side of the border in Saudi Arabia. "Let them mass whatever numbers they can, because God will protect us from evil and save Iraq," Saddam said. "To Bush's disappointment, the unprecedented U.S.-dominated buildup has failed to force Iraq to blink. At a time when the U.S. awaits impatiently for a sign indicating Iraqi readiness to compromise, Iraq is growing more and more resolved not to cede any of its rights."

CHAPTER 13

THE EVE
OF DESTRUCTION

GEORGE BUSH was convinced there could be no compromise with Iraq. Saddam, he felt, still didn't seem to understand how serious the alliance was. Over the Christmas holidays at Camp David, Bush had resolved that using military force was the right thing to do. "I've got it boiled down very clearly to good versus evil," Bush said. He had read and reread an Amnesty International report on the atrocities committed by Iraqi soldiers in Kuwait. The abuses, Bush said, were "devastating, absolutely devastating. It helps one come to a recognition that the right must prevail."

Late in the afternoon on New Year's Day, Bush's advisers began arriving in the White House family quarters, upstairs in the East Wing. Bush greeted Vice-President Dan Quayle warmly. The vice-president had just returned from the Gulf hours earlier. Tired from his long trip, he was nonetheless invigorated by his visits with American soldiers, sailors, and fliers. Before leaving the Gulf the day before, Quayle told Bush, he had had breakfast with sailors aboard the aircraft carrier USS *John F. Kennedy*. After that, he had visited with the emir of Kuwait, Sheik Jaber al-Ahmed al-Sabah, in Taif, Saudi Arabia. The American soldiers he had seen appeared strong and enthusiastic. The emir had responded very positively to his suggestion that the United States and its allies would soon need more financial support. Bush congratulated Quayle on a successful trip. Scowcroft was present, and the others arrived shortly. Dick Cheney came in with Colin Powell. Secretary of State James Baker, John Sununu, and Marlin Fitzwater completed the group. Not since December 18 had Bush met with so many of his senior advisers at one time.

Baker related the substance of his discussions with some of the European Community foreign ministers. The EC meeting scheduled for January 4 would almost certainly result in some sort of overture to Saddam, Baker predicted. Bush told the group that Gorbachev had told him that he would push right up until the January 15 deadline for some kind of agreement with Baghdad. These eleventh-hour overtures to Saddam would test the coalition, Bush said, especially the Soviet actions. "The President didn't really approve of what Gorbachev was doing at the last minute," a participant said, "but he didn't want to make a big deal of it." Bush wondered whether it would be wise for Baker to take another trip to Europe and the Persian Gulf.

Baker and Sununu reopened the question of a visit to Baghdad. Bush had rejected Saddam's invitation for Baker to come to Baghdad on January 12; it would have to be before January 3 or not at all, he had said. Now, several of the Big Eight argued that they should extend the January 3 deadline. Otherwise, the administration would appear too inflexible. If they announced that Baker would be willing to travel to Baghdad on some date earlier than January 12, the ball would be back in Saddam's court. The President agreed, but he insisted a visit by Baker to Baghdad was out of the question unless Saddam extended the invitation for a date much earlier than January 12.

Bush turned next to the role of Congress. It would convene in just two days. The first order of business was certain to be a debate over the administration's policy in the Persian Gulf. Bush said he had spoken with several members of the congressional leadership over the holidays, and he was still not convinced that the votes for a resolution supporting the Gulf policy were there. Baker was not so sure, aides said. This was precisely the situation he had envisioned when he had pushed for United Nations action in early August, despite the reservations of the Pentagon, John Sununu, and others among the President's advisers. With the Security Council having approved a resolution authorizing the alliance to use military force, the Democrats were in a real bind. "It jammed up Congress," said one of Baker's most trusted confidants. "How could our Congress not support something that Ethiopia was supporting? That the Soviet Union was supporting? You look at the nations that were supporting it. How could the United States Congress not support it?" Baker told Bush and his advisers that when it came to a vote in the Congress, he was confident the administration would prevail. The meeting concluded with a brief review of the military situation by Cheney and Powell.

On January 3, Fitzwater announced the President's decision to have Baker visit Baghdad if he were invited to do so by the Iraqi government in the immediate future. "Let's hear from them," Fitzwater said. At 11:59 A.M. on January 3 in Baghdad, Deputy Chief of Mission Joseph Wilson made the American offer official. Less than twenty-four hours later, Wilson received a call from the Iraqi foreign ministry. A statement would be forthcoming immediately, the Iraqi official said. Minutes later, Iraq's state-run television carried a brief announcement that, despite the Bush administration's "arrogant statements," Foreign Minister Tariq Aziz had agreed to meet with Secretary of State Baker. The Iraqis proposed that the meeting take place on January 9 in Geneva. Aziz explained the Iraqi reply a short while later. "I was prepared to go to Washington and to receive Minister Baker in Baghdad," he said, "if the American administration [had] acted in a courteous manner and respected the internationally recognized rules with regard to fixing heads of states' meetings with other nations' envoys." Since the Americans had behaved in such an unbecoming manner, Aziz said, he would agree to meet with Baker only on neutral territory. Joseph Wilson issued a statement welcoming the announcement. "I think as long as we're talking, as Winston Churchill said, 'Jaw, jaw, jaw, talk, talk, talk, is better than war, war, war.' So we'll see."

In Washington, the President was unhappy at the Iraqi response. As influential as he was within the Iraqi government, he argued, Aziz would not be authorized to make any decisions in Geneva. Scowcroft and Baker agreed. But there was no way to reject the Iraqi offer, they said. The Senate was scheduled to begin debate on the administration's policy in just a few hours, the President noted. The administration had to be—or at least appear to be—as flexible as possible. Bush drew the line, however, at any meeting between himself and an Iraqi envoy in Washington. That would accomplish nothing, he said. The President authorized Fitzwater to prepare and release a statement agreeing to the Iraqi proposal. Fitzwater finished it quickly and handed it to the President. "This offer [for Baker to meet with Aziz] is being made subject to the same conditions as my previous attempt," the statement said. "No negotiations, no compromises.

No attempts at face-saving, and no rewards for aggression."

On Capitol Hill, the Bush statement was greeted with immediate dismay. "I think they ought to be creating opportunities to talk to Saddam, not foreclosing on them," said Les Aspin, the chairman of the House Armed Services Committee. Aspin had been supportive of the administration's Gulf policy, but now, he said, it looked as if Bush and his advisers were guaranteeing a war. "The whole purpose originally was to see Saddam Hussein and get through the sycophantic advisers. . . . They are handling this diplomatic initiative so badly I can't believe it."

In Luxembourg on January 5, the foreign ministers of the European Community received what they regarded as an insulting statement from Tariq Aziz. The EC ministers had voted the day before to invite Aziz to come to Luxembourg to discuss the Gulf conflict and see if there were still some way to arrive at a peaceful solution. Jacques Poos, Luxembourg's foreign minister, had issued the invitation personally. Aziz had rejected it, noting that the EC ministers had refused to meet with him in Rome a month earlier to discuss the Gulf conflict. Now, Aziz charged, the EC was merely doing the bidding of the United States. "We resent the submissive policies pursued by certain European governments toward the aggressive and haughty American policies," Aziz said. "These governments should realize that he who wants to talk to Iraq should visit Baghdad and talk directly to officials there."

In Washington, President Bush's advisers in the White House and the State Department expressed quiet satisfaction with the response to the EC overture by Aziz. "We were not at all displeased," a senior State Department official said.

As dusk descended on the White House on January 5, the President's advisers huddled once again. Throughout the day, they had been passing copies of a letter back and forth, deleting language and adding language. George Bush was concerned that Saddam Hussein would not be given a clear message by Tariq Aziz no matter how forcefully Baker delivered his message in Geneva. "I think there is a question mark in [Saddam's] mind as to whether the U.S. will do its part to implement the resolutions of the Security Council," Bush said. "He listens to the debate. People tell me that he stays glued to CNN. And as he listens to these experts that are called into service for a thirty-second sound bite, he probably wonders who is speaking for the administration." Bush wanted to make sure that Saddam Hussein knew exactly who was speaking for the administration. This was a personal letter from the President of the United States to the President of Iraq. Baker would deliver the letter to Tariq Aziz in Geneva. It was a last chance, Bush said, for him to communicate with Saddam directly.

Bush approved strongly of the tone of the letter to Saddam. It had a no-nonsense quality to it: "Mr. President: We stand today at the brink of war between Iraq and the world. This is a war that began with your invasion of Kuwait; this is a war that can be ended only by Iraq's full and unconditional compliance with U.N. Security Council Resolution 678. There can be no reward for aggression. Nor will there be any negotiation. Principle cannot be compromised. However, by its full compliance [with the Security Council resolutions], Iraq will gain the opportunity to rejoin the international community."

The letter's conclusion was forceful: "Mr. President, U.N. Security Council Resolution 678 establishes the period before January 15 of this year as a pause of good will so that this crisis may end without further violence. Whether this pause is used as intended, or merely becomes a prelude to further violence, is in your hands, and yours alone. I hope you weigh your choice carefully and choose wisely, for much will depend on it." The letter was signed simply: George Bush.

On January 6, James Baker departed from Andrews Air Force Base with George Bush's letter for Saddam Hussein in a locked briefcase. Baker was not due in Geneva for another three days, but he wanted to consult with a few key allies before he sat down with Tariq Aziz.

Baker's first stop, on January 7, was London. Prime Minister John Major, who had succeeded Margaret Thatcher after her surprise ouster just weeks before, was in Saudi Arabia visiting British forces. Baker met instead with Douglas Hurd, the British foreign secretary. Under Thatcher, the British had been America's staunchest allies in the coalition against Iraq. Hurd told Baker that Major was equally committed to the alliance. If Saddam Hussein did not order the withdrawal of his army from Kuwait soon after the January 15 deadline, Hurd told Baker, Prime Minister Major would be prepared to go to war. The next few days would be difficult, Hurd and Baker agreed; the allies must hang together.

The next day, Baker met with President Mitterrand in Paris. Since the very beginning of the conflict with Iraq, a senior aide to Baker said, the French had been a "royal pain in the ass," even though Mitterrand had been among the first to deploy warships to the Gulf and had quickly sent some 30,000 troops, including several units of the French Foreign Legion. But chain-of-command orders maintained by the Central Command staff in Riyadh showed that of the thirty nations that had committed military forces to the alliance, only France had refused to submit to the command structure that placed all Allied forces under General Schwarzkopf and his Saudi counterpart, Lieutenant General Khalid ibn Sultan. Worse, aides to Baker said, even at this late hour, Mitterrand was sending signals to Baghdad that might persuade Saddam Hussein to believe that he could still link the withdrawal of his army in Kuwait to Israel's relinquishing the occupied territories of the West Bank and Gaza. Just four days earlier, Baker knew, Michel Vauzelle, a longtime ally of Mitterrand who was also the chairman of the committee on foreign affairs in the French National Assembly, had concluded what he described as a "personal peace mission" to Baghdad. Mitterrand had denied any official connection to the Vauzelle mission, but senior officials in the State Department didn't believe it.

In his meeting with Mitterrand, Baker stressed the importance of holding firm against Iraq. Mitterrand agreed. Bush had telephoned Mitterrand on January 3, the same day Marlin Fitzwater announced that Baker would be willing to meet with Tariq Aziz. In his conversation, aides said, President Bush had stressed that there could be no negotiations with Saddam Hussein until the Iraqi army was out of Kuwait and the Sabah family had returned to the emirate. There could be no negotiations prior to some movement on Saddam's part, he said. Mitterrand agreed.

In Washington, meanwhile, Chief of Staff John Sununu dispatched a White House courier to Capitol Hill with a letter from Bush. The President, who had been meeting almost daily with members of Congress, was now seeking congressional approval for war. The proposed Baker meeting with Aziz in Geneva had convinced many Americans to give the administration the benefit of the doubt. And a *Washington Post*/ABC News poll showed that seven of ten respondents approved of the United States and its allies employing military force against Iraq if Saddam Hussein refused to remove his army from Kuwait by January 15. Bush told aides that his confidence had not been misplaced: the polls had finally turned around; there was clear public support for his Gulf policy. And, Bush said, he would rather go to war with congressional support than without it. He was thus requesting a resolution authorizing the United States to use "all necessary means" to eject the Iraqi army from Kuwait if it was not withdrawn by

January 15. Bush and Baker had deliberately used the same language as U.N. Resolution 678. This way, aides explained, Congress was being asked only to authorize the President to enforce a resolution that had already been approved by the United Nations Security Council. The administration's nutcracker strategy of avoiding an outright vote or a congressional declaration of war was designed to permit the President to avoid any serious entanglement in this thorny constitutional issue. Congress, for its part, would continue to believe it had satisfactorily discharged its own obligation to the Constitution.

On the morning of January 9, James Baker, Bob Kimmitt, State Department Spokesperson Margaret Tutwiler, and John Kelly, the assistant secretary for Near Eastern and South Asian affairs, trudged into an unadorned meeting room in Geneva's posh Hotel Intercontinental. They were joined almost immediately by Tariq Aziz, Barzan Ibrahim, and an equally small delegation of Iraqi officials. News photographers allowed in for just a few minutes requested that Baker reach across the long table to shake hands with Aziz. With an unsmiling Kimmitt sitting immediately to his left, Baker obliged. But he refused to make eye contact with the Iraqi foreign minister. The photographers then left, and the meeting began.

Just minutes into the meeting, Tariq Aziz looked across the table at Baker, according to several people present, two of whom took notes. "Would you mind if I smoked?" Aziz asked. "No," Baker replied. "As long as it's not a Cuban cigar." Minutes after that, Baker removed the letter from President Bush from a folder. He told Aziz that the letter was for President Hussein. He asked the Iraqi foreign minister to deliver the letter to Saddam in Baghdad as soon as possible. Aziz indicated he wanted to read the letter first. It was three typewritten pages. The room fell silent as Aziz scanned the letter's seventeen short paragraphs. "His hands trembled," a participant in the meeting recalled, "and he was sweating as he read it." When Aziz finished reading the letter, he put it down in the middle of the conference table. He looked Baker directly in the eye, and said, "I regret that I cannot accept this letter. The tone is not appropriate for a head of state."

"The letter is frank," Baker acknowledged. "But it is appropriate." "I cannot accept it," Aziz repeated. "I regret that I cannot accept it." Baker replied in low but respectful terms to Aziz. "You are taking onto your shoulders the responsibility of being the only official of your government to have seen this letter." Again Aziz demurred. He could not convey the letter from Bush to President Hussein, he said. He was sorry.

The meeting dragged on for exactly six hours and forty-five minutes. Barzan Ibrahim, Saddam Hussein's half brother, was seated to the left of Aziz, and he fidgeted visibly at the far end of the long conference table, snorting in disgust as Tariq Aziz ticked off a long list of what he described as American-orchestrated "conspiracies" against Iraq. According to two American officials present, Barzan pounded the conference table several times as Aziz detailed the "conspiracies." The conflict over Kuwait, Aziz said, was not at all unlike the American involvement in the Second World War. The United States had attacked Japan, Aziz said, because of its fears about the potential economic threat from Tokyo. To Aziz's left, Barzan thumped the conference table. A former Marine who had served in the Second World War, Baker calmly asked: "Mr. Minister, have you never heard of Pearl Harbor?"

Aziz turned to the Palestinian question. The United Nations Security Council had passed a host of resolutions condemning Israeli treatment of the Palestinian communities in the West Bank and Gaza. Nothing had ever been done to force Israel's compliance with the resolutions, he said. It was only against Arabs, he told Baker, that "you raise the stick." The conflict between Iraq and the United States, Aziz said, was truly the result of America's "double standard" in the Middle East.

The United States had expressed its concerns about Israeli conduct in the occupied territories, Baker replied. It had condemned the deportation of Palestinians from the West Bank and Gaza, actions that had resulted in the separation of families and loved ones. But the invasion of Kuwait was a different matter. Iraqi forces had violated an international border to occupy a neighbor state; until the Iraqi forces were withdrawn, there could be no discussion of other issues. The deadline of January 15 was a real deadline. There would have to be some movement on the part of Iraq by that time, or hostilities would ensue. And, Baker said, in the event that President Hussein did not understand the size of the military force arrayed against his army in Kuwait, it was enormous. If the dispute in the Gulf were to result in armed conflict, Baker said, there should be no doubt about the outcome.

As the two foreign ministers debated, the letter from President Bush lay in the middle of the table. To several of the Americans in the room, the letter was like a totem, a symbol of the futility of these last-ditch talks between the United States and Iraq.

"Have no illusions," Baker told Aziz toward the close of the meeting. "Do you understand the forces that are arrayed against you?" "Yes," Aziz replied. "We have studied your military for years. . . . You may have the superiority, but we are going to fight with valor and with courage." Mr. Minister, Baker said a short while later, "I am not stating this as a threat. This is a fact. But if this dispute results in armed conflict, the Iraqi people will suffer gravely." Aziz nodded in assent. "Perhaps," he told Baker, "it will just come down to fate." It would be a very painful and bloody conflict, Baker said. Iraqis would suffer more than soldiers in the alliance. "No," Aziz replied, "it will not be a short war. Americans do not know how to fight in the desert."

Baker said that he had conveyed all of the points President Bush had asked him to convey. "I am prepared to stay here for as long as it takes, Mr. Minister. Do you have anything more that you need to say?" Baker asked, "or that you would like to say?" Aziz said that he, too, had conveyed his message. "Well, then," Baker said, "that's it."

The two delegations rose from the conference table. The letter from President Bush still sat in the center of it. Baker looked at the letter and then at Aziz. "Are you sure you wouldn't like to take the President's letter?" Baker asked. Aziz said that he would prefer not to. An aide to Baker retrieved the letter from the center of the table. As the two parties prepared to leave the room, Margaret Tutwiler approached Aziz. "Sir," Tutwiler said, "you know we are both expected to speak with the press. Do you want to go first?" "No," Aziz said quietly, "you go first."

Upstairs in his hotel suite, Baker telephoned President Bush. The secretary of state was exhausted. Stretched out on the bed with his head propped up against the headboard, Baker told Bush of the meeting's failure. The two men spoke for approximately fifteen minutes. Afterward, Baker and a handful of key aides worked on changes to a statement that had been drafted earlier, one that anticipated the Iraqi delegation's unwillingness to yield. Then Baker went down to deliver the news to the world. "There have been too many Iraqi miscalculations," Baker said somberly, addressing a chaotic news conference. "The Iraqi government miscalculated the international response to the invasion of Kuwait, expecting the world community to stand idly by while Iraqi forces systematically pillaged a peaceful neighbor. It miscalculated the response, I think, to the barbaric policy of holding thousands of foreign hostages, thinking that somehow, cynically doling them out a few at a time would somehow win political advantage. And it miscalculated that it could divide the international community and gain something thereby from its aggression. So let us hope that Iraq does not miscalculate again. . . . The path of peace remains open. . . . And let us all hope that [the Iraqi] leadership will have the wisdom to choose the path of peace."

In Washington, Bush sat in his small private study just off the Oval Office and watched the CNN broadcast of the Baker-Aziz press conference. Vice-President Quayle, Scowcroft, and Cheney watched with him in silence as Tariq Aziz delivered his remarks to the press. The fact that Aziz refused to accept the letter, Bush said, was a bad omen: now there was no way of getting through to Saddam.

After the press conference, in his hotel suite, Baker reflected on the hours he had just spent with Aziz. Neither man had raised his voice. Both had been respectful and patient. A former corporate attorney who respected a worthy adversary, Baker told his aides that Tariq Aziz had carried out a very difficult assignment with skill. "He delivered a very bad brief," Baker said, "very well."

Congress resumed its debate the following day. But time was running out. The U.N. deadline was only five days away. Many legislators were still angry that the President continued to believe that he could engage American military forces in a war without Congress's consent. "We have not seen this kind of arrogance in a president," Senator Edward M. Kennedy remarked, "since Watergate." But the administration's strategy had plunged the Democrats into disarray. Throughout the day, Bush had been telephoning Southern conservatives to enlist their support. So far, he was having success.

In the House, Bush's Republican allies were seeking to maximize the President's leverage by pushing for a joint resolution. The so-called Authorization for Use of Military Force Against Iraq Resolution required that Bush first come to a determination that "diplomatic and other peaceful means to obtain compliance" with the Security Council resolutions were exhausted before the military alliance could begin offensive operations. The measure gave the President wide latitude to determine when peaceful means had failed. In both chambers, lawmakers debated the likely effect of the economic sanctions. The proposed congressional resolution would require the President to make a judgment that these "efforts have not been and would not be successful" in forcing the Iraqi army to leave Kuwait.

On the afternoon of January 10, the House Armed Services Committee released a letter from William Webster on the CIA's view. "Our judgment remains that, even if the sanctions continue to be enforced for another six to twelve months," Webster wrote, "economic hardship alone is unlikely to compel Saddam Hussein to retreat from Kuwait or cause regime-threatening popular discontent in Iraq." As the debate in the House and Senate went into the evening, aides reported to John Sununu that the tide seemed to be moving in Bush's favor.

After three days of often somber and sometimes eloquent debate, the House and Senate finally voted late in the afternoon on January 12. At Camp David, Bush had watched some of the debate on television, and he told aides it was stirring, even some of the arguments against the resolution. Many members recalled their own wartime experiences. Some of those with more than a quarter century on Capitol Hill recalled the last time the Congress had authorized military action, on August 7, 1964. "Out of the seventeen thousand votes I have cast," said Charles E. Bennett, the eighty-year-old Florida Democrat who was awarded a Silver Star in the Second World War, "the only one I really regret was the one I cast for the [Gulf of] Tonkin resolution."

In the Senate, with members sitting motionless in their seats instead of milling around noisily on the floor as usual, the final tally was close: 52–47 in favor of the resolution. Two Republicans had joined 45 Democrats in opposing the resolution. In the House, the vote was 250–183, as 86 Democrats joined 164 Republicans in supporting the measure. Speaker of the House Thomas Foley had argued forcefully against support of the measure. But just minutes before the roll was called, Foley struck a note that characterized the debate over the past three days. "Let us come together after this vote without recrimination," Foley said. "We are all Americans here—not Democrats, not Republicans."

On the evening of Saturday, January 12, in Baghdad, Javier Pérez de Cuéllar, the secretary-general of the United Nations, was greeted by Tariq Aziz at Saddam International Airport. "I am bringing the will of the international community for a peaceful solution," Pérez de Cuéllar told Aziz. In the very next breath, however, he conceded that he had "no new proposals." The next day, after a meeting with Saddam Hussein, Pérez de Cuéllar was on his way back to the airport. Aides said that the secretary-general had been stonewalled by Saddam. There had been almost no give-and-take. "I don't see any reason for hope," Pérez de Cuéllar said just before his plane departed.

Late on Saturday evening, Lawrence Eagleburger, the deputy secretary of state, stepped into a side entrance of Israeli Prime Minister Yitzhak Shamir's modest home in Jerusalem. It had been announced on the radio that Eagleburger was coming to Israel, but he had insisted to his own aides and to Israeli officials that he not be photographed. He wanted the visit to be as low profile as possible.

Eagleburger was an inspired choice for the last-minute mission to Jerusalem. "He has a record of being friendly to Israel," a senior adviser to Shamir said. "He has the right mentality, and he knows how to work with us." In his conversation with Shamir, according to knowledgeable officials, Eagleburger stressed that Israel, despite its understandable and obvious security concerns, should not initiate a preemptive strike against Iraq. Shamir had made such a pledge to Bush in December, but administration officials were not sure how firm it was.

For the last twelve days, Bush had raised his fears over the possibility of an Israeli preemptive attack almost daily with aides and advisers. On January 10, Bush had called Shamir to stress the point personally. When they had talked the next day (the evening before Eagleburger's arrival in Jerusalem), Shamir had promised Bush again that Israel would not strike first at Iraq. In exchange for this pledge, Eagleburger had been authorized by Bush and Baker to be more explicit about the American pledge to defend Israel. In his remarks to the press after his January 9 meeting with Baker, Tariq Aziz had been asked whether Iraq would attack Israel in the event of war. "Yes," Aziz had said. "Absolutely, yes!" The response had escalated fears even higher in Israel, and Eagleburger had told Baker that Shamir was under pressure—not so much from the military, but from members of the inner cabinet to take a hard line against Iraq.

If Israel was attacked by Iraq, Eagleburger now told Shamir, the Bush administration would consider it a *casus belli* and respond immediately. In addition, Eagleburger said, two Patriot advanced missile batteries would be shipped to Israel shortly. HAMMER RICK, the secret communications link between Defense Secretary Cheney and Israeli Defense Minister Moshe Arens, would finally be installed. The Pentagon was also dispatching a two-star Air Force general named Mack Armstrong from the staff of the Joint Chiefs to Tel Aviv to coordinate with General Avihu Bin-Nun, the chief of staff of the Israeli air force. (General Armstrong would replace a senior Central Command Air Force official. Aides to Shamir believed that the Central Command was less responsive to Israeli concerns than officials on the Joint Chiefs of Staff and on the staff of the European Command, with whom Israel ordinarily dealt on military matters.) In the event of war, Eagleburger said, Armstrong would keep Bin-Nun and his people apprised of the progress the United States and its allies were making in destroying Saddam Hussein's Scud missiles in western Iraq.

An Iraqi attack, Eagleburger continued, should not automatically result in Israeli retaliation. Eagleburger said that while he understood Israel's security concerns, an Israeli counterattack could weaken the Allied coalition at the very moment it was prepared to crush Iraq. It was in Israel's own interest not to retaliate, Eagleburger argued. Besides, he said, the Pentagon was confident that they could neutralize Saddam's Scuds very quickly; they expected no threat from the Iraqi air force.

"It was tense," Shamir said. Despite his long friendship with Israel, Eagleburger "was not coming in a personal capacity or to ask personal favors. He came as a personal envoy of the President. He wanted a commitment that Israel would not retaliate. We did not give such a commitment."

Eagleburger told Shamir that the United States would not give the Israeli air force the IFF ("identify, friend or foe") codes used by the Allied air force in Saudi Arabia. General Bin-Nun and Defense Minister Arens had been pushing for the codes, so that if the Israeli air force had to respond to an air attack from Baghdad, it would not shoot down—or be shot down by—American and Allied pilots. If Washington refused to give Israel the IFF codes, Arens and Bin-Nun wanted the administration to allow the Israelis an air corridor across Jordan, so that Israeli war planes could respond to an attack from Baghdad and minimize the risk of encountering Allied fighter aircraft. Eagleburger was not authorized to agree to specify such a corridor. The Allied air force, he told Shamir, would destroy the Iraqi Scud missiles and their launchers in western Iraq in a very short time. Israel would just have to be patient.

Particularly important, Israeli officials said, were the calculations they would have to make if Saddam attacked with chemical weapons. There was strong sentiment within the Israeli cabinet to refrain from retaliation, Foreign Minister David Levy and other officials told Eagleburger during his visit. But if Saddam used chemical weapons against Israel, and especially if such an attack resulted in large numbers of casualties, Prime Minister Shamir would virtually be forced to retaliate.

Eagleburger met with Levy the morning after he saw Shamir, the morning of January 13. According to several knowledgeable American and Israeli officials, Levy like other members of the Shamir government, was angry at the United States. Baker had tried to keep Levy apprised of the progress of the last-minute diplomatic wrangling. He had sent Levy a long, detailed letter outlining the substance of his meeting with Tariq Aziz in Geneva, but still Levy felt that the United States was not dealing fairly with Israel.

Regular Western analysis does not fit someone like Saddam, Levy told Eagleburger. When he threatens us, we take him seriously. Baker visited Hafez al-Assad in Syria, but he did not come here because he feared it would anger Assad. The Security Council slapped us, and the United States was quiet. There is a situation today where the Americans are afraid to sit down with us because they are afraid that they will anger the Arabs. Eagleburger listened silently.

Levy asked him about the U.S. push for Israel not to retaliate if it were struck by Baghdad. "Do you really think [that] if we are attacked, we shouldn't defend ourselves?"

"I told Prime Minister Shamir yesterday that the United States—and this comes from President Bush—will regard an Iraqi attack on Israel as a *casus belli*," Eagleburger replied. Bush would immediately declare war on Iraq, Eagleburger said. "This is a presidential commitment that has never been given to another state. . . . I've been sent here to tell Prime Minister Shamir and you that once the war starts, whether Iraq attacks you or not, our intention . . . is to target as very important those things that threaten Israel."

Levy repeated Shamir's pledge that Israel would not launch a preemptive strike against Iraq. But what about retaliation? Eagleburger asked. "We are concerned that if war starts and we are in Iraqi air space that there be no conflict with the Israeli air force by mistake," Eagleburger said. "We want to prevent accidents. We know the supreme importance of retaliation for you, but these are unusual circumstances. We also think that we can destroy Iraqi targets, and that therefore there is no need for Israeli retalia-tion. If we can reach an agreement, I don't know. It will be hard for both of us. All I know is that it will be a human and political catastrophe if American airmen are killed by Israelis or the reverse, if we kill Israelis. All this is based on [whether] there are hostilities. I am not sure, but war is close." Levy replied, "We must coordinate in advance of war. We must do our national duty. . . . Tell us when the skies are clear so we can act."

In yet another meeting, with Defense Minister Arens, Eagleburger was told that Israel was not prepared to accept the Patriot batteries. They would have to be manned by American crews, and that was unacceptable.

Later in the day, Eagleburger and Paul Wolfowitz, the under secretary of defense for policy, met with senior officials of the Israeli defense forces in the Kirya, the Israeli equivalent of the Pentagon. Eagleburger and Wolfowitz promised that the United States and its allies would destroy the Scud missiles and launchers in western Iraq. According to several people present, the two U.S. officials said that Iraqi Scuds would be destroyed within forty-eight hours of the war's commencement. "Gentlemen," one of the Israelis present told Eagleburger and Wolfowitz, "it does not work this way during wartime. Simple things become complicated."

The Israeli generals said they had reason to be skeptical of the American promises. Senior military and intelligence officials in Washington had said that they would be able to identify launchings of Iraqi missiles even before they happened, because fueling and other prelaunch preparations would be detected by America's spy satellites. However, on December 20, Iraq test-fired three medium-range missiles in western Iraq, and the satellites failed to detect the launches until the first had been airborne nearly six minutes. Worse, Israeli officials complained, they had learned of the test-firings almost sixteen hours after they had occurred, when the news was broadcast by CNN. "We have to sit together," a senior official in the Kirya meeting told the two U.S. officials, "or this is not going to work." The meeting ended with a reaffirmation of Shamir's pledge that Israel would not launch a preemptive strike. But Eagleburger and Wolfowitz had won no promises that Israel would not retaliate if attacked.

On Sunday evening, January 13, in Washington, Bush gathered in the White House family quarters with Dan Quayle, Dick Cheney, Brent Scowcroft, and Colin Powell. Bush had taken to convening informal Sunday-night sessions following his return from the weekend retreat at Camp David. "He would have us come in when he came down from the mountain," Cheney said, "and we would talk about whatever was hot at the time." Sitting in a white wingback chair, Bush was calm as Scowcroft handed him a national security directive—the order that would commit more than half a million Americans to war. Bush signed the directive, but left the date and the time blank. Turning to Cheney, Bush said that he was authorized to implement the presidential order the next day, January 14, unless he heard otherwise. Cheney nodded. The meeting was over.

On January 14, a spokesman for the Soviet foreign ministry appealed to Saddam Hussein to stop his "game of wire walking" and to order his army to withdraw from Kuwait. In a telephone conversation with Saddam Hussein two days earlier, Yevgeny Primakov had been assured by the Iraqi leader that he would issue an order for his troops to leave Kuwait. "I am a realist," Saddam said, according to Primakov. "I know that I will have to withdraw." Now, on the evening of January 14, with less than forty-eight hours before the United Nations deadline was to expire, Primakov doubted the words of the Iraqi leader he had known for so long. "If Saddam Hussein has to choose whether to be trampled, as he says, or to fight," Primakov mused, "he will choose the latter."

In Paris, Prime Minister Michel Rocard conceded that an eleventh-hour appeal to Baghdad by the government of President Mitterrand had also failed. Despite his pledge to Secretary of State Baker, Mitterrand had continued to put forth proposals to the Iraqi government that compromised the terms of the twelve United Nations resolutions directed at Iraq since the August 2 invasion of Kuwait. The day before, the French ambassador to the United Nations had proposed that if Iraq were to withdraw immediately from Kuwait, with a United Nations peacekeeping force monitoring the pullout, the members of the Security Council would sponsor a broad Middle East peace conference. Secretary Baker and U.N. Ambassador Pickering sharply criticized the proposal, as did British Prime Minister John Major. It didn't matter. Baghdad had spurned the French offer. "The fact, the only one that counts, is the painful recognition that Baghdad resolutely refused all offers of dialogue compatible with the U.N. resolutions," Rocard said. "In any international police operation, the fatal moment comes when one must act. Alas, after everything we have done to avoid it, that moment has now arrived."

The United Nations deadline expired precisely at midnight Eastern Standard Time on January 15.

Just after seven in the morning on January 16, Baker joined Cheney in Scowcroft's White House suite for a regularly scheduled breakfast meeting. On this particular morning, the mood over the White House china was somber. Outside, it was still dark, and a harsh rain slashed at the streets and trees. It was a far cry from the freak, springlike weather of the day before, when protesters had gathered in Lafayette Park, across Pennsylvania Avenue from the White House, where they were joined by a group of Native Americans. The steady beating of drums could be heard distinctly throughout the presidential mansion.

Cheney told Baker and Scowcroft that he had signed the "execute order" transforming Operation Desert Shield to Desert Storm. Scowcroft assured his colleagues that Bush had not wavered. He was more convinced than ever that he was doing the right thing.

After the breakfast meeting broke up, Cheney left the White House without seeing Bush. He returned to the Pentagon, where last-minute planning for Desert Storm was continuing around the clock.

Baker and Scowcroft joined the President for the regular 8 A.M. meeting of the National Security Council, as did Quayle, Sununu, Webster, and his other senior advisers. The CIA director informed Bush that the latest overnight intelligence from the Gulf showed no evacuation of Iraqi defensive positions in Kuwait, no sign at all that Saddam had issued an order to withdraw. It was evident that the Iraqi leader just did not understand the kind of force he was up against. They had tried to warn him, Bush said. Now they would have to use the Allied force they had worked so hard to create and sustain over the past 5½ months.

Shortly after the meeting in the Cabinet Room adjourned, Bush began making phone calls. An aide interrupted with a letter from Pope John Paul II. The pontiff wrote that he was praying for peace, but that if hostilities did commence, he prayed that the United States and its allies would win quickly and with a minimum of casualties. Bush told aides that the Pope's letter was bracing. In the previous weeks, the President had consulted with several religious leaders. Edmond Browning, the presiding bishop of the Episcopal Church, had urged Bush strongly to give Saddam Hussein more time to get out of Kuwait. Dorothy Walker Bush had raised her children as Episcopalians, and George Bush had never strayed from his faith. But he was frustrated by Browning's advice. "What is the morality of not doing anything?" Bush had asked Browning. "Where were the churches when Hitler overran Poland?" he asked, brandishing the Amnesty International report. "You read this report," Bush had told Browning, "and then you tell me what to do."

In the previous weeks, Bush had also spoken with Bernard Law, the Roman Catholic cardinal in Boston, and with television preachers Robert Schuller and the Reverend Billy Graham. After accepting a call shortly before midday from German Chancellor Helmut Kohl, Bush called Graham to invite him to spend that evening at the White House. Graham, who had served as an adviser to many Presidents, readily agreed.

At the State Department, James Baker had retired to his office to make some phone calls of his own. On his final round of talks with other members of the anti-Iraq alliance, Baker had said that if diplomatic maneuvering failed and it came to war, he would notify them beforehand. Baker first called Alexander Bessmertnykh, who had replaced Shevardnadze as the Soviet foreign minister. Other calls went out to Hans-Dietrich Genscher, the German foreign minister, to Manfred Woerner, the secretary-general of NATO, and to Gianni de Michelis, the Italian foreign minister. "Most people's reaction," recalled an aide who was with Baker as he made the calls, "was 'God bless you, God bless us all. We are doing the right thing. God bless America.' They were very patriotic statements. The conversations were very brief."

In the White House, George Bush made and received several more phone calls as he worked on the draft of the speech he would deliver to the nation that evening. As dusk fell and the protesters continued their vigil across the street from the White House in Lafayette Park, Bush walked upstairs to the family residence to freshen up and change clothes. When he returned to the Oval Office little more than an hour later, the United States and its allies would be at war.

CHAPTER 14

DESERT STORM: BOMBS OVER BAGHDAD

D ESERT STORM began in the dark.

At 10:30 P.M. local time on January 16, at an airfield known as Khamis Mushayt in the southwestern corner of Saudi Arabia, ten American pilots strode across the concrete tarmac toward a line of hulking, angular shapes barely visible against the moonless sky. The pilots spoke quietly to their crew chiefs and received assurances that the planes were ready. Then they walked around the planes to check for themselves. The night was so dark that approaching from a distance they could not even see their planes. The pilots withdrew small pocket flashlights and studied the planes' hydraulic lines for signs of leaks. They double-checked the tires, then looked over the wiring to the armaments and checked the settings on their bomb fuses. Satisfied, the pilots climbed the ladders to their narrow cockpits, dropped their gear inside, and wriggled into their seats. They put on their helmets, plugged in their radio cables, and began an hour-long check of the complex avionics and flight and weapons systems of their planes. These were the newest and most secret aircraft in the arsenal of the U.S. Air Force. These were F-117As, Stealth attack fighters.

At about 11 P.M., the pilots started their engines and began checking their aircrafts' internal systems. Captain Marcel Kerdavid, Jr., was one of them. Kerdavid, thirty-three years old, from Tarrytown, New York, had never wanted to be anything but an Air Force pilot. Kerdavid couldn't believe it—on this, possibly the most important mission of his life, the first of his plane's two engines wouldn't start. Quickly, he climbed out of his cockpit and jumped into a waiting truck, which took him to another Stealth fighter about a quarter mile away. That one started and Kerdavid finished his cockpit checklist. A few minutes before midnight, he taxied out and joined up with his wingman at the end of the long runway. All ten pilots punched their clocks to begin the mission—a mission that would last six hours.

At midnight, Kerdavid's F-117A roared down the runway until it reached its takeoff speed of nearly 200 miles an hour, when Kerdavid gently lifted its nose skyward. His wingman was right behind. In precise intervals seconds apart, the eight other aircraft paired up also. Not a word was spoken between any of the pilots. Aloft, Kerdavid led his wingman to their KC-135 refueling aircraft 170 miles to the north. The two pilots located the tanker and eased their aircraft into place behind the tanker's tail. In the night sky nearby, the four other pairs of F-117As were meeting their tankers and doing the same. They were barely visible. Only their running lights were on. The pairs of F-117As followed their five tankers to a place 30 miles south of the Iraqi border. The ten Stealth pilots had not yet spoken a word to one another. Their mission called for absolute radio silence.

At about 2:30 A.M., the tankers turned away and the Stealth fighters continued forward, slipping out of Saudi airspace and into Iraq. From there, it was a half-hour flight to downtown Baghdad. Each pilot followed the flight plan that had been programmed into his navigation module, cross-checking the already agreed-upon decision points and turn points against his computer printout and written notes taken in briefings earlier that day. By now, Kerdavid and the other pilots had separated; some headed for Baghdad, others to desert radar sites. The ten pilots set their speeds, altitudes, and headings to close in on their assigned targets. They slid lower in their cockpits so they could study the instrument panel and focus on the information that would guide them in for the kill. Once the planes were within striking distance, the pilots located their targets on their cockpit displays and maneuvered them into the center of their cross hairs. Kerdavid bore down, more fearful of being hazed by his buddies for missing his crucial target than of the enemy. The pilots locked their bomb-guidance systems onto the ghostly shapes of buildings on their screens.

At 2:51 A.M. Baghdad time on January 17, the first Stealth pilot pressed a button on his control stick and his laser-guided bomb steered into an early warning radar control center about 160 miles southwest of Baghdad near a town called Nukhayb. Exactly one minute later, a second Stealth pilot released a bomb onto a similar center at an airfield in western Iraq, about thirty miles east of the Jordanian border. At precisely 3 A.M., another Stealth pilot squeezed the button on his control stick and a 2000-pound, laser-guided penetrator bomb flew unerringly to its target point, dead center in the roof of a twelve-story, antenna-topped structure the Iraqis called their International Telephone and Telegraph Building in downtown Baghdad. Following right behind his airplane at two different approach angles, two more F-117As dropped 2000-pound high-blast bombs through the hole made in the building's concrete roof. The blasts obliterated the building's top two stories.

The next most important target was the Tower for Wire and Wireless Communications—the building through which most of Baghdad's electronic telephone circuits were routed. At 3 A.M., a 2000-pound bomb went through its roof. Other F-117As were hitting the Presidential Palace and command centers that controlled early-warning radar and interceptor aircraft. There were five such centers in Iraq. One was in Baghdad, and one was at Tallil Air Base in the Euphrates Valley near Kuwait. The Stealth fighters hammered both.

The ten pilots pressed on. They struck the Iraqi Ministry of Defense and the Air Force Headquarters building in Baghdad (one of their bombs dropped straight down the air shaft of the latter). Several pilots dropped their bombs on hardened bunkers housing air defense centers at al-Taji and al-Taqaddum, west of Baghdad. One pilot clearly had the most impressive strike of the night—a 320-foot antenna tower, a concrete spire with a bulge of antennas at the top. His bomb hit exactly on the tower's top, penetrated about 10 feet, and exploded, disintegrating the antenna array but leaving the building next door untouched.

As the first bombs went off, the sky over Baghdad was suddenly bright with anti-aircraft fire. Its intensity surprised the ten pilots, several of whom began to wonder if they would make it back alive. Within a matter of minutes, Kerdavid said, the anti-aircraft fire became increasingly dense, especially at medium and low altitudes. After Moscow, Baghdad possessed the heaviest concentration of air defenses of any city in the world. It seemed to the ten Americans who delivered the first blow of Desert Storm that every one of the Iraqi batteries must be firing at once.

One by one, in less than fifteen minutes, the pilots completed their bombing runs and headed for home. Their mission had been a success.

Each of the pilots had delivered his bombs precisely onto his targets. Sixty miles north of the Saudi border they turned on their radar-signal generators so that they could be seen by friendly aircraft and would not be attacked. They came up on the radios and quickly took an inventory. No one was missing. Kerdavid remembers the relief of hearing his buddies check in. "I honestly didn't think we'd all make it home," he said. At 6 A.M., six hours after they took off, the Stealth pilots touched down safely in Saudi Arabia.

At 6:35 P.M. in Washington, George Bush was seated in his small study off of the Oval Office with Dan Quayle, Brent Scowcroft, John Sununu, and Marlin Fitzwater. Five minutes into the ABC evening broadcast, anchorman Peter Jennings reported that there had just been explosions and bursts of light over Baghdad. CNN's Bernard Shaw reported the same thing seconds later. Shaw, unlike Jennings, was in Baghdad.

Bush looked at his watch, then at Scowcroft. The timing was way off. "What's that?" Scowcroft said he didn't know. The F-117As were not to strike their targets in Baghdad before exactly 7 P.M. Eastern Standard Time. That had been designated as H-Hour, the official start of Desert Storm. U.S. forces had been authorized to attack selected targets elsewhere in Iraq a few minutes earlier. But Bush had been promised that there would be no attacks on Baghdad prior to 7 P.M.

The clock in Bush's study struck seven, and within minutes all of the television networks were reporting anti-aircraft fire and falling bombs over the capital of Iraq. "This is just the way it was scheduled," Bush said calmly.

The live reports from Baghdad were suddenly interrupted. The bomb that fell on the Tower for Wire and Wireless Communications had knocked out the international phone lines from Baghdad. Minutes later, however, CNN was reporting live again. They had arranged for a special communications link to Amman, and from there to the United States.

Scowcroft suggested that the pyrotechnics reported earlier from Baghdad had evidently come from jittery gunners in Iraqi anti-aircraft batteries around Baghdad. That was his best guess. Bush turned to Fitzwater, the genial press secretary who had been one of the President's closest advisers in the 5½ months since the invasion of Kuwait. "Go ahead and do it, Marlin."

A few minutes later, Fitzwater trudged into the White House briefing room. The United States, he told the room packed with reporters bristling with microphones and television cameras, had initiated military action with its allies to force the Iraqi army in Kuwait to withdraw. Operation Desert Storm had begun.

At a secret staging area 700 miles west of Dhahran, just as the first wave of ten F-117A pilots was heading for Iraq, a flight of eight Apache AH-64 helicopters and four MH-53J Pave Low helicopters lifted off from a darkened tarmac. They were also headed north toward Iraq. Flying just thirty feet above the ground, Lieutenant Thomas Drew, a twenty-seven-year-old pilot from the 101st Airborne based at Fort Campbell, Kentucky, was embarking on the first combat mission of his life. Drew had been training for such a mission since September, but he had not been told where the target would be or how important it would be.

The information had been withheld from Drew and his colleagues for as long as possible. Finally, just days before, they had been told that they were to strike early-warning radar systems in southwestern Iraq. The original plan called for three separate teams—red, white, and blue teams of three Apaches and two Pave Lows each. Initially, they had been assigned to strike three radar sites. At the 10 P.M. briefing on January 16, however, Drew and his colleagues were handed a revised plan. One target had been dropped. The radar facility had become inactive, intelligence officials said. So two Apaches of the blue team were assigned to the other teams, making two teams of four Apaches each. In memory of the D-Day invasion of the French coast in the Second World War, they were given the name Task Force Normandy.

The two early-warning radar systems left as targets were about thirty-five miles apart. One was located just seven miles inside Iraq; the other was fourteen miles across the Iraqi border from the Saudi desert village of Ar Ar. The two facilities provided defensive coverage of the southwestern Iraqi border and protection for Iraqi air bases and fixed launchers for Scud missiles there.

At 12:56 A.M. on January 17, the helicopters took off. The Pave Low helicopters were outfitted with global-positioning systems that could help the Apache pilots navigate in the desert in the dark. The Pave Lows were also equipped with sophisticated terrain-following radar and on-board computerized mapping systems that would enable the Apache pilots to locate their targets in even the worst weather.

Fifteen miles from the Iraqi border, Drew and the other Apache crews flew over what looked like a small Bedouin camp. Seconds later, there were surface-to-air missiles rising toward them. The missiles narrowly missed. One of the Pave Lows flying with Drew's team of Apaches shot at the Bedouins with a 7.62-mm machine gun. That was odd, Drew thought, being fired at from inside Saudi Arabia. There was no time to delay, however, so they flew on.

At 1:45 A.M., an hour and fifteen minutes before H-Hour marked the start of the air war, Lieutenant Drew and his small fleet of attack helicopters crossed the border into Iraqi airspace. Drew was the commander of the white team; he sat in the front seat of his Apache and controlled the weapons systems. Behind him sat his pilot, Chief Warrant Officer 2 Tim Zarnowski. Ten miles inside Iraq, Task Force Normandy was attacked again, this time by machine-gun fire. The helicopter pilots ignored it. They had a far more important objective. It was Drew's job to coordinate all aspects of the mission. The most important element of all, Drew had been told over and over again, was what the Air Force called "time on target." The Apache pilots had been instructed to destroy the two radar sites at precisely 2:38 A.M. No sooner, no later.

Soon after crossing into Iraqi air space, Drew and Zarnowski saw a dozen tiny white dots on their Forward Looking Infrared Radar scopes. Their range-finder told them the dots were twelve kilometers away. Five kilometers from their target site, the outlines of the radar facility became clear. Drew could see a line of squat buildings, trailers, and radar antennas. The layout, he knew, was characteristic of the Soviet-designed radar systems. They were supported by Soviet-made anti-aircraft artillery.

Just under five kilometers from the radar site, Drew got his team of four Apaches on line. Each weapons officer centered his cross hairs on the ghostly white shape of his target. Drew's first target was a trailer. His wingman would first hit a radar antenna. The two other Apaches would hit different antennas, control buildings, and the facility's communications vans. When ten seconds remained to launch time, Drew radioed to his team: "Party in ten." Five seconds passed and a pilot said, "Here's one for you, Saddam." Five seconds after that, Drew called, "Get some." Less than a second later, a swarm of missiles was screaming across the desert toward their targets.

At that same moment thirty-five miles away, the red team of Task Force Normandy was lined up on approach to the second radar site. Locking onto their targets with their Image Auto Gate Trackers, electronic rectangles on their scopes designed to find and hold targets by identifying their heat sources, the four Apache pilots of the red team released their missiles. The looping trajectories were visible for just seconds in the helicopters' thermal scopes before the targets exploded. The tiny figures of Iraqi soldiers could be seen on the Apaches' scopes, running. One of the Iraqis ran from a building that had just been attacked, apparently to warn soldiers in another building. At the very instant he opened the door to the second building, the structure exploded into flames.

Back at his target site, Lieutenant Drew ordered the white team to switch tactics. "Okay," he called over the radio, "let's do rockets." Their 2.75-inch rockets contained thousands of little fléchettes, or darts, to take out supply trucks and wiring systems. Then the Apaches mopped up with their 30-mm automatic cannons.

In a matter of minutes, Task Force Normandy had thoroughly destroyed the two targets. "Okay," an Apache pilot radioed Lieutenant Drew, "I cannot see any more targets in my area." On the red team nearby, another Apache pilot signaled a successful mission. "Okay," he radioed, "we can get us out of here." The world would think of the first bombs dropped on Baghdad as the beginning of the Gulf War. General Schwarzkopf and his staff saw the attack by Task Force Normandy as the real beginning of the war.

Even as Drew, Zarnowski, and the other members of Task Force Normandy were fleeing back to Saudi Arabia, pushing their helicopters at 160 miles per hour, a flock of American F-15E and British Tornado bombers were flying just hundreds of feet off the ground in the opposite direction. Their targets were fixed Scud missile launchers at an airfield in a sector of western Iraq designated as H-2 on American, Allied, and Israeli military maps and at desert outposts near the wadis of Amaij, al-Jaber, ar-Ratqa, and Muh Hammadi. All of the targets were in westernmost Iraq near Jordan; in fact, they were the Scud bases nearest Israel. The bombers were seeking to fulfill the pledge of the Bush administration to Israeli Prime Minister Yitzhak Shamir.

At 3:05 A.M., the first of the U.S. Navy's terrain-guided, air-breathing Tomahawk cruise missiles arrived in the Iraqi capital and struck its target. The missile had been launched one hour and twenty-four minutes earlier from the USS *San Jacinto* in the Red Sea. Minutes later, another Tomahawk missile struck a communications building in Baghdad. It had been fired from the USS *Bunker Hill* in the Persian Gulf.

These were the first two of 100 Tomahawks to be launched on the first day of Desert Storm. The missiles were fired by nine different U.S. Navy vessels, in nearly equal numbers from the Red Sea and the Persian Gulf. Before the war against Iraq concluded, U.S. Navy ships would launch 288 Tomahawk cruise missiles, which cost roughly $1 million each. Their targets were oil refineries, communications facilities, and other so-called soft targets that could be disabled or destroyed relatively easily.

After launching, a Tomahawk cruise missile rockets vertically into the air. Seconds after launch, its trajectory flattens out as the turbofan motors kick in. Inside the missile, a gyroscope senses its speed and direction and starts the missile on a computer-guided target path. A tiny radar scans the terrain below, matching the topography with a map that has been digitized and programmed into the missile's computer, which also rotates the missile's fins to steer it. As the missile draws closer to its target, optical sensors take over, comparing the topography below with the computerized picture of the expected target to enable the missile to home in.

Cruise missiles are extraordinarily accurate weapons. For each missile launched during the Gulf War, Pentagon officials said, the maps had to be specially coded by experts at the highly secretive Defense Mapping Agency just outside Washington. The Tomahawks "performed beyond anybody's wildest expectations," a Central Command official said. "I mean, [if] they programmed them to fly through the windows in some of those buildings in Baghdad, [the missiles] went through the windows inside the building and detonated. If the guys who programmed the missiles put the cross hairs right on the bolt hole on a door, you can bet your sweet last dollar that's where it impacted."

In the planning of the air campaign, senior Air Force officials had opposed the idea of such heavy reliance on the Navy's Tomahawk missiles. (They had done the same thing in the 1986 raid on Libya because they feared that the Tomahawks would not work; they had won out then despite objections from the National Security Council staff and others who wanted to use the missiles.) This time, Central Command planners had spent two full weeks working up a long target list for the Tomahawks. The targets had been selected to be struck during the first two nights of the air war. Central Command officials concluded that the Tomahawk strikes would have disabled most of Iraq's forty-four military airfields. For instance, the al-Taqaddum fighter base, which was located forty miles west of Baghdad, had been targeted for sixty Tomahawk strikes. But senior Air Force officials had vetoed those strikes, Central Command officials said, arguing that they could destroy the array of hardened fighter hangars at al-Taqaddum more effectively with bombers and ground-attack aircraft.

One senior war planner in the Central Command headquarters in Riyadh found himself directly in the middle of the conflict between the Air Force and the Navy. He wrote in his notebook: "They [the Air Force] can take care of it. Sure, When?" This official said that the position of the Air Force was impossible to justify. With the Tomahawks, he said, "we would have gotten every airplane at [al-Taqaddum], every hangar, on the first or second night. And the Air Force finally got around to hitting it on the eighth night. And the aircraft were gone by then. It was kind of a minor problem in the long term, I suppose. But the Air Force was very, very parochial in its approach to doing business. They felt they could win the war by themselves."

Twenty-five minutes after the first two Tomahawk missiles struck their targets in Baghdad, decoy drones were launched from bases in Saudi Arabia. Ten minutes later, Navy jets based on aircraft carriers in the Red Sea and the Persian Gulf launched another flight of drones. Pilotless and unarmed, the fast-flying drones were designed to draw enemy fire away from the real attack force of manned aircraft. At 3:50 A.M., the drones would reach Baghdad, where the Iraqi air defenses would detect them and begin firing away almost indiscriminately.

Meanwhile, an armada of American F-4G Wild Weasels, EF-III electronic-warfare planes, EA-6B Navy Prowlers, and F/A-18 attack jets was standing off south of the Iraqi capital. The planes were armed with high-speed HARM missiles with 145-pound warheads that would follow radar beams back to their emission point, destroying the radar facilities.

The ground-launched drones had been programmed to fly in circles around Baghdad. They were to stay up in the air long enough to attract most of the Iraqi fire and keep the Iraqi radars turned on. The Iraqi anti-aircraft batteries destroyed many of the drones, of course. Iraqi gunners reported that they had shot down dozens of Allied airplanes. But they also lost most of their Baghdad radars in the process. Their targets in sight, Allied planes launched 200 of their anti-radar missiles, and they homed in on the Iraqi radars, destroying most of them. In effect, the Iraqi radars beckoned the missiles in on themselves. The Iraqis were compelled to change the way they used their radars for the rest of the war. "That's probably one of the main reasons why I was only able to use the drones that once," Brigadier General Buster Glosson said. "They wouldn't turn their radars on anymore." The Iraqis would break the record for surface-to-air missiles fired at decoys for all wars. Intelligence analysts later counted nine surface-to-air missiles fired for every drone detected.

In keeping with Colin Powell's dictum to make the odds in their favor as long as possible, the architects of Desert Storm employed another gambit to disable and confuse the Iraqi air-defense system. According to two senior U.S. officials familiar with the matter, weeks before the commencement of the air war, a team of U.S. intelligence operatives had slipped several electronic microchips into a French-made computer printer that was being smuggled to Baghdad through Amman, Jordan. It is unclear how the intelligence officers located the printer or managed to gain access to it. But the two officials knowledgeable about these events said that the plan was for the printer to be delivered to a command bunker within the Iraqi air-defense network.

The microchips inserted into the printer carried a computer virus that was designed by U.S. intelligence technicians at the National Security Agency, the two U.S. officials said. According to computer experts, such viruses cannot ordinarily be inserted into large mainframe computer systems. Although computer "hackers" have managed to gain access to U.S. government mainframe computers in recent years, experts insist all government computers, especially those with national-security applications, are protected by elaborate electronic defenses. The experts said that the virus inserted into the Baghdad-bound printer was designed to disable the computers that allowed for coordination and communication among the Iraqi air-defense batteries. This was done by attacking the mainframe computer through a peripheral piece of equipment, the printer, which ordinarily would not be protected by the mainframe computer's electronic-security defenses.

According to one account, once the virus was inserted into the heart of the Iraqi air-defense computer system, it would have disabled it by devouring "windows" as Iraqi technicians opened their monitor screens to check on different aspects of the air-defense system simultaneously. Each time a technician opened a window on his screen, one official explained, the window would disappear and the information in it would vanish.

The two officials familiar with this operation said that it may never be known whether the virus worked as designed. The irony, however, according to senior U.S. Air Force officials who monitored the opening hours of the Desert Storm air campaign closely, was that the virus was probably not needed. Between the drones confusing the air-defense guns and the pinpoint opening attacks of the Tomahawk cruise missiles and Stealth fighters, the Iraqi air-defenses immediately around Baghdad were rendered virtually useless within the first several hours of the war.

In the first hour of Desert Storm, six "packages" of bombers, fighters, and electronic-warfare aircraft attacked Iraq. One was the squadron of F-117As. A second was the flight of twenty-two F-15Es and British Tornados, accompanied by two EF-111 radar jammers, that struck the Scud missile launchers and airfields. A third group of Air Force and Navy bombers and fighter escorts also attacked other Scud launchers and airfields in far western Iraq at H-2 and H-3 airfields. A fourth and a fifth package of bombers crossed Iraq's south-central and east-central border headed for other radar sites and airfields; one of their missions was to fire HARM missiles at the radars shooting the decoy drones. The sixth package consisted of twelve B-52 bombers, flying as low as 300 feet off the ground, and several British Tornado GR-1s whose mission was to drop cluster bombs on Iraqi airfields.

In the first three hours of Desert Storm, more than 400 combat planes and 160 tankers and command aircraft would swarm across the dark skies of the Persian Gulf theater. The operation called for a complex orchestration of split-second timing, all done with virtually no plane-to-plane communications. Months before, Lieutenant General Chuck Horner, with help from the Pentagon's Checkmate division, had created the architecture for the air war. It had been left to Buster Glosson to make it happen. A gruff, silver-haired Air Force general, Glosson was the type of leader military people call "mission-oriented." The only subordinates he tolerated were those who got the job done. "There are just some guys who can score touchdowns," Lieutenant General Horner said, in explaining why he chose Glosson. "These are the guys you call upon. These are the guys you pull off the bench." It was Glosson who had decreed that H-Hour would be 3 A.M., the time the first bomb hit the main telecommunications building in Baghdad. To effect that strike at that time, he told his superiors at Central Command headquarters, some bombs would have to be dropped and some missiles launched a little earlier. But everything was figured on H-Hour, either H-plus or H-minus so many minutes.

For instance, the Tomahawk missiles needed to be launched at H-minus 1 hour and 19 minutes for them to hit Baghdad at 3:05 A.M. Glosson had told Schwarzkopf that the first Tomahawks would be fired at 1:30 A.M., to give himself a few minutes' leeway, in the event Schwarzkopf received a last-minute order from Washington delaying the beginning of Desert Storm. The additional eleven minutes Glosson had allowed himself would guarantee that he could contact the USS *San Jacinto* and USS *Bunker Hill* before they launched their missiles.

To ensure that his F-117A Stealth fighters would be able to complete their bombing mission to Baghdad and then return, Glosson needed to have them refueled between thirty and fifty miles south of the Iraqi border. There was no way to hide the tankers from Iraqi radar, so Glosson had decided to display them prominently instead. Months earlier, beginning in September, once or twice each week, Glosson had run five KC-135 refueling tankers up to within fifty miles of the Iraqi border in what the Air Force described as a "tanker cell." The tanker pilots had been instructed to fly in a racetrack pattern for several hours within sight of Iraqi radar installations before they returned to their bases. The Iraqis undoubtedly saw the huge tankers. What they did not see, however, were the ten Stealth fighters flying just off their wings.

Most of the time, to check Iraqi reactions and see if they could pick up the F-117As, Glosson had had the Stealth pilots fly practice missions over Saudi territory and then return to the tankers. But on three occasions he had had the planes fly to within ten miles of the border and then fly another fifty miles up and down the border. On the second of these practice missions, Glosson had tried something different. He had the F-117As turn on their transponders, which emitted the IFF codes. This way the Stealth fighters would appear on a radar screen, just like any conventional aircraft. With their transponders on, the F-117As had dashed toward the Iraqi border. Then, fifteen miles away, they had turned them off and gone into

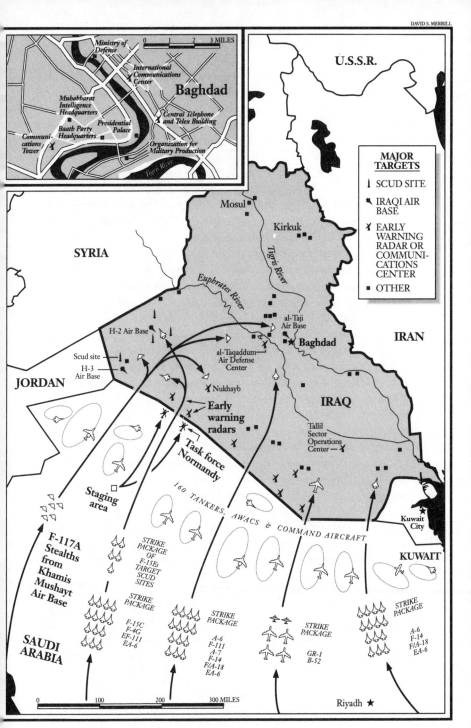

DAVID S. MERRILL

MAJOR TARGETS

⌇ SCUD SITE

➹ IRAQI AIR BASE

✕ EARLY WARNING RADAR OR COMMUNICATIONS CENTER

■ OTHER

Baghdad (inset map)

Ministry of Defense

International Communications Center

Mukhabarat Intelligence Headquarters

Baath Party Headquarters

Presidential Palace

Communications Tower

Central Telephone and Telex Building

Organization for Military Production

Tigris River

0 1 2 3 MILES

U.S.S.R.

SYRIA

Mosul

Kirkuk

Euphrates River

Tigris River

H-2 Air Base

Scud site

H-3 Air Base

JORDAN

al-Taqaddum Air Defense Center

✕ Nukhayb

Early warning radars

Task force Normandy

al-Taji Air Base

★ **Baghdad**

IRAN

IRAQ

Tallil Sector Operations Center

Staging area

160 TANKERS, AWACS & COMMAND AIRCRAFT

Kuwait City

KUWAIT

F-117A Stealths from Khamis Mushayt Air Base

STRIKE PACKAGE OF F-15Es TARGET SCUD SITES

STRIKE PACKAGE

F-15C F-4G EF-111 EA-6

STRIKE PACKAGE

A-6 F-111 A-7 F-14 F/A-18 EA-6

STRIKE PACKAGE

GR-1 B-52

STRIKE PACKAGE

A-6 F-14 F/A-18 EA-6

SAUDI ARABIA

0 100 200 300 MILES

Riyadh ★

MORE THAN 400 COMBAT AIRCRAFT HIT TARGETS IN IRAQ IN THE OPENING HOURS OF THE AIR WAR, JANUARY 17, 1991

their Stealth mode of operation. To the Iraqi radar operators, it looked like ten fighters had headed right at them and then disappeared, probably dropping down under their radar beams. A day after this exercise, Baghdad accused the allies of overflying Iraq. In fact, the F-117As had turned away, never entering Iraqi airspace. The exercise had convinced Glosson that Stealth worked. If the Iraqi radar operators had seen the planes turn away, they would have never have broadcast their accusations.

With the air war finally under way, Buster Glosson worried about how many things might still go wrong. Glosson had discussed every facet of the complex campaign with Horner. Both men were concerned by the tight sequencing of the operation. At one airport, fifty-six fighter aircraft had been scheduled to launch within forty minutes. If just one plane blew a tire or crashed on takeoff, the whole schedule would be set back. The targeting sequences required coordination to the second, not the minute. Both men knew that an error of ten seconds could result in tragedy.

As the first planes began departing their air bases, Glosson and Horner watched a large display screen at their headquarters in the basement of the Royal Saudi Air Force Headquarters building. The screen relayed information on the attack from an AWACS aircraft overhead. "The AWACS display was like a large TV screen in a bar for watching pro football," Horner said. "It goes from Israel to Tehran, from Turkey to Saudi Arabia. Everything that's flying appears on that except the Stealth [fighters]. And you might get a hit on a Stealth every now and then. I just sat there and watched planes take off and rendezvous."

"General Horner and I sat there," Glosson said, "and it was eerie how precisely it unfolded. You just don't expect to be able to do that without having some losses and some things go wrong. But that just didn't happen."

Horner had sent an aide, Ollie Olson, up to his office to watch CNN. Horner noticed that everyone was drinking coffee and munching on cookies. "Americans sent a billion cookies over there," Horner said. "The key was to go find the cookies you liked. I would go around to all the duty officers and see what kinds of cookies they had. There were some really good home-baked cookies, and the guys would try to hide those. You really had to be crafty, but nobody will ever refuse a general." At H-Hour, Horner called Olson to see what was happening. "He said, 'Okay, Bernie Shaw is under the coffee table. . . . Bernie Shaw just went off the air,'" Horner recalled. "That's when we were supposed to take down the electrical-and-communications capability. Talk about bomb-damage assessment!"

One hour and twenty minutes behind the first wave of ten F-117As, a second wave twice as large flew toward Baghdad. Their assigned "time over target" was 4:20 A.M. This second wave of Stealth fighters was led by Colonel G. T. "Greg" Gonyea. In one of the Stealth planes, nicknamed the Toxic Avenger, was a forty-five-year-old boyish-looking Air Force colonel from Orangeburg, South Carolina, named Al Whitley.

Like most pilots, Whitley carried his own personalized survival gear, a plastic bag the pilots called a "piddle-pack" for kidney relief, and a plastic doughnut he could sit on and pump up to relieve the pressure on his tailbone on long flights. On this mission, as usual, Whitley had brought along a bottle of water, a package of LifeSavers, and a Snickers candy bar. He would pop the LifeSavers into his mouth and sip water all the way to Baghdad and back. But only if he hit his two targets precisely would he allow himself the Snickers bar.

Flying this mission was Whitley's reward for a series of jobs well done. This would be Whitley's third tour in combat. In Vietnam, he had flown 143 combat missions in the F-100 aircraft and 90 more in the A-7 Corsair. In 1980, when he was a weapons-systems instructor on the A-10 Warthog tank-killer, Whitley had been asked to join a very special team. The team was supporting a top-secret airplane being built at a hangar in Burbank, California, owned by the Lockheed Corporation. People at Lockheed called the secret facility the Skunk Works. At the time only about two dozen Air Force people knew the actual nature of the project.

At the Skunk Works, Whitley had been able to watch Lockheed build the secret airplane from the ground up. He had watched his own airplane, number 786, roll off the assembly line in Burbank, and he had accompanied it as it was delivered to Tonopah Air Base, a high-security Air Force facility in the Nevada desert north of Las Vegas. Number 786 was among the very first of the Stealth fighters. The plane had been built in a remarkably short period of time—it was just 2½ years from the time the project received the go-ahead until the first plane rolled out. Its designers had made use of many existing parts from other aircraft. The wheels, for instance, had come from the F-15 fighter. The new Stealth aircraft was small enough to be a fighter. But its subsonic speed and inability to carry lots of air-to-air missiles dictated its real role. The Air Force intended to use the new jet as a penetrating fighter to launch ground-attack missiles and laser-guided bombs. It was really a radar-evading bomber. Any attack into Soviet territory would mean encountering extensive Soviet air defenses. Radar beams are best reflected back to their source by flat, perpendicular surfaces, and the Stealth fighter had been built with as many angled surfaces as possible, few of which would ever be broadside to an enemy radar.

The leading edge of the F-117A's main wing edges were angled and knife-sharp. The flat blades of the plane's turbine engines were masked with a honeycomb cover. The exhaust gases from the engines were mixed with cooling air before exiting through long, narrow slots, which made the aircraft unusually invisible to heat-seeking missiles and heat-reading radars, too. Flying on a moonless night, such as this one, the aircraft would also be invisible to the naked eye. In fact, January 16 was one of only five moonless nights in January following the expiration of the U.N. deadline, a meteorological fact that weighed heavily in the decision to start the air campaign sooner rather than later. The Stealth fighters could be seen in the daytime, however, so they flew only at night. The irony in waiting for the moonless night was that the weather would deteriorate almost immediately afterward, reducing visibility and cutting down the number of combat and support missions flown.

For Whitley, the project to build the invisible fighter-bomber had been all consuming. From 1981 to 1985, he had trained openly with his A-7 Corsair group at Nellis. That, however, was a ruse. Often, they would fly the A-7s to Tonopah, where they would then board the Stealths for night training. He had not even been allowed to tell his wife what he was doing.

After five years with the Stealth project, Whitley moved on. He did stints at the National War College and the Pentagon, and then returned to Nellis to command the 4440th Tactical Fighter Training Group, which plays the "red team" in training exercises, and then to become vice-commander of the A-10 wing there. Then he was named the Tactical Air Command's director of fighter training and tactics, and moved to Langley, Virginia. In the summer of 1990, as the conflict with Saddam Hussein was reaching the point where war seemed increasingly likely, Whitley was promoted again, this time to commander of the 37th Tactical Fighter Wing and its fifty-six

F-117As at Tonopah. Whitley had wondered whether he, too, would be drawn into the conflict in the Persian Gulf. Two days after he arrived in Nevada on August 15 with his wife, two children, and two cats, Whitley got his answer. On the morning of August 17, Whitley presented himself for the change-of-command ceremony at Tonopah. That afternoon, at 2 P.M., a priority message for Whitley came into the command post on the air base. A squadron of F-117As was needed in Saudi Arabia immediately.

Now, five months later, Whitley was flying north to Iraq. He met his refueling tanker, then silently crossed the border. The sky was pitch-black until Baghdad appeared, a low, red glow on the horizon, like a harvest moon rising. Only it wasn't a moon rising, Whitley realized, it was Baghdad's formidable anti-aircraft batteries illuminating the sky. Whitley knew immediately that the blizzard of tracers and surface-to-air missiles was the result of the work done by the first wave of Stealth fighters. "They had stirred up a hornets' nest," Whitley recalled.

As he approached the outskirts of Baghdad, Whitley saw the flashes of flak bursting, coming up all around him, orange, white, yellow. It was, Whitley said, like being in the middle of the fireworks display on the Fourth of July in your hometown. From his cockpit, Whitley could see flak bursting in the air on every side of the Toxic Avenger. Some of the anti-aircraft fire rose as high as 20,000 feet, Whitley noticed, probably from Iraq's impressive 100-mm and 85-mm batteries. There was even more flak at lower altitudes. Occasionally, he could see an unguided surface-to-air missile fly past as well.

Whitley had two targets, both command-and-control facilities. He dropped a 2000-pound bomb on his first target, then flew out over the outskirts of Baghdad to reposition for his second strike. Below him, Whitley could see the headlights of a stream of cars fleeing the city.

Despite the lethal clouds of flak exploding all around him, Whitley tried hard to concentrate on his mission. Buster Glosson's target planners had blueprints of the key Iraqi targets. They had talked to American officers who had been stationed in Iraq and to Europeans who had built the buildings and shelters. These people had helped Glosson's men draw the floor plans of the buildings they wanted destroyed. The planners also had the help of aerial photographs from spy satellites. The image resolution was so good that the target planners could identify air ducts and other details as small as one foot in length. The targeters had pinpointed not just rooftops, but the exact spot on the rooftops where they wanted Whitley and his fellow pilots to aim their bombs. Usually, they specified air-conditioning ducts, vents, or airshafts.

Whitley carried two 2000-pound bombs, which were known as GBU-27s (GBU stood for glide-bomb unit). The ordnance was guided to its target by the reflection of a laser from the aircraft. The GBU-27 was the most effective weapon in the Air Force arsenal against hardened targets—targets protected by feet of reinforced concrete. The GBU-27 was similar to the GBU-24 bombs carried by the F-111B bombers, but it was newer and more accurate. Whitley and the other Stealth pilots also carried GBU-12 bombs, 500-pounders designed more for blast effect than penetration. They were used against unprotected targets, such as fighter jets on airfields. The F-117As could carry two 2000-pound bombs or four of the smaller GBU-12s. They were all laser-guided.

Like the other Stealth pilots, Whitley was well trained in precision bombing. If he hit a target seconds too early, it could bring up concentrated anti-aircraft fire at his wingman. If he hit too late, he could be in an Iraqi gunner's sights himself. "Five seconds makes a big difference," Whitley said. "You'd better not be early or your buddies will let you know it. And you better not be late or you suffer the consequences."

He dropped the second bomb. As he headed south from Baghdad and cleared the last of the anti-aircraft fire, Whitley breathed deeply. Then he opened his Snickers bar and took a bite. He allowed himself only half the candy bar. One of his two bombs had missed its target.

At 10 P.M. Eastern Standard Time in the small, cramped, cavelike control room at CNN headquarters in Atlanta, Bob Furnad, CNN's senior executive producer, was issuing orders. On the monitor in front of him, Bernard Shaw, Peter Arnett, and John Holliman were taking turns describing the air war taking place outside the window of room 906 in Baghdad's al-Rashid Hotel. With the three main American television networks prevented from broadcasting live because of the interruption of telephone service from Baghdad, CNN had the only timely reporting from Iraq on the waging of Desert Storm. CNN had installed what was known as a "four wire" from Baghdad through Amman, Jordan, to Atlanta. One half of the "four wire" was an open line to their studios, separate from their audio and video transmission line. Reporters could simply press a button and begin talking without having to dial and have the transmission go through the normal electronic switching required on commercial calls. The arrangement cost the company $30,000 a month.

Three hours and twenty-five minutes earlier, at 6:35 P.M., Bernard Shaw had shouted into his telephone at Eason Jordan, CNN's international editor. "It's happening, it's happening," Shaw said. "Get me on. Get me on." Seconds later, he was on. From then on, George Bush, Colin Powell, and Dick Cheney, as well as millions of other Americans, and viewers in 105 other countries, stayed glued to Cable News Network. It had been Holliman's idea to hold the CNN microphone out the window of their hotel room. A former radio reporter, he knew that the sounds of the war would be more dramatic than anything they could say. "I knew the sound was just as important as the picture." For seventeen hours after the phone lines from Baghdad were cut, Shaw, Arnett, and Holliman used their "four-wire" link to Atlanta to provide a live, exclusive, and uncensored view of the war from behind enemy lines. Not since Edward R. Murrow had reported on the Battle of Britain had there been more dramatic live war coverage. Air Force planners in Riyadh and Washington made detailed notes as they watched the live CNN footage of bombs exploding and anti-aircraft fire futilely chasing American fliers high into the night sky.

In the hours immediately after the start of Desert Storm, CNN ratings topped those of CBS in twenty-five major U.S. cities. More than 200 U.S. affiliates of the three larger networks dropped them temporarily to pick up feeds of CNN's live coverage from Baghdad. At 11 P.M., Furnad was still issuing orders in the darkened control room. Just outside, Tom Johnson, former publisher of the *Los Angeles Times* and the newly appointed president of the Cable News Network, was beaming. "This," he said, "is global television at its finest."

When the first ten Stealth pilots returned to their base in Saudi Arabia not long after dawn on January 17, Major K. D. Boyer came out to shake their hands. Boyer had helped to plan the missions and dispatch the pilots. He could see they were still excited. Marcel Kerdavid said the flak had been so thick he could walk on it. Others had seen flak explode next to them and flown through the air turbulence created by flak explosions. By the end of the first night of Desert Storm, the thirty Stealth fighters sent aloft by Chuck Horner and Buster Glosson would account for 80 direct hits in central Baghdad. The F-117As would be the only manned aircraft to fly missions against central Baghdad during the entire war.

In the coming weeks, Colonel Whitley would fly nineteen combat missions without getting hit. His colleagues would each fly roughly the same number during the course of the war. By the time of the cease-fire with Iraq, Stealth fighters would fly 1,271 of the war's 110,000 combat missions, representing slightly more than 1 percent of all combat missions flown by Allied aircraft. The effectiveness of the Stealth fighters was way out of proportion to the number of missions, however. "The bottom line," Glosson said, "is that over 47 percent of the [strategic] targets destroyed in Iraq were destroyed by the F-117s."

Not long after Colonel Al Whitley entered Iraqi airspace on his way to Baghdad, Captain Jon Kelk followed, though he had a far different mission than Whitley's. The mission was air-to-air combat. At six-foot-three and not much more than 170 pounds, Kelk, with his thatch of sun-bleached blond hair, did not fit the typical image of the stocky, squared-jawed Top Gun. Articulate and easygoing, Kelk, at thirty-three, was well practiced in the art of war. He had been flying fighter aircraft for eight years.

On the night of January 16, Kelk and three other pilots formed a group known as a "four-ship." Kelk's four-ship had been assigned the code name Pennzoil. Earlier in the day, Kelk and the other three Pennzoil pilots had spent hours in the mission planning room, reviewing the details of their assignment. Besides the Iraqi radar, anti-aircraft batteries, and surface-to-air missiles, Glosson and Horner worried about another Iraqi threat—the Iraqi air force. Saddam Hussein had at his disposal more than 500 combat aircraft, many of them late-model Soviet-built MiGs and French Mirage fighters. The aircraft were based at forty-four airfields scattered throughout the country. Horner had promised his superiors that he would establish air superiority very quickly, "within a matter of days." To make good on the pledge, it would mean that Kelk and dozens of other F-15C pilots would have to sweep the skies of any Iraqi aircraft that came up to fight.

Crossing into Iraq in the early hours of January 17, Kelk and his wingmen in the four-ship of F-15Cs were hoping that the thirty Stealth fighters that had preceded them would now be evacuating the area according to plan. The last thing they needed, Kelk said, was to be going against the enemy with friendly aircraft still in the area. Kelk and his colleagues wanted to engage the Iraqis at long range, beyond visual range. Given the range of modern air-to-air missiles, if he got close enough to the enemy to dogfight, Kelk knew, he would be in hot water. As Kelk and his companions flew deeper into Iraqi airspace, they picked up an aircraft on radar forty miles to the north, a target the radar operators in an AWACS aircraft overhead could not confirm as a friendly fighter or enemy "bandit."

Kelk's leader, Captain Richard Tollini, in Pennzoil 1, radioed to Kelk in Pennzoil 3, and asked if he had seen the same thing on his radar screen. Kelk replied that he had. Kelk was closest to the target, and he locked onto it with his missile-guiding radar. "We were traveling at about 30,000 feet," Kelk said, "but I was very unsure if he was a bandit because we had pushed [over the Iraqi border] very early, and we knew there would be friendlies in the area. I had no idea what that could be if it was not a bad guy. Or maybe it could have been a Stealth, and I just happened to have really good radar that night. I didn't know."

Tollini maneuvered to concentrate on another target, instructing Kelk to take the first plane. The still unidentified aircraft had started out very low. But Kelk watched it as it climbed steadily. It seemed to be heading directly toward him and the three other F-15Cs in the Pennzoil four-ship. "It appeared that this guy was attempting to engage us," Kelk said. He needed no one's permission to fire.

Kelk pressed the trigger and fired one 12-foot radar-guided missile with an 86-pound warhead, which has a range of 25 miles. "Fox from Three," Kelk yelled into his radio, indicating he had fired his missile. Quickly, he tried to release his external fuel tanks so that he could escape quickly if necessary. The tanks failed to drop off. Kelk maneuvered away, but he had to keep pointing his aircraft at the target to guide the missile with his own aircraft's radar.

He was tense, worried, and confused. His four-ship had flown into Iraqi territory early, and the AWACS aircraft had been unable to confirm that what he had targeted was an enemy airplane. Perhaps he had fired on one of his fellow pilots. He was not certain that his missile had even struck the other aircraft. A few seconds later, however, he saw what looked like a giant sparkler. "It wasn't your classic fireball," Kelk said. "It was bluish, and it moved in circular fashion. That's not what I expected."

Kelk knew that the sparkler could also be a missile heading his way. Or the flash could have been flares or chaff that enemy fighters eject as countermeasures as they attempt to escape. Uncertain, Kelk and his wingman bolted, joining the other two F-15Cs in the Pennzoil four-ship as they continued north. Their mission required them to sweep the skies near the al-Taqaddum and al-Assad air bases west of Baghdad.

Patroling his assigned area and checking his radar for indications of hostile aircraft, Kelk finally looked down at the electronic indicator that kept track of his missiles. The indicator board showed that he had not fired any missiles. Kelk was baffled. He thought he remembered the missile coming off, the characteristic jolt and clunk it makes when it leaves the ejector rails. But he had closed his eyes when he had fired the missile, in order not to be temporarily blinded by the flash of the rocket motor.

Over the radio, Kelk could hear the pilots in another F-15 four-ship code-named Citgo. They were engaging two Iraqi MiGs. It sounded like they had the situation well in hand, however, and Pennzoil's sweep was completed, so they turned home. Slowed by the fuel tanks he had been unable to eject, Kelk limped into Saudi territory, his wingman at his side. "As soon as we were across the border," Kelk recalled, "I asked my wingman to have a look underneath me and check my missiles. He said, 'Yeah, you are missing one.'"

When he landed, Kelk claimed an unconfirmed kill. The video recorder on his F-15C had not worked, making it difficult to confirm, but Kelk was pretty certain he had shot the hostile jet out of the sky. "I figured with all the timing and where he was and the fact that my wingman saw the same thing I did, I went in the next morning [to the mission-planning room] at about 8 A.M. and confirmed it at least on a visual sighting."

Later that day, the AWACS air crew that had been monitoring that part of the Kuwait Theater of Operations confirmed that there had indeed been an enemy plane shot down. Kelk had scored the first air-combat kill of the war. Kelk was assigned to the 33rd Tactical Fighter Wing based at Eglin Air Force Base in the Florida Panhandle. In Desert Storm, the wing earned a reputation for being extremely aggressive. Of the 36 air-to-air kills recorded during Desert Storm, the pilots of the 33rd Tactical Fighter Wing would tally 16. These would occur over the course of 1,182 combat missions.

By dawn in Baghdad on the morning of January 17, key parts of Saddam Hussein's military infrastructure were buried in rubble. Electronic communications throughout most of Iraq had been severely disrupted. In central Baghdad, the Iraqi Ministry of Defense and the headquarters of the Iraqi air force were in ruins. Other buildings that were severely damaged included the headquarters for the Organization for Military Production, the National Command Center of the Baath Party, the Ministry of Justice, and the Ministry of Local Affairs. Bridges across the Tigris and Euphrates rivers had been damaged. "The great showdown has begun," Saddam Hussein announced. "The mother of all battles is under way."

CHAPTER 15

THE AIR CAMPAIGN
CONTINUES

Eight hours after the first bombs fell on Baghdad, twelve American F-16 fighter aircraft left the small NATO air base in Spangdahlem, Germany. "We departed hastily under a thin veil of secrecy; everyone knew where we were going," said Major Mike Worden, one of the pilots. At thirty-seven, Worden was a fifteen-year Air Force veteran. In the course of his career, he had flown a variety of fighter aircraft, most recently the F-16. His call sign was Wardog.

Worden and the other F-16 pilots had to fly first to the large NATO air base at Sigonella in Sicily, where they were to refuel before flying on to Turkey. Over the Mediterranean, Worden and the other pilots would link up with the F-4G Wild Weasels that constituted the other half of the 23rd Tactical Fighter Squadron. The Wild Weasel was the U.S. Air Force's premier killer of enemy anti-aircraft batteries. In Vietnam, Lieutenant General Chuck Horner had been a nonpareil Wild Weasel pilot. The motto of the Wild Weasels was "First in, last out." Pilots of other American fighter aircraft joked grimly that the motto was inaccurate. It should have been "First in, never out."

Months before the commencement of Operation Desert Storm, a group of Air Force air crews at Spangdahlem and several other NATO bases scattered across Europe had devised and proposed an operation they referred to as a "back-door slam." It involved launching American fighter aircraft out of Turkey, opening up a second major front in the air war against Baghdad. Because of President Turgut Ozal's concerns that Turkey not be drawn too deeply into the war against Iraq, the plan at one time had been rejected. But Lieutenant General Horner persisted. He wanted American aircraft from the Pentagon's European Command—especially the Wild Weasels—involved in the prosecution of the war. With as much anti-aircraft fire as he had seen the night before as he watched CNN, Horner deployed as much firepower as he could muster to disable Iraqi air defenses. That was the mission the pilots of the 23rd Tactical Fighter Squadron had in front of them as they departed Sigonella Air Base late in the afternoon on January 17.

From Sigonella, Worden and his fellow pilots flew to the NATO air base at Incirlik in southern Turkey. As planned, they had been joined en route by twelve F-4Gs that comprised the other half of their squadron. At Incirlik, they would be joined by a squadron of F-15C fighter aircraft from Bitburg, Germany, and eighteen F-111E bombers from Britain's Upper Heyford Air Base. There were also six American electronics-jamming EF-111s that had arrived from Upper Heyford, as well as F-16 aircraft from Torrejon Air Base, in Spain, EC-130 electronic-warfare aircraft from Sembach Air Force Base in Germany, AWACS aircraft from Tinker Air Force Base in Oklahoma, and KC-135 refueling aircraft from Dyess Air Force Base in Texas. This comprised what was known in Air Force terminology as a "composite wing." In theory, with aircraft of so many different capabilities, the wing would be able to establish air superiority over an enemy air force rapidly.

Two and a half hours after landing at Incirlik, Worden's colleagues were briefed on the mission, and shortly thereafter they launched the first air strike at Iraq from the north. Bad weather closed in, and Worden himself didn't get to fly until January 20.

Throughout the air campaign, the air crews of this new composite wing would divide into separate "strike packages," each assigned to one of the three raids that would be flown almost every day. The packages were huge, made up of fifty to sixty aircraft in a formation pilots called "a forty-mile-long gorilla." From Incirlik, it was more than an hour's flight to the Iraqi border, and almost another hour to Baghdad. "We'd come in with a wall of [F-15] Eagles," Worden said, "maybe eight up front. They were to go in and clear the air of enemy aircraft." Approximately four to five miles behind the F-15s, which flew at an altitude of more than 40,000 feet,

Worden and the other F-16 Wild Weasel pilots shadowed the F-4G Wild Weasels. The F-4G pilots referred to the F-16s as their "little buddies." They were there to assist in firing radar-killing missiles and to drive hostile aircraft away so that the F-4Gs could concentrate on knocking out enemy air defenses. Following them in the package would be two EF-111s to jam enemy radars. Next would be two RF-4G reconnaissance aircraft to take pre-strike photos. Behind them would be the strikers, as many as twenty-four F-16 or F-111B bombers. And covering the tail of the package were four F-15C fighters, and four more Wild Weasels.

"Our overall objective from the north," Worden said, "was to distract them from the one end of the spectrum, and to dismantle them from the other end . . . by flying as hard as we could to follow the goals that President Bush had set: to destroy Saddam Hussein's chemical, nuclear, biological, and offensive military capability [and] knock out his command-and-control."

Early in the afternoon of January 17, Captain Dave Ross was sitting in the cockpit of his B-52 bomber at the U.S. base at Diego Garcia in the Indian Ocean. Ross had originally been assigned to the first night's strike, but his aircraft had been moved back to the second night's strike package. Now, with his engines running, Ross watched the twelve returning bombers from the first strike lumber down the runway. He had already learned that the pilots had delivered their bombs onto five targets, as ordered. As he taxied out for his night mission into Iraq, Ross gave the incoming B-52 pilots a thumbs-up, revved his engines, and rolled his B-52 down the runway.

The returning B-52s had spent about thirty minutes over Iraq, dropping cluster bombs on airfields in the southern part of Iraq. Ross had been assigned to deliver his bombs to targets in northern Iraq, keeping him and the other B-52s on his wing over Iraq five times longer than his colleagues just returning. Mission planners had calculated the time over Iraq for the second wave of B-52s at precisely 2 hours and 55 minutes. It would be a low-level run, Ross knew. And it would be long. It took nearly 8 hours just to get to Iraq. Northern Iraq was more than 3,500 miles away from tiny Diego Garcia.

Ross's B-52 was a thirty-year-old, eight-engine behemoth originally built to deliver strategic nuclear weapons. The B-52s—nicknamed BUFFs, for "big ugly fat fuckers," by their crewmen—had been modified during the

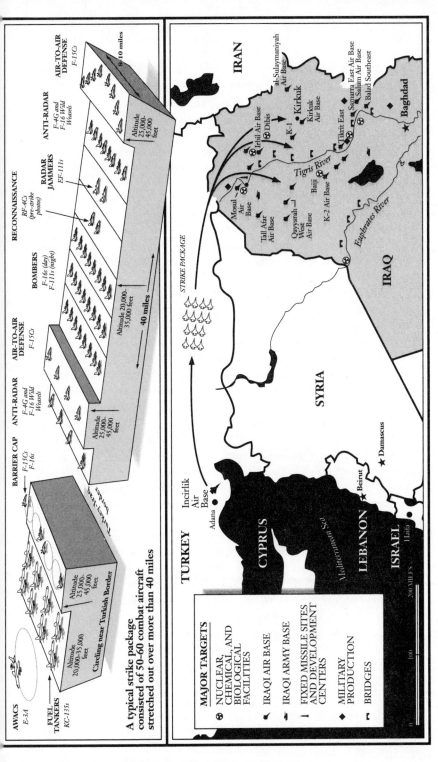

BEGINNING JANUARY 19, 1991, IRAQ'S "BACK DOOR" WAS OPENED WITH AIR RAIDS FROM TURKEY

Vietnam War for saturation or "carpet" bombing. That was a misnomer, because when the plane's 108 500- or 750-pound bombs were dropped, their path of destruction was a long, thin trail, not a rectangle. Against Iraqi airfields, the bombing pattern would be perfectly suitable. The trick was getting the BUFFs into Iraq and out again unscathed.

Soon after he crossed into Iraqi airspace at 11 P.M. on January 17, Ross and his crew were alerted by their AWACS controller overhead that Iraqi fighter aircraft were in the area. By now the B-52s had split up into formations of two and three aircraft each. Ross listened as the AWACS controller dispatched several American fighter jets flying so-called combat air patrols after the enemies. No sooner were they chased away than the AWACS controller warned Ross again about the presence of hostile aircraft. Again Ross listened as the controller directed American fighter pilots toward the enemy jets.

Halfway to their target sites in northern Iraq, Ross and the other B-52 pilots outran all of their fighters. Now they were unprotected. Suddenly, Ross was alerted by the AWACS controller that two hostile aircraft were approaching him and his B-52 partner. "They said, 'We have no more cover for you. You're on your own if you go up.' Right after that," Ross said, "they identified another set of [Iraqi] fighters and said they appeared to be coming at us. I said, 'That's it, we're going home.'" Ross called Captain John Paganoni, the commander of the other B-52 in his formation, and told him to reverse direction and head south.

Minutes later, however, the AWACS controller radioed Ross with good news. The Iraqi planes had directed their attention toward other Allied aircraft in the area. "He said, 'If you want to go, go,'" Ross recalled. "'If you want to go home, go home. I've got nothing for you. There's no coverage. There's no help for you at all up there.'"

Ross ordered Paganoni to reverse direction, and the two B-52s were soon flying north once more. The hostile aircraft worried Ross, but he was equally concerned by the anti-aircraft fire he would find over his target sites. He knew that Air Force planners had developed an attrition model for the B-52 in the Gulf War, and it was not encouraging. B-52 pilots had two choices. They could fly into Iraq at a high level, or they could approach their targets low, hugging the ground. At high levels, the lumbering B-52s stood a good chance of being identified by Iraqi radar and targeted with radar-guided surface-to-air missiles. At low levels, the big bombers could fly under the enemy radar, but they would be highly vulnerable to anti-aircraft fire, historically the biggest killer of attack aircraft. "Low-level was definitely our better option," Ross said, "but a better option yet was to stay home and watch the first round on TV."

Ross and Paganoni were trying to stay between 300 and 500 feet off the ground. The landscape of northern Iraq is mountainous, however, and Ross was trying to fly by using the plane's infrared television images of the ground racing by below him. "It was quiet," Ross said, "too quiet."

A few minutes later, near other targets in the distance that the Iraqis were trying to protect, Ross saw bursts of anti-aircraft fire. It was evident the Iraqis were prepared to put up a fight. As Ross closed in on his target, five minutes before he was to release his bombs, another Allied bomber struck an Iraqi airfield across the valley roughly five miles away. The strike caused the entire valley to erupt with anti-aircraft fire. Ross was headed straight toward the wall of flak.

At first, Ross was able to skirt along the edge of the wall of Iraqi fire as he and his wingman drove the huge bombers down the valley toward their target. But as they neared the target, the two B-52s had to weave their way through the anti-aircraft barrage.

Ross maneuvered the big bomber over the airfield. "I wanted to get the damn bombs off the airplane," he said, "period." Using his targeting monitor, Ross lined up his target and the B-52's on-board computer dropped the bombs. "When they went off, you could see buildings on the airfield light up," Ross said.

The mission called for a two-aircraft strike. But when Ross went through, Paganoni lost the element of surprise. The Iraqis now knew the altitude of the bombers. "You can't hide a B-52 coming through," Ross said. Paganoni saw the danger and veered off the target, aborting his drop. The two planes turned and sped for home. "Then we went as fast as we could. We went to the limiting speed of the aircraft exiting the country," Ross said.

Ross and Paganoni and their crews had been over Iraq for nearly three hours; their total mission time would be nearly seventeen hours.

In Washington, General Powell expressed his satisfaction at the results of the first strikes. "I am rather pleased," he said laconically, "that we appear to have achieved tactical surprise." Powell had remained in his office throughout the previous night, catnapping on his couch, so that he could monitor the progress of the war. One floor above him, Dick Cheney had done the same thing, dispatching an aide to his home for a suitcase of fresh clothing and sending out for Chinese food.

During the course of the long evening, Powell and Cheney had been transfixed by the live images that CNN was broadcasting from Baghdad. But they had also been getting periodic reports from Schwarzkopf and Horner in Riyadh. Rear Admiral Michael McConnell, the senior intelligence officer for the Joint Chiefs of Staff, had been getting firsthand reports from Glosson. Aside from the surprise over the lack of a more effective response by the Iraqi air force, all of the senior officials briefed on the allies' performance in the first hours of the air war were also astonished that there had been so few equipment failures. Powell and Cheney had told President Bush that he should expect casualties on the order of 3 percent during the first hours of the war. With so many aircraft in the skies and the scope and reputed effectiveness of the air-defense system around Baghdad, it had seemed a reasonable estimate. On the morning of January 17, Bush told Powell and Cheney he was thrilled by the performance of the evening before and encouraged by the small number of casualties. In the first twenty-four hours of combat only one U.S. Navy F/A-18 fighter attack jet from the USS *Saratoga* stationed in the Red Sea and one British Tornado aircraft had been lost. Allied casualties were three—one American pilot and two British airmen.

At 3:03 A.M. on Friday, January 18, Saddam Hussein made good on at least one of his promises. The first of eight Iraqi Scud missiles landed in Israel. Six fell in and around Tel Aviv, two in Haifa. Though no one was killed in the attacks, forty-seven people were injured and 1,587 apartments were damaged, of which 399 would have to be either demolished or completely refurbished. Of all the weapons in Saddam Hussein's arsenal, the Scud would prove to be his best. Crude and relatively cheap, the Soviet-built thirty-seven-foot-long missile was guided by ballistics—that is, it was aimed and launched into the air, then fell onto its target. The Scuds were notoriously inaccurate, but when fired at major population centers they did not need much accuracy to generate civilian terror. And although the F-15s had targeted known Scud fixed launcher sites on the first night of the war, there were two dozen more mobile Scud launchers on the loose in Iraq.

At first, senior officials in the Israeli defense forces were convinced that the worst had happened. A missile that landed in south Tel Aviv had detonated a container of heating gas, fueling speculation that Israel had come under chemical attack. American officials in Israel worried because one of the six missiles aimed at Tel Aviv had exploded 100 feet above the ground; they suspected that it was an "air burst" warhead, one that could be used to disperse chemical agents over a wide area. In fact, the warhead was a defective Scud that had broken up upon reentry into the atmosphere. Nevertheless, U.S. embassy officials began making plans to evacuate their dependents to the southern port of Eilat, out of harm's way.

Minutes after the missiles landed, Defense Minister Moshe Arens picked up HAMMER RICK, the secure communications link to the Pentagon that that had been installed five days earlier. Confidential records show that Arens and Cheney would use the link another twenty-six times during the course of the war.

According to knowledgeable officials, Arens was subdued in this first conversation. Just a few days earlier, he had rejected the American offer of two Patriot missile batteries. Israeli crews had been training with the Patriot in Texas, but they had not yet completed their course. Shortly after his arrival in Israel on January 12, Lawrence Eagleburger had offered American crews until the Israeli crews were ready. Eagleburger's offer would be the latest in the on-again, off-again attitude of the United States toward providing Patriot missiles to Israel. Three separate commitments had been made to senior Israeli officials by the Bush administration in September to provide two Patriot batteries. But the administration's pledge had been undermined by senior Pentagon officials in the fall. Israel had been told by the Pentagon that it could not have the advanced PAC II Patriot batteries, as had been promised by the White House; instead, it would be given PAC I batteries, a system designed for anti-aircraft warfare and useless against Scud missiles.

On his visit to Israel just before the start of the air war, Eagleburger had promised quick delivery of the advanced Patriot missile batteries to defend Israel. In his conversation with Cheney in the early morning hours of January 18, Arens accepted the offer of the advanced Patriot missiles. He knew the Patriot would provide a needed psychological boost for the people of Israel. Thus he told Cheney that he would welcome their dispatch and their American crews as quickly as possible. Cheney assured

Arens that U.S. airmen were on search-and-destroy missions against the Scuds. Arens remained calm, but alert. He set up a cot, and was to sleep at his office for the next two weeks.

Even as Arens was speaking to Cheney, Israeli fighter aircraft had scrambled and were circling in a long practiced defensive operation concentrating on Jerusalem. General Avihu Bin-Nun, the chief of staff of the Israeli air force, was especially concerned that in his first offensive move against the Jewish state, Saddam Hussein would order his most accurate and lethal Sukhoi-24 aircraft to attack Jerusalem. General Bin-Nun calculated that Saddam would not risk firing one of his wildly inaccurate Scuds into the holy city for fear of hitting the al-Aqsa mosque or Arab East Jerusalem.

Less than thirty minutes after Cheney and Arens concluded their conversation, President Bush telephoned Prime Minister Shamir. Despite his penchant for telephone diplomacy, Bush spoke only rarely with Shamir. Relations between the two men had been chilly for nearly a year. Shamir was at home when he took the call from Bush, but he was receiving minute-by-minute updates on the Scud attack from Azriel Nevo, his military aide. Nevo confirmed that the Scud attack on south Tel Aviv was not chemical, and Shamir passed on the information to Bush, who expressed relief, according to U.S. and Israeli officials. Bush stressed to Shamir how destructive it would be for Israel to retaliate against Iraq now. The Allied air force was concentrating even as he spoke, Bush said, on rooting out the Scud missile launchers in western Iraq. The Patriot missile batteries would be sent as soon as possible. While he recognized Israel's right to retaliate, Bush said, the exercise of that right at this juncture would only be playing into Saddam's hands. Shamir listened, but he made no commitment.

Several hours later, the twelve ministers who made up the Israeli inner cabinet—known officially as the Ministerial Committee on National Security—met. They were joined by Israel's most senior military officials. The mood, said a participant, was one of "shock, and nobody wanted to act hastily." Bin-Nun argued for retaliation. He wanted his superiors to know that if they gave the word, the Israeli air force was ready to fight. But Dan Shomron, the chief of staff of the Israeli defense forces, expressed reservations. Ehud Barak, Shomron's deputy (who would ultimately succeed him as chief of staff), also expressed doubts. Shamir listened to the discussion impassively. Then he asked Shomron and his generals to draw up retaliation plans. The entire cabinet would review them, Shamir said, at its regular weekly meeting on Sunday. Privately, Shamir hoped it would never have to come to a decision. Bush and Eagleburger had emphasized that the allies could destroy the Iraqi Scuds in a couple of days. Perhaps by Sunday, Shamir thought, the Scuds would be gone, and Israel could rest more easily. If Saddam Hussein had wanted to make a point, Shamir thought, he had already done it with the one Scud attack. Perhaps there would be no more. On that note the meeting ended.

Despite Shamir's hopes that Saddam Hussein might be satisfied with a single attack on Israel, the Scud attacks continued. Air-raid sirens howled three more times on the Jewish sabbath. Israel was facing a new and dangerous situation. A cabinet meeting could no longer wait until Sunday, Shamir thought. An emergency meeting would have to be convened on the sabbath morning, an almost unheard-of occurrence.

An agitated Moshe Arens used the HAMMER RICK a second time late Friday evening. If Israel decided to retaliate against Iraq, Arens told Cheney, the United States would have to either provide the IFF codes for Allied aircraft, or "stand down" while Israeli planes flew through a specified air corridor across Jordan to attack the Scud-missile launchers in the H-2 and H-3 sectors of the desert of western Iraq. Cheney tried to reassure Arens, but as soon as he hung up, he telephoned the President.

Bush, too, was alarmed. He understood the pressure that Shamir and his cabinet were under, but he wanted to try to make Shamir understand that there were even greater risks if Israel did retaliate against Iraq. Bush dialed Shamir and said that while he would "understand" if Israel retaliated, doing so might very well weaken the coalition and strengthen Saddam's position. Israeli sources said that Bush concluded the conversation with a direct appeal: "I urge you not to retaliate."

Shamir listened, but never pledged that Israel would forswear retaliation. He was still willing to see if the combined U.S. military effort and the newly deployed Patriots would reduce the threat.

In Washington, it was nearly midnight on Friday, January 18, when Bush telephoned Shamir once again. The President knew that the inner cabinet was to meet in exactly two hours, 10 A.M. Saturday Israeli time. He wanted Shamir to know that the American pledge to come to Israel's aid was real. The two Patriot batteries had already been loaded onto an Air Force cargo plane. They would arrive in Tel Aviv at 12:30 P.M. local time.

Shamir thanked Bush again and hung up. "He did not repeat himself," Shamir said. "He tried to be persuasive, saying that we have a joint interest." Bush did not go into great detail, Shamir said, because "we knew what we were talking about. On the other hand, he also knew there might come a time that we wouldn't listen to him and we'd join the war. There was this possibility."

At the 10 A.M. meeting of the inner cabinet, the possibility of Israeli retaliation against Iraq was debated vigorously. Participants said it may well have been the most pivotal Israeli debate of the war. Religious ministers received special dispensations from rabbis to be driven from their Jerusalem homes for such an important meeting. Driving is forbidden on the sabbath, so the ministers were chauffeured by Druse Christian drivers.

Shamir began the meeting by asking the military to present its plans for a retaliatory strike against Iraq. General Bin-Nun spoke at some length. The allies had anywhere from four to twenty aircraft near the critical airfields of H-2 and H-3 in western Iraq at any given time. The Israeli air force could flood those areas with nearly double that number, Bin-Nun said. It would mean taking over the skies of western Iraq for two to three days, but anything that moved would be destroyed. The plan presumed shuttling hundreds of Israeli fighter aircraft through the airspace of neighboring Jordan.

Dan Shomron again demurred. Such a plan as that described by Bin-Nun, he argued, would certainly weaken the anti-Iraq coalition of nations. "The choice," Shomron said, "is between the immediate and the important." Also, he argued, there was no predicting how Jordan would react to the violation of its airspace. Jordan, after all, did have a defense pact with Syria. What would Hafez al-Assad do, Shomron asked, if Israel entered the war? Shamir was convinced that if Israel retaliated, it would almost certainly mean a war with Jordan. The Israeli prime minister had reportedly met with King Hussein in a European city before the war; the king had warned Shamir that if Israel entered the conflict against Iraq, his large Palestinian population would "rip up his palace" if Jordan did not retaliate against Israel.

Just as he had the day before, Ehud Barak seconded these reservations point by point. It was important, Barak said, for Israel to keep its eye on the big picture. "We made our view known," said a participant who disagreed with General Bin-Nun. "We all agreed [that] you know how a war starts, but not always how it finishes."

Ariel Sharon, the hard-line housing minister and former minister of defense, and Yuval Neeman, the science minister who had characterized the possibility of a visit by James Baker to Baghdad as "Chamberlain and Munich," pushed hard for retaliation. Rafael Eitan, the agriculture minister who had once served as chief of staff of the Israeli defense forces, supported Sharon and Neeman, but with some reservations. The thread of the argument was picked up at times by some other members of the cabinet. "We have to react," one participant told Shamir pointedly, "because the public expects us to do so."

"The public is confused," Shamir shot back. "Don't tell me what the public wants, because the public doesn't know what it wants. The public will agree with what we decide."

David Levy, the foreign minister, agreed with Shamir and argued forcefully against the hard-liners led by Sharon. Levy had taken on Sharon before, opposing his advocacy of the Israeli invasion of Lebanon in 1982. Pounding his fist on the long table in the cabinet room, Levy addressed himself directly to Sharon. "Only when you give me answers to A, B, C, D, then I am ready to act," he said. "I want to know how will the Jordanians act, how will the Syrians act? How will the U.S. respond? . . . Can we do this without them? You have to assure me to the last detail before I consent." As the debate continued, Moshe Arens, the defense minister, interjected on both sides. He understood the danger to the alliance against Iraq if Israel responded, but retaliation was an article of faith with him. Participants said Arens was truly divided on the issue.

Until the very end of the meeting, Shamir listened in silence. Longtime colleagues and political observers were amazed that he had not yet convened a kind of "kitchen cabinet," as Golda Meir had during the Yom Kippur War. Shamir had consulted on a regular basis with Arens and to a lesser extent with Levy and with Dan Meridor, the justice minister, and a couple of trusted aides. But he had not expanded his circle of confidants. One of Israel's most conservative and hard-line prime ministers, Shamir clung as tenaciously as anyone to the principles that had guaranteed Israel's security. All the ministers now waited to hear Shamir's view. The room was hushed, and uncharacteristically, the usually terse Shamir spoke for a full fifteen minutes. "I am going to surprise you," Shamir said. "I do not think we should react. This is what Saddam wants, to transform the war into one between Arabs and Israel. What do we gain from this, just to have the satisfaction that we retaliated?" Shamir believed that the coalition arrayed against Iraq was prepared to humble or destroy one of Israel's most dangerous enemies. If Israel retaliated, Shamir said, Saddam might suddenly withdraw his tanks from Kuwait and assemble a new Arab coalition, which he would lead against Israel in a bloody confrontation on the ground. Shamir was also worried about what might happen in Jordan. The destruction of the buffer of the Jordanian monarchy would not be in Israel's interest.

The meeting ended without a vote. Shamir had had the last word. Despite the Iraqi missiles that would continue to rain on it during the coming days, Israel would exercise restraint.

Late in the morning of January 19, Captain Cesar "Rico" Rodriguez was flying what was known as a combat-air-patrol mission along Iraq's ragged southern border with Saudi Arabia. Pilots flying such missions described themselves as "cap-ing." Rodriguez was the flight leader of a four-ship of F-15Cs code-named Citgo, which had taken off from the large Saudi air base at Tabuk. Rodriguez and his three colleagues from the 33rd Tactical Fighter Wing at Eglin Air Force Base, Florida, each carried four AIM-7 Sparrow radar-guided missiles, four AIM-9 Sidewinder heat-seeking missiles, and three tanks of fuel.

After taking off at 9 A.M., Rodriguez's four-ship had joined up in a wall of F-15s, a line abreast about a mile apart. They arrived at their flying stations northeast of Tabuk and relieved planes that had been in the air for more than four hours.

South of Rodriguez, just inside the Saudi border, American AWACS and spy planes flew in long, lazy patterns. To their north, inside Iraq, were airfields that the Americans had designated as H-2 and H-3. Those and other bases located at Mudesas, al-Assad, and al-Taqaddum were among the most likely locations from which Iraqi fighters or interceptors might come up to engage Allied aircraft. Rodriguez's mission was to protect the AWACS, spy aircraft, and tankers if Iraqi fighters came south.

Not long into his mission, Rodriguez received a call from an AWACS controller. A four-ship of F-15s coming out of the Saudi base at Tabuk would join with a package of F-16s at a point well south of the Saudi-Iraqi border to fly up and attack a target just southwest of Baghdad, the controller said. Citgo's new assignment was to fly up and sweep behind this fleet of aircraft, making sure that no Iraqi fighters were on their tails as they exited Iraq.

Rodriguez topped up his tanks from a KC-135 refueling aircraft. He detailed two Citgo pilots to stay on station, protecting the AWACS. He and his wingman, Craig Underhill, would be the primary sweepers behind the attack package. Rodriguez calculated that he could reconnoiter with the package of attack aircraft just as it turned south after bombing its targets near Baghdad. Flying above them, at 30,000 feet, Rodriguez could watch the package of aircraft as they turned south, alert them if hostile aircraft were on their tail, and chase the Iraqis off if necessary. Rodriguez and Underhill headed north.

Just as the strike package was hitting its target, a radar operator aboard the AWACS aircraft radioed Rodriguez. The Iraqis apparently had seen the strike package on their radars and had launched interceptors. "Citgo 25, pop-up contact. Forty north of target," the controller said. Since Rodriguez was forty miles south of the bombing target, this meant that the Iraqi interceptors were eighty miles north of his position.

Rodriguez was searching the sky to his north with his radar. "I was scared," he later said, "thinking, it's really going to happen, sports fans."

The radar on his F-15 told Rodriguez where the friendly American strike aircraft were. Rodriguez and Underhill, who was known by his buddies as "Mole," were about a mile abreast of each other in tactical formation. Rodriguez, using his call sign Citgo 25, radioed Underhill. "Twenty-five has friendlies thirty-right, forty miles."

"Two same," Underhill replied. He had seen the same thing.

Next Rodriguez picked up two new contacts, about forty miles north of the Allied aircraft. These two aircraft were not emitting the transponder codes that indicated that an airplane was friendly, however. The AWACS controllers verified to him that the two contacts forty miles north were potentially hostile.

Rodriguez and Underhill headed down at Mach 1.1 on a descent from 30,000 feet toward the two planes to the north. It was a clear day. Rodriguez and Underhill had reached the reconnoiter point, too. Below him, Rodriguez could see the lead F-15s of the strike package heading south. Next a trickle of F-16s passed by. Rodriguez felt better. The friendlies were past. Anything left would be an enemy.

The two contacts were now twenty-five miles off the nose of Rodriguez's F-15. The contacts were chasing the strike package. Rodriguez received word that the two planes had locked their radars onto the last of the American F-16 fighter aircraft. The F-16s were bolting south, though, and the Iraqi MiGs were not close enough to shoot them.

Rodriguez and Underhill were approaching the MiGs at a sharp angle from the MiGs' left side. The radar contacts were good and clean. Quickly, Rodriguez and Underhill agreed on how they would attack. Rodriguez moved a lever on his throttle and put the cursor on his radar screen onto the hostile aircraft. Then he pushed another button on the throttle. That "locked up" the Iraqi plane with his missile-guidance radar. F-15 pilots referred to this as their "death ray." Usually, they said, when it was activated, it set off the enemy plane's radar-warning receiver, producing a high-pitched squeal in the ears of the targeted pilot.

Seconds after Rodriguez locked onto the Iraqi aircraft, the MiG turned and ran north. Evidently, he had heard the death ray. "The western leader is dragging northbound," Rodriguez radioed to Underhill.

"No contact on east guy," Underhill replied. He could not get a firm radar lock on the second MiG.

Rodriguez pushed the button on the main control stick to break his radar lock on the first Iraqi MiG. He was closer than Underhill to the second MiG, close enough to get a good radar lock. The second MiG, Rodriguez saw, was just eighteen miles away from him. It had turned suddenly and was accelerating north. The death ray had chased it off too. Rodriguez decided not to pursue it.

Rodriguez and Underhill were just about to turn for home, when the AWACS controller called again. "Two pop-up targets," the controller said, "330 for thirteen." The "330" meant that the hostile aircraft were 30 degrees to the left of their nose. Thirteen was the number of miles between Rodriguez and Underhill and the Iraqi aircraft. That was damn close, Rodriguez thought.

"I just started acting on instinct," Rodriguez said. He and Underhill both ejected their extra fuel tanks so that they would have greater speed and maneuverability. Rodriguez fixed his missile-targeting radar on the first aircraft. "I locked onto the leader right off the bat," Rodriguez said. "And he's eight miles off my nose, and he's at 10,000 feet. I'm at about 2,000 feet coming up underneath him. We're now trying to get AWACS to declare hostile bandits so we can shoot. So I call 'Hot left' to Mole, and we both turn left. And then when I get the lock on him, I call the same frequency that both AWACS and Mole are on and I say, 'Lock eight miles, 10,000.' " The aircraft targets were at 10,000 feet, just eight miles away.

"Two same," Underhill replied. He had the same fix on the potentially hostile aircraft.

Rodriguez and Underhill closed to within five miles of the jets. "Of all my overall aircraft systems, the one I really needed right then wasn't working," Rodriguez said, "and that was my radar-warning receiver that would tell me if [the enemy pilot] is locked onto me. So I suspected the worst case, and I reacted defensively. As I went into my turn, Mole has locked up the leader, and I still can't pick up a visual on them. And just as we're coming on to them, the MiGs are trying to run down a strike package of [U.S.] Navy A-7s. So I go into my defensive turn and Mole drives in . . . and just then AWACS calls 'Hostile, hostile, hostile!' And Mole, who has his guy locked up, calls 'Fox one,' meaning he just fired an AIM-7 radar missile. Mole takes his shot and starts coming toward me because he has to maintain radar illumination of the target. And I saw his missile climb up, and then the motor stops burning. And as I'm starting to hook the corner, I see this guy blow up. Mole is basically looking at me, making sure he is still illuminating the target. And he hears me call 'Splash one, splash one.' He turns around and sees a disintegrated MiG-29."

In the cockpit of his F-15, Rodriguez received a new call from the AWACS controller. "Second bandit, three miles in trail from the leader." Rodriguez looked through the first MiG's fireball and identified the second aircraft on his radar. "When I picked up the second guy, I told Mole to come right to north," Rodriguez said, "and now we'll come at this guy to engage him. The MiG is now coming in, and Mole locks him up with his radar. I pull in one direction and Mole goes on in, and then the MiG pulls an S turn." For a moment, the Iraqi's move broke their radar lock.

"He starts coming back," Rodriguez said, "and as he comes back, I start to cut the corner and start chasing him."

"Possible V.I.D. friendly," Underhill radioed Rodriguez. Underhill had visually identified the aircraft, and it looked like it might not be an Iraqi jet after all. Its profile resembled that of an American F-15.

Rodriguez refrained from firing. "As we come in, he starts turning the corner," Rodriguez said, "and now I'm getting a good look at him. And I see that he is in fact a bandit."

"Negative V.I.D. friendly," Rodriguez called to Underhill. "Hostile, hostile, hostile!"

The Iraqi pilot held the MiG fighter in a hard turn. As he came out of it, he was heading straight for Rodriguez.

As Underhill watched the dogfight from above, Rodriguez and the MiG went into a series of sharp turns. The two aircraft were just a few thousand feet apart. "I'm gaining some angles on him," Rodriguez said, "and I'm now about 40 degrees off his tail and about 4,000 feet behind him." Rodriguez closed to 3,500 feet.

In front of Rodriguez, the Iraqi pilot rolled upside-down, apparently preparing to do a downward loop called a split S that would bring him out heading in the opposite direction. But the two planes were very close to the ground.

"He started at about 9,000 feet, then he was around 4,000 feet and then at this time he's at about 1,000," Rodriguez said. "So when he's at 1,000 feet, he trys to do this maneuver that probably takes about 3,000 feet to accomplish. I'm in a pretty good position all the way around. But I know how low we're getting. I'm about 1,000 feet off the ground, and he's slightly below me. And when I see him do that, I threaten him with my nose."

Trying to evade Rodriguez, the Iraqi pilot dived downward.

"He impacts the ground," Rodriguez said. "Hits the dirt." The engagement, Rodriguez said, had taken less than two minutes.

During his first mission into northern Iraq, on January 20, Mike Worden and the other Wild Weasel pilots got their first close look at Saddam Hussein's war machine. "You would not have believed how much military hardware was scattered through that big country," he said. "It was not as dense as central Europe. But I couldn't believe that a country like this was as armed to the teeth as it was. . . . From 30,000 feet [north of Baghdad], one could count four fighter bases, and even further up north, one could look around and see a Scud storage facility, here's another weapons dump, a nuclear-research facility, a missile-development facility, and several more military facilities all at once."

Among the Wild Weasels, sixteen planes—ten F-16s and six F-4Gs— had left Incirlik on this particular mission, but six planes had had to turn back because of mechanical difficulties. They had been deployed without maintenance crews. Worden, the mission leader, flew on in one of the nine F-16s. Piloting the single remaining F-4G Wild Weasel was Lieutenant Colonel William "Mild Bill" Miller. In the backseat of Miller's F-4G was Captain Bobby "Stump" D'Amico, the Wild Weasel's electronic-warfare officer.

As the aircraft approached Turkey's southern border with Iraq, they saw that there was a deck of clouds ahead. With the other missions departing

Incirlik that afternoon, there were approximately sixty American aircraft in the immediate area of the Iraq-Turkey border.

Just inside Iraq, Worden received a radio call from Mild Bill Miller. The heart of the Wild Weasel is a piece of electronic hardware known as the APR-47, which pinpoints the location of enemy surface-to-air missile launchers and radar facilities. Locating those targets was critical to the F-16s' mission of firing high-speed anti-radar missiles at the Iraqi radars.

"APR-47," Miller called. "Dead."

"Continue," Worden radioed back. The F-4G was not a high-tech fighter like the F-15s and 16s, but it did carry a radar-guided anti-air missile. Worden thought it best to keep Mild Bill in the package.

Flying at 9½ miles a minute, the Wild Weasels, accompanied by F-15Cs from Bitburg, Germany, were now twenty miles inside Iraq. Worden's was the lead Wild Weasel. Off to the southwest of the Wild Weasels was a four-ship of F-15Cs whose call sign was Rambo. Captain Steve "Gunga Din" Dingee was their leader, flying Rambo 1. In his flight were Captain Larry Ludwig in Rambo 2, Captain Dave Prather in Rambo 3, and First Lieutenant Dave Sveden in Rambo 4.

An AWACS aircraft suddenly alerted the strike package to two scrambling Iraqi aircraft taking off from an air base about twenty miles south of Mosul. Within seconds of receiving the alert, the Rambo four-ship took off toward the two Iraqi Mirage F-1 fighter jets that had just popped up on the AWACS radar screen.

Meanwhile, Worden's group continued south toward targets near the northern Iraqi city of Kirkuk. The area was well defended by Soviet-built SA-3 and SAM surface-to-air missile batteries. "We came in," Worden recalled, "and the SAMs started coming up. But we didn't have any [functioning] F-4Gs to pinpoint the exact location. So we had to employ a degraded backup engagement plan."

There was a deck of clouds at about 27,000 feet, and dusk was falling. Without a fully functioning F-4G to guide him, Worden wanted to get beneath the cloud cover so he could at least see what was coming up at him. The anti-aircraft flak began to intensify. Worden dove. "We were running toward Kirkuk," he said, "and as I ducked under the weather, the package followed me because I'm in front, and we were looking for firings off the ground. And of course everybody's like a tree full of owls up there."

Focusing on the threat from the ground, the entire Wild Weasel package was suddenly interrupted by a call on their radios: "Break left." This meant that a missile was approaching from behind. "Several aircraft in the package began turning hard to the left," Worden said, "to evade this big smoking missile—a huge missile like a telephone pole—that came steaming up through the formation." But it was only a "friendly."

From the middle of the strike package, Captain Brad Cushman had locked in on one of the Iraqi surface-to-air missile batteries. Watching as some of the package began breaking left, Cushman called again on the radio: "Skip it, it's a HARM." The missile was American, Cushman was saying. He had just fired his HARM missile at the SAM battery below, from his F-16 Wild Weasel. The package turned back on course and headed for Kirkuk.

"Oh, thank you," Worden thought. "Thank you." He meant it.

Seconds after Cushman fired the missile, with the rest of the strike package five to six miles behind him, Worden was maneuvering his F-16 Wild Weasel into position to fire his missile. In his cockpit, Worden's audio-warning system was squealing. A surface-to-air missile battery below had illuminated his aircraft. But that meant they had also revealed themselves, and now he could shoot them too. Worden knew that the rest of the strike package was about to enter what fighter pilots called the "lethal envelope."

Banking his F-16 in a hard turn to try to break the radar lock on him, Worden flicked on his electronic-jamming equipment and slammed the button on the left side of his cockpit to eject metallic chaff and hot flares, which confuse radar and heat-seeking missiles. By the end of the air war, Worden's knuckles would be bloody from slamming the chaff and flares button so often. "They could be shooting when I shoot," said Worden. "It's like a gunfight." As Worden was evading the Iraqi radar, Captain Bob Harvey fired another missile into the target area from a different direction.

The strikers were now rolling in on their targets from 25,000 feet. As their first bombs exploded, the anti-aircraft fire intensified dramatically from all quadrants. Captain Jim Whitton, in the middle of the strike package, began his roll in on his target. His first challenge was to find his target through the barrage of flak and explosions on the ground. As he found his target and pointed the nose of his fighter downward, his audio-warning system alerted him to impending surface-to-air missile launches against his aircraft. He dispensed chaff and picked his way through the numerous fireballs of flak coming up at him. Just he released his ordnance, Whitton noticed a flash, then an explosion on the missile battery near his target. Captain Cushman's missile had found its target, the hit confirmed by the sudden absence of the squeal from Whitton's audio-warning system.

As he pulled away from the target, Whitton noticed two Iraqi MiGs scrambling off the runway ahead, below him and to the left. Seizing the opportunity, Whitton accelerated down toward the MiGs as they lifted off. Whitton fired one heat-seeking missile at each MiG as he maneuvered his aircraft through a curtain of anti-aircraft fire. When the second missile left his fighter, Whitton lit his afterburners, dispensed chaff, jettisoned his external fuel tanks, and climbed nearly straight up to escape the cauldron he had entered.

A few minutes later, Worden's watch indicated that the last bomber should have been off target by now. His Wild Weasel package could begin the trek back to Incirlik. Just then, however, Worden and the other pilots heard a loud voice over the radio, intoning, "IP [initial point] inbound"— the flight of fighter aircraft that had turned to react to the HARM missile earlier was behind schedule and had only now just hit their "initial point," where they were to begin their bombing run. The radio call alerted the F-16 Wild Weasels and F-15 Eagles to stay in the area to provide air cover and protection against the anti-aircraft batteries below.

Worden turned south one final time. Almost immediately, another of the Iraqi Soviet-built batteries illuminated Worden's plane with its radar. Worden fired a second missile and again began to take evasive maneuvers to break the anti-aircraft battery's radar lock on him.

Meanwhile the Rambo flight of F-15Cs had split in half to outflank the two Iraqi Mirages and began to descend on their prey. The Iraqi pilots were accelerating and climbing through 7,000 feet headed for the American strike package. As Captains Dingee and Ludwig in the Rambo 1 and 2 aircraft approached their missile-launch parameters, the Iraqi pilots, electronically warned of the impending approach, began to turn away. Their turn to avoid Rambo 1 and 2 brought them straight into the sights of the flanking Rambo 3 and 4 aircraft. Captain Prather and Lieutenant Sveden each fired a radar-guided missile. Each missile struck its mark, destroying the two Iraqi aircraft.

As Worden was coming out of his second evasive maneuver, he saw the fireball of a burning Iraqi fighter cartwheel down into the valley about ten miles northwest of him. In the gathering dusk, he saw two silhouettes of Prather and Sveden's victorious F-15s climbing back up to join the Wild Weasels to escort the package north and out of Iraq.

By the end of the third day of the air war, January 19, the Allied air force had flown nearly 2,000 combat sorties and suffered twelve aircraft lost in combat. By the end of the first week of the air war, there would be twenty-six downed Allied aircraft, including five non-combat losses. One fifth of the losses would be British Tornados, all but one lost on low-level attacks on Iraqi airfields. Twenty-four servicemen were missing in action: thirteen Americans, eight British, two Italians, and one Kuwaiti. Seven Americans had died, only one in combat. Five of the Americans listed as missing in action were believed to be prisoners of war inside Iraq and Kuwait.

On January 20, Lawrence Eagleburger stepped off a State Department jet at Tel Aviv's Ben-Gurion International Airport. It was his second visit to Israel in a week. Few Israeli officials had any illusions about his intentions. "I'd say he was sent here less to hold our hand," one official said, "than to stay our hand."

In a meeting with Shamir shortly after he arrived, Eagleburger was subjected to a long, angry speech. Shamir restated his pledges to President Bush. Israel would not launch a preemptive strike against Iraq, and Shamir would notify Bush personally of any decision on the part of his government to retaliate against Iraq. You want Israel not to retaliate, Shamir told Eagleburger, but you must give us the minimum of protection. There were not nearly enough of the Patriot missile batteries to protect Israel's major population centers, Shamir complained. Eagleburger replied that he would check on the matter. (Two more of the batteries would arrive in Israel by week's end.)

Shamir also complained to Eagleburger that the United States was deliberately delaying the dissemination of satellite intelligence data to Israel by as much as twenty-four hours. Shamir had been told that the explanation for the delay was purely technical, but the prime minister told Eagleburger that he believed the reason was political. The Bush administration was trying to prevent Israel from retaliating against Iraq. Eagleburger pledged that he would see what could be done to reduce the delay. (In fact, U.S. intelligence officials would continue to withhold so-called real-time satellite data from Israel throughout the war.)

Shamir had other complaints as well. For instance, General Schwarzkopf had been quoted as saying that the chances of an Israeli being struck by a

Scud missile were far less than that of a resident of Georgia being struck by summer lightning. Eagleburger pointed out that the relations between Washington and Jerusalem had been less than both parties had hoped for. But the conflict with Iraq offered both parties a rare opportunity to reinvigorate the relationship. If Shamir declined to retaliate against Iraq, Eagleburger said, according to a participant in the meeting, it could mean "turning around his whole relationship with the President and the secretary of state." Once again, Shamir made no commitment.

Despite the obvious difficulty of his mission, many Israeli officials said Eagleburger's visits served an important purpose. Both he and Paul Wolfowitz, the under secretary of defense for policy, were trusted by Shamir and his closest advisers. When they promised to check on something, such as the shipment of more modern Patriot missile batteries, it took a bit of time. This provided a measure of reassurance that Washington wanted to work with Israel, thus making it more difficult for the hawks in Shamir's cabinet to advocate immediate retaliation. "Eagleburger's [second] visit," said one knowledgeable U.S. official, "gave time for the policy of restraint to firm up."

By the end of the first full week of the air campaign, Chuck Horner and Buster Glosson were generally pleased with the way things were going. The two generals had settled into a routine. Glosson would take the graveyard shift, working until 7 A.M., when Horner would relieve him.

Coalition aircraft had hit all of the important strategic targets listed in the mammoth air-tasking order. In some cases, Allied aircraft had been able to return to targets and strike them a second time.

Glosson knew more about the targets of Desert Storm than perhaps anyone in the Central Command, officials said. Since September, Glosson's intelligence team had been plotting the location of Iraqi radars, surface-to-air missile batteries, airfields, and command-and-control centers. Glosson's target planners had sites plotted on a huge wall map in what they called the Black Hole, a room in the basement of the Royal Saudi Air Force headquarters in central Riyadh where the offensive operation had been planned throughout the fall.

In his preparations for an air war against the Iraqi forces, Glosson had been given carte blanche. "Anything I asked for," he said, "I got. I talked to the people who designed and built the command-and-control bunkers in Iraq. I . . . took the blueprints and went over the thing, hunting for the exact place to have the F-117s bomb, with the highest probability of going all the way down to the bottom of the bunker." During the 5½ months before Desert Shield was transformed into Desert Storm, Glosson had sent his people to Europe and elsewhere to persuade construction companies, design firms, and engineering outfits to allow their representatives—the people who had actually built the structures being targeted in Iraq—to talk to them. In this way, Glosson had received detailed information on all five of Saddam's primary command-and-control bunkers. He had information on Iraq's five air defense system centers. In many of the facilities he intended to target, Glosson knew where every door was located. He knew the Iraqis had a computer system called Qari (Iraq spelled backwards) to tell them which aircraft and which surface-to-air missile batteries to fire if they came under attack.

Glosson was good friends with Rear Admiral Mike McConnell, the Joint Chief's director of intelligence. The two men usually talked several times a day, which was invaluable to Glosson in two major ways.

First, McConnell always had the latest information: he met with Cheney and Powell twice a day, he frequently joined them in briefing the President, and he regularly accompanied General Tom Kelly to the daily air-war briefings in the Pentagon press room. Before pertinent bits of information found their way through Schwarzkopf to Glosson, Glosson had already heard them.

Second, even though Glosson was cleared to receive all levels of intelligence, a quick phone call to McConnell could bypass the bureaucratic channels at the Pentagon, the CIA, or the National Security Agency. Often within twenty minutes after talking with McConnell, Glosson would have a hard copy of the material he needed. Glosson would then rush the new information into the computerized attack-planning system. An hour after that, the bomber or fighter pilot who was planning that day's mission had a copy.

There were still a host of problems to be addressed. Scuds continued to fall intermittently on Israel, as well as on Saudi Arabia (where five Scuds landed the first week). Senior officers in the Central Command insisted that the missiles were not "militarily significant," but they diverted significant amounts of Allied aircraft and prevented Horner and Glosson from concentrating more intensive firepower on important Iraqi targets like Saddam Hussein's Republican Guard divisions, whose capabilities had not been seriously impaired so far.

Beginning on the evening of January 20, Horner and Glosson ordered between 600 and 700 combat aircraft into western and southern Iraq every twenty-four hours. Their sole mission was to hunt Scuds, which were proving damnably hard to find. Carried on trailerlike mobile launchers forty feet long, the Scuds were easily hidden in a building or in a wadi by day, then moved at night into firing position. U.S. intelligence analysts had guessed at the start of the war that the Iraqis had no more than two dozen mobile Scud launchers. In the end, they would revise their estimate upward to several hundred.

The great Scud hunt represented a commitment of between 25 and 30 percent of the entire coalition air force. Given the size of the coalition's commitment to the destruction of the Iraqi Scud missiles, it was difficult to support the dismissal by the Central Command of their military insignificance.

The political effect of the Scud missiles also could not be ignored, as President Bush and his advisers well knew. On January 22, a Scud missile had landed in the Tel Aviv suburb of Ramat Gan; three people had died of heart attacks and ninety-six more were injured, six of them seriously. One of the American-manned Patriot missile batteries had downed a Scud that night, but the Patriot battery hadn't stopped a second Scud, Israeli military intelligence officials said. Both American and Israeli officials said that the Patriot itself had done serious damage in Ramat Gan, though it was unclear whether it had caused any deaths or serious injuries. This was by far the most serious Scud attack on Israel. The next day another Scud landed in Haifa. Bush and his advisers knew that Israel could not be expected to hold off retaliating for very much longer.

The effort to find and destroy Scuds was delaying the thorough and rapid destruction of other targets. But General Schwarzkopf was determined not to commit any of his ground forces until the Air Force had completed its attack. It was one of the many paradoxes of this war, Schwarzkopf told aides: the mud soldier in him wanted the air war to continue a while longer.

But it was not that easy. For seven days, every pilot dispatched on a mission—and they included airmen from the United States, Saudi Arabia, Britain, France, Canada, Italy, Kuwait, Bahrain, and Qatar—had been plagued by bad weather. Meteorologists who had studied the Persian Gulf closely described the weather from January 16 to January 23 as the worst in a decade. That fact was reflected in the number and effectiveness of sorties by Allied aircraft. In seven days of war, coalition aircraft had flown just over 12,000 sorties, of which slightly more than 6,000 were combat sorties by bombers and fighter aircraft; the remainder were support missions, by refueling tankers and the like. Had the weather been better, Air Force officials said, the numbers could have been significantly higher. While U.S. pilots like Mike Worden, Dave Ross, and Jon Kelk had scored significant successes in the air war to date, many more pilots had returned to their bases, their ordnance undelivered because of the inclement weather.

Another little known fact about the air campaign was that it was, overwhelmingly, an American war. The briefings the Central Command gave news reporters each day took pains to stress the contributions of Allied fliers. But the fact was that, collectively, the allies never flew more than 15 percent of the total number of combat and support missions in the Gulf conflict. (It is true that British airmen suffered a disproportionate number of casualties in the early days of the campaign, because of the highly dangerous, low-level attack runs they made on Iraqi airfields.) Notwithstanding the courageous performances of a great many Allied airmen, the overwhelming burden for the prosecution of the air campaign was borne by the fliers of the U.S. Air Force, Navy, and Marine Corps. And that's precisely how Schwarzkopf and his senior air commanders wanted it.

As the weather began to clear just over one week into the war, Saddam Hussein ordered his army to begin flooding the Persian Gulf with slick, black crude oil. President Bush quickly condemned this as "environmental terrorism." The oil slick seemed designed to foil an expected amphibious landing by Marines on the beaches of Kuwait City.

In the United States the euphoria that had been generated by television coverage of the first twenty-four hours had begun to dissipate. Suddenly, the so-called Nintendo war characterized by smart bombs and slick gun-camera footage seemed much more messy. Downed airmen, Americans and allies, had been paraded before Iraqi television cameras reciting condemnations of the war (in clear violation of the Geneva Conventions). And with Scuds continuing to fall, the prophecy of General Colin Powell was remembered. A war with Iraq, Powell had told George Bush on August 4, two days after the invasion of Kuwait, would not be another Panama, done in a day. The intoxication of war began to give way to sober reality.

At a midmorning news conference at the Pentagon on January 23, Powell addressed the nation's somber mood directly. It was the kind of performance that none of Bush's other close advisers could have carried off. As he outlined the Pentagon strategy for the continued prosecution of the war against the Iraqi army, Powell sounded like nothing so much as a dispassionate surgeon describing the procedure for removing a noxious growth. "Our strategy to go after this army," Powell said, "is very, very simple. First we are going to cut it off. And then we are going to kill it." The United States and its allies, Powell said, would isolate the "brains of the operation." That was being done even as he spoke, with strikes at Saddam Hussein's command-and-control network. Next, they would excise deposits of food and ammunition, and then they would tie off movement of supplies and reinforcement to Iraqi troops in Kuwait. It was, as the President said to several aides, an "enormously impressive" performance.

CHAPTER 16

BUSH SETS A DEADLINE

WITH DESERT STORM well into its second week, the number of combat sorties began increasing daily. Schwarzkopf, Horner, and Glosson followed the progress of the air campaign through the eyes of the AWACS. Flying racetrack patterns above the battlefield, keeping track of all Allied aircraft was one half of the AWACS' mission. The other half involved tracking enemy aircraft, listening in on Iraqi air- and ground-forces radio transmissions, and directing Allied aircraft toward attacking Iraqi fighter aircraft. The same picture that a radar controller monitored on his screen at his tiny desk aboard the AWACS was transmitted to the Central Command headquarters in Riyadh. Despite the bad weather, at times during the first and second week of Operation Desert Storm, the skies over Iraq and Kuwait were thicker with airplanes than those over Atlanta or Chicago on a busy weekday.

Schwarzkopf, Horner, and Glosson worried that the Iraqi air force would suddenly rise to fight or that Saddam Hussein would order a Tet Offensive–type raid, swarming sixty or more attack aircraft toward Saudi Arabia or Israel. To counter such a possibility, AWACS crews were often ordered to remain aloft for longer than twelve hours. With in-flight refueling, the AWACS could fly for as long as twenty-two hours at a stretch. During the first two weeks of Operation Desert Storm, AWACS crews routinely worked nineteen hours a day. This included two hours of debriefing after each mission. After a mission, the crews got about eighteen hours of rest. The planes got little rest, however, and things sometimes broke down. The AWACS flew at more than 500 miles an hour, often in heavy winds. The rough weather during the first week of the war had also made things more difficult. Frequencies on some of the AWACS' electronic gear went bad. White noise had drowned out some radio channels. Radar visibility had sometimes been severely constricted.

Shortly after dusk fell on Iraq on January 24, the mission of the AWACS crews in the Gulf conflict promised to became significantly more complicated. Under cover of darkness, but before the heaviest American bombing raids began, an Iraqi Boeing 727 that had been converted to an airborne military command-and-control post departed from an air base near Baghdad with a Soviet-built Il-76 military transport plane. AWACS controllers watched as both crossed the border less than an hour later into western Iran. The two aircraft landed at an Iranian air base near the city of Isfahan. A day earlier, Soviet officials confirmed, Saddam had ordered the execution of his air force chief and chief of Iraqi air defenses, General Muzahim Saab Hassan. Scores of Iraqi military aircraft would follow these first two planes to Iran. Senior Iraqi officials confirmed after the war that Saddam Hussein had decided to move what was left of his air force into Iran.

Horner and Glosson instructed the AWACS crews to watch the borders of Iran, as well as those of Iraq. Iran was no friend of the United States, and it was not inconceivable that Iraqi planes could strike at coalition aircraft from bases inside Iran. "It didn't make any difference to us if they came out of Iraq or Iran," said Colonel Gary Voellger, commander of the 552nd AWACS Wing. "We'd shoot them down."

As General Schwarzkopf and his principal ground-force commanders, Army Lieutenant General John Yeosock and Marine Lieutenant General Walter Boomer, contemplated the start of a ground campaign, they were eager for Horner and Glosson to begin concentrating on tanks, artillery, ammunition stockpiles, trucks, and troop concentrations. Destroying these targets was the essence of battlefield preparation.

But some Air Force officials disagreed on the timetable. At the heart of the dispute was a basic difference over what wins wars. During the 1970s and 1980s, U.S. military tacticians had adopted the thinking of Clausewitz, who was convinced that an enemy could be defeated by striking at his "center of gravity." That much, at least, seemed to make sense. The problem was in defining that center of gravity for the Iraqis. Air commanders and ground commanders saw Iraq's center of gravity very differently. In the Army's view, the Iraqi center of gravity was its Republican Guard, the eight divisions that constituted Iraq's smartest, best-equipped and -trained, and most loyal forces. Defeat the guard, Army brass argued, and the rest of the Iraqi force would collapse and abandon Kuwait.

Much of the initial planning for the air war had come out of a little-known office in the basement of the Pentagon known only as Checkmate. Checkmate had been in existence for a decade, functioning as a shop that tried to make realistic estimates of Soviet operational capabilities. Mainly staffed by Air Force officers, it was run by an Air Force colonel named John Warden, who had published a book in 1989 entitled *The Air Campaign— Planning for Combat.* Some thought it brilliant.

Immediately after the Iraqi invasion of Kuwait, according to Major General Perry Smith, a retired Air Force general and CNN Gulf War commentator, and former Air Force Chief of Staff General Michael Dugan, the Checkmate division turned to a new task: drafting a plan for an air option against Iraq. By most accounts, it was Warden and his Checkmate staff who were responsible for the four-phased air campaign. While the plan called for a final phase in which the focus shifted to support of ground operations, strategic bombing would continue throughout the air and ground war.

Since the plan came out of the Pentagon, it met resistance at Central Command headquarters in Riyadh. By some accounts, the greatest resistance came from Lieutenant General Horner, who thought the Pentagon existed to support his war plans, and not the reverse. But there was another, more substantive issue. The Air Force had years earlier signed on to something called AirLand Battle, a way of fighting the Soviets in which the Air Force largely served to support the ground forces. Horner, some said, saw the Checkmate plan as a deviation from AirLand Battle and a return to the old ways, with the Air Force fighting its own war. But Schwarzkopf had been briefed on August 10 by the Checkmate team and he approved their plan, and Powell liked it as well.

The key, then, was to refine it to accomplish all purposes. Glosson was one air officer who had not read Warden's book. Glosson's supporters said he came to the view that the Checkmate planners' theory about the Iraqi centers of gravity was too parochial.

They regarded Iraq's center of gravity as a set of concentric circles. In the center was Saddam Hussein. Next came the command-and-control and communications network. After that came the Iraqi infrastructure, which, to the Air Force staff was electrical plants and oil refineries. Last was the military, but that meant Iraqi airplanes and weapons of mass destruction. The Republican Guard was not on the list.

Glosson argued that the center of Iraqi gravity was, first and foremost, the ability of the Iraqi leadership to command and control its military and to inform its populace. Center of Gravity 2, Glosson said, should be the enemy's facilities for research and production of biological, chemical and nuclear weapons. Center 3, he continued, should be the Iraqi military, including the Republican Guard, the air force, the Scud missile launchers, and even terrorists. Center 4, in Glosson's judgment, should be the Iraqi maintenance and resupply effort.

Glosson's supporters said it was he who readjusted the plan. But at least one high-level Central Command planner contended Glosson himself had to be "dragged kicking and screaming," by the ground commanders, to apportioning more air resources to bombing Iraq's ground forces.

Proponents of the Checkmate view argued that the intensified Scud hunting ordered by Washington had changed the attack schedule. As a result, they said, Allied ground-attack aircraft that had been scheduled on earlier missions against tactical battlefield targets in Kuwait had been delayed. The "ground pounders," Air Force officers charged, did not understand "the synergy of the focused attacks on strategic targets." They wanted to do air strikes on the Republican Guard to the exclusion of more important targets.

In Washington, General Merrill A. McPeak, the Air Force chief of staff, questioned whether the Republican Guard divisions were as important to Saddam's power base as Schwarzkopf and some of his men believed. The Republican Guard, McPeak said, had become too regularized. To be sure, they were the best of Saddam's military forces, but they were not a key element of his power base.

As the ground war approached, the arguments grew more heated. "The ground guys—General Yeosock and General Boomer—were convinced they were not getting the kind of support from the Air Force that they really wanted," said a senior Central Command official who was deeply involved the planning for the ground war. According to several participants in Central Command planning meetings in early February, the Air Force argued that it was hitting all the targets it could; Yeosock and Boomer accepted that, but contended that the targets selected by the Air Force were different than the ones they wanted. Yeosock and Boomer mainly wanted artillery and tank emplacements in the vaunted Iraqi defensive lines along Kuwait's southern border to be targeted.

Air Force officials replied that they were striking the Republican Guard as much as possible, but the targets were hard to hit from 10,000 feet in the air. The guard's T-72 tanks were heavily armored, and they were well dug in—buried to their turrets in deep sand in many cases. As for artillery—that was even more difficult to destroy. An artillery gun, after all, was nothing more than a hardened steel tube on a base. Even if a bomb managed to land right next to it, one could not tell from overhead pictures whether it had been damaged.

Yeosock and Boomer conceded the difficulty of the mission, but they asked for heavier pounding of the Republican Guard. They also said that the Air Force had not yet struck at many well-protected targets, such as artillery guns, that were in plain view of their soldiers on the front lines.

Within days, the dispute was referred to Lieutenant General Calvin Waller, the deputy commander of the Central Command. From the first week of February through the conclusion of the war, Waller would confer innumerable times with Lieutenant General Chuck Horner. From then on, Army and Marine commanders said, cooperation improved, but never to the point where the ground commanders were entirely happy with the performance of the Air Force.

One reason for the dispute, Horner said, was that the ground commanders had so many variables to contend with. "The problem was that the ground commanders didn't have a clear idea of what had to be done." One Central Command official who participated in these discussions between the ground and air commanders sided with the Army and the Marines. "I don't necessarily agree [with the Air Force]," he said, "simply because a lot of the targets they were hitting were targets of opportunity in the areas where the Republican Guard forces were. And the ground component wanted to hit some very specific things that would create the most problems for them—the artillery, for example. It took us a long time to even start focusing on artillery."

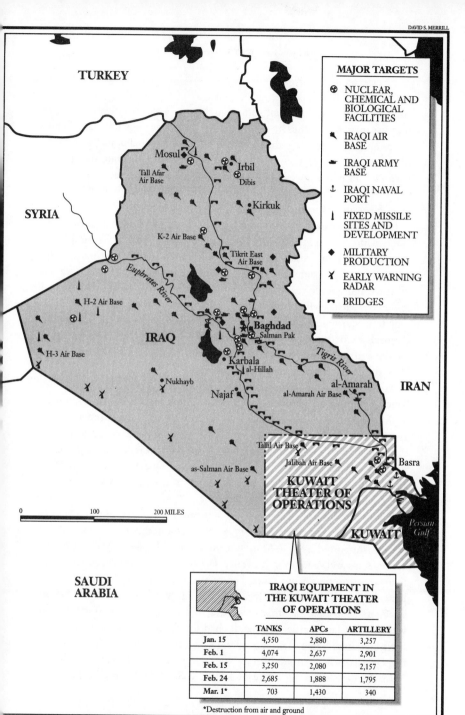

DAVID S. MERRILL

TURKEY

SYRIA

MAJOR TARGETS

⊗ NUCLEAR, CHEMICAL AND BIOLOGICAL FACILITIES

🦅 IRAQI AIR BASE

⬳ IRAQI ARMY BASE

⚓ IRAQI NAVAL PORT

▮ FIXED MISSILE SITES AND DEVELOPMENT

◆ MILITARY PRODUCTION

✗ EARLY WARNING RADAR

⌒ BRIDGES

Mosul
Tall Afar Air Base
Irbil
Dibis
Kirkuk
K-2 Air Base
Tikrit East Air Base

Euphrates River

H-2 Air Base

IRAQ

H-3 Air Base

Baghdad
Salman Pak

Karbala
al-Hillah

Tigris River

Nukhayb
Najaf

al-Amarah
al-Amarah Air Base

IRAN

Talil Air Base
Jalibah Air Base

as-Salman Air Base

KUWAIT THEATER OF OPERATIONS

Basra

Persian Gulf

KUWAIT

0   100   200 MILES

SAUDI ARABIA

IRAQI EQUIPMENT IN THE KUWAIT THEATER OF OPERATIONS

	TANKS	APCs	ARTILLERY
Jan. 15	4,550	2,880	3,257
Feb. 1	4,074	2,637	2,901
Feb. 15	3,250	2,080	2,157
Feb. 24	2,685	1,888	1,795
Mar. 1*	703	1,430	340

*Destruction from air and ground

THE AIR WAR AGAINST IRAQ TARGETED A MULTITUDE OF STRATEGIC SITES AS WELL AS GROUND FORCES

As the second week of the air campaign drew to a close, on January 30, the Iraqis surprised the allies by taking the Saudi border town of Khafji. While it was an easy conquest—the town had been all but abandoned when U.S. Marines withdrew on January 17—the attack held larger significance for the Iraqis because it showed they could surprise the allies and take Saudi territory. It would later turn out, though, that the invasion of Khafji was even more useful to the Americans than it was to the Iraqis.

In the dark of early morning on January 30, a reinforced battalion of 700 Iraqis with about 45 tanks from the respected Iraqi 5th Mechanized Division drove 10 miles south across the Saudi border and walked into Khafji. A small Saudi garrison fled minutes before the Iraqis' arrival. Khafji was an oil town and seaside resort with a population of 20,000, most of whom had left weeks earlier when Iraqi artillery had begun shelling Khafji's oil tanks. The U.S. Marines had left two weeks earlier because they were positioning themselves for their own attack farther west. "Khafji surprised us," said Colonel Ron Richard, the operations officer for the 2nd Marine Division. "For the Iraqis it was a major spoiling attack."

At the same time, two other Iraqi battalions crossed the border into Saudi Arabia about 45 miles further west. Those incursions were repulsed by Marines in armored vehicles and by Marine and Air Force anti-tank aircraft. Allied commanders believed either that the force was going to turn east and support the other force taking Khafji, or that it may have just been scouting Marine positions south of the border. One U.S. Air Force A-10 aircraft shot a Marine light armored vehicle and killed 11 Marines, in the first friendly-fire incident of the war.

The Iraqis controlled Khafji for about thirty-six hours, until they were driven out on Thursday, January 31, in a counterattack by Saudis and Qataris supported by U.S. Marine artillery and Marine Cobra helicopters and F/A 18s and A-10s. About twenty T-62 tanks were destroyed and more than 400 prisoners were taken before the remaining Iraqis fled back to Kuwait. When the Iraqis surrendered at 1:45 P.M., the victorious Saudis swaggered through the streets shouting and waving their national flag. It was the first land battle that Saudis had fought in the modern history of their kingdom. Some observers, though, said the tough fighting was led by the Qataris (whose ground forces were largely Pakistani mercenaries).

In the days after the battle of Khafji, U.S. intelligence officers would study the Iraqis' behavior. What they saw reinforced their growing belief that the Iraqis were not so formidable a foe. For instance, the Iraqis who attacked near Wafra that night got lost returning to Kuwait. "It appeared that they came out from their own barriers, got disoriented, and didn't have the navigational aids to get back and got hung up in their own mine fields," said Lieutenant Colonel Keith Alexander, the intelligence officer for the 1st Armored Division. U.S. aircraft destroyed 22 tanks while the Iraqis were pinned there.

The Khafji attacks also pointed to other weaknesses in Iraqi command and training. The Iraqis seemed unable to adjust their artillery fire to track moving Allied troops. They failed to coordinate their separate units to gather enough mass for a successful spoiling attack. The battles showed Allied commanders how vulnerable Iraqi armor was to strikes from TOW anti-tank missiles and air-dropped munitions. Lieutenant Colonel Thomas Strauss, the 1st Armored Division's operations officer, noted that one of Iraq's better mechanized divisions had been badly beaten. "When you send in the 5th Mech and they get drubbed," Strauss said, "it's got to have an effect on the rest of your units."

On February 7, Defense Secretary Cheney and General Powell left Washington for Saudi Arabia. Two hours after their departure, as their Air Force jet was over the Atlantic, Central Command headquarters in Riyadh announced that the pace of the air campaign was being accelerated. The Republican Guard divisions and artillery batteries in the Iraqi force would become primary targets, Brigadier General Richard Neal announced at a press briefing, although the pressure on Baghdad would not be decreased. On the twenty-second day of Desert Storm, American F-117A Stealth fighters had pounded targets in central Baghdad, Neal said. They were among more than 2,600 Allied air sorties flown that day, bringing the total number of sorties to 54,500.

Although the senior officers of the Central Command had tried to keep the simmering dispute between the Air Force and the Army within the headquarters building in Riyadh, word of it had evidently leaked back to Washington. Powell and Cheney had both described a ground war as "inevitable." They didn't want any old-fashioned interservice rivalry screwing it up. Shortly after their arrival in Riyadh on February 8, Powell and Cheney spent nearly eight hours with Schwarzkopf reviewing the status of the air campaign and the planning for the ground war. It was the first of three days of long meetings. There were still issues to be resolved, and some sharp questions to be asked, according to senior aides who were present. Nevertheless the first twenty-three days of Operation Desert Storm, Cheney told pilots and crew members in the hangar of an Air Force F-III bomber, constituted the most successful air campaign in the history of the world.

Five days later, tragedy struck. Two American Stealth fighter pilots each dropped a laser-guided bomb onto an underground bunker in the Amariyah neighborhood of Baghdad, killing more than 400 people, many of them women and children. The first bomb penetrated the roof of the bunker, leaving a hole about nine feet in diameter; it ripped through three layers of concrete. The second bomb came seconds after the first and penetrated forty feet down into the building, setting fire to the building's cooling and electrical systems. Exits were blocked by falling debris. Iraqi officials said that the facility, known as General Shelter 25, was operated by the General Civil Defense Administration. Constructed in 1980, the building was a large, rectangular structure with beige, white, and dark brown panels on the sides and a camouflage pattern painted on its roof. It was set somewhat apart from the surrounding houses, in a square next to a food cooperative.

U.S. intelligence officials said that the facility had military applications. It was impossible to confirm. A tour of the facility after the war indicated that the basement was divided into chambers identified variously as Isolation Room, Disposal Room, and Decontamination Room.

During the four weeks the Stealth fighters had been bombing government buildings and military installations in and around Baghdad, there had been some damage to apartment buildings and businesses. The Pentagon referred to this euphemistically as "collateral damage." Even by the estimates and complaints of the Iraqi government, however, such damage had been slight compared with the enormous amount of ordnance that had been delivered on the Iraqi capital. An extensive tour of Baghdad after the war confirmed that this was the case.

Marlin Fitzwater learned of the bombing of the bunker from a wire-service bulletin. On one of the four televisions opposite his desk in the White House, Fitzwater immediately turned on CNN. The bombing, Fitzwater knew, was a potentially devastating blow to the American public's support for the war. He felt the administration needed to demonstrate compassion for the victims while reaffirming its resolve to continue the war. But first he wanted to know whether the bunker was, in fact, a legitimate target. Richard Haass, the Middle East specialist on the National Security Council staff, assured him that it was. Pete Williams, Cheney's spokesman, confirmed Haass's report.

At his desk, Fitzwater crafted a short statement on the bombing. He then asked Roman Popadiuk, Brent Scowcroft's aide, to show it to the national security adviser. Popadiuk returned to Fitzwater's office a few minutes later. Scowcroft wanted no immediate comment.

Fitzwater felt that that would be a mistake. During the nearly six months since the invasion of Kuwait, he had talked with Bush many times about how they might best prepare the American public for the possibility of war. Bush had agreed to leave the details to Fitzwater, and Fitzwater had accepted the assignment as a personal challenge. He had spent nearly his entire professional life as a government spokesman, and he was confident of his ability to accurately assess crises and the public's likely responses. Fitzwater called Margaret Tutwiler at the State Department and read her the statement he had drafted. Tutwiler said it sounded fine to her. Fitzwater thanked her, slipped on his suit jacket and walked down the hallway to the Oval Office, the draft of the statement in his breast pocket.

The White House needed to get out in front of the story, Fitzwater told Bush, and make a statement as soon as possible. Fitzwater suggested that the President would say that the civilian casualties were tragic, but that this was a legitimate military target and that the United States had nothing to apologize for. He then asked the President whether there was any doubt that the bunker was a legitimate target. "None whatsoever," Bush replied. He then told Fitzwater he had already heard from Dick Cheney, who was adamant that any statement released by the White House should be terse; certainly, there should be no expression of compassion.

Fitzwater persisted. He told friends time and again that this was the best job he had ever had or expected to have. Now he was putting it on the line. The President must express compassion for the Iraqi victims, Fitzwater said. Bush himself had stated publicly that America's quarrel was not with the Iraqi people, but with their leader.

Bush listened carefully. Though he consulted with the Big Eight on major crises, he discussed nearly everything with Fitzwater. Bush's aides said he valued his press secretary's commonsense counsel. Aides called Fitzwater the "ninth man." If Bush did not issue a statement, Fitzwater insisted, the public's support might well be shattered along with the bunker in Baghdad. Bush told him to do it.

Minutes later, Fitzwater told aides to alert the television networks and the wire services that he would be going live on camera, something he rarely did. In the glare of the television lights, Fitzwater pulled the statement out of his breast pocket. Then he read it, exactly as he had written it.

In Baghdad and elsewhere in Iraq, the people who endured the Allied bombing campaign conducted themselves bravely. An elderly man whose daughter was killed in the bombing of the Amariyah bunker said that despite the nightly bombing, the other men in his neighborhood insisted that women and children be given places in the shelter while they took their chances outside. "There was not enough room for the men," said the man, who would not give his name. "If we had known, we would have gone in and taken the risk, but it was impossible to tell where the bombs would fall."

Many wealthy Iraqis who could afford to do so fled Baghdad and the larger cities for safer havens in the countryside. Among those who remained behind, however, many people told of sharing meager food supplies with neighbors in candlelit apartments. The candles were necessary because within the first twenty-four hours of the beginning of the war, electricity to most large cities had been cut off. Shops, markets, and restaurants—all of which relied on electricity to keep food supplies fresh—soon shut their doors. For the poorest Iraqis, food shortages began almost immediately. Rich or poor, few Iraqis apparently thought that Saddam's conflict with the West would ever result in war. The only difference was that once the war began, the rich were able to purchase goods at inflated prices on a black market that seemed to have sprung up overnight; the poor simply went without.

Many Iraqis said they could not understand how the American-led coalition chose their targets. On Haifa Street, a handsome thoroughfare, the ministries of Justice and Local Culture were bombed, as was a center for trade conventions not far away. Between those locations, however, several large monuments to Saddam and the Baath Party were left untouched. "If his quarrel was with Saddam," said a young man named Muhammad, "Bush surely had a strange way of showing this."

On the battlefield in Kuwait, Iraqi soldiers exposed in the southern desert in bunkers would tell Allied soldiers after the war that the bombing took a fearful toll on them. Few told of large numbers of deaths as a result of the bombing. But the nightly sorties, they said, especially by the big B-52 bombers, prevented sleep. The wear and tear on the soldiers' nerves, together with the lack of food and water many Iraqi units would complain of, would be cited by many of Saddam's soldiers as the principal reasons for their unwillingness to fight.

What was clear, many Iraqis said, was that after the bombing began in Kuwait and Iraq, Saddam had entered a fight that he had no chance of winning. Much anger was directed at the United States and its allies by ordinary Iraqis. But at least as much seems to have been directed at Saddam. Many Iraqis felt that they would bear all of the cost and privation of his posturing.

The bombing of the Iraqi bunker revealed a serious flaw in one of the most important aspects of Desert Storm—its intelligence gathering. The facility had been targeted months before by planners who were convinced of its military significance, but they had never received any intelligence information that the facility was not also being used as a shelter for civilians. There were other gaps in the way intelligence was gathered during the prosecution of the war, too. And the lack of information—which resulted in bitter controversy among the Central Command, the Pentagon and the CIA—impinged on what might have been the most important decision of the entire Gulf conflict: When to begin the ground war?

There had never been any doubt among Schwarzkopf's commanders (from all of the services) about the need for a battle on the desert floor, but no one wanted to get entangled in a long ground war. To this end, the war planners in Riyadh and Washington as well as the corps and division and brigade planners in the desert, had developed a plan for the ground attack that accounted for every possibility, every need, every problem. No detail was too small to escape their attention, no possible reaction by the Iraqis went uncountenanced. The planning effort was massive and unceasing. At its core, it embraced the ideal of a short war with few casualties. By mid-January, Schwarzkopf's planners were refining their ideas for the massive ground attack on the Iraqi army's flank. The attack was to be supported by the Marines to the south and by General McCaffrey's 24th

Infantry Division (Mechanized), which was to take the Euphrates River Valley. The heart of the attacking force would be the VII Corps led by Lieutenant General Fred Franks. Schwarzkopf's men had planned the operation almost down to the minute. From beginning to end, they calculated, it should take exactly 144 hours.

That goal was predicated on another very precise calculation, however. At the start of the air campaign, General McPeak had told President Bush that the Air Force could inflict losses of 50 percent on Iraqi equipment within four weeks. By Day 30 of Operation Desert Storm, McPeak said, the U.S. Air Force and its coalition partners had come close to that objective. McPeak believed that once the Allied ground forces attacked the Iraqi army, Saddam's soldiers would surrender by the thousands. McPeak compared the situation to Operation Strangle in Italy during the Second World War, when German troops, isolated for months, appeared to be primed to fight, but collapsed when the battle began.

In Riyadh, Schwarzkopf was both angered and perplexed by the information coming to him about the success of the air campaign. He was fully prepared to commit his ground forces once the fighting capability of the Iraqi army had been reduced by 50 percent. But by Day 30 of Operation Desert Storm, little more than 1,000 Iraqi soldiers had defected to the allies, and there were no firm assurances that the Iraqi army had been seriously eroded. The intelligence information, known in military jargon as "battle-damage assessments," was maddeningly imprecise. In almost every instance, the CIA's estimates differed from those of the staff of the Joint Chiefs, which differed from those of the Central Command.

The conflicting assessments obsessed Schwarzkopf. At the start of the air campaign, according to intelligence estimates at the time, the Iraqis had 4,280 tanks, 2,870 armored personnel carriers, and 3,110 artillery guns in the Kuwait Theater of Operations, which included an area extending more than 100 miles to the west of Kuwait and north of Basra to the Euphrates River in Iraq. By February 14, after four weeks of bombing, the air campaign had destroyed 1,300 tanks, Schwarzkopf's staff announced. But analysts at the CIA and at the Defense Intelligence Agency would verify only 500 to 600 tank kills.

The main information source on which all analysts relied was satellite photography. The imagery, both optical and infrared, was usually very good. The satellites swept the area from southern Kuwait to the mountains north of Baghdad once every two hours. This was done normally only with a wide-angle lens. The satellites were able to focus on a specified arc with a high-powered lens, but the area of coverage was very small. And the coverage of the area lasted only ten to twenty minutes. The close-ups, which focused on a narrow target, had to be specially ordered. These images were sent for processing to a ground station outside of Washington. Analysts in the National Photographic Interpretation Center and the CIA's Office of Imagery Analysis then evaluated hard prints. Curiously, none of the U.S. intelligence agencies had broad-band transmission capabilities to send the information to Riyadh electronically; it all had to be sent by courier on an Air Force jet dispatched from Washington each evening.

This process was much too inefficient for Schwarzkopf's intelligence staff. They tried using the TR-1, the modernized version of the U-2 spy plane, to take pictures of the battlefields. They brought hundreds of military-intelligence analysts and photo interpreters to Riyadh. These efforts almost made things worse. There were thousands of pictures to inspect and interpret.

But how to determine from photos alone whether a tank had been thoroughly disabled by a bomb? The easy calls were the so-called catastrophic kills. When a tank had blown up, its turret thrown hundreds of feet in the air and the ground around it was a big black smudge, there was universal consensus. But many Iraqi tanks were dug into fighting holes, and were hard to hit. And if one was struck by a cluster bomblet or a piece of shrapnel from a close hit, it was impossible to determine from the photographic imagery whether the tank would be able to fight again.

A great many of the air strikes against the Iraqi tanks were being assigned to American F-16 pilots flying daylight bombing runs. This was a difficult and tedious job, one that was even more dangerous when they attacked the well-defended T-72 tanks of the Republican Guard divisions. The F-16 pilots tried using other F-16s to fly ahead of the attack aircraft assigned to a tank-killing mission. They served as forward air-traffic-controllers. Using their radar, even a moderately competent pilot flying far ahead could direct his colleague onto a target. But even then, tank-killing was difficult. At 15,000 feet, where the F-16s typically started their approach on a tank-killing run, an Iraqi tank or armored personnel carrier looked like a pinhead. It took keen eyes, sometimes aided with binoculars, to even spot them. Once the target was found, the pilot would center the target in the cross hairs of his computer-aided targeting scope and put the aircraft on the proper glide path. At 10,000 feet, he would press the button on his control stick to drop the bomb. To get the kind of hit on a dug-in tank, one that would blow it up or make its ammunition explode, required nearly a direct hit. But putting that bomb directly on such a target from 10,000 feet was like putting a golf ball into the hole with a pitching wedge 100 yards away from the green.

Air Force pilots rated such targeting problems according to a criterion known as "circular error, probable." This referred to the circle around the specific target in which half of a pilot's bombs were likely to fall. One veteran pilot who flew dozens of anti-tank missions in the Gulf War estimated that the circle in which half his bombs fell on a typical mission was 110 feet. A Central Command intelligence officer estimated that the coalition aircraft were damaging Iraqi tanks on daylight runs with only 20 percent of their bombs. The other 80 percent missed.

Air Force planners eventually figured out a way to achieve a higher rate of success. Desert sand cooled rapidly at night; tanks warmed by the sun tended to retain their heat. At night, the warm tanks appeared as hot spots in infrared radar scopes. Laser-guided bombs dropped by American pilots using the infrared scopes on their F-15Es or F-111s could hit the glowing tanks precisely. It was an expensive way to destroy tanks, though, but they authorized it partly because Schwarzkopf and his generals needed to decide by mid-February how soon he could begin the ground campaign. The more answers the Air Force could provide him about the success of the air war, the sooner a decision could be made.

On February 14, the Central Command claimed 1,300 Iraqi tanks killed, or 30 percent of those in the Kuwait Theater of Operations. By February 24, the Central Command's analysts calculated, the number rose to 1,685, an increase of 385 over ten days. If true, the figure amounted to a kill-ratio of almost 40 percent of the 4,280 Iraqi tanks believed to be in the theater. In addition, the Central Command's analysts estimated, the Allied air forces had destroyed 925 of Iraq's armored personnel carriers, 32 percent of the total of 2,870. The Central Command said 1,485 artillery pieces had been damaged or destroyed, amounting to about 48 percent of the total number in the Iraqi arsenal.

There was still considerable disagreement about the success of the air war, however. At the CIA and on the staff of the Joint Chiefs in the Pentagon, skeptics wondered if the destruction of only 385 tanks over a ten-day period when the U.S. Air Force and its allies were concentrating on them was significant. The analysts also noted that the Central Command had not reached the threshold of 50 percent established by Schwarzkopf in any of the target categories. To those who would listen, General McPeak explained that bombing ground targets from the air would clearly reach a point of diminishing returns; the remaining targets were either hidden or dug in so well that they could not be destroyed by aircraft. For McPeak, the issue was simply whether the Air Force had done all it could. He believed that it had. The question of when the ground war should commence, McPeak told friends and advisers, was a matter for others to decide.

At 6:25 on Thursday evening, February 21, a White House operator reported that a call was coming in from Gorbachev in Moscow. The President was in his small study off the Oval Office about to watch the evening newscasts. An aide rushed to locate a Russian translator, while others telephoned several of Bush's senior advisers.

Five minutes later, while aides to Gorbachev kept the phone line to the White House open and waited for the translator, Bush watched as the nightly news announced a new Soviet overture to Baghdad. Bush knew that Primakov, Gorbachev's personal envoy, had traveled to Baghdad on February 11, offering to mediate the conflict. He also knew that Tariq Aziz was due to visit Moscow the next day. A deal seemed to be in the works, and he was not happy about it. Bush listened as the CNN announcer said that the Soviet intercession could result in an early end to the Gulf War. The gist of the Soviet plan, the announcer said, was this: in exchange for an announcement of Iraq's "unconditional withdrawal" from Kuwait, the Soviets would press the coalition for an immediate cease-fire.

At 6:47 P.M., with a translator finally in place, Bush accepted the call and Gorbachev came on the line. By this time, James Baker and Robert Gates had rushed to the study. During the thirty-three minute conversation, aides said, Gorbachev informed Bush of the discussions Primakov had had with Saddam Hussein. He indicated that Primakov had discussed a wide range of issues while in Baghdad. Bush replied that two fundamental conditions for a cessation of hostilities with Iraq had to be met before any deals were struck. Every Iraqi soldier had to be withdrawn from Kuwait, and the legitimate rulers of the emirate had to be allowed to return. Only after those two things occurred, Bush said, could there be discussions with Baghdad. Linking the issue of Kuwait with that of the Arab-Israeli conflict was impossible. Bush said that he would not accept any solution that afforded Saddam even the slightest appearance of victory. The Soviet offer, he said calmly, was "unacceptable." The conversation ended amicably.

Bush told aides that he understood the pressure Gorbachev was under from Kremlin hard-liners and from those within his foreign ministry who wanted to come to Iraq's assistance and maintain the Soviet Union's credibility in the Arab world. The President also knew that Gorbachev, in attempting to interpose himself in the Gulf conflict, hoped to demonstrate to the millions of Muslims in the Soviet Union that he was sensitive to their concerns about the devastation of a Muslim country. "The President wanted to tell the Soviets to get lost," said a senior adviser, "but to do it in nice way."

Soon after he hung up on Gorbachev, Bush left the White House to attend a performance of *Black Eagles,* at Ford's Theatre a few blocks away. The play was about a squadron of heroic black pilots in the Second World War.

Once Bush was gone, his most trusted advisers gathered on the second floor of the White House in the residential quarters to discuss where the United States stood in the Gulf conflict. They gathered in a spacious study, under an enormous gold chandelier. Vice-President Quayle and Defense Secretary Cheney were dressed in tuxedos. They were obliged to attend a reception that evening for Danish Queen Margrethe II. General Powell was dressed in a turtleneck and slacks. Scowcroft, Sununu, and Baker all wore suits.

At 10:30 P.M., Bush joined the group. He took a seat behind a big oak desk. The United States, Bush said, according to a participant, was at a "critical point" in the conflict. Powell said he thought the administration should set a deadline for Saddam Hussein to pull his battered forces out of Kuwait. It had failed on January 15; perhaps it would work now. But if a deadline was set, Powell said, it should be set quickly. "That's a good idea," Bush said. Baker said he did not expect that any of the coalition members would object to such a move.

The discussion turned to timing. Several participants suggested that a day should be sufficient time for the Iraqi leader to begin moving his forces out. "Okay, then," Bush said. "It's going to be noon Saturday." That would make the deadline 8 P.M., Baghdad time, February 23, Day 38 of Operation Desert Storm.

As the meeting broke up, one participant asked what would happen if Saddam Hussein surprised them and began moving out. "We monitor," General Powell said. "No problem."

CHAPTER 17

THE COUNTDOWN

F AR NORTH in the desert of western Saudi Arabia, Major General Barry McCaffrey gathered the battalion and brigade commanders of the U.S. Army's 24th Infantry Division (Mechanized) and their staffs for a fifth and final review of the war plan. This was known as a "Map-Ex," for map exercise. McCaffrey's commanders considered the exercise strong evidence that the ground war was finally at hand.

The unwieldy group huddled beneath two large tents that had been set up on a flat expanse of sand just outside the triple rolls of concertina wire and the sand berms that surrounded his division headquarters. Inside the tents, headquarters personnel had constructed a large plywood-topped table that zigged and zagged for some thirty feet on both sides; only the top and bottom ends of the table were cut straight. On both sides of the long table, they had pieced together dozens of map sheets. The maps, which were scaled one meter per 25,000 meters, described an area of 230 miles from the northwestern border of Saudi Arabia to the Euphrates River Valley in the heart of southern Iraq. Along the edges of the table were larger-scale maps. The scale was one meter per 250,000 meters. These maps, smaller in actual size, were intended to help McCaffrey's commanders put the more detailed picture into a larger perspective.

With McCaffrey's aides watching closely, junior officers from the Division Operations staff drew black greasepaint lines in the yellow of the map's desert. The more prominent were labeled Main Supply Routes Yankee and X-ray. The greasepaint lines snaked north into the heart of Iraq. There were also phase lines labeled Opus, Colt, Charger, Ram, Smash, Jet, and Viking. These divided the desert along east-west lines. Next were the objectives of McCaffrey's division. These were marked Brown, Red, Gray, and Orange. They were described with little circles. These were the targets toward which McCaffrey's mobile forces would aim. There were areas of operation marked Hammer, Stewart, Vanguard, Saber, Liberty, Cougar, Wolf, and Fox. There were battle positions marked 101, 102, and 103.

Finally, flags were placed on the map table—one for every unit in McCaffrey's division, as well as flags for the 82nd Airborne Division, the French units, and the 101st Airborne Division, which would be on McCaffrey's left flank, and for the divisions of Lieutenant General Fred Franks's VII Corps, which would be on the right flank. There were also flags for six Iraqi divisions clustered along Highway 8, the six-lane superhighway that connected Baghdad in the north with Basra in the south. Each flag was affixed to a wooden base so that it could be moved. During the course of the map exercise, the flags would be moved over and over again.

Gathered around the map table with McCaffrey were his staff chiefs for operations, intelligence, and communications. Each of McCaffrey's battle-field commanders was present as well, accompanied by his own operations officer and executive officer. There were three brigade commanders plus the aviation-brigade commander, the air-cavalry commander, and the commanders of McCaffrey's nine maneuver battalions. In addition there were the commanders of McCaffrey's six artillery battalions, the commander of the 36th Engineer Group, the chemical-warfare commander, and the commanders of two support and supply groups. Altogether, there were sixty men and women crowded around the map table. There was not a single chair anywhere. Everyone had to stand.

Sipping from a cup of coffee, McCaffrey ordered the attack to begin. As he watched silently, his commanders began taking turns maneuvering their forces on the map table by moving the tiny flags on their wooden bases. What the movement of the flags described was a high-speed attack by the heaviest armored division ever fielded by the U.S. Army. The 24th Infantry Division (Mechanized) combat team boasted nearly 25,000 soldiers, 241 M1A1 Abrams tanks, 221 Bradley fighting vehicles, 72 self-propelled 155-mm howitzers, 9 Multiple Launch Rocket System launchers, 18 Apache attack helicopters, and 6,000 wheeled vehicles. McCaffrey was planning nothing less than the most audacious cavalry charge in history. His division had more firepower than General George Patton's entire 3rd Army. In the days to come, it would charge farther, faster, and with more firepower than any armored unit had ever charged before.

The map exercise dragged on for thirty-six hours over two days before it was concluded. "Well," McCaffrey said, "I guess that's it. Anyone have any questions or comments?"

Bill Chamberlain, a lieutenant colonel who was a descendant of Colonel Joshua Lawrence Chamberlain of the famous 20th Maine Regiment that had held Little Round Top against ten-to-one odds at the Battle of Gettysburg, raised his hand. "Sir," Chamberlain said, "I just want to say that I would rather be shot in combat than go through another Map-Ex."

Out of the crowd of sweating soldiers around the map table came the voice of another battalion commander: "Sir, I agree. I, too, would rather see Bill shot than go through another Map-Ex."

McCaffrey's commanders dissolved in laughter.

Until the eve of the ground war, Schwarzkopf, his commanders, and his intelligence officers received new information about the disposition and activities of the Iraqi army in Kuwait. Reports to Central Command headquarters toward the conclusion of the air campaign indicated that Saddam Hussein's generals expected an amphibious assault on Kuwait City on the coast and another attack at the point the Americans called the "elbow" (where the southern Kuwait border bends closest to Kuwait City). Central Command intelligence officers also knew from interviews of Iraqi defectors that the Iraqis expected the main thrust of the Allied ground attack to come up the Wadi al-Batin, which defined Kuwait's western border with Iraq. Schwarzkopf wanted to reinforce these perceptions. A feint at the wadi would focus the enemy's most potent forces there, keeping them from moving defenses farther west to block the left hook of the VII Corps.

Just south of the Iraqi border, and just to the west of the point where the Wadi al-Batin enters Saudi Arabia, Colonel Randolph W. House commanded the 2nd "Blackjack" Brigade of the U.S. Army's 1st Cavalry Division. House had two jobs. One was to protect the VII Corps headquarters and logistics sites from an Iraqi attack down the wadi. The second was to feign an Allied attack there to keep the Iraqis' attention on that spot. A slight, balding man fiercely dedicated to his soldiers, House had ordered his brigade on February 7 to start using their Multiple Launch Rocket Systems and artillery to pound Iraqi positions near the wadi. "We would rush up to the berm, fire, and then pull back," House said. "We did not know what the response was going to be. And so with the chemical threat and everything else, we were always ready for some kind of an artillery response."

The response never came, House said, but Iraqi deserters soon did. The deserters told House that reinforcements were being dispatched to their area from other parts of Kuwait. The rocket and artillery fire from the Blackjack Brigade had caught the attention of Saddam's generals. The deception seemed to be working.

House stepped up the campaign. One night, he said, his soldiers approached the earthen berm that defined Kuwait's western border with Iraq with their tank guns blazing. They blew holes in the berm with demolition crews. Then they sneaked through the holes. In the dark, the soldiers inflated large plastic models of M1A1 Abrams tanks and anchored them to the ground. They also left clanging noisemakers. After retreating five kilometers, House's soldiers watched through night scopes, hoping the Iraqis would approach. But they did not take the bait.

Then on the afternoon of February 19, House got new orders: "Cross the border berm and conduct a reconnaissance in force deep into Iraq to determine enemy location, disposition, composition, strength, and intent. Let them know you are there. Elicit a response." The order also said: "Do not become decisively engaged, and do not attrit your force."

On February 20 at noon, House took his brigade ten kilometers into Iraq up the Wadi al-Batin. The wadi was a spooky place. A long, wide gully, twenty to thirty meters deep in places, it extended north from the Saudi village of Hafar al-Batin. The rims of the wadi were flat, and from some of them a soldier could see for miles. At other places, however, the wadi snaked back and forth, and soldiers inside it could not be detected by someone on the rim at all. Running along the eastern rim of the wadi was a narrow road from the Kuwaiti village of Rugei. It was called the Rugei Road. Along the sides of the wadi were washouts where water had rushed in during heavy rains; they were natural hiding spots for artillery, anti-tank guns, even tanks. Readily navigable except during heavy rains, the wadi was a likely approach for a division of Iraqi forces driving into Saudi Arabia.

As he moved farther into Iraq on the afternoon of February 20, Colonel

House found the first evidence that the Iraqi army was preparing a vigorous defense concentrated on the Wadi al-Batin. A battalion of Iraqi soldiers with Soviet-made BMP fighting vehicles and T-55 tanks engaged House's brigade. Using their own tanks, Bradley fighting vehicles, and artillery, and supported by Air Force A-10 ground-attack aircraft, House and his soldiers destroyed the Iraqi battalion and took a dozen prisoners. In doing so, they also discovered more than 100 Iraqi artillery guns that had been moved into the area at night and hidden in holes covered with camouflage netting. House's troops did not discover the Iraqi artillery until it started firing, however. "I was listening to the [A-10] pilots talk," House recalled. "At one point, one of the pilots said, 'I've counted twenty-six artillery tubes shooting at these guys.' And then eight or ten or fifteen minutes later, I heard another A-10 pilot say 'I stopped counting at a hundred.'" The A-10s destroyed the Iraqi artillery.

But House's brigade had been drawn into a trap.

Ahead of him, the first thing House saw was the scouts from his brigade's Task Force 1-5 taking direct fire in their Bradley fighting vehicles. Task Force 1-5's four companies were arrayed in a diamond formation, led by a Bradley company, and the scouts were leading them. The trailing company was a Bradley, and their two wings were tank companies. On the.brigade's radio House heard the lead scouts report: "Receiving fire, returning same." House saw the dirt puffs next to the scouts as the rounds came in.

House thought he had the situation in hand. His soldiers were returning fire, and the tank companies had stopped the enemy on their flanks. They had taken a number of Iraqi prisoners, and they were being transferred to the rear. Artillery fire was coming in, but not much. This wasn't too bad, House thought. "And all of a sudden, I'm about a thousand meters back as the brigade commander, observing with my binoculars from my command track . . . [and] the Vulcan [anti-aircraft gun] that's behind me takes a hit. And I can hear, and then I see, rounds going through my antennas, I can hear that, and then I see them impacting right on the other side of my track."

House's driver rammed his tracked vehicle into a hole. The incoming rounds were huge. They were being fired from AT-12 tank guns, highly accurate 100-mm cannons hidden in the side of the wadi. "They had let us move forward, and engaged," House said. "And then on the flank there was an AT-12 battery dug in with those guns pointed at us."

The tank round that hit the Vulcan anti-aircraft gun had decapitated its commander. Seconds later, the Bradley of Task Force 1-5's executive officer was also hit. Christopher Cichon, a staff sergeant in Alpha Company, drew his Bradley up to help the executive officer, his "X.O.," First Lieutenant Christopher Robinson. Cichon, a lanky thirty-year-old from Chicago with clear eyes and a reserved manner, filed his report later that night:

I was up neck-high out of the hatch scanning for a new target when the noise and pressure wave from the X.O.'s vehicle getting hit caused me to look back to my left rear. I saw smoke and flame coming off his turret and burning pieces going everywhere. [Alpha Company's Commander] called at that time saying "My Black-5 element is hit." Or something like that. I saw Sergeant Adeloye, the senior medic assigned to A Company, running to the X.O.'s track about the same time Specialist Jeffery Mitchell was at the side of my vehicle. Mitchell . . . said they took a bad hit. I told him medical help was there and to go back to your vehicle to help. I then started to drive away in reverse and I was surprised to see no vehicle evacuating casualties [from A-51, the executive officer's Bradley], just someone standing on the turret not really doing anything but just staring into the turret. I was expecting to see full [medical evacuation] in progress.

So I figured we've got to do something quick and guided the driver back alongside A-51 with intentions to evacuate casualties. I positioned my Bradley so as to use his vehicle [A-51] as somewhat of a shield for mine and still be able to shoot over his [Bradley's] front deck. I alerted my squad leader and soldiers on board with combatlifesaver [bag] to begin evacuation of A-51's crew.

Then I directed my gunner to shoot anything coming at us, and I was dismounting to see what was up. I checked out Sergeant Joe Thompson, the casualty laying out back before trying to get heads counted. Sergeant [Mark] Jones jumped on A-51 and got Lieutenant Robinson out of the turret. I counted the crew of A-51 then and came up short A-51's gunner. I found out from the scouts that the gunner on A-51 was dead, and a glance into the back confirmed that. So I concentrated on Sergeant Thompson, prepping him for evacuation to my vehicle. I was squatting down to lift him with some person who I don't remember, saw PFC [Ardon B.] Cooper helping someone else laying behind 51, when A-31 (my track) was hit.

I was looking across Sergeant Thompson's chest toward my vehicle, getting ready to lift him, when I saw an orange flash on my vehicle, a billowing cloud of black-gray smoke, and I saw or watched everyone hitting the ground and covering the wounded with their bodies. This is what I saw PFC Cooper doing, because his helmet was either blown off or fell off, as he was about ten feet from the explosion. And I recognized his bright-red hair. He was across the man he was trying to give aid to at the time. Also I caught a glimpse of the TOW [anti-tank missile] launch rails with the missile tubes flying off, missiles still intact on the rails. [His TOW-equipped Bradley had been hit, and the missile tubes blown off.] Parts of the vehicle started pinging and bouncing off A-51, kicking up dirt around us. I thought my gunner was dead because he was in the turret that was hit. Then I heard him yelling, "Hey, hey," and felt a great relief. . . . I also saw Sergeant Jones climb up to evac or check on my gunner. It was then that PFC Cooper stood up halfway, looked at me, and blood started running out of his nose and mouth and he fell over. I ran over to him, stuck my fingers in his mouth to ensure that his tongue was not blocking his airway, found back wounds with no exit wounds on his chest, rolled him on his side to keep his good lung up and . . . to keep him from drowning on his own blood. Then I told PFC [Daniel] Sheets to stay with him. I started sending casualties back to the scout vehicle to use it as a means of escape when it pulled out. . . . I thought, We've got to get out of here, or we all are dead meat. And I ran back to use my vehicle radio, and when I got to it, I was amazed to find it running and not knocked out. I conferred with Sergeant Jones and told him that I was going to use it to evacuate us. And I found my driver, who had gotten out to help Sgt. Jones evacuate my gunner. I told him, "The enemy thinks we are dead, let's let him think we are dead. Get in the vehicle, and when I tell you, go right and back to the rear as fast as you can."

Three of the Blackjack Brigade's vehicles had been hit by enemy fire. One tank had been damaged by a land mine. Staff Sergeant Jimmy D. Haws, twenty-eight, was dead. He was the commander of the anti-aircraft gun behind Colonel House. Sergeant Ronald Randazzo, twenty-five, the gunner in the executive officer's Bradley had also been killed. The third fatality was Private First Class Ardon B. Cooper, twenty-three. In addition, nine soldiers of the 1st Cavalry's Blackjack Brigade had been wounded.

Hours afterward, House received new orders on his radio. "You've done what we wanted you to do," a superior said. "Pull back into Saudi." In the forty-eight hours before the ground war began, Allied aircraft pounded the area along the Wadi al-Batin.

In Riyadh, as the date for the start of the ground war approached in the final days of February, General Schwarzkopf was convinced that the plan he had begun describing to aides and colleagues as the Hail Mary play would end the war quickly, with a very small number of Allied casualties. The Jedi Knights, as well as his entire planning staff and the staffs of corps and divisions, had war-gamed the plan endlessly, plotting every conceivable Iraqi action and winning Allied reaction. Since the first Jedi Knights, as the graduates from the Army's School for Advanced Military Studies were known, had arrived in Riyadh in mid-September, their number had grown. By mid-February, eighty-two SAMS graduates were scattered throughout the theater, where they were assigned to a wide array of command and planning tasks.

On February 22, a day before the Bush administration's noon deadline for the withdrawal of Iraqi forces, Schwarzkopf's massive army had already moved into position to execute the Hail Mary. A plan this daring was also risky, as Schwarzkopf well knew. By sending the VII Corps so deep into southern Iraq, he was gambling that it would not be trapped by the Republican Guard divisions Saddam Hussein had held in reserve south of Basra. To reduce the risk, Schwarzkopf had demanded some considerable embroidery. They were called "supporting attacks" or "secondary and tertiary efforts."

On the eve of the ground war, several of Schwarzkopf's key battlefield commanders were preparing to carry out these efforts. General McCaffrey's 24th Infantry Division was the heaviest American tank division in the 18th Airborne Corps positioned far to the west in the Saudi desert. The 24th was flanked on their left by the 101st Airborne Division. On McCaffrey's right flank was the 3rd Armored Cavalry Regiment, which had been assigned a narrow sector of the battlefield. To the right of that unit was the VII Corps, the mailed fist of the attack. Commanded by Lieutenant General Fred Franks, the VII Corps' four tank and mechanized divisions were assigned an area extending from the right flank of the 3rd Armored Cavalry Regiment in the west to the Wadi al-Batin, nearly seventy-five miles to the east.

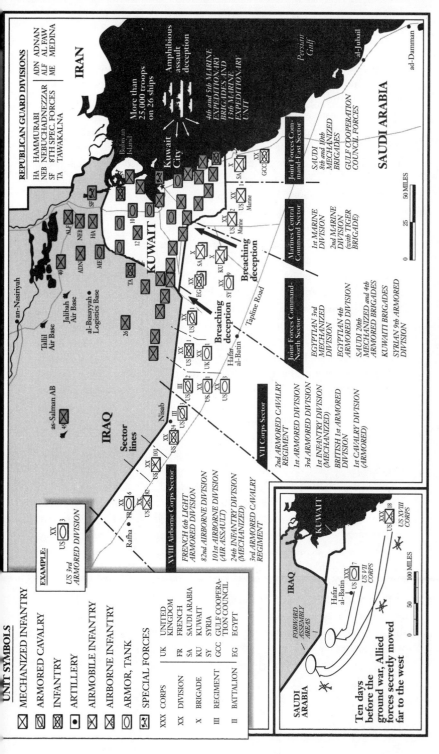

DISPOSITION OF ALLIED AND IRAQI FORCES: FEBRUARY 23, 1991

In the month before "G-Day," as the soldiers called the start of the ground campaign, Iraqi defectors and prisoners of war had provided valuable information about the quality and extent of the defensive lines they had helped construct in southern Kuwait. Intelligence analysts had drawn three important conclusions. The first was that the Iraqis had stationed nearly all their forces near roads and desert trails. Remarkably, it appeared that the Iraqis didn't want to stray too far from the road network, for fear of getting lost in their own desert. They had set up their ambushes along the roads, too, because they expected the allies to travel in the same manner. If the allies attacked from across the open desert, the Iraqis would be taken by surprise.

Their second conclusion was that Iraqi commanders were preparing for a three-pronged attack by the allies: from the sea, over the southern border of Kuwait (at the "elbow"), and at the Wadi al-Batin. The third was that the air bombardment had stopped the Iraqis from building their defensive lines farther than fifty miles west of the wadi.

The Iraqi defensive lines stretched from Kuwait City south down the coast, then turned westward to follow the border of Kuwait and Saudi Arabia toward Iraq. In some areas, the Iraqi defensive lines were daunting, consisting of two mine fields 100 to 200 meters deep bordered by concertina wire and overlooked by trenches, fighting ditches, bunkers, and revetted tanks and anti-tank guns. Behind those positions were artillery, already aimed at the places in the mine fields where the Iraqi commanders expected the allies to cross. In some places there were also fearsome fire ditches, filled with oil, ready to be ignited by a remotely detonated explosive charge.

Franks had studied this information intently. His VII Corps consisted of the 1st Armored Division, the 3rd Armored Division, and the 2nd Armored Cavalry Regiment from Germany. Schwarzkopf had also assigned to him the command of the 1st Infantry Division (Mechanized), known as the Big Red One, as well as the British 1st Armored Division. The Big Red One had trained with Franks' VII Corps in the annual NATO REFORGER exercises in Europe.

A man of no imposing physical stature, Franks had a grandfatherly demeanor that appealed strongly to his soldiers. He wore a trim mustache, almost a rebellious gesture in a straitlaced general officer corps. Yet he exuded self-confidence and a great inner calm. Franks also spoke rather quietly. At headquarters, staff officers and division liaison officers would gather for a daily briefing. As Franks spoke slowly, almost imperceptibly, everyone would start leaning forward. Soon chairs would start inching closer, as everyone strained to hear. At the conclusion of the briefing, junior officers gathered in groups and tried to reconstruct the briefing. "What did he say? What did you hear him say?" they would ask one another. Behind Franks's mild ways, colleagues said, was an exceptional tactical intellect and an iron will. Franks had lost a leg in Vietnam and used an artificial limb. But he had trained himself to walk with it so that it was not noticeable at all.

On the eve of the ground war, Franks was still hoping to reinforce any ideas Saddam Hussein's battlefield commanders had about an attack coming up the Wadi al-Batin at the "elbow" of the three borders. On February 15, Franks had ordered the 1st and 3rd Armored Divisions and the 2nd Armored Cavalry Regiment into positions far enough west to skirt the end of the Iraqi defensive lines. To get his forces into their attack positions took six days, until February 21. But the time had been spent well, Franks believed. By waiting until the last minute, Schwarzkopf and his commanders had kept the VII Corps and General Gary Luck's 18th Airborne Corps south of Kuwait and east of the Wadi al-Batin as long as possible, encouraging Saddam's generals to keep focusing on the place where the three borders met at the ancient riverbed. The skirmishing that Iraqi forces had engaged in with Colonel House's Blackjack Brigade had also increased the Iraqi generals' focus on the wadi. Then, to move his forces west into position, Franks put them on a 160-kilometer march, from east to west. The march hooked to the right. Laid out on a map, it was the exact mirror image of the way they would later attack into Iraq. That was their dress rehearsal.

As they waited for the orders to attack on February 23, the soldiers of the 1st Infantry (the Big Red One) worked over a replica of the Iraqi barrier system. They had constructed the obstacles the intelligence analysts had identified at the Wadi al-Batin and practiced breaching them over and over again. The officers had made large maps of their attack sectors on the desert floor, then walked through their moves, each officer representing his unit, others representing Iraqi units. "Okay, I'm here, facing the Iraqi 26th Division's 4th Brigade," one would say. "He maneuvers this way, I send my forces over there. He does this, I do that." Franks called these drills "rubber-duck exercises." The repeated practice and the emphasis on speed and deception all built a soldier's confidence, Franks said. His soldiers were ready to fight.

The Hail Mary plan embodied all the new concepts of maneuver warfare, emphasizing speed, deception, quick decision making, and the coordinated air and land attack doctrine known as AirLand Battle. The latter had been conceived as a way to attack deep behind the Soviet army in Europe; its practitioners would have several huge advantages in this war with Iraq. One was the desert itself, which made it hard to hide ground targets. The other was time. Instead of having only hours or days to stop a Soviet rush, the allies had had weeks to cut off the Iraqi lines of logistics and moving troops.

Because Saddam Hussein's forces had such limited intelligence-gathering capability, Schwarzkopf's planners were able to use deception on a grand scale. Since the Iraqi commanders had reacted earlier to the two large amphibious-landing rehearsals staged in operations Camel Sand and Imminent Thunder, Schwarzkopf had ordered two Marine expeditionary brigades to float ostentatiously off the coast of Kuwait. Using radio transmissions, bogus practice drills, and the like, the two Marine brigades were to act as if they were about to attack. Iraqi commanders had been seen scanning the sea nervously.

The ground commanders of Desert Storm were also to test another new idea Schwarzkopf and his senior aides believed in strongly. Some people called it decentralized battlefield management; it manifested itself in what Schwarzkopf called "mission-type orders." Taken from the German concept of *auftragstaktik*, the idea was that each commander—from the corps to the division to the brigade all the way down to the company—would be given the unit's mission, but allowed to plan it and execute it himself. Plans had been routed back to Central Command headquarters in Riyadh, where Schwarzkopf's staff synchronized the entire plan. On November 13, the corps commanders of Desert Storm had met with Schwarzkopf, and he had given them the master plan for the operation. From that point on, Fred Franks, Gary Luck, and their respective division, brigade, battalion, and company commanders had mapped out their particular part of the plan, deciding themselves how their units would prosecute the war within their sectors.

The corps and division sectors were enormously important. Each division or regiment had clearly defined boundaries. Within the division sectors, each brigade had its own sectors. The operating sectors were coterminous with one another, forming a wall of force from the beaches of Kuwait in the east to the Saudi village of Rafha 485 kilometers to the west. Each sector was from 20 to 75 kilometers wide. They curved to the northeast; each was about 260 kilometers long. On a map, the sectors lay neatly side by side. They resembled wide, parallel highways.

In the next few days, Schwarzkopf's generals knew, keeping the many different units inside their assigned sectors would be critically important. Maintaining discipline would ensure that the entire Allied force advanced through designated areas in a broad sweep north and then east, shoulder to shoulder. That way, Schwarzkopf and his senior commanders agreed, no Iraqi units would escape.

There was an even more important reason his commanders must adhere strictly to the plan. The commanders expected their forces to suppress enemy fire and overrun Iraqi positions very quickly. Allied forces would then rush to reach key targets, Schwarzkopf said. But on a battlefield where artillery could strike from twenty miles away and tanks could kill from a distance of two miles, Schwarzkopf continued, it was important that no units trespass into other units' sectors. Fratricide, or so-called friendly fire, was to be avoided by maintaining the battlefield discipline that had been a key assumption in his war planning. That did not mean that sector boundaries could not be changed if all parties agreed, Schwarzkopf said. But driving into your neighbor's sector in the night by mistake could get you killed. "You've heard the phrase 'Shit happens,' " said a senior Central Command planner and a close adviser to Schwarzkopf. "In this business, shit does not happen. You don't let it happen."

CHAPTER 18

HAIL MARY:
THE GROUND WAR BEGINS

A T CAMP DAVID on February 23, the deadline of noon, Eastern Standard Time, that George Bush had set for Saddam Hussein to withdraw from Kuwait expired. Just as when the United Nations deadline had expired thirty-eight days earlier, Saddam had not budged. Padding in the woods outside the Aspen Lodge, Bush did not even remark upon the deadline as it passed. Nine and a half hours later, the ground war began.

Like nearly all of the American soldiers who had spent the previous weeks and months in the Saudi desert, the leathernecks of the 2nd Marine Division had looked forward to the start of the ground war with a mixture of anxiety and eagerness. Anxiety because they knew that the conflict would be dangerous. Eagerness because they knew that the sooner they began fighting, the sooner they could go home.

In the far north of Saudi Arabia at 5:30 A.M. on February 24, nearly forty miles east of the Persian Gulf, forward units of the 2nd Marine Division approached the first Iraqi defensive line in a cold rain. Above them, the sky was black with soot from the wellhead fires Iraqi soldiers had set in Kuwait's al-Wafrah oil field. It was strangely quiet as the advance elements of the 2nd Marine Division approached the border in their tanks, tracked amphibious vehicles, and jeeplike Humvees, except for the roar of diesel engines and an infrequent command from a vehicle tender. To George Butler, a twenty-two-year-old corporal, and many of his Marine Corps buddies, it was all a bit confusing, all the forming up and waiting and stop-and-start movement in the rain and darkness. Even though this was to be their attack into the meanest part of the vaunted Iraqi defenses, it still didn't seem quite real.

Ahead of Butler, the 2nd Marine Division's engineer units had approached the first Iraqi mine field, cut through the barbed wire at its edge, and fired several rocket-propelled explosive charges. Known as mine-clearing line charges, or Mic-Lics, these were intended to detonate the Iraqi mines ahead. After firing the line charges, it was the job of the engineers to cut six narrow lanes through the mine fields with their tank-plows. Three battalions of Marines had been given the unenviable task of following the engineers through those six lanes, attacking the enemy behind the mine fields, and making the breach secure for the rest of the division to follow. Corporal Butler was the leader of a heavy machine-gun team in the regiment's 2nd Battalion. He was in a Humvee armed with a 50-caliber machine gun. Throughout the American military, the Humvee had replaced the venerable jeep. It had a wider wheel base and was more stable, and it was allegedly more comfortable. Each Marine also had an M-16 rifle. After the engineers cut the lanes through the mine field, Butler's unit was to lead his battalion through the center two lanes breaching the Iraqi defenses.

Muscular but normally soft-spoken and easygoing, Butler was tense and disoriented as he approached the mine field. His squad had trained to work in a wedge formation, but when they arrived at the breach lanes the engineers had cut through the Iraqi defenses, Butler saw that they were only twelve feet wide. The tanks and Humvees would have to go through in single file. In the distance, Butler watched the oil fires burn.

Butler's Humvee entered the first Iraqi mine field. His team went through surprisingly quickly. The rain was still falling. The Marines would have been even colder still, Butler thought, had they not been wearing their chemical-protection suits. The suits kept them warm, but they were getting soaked. Every Marine knew that the suit's charcoal-filter liner was worthless when wet. At the end of the first Iraqi mine field, there was a broad, open space. Ahead of him, the tanks of the engineers were preparing to breach the second mine field.

Suddenly, Iraqi mortar crews began firing. To the left of Butler's Humvee, three mortar rounds exploded. The thin-skinned Humvee afforded no protection against mortar fire. Butler looked to his section leader in another

Humvee one hundred yards away for orders. But the section leader wasn't taking fire, and he was not moving. Seconds later, ten yards to the right of Butler's Humvee, two more mortar rounds exploded. Shell fragments spattered the side of the Humvee. Butler slammed the Humvee's sliding plastic window shut. As he did so, another round hit, and Butler's arm went numb. "I've been hit," he screamed. "I'm hit!"

"Let's get the hell out of here," Butler yelled at his driver. The Humvee careened away from the incoming rounds. Mortar fire was now falling on the main part of the battalion whose flank Butler was assigned to guard. As Butler tore at his chemical-protection suit to see what was wrong with his arm, section leaders started pushing vehicles through the narrow breach lanes two at a time to escape the incoming fire. In his Humvee, Butler examined his arm. There was no blood. He had just hit his funny bone on the Humvee's window frame.

Well behind Butler, Colonel Ron Richard, the 2nd Marine Division's operations officer, was monitoring the attack closely. He knew that once his soldiers were strung out in the narrow lanes through the mine fields, there would be no place to run when artillery and mortar fire began falling on them. Richard had studied maps of the Iraqi defensive lines his intelligence people had made from overhead photos, but, up close, the Iraqi defensive belts were full of surprises. There were some oil-filled ditches the Iraqis had planned on lighting, but the Marines were skirting them. There were no high sand berms. At the rear of the mine fields, and even interspersed within them, there were plenty of fighting positions, trenches, foxholes, and bunkers. There were decoy tanks as well, some constructed of wood, others of metal. While some were no more than a steel pipe welded to a big, flat cylinder, covered with a camouflage net, many others were of ingenious design. In addition, real tanks were dug into the desert floor, with only their gun barrels peeking out. There were chicken-wire and chain-link fences in front of some of the Iraqi positions—this was an effective means of stopping anti-tank missiles, which are guided by a fine wire which they trail behind them. The fighting positions were well placed, enabling Iraqi soldiers to cover one another with interlocking fields of fire. "We were very much impressed with the defensive abilities that the Iraqis had set up," said Marine Sergeant Robert Novak from Clearwater, Florida, the leader of an anti-tank missile squad. "If they had not withdrawn, it would have been very, very hard."

Besides the difficulty of the defensive lines, Colonel Richard and his superiors knew the 1st and 2nd Marine Divisions were confronting a much larger Iraqi force. Schwarzkopf's intelligence officers had estimated that there were 188,000 Iraqi soldiers in southeastern Kuwait, the area the divisions were assigned to attack on the morning of February 24. Even if there were only half that number, Colonel Richard thought as his Marines raced through the breach lanes ahead of him, they would still have a serious fight ahead of them. Together, the 1st and 2nd Marine Divisions had fewer than 40,000 soldiers. Tactical doctrine called for an attacking force that outnumbered a defender by at least three to one. In January, Central Command officials had estimated that the two Marine divisions might sustain casualties of 30 percent or more going through the Iraqi defensive lines.

The attack plan was also an unusual one for Marines. The 1st and 2nd divisions were expected to drive through part of southern Kuwait and fight. Their primary mission was not to fight their way through to the emirate's capital (though if they could do that easily, fine). Instead, their main role in the overall plan was to attack to keep the Iraqis' attention, to hold them in place. As he listened to the radio reports of the Marines from his 2nd Division inching through the breach lanes, Richard contemplated the mission. After months of waiting, he thought, he would learn once and for all how difficult this conflict would actually be.

High above the breach in the Iraqis' forward defensive lines cut by the engineers of the 1st Marine Division, Captain Larry Buynak and his copilot, Captain Scott Carhart, could see the mortar fire off in the distance from the cockpit of their CH-46 helicopter. Like Butler and the Marines on the ground, Buynak and Carhart were wearing chemical-protection suits. They also had on air-cooled gas masks, which resembled diver's masks. Buynak and Carhart were "medevac" pilots: it was their mission to evacuate wounded Marines.

Entering Iraqi airspace, Buynak and Carhart flew between ten and twenty feet above the desert floor at over 100 miles an hour. Because they did not have a gunship escort, Buynak was "bunting," flying below ridges, power lines, and tank traps until the last second, then jerking the chopper upward. Along with the other Marine helicopters in this first hour of the ground war, Buynak and Carhart knew that they were highly exposed targets. The Iraqi army had Soviet-built anti-aircraft guns. Marine commanders had calculated that the Iraqi soldiers would use these first against low-flying helicopters, saving their surface-to-air missiles for higher-flying attack aircraft. The CH-46 was no match for the Iraqi firepower. It was a quarter century old and had only a 50-caliber machine gun with which to return fire.

As they approached the second breach cut by the engineers, Buynak and Carhart saw the artillery and anti-aircraft fire open up. "I didn't think about any of that stuff," Buynak said. "It was just like a normal training flight." As the anti-aircraft fire intensified, however, the two pilots reversed direction and headed south. It looked like "a wall of fire," Buynak said.

It took just a few minutes to return to the medevac-staging area the Marines called Lonesome Dove. It was located just inside the Saudi border not far from the elbow of the southeastern border with Kuwait. Within minutes after landing their helicopter at Lonesome Dove, Buynak and Carhart were ordered into the air again. The 1st Marine Division had called for its first medical evacuation. While Carhart went out to start the helicopter's engines, Buynak received map coordinates and requested a fighter escort.

None was available, he was told: all fighter aircraft in the area were assigned to anti-tank missions. Buynak and Carhart took off anyway. "They told us there were four of them [injured Marines] who stepped on a mine," Buynak said, "and that one wouldn't live ten minutes."

In less than two minutes, Buynak and Carhart were above the battlefield. Buynak saw no Iraqi troops or vehicles in the immediate vicinity so he set the helicopter down quickly near the wounded Marines. Immediately, with the blades of the helicopter roaring overhead, leathernecks came running toward the aircraft carrying their injured comrades. "It was right out of the *Life* magazine I saw in high school," said Buynak, thirty-seven, whose father was a Marine officer in Vietnam. "Black smoke, the guys were a mess, blown apart." There was blood everywhere, he said.

Quickly, the Marines loaded the four men aboard. The most seriously wounded had suffered compound fractures of both legs. The other three, their uniforms mostly blown or torn off, had been treated by their comrades with makeshift bandages to stanch the bleeding. In the back of the helicopter, a medic was already attending to the first of the wounded.

"We're losing them," Buynak screamed. "We're losing them!" Eight minutes after landing, Buynak was pushing the helicopter hard through the air while Carhart radioed ahead to the nearest field hospital. He covered the thirty-five miles in just fifteen minutes, as the medic in back attended to the four soldiers. En route, Buynak ordered one of his door gunners to put down his machine gun and hold an intravenous-feed bottle for the medic. Approaching the field hospital, Buynak set the helicopter down as close as possible to the waiting ambulance. Within seconds, medics hauled the doors of the aircraft open and lifted the injured Marines gently into the vehicle. Seconds later, the ambulance was speeding across the tarmac.

It would be another twenty-four hours before Buynak and Carhart got the good news. "Because of what you guys did," a doctor at the field hospital said, "those guys lived." The Marine who had been most grievously injured had lost a leg. Had Buynak and Carhart not gotten to him as quickly as they had, the doctor said, the Marine would surely have died.

By 9:20 A.M., the 2nd Marine Division was having mixed success. Of the three battalions trying to break through Iraqi mine fields and defenses, the one on the left and the one in the middle had made it.

The battalion on the left had gotten all the way through both Iraqi mine fields, and then had turned to the left and rolled in behind several Iraqi defensive positions. Many of the Iraqi tanks were dug in facing south; they were unable to maneuver at all. When the battalion rolled in behind these positions, the Iraqi forces in them were quickly destroyed. In the middle, the lead Marines of the next battalion had pushed through, their tankers heading directly toward an Iraqi brigade lying in wait ahead of them. On the right, however, the third battalion was still having trouble.

The original plan for Desert Storm had called for just one Marine Corps breach of the Iraqi lines. That breach was to have been accomplished by the 1st Marine Division, with the 2nd Marine Division following behind. It had been planned for a site just west of the Kuwait-Saudi Gulf coast highway. However, the plan had been changed after Arab members of the coalition requested a role in the opening hours of the ground campaign. Those forces were assigned two places to attack, and one of them was the site formerly assigned to the 1st Marine Division.

As a result of the change in plans, the 1st Marine Division had found a new site, forty miles to the west of the Gulf, where the southern Kuwait border turns abruptly north (that corner was called the "heel"). Twenty miles farther north and west, the 2nd Marine Division had chosen a site for its attack. It was defended by two belts of mine fields, each overlooked by

Iraqi artillery on a promontory and bordered by an oil field that spewed out noxious gases. The site was so well defended that the 2nd Marine Division commanders judged that the Iraqis would never guess that they would attack there. Nevertheless, it was something of a gamble.

From his command post in an amphibious vehicle, Colonel Larry Livingston, the commander of the 6th Marine Regiment, monitored the radio traffic with concern. A big, affable man from Ohio, Livingston had been placed in charge of the breaching operations by Major General William "Pit Bull" Keys, the commander of the 2nd Marine Division. This was not the spot that Livingston would have chosen for the breach. "There was a lot of risk. It would not have been my choice to go there. . . . It was difficult, and it was dangerous." There was a certain irony in this statement, though. Under the earlier plan, the 2nd Marine Division did not have to do a breach at all. Livingston was one of the top officers who had argued for a separate breaching operation by the 2nd Division, and this was the site he had been assigned.

The 2nd Marine Division had never practiced breaching in the States, and permission to do their own breach had not come until February 6. They had built a replica of the Iraqi defensive lines and practiced pushing through. The plan was to plow six lanes through the two mine fields, then come through fighting into southern Kuwait. To make the breach lanes, their engineers were supposed to advance to the edge of the mine field, then fire Mic-Lics, the 100-yard-long ropes of high explosive towed by a big rocket. The line charges were fired out ahead of the troops, then detonated. They would clear a path 100 yards long and 12 feet wide, detonating many but not all of the mines in their path. After the line charges came the tanks with plows, rakes, and rollers on the front. And through those long lanes in single file would pour the entire 8,000 vehicles and 19,000 men of the 2nd Marine Division.

That was the plan. But several of the Mic-Lics got hung up in the power lines that bordered their breach site. Then the plows encountered densely sown mines. As Sergeant Don Griffin watched the engineers work to clear two breach lanes, he counted four tank-plows damaged as they detonated the mines they were attempting to clear. One tank had been lifted right off the ground by the explosion. The scene, said Griffin, "was a mess." On the battalion's radio network, he listened as someone suggested that the tank drivers lower their plows another twelve inches. From his commander's hatch on his amphibious vehicle, Griffin could see the mines ahead of them, many lying right on top of the ground. All the Marines could do was bring up more tank-plows and try to get the breach lanes cleared.

As Sergeant Griffin watched the 2nd Marine Division's rightmost battalion stack up behind him while the tank-plows worked to clear the lanes ahead, he knew it was a dangerous location. The Iraqis could launch an artillery attack with chemical weapons. With so many troops concentrated in one place, there would be a lot of casualties. Even the regular Iraqi artillery, as erratic as it was, was dangerous in these circumstances.

Finally, with one breach lane cleared, a company of light armored vehicles, known as LAVs, crawled through bumper to bumper. As the column began to inch forward, an Iraqi artillery round exploded just to the right of Sergeant Delbert Pushert's thin-skinned LAV. A fragment whizzed past Pushert's face and struck his gunner, Lance Corporal David Ragas, square in the chest. "He thought he was dead," Pushert said. "I thought he was dead. He was yelling and screaming and flopping around in the turret. We thought we had a casualty." Pushert grabbed the radio, yelling to his company commander. He needed a corpsman fast, he said. The commander would not send a corpsmen through the mine field, however. Ragas ripped open his chemical-protection suit, and Pushert braced himself for the gush of blood. A heavy chunk of ragged metal clunked to the floor of their LAV. Ragas's flak jacket had saved his life.

As First Lieutenant William Redman waited to get in line for the breach, he was alerted by the 2nd Division's scouts that the breach lanes being cut on the left were contaminated by chemicals from a chemical mine. And up ahead, the scouts said, the breach teams of the battalion on the right were being delayed by small-arms fire. The commander of a rifle platoon in a tank battalion, Redman had been assigned to push through his breach lane fast and be ready to help fend off any Iraqi counterattack on the division. Chilled to the bone by the driving rain, Redman was instructed by the scouts to maneuver over to the two middle breach lanes, where they had only lost two tank-plows. They told him that his platoon had to push through quickly because a large Iraqi armored counterattack was coming. This, Redman thought, is for real.

With visibility at times less than 100 yards, the Marines had lost their support from the Navy F/A-18 attack planes. This was referred to as "close air support." While in the previous months Navy, Marine, and Air Force aviators had flown thousands of practice missions in preparation for the start of the ground campaign, the poor visibility on the morning of G-Day caused the suspension of nearly all such missions.

Meanwhile, back in Riyadh, Schwarzkopf received periodic reports from his battlefield commanders. By attacking with so much strength from the southwest, Schwarzkopf hoped to drive the Iraqi army into a retreat to the north and the east that would be focused in a pocket south of Basra. To accomplish this, Schwarzkopf knew, his soldiers would have to coordinate their movements very closely. At the far west end of the Allied front, the French-American force would protect the left flank. The 101st Airborne Division (Air Assault) would fly to the Euphrates Valley and cut the main east-west highway there, Iraqi Highway 8. General McCaffrey's division meanwhile was to skirt the end of Iraq's east-west defensive line and drive fast and deep north to the Euphrates Valley, before turning his division east. They would be in position to stop the Republican Guard divisions from escaping from Basra, or to assist in attacking them if the guard stayed in place.

On McCaffrey's right flank, General Franks's 1st and 3rd Armored Divisions and 2nd Armored Cavalry Regiment filled the middle of the Allied line. Their mission was to drive northeast into Iraq, see how the "center of gravity," the Republican Guard, reacted to their move, then attack and destroy them. The 1st Infantry Division was to remain in trail as a reserve force. Franks's VII Corps also had a tough British component, the British 1st Armored Division. Their mission was to punch through the Iraqi defenses and turn right and cut the defenders down from behind. Then they were to proceed toward Kuwait City, cutting the Iraqi forces in Kuwait in half. The British would also likely meet several of the armored divisions that Saddam kept just behind his forward defensive lines. These divisions were Saddam's linebackers, poised to respond across a wide area to any Allied attack.

On the right flank of the 1st Infantry Division, an Arab coalition force of Egyptian, Saudi, and Kuwaiti tanks was driving into southwestern Kuwait. A Syrian tank force lagged behind them. To their right, the 1st and 2nd Marine Divisions were already driving into southeastern Kuwait. Because their mission was primarily to fix the bulk of the Iraqi force in southern Kuwait into place and prevent them from attacking elsewhere, the Marines were referred to as a "supporting force" in Desert Storm. The 1st and 2nd

Divisions had been given the orders to attack first, because they would have to fight their way north while the divisions to their west could race through miles of empty desert. Their progress in the opening hours of the ground war would be critical to the coordination and success of the rest of Schwarzkopf's plan. In the twenty-four hours that the Marines would have to test the strength of the Iraqi defenses, the French-American force farthest west would secure the as-Salman Air Base. The 101st Airborne Division (Air Assault) from General Luck's 18th Airborne Corps flew north in a wave of 300 Black Hawk attack helicopters to establish a large logistics base halfway to the Euphrates. Its job was to get to the Euphrates Valley as soon as possible and cut off Highway 8, which was the Iraqi army's escape route from Basra.

Within three hours of the start of the ground campaign, the reports coming in to Schwarzkopf's headquarters staff were both encouraging and harrowing. At his command post far north in the Saudi desert, Marine Lieutenant General Walter Boomer was receiving periodic reports about the progress of the 1st and 2nd Marine Divisions through the Iraqi lines. Despite sporadic artillery fire and the four early casualties, Boomer was told by Major General Keys and his other commanders on the battlefield, the 1st and 2nd Marine Divisions were making far better progress than had been expected. They had already taken more than 1,000 prisoners of war. The condition of the Iraqi soldiers, Boomer was told, was appalling. Ill-fed, some of them without shoes, they hardly seemed to be a formidable fighting force. When he relayed these reports to Schwarzkopf, Boomer received authorization for his Marines to continue driving north.

Meanwhile, U.S. intelligence sources and members of the small Kuwaiti resistance movement inside Kuwait City were reporting a last-minute fit of bloodletting by the Iraqi forces there. One report reaching the Central Command headquarters staff described a "systematic campaign of executions . . . particularly of people they may have tortured."

Schwarzkopf conferred with Major General Robert Johnston, his chief of staff, and General John Yeosock, the commander of the Central Command's Army ground forces. All of the Allied forces were tied to the progress of the Marines, Schwarzkopf said, but since they were ahead of schedule, it seemed they should accelerate the movement of the other divisions. McCaffrey's division and Franks's corps had not been authorized by Schwarzkopf to move north from their "lines of departure," the attack points established by the Central Command, until the next morning, February 25. Johnston and Yeosock agreed that they should move earlier.

Schwarzkopf told Yeosock to relay the command. McCaffrey and Franks should prepare to begin their attacks immediately. At 9:30 A.M., Franks received a call from Yeosock. The Army ground commander was suffering acutely from an infected gallbladder, but he had refused to leave his post. The Marines were acquitting themselves so well on their end, Yeosock told Franks, that he wanted the VII Corps to begin its attack a full sixteen hours early. Could he move north by afternoon?

Franks said he could. He hung up and began issuing orders.

Minutes later, McCaffrey got a call from Yeosock. He, too, would issue orders for his division to begin moving north immediately.

On Sunday morning, February 24, President Bush invited a few of his closest aides and their spouses to attend church services with him and his wife, Barbara, at St. John's Church. Brent Scowcroft and John and Nancy Sununu were there, along with Dick and Lynne Cheney. Cheney was accompanied to St. John's by several Pentagon aides, and during the course of the service, one handed him a brief note summarizing the first written battlefield reports. The note indicated that early reports from the front were very favorable: little opposition and low casualties. Cheney handed the note surreptitiously to Bush.

After the service, the Bushes invited the group back to the White House. In the interim, Cheney had received more details from Central Command. Bush asked Cheney to give the group a description of the opening hours of the ground campaign. Cheney repeated the outlines of the assessment that had been relayed to his aides from Riyadh.

A few minutes later, in a back bedroom of the White House residence, Cheney gave Bush a more detailed report. There had been only four casualties so far, he told the President (the four Marines that had been evacuated from the battlefield by Marine captains Larry Buynak and Scott Carhart). Cheney also said that Schwarzkopf was accelerating the deployments of General Franks's VII Corps and General McCaffrey's 24th Infantry Division.

"That was a memorable moment," Cheney later said, "because that had been the key test. We didn't know for sure, but we were fairly confident

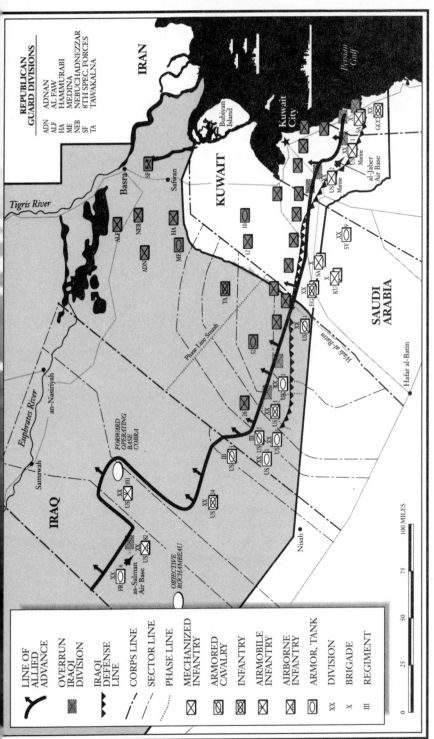

FEBRUARY 24, 1991: ALLIED TROOPS OVERRAN IRAQI DEFENSES ON THE FIRST DAY OF THE GROUND WAR

that we would do as well on the ground as we had in the air. But you didn't know until you did it exactly what the cost was going to be. But the guys had done such a good job getting through the wires, and the air [campaign] had absolutely devastated the Iraqis, that they weren't able to put up much of a fight. The biggest problems we were having in those early hours were the Iraqi prisoners."

Bush listened to the news from Cheney. He was pleased, he said, pleased and relieved.

McCaffrey's commanders and soldiers were primed for the move north. Besides the intensive map exercise they had gone through, prior to the beginning of the ground offensive scouts from the 24th Infantry Division had struck at border posts and probed their assigned routes of attack by helicopter. During that time, the scouts saw, the Iraqi border guard had deserted or melted away.

After talking to Yeosock, McCaffrey called his commanders and informed them that the time of attack had been moved up. The division would move north, he said, at 3 P.M. The actual line of departure for McCaffrey's divisions was marked as Phase Line Opus. It was twenty miles inside the Iraqi border.

The plan McCaffrey had developed called for Lieutenant Colonel Tom Leney's 2nd Squadron, 4th Cavalry to lead the way. Leney would charge far ahead of McCaffrey's three tank brigades. Leney's Bradley fighting vehicles had just returned from a deep-penetration raid into Iraq the previous night. After hearing from McCaffrey's headquarters that the attack would begin that afternoon, Leney ordered his soldiers to refuel quickly. At 10 A.M. Leney's unit was rolling north into Iraq.

The rest of McCaffrey's division also struck camp. While drivers hurried to refuel their M1A1 Abrams tanks and Bradley fighting vehicles, brigade and battalion command posts were broken down. Within hours, a long, snakelike column began forming up on the three main routes of attack.

Far to the east of McCaffrey, Major General "Pit Bull" Keys's 2nd Marine Division was contending with aggressive artillery fire. Keys calculated afterward that approximately 400 rounds fell on his division during the opening hours of the ground war. It was the threat that he and the other commanders assigned to the lead roles in the opening of the ground campaign had feared most. The Iraqis possessed highly accurate artillery guns. It would turn out, though, that their crews were so poorly trained that their fire was inaccurate.

Of course, in the week before the start of the ground war, Generals Boomer and Yeosock did not know that. They pushed the Air Force even harder to direct more combat missions against Iraq's forward-deployed artillery guns. The Air Force sent more F-16s against artillery targets. However, because their success ratio was not high, a senior Central Command official said, the ground commanders became "hostile" over what they viewed as a lack of air support. Air Force officials argued that they were trying, and even some Army and Marine officers conceded that destroying artillery from the air was an extremely difficult mission. Artillery was easy to hide in camouflage. And from 10,000 feet, the altitude at which the F-16s had to drop their bombs, direct hits on artillery were few and far between.

So, days before the ground war, Marine Corps and Army units on the front lines had begun to take matters into their own hands. Relying on satellite and spy plane photographs, Marine and Army units fired their own artillery into the target areas and then relocated quickly. American gunners were confident that they could fire and move before the Iraqis responded. The Army and the Marines also employed a more high-tech approach. Employing Multiple Launch Rocket Systems, FireFinder radar, and cluster bombs called Dual-Purpose Improved Cluster Munitions, the counterartillery effort would neutralize the Iraqi guns very quickly. The Multiple Launch Rocket System could deliver as many as twelve rockets twenty-five miles away to an area the size of four football fields, all in less than a minute. Each rocket carried 644 anti-personnel or anti-vehicle submunitions. This meant that pinpoint accuracy was not necessary. With the FireFinder radar system, soldiers could detect the first incoming enemy artillery shell, compute its ballistic path, and locate its origin with laserlike accuracy. In the days before the ground war, up and down the front, artillery teams equipped with the FireFinder had driven very close to the Iraqi border and fired at Iraqi artillery guns. The hope was that if the Iraqis returned the fire, the FireFinder would identify and then kill them. For a while, it worked. Then the Iraqis got smart and stopped firing.

. . .

By 9:30 A.M. on G-Day, the 2nd Marine Division was close to achieving its breakthrough. Of the three battalions in Colonel Livingston's regiment, the one on the left had gotten through the mine fields and was rolling up the Iraqi defenses from behind. The one in the middle was through, too, overrunning an Iraqi brigade lying in wait. The battalion on the right, however, was still in trouble. To their right, at al-Jaber airfield, an Iraqi battalion was firing onto the Marines' right flank.

Livingston broke a company of LAVs free from the center and swung them to the right to attack the Iraqi force. The small, fast, light-wheeled LAVs, which were armed with 25-mm automatic cannons, would not be enough to defeat a large Iraqi force, but the attack would buy Livingston enough time to push the rest of his Marines through the left and middle lanes of the Iraqi mine fields.

Racing ahead as they fired, the LAVs drove the Iraqis back and away from the elements of the 2nd Division still slogging through the mine fields. Then they set up blocking positions to keep them away. Livingston sent more engineers in to help the rightmost battalion, and by 10 A.M. they had punched through, too. He secured the northern side of his position and began to bring through his division's combat forces.

Livingston was worried about an attack on the division's left flank. That was where the Iraqi armored reserve would come from. Off to his left was a position assigned to the Syrians. And to the north of the Syrians was the Iraqi 1st Armored Division, in a position to drive south and hit the Marines' left flank. If the Syrians stayed close they could protect Livingston. But the Syrians had Russian-made T-62 tanks, just like the Iraqis. In a series of tense meetings, the Syrian commanders had asked over and over, "What would happen if the Marines spotted our T-62s? Could they tell Syrian tanks from Iraqis?" The Marines had answered frankly that they could not. As a result, the Syrians had refused to assume their assigned position and had then moved west to follow the Egyptians and Kuwaitis into Kuwait. The Marines' left flank was thus exposed throughout the war.

Nevertheless, the attack from the left never materialized. Instead, Iraqi soldiers patrolled the area to the right of the division's position by the hundreds or maybe thousands. Then the Tiger Brigade, a tank-heavy Army brigade sent to the Marines from the 1st Cavalry Division, finally came through the breach lanes and assumed its assigned position as the division's leftmost brigade. That addition gave the 2nd Marine Division more protection on the left and much more firepower.

But for the Marine Corps foot soldiers, the grunts of the war, southeastern Kuwait was still a very dangerous place. When George Butler's 2nd Battalion pushed through the second mine field, he saw mines of every sort lying scattered on the ground. He saw fighting trenches and tanks dug in with their guns pointed at them. There were more Iraqi tanks in flames, and Iraqi soldiers were rising cautiously out of the earthen ditches and holes on nearly all sides of him, walking toward him and the other Marines through the drizzle. Butler's platoon had passed the wire fence marking the end of the second mine field: they were finally through the breach. It would be someone else's responsibility to take charge of the Iraqi soldiers. Finally in the clear, Butler and his platoon moved into the wedge formation they had been trained to maintain. Somewhere up ahead, he knew, was their first objective. It was an Iraqi defensive position on a small hill.

Before he had traveled even 200 yards past the end of the second mine field, Butler and his platoon ran into more trenches. And more Iraqis, too. The Iraqi soldiers seemed confused, Butler said. Some fired sporadically, but most offered to surrender. Soldiers from a few ragged-looking Iraqi platoons started marching north, toward Basra.

Once again, Butler and his team ignored the Iraqi soldiers and pushed on toward their objective. Butler's team leader told him to blanket the hill with heavy machine-gun fire to cover an approaching Marine unit. But the Marines that Butler could see zigzagging toward the hill turned out to be a Marine fire squad that was providing covering fire for another attacking unit that was out of sight. Butler's team was firing into the attackers, he figured out later. "I had no idea what was going on, honestly," Butler said. "All I know was that our team leader said, 'Go ahead, rock 'n' roll, blanket the hill with fire.'"

Fortunately, their fire hit no one. More Iraqis crawled out of ditches and fighting positions to surrender.

Ahead of Butler's position, the Marines that were providing the covering fire belonged to a platoon from the middle battalion's Fox Company. One of its fire teams was led by Corporal James Disbro, twenty-three. Disbro's platoon had advanced toward the hill when Disbro, standing up in his track's hatch, heard bullets whizzing over his head and saw other rounds kicking up dirt near a Humvee behind him. "They're firing at us," he yelled.

Disbro's platoon leader had ordered his Marines out of their amphibious tracked vehicle, and seconds later, as they opened up on the Iraqi position with a 50-caliber machine gun, the Iraqi soldiers returned the fire. The Marine squads crawled and ran toward the Iraqis. "We laid down a base of fire," Disbro said, "and they were firing at us, and I started thinking, 'Where's the air support they promised us?' I was waiting for planes to come in and bomb them." Twenty minutes later, a Marine Corps Cobra helicopter began spraying the hill in front of Disbro with machine-gun fire. Minutes after that, Disbro said, white flags started fluttering in the breeze.

With the hill taken, Butler's team moved on. They encountered a network of trenches. Butler thought they had already been searched, but suddenly six Iraqi soldiers came out. Tense and frightened, Butler and his team tossed several grenades into the trenches. Still more Iraqis came out, dragging others who had been wounded by the grenades. Several of the soldiers, Butler saw, were obviously dying.

And still more Iraqi soldiers dragged themselves from the trenches. Soon Butler's platoon was flooded with them. Some were badly wounded, and many who weren't were so weak from lack of food and water that they could hardly stand. After disarming them, Butler told two Iraqi soldiers to take some of the less badly wounded to a collection point. The two soldiers walked five paces, Butler said, and then nearly fainted. One wounded Iraqi had a huge shrapnel wound in his chest. He begged for water. Butler's platoon was not supposed to give out their water, however. Butler fumed. Clearing trenches and taking charge of prisoners was not the job of his platoon. But the line companies that were supposed to do it were nowhere in sight. "We tried to ignore the crying," Butler said, "but it was hard to do."

Later that day, Marines from the 2nd Division captured an Iraqi general, a brigade commander, and the commander's operations officer. They blindfolded the three Iraqis and took them to Major General Keys and Colonel Richard. Through an interpreter, the Iraqi general gave Keys and Richard the answer to one of the chief mysteries of the war: Why had the Iraqis not used chemical artillery weapons? The Iraqi general said the soldiers in his area had never intended to use chemical weapons. They were afraid, he said, that the gas might get out of control and kill them. The general also told Keys and Richard that the main Iraqi resistance was yet to come.

With more Marines flooding through the breach lanes as the morning drew on, the offensive against the Iraqi force deployed in southern Kuwait began to accelerate. Within hours, the 2nd Marine Division would destroy what remained of two brigades of Iraqi infantry, tanks, and artillery, and by the end of the day, the 2nd Division would destroy two more Iraqi brigades and capture roughly 5,000 prisoners.

By midafternoon, McCaffrey's 24th Infantry Division had crossed the sand berms into Iraq and paused briefly to orient themselves. The order of battle established by McCaffrey was: Colonel Paul Kern's 2nd Brigade was to lead in this early phase of the division's move north; Kern's brigade was on the division's east flank. Colonel John LeMoyne's 1st Brigade was in the center and slightly behind Kern. On the western flank, and slightly ahead of LeMoyne's M1A1 tanks, was Colonel Ted Reid's 197th Brigade.

The division began driving north into the teeth of a gathering sandstorm. The engineer companies that had led McCaffrey's division through the sand berms had marked the three main trails with a series of three six-foot-long metal stakes bound together into a tripod. From each tripod hung a flashing battery-powered highway danger light. In the driving sand, the flashing lights would enable the heavy fuel tankers and supply trucks far to the rear of the three long columns make their way north. "That turned out to be a real winner," Paul Kern said. "You conceal things so you don't give away plans before you execute, but there are some things you ought to do to make life easy for yourself, and marking the route like that plainly is one of the things that helped. The critical piece of this operation was to keep the logistics moving at the pace of the armored forces."

In the driving sand long after nightfall, the long lines of tanks, Bradleys, Humvees, fuel wagons, and supply trucks snaked north through the desert. Shortly before two in the morning, about sixty miles into Iraq, Kern's map indicated a broken line running from east to west. It was a steep escarpment. "The sandstorm was still blowing, and we just flat couldn't find a route up that escarpment," Paul Kern said. "Every time we turned to go further east to find a way, we'd get stuck in a wadi. So I just kept going up one wadi. The scouts were in another wadi. The division commander was following me, wondering where the hell I was going. We just could not find a route in that sandstorm. About 4 A.M., I finally said, 'I'm holding here until we get some more light.' At first light, we found the one route up the escarpment."

Meanwhile, farther west, Ted Reid's 197th Brigade had moved all night through some of the worst terrain in the desert. He had had to cross fields of lava rock that stretched for miles. By first light on February 25, Kern's brigade was in sight of their first objective. It was listed on division maps as Objective Brown. It comprised three Iraqi logistics bases. With the sun up shortly after 6 A.M., Reid called in air strikes. His brigade attacked a few minutes later. "We met some resistance," Reid recalled. "It was mainly fire the obligatory ten rounds and then surrender. We took seventy-nine prisoners. We found out, interestingly enough, that they did not expect us to attack in that direction. That's the first indication we had that they absolutely figured that no U.S. units would go through that terrain."

At 3 that afternoon, the 1st Infantry Division attacked, too. Two months before the ground war started, VII Corps commander Lieutenant General Fred Franks had designated the Big Red One from Fort Riley, Kansas, as the division to make the breach of the Iraqi defenses for the rest of the corps. By G-Day, the 1st Infantry's commanders had all they needed. From overhead photos, they had drawn a plan of the Iraqi defenses that showed every fighting trench, tank, and artillery emplacement.

At the point of attack, about ten miles from the end of their fortifications, the Iraqi defenses were manned by a ragged brigade of reservists. After days of air bombardment that force had diminished to 1,000 men at most. After a thirty-minute artillery barrage of 11,000 shells, many Iraqis came south with their hands raised. But some chose to fight.

The mine plows and engineer vehicles of the Big Red One rolled forward. They cut eight lanes through the thinly seeded mine fields, then headed for the Iraqi trenches. When they reached the trenches, they rolled right over them. Iraqis scattered. Some came out waving flags, some fired shots at the tanks and then surrendered. Some ran away, and a smaller number stayed and fought back. The tanks turned left and right, rolling along the side of the trenches, plowing them under. Iraqis who chose not to surrender were plowed under, too. Colonel Lon Maggart, the commander of the 1st Brigade, one of two that cut the breach lanes, later estimated that between 80 and 250 Iraqis had been buried alive. Lieutenant Colonel Terry Bullington, the division's operations officer, guessed that the number was smaller than that. The division's officers and the Pentagon defended the practice, saying it was no worse than killing a resisting enemy with hand grenades or with bayonets in the gut. The Army said it was the only instance in the war of live enemy burials.

CHAPTER 19

G-PLUS-ONE

D AWN ON THE second day of the ground campaign promised a gray, windy day. It was Monday, February 25, but many of the soldiers who kept diaries referred to it as G-Plus-One.

Three hundred miles west of the Persian Gulf, the fast mechanized division composed of French forces and one brigade of the 82nd Airborne Division had raced 60 miles north into Iraq across a rocky desert floor. This was the 6th Light Armored Division, called the Daguet Division, combining American paratroopers with a variety of French armor. Its two light tank regiments were equipped with AMX-10RCs, small, fast, six-wheeled vehicles with 105-mm guns. "They just flew," said Colonel Bob Kee, the American liaison officer to the French forces. "They can go fifty miles an hour, and at times they were going that fast."

The Daguet Division also had a regiment of sixty fast attack helicopters, which were critical to the mission Central Command had assigned to the Daguet. To protect the long left flank of the 18th and the VII Corps, the Dauget Division had to watch for an Iraqi counterattack coming down from Baghdad and hooking in from the west. On the morning of G-Plus-One, the Daguet's helicopters were scouring the desert of southwestern Iraq, looking for any signs of an Iraqi approach.

The Daguet had already overrun a brigade of Iraq's 45th Infantry Division in an area about 30 miles north of the border that had been designated as Objective Rochambeau. But it was also required to take as-Salman Air Base 40 miles farther north. Located in the center of the division's assigned sector, the airfield would serve as its logistics and command base as it screened the western flank of the 18th and VII Corps. After a brief skirmish, the Allied force took the village of as-Salman and the Iraqi military garrison there. As a result, however, the Daguet and its brigade of the 82nd Airborne had more Iraqi prisoners than could be readily dealt with. The French-American force was equipped to handle as many as 500 prisoners a day, but in seizing Objective Rochambeau and as-Salman, they had already taken 1,500. Their progress had been slowed by the procession of prisoners from the village of as-Salman, as well as by the sheer mass of their force. "For the first twenty-four hours," said Colonel Kee, "the road north looked like the L.A. freeway. It was bumper to bumper."

Schwarzkopf and his generals were pleased by the French-U.S. success. The French had been a big question mark in the coalition ever since its creation in August. At the time of the invasion of Kuwait, the French defense minister was Jean-Pierre Chevènement. A founding member of the French-Iraqi Friendship Society, Chevènement had opposed sending French forces to Saudi Arabia, had been unwilling to sanction French air raids on targets inside Iraq, and had opposed France's U.N. Security Council vote authorizing the use of force against Iraq. On January 29, Chevènement had resigned. His replacement was Pierre Joxe, a vocal opponent of the Iraqi aggression. With Joxe's appointment, as well as the performance of the Daguet Division, the questions about the role of the French participation had been substantially resolved.

To the east of the French-U.S. force was the sector assigned to the 101st Airborne Division (Air Assault). They were part of General Gary Luck's 18th Airborne Corps, which also comprised the Dauget Division, General Barry McCaffrey's 24th Infantry Division (Mechanized), and the 3rd Armored Cavalry Regiment. Schwarzkopf and Luck had assigned the 101st a key mission. Made up of infantrymen and lightweight vehicles, all transportable by helicopter, the 101st was capable of being dropped onto a site to seize and hold it until heavier forces arrived. With its armada of 300 UH-60 Black Hawk helicopters, the 101st Division's job was to get to the Euphrates Valley and cut all traffic and communications lines along Highway 8, the six-lane highway connecting Basra with Baghdad. This would prevent or at least interrupt the movement of Iraqi reinforcements from

Baghdad. It would also prevent Iraqi soldiers in the divisions near Basra from escaping.

Because of the rain and limited visibility in the opening hours of the ground war on February 24, some of the officers in the 101st had urged that the mission be delayed a few hours. One of their observation helicopters had already had an accident in the rain and the dark. They were overruled by General J. H. Binford Peay, the commanding officer of the 101st. On Peay's orders, the Black Hawks began to take off at 7:25 A.M. on G-Day from seventeen different departure areas. They carried four battalions of infantrymen northward into Iraq.

These soldiers had created a vast new base that was listed on the maps of Central Command as Forward Operations Base Cobra, which would extend across approximately 200 square kilometers in an area of desert ninety-three miles north of Iraq's southern border with Saudi Arabia. The logistics base was nearly half the size of the 101st Division's permanent home in Fort Campbell, Kentucky. Within twenty-four hours, the new base had 200,000 gallons of fuel on hand. It could easily accommodate another 200,000. The base was to play a critical role as a helicopter refueling depot to support the VII Corps and 18th Airborne Corps as they mounted attacks deeper into Iraq, north toward the Euphrates River, and later, eastward toward Iraqi armored forces guarding Kuwait.

Slightly more than twenty-four hours into the ground campaign, on February 25, the infantrymen of the 101st Division were constructing twenty-five refueling areas within the Cobra base for the tanks and Bradley fighting vehicles that were grinding north behind them. As the Army specialists hurried to ready Cobra for operations, other soldiers patrolled the perimeter of the base. On the eastern side of the base, one battalion encountered a heavily defended garrison full of Iraqi soldiers. The soldiers belonged to a reserve battalion of Iraq's 45th Infantry Division, other elements of which had been taken prisoner at Objective Rochambeau and as-Salman the day before.

The battalion from the 101st pounded the garrison with artillery fire, followed by air strikes from Apache helicopters. Armed with laser-guided missiles, ground-attack rockets, and a 30-mm automatic cannon, the Apache was an effective battlefield-support weapon. Within fifteen minutes of the start of the attack, the Iraqi commander was captured. The rest of his soldiers quickly surrendered. The battalion returned with 400 Iraqi prisoners.

General Peay had taken no chances in securing the Cobra base. It was too important to the success of the ground-campaign plan. On February 23, the day before the ground war began, Peay had dispatched four long-range surveillance teams into Iraq to scout for concentrations of Iraqi soldiers. The four teams were composed of six men each. Every one of the soldiers had been trained to operate behind enemy lines, to act as the eyes and ears of his division commander.

Within hours of their arrival under the cover of night at Objective Cobra, as the scouts called it, three of the four teams had investigated the location, identifying the Iraqi garrison to the east. The fourth team had begun scouting nearby sections of a two-lane highway that led from the Saudi town of Rafha north to Highway 8.

On G-Plus-One, the fourth team of scouts had been spotted by Iraqi civilians. On foot, the surveillance team had issued an immediate call to the crews of two Black Hawk helicopters and two Apaches (the helicopters had been standing by in case of just such an emergency). The four helicopter pilots had raced north to recover the six-man team. As the commandos scrambled aboard the first Black Hawk to arrive, the pilot saw Iraqi military vehicles approaching at high speed, just a half mile away. It was a narrow escape.

Fifty miles north of the Cobra logistics base, sixty of the 101st Airborne's enormous Chinook helicopters dropped out of the soot-gray sky just minutes after first light. The Chinooks were loaded with soldiers, Humvees, and tons of equipment. Central Command maps called the location Landing Zone Sand. The soldiers were part of a heavy infantry force known as the Rakkasans, which means "falling umbrellas" in Japanese. The regiment had earned the name as an occupation force in Japan after the Second World War.

The original plan had called for the Rakkasans to leave for Landing Zone Sand under cover of darkness the evening of February 25, but the weather forecast was so bad that Peay had decided to send them early. The Rakkasans were to drive 40 kilometers north to a point next to Highway 8 to join other battalions of infantrymen being flown in by helicopters. Just hours after arrival at Landing Zone Sand, Lieutenant Colonel Tom Greco began to lead his troops north across the Euphrates Valley toward Highway 8. The rains turned their route to deep, sticky mud, hampering their progress.

By 10 A.M., to the east of General Peay's 101st Division, the 1st and 2nd brigades of McCaffrey's 24th Infantry Division (Mechanized) were atop the escarpment that had so bedeviled them the night before. Meanwhile Colonel Ted Reid's 197th Brigade had made it halfway to the Euphrates. Reid was positioned just east of Peay's Cobra base. Farther east, on the right flank of the 24th Infantry Division, was the 3rd Armored Cavalry Regiment. So far, the composite parts of General Schwarzkopf's field army were coordinating well, and Hail Mary was unfolding according to plan. "It was just like a parade," Lieutenant Colonel B. J. Craddock said. "The only problem was weather. We faced, in my opinion, the worst weather we had the whole time we were over there, what with the sandstorm followed by the rainstorm."

As Reid's brigade pushed farther north, the rain continued to fall. The routes that Reid and several of the other commanders had studied during their map exercises turned out, in many instances, to be little better than goat trails; in the rain, Reid discovered, they quickly turned into alleys of mud.

East of Reid's brigade, Colonel Paul Kern's 2nd Brigade was moving forward with trepidation. On his map the area ahead of him appeared to be scored by deep wadis. But as far as Kern could see in the rain, the ground ahead was flat and wide. He was perplexed. The reconnaissance photographs he had been shown just days before had indicated clearly that this part of the desert was traversed by several deep, dried-up riverbeds. Perhaps, Kern thought, the shadows and the colors of the desert made a shallow wadi look 100 feet deep.

Moving ahead warily, Kern's brigade encountered an Iraqi compound—an electronic-warfare facility with antennas on the roof, flanked by several fighting bunkers. Kern ordered the compound saturated with artillery fire. Iraqi soldiers soon ran from the buildings.

As his soldiers began disarming the Iraqis, Kern noted that they fell into essentially two classes. One group of prisoners had retreated from the Kuwait border; they were in very poor shape. The second was made up of men assigned to air-defense units based in the area. Kern's brigade took about 300 prisoners. Most, Kern and his men believed, were from Iraq's 26th and 35th Infantry Divisions.

Thirty-five miles north of Kuwait's border with Saudi Arabia, at 10:15 A.M., advance units of the 1st Marine Division were skirting the fires of the al-Burgan oil field when they received a nasty surprise. Of all the forces penetrating Iraqi-held territory, the Marines had the toughest time. First, it had been slow picking their way through the densely seeded mine fields. Then, at 6 P.M. the evening before, when leathernecks from Marine Task Force Papa Bear had called for artillery fire, the incoming rounds landed near a prisoner-of-war compound in another zone assigned to Marine Task Force Ripper. A Marine and a Navy corpsman were injured. Two Iraqi POWs were killed, and twenty-three prisoners were injured.

Fog had flanneled the 1st Marine Division until the next morning. Then it lifted. A short distance from the division's command post, or CP, First Lieutenant Mike Dunlop heard the unmistakable clanking of armored treads. He couldn't tell if they were friend or foe, or even which direction the noise was coming from. Suddenly someone yelled, "Enemy on the perimeter!" Machine guns began to chatter, TOW missiles were fired. "They're headed to the CP!" someone else shouted. An Iraqi counterattack, in the form of a mechanized brigade and some infantrymen, had emerged from the one place American tacticians had considered unlikely—the al-Burgan oil field. With blazing wells belching black smoke and a maze of pipelines snaking across the sand, the oil field had been virtually written off by Marine battle planners as a source of trouble.

In the command post, which was no more than a cluster of Humvees with tent extensions attached to them, Colonel Greg Pepin, an Army artillery liaison officer attached to the Marines, was jolted by the explosion of several Iraqi artillery shells dropping just 100 yards away.

An instant later, tanks from Iraq's 5th Mechanized Brigade and 26th Armored Brigade came wheeling out of the darkness of the burning oil field, storming right at the Marines. "It was dicey," Pepin said. It was a moment that called for air support, but in the black skies created by the oil field fires, there was none. By good fortune, however, the Marines' howitzers were pointed directly at the oncoming Iraqi tanks. Quickly but steadily, the Americans lowered their guns and fired. Several of the Iraqi tanks were hit dead-center and Marines with shoulder-fired anti-tank weapons also opened up, while Cobra helicopter gunships and LAVs took after the fleeing Iraqi tanks.

A half mile away, Lieutenant Dunlop reacted swiftly. He ordered the tanks of Charlie Company to halt the Iraqi advance. The first troops they saw were infantrymen in Chinese-made armored personnel carriers (APCs), with T-55 tanks in a staggered column behind them. Dunlop counted fifteen tanks and fifteen to twenty APCs. Sergeant Karl Falls, a ten-year veteran from Slater, Missouri, and a tank commander, called the counterattack "the battle for breakfast," because his platoon had been eating their rations, or MREs (for "meals, ready to eat"), and shaving when they got the word the enemy was inside their perimeter. "We thought, 'We're going to get shot by our own people,' " he said. Lance Corporal Keith Beer, a twenty-year-old ammo loader, found his tank chasing Iraqis. "We came up over a ridge—nothing," said Beer. "We came up over another ridge and there were thirty or forty enemy vehicles. Everybody started shooting." Beer began throwing fifteen- to twenty-pound rounds into the tank's guns "like it was an Olympic sport." Several empty Iraqi tanks had been positioned in front as decoys, while those in back were doing the actual firing. Most of the Iraqi force was eliminated in about twenty minutes, but the Americans continued to fire for another hour. Just as the shooting was over, a white dove flew in and landed on the gun of Charlie tank 1-3.

The 1st Marine Division had processed 600 Iraqi prisoners of war the evening before. Across the battlefield, the reports of thousands of such prisoners were being passed across the Allied radio networks. It was stunning news. But for Colonel Pepin, the sudden barrage of artillery fire and the surprise tank charge suggested that at least some Iraqis still had some fight left in them.

Well to the rear of his advancing columns, Lieutenant General Fred Franks was watching the progress of his 1st and 3rd Armored Divisions, his 1st Infantry Division, his 2nd Armored Cavalry Regiment, and his British 1st Armored Division. Franks intended to push his divisions north for 120 kilometers parallel to Kuwait's western border with Iraq, all the while watching to see what the Republican Guard did. If the Republican Guard stayed in place north of Kuwait, he would turn his divisions east, toward them and the Persian Gulf.

Franks knew they had a long way to go. The lead elements of his 3rd Armored Division had advanced just 29 kilometers into Iraq on G-Day. The heavy divisions were so large and moved so slowly that it was not until nearly noon on G-Plus-One that the last elements of the 3rd Armored Division crossed into Iraq.

Advancing through the desert, the 3rd Division's brigades had finally formed up, the 2nd Brigade to the left and the 1st to the right. Side by side, with their smaller interior units positioned in fighting wedges, the two brigades stretched for 20 kilometers across the desert. Schwarzkopf's war plan called for the 1st and 2nd brigades to drive rapidly toward a position marked as Objective Collins, where the two brigades were to tighten up their ranks and synchronize their drive eastward toward the Republican Guard divisions. To their rear, the 3rd Division's 3rd Brigade tagged along in reserve, its tank drivers and soldiers straining to see ahead in the driving rain.

In the afternoon, the 3rd Brigade swept through a small desert town that the 1st and 2nd brigades had bypassed. They made a rapid sweep of the village, capturing 270 very surprised and disheartened Iraqi soldiers.

As the 3rd Brigade continued north in the rain, Sergeant First Class William Paslay had to keep wiping his goggles to see. A platoon sergeant in a tank battalion, Paslay stood in the turret of his M1A1 Abrams tank, peering forward through the fog and rain. The precipitation ran down his face and dripped off his chin. Like other Allied soldiers and commanders all across the front, Paslay and his colleagues were astounded by the numbers of Iraqi prisoners they were taking. The commanders of Desert Storm worried that the prisoners would slow down the attack plan considerably. "We started taking prisoners," said Sergeant First Class Dale Orndorf, forty-six, a seventeen-year Army veteran riding in a headquarters command vehicle near Paslay's tank. "Then we started not taking prisoners. There were so many. We'd throw them some water and MREs and keep going."

Just to the west of the 3rd Armored Division, the 1st Armored Division ran into elements of a brigade of the Iraqi 26th Infantry Division. They rolled them up with ease. Almost a reserve force, the Iraqi division had been assigned only support roles, never combat missions, during the Iran-Iraq war. Two brigades of the 26th Infantry Division had been deployed to the south, manning the western tip of the Iraqi defensive lines, and one brigade was to the north. It was this latter brigade that the 1st Armored Division came upon, scattered in fighting positions at desert crossroads and villages. "They had some pretty good defenses that could probably have taken out 10 percent of our division," said Lieutenant Colonel Keith Alexander, the division's intelligence officer, "if they had fought hard enough and timed it well."

Instead, the half-dozen engagements during the course of the six-hour battle developed into routs. Alexander had used intelligence photos from satellites and spy planes to draw plastic overlays spotting every enemy fighting position. Unit commanders would lay the overlays on their maps, and see exactly the location of every tank revetment and trench and fighting hole. As the division's brigades rolled up close to enemy positions, which were usually at road junctions, they pounded the Iraqis with artillery. Then the division's brigade commanders ordered their M1A1 Abrams tanks into action. With the M1A1's superb long-range targeting system, the Americans could see, identify, and shoot Iraqi tanks and fighting vehicles far beyond the Iraqi tank-gun range. Often, the Iraqis simply did not know what had hit them.

Toward the end of the afternoon engagement, Iraqis were surrendering in droves. The men of the 1st Armored Division congratulated one another. "We got to practice on a third-stringer," said Alexander. "We were the New York Giants scrimmaging the JayVees from some high school called the Iraqi 26th Division."

From that battle, and from most of the other lopsided engagements with Iraqi forces in the first thirty-six hours of the ground war, American commanders began to reach several early conclusions. By deploying some of his least battle-ready troops (such as the 26th Division) on the front lines, Saddam Hussein had made a strategic blunder. He was sacrificing both soldiers and any possibility of receiving accurate intelligence from his front-line troops on the direction, size, and scope of the Allied offensive. Those Iraqi soldiers who did not flee or who were not killed or taken prisoner in the first hours of the Allied ground campaign may well have relayed information to Saddam's more able military commanders in the rear. But they were such unskilled soldiers and had such little training, U.S. officials said, that whatever information they did convey was almost certainly incomplete or erroneous.

· · ·

On G-Plus-One, Captain Eric Salomonson, twenty-eight, and First Lieutenant John Marks, twenty-six, destroyed twenty-three Iraqi tanks. Despite the black smoke from the oil field fires, the rain, and the fog, Salomonson, Marks, and the other pilots assigned to the 144 A-10 ground-attack aircraft deployed in Operation Desert Storm were among the most important contributors to the Allied success. The A-10s killed many Iraqi tanks long before American or Allied tankers could even approach to within range. The A-10 Warthog had been designed and built with two objectives. It was a killer of enemy armor, and it could provide highly effective close support for American ground troops. In Desert Storm, the A-10 succeeded brilliantly at both missions. Although the 144 A-10s deployed in the Kuwait Theater of Operations flew only about 30 percent of the combat sorties during Operation Desert Storm, Air Force officials said they accounted for more than 50 percent of the destruction of Iraqi equipment.

Typically, the A-10 flies at 420 miles an hour on combat runs. That is slow for jets, but ideal for ground troops who need air cover. In addition to its 30-mm cannon, which fires heavy depleted-uranium bullets, the A-10 can carry up to eight tons of ordnance. It can drop laser-guided bombs, fire Maverick anti-tank missiles, or employ its 30-mm gun. Theoretically, the A-10 can fly combat missions circling "on station" for two hours at battlefields more than 250 miles from its base.

The A-10s were also the first aircraft deployed when, during the air campaign, the Bush administration ordered Schwarzkopf to step up his efforts to locate and destroy the Scud missile launchers in western Iraq. Their long "play time"—they could spend thirty to forty-five minutes over a target—made them ideal for hunting the mobile Scud launchers. Finally, the A-10 was built to fly even if heavily damaged. In one attack early in Desert Storm, an A-10 survived after Iraqi ground fire ripped a ragged six-foot hole in its wing.

On February 25, neither Eric Salomonson nor John Marks thought he would be able to fly because of poor visibility. They had started their engines, then gone back to the squad room of the 76th Tactical Fighter Squadron at King Fahd Airport in eastern Saudi Arabia to wait. A sign on the wall read: "Kill 'em all—Let Allah sort 'em out."

Then the call came. A patrol squadron had discovered "a lot of tanks," Salomonson said. They were the best Soviet models, T-72s, the report said. Evidently, Salomonson and Marks were told, the tanks had pulled far to one side of a dirt road in an attempt to hide from Allied aircraft.

Aloft, Salomonson and Marks flew their A-10s north to the area where the tanks had been seen. It was south of Kuwait City, just ahead of the most forward units of the 1st and 2nd Marine Divisions. Crossing the southern border of Kuwait, Salomonson and Marks made radio contact with several other A-10 pilots. Next they spoke with one of the U.S. Army's forward air controllers. "He told us we were well clear of friendlies [coalition troops]," Salomonson said. "Another pair of A-10 pilots joined us. We took the west, they took the east, and we saw the tanks."

Salomonson and Marks attacked without waiting. First, they fired Maverick heat-seeking missiles. They held off using the 30-mm cannon. "You've got to get a little closer with the gun," Salomonson said, "a mile and a half or so, generally after you've shot the Mavs."

On their first run, Salomonson and Marks each fired a full complement of four Mavericks. They destroyed six of the Iraqi tanks. But two of the Mavericks missed their targets, "going stupid," as Salomonson and Marks put it. The raid had taken less than ten minutes. "We still had plenty of time and gas to strafe with the gun," said Marks, "so we engaged other tanks, using high-angle deliveries."

Short on fuel and ammunition, Salomonson and Marks finally decided they had to head south. They flew to King Khalid Military City in north-central Saudi Arabia to refuel and restock their ammunition. There Salomonson and Marks were told that they would be placed on a thirty-minute alert. That meant that they should be prepared to fly again on a half hour's notice. But as they walked into the operations building, a lieutenant colonel handed them a message. The pilot of a Marine Harrier jet had just radioed in, reporting that his aircraft had been struck by ground fire in Kuwait. The jet was on fire, and the Marines on the ground below were requesting immediate air support against tanks that lay ahead.

Within twenty minutes, Salomonson and Marks were airborne again. It was still raining, and the smoke from the oil field fires gave them a visibility ceiling of between 8,000 and 10,000 feet as they approached the sector in Kuwait where they had been asked for air support. The flat windshield of their A-10s further reduced their visibility in the rain. Salomonson and Marks strained to see.

"Look, are you guys gonna come in or not?" a Marine forward air controller radioed.

Marks and Salomonson still could not locate their targets. Minutes later, an F/A-18 Hornet pilot "smoked" the target site with white phosphorus from a ground-attack missile.

In the fog and smoke, Marks and Salomonson saw the marker and decreased their altitude, scanning their infrared screens and readying their Maverick missiles. Below them was a line of Iraqi tanks, partially concealed behind revetments, which were perpendicular to a narrow dirt track road that ran west from the outskirts of Kuwait City. "It became readily apparent," Salomonson said, "that this was going to be tough hunting, because the tanks weren't real hot." That would make them difficult to locate on the infrared screens of the A-10.

Finally, Salomonson and Marks were able to target the tanks. Both pilots delivered their missiles quickly. Salomonson scored direct hits with his four missiles. Marks killed two with his. A burning chunk of metal from one of the exploding tanks had caused one of his missiles to miss, Marks said. Because the targets were relatively "cold" and the visibility was poor, Salomonson and Marks had to fly closer and lower to attack than was usual. Very quickly, Iraqi anti-aircraft batteries opened up at them, followed by surface-to-air missiles. "The sky just exploded," Marks said. "We moved out of there pretty quick. We were out of Mavs and just about out of gas. I said, 'Hey, we're still alive, let's get out of here!' "

They refueled and picked up more ammunition, and were sent back to the battle. They saw about a dozen more tanks. A Marine forward air controller radioed them: "They're all enemy. Go for it!" They fired their missiles and strafed the tanks several times within the three-mile radius of their target area. Seven tanks were reduced to burning hulks.

The final results after three sorties and nearly twelve hours in the cockpit: 23 Iraqi tanks destroyed, 17 with missiles, 6 with 30-mm guns. Another 10 tanks damaged by guns. Recalled Salomonson, "It was an A-10 driver's dream."

Late in the afternoon, Lieutenant General Franks summoned his chief of staff, his senior division intelligence officer, his fire-support coordinator, and his brigade commanders to meet him at his mobile headquarters.

During the first full day of Allied ground attack, Franks noted, the Republican Guard divisions clustered to the southwest of the city of Basra had not moved. There were three divisions that seemed the most threatening: the Tawakalna, the Medina Luminous, and the Hammurabi. Each was at least 13,000 men strong, with 350 Soviet T-72 tanks and cadres of combat soldiers who were young, smart, and well trained. They were positioned where they could try to block the advance of the VII Corps as it approached Kuwait. Like General Yeosock and Marine General Boomer, Franks had never wavered in his view of the importance of the Republican Guard. It was, he believed, the true center of gravity of Saddam Hussein's army.

If the elite Iraqi divisions were not going to come out and fight, Franks intended to take the battle to them. His headquarters staff had developed seven different plans for moving his VII Corps to engage the Republican Guard. To meet the guard north of Kuwait, Franks had originally intended to use the 1st and 3rd Armored Divisions while he held the 1st Infantry Division, the Big Red One, back at the border as a reserve force. Now Franks decided he would pursue the Iraqis with all haste and might, so he added the Big Red One to his punch. He ordered all three divisions, with more than 1,000 tanks and 50,000 men, to halt their drive to the northeast, wheel to the east, and drive toward Saddam's elite force. At the same time, Franks had the fourth force in VII Corps, the British 1st Armored Division, turn due east toward the Gulf and the belly of Kuwait. This would make four full, heavy armored divisions smashing at the Iraqi forces south of Basra and inside Kuwait.

The 1st Armored Division was scheduled to attack the crossroads village of al-Busayyah, where there was a large supply depot that the Iraqis would want to defend vigorously. The depot contained enough fuel, ammunition, and food to support an entire armored corps. But Franks believed now that it was more important to get his forces moving and to drive them east to strike at the Republican Guard. While al-Bussayah would be hit, it would largely be bypassed. The 1st Armored's commander, Major General Ronald Griffith, agreed.

Franks ordered the 2nd Armored Cavalry Regiment to get out in front of the VII Corps to locate the leading edge or flank of the Republican Guard forces, engage them, and then hold them in place for the heavier forces moving up behind them. His heavier forces, Franks hoped, would crush the Iraqi army's center of gravity soon after they were engaged.

Northwest of Franks's 1st Armored Division, which had begun to shell al-Busayyah, Lieutenant Colonel Tom Greco's Rakkasan task force was slogging through the mud of the Euphrates Valley. Sometimes it was ankle deep, sometimes almost knee deep. The soldiers staggered along under their sixty-pound rucksacks. They were also carrying heavy ammunition belts, rifles, and TOW anti-tank missiles.

Forty kilometers to their north, the lighter elements of their brigade were already arriving at Area of Operations Eagle, just to the side of the division's main objective that day, the east-west Iraqi Highway 8 that ran through the Euphrates Valley. One of the soldiers dropped into the Eagle area was Jason Davis, a twenty-nine-year-old sergeant from Apopka, Florida. In the mud of a cultivated field outside the village of al-Khidr near Highway 8, Davis saw a cluster of Bedouin tents to the west. The tents belonged to a small family. Davis and his squad approached rapidly and in silence. One Bedouin had a rifle. The Americans took the man prisoner. A husband and wife and two little girls, surrounded by their goats, cowered inside the house. Davis's squad left them alone and moved on through the mud to join their lieutenant and the platoon. They came upon a car, a Nissan, abandoned on a road with its engine still running, its radio still on. Davis figured the driver must have seen sixty helicopters landing in this field, and the guy just left his car there running and ran.

The platoon leader took Davis's squad off to reconnoiter the area. Davis was making his way through a deep irrigation ditch when he spotted an Iraqi military truck stop about fifty meters ahead of him. Four soldiers jumped out waving their rifles.

"What do you want us to do, sir?" Davis asked by radio.

"Take them out," his platoon leader replied.

Lying in the mud, Davis noticed two Iraqi soldiers moving closer to his position. Just then, a second truck, much larger than the first, pulled up. More Iraqi soldiers jumped out. Davis and his squad began firing.

"Everybody's shooting," Davis recalled, "and we're being shot at. Bullets are going everywhere." He noticed some Iraqis flanking around on their left to attack them from behind. But the way Davis's squad was positioned lying in the ditch, if he fired lying down he would have shot his own men. His only choice was to stand up and fire. "So I just stood up and stopped the individuals coming around to our rear." It was purely an act of self-preservation, according to Davis. "If somebody hadn't done something at the time, nine of us would have come home in body bags." After the war, Davis would receive a Bronze Star with a V for valor.

All along Highway 8, as the second day of the ground campaign drew

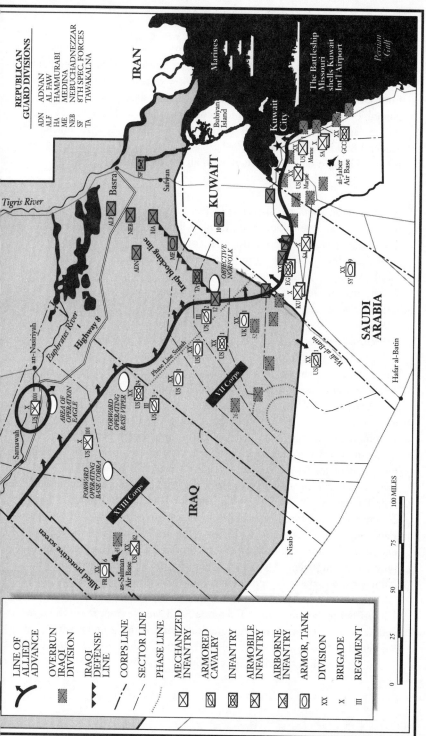

FEBRUARY 25, 1991: BY THE END OF THE SECOND DAY, ALLIED FORCES HAD TAKEN HALF OF THE KUWAIT THEATER

to a close, there were scattered fights. As Iraqi military convoys attempted to crash through the American roadblocks, they were fired upon by soldiers from Davis's brigade of the 101st Airborne. Most deadly were the wire-guided TOW missiles fired from launchers mounted on Humvees. Seeing the carnage, some Iraqi soldiers turned their vehicles around and fled. General Binford Peay's soldiers had seized and secured Highway 8. Nothing would move on the road now without his permission.

At 8:20 P.M., in Dhahran, Specialist Ruben Carranzas was trying to nap on his cot in a converted water-bottling plant about the size of a football field. The building had a concrete floor. Its concrete walls were reinforced by steel beams. A few yards away from Carranzas, Michael Trout, Beverly Clark, Michael Anderson, and several of their colleagues from the 14th Quartermaster Detachment were playing a game of Trivial Pursuit. The 14th Quartermaster Detachment was a reserve unit from Greensburg, Pennsylvania. The unit had arrived in Saudi Arabia just seven days earlier, on February 18. Its mission was to assist with water purification.

Two miles away from the converted barracks where the 14th Quartermaster Detachment was housed while they waited for their water-purification equipment and a mission assignment, the men and women of the U.S. Army's Alpha Battery, 2nd Battalion, 7th Air Defense Artillery Regiment were scanning their radar screens anxiously. The Alpha Battery was surrounded by a rectangular earthen berm topped with barbed wire. Just inside the berm were foxholes protected with plastic liners to be used in the event of an Iraqi chemical-weapons attack. There were also sand-bagged bunkers. In the very center of the Alpha Battery's position were four Patriot missile launchers. The Patriot launcher resembled a large commercial dumpster. It was tipped at a 45-degree angle toward the sky. Each launcher contained two missiles. A few yards away from the launchers were communications vans, a rotating radar dish, and a generator to power the equipment. A powerful computer linked the radar dish to the launcher and to the radar screens and gunners in the communications vans.

At 8:21 P.M., other Patriot batteries north of Dhahran and closer to the Kuwait border reported the launch of a Scud missile from somewhere in southern Iraq. The day before, after the start of the ground war, Iraqi soldiers had fired three Scud missiles into Saudi Arabia; two had landed in Riyadh, one at King Khalid Military City.

Carranzas and a friend, Specialist Kelly George, had done extra guard duty earlier that evening outside the converted water-bottling plant. They'd responded to several false alerts of Scud attacks. With the start of the ground war, Carranzas said, the level of tension among nearly everyone he spoke to in Dhahran had increased significantly. "There were all kinds of rumors going around that day about terrorist groups in the area," Carranzas said. "That left some of the guys shaky. I had more fear of a sniper attack or something."

As he tried to doze on his cot after a quick dinner of Vienna sausages and Spam, Carranzas could hear the game of Trivial Pursuit going on a few yards away. "A mouse had run by," Carranzas recalled, "and one of the guys had killed it with his boot. My friend Michael Trout got up and walked away from the group, I think he felt squeamish." At that moment, Carranzas said, they heard the Scud alert warning.

At 8:22 P.M. at Alpha Battery two miles away, Sergeant David Trujillo from Cheyenne, Wyoming, knew that the Scud was traveling south, perhaps toward Dhahran. Farther to the north, Delta Battery, another Patriot unit, had identified the launch of the missile. "We had it tracked as soon as it cleared airspace," Trujillo said. "Delta gave a handoff to us. [It was] between Alpha and Charlie [batteries]. I was in there [in the Patriot tracking-system center]. The chief was in there. I didn't see a thing. I didn't see a thing."

At 8:23 P.M., the Scud missile landed on the converted water-bottling plant and fell through the roof. Part of the missile struck the group playing Trivial Pursuit. Smaller fragments struck Ruben Carranzas. "I got blown out of my bunker about twenty feet to the front of the warehouse, where I landed on a cot," Carranzas said. "I felt blood gushing out of my ear. Shrapnel covered my face. I couldn't see anything. My face was covered with blood. I could hear people screaming and crying out for help."

At the Alpha Battery, Sergeant Trujillo heard the explosion and yelled at the Patriot gunners, "Did we shoot?"

"We didn't shoot," a soldier replied. "I stood down."

In the barracks of the 14th Quartermaster Detachment, Michael Anderson's leg was crushed under debris; he would later have to have it amputated. Around him, Beverly Clark and twelve other members of his unit lay dead. These reservists had joined the unit in August after the Iraqi invasion of Kuwait. Thirteen of the sixty-nine members of the 14th Quartermaster Detachment perished. Fifteen U.S. Army reserve soldiers who had been sharing the large barracks were also killed. The twenty-eight fatalities were the largest number of casualties from a single attack in Operation Desert Storm.

A few yards away from where Ruben Carranzas lay bleeding, Michael Trout, the specialist who had left the group playing Trivial Pursuit, was not seriously injured, although afterward he had hearing problems. "I was walking around half in shock," Trout said. "One guy yelled to me to help him, and I helped pick him up and put him on a cot. Then I helped another guy look for his glasses because he said he could not see without them. That is when I heard the ammunition going off. It just sounded like tons of bullets going off." Pentagon sources confirmed that, despite regulations about storing ammunition close to the living quarters of military personnel, the facility assigned to the 14th Quartermaster Detachment had been used as a storage depot for thousands of rounds of M-16 ammunition. For security reasons, the ammunition had been stored inside the barracks, near sleeping cots and lockers. The Pentagon officially listed the twenty-eight people killed in the attack as victims of the Iraqi missile. Members of the 14th Quartermaster Detachment, however, said they believed at least one specialist, and perhaps more, had been killed by the exploding ammunition rounds, which had been detonated by the fire caused by the missile's explosion.

As emergency medical crews rushed into the flaming barracks, Second Lieutenant John Kruthaupt of Cincinnati, Ohio, was sitting with several colleagues in an abandoned mosque that members of the Alpha Battery had converted to living quarters. "I heard three concussions," Kruthaupt said. "We thought it was a fuel tank that had fallen."

Back at Alpha Battery, David Trujillo was shocked and angry. "Nothing came up on the [radar] screen," he said. It would take Army investigators three months to explain the Patriot battery's critical failure. The Scud missile was intact when it struck the barracks, the investigators ultimately determined, and a software failure in the Alpha Battery's computer had rendered its radar system inoperable on the evening of February 25. "The radar system never saw the incoming missile," Colonel Bruce Garnett said months later. The failure, Garnett and the other investigators agreed, was the result of long use of the radar system and corresponding stress on its batteries. Eight hours of use was considered optimal for the Patriot system; but, because of the Scud threat, many Patriot batteries operated their radars for eighteen to twenty hours straight.

The Scud missile that killed the twenty-eight soldiers was the seventy-first fired by Saddam Hussein's soldiers during the war. Saddam would order the firing of just one more Scud before the conflict ended. It would land harmlessly in the Persian Gulf near Qatar the next morning.

CHAPTER 20

THE REPUBLICAN GUARD FIGHTS BACK

O N T H E T H I R D day of the ground war, Tuesday, February 26, a cold front blew in, bringing sandstorms. It had rained all of the previous night and into the early morning hours. The soldiers of Lieutenant General Franks's VII Corps were miserable. They had slept where they could, slouched inside their vehicles or outside on the decks of their tanks, curled up in sleeping bags in the pouring rain. Now, with the blowing sand, the soldiers put goggles on and wrapped T-shirts and towels around their necks and faces. As the ranks of M1A1 Abrams tanks and Bradley fighting vehicles lurched forward, hundreds of soldiers peered out across the desert from their turrets and hatches. There was not much to see, however. Visibility was about zero.

For the past two days, Captain H. R. McMaster's Eagle Troop, a company in the 2nd Armored Cavalry Regiment, had driven north through the Iraqi desert encountering virtually no opposition. Instead, an extraordinary number of Iraqi soldiers had waved and given the thumbs-up sign as they walked south to surrender. Scouts had searched the Iraqis for concealed weapons and given them food. McMaster had wondered where they came from and whether his soldiers would ever see battle, since there were no enemy positions in sight.

McMaster was not happy. The previous night, he had been at his squadron's command center, where he had heard a rumor that his unit would be moved to the rear to become part of the corps reserve. "The sun had set and the weather changed as if to become consistent with my mood," McMaster later wrote in a personal memoir. He had returned to his troop command vehicle in a driving rain, protected only by a captured Iraqi poncho. Once inside, in his drenched chemical suit, he fell asleep on a narrow wooden shelf beneath the radios. He had hardly dozed, it seemed, when he was awakened with word of a new order. Eagle Troop was instructed to stay in place, reorienting its defense to the east. It did not sound to McMaster as if the day would bring much action.

In the early morning light, however, three Iraqi armored vehicles, known as MT-LBs, approached the perimeter of McMaster's Eagle Troop. "Contact east," radioed McMaster's soldiers on guard duty. "Three MT-LBs." McMaster raced ahead in his tank, but by the time he was in position to fire, Bradley fighting vehicles from the adjacent Ghost Troop had destroyed two of the Iraqi vehicles. The third one was escaping, but McMaster thought he might be able to shoot it with his tank's 120-mm cannon. McMaster radioed 1st Platoon Sergeant Robert Patterson. "Red 4, this is Black 6," McMaster said. "Does that MT-LB have my name on it?"

"Roger," Patterson replied. "Your name's written all over it."

McMaster's gunner, Staff Sergeant Craig Koch, then peered into his scope. He moved the handgrips that aimed the tank's main gun and laid the cross hairs squarely over the retreating Iraqi vehicle. The gun was loaded.

"Fire!" McMaster yelled.

Koch pulled the trigger. "On the way," he replied.

A second later, the Iraqi armored vehicle was in flames. Good, McMaster thought. At least these scouts would not be reporting Eagle Troop's position back to their headquarters.

A few miles north of McMaster, yet another cavalry unit was operating. This one, part of the 3rd Armored Division, was already moving east. It was guarding the southern flank of the 3rd Armored Division, acting as a visual contact and a buffer between it and the 2nd Armored Cavalry. Captain Gerald Davie was the commander of Alpha Troop in the 4th Squadron, 7th Cavalry. Along with all of the other Allied units in his sector, Davie's Alpha Troop had headed out on the morning of February 26. As they moved ahead tentatively through the desert storm, the sand whipped around the commanders of Davie's Bradley fighting vehicles as they stood in their hatches. Davie tried to keep his troop's three platoons of six Bradleys each in their formations by issuing a stream of radio instructions while he navigated with the unit's only Global Positioning Satellite device, known as a GPS. Of all the electronic weapons of the U.S. ground forces, the GPSs were the ones most worth their price. Costing only $5,000 each, the book-size receivers with number pads looked like large hand-held calculators. They used satellite signals to tell the user his location within 100 yards. Soldiers could punch in data and find out the distance and direction to any number of waypoints, and could even find out how well they were keeping to the prescribed route. With them, American soldiers could navigate across hundreds of miles of featureless Iraqi desert, where even the Iraqis found it impossible to go. Without them, they would have been lost. Davie ordered his 3rd Platoon into the lead and pulled his 2nd Platoon into position about 500 meters behind them. The 2nd Platoon's job was to keep the troop from wandering off into the sandstorm while the 3rd Platoon concentrated on finding the enemy. The 2nd Platoon would provide fighting depth if and when the enemy was engaged. Unlike McMaster's troop in the 2nd Armored Cavalry Regiment, Davie's unit had no tanks, only the more lightly armored Bradleys. While the armor of the Bradley fighting vehicle would stop small-arms fire, it was vulnerable to fire from heavy machine guns, shoulder-fired rockets, and the big guns of the Republican Guard's T-72 tanks.

By midafternoon, Davie's troop was within twenty miles of Kuwait's western border with Iraq. Until now, contact with the enemy had been light, and most of Davie's men were optimistic that they would come through the war unscathed.

Although thousands of Saddam Hussein's regular troops were surrendering to Allied forces while thousands more beat a ragged retreat back behind Iraqi lines, the Republican Guard divisions were not running away. Since the invasion of Kuwait, the eight divisions of Republican Guard forces had been kept well behind the lines, well fed and far better protected than the half-starved and shell-shocked Shiite soldiers in southern Kuwait.

On the second day of the ground campaign, despite the extensive damage done to their communications capabilities, Saddam's battlefield commanders in Kuwait had somehow managed to get word to higher headquarters on the position and movement of Franks's VII Corps attack. Saddam's generals had responded by sending their best armored units out to the west, into positions to try to block the advance of the VII Corps. The first unit to move west was the Iraqi 12th Armored Division, a brigade of which positioned itself along a road about fifty miles west of Kuwait's border with Iraq. From there, it hoped to slow or stop the eastward rush of the VII Corps while Republican Guard units came down from the north and attacked Franks's forces on their northern flank.

This plan was apparently based on the assumption that the VII Corps was attempting only a shallow foray into Iraq before it turned southeast toward Kuwait City. In fact, Franks was driving the bulk of the VII Corps farther north. And when he ordered the force to turn east, they were poised to strike not at Kuwait City, but at the Republican Guard divisions hunkered down north of Kuwait and south of Basra.

After the 2nd Armored Cavalry Regiment overran a brigade of the Iraqi 12th Armored Division on Monday afternoon, however, the Republican Guard generals finally realized that the VII Corps was heading not toward Kuwait City, but directly toward their own position. The 2nd Armored Cavalry Regiment had shredded the Iraqi force with air attacks and artillery. Then Franks's VII Corps rolled through, continuing its drive eastward. When the Iraqi generals realized their mistake, the mission of the Republican Guard became critically important. With so many Iraqi units fleeing to the north behind them, the Republican Guard divisions would have to block the VII Corps and prevent them from breaking through into northern Kuwait and southeastern Iraq and rolling up the retreating Iraqi army. Just to the west of the Kuwait border, running on a northeasterly line all the way to Basra, ran the so-called Iraq Pipeline through Saudi Arabia, usually referred to as the IPSA Pipeline. Next to it was the IPSA pipeline road.

Late in the day on February 26, three Republican Guard divisions had established a blocking line just west of the pipeline road. Farthest to the south was the Tawakalna. To their north and east were the Medina Luminous, and to their northeast was the Hammurabi division.

The Adnan, another Republican Guard division, was farther to the north, in the Euphrates Valley. The Adnan was poised there to attempt an attack on the northern flank of the VII Corps as it came through that area.

Lieutenant Colonel Keith Alexander, the 1st Armored Division's senior intelligence officer, had studied the Iraqi positions closely and later debriefed officers from the Medina division. "We may look at these guys and say they're a third-rate outfit," Alexander said, "but I'll tell you that whoever made that decision to block the VII Corps was a first-rate strategist."

McMaster had received two orders that day to move eastward, but only for short distances. Then they would stop. Meanwhile, the Iraqi high command was still moving to shore up the Republican Guard force with brigades of regular armored divisions. Two among these were the Iraqi 17th Armored Division and other elements of the 12th Armored Division. They were trying, as Alexander explained, "to make a strong line."

It would be the two U.S. armored cavalry units, Davie's troop with the 3rd Armored Division and McMaster's troop with the 2nd Armored Cavalry Regiment, that would hit the Iraqi line first. Since the days when it fought on horseback, the U.S. Army has used its cavalry as a swift, lightweight force to scout enemy positions, lead its advances, and guard its flanks. In the modern mechanized army, the cavalry has remained fast and light. But it has also embraced a variety of new configurations. Some cavalry units are helicopter-borne. Smaller cavalry units, like Davie's 4th Squadron of the 7th Cavalry, rode only in Bradley fighting vehicles. Others, like the 2nd Armored Cavalry Regiment, were the size of a hefty brigade and had about 120 M1A1 tanks as well. But the trademarks of the cavalry, no matter how it was configured, were still lightness and speed.

As Lieutenant General Franks drove his VII Corps toward the heart of the Republican Guard's strength, the 2nd Armored Cavalry and McMaster's Eagle Troop were in the lead. At 3:25 P.M., McMaster received orders to drive toward a north-south grid line identified on Central Command maps as 70 Easting. Eagle Troop comprised 140 soldiers, nine M1A1 Abrams main battle tanks, twelve Bradley fighting vehicles, two 4.2-inch mortar carriers, and several more armored vehicles for command, communications, and artillery-fire support and troop transport. On either side of McMaster, other troops of the 2nd Armored Cavalry Regiment—named Ghost, Iron, Killer, Bull, and Apache—were similarly equipped. With the driving sand and the low cloud cover, the cavalry troops had had little helicopter or close air support. When they engaged the enemy, they knew there would be little or no warning.

At 3:56 P.M., Eagle Troop was driving east through the blowing sand when one of McMaster's Bradleys picked up four enemy soldiers who

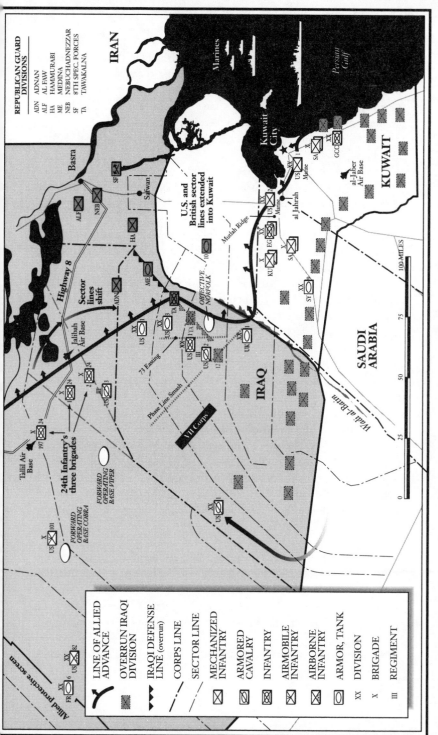

FEBRUARY 26, 1991: ON THE THIRD DAY, VII CORPS WHEELED TO THE EAST TO ATTACK THE REPUBLICAN GUARD

surrendered in a bunker complex to their north. They loaded the Iraqis onto the front of their Bradley and were taking them to the rear when another Bradley came under heavy machine-gun fire from a village east of the bunkers. McMaster brought his nine tanks on line quickly. All fired simultaneously into the village's dun-colored, concrete-block buildings. Several buildings burst into flames. Eagle Troop continued east, skirting the village.

Twenty minutes later, McMaster's scouts spotted two enemy tanks. They fired TOW anti-tank missiles at them. "Tank!" McMaster heard Staff Sergeant Cowart Magee yell on the platoon's radio network. "We hit a tank!"

At 4:18 P.M., McMaster moved to the point of the Eagle Troop formation. The sandstorm had not abated. McMaster's tank crested a slight rise, and McMaster's gunner, Staff Sergeant Koch, yelled, "Tanks, direct front!"

Squatting just ahead of McMaster's M1A1, dug in and protected by large mounds of dirt, were eight Iraqi tanks from the Tawakalna division of the Republican Guard. The Iraqis, evidently, had anticipated that the Americans would bypass the town. They had been waiting behind it to the east, apparently with the intention of ambushing them on their flank as they came through. McMaster saw that the Iraqi tanks were positioned on the back of a gentle incline, in a classic "reverse-slope" defense. This enabled the Iraqi gunners to target the M1A1 tanks of the Eagle Troop on their vulnerable underbelly. Because the Americans had destroyed the Iraqi scouts in their MT-LB vehicles earlier in the day, however, the Iraqi tankers had had no warning of the approach of McMaster and his Eagle Troop.

In the cramped interior of McMaster's M1A1 tank, Staff Sergeant Koch pushed the button on his laser range-finder. The display beneath the red cross hairs indicated that the tank in his gun sight was exactly 1,420 meters away.

"Fire," McMaster ordered.

Koch pulled the trigger. The gun breach recoiled in the turret, and the inside of the big tank filled with the acrid smell of burned gunpowder. The enemy tank exploded in a fireball.

Koch swung the cross hairs onto another Iraqi tank. This one was much closer. As Koch checked the range, the Iraqi tank rotated its turret toward McMaster's M1A1.

Beneath him in the tank, Private Jeffrey Taylor, McMaster's loader, grabbed a sabot round from the ready-rack and slammed it into the breach. "Up!" he screamed, indicating the gun was loaded and ready for firing.

Koch squeezed the trigger again.

McMaster watched as the turret of the Iraqi tank was ripped from the vehicle in a hail of sparks.

McMaster's driver, Private First Class Christopher Hedenskog, slowed the M1A1 to twenty kilometers per hour. He had spotted an enemy mine field and was trying to wend his way around it. As Hedenskog negotiated the terrain, two Iraqi T-72s fired at McMaster's tank. McMaster saw the rounds fall short, one on either side of him. In the meantime, Taylor had loaded another sabot round into the M1A1's gun. Koch fired again. Ahead of McMaster, a third Iraqi tank exploded.

Seconds later, McMaster's two platoons with four M1A1 tanks each crested the ridge. The gunners picked their targets quickly. Within seconds, eight more Iraqi tanks were burning below McMaster on the side of the hill. Eagle Troop pushed forward, cutting a swath roughly five kilometers wide through the Tawakalna division, destroying several more T-72 tanks and Iraqi armored vehicles. As McMaster's tanks ground forward, Iraqi anti-personnel mines exploded harmlessly beneath their tracks.

At 4:22 P.M., McMaster's Eagle Troop was even with the Iraqis' first line of defense. All of the Iraqi tanks directly in front of him were in flames. But there were more behind them and on either side. The Tawakalna division had been waiting with thirty T-72s and fourteen Soviet-built armored fighting vehicles, and several hundred infantry were in buildings and trenches nearby.

Thanks to the sandstorm and the lack of advance warning from Iraqi scouts, McMaster and the other cavalry troops had surprised the soldiers of the Tawakalna division. But the fight wasn't over. To McMaster's right, the 3rd Platoon took direct fire from a bunker that housed a Soviet-made 23-mm anti-aircraft gun. It was a particularly effective weapon, one the Iraqis favored for coastal defenses. Gunners from the 3rd Platoon fired two TOW anti-tank missiles, destroying the bunker that housed the anti-aircraft gun.

Seconds later, Sergeant Timothy Hovermale spotted a T-72 tank as it fired at the Bradley fighting vehicle he was riding in. The Iraqi round just missed Hovermale's Bradley, kicking dirt into the air. As the T-72 gunner reloaded, Hovermale shot the Iraqi tank with a TOW missile. Over the intercom of Hovermale's Bradley, Sergeant Willie Digbie yelled for help in reloading the TOW missile launcher. Digbie had just fired two missiles. There were none left on top in the ready-rack. Inside the Bradley Digbie's crew members pulled out more missiles to reload the launcher, but they could not get their hatch open. Finally, one kicked at the hatch release until it snapped. Then he and another soldier jumped out and reloaded the TOW launcher with fresh missiles as small-arms fire whizzed past them. When they were done, they jumped back into the Bradley behind Digbie.

The Iraqi camp was in panic as explosions sent chunks of metal overhead. In the swirling dust, the angry Iraqi infantry fired assault rifles and machine guns at the Bradleys, but the fire had no effect on the armored vehicles. Some Iraqis played dead, then jumped up behind their tanks and fired their rifles or rocket-propelled grenades. The Bradleys suppressed them or cut them down with 25-mm cannon fire and machine guns.

McMaster received a radio call from First Lieutenant John Gifford at the command post. McMaster and his Eagle Troop were well past the 70 Easting line. In the orders issued a little more than an hour ago, 70 Easting had been described as the limit of McMaster's line of advance. This was no time to stop firing, McMaster thought, and become sitting targets for a still potent Iraqi fighting force. "I can't stop," McMaster radioed. "We're still in contact [with the enemy]. Tell them I'm sorry."

Gifford said he understood.

McMaster saw more Iraqi tanks and armored fighting vehicles in the distance. Seventeen T-72s were parked in a coil two kilometers ahead to the east. As McMaster drove up a sloping hill, more of the Iraqi reserve force came into view. The Americans blasted away at them.

At 4:40 P.M., McMaster's Eagle Troop reached a spot on the edge of the enemy's defensive perimeter, just beyond the range of the seventeen T-72 tanks. McMaster called a halt. They had arrived at a line described on Central Command maps as 73 Easting.

McMaster had exceeded his limit by four kilometers. The sand was blowing so hard that he could see only those tanks next to his own. McMaster's platoon leaders radioed to report that they had suffered no casualties during the battle. The engagement had lasted exactly twenty-two minutes. Around him, McMaster's soldiers began treating wounded Iraqi soldiers. A radio operator called Iron Troop, which was still advancing approximately five kilometers behind Eagle Troop, to provide Eagle's precise location, so that Iron Troop did not mistake them for Iraqis and begin firing on them. McMaster jumped on top of his tank to give his crew room to

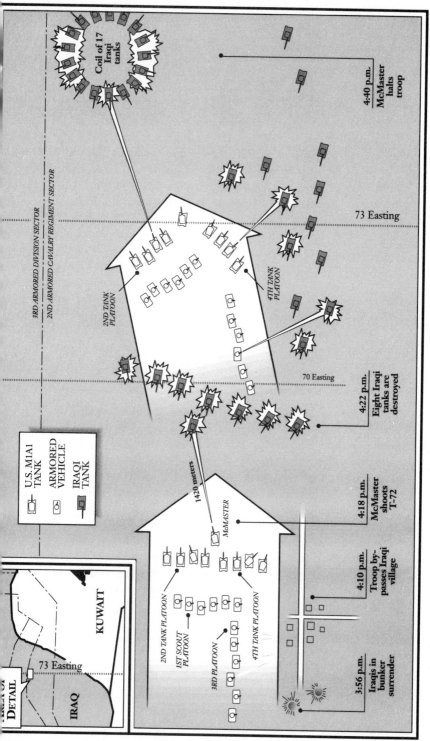

ON FEBRUARY 26, 1991, CAPTAIN MCMASTER'S EAGLE TROOP FOUGHT "THE BATTLE OF 73 EASTING"

reload the ammunition ready-rack and to survey the scene. The action had seemed to last only seconds. He had felt no significant emotions during the fight, but he had not eaten all day, and he was ravenously hungry. McMaster tore into a package of MREs and devoured the cold potatoes and ham.

To the east, the soldiers of Eagle Troop could still see more tanks of the Tawakalna division beyond 73 Easting. Using their thermal sights to cut through the driving sand, the soldiers saw that the supply base and head-quarters of the Iraqi fighting force lay a considerable distance ahead of them, across a seemingly endless sea of white-capped dirt mounds. The Iraqis fired sporadically at McMaster and his soldiers, and Eagle Troop returned the fire, targeting the Iraqi tanks with TOW missiles and drop-ping air-burst mortar rounds on the infantry. The mortar rounds spread a hail of shrapnel from a relatively low altitude.

McMaster saw that the Iraqi soldiers showed no sign of giving up. Indeed, as dusk fell, the Iraqis launched a counterattack, attempting to use the gathering dark and blowing sand as cover. Through their thermal sights, McMaster's tankers were able to identify the advancing Iraqi vehi-cles as they drew within range of their guns. One by one, the Soviet-built T-72 tanks and armored fighting vehicles blossomed into balls of flame on the horizon.

Well to the east that afternoon, in the desert south of Kuwait City, the leading task forces of the 1st Marine Division were making a ten-mile surge north to assume control of Kuwait International Airport by nightfall. Origi-nally, the 1st and 2nd Marine Divisions had been assigned to tie up the roving divisions and brigades of Iraqi armored forces in the south of Kuwait while the VII Corps struck deep at the Republican Guard in the north. But most of the Iraqis had already vanished, and the Marine divisions had pressed the attack toward the outskirts of the capital.

At thirty-two minutes past midnight on the morning of February 26, Baghdad Radio had briefly announced that Iraq would comply with the United Nations resolutions. Iraqi forces had "performed their Jihad duty of refusing to comply with the logic of evil, imposition, and aggression," the announcement had said. "They have been engaged in a valiant battle, which will be recorded in history in letters of light." That afternoon, a longer statement was read declaring a troop withdrawal. Most of the Iraqi soldiers in southern Kuwait appeared to be either on the run or prepared to surrender peacefully. But not all of them.

The soldiers of Corporal George Butler's platoon in the 2nd Marine Division had not heard the news of the Iraqi concession. As far as they were concerned, the war was still on. Until Iraqi soldiers actually climbed out of their tanks and fighting vehicles and dropped their weapons, they were still to be regarded as the enemy. Driving north, Butler's fire team was leading his battalion in its squad of Humvees, looking for Iraqis. If they found Iraqi tanks or armored vehicles, the Marines' tanks would come ahead and shoot them. On Butler's side, Marine tanks had been chasing several Iraqi tanks in a game of hide-and-seek: about every two kilometers, the Marine tanks would see a tracked vehicle and shoot at it.

Butler's fire team spotted an Iraqi tank and scooted into a depression while the Marine tanks went forward to take care of it. As they emerged from the hole, two Iraqi armored personnel carriers suddenly approached them from the rear and opened fire. First, Butler saw muzzle flashes, then, "we saw green tracers everywhere. Over our heads and on the side and hitting the ground, everywhere."

Butler's section leader darted forward in his Humvee, looking for a place to hide. Butler wanted to follow, but his driver had frozen with fear. He could not make his hand move the shift lever. Butler screamed at his driver. Then Butler's corpsman panicked, and Butler had to restrain him. Butler shook the man hard and told him to shut up. "We were in the kill zone," Butler said. "Our training was to get out of the kill zone—that's the first thing you do."

Butler turned around and began firing at the Iraqi armored vehicles. "It was one of those things," Butler said. "[You] just turn around and fight. That's your cover." Within seconds, all of Butler's fire team had followed suit and opened up on the Iraqis. They stopped one of the armored vehicles dead in its tracks. The other one retreated to safety. Amazingly, none of the Marines had been hit.

The most critical objective of the 2nd Marine Division on the third day of the ground campaign fell to its 3rd Brigade, the heavily armored Tiger Brigade, on loan to the Marines from the U.S. Army. Its mission was to take control of a highway intersection at the village of al-Jahra about twenty kilometers west of Kuwait City. It was there that the main highway west from Kuwait City met the highway north to Basra and two others. When they drove into Kuwait on August 2, it was al-Jahra that the Iraqis had invaded first. This was where the Iraqis would try to flee from Kuwait City.

One third of the Tiger Brigade was under the command of Lieutenant Colonel Michael Johnson. His battalion was advancing on al-Jahra with another battalion-sized task force on its left flank. To their rear was still another tank battalion. Ahead of Johnson, his scouts scoured the desert for signs of the enemy from the hatches of their Bradley fighting vehicles. The ground was covered with mines and other unexploded munitions, both Iraqi and Allied. "God, the place was littered with them," said Johnson, after the war. "Archaeology three hundred years from now is certainly going to be exciting."

Johnson had placed his scouts three kilometers ahead of the task force, a distance that allowed him about fifteen minutes to react to whatever the scouts encountered. The battalion traveled in a box formation, with two companies in front and two behind. Johnson was also accompanied by eight fuel trucks and six fully loaded ammunition trucks, as well as first-aid stations and armored ambulances and recovery vehicles. "We were told," Johnson recalled, " 'You guys get up there and take that intersection. You've got a hell of a fight on your hands.' "

Hurrying to al-Jahra, Johnson's lead company, with twenty tanks and fifteen Bradley fighting vehicles, rolled right past several dug-in and camouflaged Iraqi T-72 tanks. When Johnson's battalion was nearly past the tanks, a captain in the battalion's trailing company spotted them. The Iraqi tanks were just a few hundred meters away, and they were not moving. But the captain noticed a soldier in the turret of one of the tanks. Suddenly, two more Iraqi soldiers appeared, and one began firing at Johnson's fuel trucks with his 12.7-mm machine gun.

The captain ordered his nearest Bradley to engage the tank, and the Bradley charged it. Shooting its 25-mm cannon from 400 meters away, the Bradley's gunner put several armor-piercing rounds into the left side of the Iraqi tank, in a vulnerable spot just below the turret. The tank exploded in a ball of orange flame. Why the Iraqis never fired their main tank cannon, Johnson would never know.

Johnson's scouts next encountered a few scattered Iraqi military vehicles. Inside were soldiers who apparently had not received word that the Americans had moved north with their allies. But these soldiers were no more than remnants of platoons. The best Johnson could figure, he was hitting bits and pieces of Iraqi units that made up Saddam Hussein's armored reserve, the tanks that were supposed to pounce if the allies broke through the defensive lines. But they were guarding only roads and intersections, apparently in the belief that the attack on Kuwait City would have to come up the coast road or from the west on the main highway. Since they could not operate off the roads, they assumed that the allies could not either. Moreover, they knew how easy it was to get lost in the vast desert.

Johnson's scouts drove forward in the lead, and when they saw Iraqi vehicles, they shot them. "Kicking over anthills," Johnson called it. "They were seeing what they could stir up." Then they kicked over a big one. "Hey, sir," a scout radioed not far from al-Jahra, "I'm pinned by about ten tanks." Johnson ordered his two lead armor companies to advance quickly to get on line with the scouts. When they moved a bit farther north, the two companies discovered there were not ten but twenty Iraqi tanks.

Johnson radioed his brigade commander, Colonel John Sylvester. "I've got twenty tanks coming from the east toward the west," Johnson said. "I've got them all in sight."

"Kill them," Sylvester radioed back.

Johnson replied immediately: "It would be my pleasure."

Within five minutes, the tanks and Bradleys of Michael Johnson's battalion destroyed all twenty of the Iraqi tanks. "That was what we call a counterattack, because it makes us feel better," Sylvester reflected afterward. "I'm not sure whether it was a counterattack, or whether it was twenty tanks trying to get the hell out of Dodge."

From that point all the way to al-Jahra, Johnson's battalion chased the enemy. Continuing in the box formation and moving twenty-five kilometers per hour, they pursued Iraqi tanks and armored fighting vehicles trying to escape Kuwait. At a point just west of al-Jahra, Johnson and the other battalions of the Tiger Brigade approached a network of cloverleafs where the two main highways from eastern and western Kuwait joined two other highways leading north to Iraq. Johnson's battalion was assigned to take one intersection, where the stream of Iraqi military vehicles racing toward Basra was heavy. Within hours, Johnson's soldiers destroyed fifty-five vehicles. These included trucks, tracked fighting vehicles, and rocket and missile launchers.

The other battalions of the Tiger Brigade climbed up the back of a long spine of hills some 300 feet high known as the Mutlah Ridge. It overlooked the four-lane highway that ran from the cloverleafs north toward Iraq. In order to gain the ascent of the Mutlah Ridge, one battalion of the Tiger Brigade had to fight its way through a mine field and several entrenched Iraqi tank positions, destroying thirty-three Iraqi tanks and armored vehicles and taking 720 prisoners in the process.

When the Tiger Brigade finally assumed control of the Mutlah Ridge, its soldiers gazed down on a shocking scene of destruction. The pass through the Mutlah Ridge was littered with hundreds of blackened and burned-out vehicles that had been incinerated the previous night by Marine and Air Force pilots in ground-attack aircraft. It was a three-mile-long purgatory of abandoned, burned, and wrecked trucks, buses, jeeps, cars, and armored personnel carriers. Many were loaded with loot from Kuwait City: living room furniture, filing cabinets, television sets, videocassette recorders, clothing and shoes, perfume and cigarettes. In some vehicles charred bodies could be seen.

The attack aircraft had destroyed the lead vehicles and the ones in the rear; the rest had been abandoned by their drivers or driven into the soft sand in futile attempts to escape. American soldiers later found thousands of footprints leading away from the wreckage in all directions.

On the evening of February 26, as the Tiger Brigade consolidated its position on the Mutlah Ridge, fifty-four more Iraqi vehicles attempted to flee through the pass. Ten of these were armored vehicles; the rest were rocket launchers, missile launchers, and supply trucks. Those vehicles not destroyed by the guns of the Tiger Brigade soon encountered a mine field laid by Iraqi soldiers adjacent to the roadway. None of the fifty-four Iraqi vehicles that attempted to run the Mutlah pass that evening survived. The road between the Mutlah pass and Basra would soon become known to the world as the Highway of Death.

The Allied air bombardment that had resulted in the massive destruction of vehicles in the Mutlah pass northwest of Kuwait City was orchestrated by none other than Major John Feeley. To protect those civilians who assisted in smuggling him out of the Gulf with false identification papers, Feeley and his superiors refused to discuss the specifics of his escape. But soon after Feeley returned to the United States, General Schwarzkopf had telephoned him and ordered him to report to Riyadh. There Feeley was thrown into the thick of the war-planning effort. "I got in and met the Jedi

Knights and saw some of my friends there," Feeley said. "And then I was put in charge of a group that was going to be called the combat-assessment cell, which was going to have to brief General Schwarzkopf every day on what the Iraqis were going to do over the next three days."

After the start of the war, Feeley's combat-assessment cell and Schwarz-kopf's battlefield commanders were receiving information on the disposition of the Iraqi army from a wholly new intelligence source, one that had never before been available because it was in the prototype stage of development. When the war began, the Joint Surveillance Target Attack Radar System (J-Stars) was so new that it had not even concluded the elaborate series of tests the Army and the Air Force had demanded of its creators. The J-Stars program was developed by Grumman Melbourne Systems, a division of the Grumman Corporation, for both the Army and the Air Force. Proponents of J-Stars said it was able to detect, locate, identify, and target ground forces on a battlefield in any weather, twenty-four hours a day.

As elaborate as it sounded, the J-Stars hardware was unprepossessing in appearance. Grumman technicians had installed the sophisticated J-Stars electronics into two used Boeing 707 aircraft. (One had been acquired from American Airlines; it had just over 50,000 flying hours on it. The other was a former Korea Air Lines 707, with approximately 30,000 hours of flight time.)

It may not have looked like much, but the J-Stars aircraft provided a critical link in the intelligence chain that modern battlefield commanders had never had before. Between the high-flying satellites and low-level reconnaissance aircraft, the J-Stars aircraft was designed to provide a picture of battles and battlefield conditions as they were developing. Just as the AWACS aircraft downloaded its constantly changing picture of the air campaign, the J-Stars aircraft was equipped with two electronic down-links (one to the Air Force, the other to the Army) that provided real-time information on troop movements, enemy deployments, and the like. Proponents of the J-Stars program referred to the two prototype aircraft as upside-down AWACS.

In Germany, just before the VII Corps was deployed to Saudi Arabia in the first week of December 1990, Lieutenant General Fred Franks had seen a demonstration of the J-Stars program and was deeply impressed. Soon after his arrival in the desert, Franks suggested to General Schwarzkopf that he requisition the two prototype aircraft for use in Desert Storm.

Schwarzkopf had agreed enthusiastically, and on January 11, 1991, the two J-Stars aircraft departed for Saudi Arabia, their teams of Grumman technicians with them. It marked the first time that an American military aircraft still in development would be used in combat.

On the night of February 25, Major Feeley was manning an operations desk at the headquarters of the Central Command in Riyadh. He and his colleagues had had word from Pentagon intelligence sources earlier in the day that there might be a large-scale retreat by Iraqi forces from Kuwait City that evening. With Feeley were a colonel from the Defense Intelligence Agency (DIA) and a major who was a project officer assigned to the J-Stars program. The DIA colonel had an open line to Central Command air bases where Allied warplanes were on alert. The major assigned to the J-Stars project had another line to the ground station where the J-Stars aircraft aloft that night was downloading its continuous reports on the battlefield and the area around Kuwait City and south of Basra. "The major came in with the [J-Stars] photos," Feeley said, "and he pointed out that the retreat was starting to develop. Those [radar] pictures were starting to light up. The best way I can explain it is if you picture yourself flying over Los Angeles at night, when you can pick up the 405 freeway and the major traffic arteries."

Feeley had driven through the Mutlah pass and knew the road and the surrounding terrain. "We were set up to react quickly," Feeley said. "We looked at the maps, the targeting folks were next to me. All of us were right there, and we were able to make things start happening."

There was a cloverleaf intersection just south of the Mutlah Ridge. Feeley suggested that the air bombardment focus on that location. By destroying the lead vehicles in the Iraqi military convoy there, it would block the vehicles behind from escaping. "Striking there would have trapped them in the city," Feeley said. "We went to the bosses in the war room, but Schwarzkopf didn't want them trapped in Kuwait City; he didn't want to fight in the city. So we moved the target area a little farther north to the ridge. That gave the Air Force some good targets, and we were able to guide them in even though there was very heavy cloud cover that night."

In the J-Stars aircraft aloft, the Iraqi convoy looked like an enormous green slug, slithering northwest toward the Iraqi border through the Mutlah pass. Within minutes of the decision by Schwarzkopf and Air Force commanders, American warplanes swarmed toward the Mutlah pass. Below them were missile launchers, military trucks, armored vehicles. The rules of engagement allowed the Iraqi soldiers to surrender, but not with their weapons. American ground-attack aircraft destroyed the lead vehicles in the Iraqi convoy. It came to a grinding halt. As Iraqi soldiers fled on foot, the American pilots returned again and again to destroy the long line of Iraqi vehicles. "We hit the jackpot," Feeley said. "But we didn't really realize the damage we had done until the newsmen and our first units reached the highway [the next morning]. We were in shock."

Far to the west of the Marines and the Tiger Brigade, McCaffrey's 24th Infantry Division (Mechanized) was still driving north. Theirs was to be the deepest penetration into Iraq by a heavily armored Allied force. McCaffrey's objective was to reach Highway 8 and assume control of the six-lane highway, reinforcing the lighter force of General Binford Peay's 101st Airborne Division (Air Assault). Advancing deeper into Iraq, McCaffrey's soldiers scattered Iraqi positions with rockets and long-range artillery, stunning them with an attack in such an unexpected quarter of the battleground. "They had no earthly idea where it was coming from," said Colonel John LeMoyne, the commanding officer of the 24th Division's 1st Brigade. "We spent the first two hours picking up deserters and stragglers and reassuring Bedouin herders that we weren't going to hurt them."

A decade earlier, LeMoyne had served a tour as an adviser to the Saudi army. From weekend camping trips in the desert, he had come to know and love the Bedouin nomads. When one of his companies of tanks roared out of the sandstorm into a Bedouin encampment early on February 26, the shepherds were terrified. LeMoyne ordered the company to halt long enough to build a fire and brew up tea for the frightened Bedouins. To his west, a battalion ran through some Iraqi soldiers disguised as Bedouins. They were captured and disarmed.

There were pockets of fierce resistance, however. Some Iraqis positioned in revetments and bunkers attempted to shoot at Lieutenant Colonel B. J. Craddock's battalion, but he retaliated with artillery fire and bore down on their positions with his tanks. The Iraqis dove into their bunkers and came out firing machine guns and small arms, trying to shoot rocket-propelled grenades into the back of Craddock's tanks. The tanks grouped themselves into a diamond formation and started shooting the Iraqis with machine-gun fire. When the Iraqis refused to come out of their bunkers, the tanks fired rounds from their 120-mm cannons. Some of the Iraqi bunkers had so much ammunition that they exploded in huge orange fireballs.

Craddock's companies reached Highway 8 about 6 P.M. He placed his mechanized company astride the six-lane thoroughfare, with two tank companies in front. The Iraqis fleeing Basra in military trucks and armored-vehicle transporters had no idea the Americans were there. "They would just roll right in, fifty to a hundred trucks, and they kept coming," Craddock said. "There were heavy equipment transporters with armored vehicles on them. Great landmarks. Those things burned all night long."

Farther east, Paul Kern's 2nd Brigade moved up to a position about fifteen miles southwest of Jalibah Air Base. His tanks and fighting vehicles refueled just after midnight. They would grab a few hours' sleep before an assault on the airfield scheduled for 5 A.M. Wednesday.

General McCaffrey's 197th Brigade, commanded by Colonel Ted Reid, had been pressed into service with the 24th Infantry Division (Mechanized) after a National Guard brigade that was to have been assigned to McCaffrey had proven unready for deployment. The 197th Brigade had not yet been assigned any Bradley fighting vehicles; it still depended on the Korean War–vintage M-113 armored personnel carrier. The M-113s were old and afforded little protection, but Reid had mounted new Mark-19 automatic grenade launchers on them, transforming them into potent weapons. The Mark-19 was accurate to 2,000 yards and poured out a heavy volume of fire.

Because the sandstorm precluded air support for most ground forces, McCaffrey's soldiers were moving north blindly. "Rommel said never maneuver in a sandstorm. I found out why," said Lieutenant Colonel Tom Leney, commander of one of McCaffrey's lead cavalry units. "We hit the Great Dismal Bog. The storm had blown white sand over all of it and made it look like white hardpan. But as we progressed, the tracks churned it up and broke through. And then when we stopped or tried to turn we were in trouble."

Leney ordered a cavalry troop to move east across the bog and determine whether that terrain would support the whole 197th Brigade. It would not. More vehicles bogged down. Searching for a way through the bog, commanders in the most forward units reported that the terrain was even worse the farther east they went.

After Leney warned that the bog seemed impassable, Reid ordered his other units to try a passage still farther east. Eventually, the 197th Brigade found a slender elevated track that allowed them to traverse the bog, although several dozen vehicles became stuck. The 197th had to blow up one of its tanks that was judged irrecoverable.

Once they were through the bog, Reid's brigade moved on to attack and destroy the headquarters complex of the Iraqi army's 3rd Commando Regiment. The Iraqis put up stiff resistance with 50-caliber machine guns mounted on trucks. The M-113 grenade launchers were more effective, however. "The brigadier general we captured told us he thought it was Iraqi forces when he heard all the movement out there," Reid said. "I think we totally surprised them." His brigade rolled onto Highway 8 and swung into a blocking position facing northwest, defending against any Iraqi reinforcements that might be shifted out of the key town of an-Nasiriyah or nearby Tallil Air Base.

Not long after nightfall that same day, Captain Gerald Davie was taking stock of his losses. Like H. R. McMaster's unit, Davie's cavalry troop had stumbled onto the Tawakalna division of the Republican Guard. Unlike McMaster's unit, Davie had no tanks. McMaster's soldiers would call their fight "the battle of 73 Easting." Davie's men simply referred to their engagement with the Tawakalna division as "when it happened."

The battle began as Davie's troop was advancing through the sandstorm. Davie could see only 200 or 300 meters with the naked eye, and no more than 900 meters even with his Bradley fighting vehicle's thermal sights. Somewhere off to his left was the battalion of the U.S. 3rd Armored Division that he was protecting with his scouts. Off to the right was the U.S. 2nd Armored Cavalry Regiment. Directly ahead were the T-72 tanks and BMPs (Iraqi armored fighting vehicles) of the Tawakalna division. It was Davie's 3rd Platoon, in the lead position, that saw the Iraqi soldiers first. "I have Iraqi infantry, and I have Iraqi BMPs to my front," came the radio call from the 3rd Platoon. Their Bradleys started shooting with their 25-mm cannons, and Davie ordered the 3rd Platoon to shift into a fighting line, his Bradleys one abreast of the other. Davie could see some explosions from the BMPs being hit by the 25-mm high-explosive rounds. Tracers flew in both directions. Through his thermal sights he saw other shapes. He guessed that they were BMPs.

Davie ordered the 2nd Platoon to attack the Iraqis alongside the 3rd Platoon; the 1st Platoon stayed back as a reserve. Their thirteen Bradleys—six in each platoon, plus his own—advanced in an even line. In the swirling sand, Davie could see only one or two vehicles to either side. Suddenly the enemy was everywhere. To the far left, there were Iraqi infantry as close as 75 meters away. Within 250 meters, there were armored vehicles. Directly ahead and to the right of Davie, there were more armored vehicles 300 meters to 600 meters away. What Davie did not know was that many of these vehicles were T-72 tanks.

The Iraqi soldiers and vehicles were hiding in holes, little showing except their gun barrels. They made tiny targets. Davie was especially concerned by the threat posed by Iraqi infantrymen firing rocket-propelled grenades. Davie's soldiers were firing at what they saw in their thermal sights. The Iraqis were returning the fire vigorously. Within seconds, the brief encounter had turned into a full-blown firefight. Davie's soldiers had no place to retreat. Then enemy artillery started landing around them. "We didn't know how badly we were into it," Davie said. "At that point, we were really just fighting for our lives. To try and turn and go back would have been the most dangerous thing to do."

Just minutes into the engagement, Alpha 24, a Bradley fighting vehicle in Davie's Alpha Troop, was hit by a tank round. One of the crew members in another Bradley saw the hit and began screaming over the radio for a medic. His pleas tied up the troop's radio net for minutes. Davie tried to talk the panicked soldier off the radio by telling him that a medic was on his way.

To Davie's left the crews of Bradley fighting vehicles Alpha 25 and Alpha 26 were trying to help the stricken Alpha 24. Command Sergeant Major Ronald Sneed, a veteran who had spent five years in Vietnam with the 173rd Airborne Brigade, had raced forward to Alpha 24 to help evacuate the wounded. Iraqi infantrymen were only 75 meters away from the disabled Bradley. Less than 200 meters away, an Iraqi T-72 began firing. Davie's soldiers could see the tank rounds from the T-72 just missing the top of the turrets of their Bradleys, and machine-gun rounds were whipping past. Alpha 25 and Alpha 26 returned the fire while their drivers maneuvered to retrieve their wounded comrades who were on the ground alongside Alpha 24. A T-72 tank round hit near Sneed's vehicle, knocking him to the ground.

Sneed saw that Staff Sergeant Kenneth Gentry, Alpha 24's gunner, was badly wounded. Sergeant First Class Raymond Egan's left leg was a mess. On the ground alongside Alpha 24, two medics, Sergeant Tifari Houston and Specialist Bryan Moore, worked on Gentry as Iraqi tracer rounds

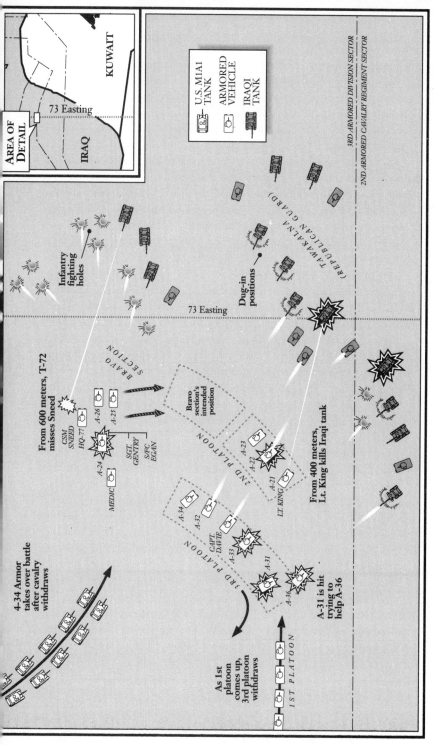

ON FEBRUARY 26, 1991, CAPTAIN DAVIE'S ALPHA TROOP BATTLED FORWARD FORCES OF THE TAWAKALNA

AREA OF DETAIL

IRAQ

KUWAIT

73 Easting

U.S. M1A1 TANK

ARMORED VEHICLE

IRAQI TANK

3RD ARMORED DIVISION SECTOR

2ND ARMORED CAVALRY REGIMENT SECTOR

TAWAKALNA (REPUBLICAN GUARD)

Infantry fighting holes

Dug-in positions

73 Easting

From 600 meters, T-72 misses Sneed

CSM SNEED

HQ-77

A-26   A-25

BRAVO SECTION

Bravo section's intended position

SGT. GENTRY

S/FC EGAN

A-24

MEDIC

A-23

A-22   A-21

2ND PLATOON

LT. KING

From 400 meters, Lt. King kills Iraqi tank

A-34

A-32

CAPT. DAVIE

A-33

A-31

3RD PLATOON

A-36

A-31 is hit trying to help A-36

4-34 Armor takes over battle after cavalry withdraws

As 1st platoon comes up, 3rd platoon withdraws

1ST PLATOON

whizzed past. Gentry would die within fifteen minutes, however.

In his Bradley, Davie knew only that one of his vehicles had been hit, and that medics had been summoned. Because the crews of Alpha 25 and Alpha 26 were out of the vehicles tending to their wounded colleagues, Davie could not raise them on the radio. The two Bradleys were too far away to be seen in the driving sand.

Davie's troop had stopped dead. He saw one of his Bradleys fire a TOW missile. Davie assumed that the soldiers had fired the missile because they were out of 25-mm ammunition. But the soldiers reported on the radio that they had hit a T-72 tank. For the first time, Davie realized that his lightly armored Bradleys were up against the best of the Iraqi tank corps. "There was a stout defense in front of us," Davie said, "and our thoughts were turning to what do we do now and how are we going to get out of this."

Before he could issue orders to move, another of Davie's Bradleys, Alpha 33, was hit by a 14.5-mm round from an Iraqi machine gun. It penetrated the turret of the Bradley and wounded its commander, Sergeant James Strong, badly in the hip. The Bradley's gunner, Corporal Efrem Zimbalist Evans, was on the troop's radio net immediately. "Sergeant Strong's been hit," Evans yelled, "and he's bleeding." While he repeated his summons for help, Evans continued to fight. "At this time we were fighting for our lives, so it was difficult to get a medic to [Sergeant Strong]," Davie said. "We were ten times too close to the enemy than we would choose to be. Actually, we were in what would be called their 'kill sack,' right where they wanted us to be."

With the battle growing increasingly desperate, Davie ordered the 1st Platoon, which until now had been his reserve, up onto the fight line. Davie's two platoons in front started to withdraw under the 1st Platoon's guard. "At this point it was not quite every vehicle for himself, but it seemed that way," Davie said. "Over the radio it got very chaotic because people were calling for medics, and transmissions began to get garbled over the radio. People were excited, and it was hard to understand what anyone was saying."

With the Bradley fighting vehicles of the 1st Platoon providing covering fire, Davie's soldiers began to withdraw from the engagement. They had done their job, and they had gotten hurt badly doing it. "We had made contact with our enemy," Davie said, "but now we wanted to break contact and pass it to 4-34 Armor," the armored battalion behind them.

The 4th Battalion, 34th Armor Regiment, was slow coming forward, however. "Why didn't they come up and help?" Davie wondered. "We were a little bit sore at them. Nothing can really hurt them—and nothing did."

For Davie's 3rd Platoon, the bloody fight was not over yet. As the 3rd Platoon's Bradleys continued pulling back, Alpha 36 was hit, first by small arms fire that disabled its transmission and stopped it dead, then by a Sagger anti-tank rocket. Alpha 31 came forward and rescued the crew of Alpha 36, but as Alpha 31 was withdrawing, it was hit by two tank rounds, and suddenly more men were wounded.

Seconds later, Alpha 22 was hit by a tank round. The blast killed Sergeant Edwin Kutz, Alpha 22's gunner. Another Bradley immediately pulled alongside Alpha 22 to help evacuate the Bradley's crew. As they were withdrawing from the Iraqi line, Davie and Lieutenant Daniel King, the leader of the 2nd Platoon, approached Alpha 22. Davie was told that Sergeant Kutz was dead. His soldiers tried to remove Kutz's body from the turret but they were unable to do so.

In the turret of his Bradley, Davie saw still more Iraqi soldiers running in front of him. Davie fired at them with the Bradley's machine gun. He got one soldier in his sights and killed him. "I felt glad when I killed him," Davie later said. "I did not have any feelings of remorse, then or now."

Davie's crew climbed back on board, and they drove to the rear, masking their withdrawal with smoke grenades. Davie and Lieutenant King raced westward at thirty miles an hour. It was getting dark. They had been in battle for an hour and fifteen minutes.

As night fell, Davie and his executive officer tried to account for their losses. Bradley fighting vehicles were still straggling toward the rear. Davie finally reported that every one of his soldiers was accounted for. Two soldiers, Staff Sergeant Kenneth Gentry and Sergeant Edwin Kutz, had been killed. Twelve others were wounded, several of them seriously. Four of Davie's vehicles were no longer fit for combat. Three others remained stranded on the battlefield.

The following morning, Davie's soldiers would retrieve the body of Sergeant Kutz. Davie saw that of the thirteen Bradleys he had had on the front line during the battle with the Iraqi force, twelve had been hit by Iraqi artillery rounds, shrapnel, small-arms fire, or worse. "There was a lot of metal flying around," Davie said. Of the thirty-six Purple Hearts that would be awarded to the soldiers of the 3rd Armored Division, fourteen would go to the men in Davie's troop who had been killed and wounded in those seventy-five minutes of fighting.

The 1st Brigade of the 3rd Armored Division picked up the battle from Davie's soldiers. With its heavy armor, the 1st Brigade pursued the main force of the Tawakalna division, as well as elements of the Iraqi 52nd, 10th, and 17th Divisions. Gunners from the 1st Brigade bombarded the Iraqi force with 155-mm artillery and tank-killing bomblets from their Multiple Launch Rocket Systems. Then, American A-10 Thunderbolt aircraft and Apache AH-64 attack helicopters took their turn at the Iraqi T-72 tanks.

By 6:40 P.M., the soldiers of the 1st Brigade reported that they had destroyed twenty-three Iraqi tanks. Some of the 1st Brigade's M1A1 tank gunners reported killing as many as five Iraqi tanks in just a few minutes. Others reported finding only the carcasses of destroyed or abandoned tanks as they rolled through the Iraqi lines.

In the days following the battle, members of the Army Medical Corps conducted a radiation check on the vehicles that had been shot in Davie's troop. Because American M1A1 tanks fired anti-tank rounds that contained depleted uranium, and Iraqi tanks did not, any vehicle struck by an M1A1 tank's sabot round would carry a telltale radiation signature. The corpsmen found that the ragged edges of the holes in Alpha 24, 31, and 22 were "hot." Some of Davie's soldiers had told him they saw the tanks of 4-34 Armor firing as they approached to take over the battle, and they feared they might hit Alpha Troop's vehicles by mistake. It turned out they were right. An investigation by the 3rd Armored Division in March 1991 concluded that two of Davie's vehicles were probably hit by 4-34 Armor and one by either 4-34 Armor or the 2nd Armored Cavalry Regiment. Sergeants Gentry and Kutz had been killed by "friendly fire."

CHAPTER 21

THE BIG RED ONE
PRESSES THE ATTACK

Five-thirty p.m., February 26: a bad hour in a wretched day. Lieutenant Colonel Pat Ritter stood in the commander's turret of M1A1 tank HQ-66 as it roared across the bleak, flat, muddy-sand landscape, a landscape fast becoming indistinct in the dimming gray light. An incessant rain, driven by a cold, hard northwest wind, had pelted his face and run down his flak jacket all the previous night, soaking his pants and his boots and making it impossible to sleep. Then when the rain stopped that morning, a dense fog rolled in; when that lifted, the wind brought a sandstorm so fierce that his tanks nearly lost their way to their fuel trucks. His men, now strung out behind him in a mile-long train of fifty-eight sand-colored tanks, had been on the move since daybreak. Even the high-octane adrenaline that had kept them going for the past two sleepless days seemed to be running low. And just when he had thought they would stop and get some rest and respite from battle, he had gotten some worrisome news instead.

Somewhere up ahead in this soggy desert called southeastern Iraq, the smaller and lightly armored U.S. 2nd Cavalry Regiment had smacked dead into a division of the Republican Guard, the toughest, best-led and best-equipped tank forces of the Iraqi army. Ritter's men could hear the 2nd Cavalry on the tactical radio now—an unnerving mix of dead calm and excited and frantic voices calling for medics and "evacs"; others calling out their targets, the dreaded Iraqi T-72 tanks. It had been decided—at a level that soldiers call "echelons above reality"—that the 1st Infantry Division, the Big Red One, which had just fought its way through the western end of the Iraqi defenses and was then supposed to become the corps reserve force, would drive forward instead through fifty miles of desert, find and relieve the 2nd Armored Cavalry Regiment, and take up their battle. This had been relayed to Ritter and his comrades over a paper map under a hastily thrown up tarp attached to one side of a command vehicle in a wind so strong that four men had to hold the corners so it would not be ripped away. Ritter and the other two battalion commanders in his brigade were told that they would have to locate the 2nd Cavalry in the pitch-black night, edge through the regiment's rear forces while it was fighting the Iraqis, pick up the running tank battle, and continue until the Tawakalna division was destroyed. They had been too stunned to ask many questions.

Months later, Ritter would sit in his quiet office in Fort Riley, Kansas, barely close his eyes and still see the explosions and artillery and tracers and burning tanks from that middle-of-the-night operation. He would still remember his soldiers being wounded, and the one soldier who died. His men would call it "fright night."

Ritter and his men had never done anything like this before. Never had anyone else, as far as he knew. Each of the pieces of this maneuver would be difficult, and dangerous as hell. As he received his orders, Ritter recalled what he had learned from other officers in the brigade about night attacks. Once when they were at the Army's National Training Center, a huge slab of California desert where the Army learns to fight, Lieutenant Colonel Sidney "Skip" Baker, a Vietnam veteran and gritty battalion commander, had asked permission to try a night attack. Even in the controlled environment of the training center, they were not allowed to try. Too dangerous, they were told. And that was just a textbook night attack. In this case, Ritter and his tank soldiers would have to come into contact with the 2nd Cavalry and pass through them while they were still fighting. It was dangerous enough to pass through friendly forces from behind when they were *not* fighting, because of the likelihood they would mistake some of their own side's tanks for an enemy attacking from the rear—and fire away. Then, to move out in front of the 2nd Cavalry and pick up their targets and their battle . . . and at night? Well, Lieutenant Colonel Greg Fontenot, the commander of the 2nd Battalion, 34th Armor, which would be fighting at Ritter's side, was already calling this operation "a leap of faith."

For Ritter, it would be more than that: it would be his baptism and first communion, too. A sandy-haired forty-two-year-old, he had taken command of his battalion only the previous June and was probably the youngest battalion commander in the whole U.S. Army. And if he wasn't, he sure looked like it. With a cherubic face and a heavy dose of naïve enthusiasm, he might easily be taken for one of his own young soldiers, rather than for the commander of 450 of them. Yet, except for one week-long practice run in the Saudi desert ten days before, he had never commanded his men in any full-scale battle maneuvers at all. There simply wasn't enough space at Fort Riley for whole battalions to practice warfare. Since he had joined the Army twenty years before, Ritter had been wondering about real combat. What would it be like: the noise, the light, the smell, the confusion? Would he measure up? How scared would he be? In his battalion of 450 men, only 9 guys had been in combat before, and he was not one of them.

Nonetheless, it was surprising how well things had gone so far. Two days earlier, the Big Red One's breach of the Iraqi defenses, fifty miles west of the point where Kuwait, Iraq, and Saudi Arabia meet, had been smooth and fast, even better than they had dared hope. Most soldiers had believed they would take at least 30 percent casualties. Indeed, before the ground war, the other divisions joked that while the 1st Infantry Division had needed three transport planes to get to Saudi Arabia, they'd need only one to get back. That only made things worse: if they were going to die, the jokes should be their own, they thought. "I was really scared," said Captain Juan Toro, months later. He expected twenty or thirty Iraqi tanks to come roaring down right at him as he crept through the breach. "I hated every goddamn minute of it," recalled Captain Robert Burns. But as it turned out, the intelligence—that is, the intelligence the division obtained for itself, not what it got from higher headquarters—had been superb for locating the enemy and for finding the best point to breach the defenses. They had maps showing exactly where every Iraqi trench, fighting hole, and artillery gun was. And when they drove through the Iraqi defenses, cutting their eight attack lanes with their mine plows through the mine fields, they found the trenches to be shallow and rarely arrayed in depth, right where their maps had indicated. They found the Iraqi mines to be sparse; far worse were all the unexploded U.S. munitions scattered about from the thirty-minute pre-breach artillery bombardment. They found the Iraqi artillery and mortar and gunfire sporadic and inaccurate, and the Iraqis surrendered in droves. After the tank plows made the breach lanes, they swung left and right and plowed right over the Iraqi bunkers and trenches. The commanders had told the soldiers that the Iraqis had three options: to fight and be killed, to surrender, or to not come out and be buried in their bunkers. And a few, perhaps many, were buried alive.

In the whole breach operation of 3½ hours, one American soldier had been killed defusing an enemy mine and another wounded by artillery shrapnel. Neither was in Ritter's battalion. There had been a couple of moments, though, when the hairs on his neck had stood right on end.

One of those moments came right after the breach on February 24. As soon as it was made, Skip Baker's 5-16 Battalion (5th Battalion, 16th Armor) and Greg Fontenot's 2-34 Battalion were to hold the ground on the Iraqi side. Ritter's 1-34 Battalion (1st Battalion, 34th Armor) was to surge ahead. Ritter had fifty-eight tanks in his four companies, a mortar platoon, and a scout platoon with six fast and light Bradley fighting vehicles. They were to all shoot through the breach lanes as fast as possible and assault an Iraqi company known to be lying in wait just behind the defensive lines. The fear, of course, was that the Iraqi company would use its tanks or artillery to smash the 1st Infantry Division's vehicles as they crept along in file through the narrow breach lanes. If that happened, they would be little more than a 7,000-vehicle American traffic jam, sitting ducks for a punishing artillery barrage.

Ritter set his troops into a combat diamond, a formation that put his most experienced tank company, Charlie Company, to the front, Alpha and Bravo Companies to the sides, and Delta Company to the rear in reserve. They crept forward waiting for artillery to soften up the Iraqi tank company. But the artillery wasn't coming—there were too many other targets, the gunners said. Just then an air liaison officer radioed and told Ritter he had four F-16s coming into the area. Ritter called for one artillery smoke round and it hit dead center into the Iraqi company. "Does the lead F-16 see the target?" he asked the air liaison. "Wait . . . negative," came the reply. So Ritter called for another smoke round, asking the liaison if the F-16 saw it now. "He still doesn't have it," came the reply. Suddenly Iraqi artillery rounds began exploding all around Delta Company as it struggled through the breach lanes. Now Delta's commander was yelling into the radio, "Let's get the fuck out of here!" and Ritter was calling off the air support and the artillery and his driver was gunning their tank. As the battalion leapt forward at twenty miles an hour, Ritter's lanky gunner, Staff Sergeant Kevin Draper, jabbed Ritter with his elbow, a prearranged signal that meant an Iraqi target lay ahead. Ritter peered through his sight, saw a metal vehicle of some sort, and told Draper to fire. And at that moment, to Ritter's amazement, forty-four of his tanks blasted their 120-mm main guns at once. The shock was so sudden, the noise so great, his heart nearly stopped.

At first, Ritter thought he'd mistakenly hit the intercom button and given the "fire" command to the whole battalion. But later he decided that just when his gunner acquired his target, the rest of the company had spotted theirs, and when the "old man" fired, they all fired too. Everyone kept on shooting, and there was so much ammunition flying Ritter nearly told them to stop. When they rolled up to the Iraqi company, there were no tanks to be seen, but eighty Iraqis and their commander were standing with their hands up. Much later, Ritter would say he was too busy to be scared. But at the end of that breach and attack, he recalled, there was a moment of grand and almost heady relief. He was okay, his men were all alive and unhurt, and they had done their job well.

That first night, as they waited in the desert just north of the breach lanes, three Iraqi infantry soldiers approached their company about 800 yards away. It was strange: the Iraqis would move, then stay still for a while, then move again. The whole tank company quietly watched them through their thermal sights, which picked up heat from tanks, trucks, even bunkers and birds and men, and turned them into a visual TV image much like a daylight scene. But thermal sights could not detect hand-carried anti-tank rockets and launchers or Soviet rocket-propelled grenades made of cold metal. These dismounted infantrymen—"dismounts" the soldiers called them—were dangerous. On the battlefield they were tiny targets. They could hide in a hole or a trench, then creep up on a clumsy, half-blind tank and shoot it in the side or rear with an anti-tank rocket. Those could be deadly.

What were these dismounts up to? Ritter wondered. Were they spies? Were they armed with rocket-propelled grenades? Could they be captured? Were they approaching to surrender? Despite the danger, Ritter found himself ruled by a strong emotion—he really didn't want to kill them. As the dismounts moved into view, he told Draper, his gunner, to fire ten meters to their left, and the Iraqis hit the dirt. But in minutes they were up again and moving. "Fire ten meters to the right of them," he told Draper. "Let's try to pin them down." This time they stayed down, and while Draper watched them, Ritter, exhausted, tried to doze off. But soon, Draper was jabbing him with his elbow. "Sir, they're up and moving," he said, toward a lightly armored Bradley fighting vehicle. "That's enough," said Ritter. "Shoot them." Ritter's tank crew watched them. And in the eerie black and green screen of the thermal sights, they saw one of the bodies turn from green to black, go cold as its life drained out. Ritter's men were dead quiet. None of them had ever killed anyone before. "No soldier wants to kill someone. Nobody wants to do that," Ritter said. But, he thought at the time, "We're really in this now."

Now, on February 26, as the tank battalions groped their way through the desert night toward the rear of the 2nd Armored Cavalry, a howling wind came up, and thunderstorms lashed them and lightning slashed the sky. For most of the 100-mile march, Ritter had kept his men in a combat diamond formation, the same companies in the same positions to reduce confusion and stress. Yet inside the tanks the men were tired and miserable. The M1A1 hatches, even when closed, leaked profusely. In addition, because the tank commander and loader usually stood up in their turrets looking out, they were cold; meanwhile, the tanks' heaters cooked the gunners, who stripped off their chemical protective suits and fireproof underwear for relief. Down in the cramped, six-foot-wide, wet compartment Ritter struggled with a huge, crumpled map as the tank bounded along. The map's scale of 1:250,000 was about five times bigger than he was used to, but it was what they needed for the vast distances in Iraq. Having been given a series of waypoints by his brigade commander, he was trying to plot the path to the 2nd Cavalry and the enemy beyond them. His intelligence officer had given him a set of points showing the centers of mass for the battalions of dug-in Republican Guard tanks and armored personnel carriers waiting in ambush. But first, they had to find the 2nd Cavalry.

A few hundred yards from Ritter's tank, Captain James Bell, a lanky thirty-year-old from North Carolina, commanded Charlie Company from tank C-66. Bell was not happy. Sure orders were orders, but why so abrupt, he wondered. And why over the radio? Why hadn't they discussed this night attack idea a little with the company commanders? Maybe they could have talked about how to do it, figured out some night recognition signals with flashlights, for instance. Hell, why not do a day attack instead? And where were these Iraqis anyway? They had had such great intelligence at the breach—maps and plastic overlays showing every single Iraqi fighting position. Now they were going to hit the Iraqis at night, and no one seemed to have any intelligence at all. The map he had with its huge scale was almost worthless.

Bell didn't know it, but their brigade commander, Colonel Lon Maggart, had even bigger worries. When Maggart got the vague orders to attack, two conflicting voices began screaming in his brain. One said, "Jesus Christ, we're going into the middle of the Tawakalna in the middle of the night with no intelligence? Good Lord, I'm not sure we're gonna come out of it!" The other voice was calmer: "Well, let's get organized and get in the right formation and just go in and tear them apart." But how? The intelligence officers at the main division headquarters had one plastic overlay with purported Iraqi positions, but it was two days old. Maggart got to look at it for about thirty seconds in one meeting, and that was it. He never got a copy.

At least Bell got a copy. As his tank drove through the desert a Humvee from headquarters came up, flagged him down, and handed him a clear plastic sheet with some marks on it. He laid it on his map, but all it showed him was a big circle where the Iraqis were likely to be. Bell's gunner struggled in the dim light of the tank turret to fit the maps and overlays together to come up with a set of coordinates leading to the Iraqi zone. Bell handed the coordinates to his executive officer, Lieutenant Mike Hazelwood. "They're not perfect, but they're close," Bell said. They headed, nearly blind in the stormy dark, for the rear of the 2nd Armored Cavalry.

Then they had a bit of luck. A voice came up on the radio net that Ritter had never heard before, the cool and steady voice of the operations officer of the 2nd Cavalry's 3rd Squadron. George Webb, "Wolfpack 3," took map locations from Ritter's men and gave them precise directions to his units. He explained how the rear vehicles of the cavalry would be marked with glowing orange chemlights and how they would make a path so that Ritter's battalion could safely drive through the regiment. Ritter could hear his company commanders and tank commanders on the radio net after that, and there was a new calm in their voices. If he ever met George Webb in a bar after the war, he thought, he would buy that guy and everyone else drinks for the rest of the night. As Webb talked them into the rear, they could see the battle ahead. They passed burning Iraqi vehicles. In the distance were the flashes and muffled explosions of tanks being hit. Ritter punched waypoints 508, 533, and 512 into his Global Positioning System computer, got the bearing and range to the first objective in Iraqi territory, and his battalion crept through. They were into it now.

At least, thought Bell, the exhausted soldiers were wide awake now. The threat of combat had a way of doing that. Hours earlier, just as they were getting the order that they would be taking over the battle, some of his soldiers were able to tune in on the brigade radio net to one unit of the 2nd Armored Cavalry. What they heard was not encouraging. In Charlie Company's tank C-31, Sergeant First Class Ralph Martin heard the excited voices talking about casualties—of vehicles being hit and evacuations and bringing medics forward, and maybe of people being killed. He also heard them mention T-72s, which gave him chills, for the Soviet-made T-72 was one tank Martin and his men knew about. Back at Fort Riley, Captain Bell had gone to a secret briefing on the T-72 and returned so sobered he got permission for all his men—even those not cleared for secret briefings—to attend. They were told that the T-72 was almost unbeatable. While its main gun range was no more than 2,800 meters (200 meters less than the probable kill range of the M1A1), the T-72 was built so close to the ground that it would be very hard to hit. When they were dug deep into the sand in a fighting position with only their guns poking out, they would be impossible to see until the Americans were well within their gun range. In addition, the way the T-72's engine and exhaust systems were covered, the tank put out very little heat and would be hard to detect in the thermal sights that gave the American tank such an advantage. Private First Class Enrique Palacios, an eighteen-year-old loader in tank C-33, walked out of the briefing thinking, God, when we go against this tank, someone's going to die. He pictured his company shooting at T-72s and nothing happening. "And then, when they shot us there would be nothing left," he said.

The secret briefers also told them about the Soviet-made BMP, an armored fighting vehicle with a main gun, a machine gun, and AT-5 anti-tank missiles. While the 73-mm main gun wasn't much to worry about—it had a range of only 800 yards—the AT-5 was a nasty weapon. A BMP could hide in a small hole with only its AT-5 peeking out; the missile had a range of 4,000 meters, a good 1,000 meters farther than the range of the M1A1 tank gun. The Kuwaitis had some new BMPs that the Iraqis probably had captured; these had 30-mm cannons that could shoot holes right through Bradley fighting vehicles.

While Ritter's battalion crept through the lanes opened by the 2nd Cavalry, U.S. artillery guns roared and the shells screamed overhead as the cavalry pounded Iraqi positions. Then the Multiple Launch Rocket Sys-

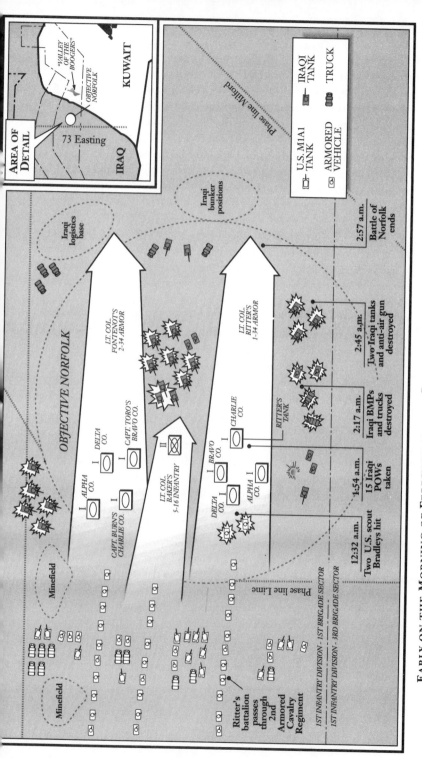

EARLY ON THE MORNING OF FEBRUARY 27, 1991, LIEUTENANT COLONEL PAT RITTER'S BATTALION FOUGHT ITS WAY THROUGH OBJECTIVE NORFOLK

tems opened up. Off to Ritter's left, Greg Fontenot's 2-34 Battalion was passing through the 2nd Cavalry under the same black and stormy sky. Many of his soldiers never even saw the cavalry's Bradleys and tanks as they passed through a large hole in the lines. Captain Robert Burns, 2-34's Charlie Company commander, saw one Bradley with two tired soldiers standing behind it, and thought, That must be them. They were parked right behind a burned-out turretless T-72, its unmistakable long cannon with the gas ejector on its tip lying nearby. As Burns's tank drove past, he smelled the sickening stench of the smoldering tank and human flesh burning inside.

Captain Juan Toro's Bravo Company was on the right side of Fontenot's battalion, driving forward. Toro had his ten main tanks on a shoulder-to-shoulder line, with four Bradleys behind them. As the connecting link between Ritter's and Fontenot's battalions, he was doing his best to stay close to Ritter's battalion to the right. The rest of 2-34 was supposed to link up with Toro and spread out to the left in one long line of tanks abreast. They would then plow through the Iraqis somewhere ahead. At least that was the plan. But the rest of the battalion couldn't find Toro. Toro told Staff Sergeant John McKinn, the commander of his leftmost tank, to put a chemical light on his antenna so the battalion could find them. The suggestion was met with silence. McKinn, a forty-seven-year-old seventeen-year veteran, was not about to put a light on his tank as they headed into the Iraqis. Toro shot some flares into the air instead.

Suddenly, Toro's company sighted two Iraqi BMPs and shot them; and then his tanks were firing fusillades with their machine guns at Iraqi trucks and dismounts. Charlie Company found Toro's Bravo Company in the dark, coming up from behind, but couldn't fire because Bravo's engineers and supply trucks were 300 meters in front of them. Then Charlie Company saw Iraqi trenches straight ahead, and there were dismounts everywhere. Burns, the Charlie Company commander, drove ahead and saw one Iraqi right in front of his tank. But he couldn't shoot him, because Toro's men were right behind the Iraqi. Burns stared at the soldier: Surrender, or I'll run you over, he thought. But the man wouldn't surrender. And suddenly there were Iraqis right off his tank's grill, only fifteen yards away, and then he heard a Bradley machine gun open up and the Iraqis went down. Tracers were everywhere, ricocheting off the ground and filling the sky. Somehow, in the dark, Charlie Company got off to the side of Bravo and opened fire on the dismounts.

In Toro's tank, there was mayhem. Everyone was shouting at once. His loader was telling him there were dismounts to the left and the gunner was seeing targets in his thermal scope. Toro saw an Iraqi tank right in front, and then his driver yelled that there was an Iraqi command vehicle besides. Toro decided to shoot the command vehicle, called a PC, with a High Explosive Anti-Tank round. "Gunner, HEAT, PC, identify," he yelled to his crew. The loader threw in a shell and screamed "Up!" and the gunner pulled his trigger . . . and nothing happened. Toro yelled, "Right trigger," and the gun misfired again. Toro pulled his own trigger, and there was a boom. Now Toro knew both of his gunner's triggers were broken.

Meanwhile, Toro's executive officer was on the battalion radio net trying to tell Burns that Burns's tracers were coming toward Bravo and all the platoon leaders were on the company radio net yelling to Toro that tracers were coming at them from behind. Toro's radio voice scrambler went haywire and he was losing his ability to talk to his men securely; his loader was trying to find a working scrambler and all Toro could think was: How am I going to control the company now? What am I going to do, get down and run from tank to tank? All the while, his company was firing at Iraqi tanks: first with TOW missiles and then one platoon fired a four-round main gun volley and the other platoons were shooting also.

In McKinn's tank, there was an unnatural calm. They'd had more panic on the gun range than out here, McKinn later thought. The men would see a target, get the range, ask another tank to confirm the range, and then shoot. And then do it again. They were very professional tank killers.

It took until midnight to get the battalion on a line abreast. To Burns, it was a spectacular sight to see every combat vehicle fender to fender on a north-south line that disappeared into the night, all driving east and firing into the Iraqi stronghold. Strangely, there was a long period of quiet, maybe thirty minutes. Then Delta Company in Fontenot's battalion saw an entire Iraqi tank platoon and opened fire. There was the boom and flash of the cannon and the red tracer streak as the shells flew through the night and the sharp, white steel-on-steel flash as the tungsten dartlike rounds hit the enemy tanks and then a second of quiet. Suddenly, two forks of fire would burst out of the hatch of a T-72 and it would explode, the turret blowing off and ammunition rocketing into the air like fireworks. Burns watched Delta's battle. With the explosions Burns could see all his tanks lit up like it was daylight, and he'd wait for the Iraqis to return fire. And it wouldn't come—or, some said later, it did come, it just missed badly.

That night Toro saw something he would never forget. He drove right by a blazing Iraqi tank and when he got too close to turn away, so close he could read its bumper number and feel the heat from its fire, he saw the tank commander still in the hatch. Toro was a tank commander too.

Off to the right, Pat Ritter's men were also rolling forward. Jim Bell's Charlie Company spotted two dug-in BMPs. At 3,600 meters they were tiny targets in the scope, too small to shoot, it seemed. Their buddies in Alpha Company suddenly shot the BMPs at about 3,000 meters. Those were great shots, thought Bell. They just might outgun the dreaded Iraqi T-72s, after all.

Out in front the battalion scouts crept along in lightly armored Bradley fighting vehicles, firing their machine guns at shapes and shadows. "Reconnaissance-by-fire," it was called, and it was scary as hell. Behind them in tank C-31 was Sergeant First Class Ralph Martin, a smart and serious thirty-five-year-old platoon leader from Missouri who was so good he had been given a job usually reserved for a second lieutenant. Martin was watching over the scouts, looking for enemy to their front or side, to protect them if necessary with gunfire. Suddenly, the first scout was lit up by a violent explosion—it had been hit.

In Martin's tank, chaos reigned. Martin's gunner, who had been staring through his thermal sights looking for Iraqis, was frantically whipping the main gun and its sights back and forth, trying to find what had shot the Bradley. He was screaming "Where? Where? Where?!" Martin couldn't tell him. The gunner swung his thermal sights onto the Bradley. He could see it burning and then, incredibly, he could see its hatches open and men stumble out and fall to the ground.

To Ritter, all this was a horror movie. Here he was, barely half an hour into the battle, and Bradley number HQ-232 had gone up in a sickening flash. My God, he thought, I've just had five soldiers killed. Ten seconds passed, and Ritter heard his scout platoon leader, Lieutenant Glen Burnham, say that Bradley 232 had been hit and he was moving to cover it. Ritter ordered Bravo Company to move up to secure the burning Bradley. Burnham was talking Ritter up into the area on the radio when Ritter felt Draper's sharp elbow. "Sir, I got an enemy BMP," Draper said. It had pulled out of its hole and was trying to get a shot at Burnham as he moved across the field. Ritter didn't hesitate: "BMP, identified, fire!" he yelled to

Draper. Their hit was dead center. A second BMP pulled out and hid behind the now burning BMP, so Ritter couldn't get a shot on it. Ritter heard a boom. A tank in Alpha Company, to the right, had sighted it and killed it.

Burnham was so calm on the radio net as he maneuvered Ritter forward that ten minutes passed before Ritter realized something was wrong with Burnham's voice; then it dawned on Ritter: Burnham was hit too. When Burnham had turned left to move toward Bradley 232, his gun was still facing to the right. Just then, a heavy machine-gun round crashed through the left rear of Burnham's turret. The round went in, through gunner Sergeant David Douthit's back and neck, came out his chest, slammed into the turret drive, and smashed Burnham's leg. Douthit was killed instantly. As Ritter was trying to absorb this, Bravo Company came up on the radio net. They had reached the burning Bradley, and the five soldiers were alive. Ritter didn't believe it. "This is Demon 6," he yelled into the radio, "Say again." There were no torso hits, Bravo said, the soldiers were wounded only in the legs and arms. "Say again!" said Ritter. He couldn't believe it. He had seen the flash of the round hitting the Bradley, a catastrophic vehicle kill—yet somehow they had survived.

The battalion, however, was stopped dead. Ritter pulled the scouts back, behind the tanks. Private First Class Palacios, the diminutive loader in tank C-33, saw that there was a new seriousness among the men, an intensity verging on vengeance. Only moments before they had been gabbing and joking on the radio net to ease their jitters. Now it was different. The Iraqis of the Republican Guard were not simply surrendering, like those they had encountered at the breach. Many of them wanted to fight, and would fight to the death.

The battalion drove forward and began to kill. Bravo Company on the left was shooting armored vehicles called BTRs, trucks, bunkers, and tanks. Alpha Company on the right was hitting tanks. An examination of the battlefield later would show they had destroyed fifteen T-72s, eleven armored fighting vehicles, one anti-aircraft gun, and four trucks. In the center of the battalion formation where Ritter stationed himself, Charlie Company was shooting at Iraqi T-72s, T-59 tanks, and anything else that moved. They hit a bunker filled with 155-mm artillery ammunition, which exploded in a startling blast. Ritter's tank drove right past a T-72 dug into a fighting hole only 250 meters away. Ritter never saw it, but before the T-72 could take a bead on him, Alpha Company took it out. Even Delta Company, the reserve company following in the rear, started to fire. Delta tanks saw two Iraqis crawling toward a tank and shot them. Another tank was tracking an Iraqi soldier as he stole through the company in three-second rushes. Just as the Delta tank was about to shoot him, the Iraqi jumped behind a sage bush and a Bravo Company tank ran over him. The tankers saw the tank's track glow warmly in their thermal sights from the doomed man's body heat.

Over in Fontenot's 2-34 Battalion, Staff Sergeant McKinn could hear the Iraqis screaming and crying. It seemed his company was running right over them, and he could hear the wounded ones crying while others were yelling what sounded like "Allah . . . Allah!" It was an eerie, awful sound.

The Americans were exhausted. Captain Toro had gotten too far out in front of Bravo Company; when the company stopped to engage targets, he realized he had to get out of the way. But before he could move, he looked ahead and there, in front of his tank, were groups of Iraqi infantrymen coming toward him. Toro forgot that his gunner's triggers no longer worked. He dropped down in the turret and yelled at his gunner to train the co-axial machine gun on the Iraqi troops. But his gunner—hands on the triggers, head against the tank wall—was fast asleep. It hardly mattered. By this time, the Iraqis were in no mood to continue the fight.

And then they were through Objective Norfolk. It had taken more than four hours. Ritter's intelligence officer had saved one warm Sharp's nonalcoholic beer, the only kind the soldiers could get in Saudi Arabia; when they stopped moving, he hopped down and walked over to Ritter's tank. "Here, boss," he said, "I've been saving this for you." Ritter popped the top, turned it up, and sucked the bottom out. It was the best beer he'd ever had.

But the celebration was premature. Just as the black night was turning to a muddy dawn, tanks in Ritter's battalion's Alpha Company spotted what appeared to be two Iraqi T-62 tanks to their southwest firing machine guns in their direction. Alpha Company returned the fire, destroying the two vehicles. Two hours later, the morning light would show that they were two Bradleys from another brigade which had strayed a kilometer out of their zone, and were firing at Iraqis. One soldier was killed in the incident. Months later Ritter would learn that the two Bradleys that he had lost during the battle of Norfolk might also have been hit by "friendly fire."

CHAPTER 22

TRIUMPH WITHOUT VICTORY

A T 1:54 A.M. on February 27, despite a driving rain, artillery gunners from Colonel Dan Zanini's Bulldog Brigade of the U.S. 1st Armored Division were shelling elements of Iraq's Tawakalna division. The Bulldog Brigade had charged through the northernmost positions of the Tawakalna the previous afternoon and evening. Now Zanini's soldiers were chasing the Tawakalna. The Iraqi forces ahead of Zanini's Bulldog Brigade were stubbornly withdrawing, and many of the Iraqi soldiers continued firing as they retreated.

The Bulldog Brigade's artillery barrage was intended to prepare, or "soften up," the enemy for a tank charge that would follow. The artillery gunners, to the rear of the Bulldog Brigade, were firing over the heads of Zanini's soldiers onto the Iraqi force to the east of them. That was always risky, because some shells might fall short, and if artillery rounds fell on them, the soldiers of the Bulldog Brigade would not know whose artillery it was—their own or the enemy's.

At 3:07 A.M., that is exactly what happened. Artillery rounds began dropping into the middle of the tactical-operations center of a light cavalry unit ahead of Colonel Zanini. Known as the 1-1 Cavalry, it was part of the 1st Armored Division. It served, in the words of Captain John Heck, the commander of 1-1 Cavalry's Bravo Troop, as the division's "eyes and ears." The 1-1 Cavalry possessed thirty-nine Bradley fighting vehicles, twenty helicopters, and six mortar vehicles. The 1-1 Cavalry boasted 182 soldiers, among whom were several groups of soldiers known as Long-Range Surveillance Detachment teams. Each team consisted of six soldiers in two Humvees; their mission was to range far ahead of the division as it advanced, scouting the terrain and the enemy.

In the earliest hours of February 27, a few miles ahead of the bulk of the 1st Armored Division, John Heck's Bravo Troop had encountered a number of Iraqi armored fighting vehicles and jeeps, probably from the Medina Luminous division of the Republican Guard. After Heck's soldiers destroyed nine of the vehicles, he received orders to remain where he was, so that heavier units could advance in front of him to pursue the attack. However, Heck's luck ran out. Fearing that the advancing friendly troops would mistake Bravo Troop in the night for the enemy, Heck ordered his soldiers to close in tightly together to make a smaller target. That was precisely where the artillery rounds began falling at 3:07 A.M. The rounds were actually canisters that spit out clusters of small munitions designed to penetrate light armor and to injure soldiers. Twenty-three of Heck's men were wounded instantly. "I was probably twenty-five meters behind a Bradley," Heck said, "and all of a sudden, we just lost sight of them. There was just that much stuff coming down on us. We had to close the hatches real quick. My Bradley got hit. In the squadron TOC [tactical-operations center] area, almost every vehicle got hit. Fourteen wheeled vehicles were destroyed. . . . It seemed like machine guns going off right by your ears continuously."

Twenty meters away, Sergeant Russell Wayne saw Staff Sergeant Michael Murray, his surveillance-team leader, get hit. The bomblet went through the roof of Murray's Humvee. The round exploded on the inside of the door and ripped it off. Seconds later, Murray's Humvee was in flames.

Wayne and his gunner immediately ran forward to help. Inside the Humvee, Murray's gunner had shrapnel buried in his side and in his hip. His right arm was badly injured. Murray's jacket was on fire, and another soldier was trying to put the fire out. Wayne reached to move the gunner, but the man's body was soaked with blood. Wayne thought the gunner was dead. "I turned Sergeant Murray around to look more at me," Wayne said, "because I didn't want him to look at [his gunner]. There was a lot of screaming, a lot of confusion."

Both Wayne and his gunner were trained as medics. While Wayne attended to Sergeant Murray, Wayne's gunner ran to his Humvee to retrieve their first-aid kits. The two men were already working on Murray and his gunner in the shattered Humvee when the platoon medics came up in their vehicle and began attending to the wounded. Soon the wounded soldiers were being evacuated to the rear. Of the twenty-three soldiers injured in the early morning hours of February 27, all would survive.

Afterward, the story would spread that it was so-called friendly fire that had fallen on Heck's Bravo Troop. The bomblets were of the same general type fired by U.S. artillery gunners. Another reason for these suspicions was that Lieutenant Colonel Bill Reese, the commander of 1-1 Cavalry, had gone on the division radio net when the artillery shells began falling and yelled "Check fire!" several times. The firing had stopped. Reese said later that the artillery gunners of the 1st Armored Division had answered that they had not fired. The Army accepted that explanation.

It would take the Pentagon a full six months after the conclusion of the Gulf conflict to examine the issue of friendly fire. The Pentagon would conclude that of the 148 American servicemen and women who perished on the battlefield in the Gulf conflict, 35 had been killed inadvertently by their comrades. Fully 23 percent of the Americans killed in action and 15 percent of those wounded were victims of friendly fire. These percentages were roughly ten times higher than those recorded in any other U.S. war in this century. But those numbers did not tell the whole story. Eleven more Americans were killed when unexploded Allied munitions later blew up on them, hiking the friendly-caused casualty rate to 31 percent. And another 18 American soldiers were killed by unexploded enemy ordnance. Most soldiers said that the thousands of unexploded mines and bomblets they encountered were more dangerous than enemy fire. The Pentagon's analysts would attribute the high percentages to several factors. A battle-field crowded with numerous coalition forces was complicated by Allied tactics that relied heavily on rapid maneuverability, often at night and in conditions of exceedingly poor visibility. In addition, technology that would enable soldiers to distinguish friend from foe had lagged far behind the technology that allowed soldiers in the Gulf conflict to kill their presumed foe from great distances.

Dawn promised only slightly better weather than the Allied soldiers had endured during the first three days of the ground campaign. A damp, gray morning shot through with ribbons of desert fog, it afforded visibility of just over a mile. These were difficult conditions for pitched battle, but perfect for ambush-type attacks.

At first light, the entire U.S. 1st Armored Division was already moving forward, three brigades abreast. Their tanks were spaced thirty meters apart. The advancing division occupied a sector of desert fifteen miles wide. Intelligence reports said that ahead of them the Iraqis had established a line of defenses that extended from north to south directly across their path. In some places, the Iraqi tank line appeared to be a brigade deep. The line included tanks from the 2nd Armored Brigade from the Republican Guard's Medina Luminous division, shored up by units from the 17th Armored Division, the 12th Armored Division, and the Medina's 14th Mechanized Brigade. To the intelligence officers of the U.S. 1st Armored Division, it appeared that Saddam Hussein was making a last-ditch effort to prevent the VII Corps, of which the 1st Armored was a key part, from cutting off the retreat of his army through northern Kuwait.

Nonetheless, across the Allied lines shortly after dawn, generals, tank commanders, and infantrymen all felt that the conflict with Iraq was heading swiftly toward conclusion. Two of the heavy divisions under General Franks's command, the U.S. 3rd Armored Division and the U.S. 1st Infantry Division, had by now shattered the main body of the Tawakalna division of the Republican Guard. Roughly on line with them to the south, the British 1st Armored Division, also under the command of General Franks, had routed remnants of Iraqi infantry and armored units that lay in their path. Many were fleeing toward northern Kuwait and Basra, in southern Iraq. In addition, the Adnan division of the Republican Guard had fled toward the Euphrates. The Hammurabi division was laying back behind the Medina Luminous, and it was not clear whether they would run or fight. But General Franks had a plan to trap them all.

Farther south, the 1st Marine Division reported at 6:57 A.M. that it had secured Kuwait International Airport. The 1st and 2nd Marine Divisions would then turn toward consolidating their strength south and west of Kuwait City. The 2nd Marine Division linked up with the Arab coalition forces later that day, and the Arab soldiers, led by the Kuwaitis, liberated the emirate's capital. The Kuwaiti flag would be raised on public buildings and Kuwaitis would begin to celebrate in the streets of their capital city.

·　·　·

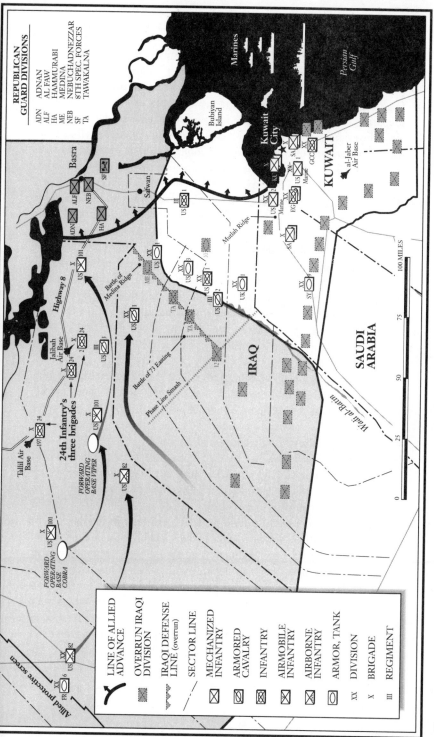

FEBRUARY 27, 1991: BY THE END OF THE FOURTH DAY, THE REPUBLICAN GUARD WAS DEFEATED OR FLEEING TO BASRA

Far to the north of Frank's VII Corps, McCaffrey's 24th Infantry Division (Mechanized) was deep in the Euphrates River Valley; his brigades were poised to destroy what they could of Iraqi forces and installations along Highway 8. Ted Reid's 197th Brigade was sitting astride the highway, preparing to attack Iraq's Tallil Air Base a few miles to the north. The airfield was the center of a ten-mile-square network of deep, well-camouflaged bunkers full of weapons, ammunition, and other supplies that had been reserved specifically to provision and maintain Iraq's army in Kuwait.

On the morning of February 27, Paul Kern and his soldiers in the 2nd Brigade were just southwest of Iraq's Jalibah Air Base, which was forty miles southeast of Tallil. Meanwhile, John LeMoyne's 1st Brigade had crossed Highway 8 late on February 26 and blocked another, smaller highway that ran alongside the Euphrates River. In the early hours of February 27, LeMoyne and his soldiers had prevented hundreds of Iraqi forces from fleeing with their equipment back to Basra. "Until one or two in the morning," LeMoyne said, "we were clearing those areas, shooting trucks, catching convoys on the roads, policing up POWs." In the gray dawn, LeMoyne, too, felt that this would be the critical day of the conflict. "The wind had died down, and we had good weather," he said. "The Iraqis were in an absolute panic."

As the brigades under the command of Ted Reid, Paul Kern, and John LeMoyne moved off into the desert, General McCaffrey abandoned his M1A1 Abrams tank for his "jump command post," a Black Hawk helicopter that would enable him and his aides to obtain a broader picture of the battlefield. McCaffrey had already issued his orders. At 5 A.M., Kern was to begin his attack on Jalibah Air Base. At 6 A.M., LeMoyne's brigade would begin rolling east down Highway 8. His mission was to clear the route and protect Kern's northern flank from any Iraqi counterattack. Reid's 197th Brigade was to launch a battalion-size attack on Tallil Air Base, but McCaffrey's orders called for Reid to delay until later in the day.

To clear the Jalibah airfield, Kern's soldiers had begun pounding it with heavy artillery fire at 5 A.M. and kept it up for precisely sixty minutes. In the predawn darkness, the Iraqi defenders at Jalibah thought they were being attacked by air, so they retaliated with all of their anti-aircraft guns. About 5:45 A.M., Kern called in A-10 ground-attack aircraft, which very quickly destroyed an Iraqi tank company on the airfield. At 6 A.M., following McCaffrey's orders to the letter, Kern had his four tank companies and four companies of Bradley fighting vehicles begin their assault.

At 8:30 A.M., Kern radioed McCaffrey in his helicopter to report that his soldiers had assumed control of Jalibah. There had been roughly 1,000 Iraqi defenders there, Kern said; his men had taken most of them prisoner. Twenty-four Iraqi T-55 tanks had been destroyed, in addition to all the fixed-wing aircraft that had been left on the tarmac. Kern said that approximately 150 Iraqi soldiers—most of whom were inside bunkers that had been shattered by artillery fire and tank rounds—had been killed during the battle.

From his position north of the air base at Jalibah, John LeMoyne could see the explosions as Kern's soldiers prosecuted the attack. Straddling Highway 8, LeMoyne's men stopped a few stray Iraqi military trucks. They found still more trucks and soldiers hidden in drainage tunnels beneath the highway. At first light, helicopters and artillery attached to LeMoyne's brigade had destroyed a larger convoy of about thirty vehicles. The Iraqis to the southeast apparently had no idea LeMoyne's troops were on the road. A half-dozen trucks drove out of Jalibah Air Base, fleeing Kern's attack.

While they moved forward to position themselves for their attack on Tallil Air Base, Ted Reid and his soldiers attacked a major Iraqi logistics site just outside of the base. In addition to destroying bunkers, ammunition stores, and other hardware, Reid's troops captured 1,290 Iraqi soldiers and civilians. At 10:30 A.M., Reid finally received word from McCaffrey to begin his tank attack on Tallil. Reid, however, was low on fuel—he would be unable to begin the attack for several hours.

Meanwhile, to the southeast of McCaffrey's three brigades, approximately twenty kilometers west of the Iraq-Kuwait border, Major General Ronald Griffith's 1st Armored Division was preparing to strike head-on at a series of blocking formations formed by the Medina Luminous division and battalion-sized elements of ten other Iraqi divisions. The U.S. 1st Armored Division's three brigades occupied a sector of desert fifteen miles wide. Inside that sector, the three brigades advanced eastward side by side, their full force of 317 tanks and 278 Bradley fighting vehicles nearly shoulder to shoulder. On the south end of the advancing line was Colonel Zanini's 3rd or Bulldog Brigade. On the morning of February 27, it had overrun the northern half of the Tawakalna and was now in pursuit of elements of the Iraqi 17th Division and the 14th Mechanized Brigade of the Medina Luminous division. To the north of Zanini was Colonel James Riley's 1st Brigade, the Phantom Brigade. His men faced elements of the Medina and the Iraqi 52nd Division.

To the north of Riley, occupying the northern third of the advancing line, was the 1st Armored Division's 2nd Brigade, called the Iron Brigade. The Iron Brigade's commander, Montgomery Meigs, came from a long line of distinguished military men; his namesake had been the quartermaster general of the Union Army during the Civil War. Meigs had 166 tanks with which to attack, which were divided among four battalions, three armored and one mechanized. In addition, Meigs had an artillery and a maintenance battalion. In total, Meigs's Iron Brigade contained some 3,000 vehicles, which consumed in excess of 100,000 gallons of diesel fuel each day. That thirst for fuel, combined with the Army's shortage of heavy tankers, had cost Meigs and the rest of the 1st Armored Division somewhere between twelve and eighteen hours in lost time the day before, when they had had to wait for their refueling tankers. The tankers had to make a 400-kilometer round trip to Saudi Arabia to bring fuel for the division. After the war, the 1st Armored Division's senior officers would state unequivocally that the Army's overland fuel supply capacity was "broken." While Meigs had waited for fuel the day before, the Medina Luminous division had been able to set up its fighting positions, while still other Iraqi units had fled Kuwait.

At approximately 8 A.M. Meigs was monitoring the movement forward of his Iron Brigade. A company of M1A1 Abrams tanks was screening his left flank when his soldiers spotted five Iraqi tanks. Meigs's Delta Company and one platoon from Alpha Company gave chase. "We fired two main-gun rounds, and the whole company fired about twenty main-gun rounds at the five tanks," Private First Class Michael Riley, a lanky twenty-year-old tank driver from Sacramento, California, said. "A lot of people were shooting a dead tank already, just because it was there. It happened all through the whole war. We had a rule: if it wasn't burning, it wasn't dead."

Tanks from Charlie Company joined Delta Company and the platoon from Alpha Company to pursue Iraqi infantrymen armed with shoulder-fired anti-tank weapons. Suddenly, all three units came under heavy Iraqi artillery fire from the north, outside their assigned operating sector. Michael Riley and the other tank drivers knew they could not turn north into that sector because of the presence of the 3rd Armored Cavalry Regiment. With such limited visibility, the two American units could very easily become engaged in a firefight with each other. Shifting the massive M1A1 tanks into reverse, Riley and his colleagues retreated about 1,000 yards, behind a low ridge. The Iraqi artillery gunners surprised them, however, by correctly recalculating the distance and dropping more ordnance on their new position. They moved to the rear again. And again the Iraqi gunners found them. "We'd say, 'Okay, we've got to be out of range now,' " Riley recalled. "And we'd sit there, and all of a sudden you'd see rounds go, *chung, chung.* And we'd say, 'Run, run!' We were running backwards. We could go about twenty-five miles an hour in reverse, and I didn't give a shit what I ran into. The Army basically had twenty-eight tanks going in reverse as fast as they could go."

Miraculously, the big tanks avoided backing into any Iraqi bunkers or Bedouin ruins, which littered the area. The battalion called in Apache helicopter gunships, 155-mm artillery, and Multiple Launch Rocket Systems to suppress the Iraqi artillery. Afterward, division intelligence officers would conclude that the artillery fire had come from the Adnan division of the Republican Guard. Meigs's intelligence officers calculated that the Adnan division's gunners, firing their towed 122-mm howitzers and the feared South African G-5 and Austrian GHN-145 artillery pieces, had delivered approximately 1,000 rounds of artillery onto the units of the Iron Brigade before retreating toward Basra.

As the Apache helicopters, artillery, and rockets hammered away at the Adnan division, Meigs's tankers tried to grab a few minutes of rest before continuing the attack. They were wet, cold, and tired. They had been driving in their cramped tank quarters for more than three days. The M1A1 Abrams tank was heated to ward off the cold of the desert night, and its ride was well cushioned as it raced across the bumpy desert floor. But to see where they were going and watch for the enemy, the tank commander and his loader had to stand up and look out their turret hatches. They were quickly soaked by the pouring rain. The water had run down their faces and into their chemical-protection suits, filling their boots. "You're just saturated with water," said Sergeant Jeffrey Reamer, the commander of an M1A1 tank in the 1st Armored Division's 1-35 Armor Battalion. "And you still have to do your job. Every tank commander I know, their ankles swelled up because they had to stand in the rain for so long." Below in the turret and just forward of the tank commander sat the gunner. He was protected from the elements. But because the tank commander and the loader insisted that the heat be turned up as high as possible to keep them warm, the gunners baked in the tanks' interiors. Up front, the driver sat all alone in a reclining seat in a hole hardly bigger than a race-car cockpit. Above him was a heavy round hatch. The seal around it leaked profusely, and the M1A1 drivers sat in the pools of water that collected on their plastic seats.

At 11:40 A.M., the Iron Brigade's 166 M1A1 tanks were ordered to get into formation and move to attack. Within several minutes, in each battalion all of Meigs's tanks were lined up abreast, 100 meters apart. At 12:05 P.M., the brigade moved out, driving almost due east. The tankers said they had never seen anything like it, a full brigade of American tanks stretching into the smokelike fog that clung to the desert floor. Meigs's long front of tanks rolled across the desert at between five and eight miles per hour. The rain had stopped, but the sky was hazy and overcast. The area was not tabletop flat. Rather, there were long upward and downward slopes, and the tankers could not see more than 1,000 meters ahead at times as they rolled up and down the long hills.

Meigs and his tank commanders did not know it yet, but the 2nd Brigade of the Medina Luminous division was waiting for them behind one of these slopes. Once again, American soldiers would confront Iraqi tanks dug into a classic reverse-slope defense. The Iraqi defensive line extended almost ten kilometers. The American tankers who confronted it would later call this the battle of Medina Ridge—it would be the largest tank battle of the Gulf War.

As Meigs and his tankers pressed ahead, their eyes strained to make sense of the green and black images that flickered on their thermal scopes. There were no indications of telltale hot spots, the infrared signatures that identified enemy vehicles.

At 12:17, a tank gunner in Charlie Company identified four Iraqi armored fighting vehicles. The M1A1's laser range-finder indicated that the vehicles were approximately 3,500 meters ahead. They were moving north to south, left to right across the range-finder screen. The M1A1 moved closer, and the tank commander ordered his gunner to fire. The gunner destroyed one of the Iraqi vehicles, then another. A short distance away, another M1A1 from Delta Company destroyed the other two Iraqi fighting vehicles.

Suddenly, dozens of Meigs's tankers began seeing "hot spots," images of Iraqi tanks, on their thermal sights. They were in a ragged line, set on an angle so U.S. tankers on the left saw them first. These were T-72 tanks. Meigs and his men saw that the Iraqi tanks were ranged ahead of them

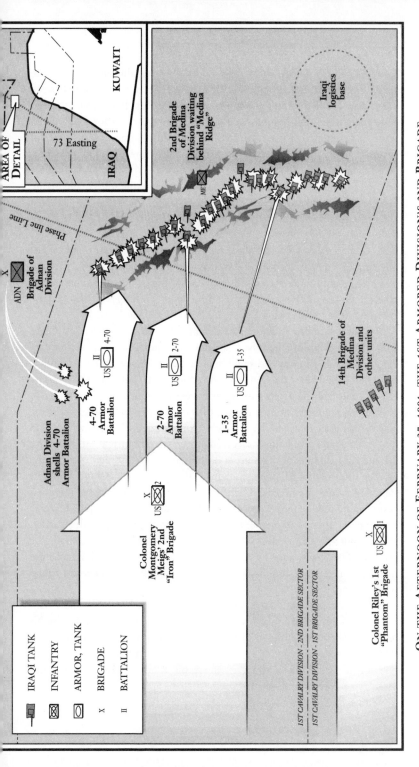

On the Afternoon of February 27, 1991, the 1st Armored Division's 2nd Brigade Destroyed the 2nd Brigade of the Medina Division in Forty Minutes

Legend:
- Iraqi Tank
- Infantry
- Armor, Tank
- x Brigade
- II Battalion

2nd Brigade of Medina Division waiting behind "Medina Ridge"

Iraqi logistics base

Brigade of Adnan Division — ADN

Phase line Lime

73 Easting

IRAQ

KUWAIT

AREA OF DETAIL

Adnan Division shells 4–70 Armor Battalion

4–70 Armor Battalion — US 4-70

2–70 Armor Battalion — US 2-70

1–35 Armor Battalion — US 1-35

Colonel Montgomery Meigs' 2nd "Iron" Brigade — US 2

14th Brigade of Medina Division and other units

Colonel Riley's 1st "Phantom" Brigade — US 1

1ST CAVALRY DIVISION - 2ND BRIGADE SECTOR
1ST CAVALRY DIVISION - 1ST BRIGADE SECTOR

between a series of low rises. The tanks were not dug deeply into the ground. Instead they had mounds of sand and dirt piled in front of them, but it was a futile attempt at protection. The M1A1's dartlike sabot round could penetrate sand mounds as easily as if they were cotton candy. The Iraqis had stationed observers on several sand ridges. There were also Iraqi armored fighting vehicles in the distance. The line of Iraqi tanks was positioned on an angle relative to the Americans. Carefully, M1A1 gunners set the cross hairs of their thermal imaging scopes on the spots made by the vehicles' heat signatures. Then they began firing.

In the Iron Brigade's 4-70 Armor Battalion, Private First Class Michael Riley was driving tank C-21, which his crew had named the Four Horsemen. Looking through his "vision blocks" (three slots about eight inches long and two inches wide), Riley could see the Iraqi tanks clearly after the first M1A1 sabot rounds were fired. "I pull out from behind the commanding officer's tank, and I see about ten or eleven burning vehicles on the horizon," Riley said. "All I hear is all hell is breaking loose."

Not far from Riley, Specialist Shannon Boldman was in tank C-24, which his crew had dubbed the Claw of Contempt. The twenty-two-year-old gunner and his crew had spent many practice sessions calibrating their main gun. They knew the gunnery procedures cold. The cramped quarters of the gun turret required a minuet of precision. Once he saw a target in his thermal scope, the gunner rotated the tank's turret and laid the red cross hairs of his laser range-finder squarely on the target. By pressing a button on his handgrips, the gunner received a precise readout that indicated the distance of his target at the bottom of the range-finder screen. Next to the gunner, the loader pulled a shell from the ready-rack behind him and slammed it into the breech. Then he had to lock the round in. The tank commander and the tankers coordinated their action with a rapid and terse exchange of orders and answers, culminating with the commander's order, "Fire," and the gunner's answer, "On the way." The gun boomed, the breech kicked back, and the smell of gunpowder suffused the tank as the metal cap of the tank round was ejected from the breech and a new round was inserted.

Boldman had practiced the drill on the gunnery range in Germany with mind-numbing repetition. Now, with the sight of enemy T-72s, he and his fellow soldiers were pumped with adrenaline and gripped by fear. All order was lost. "It was 'I've got an enemy tank!' " Boldman recalled, "and someone would say 'Fuckin' shoot it, shoot the motherfucker!' " Boldman's loader slammed another 40-pound shell into the breech of the M1A1 and yelled to Boldman, "Up!" That meant the gun was ready to fire again. "My loader, he's yelling, 'You're up, man, shoot it, shoot it,' " Boldman said. "He's hyper, he's ready to kill something. Okay, so I squeeze the trigger. I see the turret of the target fly twenty feet up in the air. You can see it with the daylight scope. With the thermal [scope], you just see a great big hot spot blowing off. My driver is looking at it. He says, 'Goddamn, is that the one you shot?' I say I got it. He says, 'Goddamn, man, wow!' Then we were having a ball in the turret. It happened so quickly, we didn't have time to be scared."

As Boldman's loader kept the main gun supplied with sabot rounds, the smell of gunpowder in the cramped turret of tank C-24 grew stronger. Staff Sergeant Jeffrey Jordan ordered Boldman to shoot a tank just ahead of them. "That one's on fire," Boldman said.

"Shoot it again," Jordan ordered. "Shoot it again!"

Boldman squeezed the trigger hard. "On the way," he yelled back.

As his tank drove ahead slowly, Boldman laid the cross hairs of his laser range-finder on still more Iraqi tanks, firing round after round. "I just kept going from target to target," Boldman said, "left to right. And it was just like, there's another tank, 'Shoot it,' boom, there's another one, 'Shoot it,' boom. That was how it went."

Often, the American tankers said, the first indication that their sabot rounds had struck an Iraqi tank was a flash of sparks. As it left the main gun of the M1A1 tank, the sabot round was traveling at 8,400 miles per hour. The hail of sparks resulted when the round struck the armored glacis of the enemy tank. If the dartlike round pierced the armor, it would often ricochet around the inside of the tank. Or sometimes, tank gunners said, the sabot round would enter one side of an Iraqi tank and fly out the other. Twin tongues of flame often leapt out of the shattered tank from its two top turret hatches. Perhaps five to ten seconds after that, the tank exploded as its fuel or ammunition ignited. A minute or two later, there might be a secondary explosion as more ammunition ignited.

At 12:31 P.M., Montgomery Meigs wrote in his log: "Enemy is direct front from 1,000 to 2,500 meters. Killed twenty to thirty armored vehicles." Seven minutes later, Meigs wrote: "Initial contact complete. Now cleaning up enemy. 600 to 800 meters beyond there is another enemy force."

Iraqi artillery rounds fell around the advancing Iron Brigade, but the gunners were not accurate. Meigs ordered the brigade to press ahead. "I fired four more rounds," Boldman said. "I put two into one tank and hit two other tanks. And then we moved into the battle area and through it. By that time we were pinpointing our targets more. There was a report that there were sixty-seven Iraqi vehicles in a wadi behind [the targets we saw], and it was really six to seven. But we were scared, because we thought we were heading for sixty-seven Iraqi vehicles, and we'd already fired some rounds."

The advance elements of the Iron Brigade passed through the first lines of burning Iraqi tanks. From the cockpit of his tank, Private First Class Riley saw an Iraqi infantryman crawling out of a hole. Riley's gunner aimed the tank's main gun at the Iraqi soldier, and the man started taking his shirt and pants off, apparently trying to indicate that he had no concealed weapons on him. By the time they moved past the frightened soldier, Riley said, he was standing naked in the desert.

The Iron Brigade had caught the Iraqis at lunch. As they rolled past burning tanks and upended fighting vehicles, soldiers saw cooking utensils and half-finished plates of chicken and rice. "Since we didn't get hit," Sergeant Jeffrey Reamer said, "we thought they didn't fire at us. But six or seven of those [Iraqi] tanks had auto-loaders." T-72 auto-loaders spit the shell cap out of the breech and onto the ground once a round was fired. Reamer saw several burning Iraqi tanks with three or four spent shell caps on the ground beside them. "That means they fired," Reamer said. "But they just couldn't hit us." After the battle, the Americans judged the maximum range of the T-72s to be 1,800 meters. The M1A1s were getting hits at nearly twice that distance. The M1A1 thermal sights picked up Iraqi tanks at 4,000 meters, well beyond visual range in the damp and fog. "One Iraqi platoon sergeant we captured said they couldn't see us," Meigs said. "They were shooting at our muzzle flashes."

As the lead tanks of the Iron Brigade closed in, the battlefield suddenly shrank. In his M1A1, Sergeant Anthony Widner, a twenty-eight-year-old from Alabama, fired two rounds at a T-72 tank and watched it explode. Then he pivoted the main gun quickly to his left and shot another T-72, which was just 700 meters away. There was so much talk on the radio net that Widner could not communicate with his driver and his loader through his headgear. They had to remove their headsets. "My driver was yelling 'There's one to the left, there's one to the right,'" Widner said. "My loader was yelling 'Shoot him, shoot him, shoot him again!'"

Then artillery fire started falling on them. "Artillery to the front, artillery to the rear." Widner heard the warning over the frantic chatter on his company's radio net. "One was friendly, and the other was enemy," Widner said of the two artillery barrages. "Someone said it was 200 meters away. I heard that, and I knew it was out there, and I got real serious. Someone wanted to move, and he was told there was nowhere to go. If you go forward you'll get hit, and if you move back you'll get hit." Sergeant Reamer added, "When the artillery was dropping, the guys kept coming up on the radio.... They were calling to turn it off. Our battalion artillery guy came and said, 'What makes you think it's ours?' "

Minutes later, American gunners using their FireFinder radar locked onto the location of the Iraqi artillery and began to pour fire onto it. The Iraqi artillery soon fell silent. Now it was just tank on tank.

At 12:47 P.M., Meigs noted in his log, "2nd Brigade destroyed forty armored vehicles." Private First Class Michael Riley's tank C-21 came over a little hill, and on the other side an Iraqi T-72 tank was waiting, just 550 meters away. "We came up over the top of it and came down," Riley said. "Whoosh, and all of a sudden my gunner says, 'Is that a tank? I can't tell.' " The Iraqi tank wasted no time in firing. From his driver's cockpit in the M1A1, Riley watched in alarm. "The whole horizon lights up, and the round went right past us.... I was looking dead into the muzzle when it fired," Riley said. "Needless to say, I was yelling and screaming and trying to crawl out of the hatch. That was the first time I really got scared. I wanted to get out of the tank right then."

An instant after the Iraqi tank fired, another M1A1 from the Iron Brigade's Alpha Company skittered in front of tank C-21. "I'm yelling, 'Shoot them, shoot it!' " Riley said. "And the gunner's going, 'I can't see it, I can't see it!' And the loader's going, 'It's Iraqi!' And the tank commander's going, 'You can't fire, Alpha Company's tank is in the way!' "

With the other M1A1 past them, Riley was staring at the Iraqi T-72 below and in front of him again when he saw an American HEAT round strike the side of the tank's turret. The T-72 tank was knocked on its side. The HEAT round had been fired by another M1A1 just down the line from Riley's tank.

By 1 P.M., it was over. The head-to-head battle between the Iron Brigade of the U.S. 1st Armored Division and the 2nd Brigade of the Medina Luminous division had taken forty minutes, of which just fifteen minutes had seen intense shooting. The Iron Brigade destroyed the 2nd Brigade of the Medina, as well as a portion of a battalion from the Medina's 14th

Mechanized Brigade. In all, Montgomery Meigs's soldiers destroyed sixty Iraqi T-72 tanks, nine T-55 tanks, thirty-eight armored personnel carriers, and five SA-13 air-defense guns. An intelligence officer with the Iron Brigade estimated that 340 Iraqi soldiers had been killed in the battle; 55 Iraqi soldiers were taken as prisoners.

"That battle lasted such a short time we never really got a chance to get momentum," Sergeant Reamer said. "Somebody called in a spot report about a vehicle trying to get away, and the brigade commander came up on the radio net and said, 'If he tries to get away and doesn't surrender, kill him.' And, you know, for a while there, you didn't feel like you were in a war. But when you heard that come across—when you heard the brigade commander say to take somebody's life, it made you remember that this was war."

At 3 P.M., as the tankers from the Iron Brigade were policing the battle scene, a company of six Apache helicopters took off from the rear of the 1st Armored Division. In the lead Apache, which had been given the name Excalibur, Captain John Arnold, the thirty-two-year-old commander of the Apache's Bravo Company, occupied the front seat. John Watson, a rangy forty-six-year-old Chief Warrant Officer 3, had the backseat. Watson, as is the custom in Apaches, flew the aircraft. Arnold directed and fired the weapons from the front seat. Since he was also the company commander, Arnold coordinated the movements and tactics of the company's five other Apaches and three OH-58 Kiowa scout aircraft. Arnold and Watson had flown together since 1989. Between them they had fifteen years of flying experience. Sometimes, they said, it seemed as if they could read each other's minds.

In the weeks and months before the war, Bravo Company had developed new tactics that they hoped to use against Iraqi tanks and armored vehicles. The Apache helicopter was a ground-attack aircraft; tanks and fighting vehicles were its principal targets. The tactics developed by Arnold, Watson, and the other Bravo Company pilots were considerably different from the ones they had practiced in Europe. There the Apache pilots had been trained to fly low, using hills for cover, and popping up to fire. In the desert there were few hills high enough for the Apaches to hide behind. To compensate, Bravo Company had devised what they called high-energy and low-energy tactics. In both approaches the pilots lined up their six helicopters shoulder to shoulder, in three teams of two. In low-energy tactics, the two helicopters in a team would fly 300 to 500 meters apart; there would be an 800- to 1,000-meter spread between teams. The helicopters flew just 30 feet off the ground, creeping forward just fast enough to leave the dust from their rotor wash behind them. It was not foolproof, but in the relative flatness of the desert terrain, the tactic gave the Apache pilots as much of a chance to pull off a surprise attack as they could reasonably hope for. The pilots of Bravo Company had practiced this tactic so often during the weeks before the war that they could fly a whole mission with virtually no radio communication.

Low-energy tactics were for nighttime, when they were nearly invisible. The high-energy tactics were for daytime use, when they would want to move faster. They called for the two-Apache teams to spread out, with about 1½ kilometers between them. Then they would circle and fly in at the target at speeds of 40 miles an hour. The idea was to get close, shoot, and get away fast. The weather had been so bad and the visibility so poor, however, that Arnold, Watson, and the other Apache pilots worried that they might never be given the opportunity to test their new tactics in the desert. Whole battalions of Apaches that were supposed to operate in the Euphrates Valley had been grounded for the first three days of the ground war because of sandstorms. Other Apache units had been deployed to suppress artillery fire and attack a few Iraqi tank companies. But because of the high winds and heavy rain during the first three days of the ground campaign, the Apache fleet had seen far less use than General Schwarzkopf and his battlefield commanders would have liked.

At 2 P.M. on February 27, the Apache battalion that included Captain John Arnold's Bravo Company was briefed on its mission. At last, Arnold, Watson, and the rest of the Apache pilots in Bravo Company would get to try their tactics on the Iraqi army. The Apache battalion had been placed under the command of the 1st Armored Division only that morning. The pilots had arrived about noon and set their aircraft down at the division's rear. Alpha Company lifted off at 2:30 P.M., Bravo at 3 P.M., and Charlie at 3:30 P.M.

Fuel was short. With less than a full load of ordnance, the Apaches flew approximately 40 kilometers to the battle area. Each Apache was armed with eight laser-guided Hellfire anti-tank missiles and thirty-eight 2.75-inch rockets, some carrying bomblets that dropped from the rocket above the target. Even the Apaches' 30-mm gun was laser-directed. The laser accounted for the speed of the aircraft, the wind, and the aircraft's movement for seven seconds prior to firing. Attached to the pilot's helmet was a two-inch-square semi-transparent monocle that extended about an inch or two in front of the pilot's right eye. Projected onto the monocle was the targeting information that came from the Apache's infrared targeting systems. There was also a cross hair–type targeting device. All of the Apache's weapons systems were linked electronically to the monocle. All a weapons officer had to do was look at a target, lay the cross hairs on it, and fire his weapon of choice.

The first Apache pilot to see a target would illuminate it with his laser and indicate its direction and distance to the other pilots. Apache pilots could laser their own targets, or laser them for one another. Either technique worked because the Apache pilot could guide his weapons toward a target using any helicopter's reflected laser energy. Approaching a target, Arnold, Watson, and the other Apache pilots agreed, they would attempt to fire their weapons from 4,000 meters away if the target was protected by air-defense systems. If the target was unprotected, they would attempt to close to within 2,000 meters. The main reason for getting so close, the pilots explained, was to make sure, given the notoriously poor visibility in the desert, that they did not target Allied forces. "My biggest worry," Arnold confessed, "was fratricide."

As the pilots of Bravo Company headed for the battlefield in eastern Iraq, the weather was so bad that they switched to their Forward Looking Infrared Radar scopes and the Apache targeting systems designed for use on night missions. Approaching the battlefield, Watson and Arnold saw lots of little dots appear on their infrared radar scopes. Each dot, the pilots knew, indicated a tank or armored vehicle. The heat emissions from the vehicles' engines yielded the immediately recognizable heat signatures on the Apache scopes. In the briefing they had been given before their mission, Watson, Arnold, and the other Apache pilots had been told that the Iraqi forces they would be attacking belonged to the Medina Luminous division of the Republican Guard. Meigs's Iron Brigade had destroyed the 2nd Brigade and a few smaller units of the Medina; other armored units were still behind them.

Arnold and Watson could see there were enough tanks and armored vehicles to make up a full battalion of the Medina. Some were still dug in, others were crawling out of their holes, and still others were already heading north to escape. There were at least fifty targets.

Arnold ordered his Bravo Company out of its regular flight formation and put them on line for attack. The six Apaches dropped down to 30 feet and crept forward. This was the low-energy drill they had practiced since their arrival in the desert. Now it was for real. The Apaches dropped lower still. By now, the helicopters were so close to the ground that their windscreens were being spattered with mud. The pilots selected their targets. Each team was assigned a pie-shaped targeting sector about three degrees wide.

Bravo Company closed to within 5,000 meters of the Medina Luminous division, and still the Iraqis showed no sign that they could see them—let alone that they realized an attack was imminent. From 3,000 meters out, the Bravo Company pilots unleashed their Hellfire missiles. On the forward-looking infrared scopes in the cockpits of the six Apache helicopters, Arnold, Watson, and the other pilots watched as one white dot after another exploded in a tiny electronic flash. Within twenty minutes, the Apache pilots from Bravo Company destroyed thirty Iraqi tanks, eleven armored fighting vehicles, and another dozen trucks and artillery pieces. "We stayed in the area for an hour, as long as we could," Arnold said. "I had to order my guys to leave. One of them had eighty pounds of fuel—that's eight gallons—left when we landed."

By late afternoon, rumors of an imminent cease-fire began skipping across the radio networks of the Allied armies. Nonetheless, from north to south across their sector of the front, under orders from Lieutenant General Franks, the U.S. 1st Armored Division, the U.S. 3rd Armored Division, the U.S. 1st Infantry Division, the 2nd Armored Cavalry Regiment, and the British 1st Armored Division pressed their attack eastward toward northern Kuwait.

South of Lieutenant General Franks's four heavy divisions, the 1st and 2nd Marine Divisions advanced to the outskirts of Kuwait City and pulled to the side of several traffic-choked roadways, so that Kuwaiti soldiers and other Arab forces in the coalition could proceed ahead of them to begin the liberation of the emirate's capital.

A large part of the Medina Luminous division was now destroyed. Its remaining elements—as well as the Adnan and Hammurabi divisions of the Republican Guard, and units of the 17th, 52nd, 10th, 12th, and other Iraqi divisions—had fled into an area south of Basra and north of Kuwait that

Franks called the Basra pocket. He pushed his battlefield commanders to begin a double envelopment of the Iraqi forces in that area. Franks wanted to have the 1st Cavalry Division sprint forward and envelop the Iraqi force from the north while the 1st Infantry Division, the Big Red One, pushed farther east and surrounded them from the south. Then the 1st and 3rd Armored Divisions would press ahead and drive into the Iraqi divisions in the Basra pocket from the west.

Shortly before 4 P.M., the U.S. 1st Infantry Division was racing toward a position astride Kuwait's Highway 8. The 1st Infantry Division had been instructed to seize the road in an area forty miles north of Kuwait City which was identified on Central Command maps as Objective Denver. To their south, the British 1st Armored Division had been given a larger sector. The mission of the British division was to push east as rapidly as possible and defeat the Iraqi 52nd Armored Division, so that General Franks's enveloping forces would not be vulnerable to a flank attack. Earlier in the day, the British division had overrun elements from at least three Iraqi divisions and crossed into Kuwait from the west.

By 7 P.M., a cavalry unit of the 1st Infantry Division reached Highway 8 and took control of the area. Now it was up to the 1st Cavalry Division to surround the Iraqis on the north. But the 1st Cavalry Division, a tank-heavy force of three brigades, had a mission that was almost impossible. Only the previous morning, on February 26, the 1st Cavalry Division had been released from its duty of protecting the VII Corps headquarters in Saudi Arabia. General Franks had ordered the cavalry division on a full-bore, 250-kilometer run from the Saudi-Iraqi border north along the left edge of the U.S. 1st Armored Division's sector in a big left hook. The cavalry division was to overtake the U.S. 1st Armored Division and push out ahead of it, sealing the north end of the Basra pocket.

Because of the tank battle between Meigs's Iron Brigade and the 2nd Brigade of the Medina Luminous division, however, Franks had been reluctant to have the 1st Cavalry Division push through. It was too dangerous. Conferring with his aides and commanders on the evening of February 27, Franks decided to have the 1st Cavalry Division move out in front of the 1st Armored Division and begin the double envelopment early on February 28.

That same evening, at an air base in the Saudi desert, a U.S. Air Force C-141 transport plane unloaded two bombs that had been built in a highly secret crash program. The bombs were made for one purpose only—to penetrate the dense concrete roofs of Saddam Hussein's best-protected command-and-control bunkers. It was rumored that there were several, but there was one where it was judged Saddam was most likely to be hiding. That was at the al-Taji airfield northwest of Baghdad.

In the twenty-three days that it took to manufacture the nineteen-foot-long GBU-28 bombs from old, eight-inch howitzer barrels, the designers could not be certain that they would work. Intelligence information indicated that the bunker at al-Taji might be protected by as much as twenty feet of concrete and dirt. So immediately after the first bomb was finished on February 17 it was rushed to Holloman Air Force Base in New Mexico and loaded onto a high-speed sled aimed at a twenty-two-foot-thick chunk of concrete. The bomb slammed into the concrete, and as the dust rose from the impact the test team rushed to the scene. All they found was rubble. The bomb had smashed through it and passed on, ending up a half mile away. "Do you want to use it again?" a team member called back to the test site. The bomb was hardly scratched.

Two F-111F pilots from the 48th Tactical Fighter Wing dropped the two GBU-28s, one behind the other, on the command bunker at al-Taji later on the night of February 27. Surveillance cameras on the planes recorded smoke billowing from the entrances to the facility. Without question, the bombs had worked. There would be intelligence reports that several top-level Iraqi commanders had been killed. But Saddam Hussein was not among them.

At 10 P.M. on February 27, Fred Franks realized there might have to be a radical change in plans. A senior Army aide in Riyadh called Franks to warn him that the rumors that had been circulating all day might well be true: there could be a cease-fire declared as early as tomorrow morning.

At 11:30 P.M., General Yeosock, commander of all Army ground forces in the war theater, called Franks to say the cease-fire might take effect as early as 5 A.M. the next day. At 2:30 A.M. on February 28 it would become official: the cease-fire would occur at 8 A.M. Franks pushed his forces forward anyway. If the cease-fire was to take effect at 8 A.M., he said, he would press the attack until exactly 7:59.

In the Euphrates Valley, beneath gray-black skies shortly before nightfall on February 27, Colonel Ted Reid's 197th Brigade was mopping up what was left of the Iraqi opposition at Tallil Air Base. After his M1A1 Abrams tanks and M-113s had refueled earlier in the day, Reid and his soldiers began their attack on the air base at approximately 3 P.M. Reid's scouts had reported back on the radio that the twenty-five-foot-high earthen berm surrounding the air base was reinforced by concrete. Several of the scouts had come under heavy fire from Iraqi air-defense guns, and they had pulled back from the air base while Reid ordered two of his tank companies around to the northeast side of the air base. Reid's plan was as audacious as it was simple: while the Iraqi defenders were concentrating on the perimeters of the air base, Reid intended to send his M1A1 tanks crashing through the front gates.

The tank charge found the Iraqis in disarray. As the massive M1A1 tanks rumbled into the air base in high gear, the Iraqi defenders were still firing at American soldiers outside the base. Quickly, they turned their fire on targets inside the base; several of Reid's soldiers said that the Iraqis may well have killed many of their own men.

Reid's soldiers swept the airfield carefully. They destroyed six Soviet-built MiG fighter aircraft, two Soviet T-55 tanks, and innumerable air-defense weapons and ammunition bunkers. Just after 6 P.M., Reid ordered his 197th Brigade to pull out. He left a heavily armored task force behind to protect his rear. Then he radioed General McCaffrey to report on his actions. With night upon them, the soldiers of the 197th Brigade rolled east down Highway 8 toward Basra. Reid's brigade would serve as the reserve force for McCaffrey's division. McCaffrey's two other brigades, led by Paul Kern and John LeMoyne, were in front. They would take up the attack next.

By the evening of February 27, Kern and LeMoyne had traveled another forty-five miles east through the Euphrates Valley along Highway 8. They had spent the better part of the afternoon destroying Iraqi trucks and abandoned equipment, including anti-aircraft guns and artillery pieces. Soldiers from both brigades had encountered thousands of retreating Iraqi soldiers on the highway. If the Iraqis refused to stop when ordered, the Americans fired a 25-mm sabot round, a high-velocity armor-piercing bullet, through the engine blocks of the retreating Iraqi vehicles. Invariably, the Iraqi soldiers then came out of the truck with their hands up. The soldiers from Kern's and LeMoyne's brigades waved the Iraqis farther up the highway to the west, carrying their white flags and looking generally bedraggled and dispirited.

Shortly before midnight, sporadic Iraqi artillery and mortar fire fell on LeMoyne's soldiers. They also came under attack briefly from retreating Iraqi soldiers firing grenade launchers. LeMoyne's soldiers retaliated furiously. "They shoot one round, we shoot back 72 rounds," LeMoyne said. "They shoot one round, we shoot back 128. We never got a repeat on a round coming in." At midnight, McCaffrey radioed LeMoyne to inquire about his fuel situation. How far could he and his brigade continue in the next few hours? McCaffrey asked.

"I can go to Basra," LeMoyne replied.

McCaffrey paused, then rejected the idea. On Central Command maps, there was a north-south grid line marked o/o. LeMoyne was just about there. Call a halt at o/o, McCaffrey told LeMoyne. "We'll go [to Basra] tomorrow."

Meanwhile, Pat Ritter's brigade of the Big Red One had entered what Major Glen Slay called the Valley of the Boogers. Slay was Ritter's operations officer, a slang-slinging southerner to whom everything bad was a "booger." And this awful place was full of Iraqi boogers.

It was unlike any place they had seen. Everywhere else, the desert was flat as a pool table, and you could drive across it at forty miles per hour. But here, just inside northern Kuwait, a wide valley floor turned bumpy and then there were wadis, ditches, pits, ravines, and old mines filled with oil and rainwater. The battalion could not drive in a straight line, and little by little, as darkness descended once more, they fell out of their combat formations and into single lines that weaved and zigzagged their way across and around the hills and ditches. Men who had not been scared going through the previous night's battle got scared. It was perfect territory for a road ambush. Here and there were Iraqi vehicles, and Iraqi soldiers came out of the night and surrendered or shot at them and disappeared. There were a million places to be trapped, for Iraqis to kill them from. The whole brigade was in a single file inching its way along a narrow, winding road, to God knew where.

Standing in his turret, Ritter found that the cloud cover rendered his night-vision goggles useless. As he dropped down in the tank to look at his Global Positioning System he felt his tank dive into a ditch and he jumped up just in time to grab the ankle of Specialist Rob Foster. Foster, his loader, had been thrown out of the hatch. With one hand on his M-16 rifle and the other on his loader's leg and his face jammed into the rear of his machine gun, Ritter could hear his loader screaming, "I've got 'em, I've got 'em." "Got what?" Ritter yelled. "Seven Iraqis in the bottom of the hole." The driver slammed the tank into reverse, and as it reared backward Foster shot into the hole with his M-16. Then Ritter felt his gunner's now familiar elbow jab. He peered into his thermal sights and everywhere, it seemed, were Iraqi dismounts.

Finally, the battalions were so mixed up and so vulnerable that the commanders called the tanks into circles, and told them they would spend the night there. In his tank nearby, Major Slay found a quiet moment and could stand it no longer. "I've got to go to the bathroom," he told Ritter and stood up on the back of the tank. And no sooner was up there than three mortar rounds landed. Boom, boom, boom. "Boogers," groaned Slay, "Won't even let a guy take a leak," as he leapt back into his tank. Sergeant Martin, Captain Bell, and Slay pulled up next to Ritter in their tanks, and the four of them began to fire their 7.62-mm machine guns. They must have fired 3,000 rounds that night, just trying to keep the Iraqis away. All Ritter could think was, Leave us alone. Just please go away. But they would not.

The next morning would be February 28. The cease-fire rumored since the previous evening was set for 8 A.M.. Meanwhile, 116 tanks and Bradleys were surrounded by untold Iraqis in a place where maneuver was impossible. The Americans formed their defenses and waited out the night. As dawn broke, the Iraqis started advancing toward them. The Americans stared at them through their sights, fingers on their triggers. But the Iraqis were waving pieces of paper, the leaflets dropped by Allied airplanes, and carrying white flags. They were stumbling forward toward Ritter's battalion by the tens, scores, and hundreds across the muddy earth. They had the battalion surrounded, and they were giving up. It was all over.

A few minutes before 1 A.M. on Thursday, February 28, one of General Norman Schwarzkopf's secure telephones rang in his headquarters in Riyadh. It was the hotline from the White House.

Like Colin Powell, George Bush had a secure red telephone on his desk that connected him directly with Schwarzkopf. No dialing was necessary. Simply by picking up the handset, Bush or Powell would cause Schwarzkopf's phone to ring 7,000 miles away. Powell and Schwarzkopf had made a point of using the secure communications link at least once a day during the six months of the Gulf conflict. Bush had used his red phone only sparingly. He told aides it was neither proper nor necessary for him to be querying his senior battlefield commander about the way he was going about his job; Powell and Cheney had kept Bush apprised of the war's progress each day, and he was pleased and gratified at the way things were going. Throughout the day on February 27, however, and into the early morning hours of February 28, the secure phone link from the White House to the headquarters of Central Command had been employed time and again.

Bush was being pressured by Arab members of the coalition, primarily Saudi Arabia and Egypt, to bring the fighting to an end quickly. The pressure from the Saudis had been especially intense, administration officials said. The last thing King Fahd wanted on his northern border was an Iraq suddenly in the advanced stages of disintegration. Fahd was especially concerned that in such a situation the Shiite Muslim majority of Iraq, which was concentrated around Basra and close to the Saudi border, might split from Iraq and establish its own state, modeled more or less on the radical Shiite regime in Tehran. Both Fahd and President Hosni Mubarak of Egypt agreed that the territorial integrity of Iraq must be preserved at all costs. Both Arab leaders had expressed their wishes in the months before the war that Saddam Hussein be replaced by another Sunni Muslim—one less obstreperous than Saddam, but another Sunni dictator nonetheless. Failing the ouster of Saddam, however, both Fahd and Mubarak said that they were prepared to live with the Iraqi despot, so long as his weapons of mass destruction and his million-man army were destroyed.

Bush and Scowcroft strongly endorsed this view. Aides said that the President had also come to accept the fact that he might have to live with a conclusion to the Gulf conflict that left Saddam Hussein in power.

At home, the administration was also beginning to come under fierce criticism for its conduct of the war. Television footage of the so-called highway of death had appalled many people. Americans, these critics said, do not engage in "turkey shoots." Aides to Schwarzkopf said that he was furious over the press reports and commentary suggesting that Allied pilots had wantonly destroyed civilians fleeing Kuwait City in vehicles on the highway north to Basra. The rules were clear, Schwarzkopf said, according to a senior adviser: the allies would not attack any Iraqi soldier who left his vehicle and offered to surrender; those fleeing in tanks, trucks, armored fighting vehicles, or any other vehicle with military applications were to be considered legitimate targets and struck if they refused to surrender.

Bush told aides that he understood and supported Schwarzkopf's policy. He rejected the criticisms of wanton killing. Still, the pressure from the two key members of the coalition, Saudi Arabia and Egypt, had to be appreciated for what it was, Bush told Cheney and Powell. If Schwarzkopf was confident that he had achieved his military objectives, then it made sense to end the war sooner rather later. Bush knew that Schwarzkopf's original war plan had called for a ground campaign lasting 144 hours. But every report he had been given, from the very first word relayed by Cheney during the church service just four days earlier, had indicated that Schwarzkopf's soldiers were ahead of schedule.

Powell and Cheney had suggested during discussions with Bush earlier in the day on February 27 that they stay in close touch with Schwarzkopf to see how the fourth day of the ground campaign progressed. All parties agreed that if Schwarzkopf said he needed more time to prosecute the war, he would have it. But participants in the discussion said that this was not expected; at most, Schwarzkopf might request a few more hours.

With Bush and several aides still conferring in the Oval Office, Powell picked up the red telephone handset that connected the White House with Central Command headquarters. As Schwarzkopf listened, Powell relayed the substance of the discussion that had been taking place among Bush and his aides.

What did Schwarzkopf think about declaring a cease-fire within the next few hours? Powell asked. One of the President's aides had suggested 5 A.M.

Schwarzkopf suggested a time several hours later, an aide who was present said. The M1A1 tanks of the 1st and 3rd Armored Divisions had been refueled only within the past few hours. In a few more hours, they would be able to make much more progress against Saddam's Republican Guard forces. Other units had also outrun their fuel tankers late in the day on February 27, Schwarzkopf said. Once they were all up and moving again, he said, General Franks's heavy tanks would be able to seal off the Republican Guard and the other Iraqi units in the Basra pocket, and General McCaffrey's 24th Infantry Division (Mechanized) would be able to roll up any other units that tried to escape out of Basra on Highway 8. "Schwarzkopf definitely wanted a few more hours," a senior Central Command official said. "The situation wasn't at all clarified yet."

In Washington, aides to the President suggested a cease-fire at 8 A.M. local time, but urged that Allied forces actually stop hostilities at 5 A.M.

Powell relayed the proposal. It did not go unnoticed that a cease-fire at that time would terminate the ground war after exactly 100 hours.

I have no problem with that, Schwarzkopf replied.

At 2:30 A.M., General Barry McCaffrey walked out of the temporary tent headquarters that was tied up to the Black Hawk helicopter he used as his airborne command post. "It's all over," McCaffrey said. "They've told us to hold in place. A cease-fire is scheduled to take effect at 8 A.M."

McCaffrey and his aides were camped in an onion field just off Highway 8, twenty-seven miles west of Basra. Paul Kern's 2nd Brigade was on the right flank of McCaffrey's division. The U.S. 3rd Armored Cavalry Regiment was to the right of Kern's brigade. Ted Reid's 197th Brigade was moving eastward on Highway 8 to assume a position as the division's reserve force. McCaffrey had already issued orders for his entire division to begin firing their artillery and Multiple Launch Rocket Systems for a period of fifteen minutes. The barrage was to commence at 4:45 A.M. At precisely 5 A.M. McCaffrey's two tank brigades led by John LeMoyne and Paul Kern were to begin their attack on the Hammurabi division of the Republican Guard. Their attack was to be complemented by a charge of the 3rd Armored Cavalry Regiment. At the same time, General Binford Peay's 101st Airborne Division (Air Assault) was to attack with a fleet of Black Hawk helicopters, dropping soldiers on the last unguarded road leading north out of Basra, a paved highway that ran north along the Iranian border. McCaffrey's battle plan was designed to prevent those elements of Saddam's army north of the Basra pocket from escaping with their weapons to fight again another day.

McCaffrey's orders forced him to scrap those plans. But he had also been instructed that offensive operations were not to cease until 5 A.M. At 4 A.M., as he had ordered earlier, McCaffrey's nine battalions of artillery and Multiple Launch Rocket Systems fired a thirty-minute barrage of fire onto the positions occupied by the Hammurabi division east of their onion field.

At first light, Kern's 2nd Brigade, accompanied by the 3rd Armored Cavalry Regiment, pushed ahead to the east. Before there could be a proper cease-fire, McCaffrey said, he had to know what the enemy's exact position was. "What was unclear," Kern said, "was where the demilitarized zone was. So we kept pushing out. We spent the day clearing this whole area and moving up. We captured a considerable amount of T-72s, BMPs, artillery pieces. There must have been eight artillery battalions out there in front of us. We had focused most of our own artillery fire on the [Iraqi] artillery units, and they just abandoned their equipment and ran away. The Iraqis we found weren't in any mood to fight."

In LeMoyne's 1st Brigade, the sudden end of the war felt strange. "We got the word of the cease-fire," LeMoyne said, "and there was initially a sense of profound relief." LeMoyne had ordered his brigade's scouts out in front and placed combat teams behind them. Shortly after dawn, an Iraqi T-72 tank approached the scouts cautiously. "It just drove up to us and surrendered," LeMoyne said. "The crew got off. They weren't tankers. They had stolen that tank to get away. Particularly during the hours of darkness, when guys could sneak away from Basra, a lot of vehicles were driving north and we were picking them up." To the east of them, the Adnan division and the Al Faw division, both Republican Guard infantry forces, were able to flee unmolested; LeMoyne's soldiers were prohibited from stopping or disarming them. "Those two divisions never fired a round [at us]," LeMoyne said. "They simply fled en masse." As glad as they were that the hostilities had ended, LeMoyne's soldiers began to feel as if they had not completed the job they had been sent to do. "You start thinking about it," LeMoyne said. "We hadn't got them all. You know, those bastards got away."

CONCLUSION

A T 11:30 A.M. on March 3, General H. Norman Schwarzkopf and his Saudi counterpart, Lieutenant General Khalid ibn Sultan, took their seats in the center of a long table beneath a large tent that had been erected at a remote air base in southern Iraq. The Safwan airfield was occupied by Major General Ronald Griffith's U.S. 1st Infantry Division. Across the table from Schwarzkopf and Khalid were Iraqi Lieutenant General Sultan Hashim Ahmad and his aide, Lieutenant General Salah Abud Mahmud. Schwarzkopf calmly instructed the Iraqi generals in the terms of the cease-fire.

Within hours after the talks ended, Iraqi Shiites in Basra rose up against Baghdad's rule. In northern Iraq, Kurds too began to rebel violently, driving Iraqi garrison forces first out of small mountain villages and ultimately out of the city of Kirkuk.

It would require several days, but eventually, Saddam Hussein would redeploy the very same Republican Guard forces that had not been disarmed in the Basra pocket to quell the twin rebellions. Refugees from both areas would tell tales of atrocities, of Shiite rebels hung from the big guns of T-72 tanks, of tanks and mortar fire on apartment houses and private residences, of Iraqi helicopter gunships slaughtering thousands of defenseless Kurds on frozen mountainsides. Many infants and children were among the victims.

Just miles away, in their bases in southern Iraq, and later at emergency-relief camps established on Iraq's northern border with Turkey, American soldiers would stand by, angry and helpless. For the tank crews in Colonel Montgomery Meigs's brigade of the U.S. 1st Armored Division, the cease-fire was a galling frustration. Iraqis defiantly strode in front of them, and taunted them. "We could see them out there at 600 and 700 meters, waving at us, waving their weapons, and just walking away. These were the guys who had been shooting at us earlier," said Sergeant Anthony Widner. "They came back and right in front of us. They went to their bunkers and got food. They dismounted, [they numbered approximately] 120 men. They could have given us a lot of trouble. So we got the order to move forward and take them. They were real smart-ass, they had a bad attitude. That's when everybody said, 'We should have finished those bastards.' "

For a military operation that had been born of such extraordinarily deft and successful diplomacy and then prosecuted with such skill and vision, it was a tragic conclusion, one that no amount of postwar celebration could disguise. There could be no doubt that America and its allies had triumphed over Iraq's army on the battlefield. But inasmuch as victory suggests the decisive defeat of an opponent, there was none. This triumph without victory was perhaps the most striking irony of the entire conflict.

Before the war began, and during the forty-two days of hostilities, President Bush had refused to second-guess General Schwarzkopf and his battlefield commanders. He had issued no orders from the Oval Office instructing them to strike specific targets. Virtually to a man, every American commander in the Gulf conflict expressed gratitude and satisfaction over the fact that their President and commander-in-chief had allowed them to fight the war as they saw fit. Toward the end of the conflict, however, because of the pressure brought to bear on the Bush administration by Saudi Arabia and Egypt, the two most important members of the American-led coalition, the President had begun pushing his military advisers for an answer as to how soon offensive operations against the Iraqis could be ended. Aides to the President said he would not have ordered the cessation of hostilities when he did if he had received strong objections from Schwarzkopf. Bush himself was adamant on the point. "I was very careful in being sure that the military supported the cessation of fighting," he told *U.S. News.* "It was stated to me clearly by General Powell, who indeed talked on the phone to General Schwarzkopf from my office, that the time had come to stop the fighting. The goal was to kick Iraq out of

Kuwait, and the goal, in the opinion of our top fighters, had been achieved. There were no pressures brought upon the President of the United States to stop hostilities before our top command recommended that hostilities be stopped."

Aides stated further that Bush could have resisted pressure from Saudi Arabia and Egypt if it meant extending the period of hostilities another twenty-four hours or so. "At that point," said a senior adviser, "we could have stiff-armed them." Still other advisers provided another explanation for the timing of the cease-fire. In Moscow, Mikhail Gorbachev was under increasing pressure from Kremlin hard-liners as the war continued. Some advisers worried that if all of central Baghdad were reduced to rubble, it might be enough of an excuse for Gorbachev's opponents in the military and the KGB to move against him. With no strong dissent from Schwarzkopf on the timing of the cease-fire, these aides said, the real reason for Bush's decision to quit early might have been to protect Gorbachev.

While it may be true that no one had ordered Schwarzkopf to stop fighting, aides to Schwarzkopf said that the general wanted at least several more hours to prosecute the war, to clarify the situation on the battlefield, and to disarm the forces of the Republican Guard that Lieutenant General Fred Franks and his other battlefield commanders nearly had surrounded. On the battlefield itself, brigade commanders and their superiors were still confused about the location of key enemy units when they received word of an impending cease-fire. No provisions had been made for a demilitarized zone or *cordon sanitaire,* an area of the desert recognized by both the Iraqis and the Allied forces where conflict should not occur.

After the war, it was easy to argue that the allies should have further pursued the Republican Guard, destroyed them, and occupied southern Iraq if necessary to prevent Saddam's crushing of the Shiites. But it is difficult to see how such efforts would have succeeded militarily. Neither the U.S. military nor America's political leaders wanted to occupy large chunks of Iraq indefinitely. None of the commanders, including Franks, wanted to follow the Iraqis into Basra itself and risk engaging in street battles to pry them out, fighting that would have cost many American soldiers and Iraqi civilians their lives. Some high-level Army officers also said that if they had continued with Franks's double envelopment and trapped the Iraqis in the Basra pocket the ensuing slaughter would have been inimical to American interests and morale. But several commanders did believe that had the Republican Guard been trapped in the Basra pocket, they might have been forced to surrender and give up their tanks and weapons.

Indeed, the cease-fire agreed to by President Bush had left the battlefield situation so confused that two days afterward, on March 2, General Barry McCaffrey's 24th Infantry Division (Mechanized) found itself in one of the largest tank battles of the war. Elements of the Hammurabi division of the Republican Guard had attempted to escape through the Rumaila oil field with hundreds of vehicles and heavy transporters, many of them carrying undamaged T-72 tanks. After Iraqi soldiers fired at Colonel John Le-Moyne's 1st Brigade, General McCaffrey ordered LeMoyne and his other commanders to respond in kind. "It wasn't a gaggle running for it," Le-Moyne said. "This was tanks and BMPs lined up in a combat-movement profile, with tanks forward and thin-skinned vehicles to the rear. As far as we knew at that point, all the bridges over the Euphrates were down and the only way out of that oil field would be to drive right through us."

At the end of nearly two hours of attack, McCaffrey reported destroying 30 Iraqi tanks, 65 armored personnel carriers, and 400 trucks. The Hammurabi division, however, was estimated to have had 350 tanks at the start of the war. Days later, the Hammurabi's remaining tanks rolled through town after town in southern Iraq, their guns smashing the Shiite rebellions.

The terms of the cease-fire had also allowed the Iraqi army to fly helicopters. General Schwarzkopf insisted that the Iraqis fly no fixed-wing aircraft, but he assented to the use of the helicopters when the Iraqi generals said they needed them to transport wounded soldiers and for other tasks. Schwarzkopf said days afterward that he was "suckered" by the Iraqis. By then, Saddam Hussein's soldiers were firing from the helicopters at the hapless Kurds in the mountains of northern Iraq. It is certain that Saddam's Republican Guard would have quelled the Kurdish uprising ultimately. But in the difficult terrain of the mountains, the helicopters turned what might have been a negotiated truce into a massacre. While the Bush administration sent aid to the Kurdish refugees (after an embarrassing international outcry), it never raised a finger to prevent the slaughter by soldiers in helicopters.

On several occasions prior to and during the war, Bush made it plain that the quarrel of the international community was not with the people of Iraq, but with Saddam Hussein. Rise up and remove him, Bush said, and Iraq will be at peace with the world. During the course of the slaughter of the Shiites and Kurds in the aftermath of the war, Iraqi opposition figures reminded the Bush administration of the President's words of encouragement.

Aides to the President pointed out that Bush had said that if the Iraqi people "and the army" rose up, the international community would support them. Because the Iraqi army never rose up and rebelled, these presidential aides explained, the United States was unable to come to the aid of the Kurds and the Shiites. It was a weak excuse. It was also the case that the administration was unwilling to deal directly with any Iraqi opposition figures not specifically approved by King Fahd and, to a lesser extent, Egyptian President Hosni Mubarak. Fear of radical Shiite fundamentalism and Kurdish separatism may well have stayed Washington's hand. In addition, there was little sentiment among the American public for having U.S. troops become embroiled in a centuries-old ethnic conflict.

The sentiment was shared by President Bush. "The battles between the Kurds and the Baath Party have been going for a long, long time," Bush told *U.S. News*. "To solve that problem forever was not part of the United Nations' goals, nor was it the goal of the United States. We deplore killings, of course. But to tie the Kurdish or Shiite problem into the handling of the aggression of Iraq is simply a bit revisionistic. It is disappointing that Saddam Hussein remains in power and is still brutal and powerful. But that in no way diminishes the highly successful effort to stop the aggression against Kuwait."

An examination of the forty-two days of Desert Storm yields some surprising conclusions. One week before the commencement of the air campaign on January 16, 1991, a Pentagon spokesman stated that Allied soldiers would face an estimated force of 540,000 Iraqi troops in the Kuwait Theater of Operations (KTO), a zone defined by the Pentagon as the area south of the 31st parallel of latitude and east of the 45th line of longitude. The KTO encompassed all of Kuwait and a portion of southeastern Iraq three times larger than Kuwait itself. After the war, General Schwarzkopf would testify to two committees of Congress that his army had confronted forty-three Iraqi divisions. Those divisions, Schwarzkopf said, boasted 623,000 Iraqi soldiers. Of these the Central Command estimated that 65,000 were taken prisoner during the conflict. The Pentagon further asserted that about four divisions, or 60,000 soldiers, had escaped. The CIA said the number was even greater. The Defense Intelligence Agency estimated that another

100,000 Iraqi soldiers perished in the war, but it conceded that the number might be wrong by as much as 50 percent in either direction. In other words, there could have been as few as 50,000 or as many as 150,000 Iraqis killed.

Given the rapidity and confusion of the Gulf War and the fact that Allied forces did not engage in Vietnam-style "body counts," such uncertainty is understandable. But even allowing for those factors, it is difficult to make sense of the Pentagon's estimates of the number of Iraqi soldiers present in the KTO and those killed there. Several respected analysts believe that the number of Iraqi soldiers present on the battlefield in the KTO at the time the ground war began was well below both the Pentagon's estimate of 540,000, and the 623,000 claimed by General Schwarzkopf.

American estimates of the Iraqi order of battle were derived from satellite photographs and intercepts of electronic communications between Iraqi units in the KTO. The aerial photos were most useful for determining the disposition of Iraqi equipment and defensive barriers. The satellite imagery could not count soldiers, however. Nevertheless, U.S. intelligence analysts concluded that there were 142 separate "brigades." This amounted to 43 divisions, of which approximately 25 were infantry divisions assigned to the front lines of defense in southern Kuwait. The analysts, however, ascribed to the Iraqi forces the manpower of their American counterparts, a practice that overestimated the fighting strength of the Iraqis.

Sources familiar with Iraqi force levels said that almost without exception the Iraqi front-line units were poorly trained and poorly led, made up of the least educated men from the countryside and the cities. Many of these divisions were created for the war as the army was mobilized; the units were provisional, and at least fifteen were disbanded after the war ended. "A lot of those divisions were under strength, called up rapidly, and not filled up," said Ahmed Hashim, a Washington-based consultant on Middle Eastern affairs who spent five years studying the Iraqi army for a doctoral dissertation on the Iran-Iraq war at the Massachussets Institute of Technology that was completed two months before Iraq invaded Kuwait. His assessment of the strength of the Iraqi army was derived from Middle Eastern sources, from publications, and from sources who fought in the Iraqi army. Hashim convincingly argued that about 70 percent of Saddam's front-line forces were Shiites, 20 percent Kurds. He called these forces Saddam Hussein's "throwaway divisions." Many Iraqis, knowing they were being sacrificed, deserted while others surrendered en masse.

At peak levels, Iraqi infantry divisions were significantly smaller than the typical divisions of Western armies. An American division ordinarily comprises three combat brigades totaling about 16,000 soldiers. A fully manned Iraqi infantry division had just two brigades of between 6,000 and 8,000 men. It was likely, moreover, that many of the rapidly formed Iraqi "divisions" were really only brigades made up of between 1,000 and 5,000 soldiers. By Hashim's estimate, Kuwait's border defenses at their greatest strength were manned by 75,000 to 150,000 soldiers. According to U.S. intelligence estimates, the Iraqis had arrayed eight armored divisions plus three brigades behind their defensive lines, an army of about 120,000 men. Behind these divisions were eight Republican Guard divisions, a force of 100,000 well-armed and well-trained soldiers. The Republican Guard divisions were more likely to be manned at full levels. Thus, the peak number of soldiers in the Kuwait Theater of Operations, according to Hashim, was somewhere between 300,000 and 370,000—a significant difference from the numbers estimated by the Pentagon and by Schwarzkopf.

On the eve of the war, it was likely that the number of Iraqi soldiers on the battlefield was smaller still. During the Iran-Iraq war, front-line soldiers enjoyed a liberal leave policy. They were allowed to spend one week at home for each three on the front. Documents captured at the conclusion of the Gulf War indicated that a similar leave policy had been in effect for front-line units. But interviews with Iraqi prisoners of war and defectors suggested that many Iraqi soldiers who left the front on leave never returned. It was likely, according to U.S. intelligence officials, that, as a result of desertion, some front-line Iraqi units suffered attrition rates of between 20 and 50 percent before and during the Allied air campaign. If true, that would have reduced the front-line forces to as few as 50,000 soldiers on the eve of the commencement of the ground campaign. On February 24, then, when the ground war began, Saddam Hussein may well have had as few as 300,000 soldiers in the Kuwait Theater of Operations. Citing the information provided by his own sources, Hashim believed the number was even smaller, and that perhaps as few as 200,000 soldiers remained in the KTO by the time the ground war began.

Such low estimates of the size of the Iraqi force appear to jibe with other facts known about the war. It appeared that about 4½ of Saddam Hussein's eight Republican Guard divisions—the Adnan, the Nebuchadnezzar, the Al Faw, the 8th Special Forces, and part of the Hammurabi—escaped the Allied onslaught. This amounted to a force of well over 60,000 men. Many of these were forces that Lieutenant General Fred Franks had intended to trap in the Basra pocket. All were integral elements of the "center of gravity" that General Schwarzkopf and his commanders had targeted prior to the war.

Postwar reconstructions and interviews suggested that at least half of the soldiers from Iraq's eight to ten armored and mechanized divisions escaped. This would amount to a total of perhaps 50,000 men. When added to the 60,000 soldiers from the Republican Guard divisions who are believed to have escaped, the number of escaped Iraqi forces jumps to 110,000. The Pentagon's count of 65,000 captured Iraqis seems reasonable. Hashim and other analysts suggested that perhaps another 25,000 to 50,000 Iraqi soldiers were killed and wounded. Those numbers would bring the total Iraqi force level on the eve of the ground war to somewhere between 200,000 and 225,000 soldiers.

The Central Command and the Pentagon have been reluctant to estimate the numbers of Iraqi military casualties. They note correctly that the Allied forces never engaged in a "body count." The Allied air campaign targeted only Iraqi strategic centers and airfields, logistics sites, and war equipment—never soldiers. But the estimate by the Central Command and the Pentagon that 100,000 Iraqi soldiers perished in the war is difficult to countenance. The first and most obvious problem with the estimate is the historical ratio of dead to wounded in modern battles. Typically in modern warfare, military historians have found that the wounded have outnumbered the dead by ratios of between 3:1 and 4:1. If 100,000 Iraqis died, another 300,000 to 400,000 Iraqis would likely have been wounded. Evidence, however, from postwar interviews with Iraqi soldiers, Allied medics, and other sources indicated that the number of Iraqi wounded on the battlefield was probably in the tens of thousands.

Military analysts have long known that average daily personnel-casualty rates for ground forces have declined significantly over the past 300 years for forces of roughly comparable size. According to George W. S. Kuhn, a Washington, D.C., defense analyst, improvements in the effectiveness of battlefield weapons have been more than offset by other improvements. For example, better communications have allowed soldiers to disperse widely over the battlefield. Movement across larger battle areas is increasingly rapid because of improved vehicles. Soldiers are better protected by both vehicle armor and body armor.

During the prosecution of Operation Desert Storm, Kuhn completed a detailed four-year study for the Defense Department on the patterns of battle-casualty rates associated with patterns of modern ground operations. His study encompassed campaigns of the Second World War, the Korean War, the Arab-Israeli wars, and hundreds of mock battles fought at the U.S. Army's National Training Center. After finishing this study, Kuhn independently examined the numbers released by the Pentagon and other public records on the conduct of Operation Desert Storm. He scrutinized the figures released on Iraqi tanks, artillery, and armored personnel carriers that had been destroyed by air and ground forces during the forty-two days of conflict in January and February. He allowed for the character and numbers of other types of targets, such as command and logistics sites and headquarters. He noted reports of the character of the bombing campaign, of Iraqi shelters, and of the fighting on the Iraqi defensive lines and the armored engagements in the ground war. He also considered the count of prisoners of war, and the range of possible sizes for the Iraqi force in the KTO.

Given the extraordinarily mobile and rapid nature of the ground campaign, Kuhn concluded that the maximum probable rate of Iraqi wounded during the four-day ground campaign was almost certainly no more than 10 percent; a more realistic figure would be around 5 percent. If Kuhn is correct and if there were 540,000 Iraqis in the KTO, as the Pentagon asserted, the maximum probable number of wounded would be 54,000, but a more reasonable maximum would be 27,000. Using the historical ratio of wounded to killed in modern wars of 3:1 to 4:1, that yields a maximum number of killed ranging from 6,500 to 18,000 during the ground campaign.

If there were 250,000 Iraqis in the Kuwait Theater of Operations, as Ahmed Hashim estimated, Kuhn's patterns of rates for this type of ground operation suggest that there would have been 12,500 to 25,000 Iraqi soldiers wounded and another 3,000 to 8,000 killed during the ground campaign. Those numbers correlate with a separate approach Kuhn took in his analysis. Kuhn calculated the probable number of casualties from the numbers of weapons, vehicles, and other targets the Pentagon has said were destroyed in the air and ground campaigns. Working from the Pentagon counts, the air campaign in the KTO may have killed some 5,000 to 10,000 Iraqis, while the four-day ground campaign added perhaps another 3,000 to 7,000 dead. Combining the two analyses, and assuming Hashim's figure of 250,000 Iraqi troops in the KTO, the air and ground campaigns against the Iraqi forces in the Kuwait Theater of Operations may have accounted for a maximum total of perhaps 8,000 to 18,000 Iraqi dead. Kuhn suspected that the numbers may be lower.

Anthony H. Cordesman, a highly regarded defense analyst and the co-author of two authoritative books on the Iran-Iraq war, placed the number of Iraqi casualties from the war at a maximum of 25,000 killed and 50,000 wounded. Cordesman insisted that these were only guesstimates, and he conceded that they were probably "on the high side." Cordesman's estimate is somewhat higher than George Kuhn's but significantly lower than that of the Pentagon. Cordesman concluded that the ratio of dead to injured in the Iraqi army may have been higher than in other wars because the Iraqi medical services in the rear broke down, contributing to a higher-than-usual number of Iraqi fatalities on the front lines. In any event, Cordesman also does not believe there were 540,000 or 623,000 Iraqi soldiers in the KTO. Cordesman noted that those force-size numbers were nominal ones associated with fully manned divisions—a worst-case Pentagon planning estimate. "Those are the numbers that were cited," he said, "but it becomes more and more difficult to support them."

Anecdotal evidence from postwar interviews with Iraqi soldiers also supports a conclusion that there were not as many killed as the Pentagon has suggested. Iraqi prisoners talked of being terrified by bombing attacks, but not of being slaughtered by them. They told how they protected themselves by hiding in ditches next to their tanks or in their bunkers. Convoy drivers spoke of running from their vehicles when they came under air attack. Historically, bombing attacks against dug-in infantry have rarely produced high casualty rates. In this case, however, they prompted wholesale desertion.

On the Allied side, soldiers spoke of seeing dead Iraqis, but most admitted to seeing tens or scores of corpses—not thousands. In the biggest tank battle of the war, in which the U.S. 1st Armored Division destroyed about 100 Iraqi tanks and armored personnel carriers, an intelligence officer from the division estimated that about 340 Iraqis had died. In fact, there were few other heavy force-on-force battles. The Tawakalna division was largely overrun by the U.S. 1st and 3rd Armored Divisions after several sharp skirmishes with cavalry; the Marines made short work of a battalion of Iraq's 5th Mechanized Division in the al-Burgan oil field fight. In several other fights, the anecdotal evidence suggested that hundreds of Iraqis died in each, but not thousands. As soldiers from the U.S. 1st and 2nd Marine Divisions swept through the heavily defended southeastern quarter of

Kuwait, for instance, officers reported that their units had destroyed 2,080 tanks, armored personnel carriers, and artillery pieces. Their count after four days of fighting was 1,510 Iraqi soldiers killed in those battles. Even the so-called highway of death west of Kuwait City was really more of a highway of destruction and panic, Anthony Cordesman concluded. He walked the highway through the Mutlah pass after the war. "It was an incredibly impressive achievement of air power," Cordesman said, "but it was not a highway of death." When the lead and rear vehicles came under attack, most of the drivers and passengers fled the scene. Cordesman said that most of the vehicles he saw were intact and abandoned. "There weren't that many bodies, and on the other vehicles, there certainly wasn't any blood."

These numbers, if true, reveal the genuine triumph of American and Allied soldiers and airmen, their battlefield commanders, and the generals and their aides who planned and directed the war effort against Iraq. The goal of the Jedi Knights, with their doctrine of maneuver, was to confuse and terrorize the Iraqis and to force them to surrender or flee, but to avoid battles where possible. In conception and execution, the Allied war plan did just that. A devastating air campaign took away the enemy's intelligence sources, leaving him bewildered and fearful, and exhausted from relentless bombing. Feints and deception kept the Iraqis pinned in place, while the ground forces swept around their defenses and rolled them up from behind. Only the Republican Guard stood and fought, and they were stunned and ultimately destroyed by the range and accuracy of superior American weaponry, which allowed soldiers to kill their opponents from long distances, before the enemy was even in a position to fix his sights on a target and fire on it.

In its emphasis on high technology, the Pentagon has been amply vindicated by the Gulf War. The performance of the F-117A Stealth fighter appears to have silenced its critics. Although Baghdad's air-defense radars were formidable, the F-117A defeated them with ease, delivering its ordnance with extraordinary accuracy. Postwar examination of the destruction wrought by the Stealth fighters in central Baghdad confirmed that so-called collateral damage—damage to structures in the immediate vicinity of bombing targets—was remarkably light. A team of reporters sent to Baghdad after the war published an account of their visit in *The Nation* magazine. They concluded that the injuries from such damage were remarkably light. At the worst, reporters found, the bombing might have killed 3,000 civilians, but the number probably was much smaller.

There has nevertheless been some thoughtful criticism of target selection in Baghdad, both from inside the Pentagon and from without. Analysts concluded that at the end of the war on February 28, only 15 percent of Iraq's electricity-delivery grid remained functional; by contrast, at the conclusion of the Second World War, Germany had *lost* only 15 percent of its electrical grid. The damage shut down most of Iraq's sewage and water treatment plants, leaving the Iraqi people susceptible to the rapid spread of cholera, typhoid and other diseases. The U.S. Census Bureau's Center for International Research estimated that the poor health conditions contributed to 70,000 civilian Iraqi deaths after the war.

Air Force officials said that they had to target the Iraqi electrical grid because of its critical importance to the facilities in which Saddam Hussein continued to develop his weapons of mass destruction. American intelligence officials confirmed that, because there was so little certainty about the location and even the existence of several nuclear-development and chemical-weapons facilities, the Iraqi electrical grid had to be virtually destroyed. The secret nuclear-weapons complex at al-Atheer forty miles south of Baghdad is perhaps the best example of the problems the United States and its allies had in identifying such facilities; its existence was never confirmed until long after hostilities were concluded.

Indeed, inspectors from the United Nations and the International Atomic Energy Agency (IAEA) were startled to discover in their postwar inspections just how advanced the Iraqis were in their efforts to develop both nuclear and hydrogen bombs. By the early 1980s, the Iraqis were fully engaged in what one analyst called the equivalent of the Manhattan Project, the mammoth American effort during the Second World War to build an atomic bomb. David Kay, one of the two chief inspectors on the U.N. teams, said the Iraqi program employed 15,000 to 20,000 scientists and engineers and technicians and cost Iraq billions of dollars while it was fighting its war with Iran. By August 1990, on the eve of Saddam Hussein's invasion of Kuwait, Iraq was only twelve to eighteen months away from producing its first nuclear bomb—not five to ten years, as some experts had previously thought.

Among the 45,000 pages of documents the U.N. team found was one linking an unspecified surface-to-surface missile program with the nuclear program. It was a memo from the Ministry of Defense to the Iraqi Atomic Energy Commission that spoke of using a concrete warhead device to test

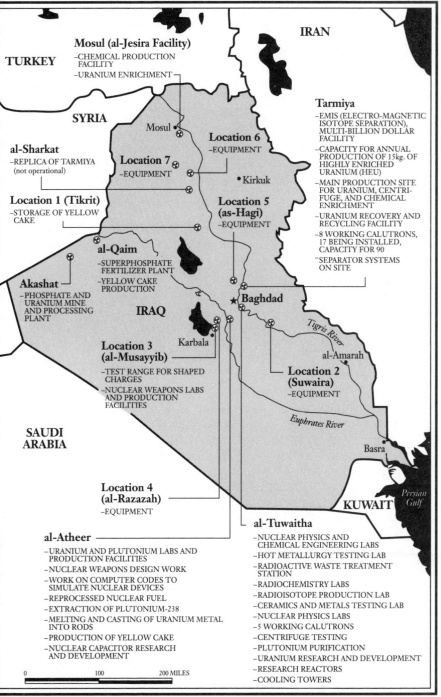

TURKEY

Mosul (al-Jesira Facility)
–CHEMICAL PRODUCTION FACILITY
–URANIUM ENRICHMENT

IRAN

SYRIA

Mosul

al-Sharkat
–REPLICA OF TARMIYA (not operational)

Location 7
–EQUIPMENT

Location 6
–EQUIPMENT

Kirkuk

Tarmiya
–EMIS (ELECTRO-MAGNETIC ISOTOPE SEPARATION), MULTI-BILLION DOLLAR FACILITY
–CAPACITY FOR ANNUAL PRODUCTION OF 15kg. OF HIGHLY ENRICHED URANIUM (HEU)
–MAIN PRODUCTION SITE FOR URANIUM, CENTRI-FUGE, AND CHEMICAL ENRICHMENT
–URANIUM RECOVERY AND RECYCLING FACILITY
–8 WORKING CALUTRONS, 17 BEING INSTALLED, CAPACITY FOR 90
–SEPARATOR SYSTEMS ON SITE

Location 1 (Tikrit)
–STORAGE OF YELLOW CAKE

Location 5 (as-Hagi)
–EQUIPMENT

al-Qaim
–SUPERPHOSPHATE FERTILIZER PLANT
–YELLOW CAKE PRODUCTION

Akashat
–PHOSPHATE AND URANIUM MINE AND PROCESSING PLANT

IRAQ

Baghdad

Karbala

Location 3 (al-Musayyib)
–TEST RANGE FOR SHAPED CHARGES
–NUCLEAR WEAPONS LABS AND PRODUCTION FACILITIES

Tigris River

al-Amarah

Location 2 (Suwaira)
–EQUIPMENT

Euphrates River

SAUDI ARABIA

Basra

Location 4 (al-Razazah)
–EQUIPMENT

KUWAIT

Persian Gulf

al-Tuwaitha
–NUCLEAR PHYSICS AND CHEMICAL ENGINEERING LABS
–HOT METALLURGY TESTING LAB
–RADIOACTIVE WASTE TREATMENT STATION
–RADIOCHEMISTRY LABS
–RADIOISOTOPE PRODUCTION LAB
–CERAMICS AND METALS TESTING LAB
–NUCLEAR PHYSICS LABS
–5 WORKING CALUTRONS
–CENTRIFUGE TESTING
–PLUTONIUM PURIFICATION
–URANIUM RESEARCH AND DEVELOPMENT
–RESEARCH REACTORS
–COOLING TOWERS

al-Atheer
–URANIUM AND PLUTONIUM LABS AND PRODUCTION FACILITIES
–NUCLEAR WEAPONS DESIGN WORK
–WORK ON COMPUTER CODES TO SIMULATE NUCLEAR DEVICES
–REPROCESSED NUCLEAR FUEL
–EXTRACTION OF PLUTONIUM-238
–MELTING AND CASTING OF URANIUM METAL INTO RODS
–PRODUCTION OF YELLOW CAKE
–NUCLEAR CAPACITOR RESEARCH AND DEVELOPMENT

0   100   200 MILES

N. INSPECTORS UNCOVERED CONCLUSIVE EVIDENCE THAT PRIOR TO THE GULF
WAR IRAQ WAS WITHIN TWO YEARS OF DEVELOPING A CRUDE ATOMIC BOMB

the missile. "The people who ought to be scared about this are not the Israelis," Kay said. "It's the other Arab states. This was a long-term program to provide regional dominance, and a deterrence to keep the superpowers out."

Since the end of the war, Saddam Hussein has taken steps to quickly rebuild his army. Of the sixty to seventy divisions he had prior to the war, twenty to twenty-five never were engaged in the Kuwait Theater of Operations. Besides the 4½ Republican Guard divisions that escaped virtually unharmed, one—the four-brigade Baghdad Division—saw almost no action. An estimated 700 Iraqi tanks escaped destruction. They became the nucleus of a new army.

At the end of the war, Saddam abolished his 800,000-man Popular Army, a ragtag militia that many Iraqis had taken to calling "the unpopular army." He has since set about reconstituting his army of sixty to seventy divisions into a leaner but more capable and mobile force of approximately forty divisions, with 300,000 to 400,000 men. He has eliminated the twenty-five "throw-away divisions" that were overrun on the front lines in southern Kuwait. The Republican Guard is being rebuilt and enlarged, probably to a force of between twelve and fourteen divisions. Other armored and mechanized forces will be kept at their former level of between six and eight divisions. These forces will all be supplied with tanks, including at least 500 T-72s and thousands of armored personnel carriers.

One of the mysteries of the ground war was the whereabouts of the Iraqi army's armored personnel carriers (APCs) and infantry fighting vehicles (IFVs). For desert warfare, these tracked and wheeled armored vehicles with large-caliber rapid-firing guns are second only to the tank in fearsomeness. Iraq was said to have some 6,000 APCs and IFVs, but Allied intelligence counted only 2,800 in the KTO, of which an estimated 1,400 escaped. The Central Command estimates defy logic, since most mechanized armies travel with roughly an equal number of tanks and APCs. Central Command also claimed to have counted 4,500 tanks in the KTO, of which 3,800 were destroyed and 700 escaped. One explanation would be that many APCs and IFVs were counted as tanks. If so, that would mean there were fewer tanks and more APCs in the theater, and fewer tanks and more APCs were destroyed. But the answer may never be known.

The International Institute for Strategic Studies in London estimated that as of October 1991 the Iraqi army had about 2,300 tanks and 4,400 armored vehicles. Ahmed Hashim disagreed, putting the number of tanks at between 1,700 and 2,600. What is certain is that, less than a year after the war had ended, Iraq already had rebuilt its army to a size more potent than that of any of its neighboring countries.

If anyone lost the war besides the Iraqi army, it was the American and international press. Disorganized, anarchic by nature, and chronically competitive among themselves, the news reporters assigned to cover Desert Storm were no match for the machine of the U.S. Central Command and the Pentagon. The mismatch was compounded by the fact that Saudi Arabia was openly hostile to the press. There was thus virtually no way to circumvent the restrictions imposed by the military. Reporters were forced to cover the war in "combat pools," small groups of reporters sent to Pentagon-approved sites where they reported and wrote stories for all reporters in the country.

As a result, the news that came from the Persian Gulf War was the news the military wanted presented. It was not that reporters did not want to do a better job or were not willing to risk their lives to get better stories; indeed, many reporters in the Gulf seethed with the knowledge that their coverage was inadequate. But they simply could not get to the story to cover it.

One consequence of this was that the press as an institution fell still further in the public's esteem. Journalists poorly prepared to cover war, high technology, and international diplomacy were assigned to cover the conflict in the Gulf. A great many embarrassed the profession. By contrast, briefers provided to the press by the military seemed, more often than not, professional, knowledgeable, and worthy of trust. The situation became so bad that "Saturday Night Live" aired a skit satirizing the performance of the press corps assigned to cover Desert Storm and lauding the military.

More seriously, the American public, because of the shackling of the press, learned little of the heroics of soldiers like those in Captain Gerald Davie's cavalry troop or Colonel Randolph House's brigade who defended and rescued their comrades during vicious firefights. The taxpayers who bore the burden of the cost of Desert Storm were told of virtually none of the battles of the war, where they were fought, or how tough they were. The combined cost of Desert Shield and Desert Storm is estimated at somewhere between $60 billion and $70 billion, budget analysts and government officials said. Cash contributions from other countries were expected to cover roughly $42 billion of that amount, though other "in kind" contributions of fuel, food, and other goods will defray that further. Whatever the final cost, it is clear that the American taxpayer had a substantial investment in the war. And yet for all of the air time and newsprint and magazine coverage devoted to the war, only an extremely incomplete and limited picture of the war was conveyed to the people on whose support the effort relied.

Perhaps the most troubling aspect of the conflict was the Bush administration's desire to circumvent Congress by seeking United Nations approval for intervention in the Middle East. The decision to secure the approval of the U.N. Security Council before moving against Iraq was at least partly rooted in the calculations of domestic politics, according to several advisers to President Bush. While there was nothing improper in that, Bush and his advisers have since attempted to cloak their motives in rhetoric about their lofty aspirations for a rejuvenated world body. In fact, the Bush administration's reliance on the United Nations has been highly selective. In its postwar diplomacy in the Middle East and in its attempts to broker a conclusion to the Ethiopian civil war, to cite just two examples, the administration all but ignored the United Nations.

When the administration moved closer to a showdown with Saddam Hussein, as the United Nations' January 15 deadline approached, there was virtual hostility on the part of the President and his men toward the constitutional requirements that govern the nation's conduct of foreign policy, especially as it may lead to war. Like each of his predecessors since Richard Nixon, George Bush believed that the War Powers Resolution passed by Congress in 1973 was unconstitutional. Also like his predecessors, Bush refused to test the resolution's constitutionality in the courts. The problem with the War Powers Resolution was that it was so riddled with loopholes that the executive branch has found it a simple matter to ignore its strictures. The White House was convinced that it could proceed toward war with Iraq without the consent of Congress, with or without the resolution. Indeed, the resolution has served as a smokescreen, obscuring the true state of relations between the executive and legislative branches. There is virtually no meaningful debate among constitutional scholars about the fact that it is Congress alone that has the authority to put the nation into war. That Congress has virtually abdicated its constitutional responsibilities in so many areas does not mean that its war-making authority is thereby conferred upon the executive branch. The President is authorized by the Constitution to commit military forces only where the defense of the nation is at issue. Where offensive military operations are contemplated, the Constitution clearly requires the consent of Congress.

George Bush's remarkable success in constructing the international coalition against Iraq should not obscure this point. Although he ultimately sought and received the approval of the Congress, Bush has stated that he believed such approval was not needed. In the twentieth century, wars begun by Presidents have been responsible for most of the armed conflicts in which the United States has been engaged; since the Second World War, Presidents have led the United States into every armed conflict. On this crucial matter, the genesis and manner of American intervention in the Persian Gulf have only deepened the debate over how the United States ought to properly and democratically decide whether or not to commit the republic to war.

THE COMPLETE U.N. RESOLUTIONS

RESOLUTION 660
August 2, 1990

The Security Council,

Alarmed by the invasion of Kuwait on 2 August 1990 by the military forces of Iraq,

Determining that there exists a breach of international peace and security as regards the Iraqi invasion of Kuwait,

Acting under Articles 39 and 40 of the Charter of the United Nations,

1. *Condemns* the Iraqi invasion of Kuwait;

2. *Demands* that Iraq withdraw immediately and unconditionally all its forces to the positions in which they were located on 1 August 1990;

3. *Calls upon* Iraq and Kuwait to begin immediately intensive negotiations for the resolution of their differences and supports all efforts in this regard, and especially those of the League of Arab States;

4. *Decides* to meet again as necessary to consider further steps to ensure compliance with the present resolution.

VOTE: 14 for, 0 against, 1 abstention (Yemen)

RESOLUTION 661
August 6, 1990

The Security Council,

Reaffirming its resolution 660 (1990) of 2 August 1990,

Deeply concerned that that resolution has not been implemented and that the invasion by Iraq of Kuwait continues with further loss of human life and material destruction,

Determined to bring the invasion and occupation of Kuwait by Iraq to an end and to restore the sovereignty, independence and territorial integrity of Kuwait,

Noting that the legitimate Government of Kuwait has expressed its readiness to comply with resolution 660 (1990),

Mindful of its responsibilities under the Charter of the United Nations for the maintenance of international peace and security,

Affirming the inherent right of individual or collective self-defence, in response to the armed attack by Iraq against Kuwait, in accordance with Article 51 of the Charter,

Acting under Chapter VII of the Charter of the United Nations,

1. *Determines* that Iraq so far has failed to comply with paragraph 2 of resolution 660 (1990) and has usurped the authority of the legitimate Government of Kuwait;

2. *Decides*, as a consequence, to take the following measures to secure compliance of Iraq with paragraph 2 of resolution 660 (1990) and to restore the authority of the legitimate Government of Kuwait;

3. *Decides* that all States shall prevent;

(a) The import into their territories of all commodities and products originating in Iraq or Kuwait exported therefrom after the date of the present resolution;

(b) Any activities by their nationals or in their territories which would promote or are calculated to promote the export or transshipment of any commodities or products from Iraq or Kuwait; and any dealings by their nationals or their flag vessels or in their territories in any commodities or products originating in Iraq or Kuwait and exported therefrom after the date of the present resolution, including in particular any transfer of funds to Iraq or Kuwait for the purposes of such activities or dealings;

(c) The sale or supply by their nationals or from their territories or using their flag vessels of any commodities or products, including weapons or any other military equipment, whether or not originating in their territories but not including supplies intended strictly for medical purposes, and, in humanitarian circumstances, foodstuffs, to any person or body in Iraq or Kuwait or to any person or body for the purposes of any business carried on in or operated from Iraq or Kuwait, and any activities by their nationals or in their territories which promote or are calculated to promote such sale or supply of such commodities or products;

4. *Decides* that all States shall not make available to the Government of Iraq or to any commercial, industrial or public utility undertaking in Iraq or Kuwait, any funds or any other financial or economic resources and shall prevent their nationals and any persons within their territories from removing from their territories or otherwise making available to that Government or to any such undertaking any such funds or resources and from remitting any other funds to persons or bodies

within Iraq or Kuwait, except payments exclusively for strictly medical or humanitarian purposes and, in humanitarian circumstances, foodstuffs;

5. *Calls upon* all States, including States nonmembers of the United Nations, to act strictly in accordance with the provisions of the present resolution notwithstanding any contract entered into or licence granted before the date of the present resolution;

6. *Decides* to establish, in accordance with rule 28 of the provisional rules of procedure of the Security Council, a Committee of the Security Council consisting of all the members of the Council, to undertake the following tasks and to report on its work to the Council with its observations and recommendations:

(a) To examine the reports on the progress of the implementation of the present resolution which will be submitted by the Secretary-General;

(b) To seek from all States further information regarding the action taken by them concerning the effective implementation of the provisions laid down in the present resolution;

7. *Calls upon* all States to cooperate fully with the Committee in the fulfillment of its task, including supplying such information as may be sought by the Committee in pursuance of the present resolution;

8. *Requests* the Secretary-General to provide all necessary assistance to the Committee and to make the necessary arrangements in the Secretariat for the purpose;

9. *Decides* that, notwithstanding paragraphs 4 through 8 above, nothing in the present resolution shall prohibit assistance to the legitimate Government of Kuwait, and *calls upon* all States:

(a) To take appropriate measures to protect assets of the legitimate Government of Kuwait and its agencies;

(b) Not to recognize any regime set up by the occupying Power,

10. *Requests* the Secretary-General to report to the Council on the progress of the implementation of the present resolution, the first report to be submitted within thirty days;

11. *Decides* to keep this item on its agenda and to continue its efforts to put an early end to the invasion by Iraq.

VOTE: 13 for, 0 against, 2 abstentions (Cuba and Yemen)

RESOLUTION 662

August 9, 1990

The Security Council,

Recalling its resolutions 660 (1990) and 661 (1990),

Gravely alarmed by the declaration by Iraq of a "comprehensive and eternal merger" with Kuwait,

Demanding, once again, that Iraq withdraw immediately and unconditionally all its forces to the positions in which they were located on 1 August 1990,

Determined to bring the occupation of Kuwait by Iraq to an end and to restore the sovereignty, independence and territorial integrity of Kuwait,

Determined also to restore the authority of the legitimate Government of Kuwait,

1. *Decides* that annexation of Kuwait by Iraq under any form and whatever pretext has no legal validity, and is considered null and void;

2. *Calls upon* all States, international organizations and specialized agencies not to recognize that annexation, and to refrain from any action or dealing that might be interpreted as an indirect recognition of the annexation;

3. *Further demands* that Iraq rescind its actions purporting to annex Kuwait;

4. *Decides* to keep this item on its agenda and to continue its efforts to put an early end to the occupation.

VOTE: Unanimous (15–0)

RESOLUTION 664
August 18, 1990

The Security Council,

Recalling the Iraqi invasion and purported annexation of Kuwait and resolutions 660, 661 and 662,

Deeply concerned for the safety and well-being of third state nationals in Iraq and Kuwait,

Recalling the obligations of Iraq in this regard under international law,

Welcoming the efforts of the Secretary-General to pursue urgent consultations with the Government of Iraq following the concern and anxiety expressed by the members of the Council on 17 August 1990,

Acting under Chapter VII of the United Nations Charter,

1. *Demands* that Iraq permit and facilitate the immediate departure from Kuwait and Iraq of the nationals of third countries and grant immediate and continuing access of consular officials to such nationals;

2. *Further demands* that Iraq take no action to jeopardize the safety, security or health of such nationals;

3. *Reaffirms* its decision in resolution 662 (1990) that annexation of Kuwait by Iraq is null and void, and therefore demands that the Government of Iraq rescind its orders for the closure of diplomatic and consular missions in Kuwait and the withdrawal of the immunity of their personnel, and refrain from any such actions in the future;

Appendix A

4. *Requests* the Secretary-General to report to the Council on compliance with this resolution at the earliest possible time.

VOTE: Unanimous (15–0)

RESOLUTION 665
August 25, 1990

The Security Council,

Recalling its resolutions 660 (1990), 661 (1990), 662 (1990) and 664 (1990) and demanding their full and immediate implementation,

Having decided in resolution 661 (1990) to impose economic sanctions under Chapter VII of the Charter of the United Nations,

Determined to bring an end to the occupation of Kuwait by Iraq which imperils the existence of a Member State and to restore the legitimate authority, the sovereignty, independence and territorial integrity of Kuwait which requires the speedy implementation of the above resolutions,

Deploring the loss of innocent life stemming from the Iraqi invasion of Kuwait and determined to prevent further such losses,

Gravely alarmed that Iraq continues to refuse to comply with resolutions 660 (1990), 661 (1990), 662 (1990), and 664 (1990) and in particular at the conduct of the Government of Iraq in using Iraqi flag vessels to export oil,

1. *Calls upon* those Member States cooperating with the Government of Kuwait which are deploying maritime forces to the area to use such measures commensurate to the specific circumstance as may be necessary under the authority of the Security Council to halt all inward and outward maritime shipping in order to inspect and verify their cargoes and destinations and to ensure strict implementation of the provisions related to such shipping laid down in resolution 661 (1990);

2. *Invites* Member States accordingly to cooperate as may be necessary to ensure compliance with the provisions of resolution 661 (1990) with maximum use of political and diplomatic measures, in accordance with paragraph 1 above;

3. *Requests* all States to provide in accordance with the Charter such assistance as may be required by the States referred to in paragraph 1 of this resolution;

4. *Further requests* the States concerned to coordinate their actions in pursuit of the above paragraphs of this resolution using as appropriate mechanisms of the Military Staff Committee and after consultation with the Secretary-General to submit reports to the Security Council and its Committee established under resolution 661 (1990) to facilitate the monitoring of the implementation of this resolution;

5. *Decides* to remain actively seized of the matter.

VOTE: 13 for, 0 against, 2 abstentions (Cuba and Yemen)

RESOLUTION 666
September 13, 1990

The Security Council,

Recalling its resolution 661 (1990), paragraphs 3 (c) and 4 of which apply, except in humanitarian circumstances, to foodstuffs,

Recognizing that circumstances may arise in which it will be necessary for foodstuffs to be supplied to the civilian population in Iraq or Kuwait in order to relieve human suffering,

Noting that in this respect the Committee established under paragraph 6 of that resolution has received communications from several Member States,

Emphasizing that it is for the Security Council, alone or acting through the Committee, to determine whether humanitarian circumstances have arisen,

Deeply concerned that Iraq has failed to comply with its obligations under Security Council resolution 664 (1990) in respect of the safety and well-being of third State nationals, and reaffirming that Iraq retains full responsibility in this regard under international humanitarian law including, where applicable, the Fourth Geneva Convention,

Acting under Chapter VII of the Charter of the United Nations,

1. *Decides* that in order to make the necessary determination whether or not for the purposes of paragraph 3 (c) and paragraph 4 of resolution 661 (1990) humanitarian circumstances have arisen, the Committee shall keep the situation regarding foodstuffs in Iraq and Kuwait under constant review;

2. *Expects* Iraq to comply with its obligations under Security Council resolution 664 (1990) in respect of third State nationals and reaffirms that Iraq remains fully responsible for their safety and well-being in accordance with international humanitarian law including, where applicable, the Fourth Geneva Convention;

3. *Requests,* for the purposes of paragraphs 1 and 2 of this resolution, that the Secretary-General seek urgently, and on a continuing basis, information from relevant United Nations and other appropriate humanitarian agencies and all other sources on the availability of food in Iraq and Kuwait, such information to be communicated by the Secretary-General to the Committee regularly;

4. *Requests* further that in seeking and supplying such information particular attention will be paid to such categories of persons who might suffer specially, such as children under 15 years of age, expectant mothers, maternity cases, the sick and the elderly;

5. *Decides* that if the Committee, after receiving the reports from the Secretary-General, determines that circumstances have arisen in which there is an urgent humanitarian need to supply foodstuffs to Iraq or Kuwait in order to relieve human suffering, it will report promptly to the Council its decision as to how such need should be met;

6. *Directs* the Committee that in formulating its decisions it should bear in mind that foodstuffs should be provided through the United Nations in cooperation with the International Committee of the Red Cross or other appropriate humanitarian agencies and distributed by them or under their supervision in order to ensure that they reach the intended beneficiaries;

7. *Requests* the Secretary-General to use his good offices to facilitate the delivery and distribution of foodstuffs to Kuwait and Iraq in accordance with the provisions of this and other relevant resolutions;

8. *Recalls* that resolution 661 (1990) does not apply to supplies intended strictly for medical purposes, but in this connection recommends that medical supplies should be exported under the strict supervision of the Government of the exporting State or by appropriate humanitarian agencies.

VOTE: 13 for, 0 against, 2 abstentions (Cuba and Yemen)

RESOLUTION 667
September 16, 1990

The Security Council,

Reaffirming its resolutions 660 (1990), 661 (1990), 662 (1990), 664 (1990), 665 (1990) and 666 (1990),

Recalling the Vienna Conventions of 18 April 1961 on diplomatic relations and of 24 April 1963 on consular relations, to both of which Iraq is a party,

Considering that the decision of Iraq to order the closure of diplomatic and consular missions in Kuwait and to withdraw the immunity and privileges of these missions and their personnel is contrary to the decisions of the Security Council, the international Conventions mentioned above and international law,

Deeply concerned that Iraq, notwithstanding the decisions of the Security Council and the provisions of the Conventions mentioned above, has committed acts of violence against diplomatic missions and their personnel in Kuwait,

Outraged at recent violations by Iraq of diplomatic premises in Kuwait and at the abduction of personnel enjoying diplomatic immunity and foreign nationals who were present in these premises,

Considering that the above actions by Iraq constitute aggressive acts and a flagrant violation of its international obligations which strike at the root of the conduct of international relations in accordance with the Charter of the United Nations,

Recalling that Iraq is fully responsible for any use of violence against foreign nationals or against any diplomatic or consular mission in Kuwait or its personnel,

Determined to ensure respect for its decisions and for Article 25 of the Charter of the United Nations,

Further considering that the grave nature of Iraq's actions, which constitute a new escalation of its violations of international law, obliges the Council not only to express its immediate reaction but also to consult urgently to take further concrete measures to ensure Iraq's compliance with the Council's resolutions,

Acting under Chapter VII of the Charter of the United Nations,

1. *Strongly condemns* aggressive acts perpetrated by Iraq against diplomatic premises and personnel in Kuwait, including the abduction of foreign nationals who were present in those premises;

2. *Demands* the immediate release of those foreign nationals as well as all nationals mentioned in resolution 664 (1990);

3. *Further demands* that Iraq immediately and fully comply with its international obligations under resolutions 660 (1990), 662 (1990) and 664 (1990) of the Security Council, the Vienna Conventions on diplomatic and consular relations and international law;

4. *Further demands* that Iraq immediately protect the safety and well-being of diplomatic and consular personnel and premises in Kuwait and in Iraq and take no action to hinder the diplomatic and consular missions in the performance of their functions, including access to their nationals and the protection of their person and interests;

5. *Reminds* all States that they are obliged to observe strictly resolutions 661 (1990), 662 (1990), 664 (1990), 665 (1990) and 666 (1990);

6. *Decides* to consult urgently to take further concrete measures as soon as possible, under Chapter VII of the Charter, in response to Iraq's continued violation of the Charter, of resolutions of the Council and of international law.

VOTE: Unanimous (15–0)

RESOLUTION 669
September 24, 1990

The Security Council,

Recalling its resolution 661 (1990) of 6 August 1990,

Recalling also Article 50 of the Charter of the United Nations,

Conscious of the fact that an increasing number of requests for assistance have been received under the provisions of Article 50 of the Charter of the United Nations,

Entrusts the Committee established under resolution 661 (1990) concerning the situation between Iraq and Kuwait with the task of examining requests for assistance under the provisions of Article 50 of the Charter of the United Nations and making recommendations to the President of the Security Council for appropriate action.

VOTE: Unanimous (15–0)

RESOLUTION 670
September 25, 1990

The Security Council

Reaffirming its resolutions 660 (1990), 661 (1990), 662 (1990), 664 (1990), 665 (1990), 666 (1990), and 667 (1990);

Condemning Iraq's continued occupation of Kuwait, its failure to rescind its actions and end its purported annexation and its holding of third State nationals against their will, in flagrant violation of resolutions 660 (1990), 662 (1990), 664 (1990), and 667 (1990) and of international humanitarian law;

Condemning further the treatment by Iraqi forces of Kuwaiti nationals, including measures to force them to leave their own country and mistreatment of persons and property in Kuwait in violation of international law,

Noting with grave concern the persistent attempts to evade the measures laid down in resolution 661 (1990),

Further noting that a number of States have limited the number of Iraqi diplomatic and consular officials in their countries and that others are planning to do so,

Determined to ensure by all necessary means the strict and complete application of the measures laid down in resolution 661 (1990),

Determined to ensure respect for its decisions and the provisions of Articles 25 and 48 of the Charter of the United Nations,

Affirming that any acts of the Government of Iraq which are contrary to the above-mentioned resolutions or to Articles 25 or 48 of the Charter of the United Nations, such as Decree No. 377 of the Revolution Command Council of Iraq of 16 September 1990, are null and void,

Reaffirming its determination to ensure compliance with Security Council resolutions by maximum use of political and diplomatic means,

Welcoming the Secretary-General's use of his good offices to advance a peaceful solution based on the relevant Security Council resolutions and noting with appreciation his continuing efforts to this end,

Underlining to the Government of Iraq that its continued failure to comply with the terms of resolutions 660 (1990), 661 (1990), 662 (1990), 664 (1990), 666 (1990) and 667 (1990) could lead to further serious action by the Council under the Charter of the United Nations, including under Chapter VII,

Recalling the provisions of Article 103 of the Charter of the United Nations,

Acting under Chapter VII of the Charter of the United Nations,

1. *Calls upon* all States to carry out their obligations to ensure strict and complete compliance with resolution 661 (1990) and in particular paragraphs 3, 4 and 5 thereof;

2. *Confirms* that resolution 661 (1990) applies to all means of transport, including aircraft;

3. *Decides* that all States, notwithstanding the existence of any rights or obligations conferred or imposed by any international agreement or any contract entered into or any licence or permit granted before the date of the present resolution, shall deny permission to any aircraft to take off from their territory if the aircraft would carry any cargo to or from Iraq or Kuwait other than food in humanitarian circumstances, subject to authorization by the Council or the Committee established by resolution 661 (1990) and in accordance with resolution 666 (1990), or supplies intended strictly for medical purposes or solely for UNIIMOG [the United Nations Iran-Iraq Military Observer Group];

4. *Decides further* that all States shall deny permission to any aircraft destined to land in Iraq or Kuwait, whatever its State of registration, to overfly its territory unless:

(a) The aircraft lands at an airfield designated by that State outside Iraq or Kuwait in order to permit its inspection to ensure that there is no cargo on board in violation of resolution 661 (1990) or the present resolution, and for this purpose the aircraft may be detained for as long as necessary; or

(b) The particular flight has been approved by the Committee established by resolution 661 (1990); or

(c) The flight is certified by the United Nations as solely for the purposes of UNIIMOG;

5. *Decides* that each State shall take all necessary measures to ensure that any aircraft registered in its territory or operated by an operator who has his principal place of business or permanent residence in its territory complies with the provisions of resolution 661 (1990) and the present resolution;

6. *Decides further* that all States shall notify in a timely fashion the Committee established by resolution 661 (1990) of any flight between its territory and Iraq or Kuwait to which the requirement to land in paragraph 4 above does not apply, and the purpose for such a flight;

7. *Calls upon* all States to cooperate in taking such measures as may be necessary, consistent with international law, including the Chicago Convention, to ensure the effective implementation of the provisions of resolution 661 (1990) or the present resolution;

8. *Calls upon* all States to detain any ships of Iraqi registry which enter their ports and which are being or have been used in violation of resolution 661 (1990), or to deny such ships entrance to their ports except in circumstances recognized under international law as necessary to safeguard human life;

9. *Reminds* all States of their obligations under resolution 661 (1990) with regard to the freezing of Iraqi assets, and the protection of the assets of the legitimate Government of Kuwait and its agencies, located within their territory and to report to the Committee established under resolution 661 (1990) regarding those assets;

10. *Calls upon* all States to provide to the Committee established by resolution 661 (1990) information regarding the action taken by them to implement the provisions laid down in the present resolution;

11. *Affirms* that the United Nations Organization, the specialized agencies and other international organizations in the United Nations system are required to take such measures as may be necessary to give effect to the terms of resolution 661 (1990) and this resolution;

12. *Decides* to consider, in the event of evasion of the provisions of resolution 661 (1990) or of the present resolution by a State or its nationals or through its territory, measures directed at the State in question to prevent such evasion;

13. *Reaffirms* that the Fourth Geneva Convention applies to Kuwait and that as a High Contracting Party to the Convention Iraq is bound to comply fully with all its terms and in particular is liable under the Convention in respect of the grave breaches committed by it, as are individuals who commit or order the commission of grave breaches.

VOTE: 14 for, 1 against (Cuba)

RESOLUTION 674
October 29, 1990

The Security Council,

Recalling its resolutions 660 (1990), 661 (1990), 662 (1990), 664 (1990), 665 (1990), 666 (1990), 667 (1990) and 670 (1990),

Stressing the urgent need for the immediate and unconditional withdrawal of all Iraqi forces from Kuwait, for the restoration of Kuwait's sovereignty, independence and territorial integrity and of the authority of its legitimate government,

Condemning the actions by the Iraqi authorities and occupying forces to take third-State nationals hostage and to mistreat and oppress Kuwaiti and third-State nationals, and the other actions reported to the Security Council, such as the destruction of Kuwaiti demographic records, the forced departure of Kuwaitis, the relocation of population in Kuwait and the unlawful destruction and seizure of public and private property in Kuwait, including hospital supplies and equipment, in violation of the decisions of the Council, the Charter of the United Nations, the Fourth Geneva Convention, the Vienna Conventions on Diplomatic and Consular Relations and international law,

Expressing grave alarm over the situation of nationals of third States in Kuwait and Iraq, including the personnel of the diplomatic and consular missions of such States,

Reaffirming that the Fourth Geneva Convention applies to Kuwait and that as a High Contracting Party to the Convention Iraq is bound to comply fully with all its terms and in particular is liable under the Convention in respect of the grave breaches committed by it, as are individuals who commit or order the commission of grave breaches,

Recalling the efforts of the Secretary-General concerning the safety and well-being of third-State nationals in Iraq and Kuwait,

Deeply concerned at the economic cost and at the loss and suffering caused to individuals in Kuwait and Iraq as a result of the invasion and occupation of Kuwait by Iraq,

Acting under Chapter VII of the Charter of the United Nations,

Reaffirming the goal of the international community of maintaining international peace and security by seeking to resolve international disputes and conflicts through peaceful means,

Recalling the important role that the United Nations and its Secretary-General have played in the peaceful solution of disputes and conflicts in conformity with the provisions of the Charter,

Alarmed by the dangers of the present crisis caused by the Iraqi invasion and occupation of Kuwait, which directly threaten international peace and security, and seeking to avoid any further worsening of the situation,

Calling upon Iraq to comply with the relevant resolutions of the Security Council, in particular its resolutions 660 (1990), 662 (1990) and 664 (1990),

Reaffirming its determination to ensure compliance by Iraq with the Security Council resolutions by maximum use of political and diplomatic means,

1. *Demands* that the Iraqi authorities and occupying forces immediately cease and desist from taking third-State nationals hostage, mistreating and oppressing Kuwaiti and third-State nationals and any other actions, such as those reported to the Security Council and described above, that violate the decisions of this Council, the Charter of the United Nations, the Fourth Geneva Convention, the Vienna Conventions on Diplomatic and Consular Relations and international law;

2. *Invites* States to collate substantiated information in their possession or submitted to them on the grave breaches by Iraq as per paragraph 1 above and to make this information available to the Security Council;

3. *Reaffirms* its demand that Iraq immediately fulfil its obligations to third-State nationals in Kuwait and Iraq, including the personnel of diplomatic and consular missions, under the Charter, the Fourth Geneva Convention, the Vienna Conventions on Diplomatic and Consular Relations, general principles of international law and the relevant resolutions of the Council;

4. *Also reaffirms* its demand that Iraq permit and facilitate the immediate departure from Kuwait and Iraq of those third-State nationals, including diplomatic and consular personnel, who wish to leave;

5. *Demands* that Iraq ensure the immediate access to food, water and basic

services necessary to the protection and well-being of Kuwaiti nationals and of nationals of third States in Kuwait and Iraq, including the personnel of diplomatic and consular missions in Kuwait;

6. *Reaffirms* its demand that Iraq immediately protect the safety and well-being of diplomatic and consular personnel and premises in Kuwait and in Iraq, take no action to hinder these diplomatic and consular missions in the performance of their functions, including access to their nationals and the protection of their person and interests and rescind its orders for the closure of diplomatic and consular missions in Kuwait and the withdrawal of the immunity of their personnel;

7. *Requests* the Secretary-General, in the context of the continued exercise of his good offices concerning the safety and well-being of third-State nationals in Iraq and Kuwait, to seek to achieve the objectives of paragraphs 4, 5 and 6 above and in particular the provision of food, water and basic services to Kuwaiti nationals and to the diplomatic and consular missions in Kuwait and the evacuation of third-State nationals;

8. *Reminds* Iraq that under international law it is liable for any loss, damage or injury arising in regard to Kuwait and third States, and their nationals and corporations, as a result of the invasion and illegal occupation of Kuwait by Iraq;

9. *Invites* States to collect relevant information regarding their claims, and those of their nationals and corporations, for restitution or financial compensation by Iraq with a view to such arrangements as may be established in accordance with international law;

10. *Requires* that Iraq comply with the provisions of the present resolution and its previous resolutions, failing which the Security Council will need to take further measures under the Charter;

11. *Decides* to remain actively and permanently seized of the matter until Kuwait has regained its independence and peace has been restored in conformity with the relevant resolutions of the Security Council;

12. *Reposes* its trust in the Secretary-General to make available his good offices and, as he considers appropriate, to pursue them and to undertake diplomatic efforts in order to reach a peaceful solution to the crisis caused by the Iraqi invasion and occupation of Kuwait on the basis of Security Council resolutions 660 (1990), 662 (1990) and 664 (1990), and calls upon all States, both those in the region and others, to pursue on this basis their efforts to this end, in conformity with the Charter, in order to improve the situation and restore peace, security and stability;

13. *Requests* the Secretary-General to report to the Security Council on the results of his good offices and diplomatic efforts.

VOTE: 13 for, 2 against (Cuba and Yemen)

RESOLUTION 677
November 28, 1990

The Security Council,

Recalling its resolutions 660 (1990) of 2 August 1990, 662 (1990) of 9 August 1990 and 674 (1990) of 29 October 1990,

Reiterating its concern for the suffering caused to individuals in Kuwait as a result of the invasion and occupation of Kuwait by Iraq,

Gravely concerned at the ongoing attempt by Iraq to alter the demographic composition of the population of Kuwait and to destroy the civil records maintained by the legitimate Government of Kuwait,

Acting under Chapter VII of the Charter of the United Nations,

1. *Condemns* the attempts by Iraq to alter the demographic composition of the population of Kuwait and to destroy the civil records maintained by the legitimate Government of Kuwait;

2. *Mandates* the Secretary-General to take custody of a copy of the population register of Kuwait, the authenticity of which has been certified by the legitimate Government of Kuwait and which covers the registration of the population up to 1 August 1990;

3. *Requests* the Secretary-General to establish, in co-operation with the legitimate Government of Kuwait, an Order of Rules and Regulations governing access to and use of the said copy of the population register.

VOTE: Unanimous (15–0)

RESOLUTION 678
November 29, 1990

The Security Council,

Recalling, and reaffirming its resolutions 660 (1990) of 2 August 1990, 661 (1990) of 6 August 1990, 662 (1990) of 9 August 1990, 664 (1990) of 18 August 1990, 665 (1990) of 25 August 1990, 666 (1990) of 13 September 1990, 667 (1990) of 16 September 1990, 669 (1990) of 24 September 1990, 670 (1990) of 25 September 1990, 674 (1990) of 29 October 1990 and 677 (1990) of 28 November 1990,

Noting that, despite all efforts by the United Nations, Iraq refuses to comply with its obligation to implement resolution 660 (1990) and the above-mentioned subsequent relevant resolutions, in flagrant contempt of the Security Council,

Mindful of its duties and responsibilities under the Charter of the United Nations for the maintenance and preservation of international peace and security,

Determined to secure full compliance with its decisions,

Acting under Chapter VII of the Charter of the United Nations,

1. *Demands* that Iraq comply fully with resolution 660 (1990) and all subsequent relevant resolutions, and decides, while maintaining all its decisions, to allow Iraq one final opportunity, as a pause of goodwill, to do so;

2. *Authorizes* Member States cooperating with the Government of Kuwait, unless Iraq on or before 15 January 1991 fully implements, as set forth in paragraph 1 above, the foregoing resolutions, to use all necessary means to uphold and implement resolution 660 (1990) and all subsequent relevant resolutions and to restore international peace and security in the area;

3. *Requests* all States to provide appropriate support for the actions undertaken in pursuance of paragraph 2 of the present resolution;

4. *Requests* the States concerned to keep the Security Council regularly informed on the progress of actions undertaken pursuant to paragraphs 2 and 3 of the present resolution;

5. *Decides* to remain seized of the matter.

VOTE: 12 for, 2 against (Cuba and Yemen), 1 abstention (China)

RESOLUTION 686
March 2, 1991

The Security Council,

   Recalling and reaffirming its resolutions 660 (1990), 661 (1990), 662 (1990), 664 (1990), 665 (1990), 666 (1990), 667 (1990), 669 (1990), 670 (1990), 674 (1990), 677 (1990) and 678 (1990),

   Recalling the obligations of member states under Article 25 of the Charter,

   Recalling paragraph 9 of resolution 661 (1990) regarding assistance to the Government of Kuwait and paragraph 3 (c) of that resolution regarding supplies strictly for medical purposes and, in humanitarian circumstances, foodstuffs,

   Taking note of the letters of the Foreign Minister of Iraq confirming Iraq's agreement to comply fully with all of the resolutions noted above (S/22275), and stating its intention to release prisoners of war immediately (S/22273),

   Taking note of the suspension of offensive combat operations by the forces of Kuwait and the member states cooperating with Kuwait pursuant to resolution 678 (1990),

   Bearing in mind the need to be assured of Iraq's peaceful intentions, and the objective in resolution 678 (1990) of restoring international peace and security in the region,

   Underlining the importance of Iraq taking the necessary measures which would permit a definitive end to the hostilities,

   Affirming the commitment of all member states to the independence, sovereignty and territorial integrity of Iraq and Kuwait, and noting the intention expressed by the member states cooperating under paragraph 2 of Security Council resolution 678 (1990) to bring their military presence in Iraq to an end as soon as possible consistent with achieving the objective of the resolution,

Acting under Chapter VII of the Charter of the United Nations,

1. *Affirms* that all 12 resolutions noted above continue to have full force and effect;

2. *Demands* that Iraq implement its acceptance of all 12 resolutions noted above and in particular that Iraq:

(a) Rescind immediately its actions purporting to annex Kuwait;

(b) Accept in principle its liability under international law for any loss, damage or injury arising in regard to Kuwait and third states, and their nationals and corporations, as a result of the invasion and illegal occupation of Kuwait by Iraq;

(c) Immediately release under the auspices of the International Committee of the Red Cross, Red Cross Societies or Red Crescent Societies, all Kuwaiti and third-country nationals detained by Iraq and return the remains of any deceased Kuwaiti and third-country nationals so detained; and

(d) Immediately begin to return all Kuwaiti property seized by Iraq, to be completed in the shortest possible period;

3. *Further demands* that Iraq:

(a) Cease hostile or provocative actions by its forces against all member states, including missile attacks and flights of combat aircraft;

(b) Designate military commanders to meet with counterparts from the forces of Kuwait and the member states cooperating with Kuwait pursuant to resolution 678 (1990) to arrange for the military aspects of a cessation of hostilities at the earliest possible time;

(c) Arrange for immediate access to and release of all prisoners of war under the auspices of the International Committee of the Red Cross and return the remains of any deceased personnel of the forces of Kuwait and the member states cooperating with Kuwait pursuant to resolution 678 (1990); and

(d) Provide all information and assistance in identifying Iraqi mines, booby traps and other explosives as well as any chemical and biological weapons and material in Kuwait, in areas of Iraq where forces of member states cooperating with Kuwait pursuant to resolution 678 (1990) are present temporarily, and in adjacent waters.

4. *Recognizes* that during the period required for Iraq to comply with paragraphs 2 and 3 above, the provisions of paragraph 2 of resolution 678 (1990) remain valid;

5. *Welcomes* the decision of Kuwait and the member states cooperating with Kuwait pursuant to resolution 678 (1990) to provide access and to commence immediately the release of Iraqi prisoners of war as required by the terms of the Third Geneva Convention of 1949, under the auspices of the International Committee of the Red Cross;

6. *Requests* all member states, as well as the United Nations, the specialized

agencies and other international organizations in the United Nations system, to take all appropriate action to cooperate with the Government and people of Kuwait in the reconstruction of their country;

7. *Decides* that Iraq shall notify the Secretary-General and the Security Council when it has taken the actions set out above;

8. *Decides* that in order to secure the rapid establishment of a definitive end to the hostilities, the Security Council remains actively seized of the matter.

VOTE: 11 for, 1 against (Cuba), 3 abstentions (Yemen, China, and India)

RESOLUTION 687
April 2, 1991

The Security Council,

Recalling its Resolutions 660 (1990), 661 (1990), 662 (1990), 664 (1990), 665 (1990), 666 (1990), 667 (1990), 669 (1990), 670 (1990), 674 (1990), 677 (1990), 678 (1990), 686 (1991) [and]

Welcoming the restoration to Kuwait of its sovereignty, independence, and territorial integrity and the return of its legitimate Government,

1. *Affirms* all 13 resolutions noted above, except as expressly changed below to achieve the goals of this resolution, including a formal cease-fire;

2. *Demands* that Iraq and Kuwait respect the inviolability of the international boundary and the allocation of islands set out in the "Agreed Minutes Between the State of Kuwait and the Republic of Iraq Regarding the Restoration of Friendly Relations and Related Matters," signed at Baghdad on 4 October 1963 . . . ;

3. *Calls on* the Secretary-General to lend his assistance to make arrangements with Iraq and Kuwait to demarcate the boundary between Iraq and Kuwait . . . ;

4. *Decides* to guarantee the inviolability of the above-mentioned international boundary and to take as appropriate all necessary measures to that end in accordance with the Charter;

5. *Requests* the Secretary-General, after consulting with Iraq and Kuwait, to submit within three days to the Security Council for its approval a plan for the immediate deployment of a United Nations observer unit to monitor the Khor Abdullah and a demilitarized zone, which is hereby established, extending 10 kilometers into Iraq and 5 kilometers into Kuwait from the boundary . . . ;

6. *Notes* that the deployment of the United Nations observer unit as soon as possible will establish the conditions for the forces of the member states cooperating with Kuwait in accordance with resolution 678 (1990) to bring their military presence in Iraq to an end consistent with resolution 686 (1991);

7. *Invites* Iraq to reaffirm unconditionally its obligations under the Geneva Protocol for the Prohibition of the Use in War of Asphyxiating, Poisonous or Other Gases, and of Bacteriological Methods of Warfare . . . and to ratify the

Convention on the Prohibition of the Development, Production and Stockpiling of Bacteriological (Biological) and Toxin Weapons and on Their Destruction . . . ;

8. *Decides* that Iraq unconditionally accept the destruction, removal, or rendering harmless, under international supervision, of:

(a) all chemical and biological weapons and all stocks of agents; and all related subsystems and components and all research, development, support and manufacturing facilities;

(b) all ballistic missiles with a range greater than 150 kilometers and related major parts, and repair and production facilities;

9. *Decides,* for the implementation of paragraph 8 above, the following:

(a) Iraq shall submit to the Secretary-General, within 15 days of the adoption of this resolution, a declaration of the locations, amounts and types of all items specified in paragraph 8 and agree to urgent, on-site inspection as specified below;

(b) the Secretary-General, in consultation with the appropriate governments and, where appropriate, with the director general of the World Health Organization, within 45 days of the passage of this resolution, shall develop, and submit to the Council for approval, a plan calling for the completion of the following acts within 45 days of such approval:

(i) The forming of a special commission which shall carry out immediate on-site inspection of Iraq's biological, chemical and missile capabilities . . . ;

(ii) The yielding by Iraq of possession to the special commission for destruction, removal or rendering harmless . . . of all other items notified under paragraph 8 (a) above . . . and the destruction by Iraq, under supervision of the special commission, of all its missile capabilities including launchers as specified under paragraph 8 (b) above;

10. *Decides* that Iraq shall unconditionally undertake not to use, develop, construct or acquire any of the items specified in paragraphs 8 and 9 above and requests the Secretary-General, in consultation with the Special Commission, to develop a plan for the future ongoing monitoring and verification of Iraq's compliance with this paragraph, to be submitted to the Council for approval within 120 days of the passage of this resolution;

11. *Invites* Iraq to reaffirm unconditionally its obligations under the Treaty on the Non-Proliferation of Nuclear Weapons . . . ;

12. *Decides* that Iraq shall unconditionally agree not to acquire or develop nuclear weapons or nuclear-weapons-usable material or any subsystems or components or any research, development, support or manufacturing facilities related to the above; to submit to the Secretary-General and the Director-General of the International Atomic Energy Agency within 15 days of the adoption of this resolution a declaration of the locations, amounts and types of all items specified above; to place all of its nuclear-weapons-usable materials under the exclusive control, for custody and removal, of the IAEA, with the assistance and cooperation of the

Special Commission as provided for in the plan of the Secretary-General discussed in paragraph 9 (b) above; to accept, in accordance with the arrangements provided for in paragraph 13 below, urgent, on-site inspection and the destruction, removal, or rendering harmless of all items specified above; and to accept the plan discussed in paragraph 13 below for the future ongoing monitoring and verification of its compliance with these undertakings;

13. *Requests* the Director-General of the International Atomic Energy Agency . . . to carry out immediate on-site inspection of Iraq's nuclear capabilities based on Iraq's declarations and the designation of any additional locations by the special commission; to develop a plan for the submission to the Security Council within 45 days calling for the destruction, removal or rendering harmless of all items listed in paragraph 12 above, to carry out the plan within 45 days following approval by the Security Council; and to develop a plan . . . for the future ongoing monitoring and verification of Iraq's compliance with paragraph 12 above . . . ;

14. *Takes note* that the actions to be taken by Iraq in paragraphs 8, 9, 10, 11, 12 and 13 of this resolution represent steps toward the goal of establishing in the Middle East a zone free from weapons of mass destruction and all missiles for their delivery and the objective of a global ban on chemical weapons;

15. *Requests* the Secretary-General to report to the Security Council on the steps taken to facilitate the return of all Kuwaiti property seized by Iraq, including a list of any property which Kuwait claims has not been returned or which has not been returned intact;

16. *Reaffirms* that Iraq . . . is liable under international law for any direct loss, damage, including environmental damage and the depletion of natural resources, or injury to foreign governments, nationals and corporations, as a result of Iraq's unlawful invasion and occupation of Kuwait;

17. *Decides* that all Iraqi statements made since August 2, 1990, repudiating its foreign debt are null and void, and demands that Iraq scrupulously adhere to all of its obligations concerning servicing and repayment of its foreign debt;

18. *Decides* to create a fund to pay compensation for claims that fall within paragraph 16 above and to establish a commission that will administer the fund;

19. *Directs* the Secretary-General to develop and present to the Council for decision, no later than 30 days following the adoption of this resolution, recommendations for the fund to meet the requirement for the payment of claims established in accordance with paragraph 18 above and for a program to implement the decisions in paragraphs 16, 17, and 18 above, including: administration of the fund; mechanisms for determining the appropriate level of Iraq's contribution to the fund based on a percentage of the value of the exports of petroleum and petroleum products from Iraq not to exceed a figure to be suggested to the Council by the Secretary-General, taking into account the requirements of the people of Iraq and in particular humanitarian needs, Iraq's payment capacity as assessed in conjunction with the international financial institutions taking into consideration

external debt service, and the needs of the Iraqi economy; arrangements for ensuring that payments are made to the fund . . . ;

20. *Decides,* effective immediately, that the prohibitions against the sale or supply to Iraq of commodities or products, and prohibitions against financial transactions related thereto, contained in resolution 661 (1990) shall not apply to foodstuffs notified to the committee established in resolution 661 (1990) or, with the approval of that Committee, under simplified and accelerated procedures, to materials and supplies for essential civilian needs as identified in the report of the Secretary-General dated 20 March 1991, and in any further findings of humanitarian need by the Committee;

21. *Decides* that the Council shall review the provisions of paragraph 20 above every 60 days in light of the policies and practices of the Government of Iraq, including the implementation of all relevant resolutions of the Security Council, for the purpose of determining whether to modify further or lift the prohibitions referred to therein;

22. *Decides* that upon the approval of the Security Council of the program called for in paragraph 19 above and of the completion by Iraq of all actions contemplated in paragraphs 8, 9, 10, 11, 12 and 13 above, the prohibitions against financial transactions related thereto contained in resolution 661 (1990) shall have no further force or effect;

23. *Decides* that, pending action by the Security Council under paragraph 22 above, the committee established under resolution 661 shall be empowered to approve, when required to assure adequate financial resources on the part of Iraq to carry out the activities under paragraph 20 above, exceptions to the prohibition against the import of commodities and products originating in Iraq;

24. *Decides* that, in accordance with resolution 661 (1990) and subsequent related resolutions and until a further decision is taken by the Council, all states shall continue to prevent the sale or supply, or promotion or facilitation of such sale or supply, to Iraq by their nationals, or from their territories or using their flag vessels or aircraft, of:

(a) arms and related matériel of all types, specifically including the sale or transfer through other means of all forms of conventional military equipment, including for paramilitary forces, and spare parts and components and their means of production, for such equipment;

(b) items specified and defined in paragraph 8 and paragraph 12 above not otherwise covered above;

(c) technology under licensing or other transfer arrangements used in the production, utilization or stockpiling of items specified in subparagraphs (a) and (b) above;

(d) personnel or materials training or technical support services relating to the design, development, manufacture, use, maintenance or support of items specified in subparagraphs (a) and (b) above;

25. *Calls upon* all states and international organizations to act strictly in accordance with paragraph 24 . . . ;

26. *Requests* the Secretary-General . . . to develop within 60 days, for approval of the Council, guidelines to facilitate full international implementation of paragraphs 24 and 25 above and paragraph 27 below . . . ;

27. *Calls upon* all states to maintain such national controls and procedures and to take such other actions consistent with the guidelines to be established by the Security Council under paragraph 26 above as may be necessary to insure compliance with the terms of paragraph 24 above, and calls upon international organizations to take all appropriate steps to assist in insuring such full compliance;

28. *Agrees* to review its decisions in paragraphs 22, 23, 24 and 25 above, except for the items specified and defined in paragraphs 8 and 12 above, on a regular basis and in any case 120 days following passage of this resolution, taking into account Iraq's compliance with this resolution and general progress toward the control of armaments in the region;

29. *Decides* that all states, including Iraq, shall take the necessary measures to ensure that no claim shall lie at the instance of the Government of Iraq, or of any person or body in Iraq, or of any person claiming through or for the benefit of any such person or body, in connection with any contract or other transaction where its performance was affected by reason of the measures taken by the Security Council in resolution 661 (1990) and related resolutions;

30. *Decides* that, in furtherance of its commitment to facilitate the repatriation of all Kuwaiti and third-country nationals, Iraq shall extend all necessary cooperation to the International Committee of the Red Cross, providing lists of such persons, facilitating the access of the International Committee of the Red Cross to all such persons wherever located or detained and facilitating the search by the International Committee of the Red Cross for those Kuwaiti and third-country nationals still unaccounted for;

31. *Invites* the International Committee of the Red Cross to keep the Secretary General apprised as appropriate of all activities undertaken in connection with facilitating the repatriation or return of all Kuwaiti and third-country nationals or their remains present in Iraq on or after August 2, 1990;

32. *Requires* Iraq to inform the Council that it will not commit or support any act of international terrorism or allow any organization directed toward commission of such acts to operate within its territory and to condemn unequivocally and renounce all acts, methods, and practices of terrorism;

33. *Declares* that, upon official notification by Iraq to the Secretary-General and to the Security Council of its acceptance of the provisions above, a formal cease-fire is effective between Iraq and Kuwait and the member states cooperating with Kuwait in accordance with resolution 678 (1990);

34. *Decides* to remain seized of the matter and to take such further steps as may

be required for the implementation of this resolution and to secure peace and security in the area.

VOTE: 12 for, 1 against (Cuba), 2 abstentions (Ecuador and Yemen)

RESOLUTION 688
April 5, 1991

The Security Council,

Mindful of its duties and its responsibilities under the Charter of the United Nations for the maintenance of international peace and security,

Also mindful of Chapter I, Article 2, paragraph 7 of the Charter of the United Nations,

Gravely concerned by the repression of the Iraqi civilian population in many parts of Iraq, including most recently in Kurdish populated areas which led to a massive flow of refugees toward and across international frontiers and to cross border incursions, which threaten international peace and security in the region,

Deeply disturbed by the magnitude of the human suffering involved,

Taking note of the letters sent by the representatives of Turkey and France to the United Nations dated 2 April 1991 and 4 April 1991, respectively (S/22435 and S/22442),

Reaffirming the commitment of all Member States to the sovereignty, territorial integrity and political independence of Iraq and of all States in the area,

Bearing in mind the Secretary-General's report of 20 March 1991 (S/22366),

1. *Condemns* the repression of the Iraqi civilian population in many parts of Iraq, including most recently in Kurdish populated areas, the consequences of which threaten international peace and security in the region;

2. *Demands* that Iraq, as a contribution to remove the threat to international peace and security in the region, immediately end this repression and express the hope in the same context that an open dialogue will take place to ensure that the human and political rights of all Iraqi citizens are respected;

3. *Insists* that Iraq allow immediate access by international humanitarian organizations to all those in need of assistance in all parts of Iraq and to make available all necessary facilities for their operations;

4. *Requests* the Secretary-General to pursue his humanitarian efforts in Iraq and to report forthwith, if appropriate on the basis of a further mission to the region, on the plight of the Iraqi civilian population, and in particular the Kurdish population, suffering from the repression in all its forms inflicted by the Iraqi authorities;

5. *Requests* further the Secretary-General to use all the resources at his disposal,

including those of the relevant United Nations agencies, to address urgently the critical needs of the refugees and displaced Iraqi population;

6. *Appeals* to all Member States and to all humanitarian organizations to contribute to these humanitarian relief efforts;

7. *Demands* that Iraq cooperate with the Secretary-General to these ends;

8. *Decides* to remain seized of the matter.

VOTE: 10 for, 3 against (Cuba, Yemen, and Zimbabwe), 2 abstentions (China and India)

RESOLUTION 689
April 9, 1991

The Security Council,

Recalling its resolution 687 (1991),

Acting under Chapter VII of the Charter of the United Nations,

1. *Approves* the report of the Secretary-General on the implementation of paragraph 5 of Security Council resolution 687 (1991) contained in document S/22454 and Add. 1–3 of 5 and 9 April 1991, respectively;

2. *Notes* that the decision to set up the observer unit was taken in paragraph 5 of resolution 687 (1991) and can only be terminated by a decision of the Council; the Council shall therefore review the question of termination or continuation every six months;

3. *Decides* that the modalities for the initial six-month period of the United Nations Iraq-Kuwait Observation Mission shall be in accordance with the above-mentioned report and shall also be reviewed every six months.

VOTE: Unanimous (15–0)

RESOLUTION 692
May 20, 1991

The Security Council,

Recalling its resolutions 674 (1990) of 29 October 1990, 686 (1991) of 2 March 1991 and 687 (1991) of 3 April 1991, concerning the liability of Iraq, without prejudice to its debts and obligations arising prior to 2 August 1990, for any direct loss, damage, including environmental damage and the depletion of natural resources, or injury to foreign Governments, nationals and corporations as a result of Iraq's unlawful invasion and occupation of Kuwait,

Taking note of the Secretary-General's report of 2 May 1991 (S/22559), submitted in accordance with paragraph 19 of resolution 687 (1991),

Acting under Chapter VII of the Charter of the United Nations,

1. *Expresses its appreciation* to the Secretary-General for his report of 2 May 1991;

2. *Welcomes the fact* that the Secretary-General will now undertake the appropriate consultations requested by paragraph 19 of resolution 687 (1991) so that he will be in a position to recommend to the Security Council for decision as soon as possible the figure which the level of Iraq's contribution to the Fund will not exceed;

3. *Decides* to establish the Fund and the Commission referred to in paragraph 18 of resolution 687 (1991) in accordance with section I of the Secretary-General's report, and that the Governing Council will be located at the United Nations Office at Geneva and that the Governing Council may decide whether some of the activities of the Commission should be carried out elsewhere;

4. *Requests* the Secretary-General to take the actions necessary to implement paragraphs 2 and 3 above in consultation with the members of the Governing Council;

5. *Directs* the Governing Council to proceed in an expeditious manner to implement the provisions of section E of resolution 687 (1991), taking into account the recommendations in section II of the Secretary-General's report;

6. *Decides* that the requirement for Iraqi contributions will apply in the manner to be prescribed by the Governing Council with respect to all Iraqi petroleum and petroleum products exported from Iraq after 2 April 1991 as well as such petroleum and petroleum products exported earlier but not delivered or not paid for as a specific result of the prohibitions contained in Security Council resolution 661 (1990);

7. *Requests* the Governing Council to report as soon as possible on the actions it has taken with regard to the mechanisms for determining the appropriate level of Iraq's contribution to the Fund and the arrangements for ensuring that payments are made to the Fund, so that the Security Council can give its approval in accordance with paragraph 22 of resolution 687 (1991);

8. *Requests* that all States and international organizations cooperate with the decisions of the Governing Council taken pursuant to paragraph 5 of the present resolution, and also requests that the Governing Council keep the Security Council informed on this matter;

9. *Decides* that, if the Governing Council notifies the Security Council that Iraq has failed to carry out decisions of the Governing Council taken pursuant to paragraph 5 of the present resolution, the Security Council intends to retain or to take action to reimpose the prohibition against the import of petroleum and petroleum products originating in Iraq and financial transactions related thereto;

10. *Decides also* to remain seized of this matter and that the Governing Council will submit periodic reports to the Secretary-General and the Security Council.

VOTE: 14 for, 0 against, 1 abstention (Cuba)

RESOLUTION 699
June 17, 1991

The Security Council,
  Recalling its resolution 687 (1991),
  Taking note of the report of the Secretary-General of 17 May 1991 (S/22614), submitted to it in pursuance of paragraph 9 (b) of resolution 687 (1991),
  Also taking note of the Secretary-General's note of 17 May 1991 (S/22615), transmitting to the Council the letter addressed to him under paragraph 13 of the resolution by the Director-General of the International Atomic Energy Agency (IAEA),
  Acting under Chapter VII of the Charter of the United Nations,

  1. *Approves* the plan contained in the report of the Secretary-General;
  2. *Confirms* that the Special Commission and the IAEA have the authority to conduct activities under section C of resolution 687 (1991), for the purpose of the destruction, removal or rendering harmless of the items specified in paragraphs 8 and 12 of that resolution, after the 45-day period following the approval of this plan until such activities have been completed;
  3. *Requests* the Secretary-General to submit to the Security Council progress reports on the implementation of the plan referred to in paragraph 1 every six months after the adoption of this resolution;
  4. *Decides* to encourage the maximum assistance, in cash and in kind, from all Member States to ensure that activities under section C of resolution 687 (1991) are undertaken effectively and expeditiously; further decides, however, that the Government of Iraq shall be liable for the full costs of carrying out the tasks authorized by section C; and requests the Secretary-General to submit to the Council within 30 days for approval recommendations as to the most effective means by which Iraq's obligations in this respect may be fulfilled.

VOTE: Unanimous (15–0)

RESOLUTION 700
June 17, 1991

The Security Council,
  Recalling its resolutions 661 (1990) of 6 August 1990, 665 (1990) of 25 August 1990, 670 (1990) of 25 September 1990 and 687 (1991) of 3 April 1991,

Taking note of the Secretary-General's report of 2 June 1991 (S/22660) submitted pursuant to paragraph 26 of resolution 687 (1991),

Acting under Chapter VII of the Charter of the United Nations,

1. *Expresses its appreciation* to the Secretary-General for his report of 2 June 1991 (S/22660);

2. *Approves* the Guidelines to Facilitate Full International Implementation of paragraphs 24, 25, and 27 of Security Council resolution 687 (1991), annexed to the report of the Secretary-General (S/22660);

3. *Reiterates* its call upon all States and international organizations to act in a manner consistent with the Guidelines;

4. *Requests* all States, in accordance with paragraph 8 of the Guidelines, to report to the Secretary-General within 45 days on the measures they have instituted for meeting the obligations set out in paragraph 24 of resolution 687 (1991);

5. *Entrusts* the Committee established under resolution 661 (1990) concerning the situation between Iraq and Kuwait with the responsibility, under the Guidelines, for monitoring the prohibitions against the sale or supply of arms to Iraq and related sanctions established in paragraph 24 of resolution 687 (1991);

6. *Decides* to remain seized of the matter and to review the Guidelines at the same time as it reviews paragraphs 22, 23, 24, and 25 of resolution 687 (1991) as set out in paragraph 28 thereof.

VOTE: Unanimous (15–0)

RESOLUTION 705
August 15, 1991

The Security Council,

Having considered the note of 30 May 1991 of the Secretary-General pursuant to paragraph 13 of his report of 2 May 1991 (S/22559) which was annexed to the Secretary-General's letter of 30 May 1991 to the President of the Security Council (S/22661),

Acting under Chapter VII of the Charter of the United Nations,

1. *Expresses its appreciation* to the Secretary-General for his note of 30 May 1991 which was annexed to his letter to the President of the Security Council of the same date (S/22661);

2. *Decides* that in accordance with the suggestion made by the Secretary-General in paragraph 7 of his note of 30 May 1991, compensation to be paid by Iraq (as arising from section E of resolution 687) shall not exceed 30 percent of the annual value of the exports of petroleum and petroleum products from Iraq;

3. *Decides further,* in accordance with paragraph 8 of the Secretary-General's note

of 30 May 1991, to review the figure established in paragraph 2 above from time to time in light of data and assumptions contained in the letter of the Secretary-General (S/22661) and other relevant developments.

VOTE: Unanimous (15–0)

RESOLUTION 706
August 15, 1991

The Security Council,

Recalling its previous relevant resolutions and in particular resolutions 661 (1990), 686 (1991), 687 (1991), 688 (1991), 692 (1991), 699 (1991) and 705 (1991),

Taking note of the report (S/22799) dated 15 July 1991 of the inter-agency mission headed by the executive delegate of the Secretary-General for the United Nations inter-agency humanitarian program for Iraq, Kuwait and the Iraq/Turkey and Iraq/Iran border areas,

Concerned by the serious nutritional and health situation of the Iraqi civilian population as described in this report, and by the risk of a further deterioration of this situation,

Concerned also that the repatriation or return of all Kuwaitis and third-country nationals or their remains present in Iraq on or after 2 August 1990, pursuant to paragraph 2 (c) of resolution 686 (1991), and paragraphs 30 and 31 of resolution 687 (1991) has not yet been fully carried out,

Taking note of the conclusions of the above-mentioned report, and in particular of the proposal for oil sales by Iraq to finance the purchase of foodstuffs, medicines and materials and supplies for essential civilian needs for the purpose of providing humanitarian relief,

Taking note also of the letters dated 14 April 1991, 31 May 1991, 6 June 1991, 9 July 1991 and 22 July 1991 from the Minister of Foreign Affairs of Iraq and the Permanent Representative of Iraq to the Chairman of the committee established by resolution 661 (1990) concerning the export from Iraq of petroleum and petroleum products,

Convinced of the need for equitable distribution of humanitarian relief to all segments of the Iraqi civilian population through effective monitoring and transparency,

Recalling and reaffirming in this regard its resolution 688 (1991) and in particular the importance which the Council attaches to Iraq allowing unhindered access by international humanitarian organizations to all those in need of assistance in all parts of Iraq and making available all necessary facilities for their operation, and in this connection stressing the important and continuing role played by the Memorandum of Understanding between the United Nations and the Government of Iraq of 18 April 1991 (S/22663),

Recalling that, pursuant to resolutions 687 (1991), 692 (1991) and 699 (1991), Iraq is required to pay the full costs of the Special Commission and IAEA in carrying out the tasks authorized by section C of resolution 687 (1991), and that the Secretary-General in his report to the Security Council of 15 July 1991 (S/22792), submitted pursuant to paragraph 4 of resolution 699 (1991), expressed the view that the most obvious way of obtaining financial resources from Iraq to meet the costs of the Special Commission and the IAEA would be to authorize the sale of some Iraqi petroleum and petroleum products; recalling further that Iraq is required to pay its contributions to the Compensation Fund and half the costs of the Iraq-Kuwait Boundary Demarcation Commission, and recalling further that in its resolutions 686 (191) and 687 (1991) the Security Council demanded that Iraq return in the shortest possible time all Kuwaiti property seized by it and requested the Secretary-General to take steps to facilitate this,

Acting under Chapter VII of the Charter of the United Nations,

1. *Authorizes* all States, subject to the decision to be taken by the Security Council pursuant to paragraph 5 below and notwithstanding the provisions of paragraphs 3 (a), 3 (b) and 4 of resolution 661 (1990), to permit the import, during a period of 6 months from the date of passage of the resolution pursuant to paragraph 5 below, of petroleum and petroleum products originating in Iraq sufficient to produce a sum to be determined by the Council following receipt of the report of the Secretary-General requested in paragraph 5 of this resolution but not to exceed 1.6 billion United States dollars for the purposes set out in this resolution and subject to the following conditions:

(a) Approval of each purchase of Iraqi petroleum and petroleum products by the Security Council Committee established by resolution 661 (1990) following notification to the Committee by the State concerned;

(b) Payment of the full amount of each purchase of Iraqi petroleum and petroleum products directly by the purchaser in the State concerned into an escrow account to be established by the United Nations and to be administered by the Secretary-General, exclusively to meet the purposes of this resolution;

(c) Approval by the Council, following the report of the Secretary-General requested in paragraph 5 of this resolution, of a scheme for the purchase of foodstuffs, medicines and materials and supplies for essential civilian needs as referred to in paragraph 20 of resolution 687 (1991), in particular health related materials, all of which to be labelled to the extent possible as being supplied under this scheme, and for all feasible and appropriate United Nations monitoring and supervision for the purpose of assuring their equitable distribution to meet humanitarian needs in all regions of Iraq and to all categories of the Iraqi civilian population, as well as all feasible and appropriate management relevant to this purpose, such a United Nations role to be available if desired for humanitarian assistance from other sources;

(d) The sum authorized in this paragraph to be released by successive decisions of the Committee established by resolution 661 (1990) in three equal portions after the Council has taken the decision provided for in paragraph 5 below on the implementation of this resolution, and notwithstanding any other provision of this paragraph, the sum to be subject to review concurrently by the Council on the basis of its ongoing assessment of the needs and requirements;

2. *Decides* that a part of the sum in the account to be established by the Secretary-General shall be made available by him to finance the purchase of foodstuffs, medicines and materials and supplies for essential civilian needs, as referred to in paragraph 20 of resolution 687, and the cost to the United Nations of its roles under this resolution and of other necessary humanitarian activities in Iraq;

3. *Decides further* that a part of the sum in the account to be established by the Secretary-General shall be used by him for appropriate payments to the United Nations Compensation Fund, the full costs of carrying out the tasks authorized by Section C of resolution 687 (1991), the full costs incurred by the United Nations in facilitating the return of all Kuwaiti property seized by Iraq, and half the costs of the Boundary Commission;

4. *Decides* that the percentage of the value of exports of petroleum and petroleum products from Iraq, authorized under this resolution to be paid to the United Nations Compensation Fund, as called for in paragraph 19 of resolution 687 (1991), and as defined in paragraph 6 of resolution 692 (1991), shall be the same as the percentage decided by the Security Council in paragraph 2 of resolution 705 (1991) for payments to the Compensation Fund, until such time as the Governing Council of the Fund decides otherwise;

5. *Requests* the Secretary-General to submit within 20 days of the date of adoption of this resolution a report to the Security Council for decision on measures to be taken in order to implement paragraphs 1 (a), (b) and (c), estimates of the humanitarian requirements of Iraq set out in paragraph 2 above and of the amount of Iraq's financial obligations set out in paragraph 3 above up to the end of the period of the authorization in paragraph 1 above, as well as the method for taking the necessary legal measures to ensure that the purposes of this resolution are carried out and the method for taking account of the costs of transportation of such Iraqi petroleum and petroleum products;

6. *Further requests* the Secretary-General in consultation with the International Committee of the Red Cross to submit within 20 days of the date of adoption of this resolution a report to the Security Council on activities undertaken in accordance with paragraph 31 of resolution 687 (1991) in connection with facilitating the repatriation or return of all Kuwaiti and third-country nationals or their remains present in Iraq on or after 2 August 1990;

7. *Requires* the Government of Iraq to provide to the Secretary-General and appropriate international organizations on the first day of the month immediately

following the adoption of the present resolution and on the first day of each month thereafter until further notice, a statement of the gold and foreign currency reserves it holds whether in Iraq or elsewhere;

8. *Calls upon* all States to cooperate fully in the implementation of this resolution;

9. *Decides* to remain seized of the matter.

VOTE: 13 for, 1 against (Cuba), 1 abstention (Yemen)

RESOLUTION 707
August 15, 1991

The Security Council,

Recalling its resolution 687 (1991), and its other resolutions on this matter,

Recalling the letter of 11 April 1991 from the President of the Security Council to the Permanent Representative of Iraq to the United Nations (S/22485) noting that on the basis of Iraq's written agreement (S/22456) to implement fully resolution 687 (1991) the preconditions established in paragraph 33 of that resolution for a cease-fire had been met,

Noting with grave concern the letters dated 26 June 1991 (S/22739), 28 June 1991 (S/22743) and 4 July 1991 (S/22761) from the Secretary-General, conveying information obtained from the Executive Chairman of the Special Commission and the Director-General of the IAEA which establishes Iraq's failure to comply with its obligations under resolution 687 (1991),

Recalling further the statement issued by the President of the Security Council on 28 June 1991 (S/22746) requesting that a high-level mission consisting of the Chairman of the Special Commission, the Director-General of the IAEA, and the Under-Secretary-General for Disarmament Affairs be dispatched to meet with officials at the highest levels of the Government of Iraq at the earliest opportunity to obtain written assurance that Iraq will fully and immediately cooperate in the inspection of the locations identified by the Special Commission and present for immediate inspection any of those items that may have been transported from those locations,

Dismayed by the report of the high-level mission to the Secretary-General (S/22761) on the results of its meetings with the highest levels of the Iraqi Government,

Gravely concerned by the information provided to the Council by the Special Commission and the IAEA on 15 July 1991 (S/22788) and 25 July 1991 (S/22837) regarding the actions of the Government of Iraq in flagrant violation of resolution 687 (1991),

Gravely concerned also by the evidence in the letter of 7 July 1991 from the Minister of Foreign Affairs of Iraq to the Secretary-General and in subsequent statements and findings that Iraq's notifications of 18 and 28 April were incomplete and that it had concealed activities, which both constituted material breaches of its obligations under resolution 687 (1991),

Noting also from the letters dated 26 June 1991 (S/22739), 28 June 1991 (S/22743) and 4 July 1991 (S/22761) from the Secretary-General that Iraq has not fully complied with all of its undertakings relating to the privileges, immunities and facilities to be accorded to the Special Commission and the IAEA inspection teams mandated under resolution 687 (1991),

Affirming that in order for the Special Commission to carry out its mandate under paragraph 9 (b) (i), (ii) and (iii) of resolution 687 (1991) to inspect Iraq's chemical and biological weapons and ballistic missile capabilities and to take possession of them for destruction, removal or rendering harmless, full disclosure on the part of Iraq as required in paragraph 9 (a) of resolution 687 (1991) is essential,

Affirming that in order for the IAEA, with the assistance and cooperation of the Special Commission, to determine what nuclear-weapons-usable material or any subsystems or components or any research, development, support or manufacturing facilities related to them need, in accordance with paragraph 13 of resolution 687 (1991), to be destroyed, removed or rendered harmless, Iraq is required to make a declaration of all its nuclear programs including any which it claims are for purposes not related to nuclear-weapons-usable material,

Affirming that the aforementioned failures of Iraq to act in strict conformity with its obligations under resolution 687 (1991) constitutes a material breach of its acceptance of the relevant provisions of resolution 687 (1991) which established a cease-fire and provided the conditions essential to the restoration of peace and security in the region,

Affirming further that Iraq's failure to comply with its safeguards agreement with the International Atomic Energy Agency, concluded pursuant to the Treaty on the Non-Proliferation of Nuclear Weapons of 1 July 1968, as established by the resolution of the Board of Governors of the IAEA of 18 July 1991 (GOV/2532),[1] constitutes a breach of its international obligations,

Determined to ensure full compliance with resolution 687 (1991) and in particular its section C,

Acting under Chapter VII of the Charter of the United Nations,

1. *Condemns* Iraq's serious violation of a number of its obligations under section C of resolution 687 (1991) and of its undertakings to cooperate with the Special Commission and the IAEA, which constitutes a material breach of the relevant provisions of resolution 687 which established a cease-fire and provided the conditions essential to the restoration of peace and security in the region;

2. *Further condemns* non-compliance by the Government of Iraq with its obliga-

1. A/45/1037; S/28812, appendix.

tions under its safeguards agreement with the International Atomic Energy Agency, as established by the resolution of the Board of Governors of 18 July, which constitutes a violation of its commitments as a party to the Treaty on the Non-Proliferation of Nuclear Weapons of 1 July 1968;

3. *Demands* that Iraq

(i) provide full, final and complete disclosure, as required by resolution 687 (1991), of all aspects of its programs to develop weapons of mass destruction and ballistic missiles with a range greater than 150 kilometers, and of all holdings of such weapons, their components and production facilities and locations, as well as all other nuclear programs, including any which it claims are for purposes not related to nuclear-weapons-usable material, without further delay;

(ii) allow the Special Commission, the IAEA and their Inspection Teams immediate, unconditional and unrestricted access to any and all areas, facilities, equipment, records and means of transportation which they wish to inspect;

(iii) cease immediately any attempt to conceal, or any movement or destruction of any material or equipment relating to its nuclear, chemical or biological weapons or ballistic missile programmes, or material or equipment relating to its other nuclear activities without notification to and prior consent of the Special Commission;

(iv) make available immediately to the Special Commission, the IAEA and their Inspection Teams any items to which they were previously denied access;

(v) allow the Special Commission, the IAEA and their Inspection Teams to conduct both fixed wing and helicopter flights throughout Iraq for all relevant purposes including inspection, surveillance, aerial surveys, transportation and logistics without interference of any kind and upon such terms and conditions as may be determined by the Special Commission, and to make full use of their own aircraft and such airfields in Iraq as they may determine are most appropriate for the work of the Commission;

(vi) halt all nuclear activities of any kind, except for use of isotopes for medical, agricultural or industrial purposes until the Security Council determines that Iraq is in full compliance with this resolution and paragraphs 12 and 13 of resolution 687 (1991), and the IAEA determines that Iraq is in full compliance with its safeguards agreement with that Agency;

(vii) ensure the complete implementation of the privileges, immunities and facilities of the representatives of the Special Commission and the IAEA in accordance with its previous undertakings and their complete safety and freedom of movement;

(viii) immediately provide or facilitate the provision of any transportation, medical or logistical support requested by the Special Commission, the IAEA and their Inspection Teams;

(ix) respond fully, completely and promptly to any questions or requests from the Special Commission, the IAEA and their Inspection Teams;

4. *Determines* that Iraq retains no ownership interest in items to be destroyed, removed or rendered harmless pursuant to paragraph 12 of resolution 687 (1991);

5. *Requires* that the Government of Iraq forthwith comply fully and without delay with all its international obligations, including those set out in the present resolution, in resolution 687 (1991), in the Treaty on the Non-Proliferation of Nuclear Weapons of 1 July 1968 and its safeguards agreement with the IAEA;

6. *Decides* to remain seized of this matter.

VOTE: Unanimous (15–0)

AUTHORIZATION FOR USE OF MILITARY FORCE

(Joint Congressional Resolution of January 12, 1991)

The following is the text of the joint resolution approved by the Senate and the House of Representatives on January 12, 1991, regarding the use of force in the Persian Gulf. The vote in the Senate was 52–47; in the House it was 250–183.

To authorize the use of United States Armed Forces pursuant to United Nations Security Council Resolution 678.

Whereas the Government of Iraq without provocation invaded and occupied the territory of Kuwait on August 2, 1990, and

Whereas both the House of Representatives (in H.J. Res. 658 of the 101st Congress) and the Senate (in S. Con. Res. 147 of the 101st Congress) have condemned Iraq's invasion of Kuwait and declared their support for international action to reverse Iraq's aggression; and

Whereas Iraq's conventional, chemical, biological, and nuclear weapons and ballistic missile programs and its demonstrated willingness to use weapons of mass destruction pose a grave threat to world peace; and

Whereas the international community has demanded that Iraq withdraw unconditionally and immediately from Kuwait and that Kuwait's independence and legitimate government be restored; and

Whereas the U.N. Security Council repeatedly affirmed the inherent right of individual or collective self-defense in response to the armed attack by Iraq against Kuwait in accordance with Article 51 of the U.N. Charter; and

Whereas in the absence of full compliance by Iraq with its resolutions, the U.N. Security Council in Resolution 678 has authorized member states of the United

Nations to use all necessary means, after January 15, 1991, to uphold and implement all relevant Security Council resolutions and to restore international peace and security in the area; and

Whereas Iraq has persisted in its illegal occupation of, and brutal aggression against Kuwait; Now, therefore, be it

Resolved by the Senate and House of Representatives of the United States of America in Congress assembled,

Section 1.
SHORT TITLE

This joint resolution may be cited as the "Authorization for Use of Military Force Against Iraq Resolution."

Section 2.
AUTHORIZATION FOR USE OF U.S. ARMED FORCES

(a) *Authorization.* — The President is authorized, subject to subsection (b), to use United States Armed Forces pursuant to United Nations Security Council Resolution 678 (1990) in order to achieve implementation of Security Council Resolutions 660, 661, 662, 664, 665, 666, 667, 669, 670, 674, and 677.

(b) *Requirement for determination that use of military force is necessary.* — Before exercising the authority granted in subsection (a), the President shall make available to the Speaker of the House of Representatives and the President pro tempore of the Senate his determination that—

(1) the United States has used all appropriate diplomatic and other peaceful means to obtain compliance by Iraq with the United Nations Security Council resolutions cited in subsection (a); and (2) that those efforts have not been and would not be successful in obtaining such compliance.

(c) *War powers resolution requirements.* —

(1) *Specific statutory authorization.* — Consistent with section 8(a) of the War Powers Resolution, the Congress declares that this section is intended to constitute specific statutory authorization within the meaning of section 5(b) of the War Powers Resolution.

(2) *Applicability of other requirements.* — Nothing in this resolution supersedes any requirement of the War Powers Resolution.

Section 3.
REPORTS TO CONGRESS

At least once every 60 days, the President shall submit to the Congress a summary on the status of efforts to obtain compliance by Iraq with the resolutions adopted by the United Nations Security Council in response to Iraq's aggression.

INDEX

ABOUT U.S. NEWS & WORLD REPORT

U.S. News & World Report was founded by David Lawrence, a prominent Washington journalist, in 1933 as a weekly newspaper called *United States News*. In 1940, Lawrence transformed his paper into a weekly magazine. Six years later, he founded *World Report*, a magazine largely devoted to international affairs. After the Second World War, when the line separating domestic and foreign news began to blur, Lawrence merged his two publications into a single magazine called *U.S. News & World Report*. Upon his death in 1973, the magazine became employee-owned. Since 1984, it has been owned by Mortimer B. Zuckerman, chairman and editor-in-chief. From the magazine's Washington, D.C., headquarters, it maintains a worldwide network of bureaus and correspondents and has an international readership of more than 13.5 million people. The recipient of many distinguished prizes for its journalism, *U.S. News & World Report* won a National Magazine Award for feature writing in 1991.